S0-CDQ-468

Microsoft® Office Professional

for Windows® 3.1
Illustrated Enhanced Edition

Microsoft® Office Professional
for Windows® 3.1
Illustrated Enhanced Edition

Michael Halvorson
Marie L. Swanson
Elizabeth Eisner Reding
David W. Beskeen • Steven M. Johnson

CTI
A DIVISION OF COURSE TECHNOLOGY
ONE MAIN STREET, CAMBRIDGE MA 02142

an International Thomson Publishing company I(T)P

Albany • Bonn • Boston • Cincinnati • London • Madrid • Melbourne • Mexico City
New York • Paris • San Francisco • Singapore • Tokyo • Toronto • Washington

Microsoft Office Professional for Windows 3.1—Illustrated Enhanced Edition is published by CTI.

Managing Editor: Marjorie Hunt
Senior Product Manager: Nicole Jones Pinard
Production Editor: Roxanne Alexander
Text Designer: Leslie Hartwell
Cover Designer: John Gamache

©1996 by CTI.
A Division of Course Technology — I(T)P

For more information contact:
Course Technology
One Main Street
Cambridge, MA 02142

International Thomson Publishing Europe
Berkshire House 168-173
High Holborn
London WCIV 7AA
England

Thomas Nelson Australia
102 Dodds Street
South Melbourne, 3205
Victoria, Australia

Nelson Canada
1120 Birchmount Road
Scarborough, Ontario
Canada M1K 5G4

International Thomson Editores
Campos Eliseos 385, Piso 7
Col. Polanco
11560 Mexico D.F. Mexico

International Thomson Publishing GmbH
Königswinterer Strasse 418
53277 Bonn
Germany

International Thomson Publishing Asia
211 Henderson Road
#05-10 Henderson Building
Singapore 0315

International Thomson Publishing Japan
Hirakawacho Kyowa Building, 3F
2-2-1 Hirakawacho
Chiyoda-ku, Tokyo 102
Japan

All rights reserved. This publication is protected by federal copyright law. No part of this publication may be reproduced, stored in a retrieval system, or transmitted in any form or by any means, electronic, mechanical, photocopying, recording, or otherwise, or be used to make any derivative work (such as translation or adaptation), without prior permission in writing from Course Technology.

Trademarks

Course Technology and the open book logo are registered trademarks of Course Technology.

Microsoft and Microsoft Mail are registered trademarks of Microsoft Corporation.

I(T)P The ITP logo is a trademark under license.

Some of the product names in this book have been used for identification purposes only and may be trademarks or registered trademarks of their respective manufacturers and sellers.

Disclaimer

Learning Mail is an educational product designed to teach Microsoft Mail. It is a simulation only, and cannot be used to send or receive electronic mail.

CTI reserves the right to revise this publication and make changes from time to time in its content without notice.

0-7600-4034-6

Printed in the United States of America

10 9 8 7 6 5 4

From the Illustrated Series Team

At Course Technology we believe that technology will transform the way that people teach and learn. We are very excited about bringing you, instructors and students, the most practical and affordable technology-related products available.

The Development Process

Our development process is unparalleled in the educational publishing industry. Every product we create goes through an exacting process of design, development, review, and testing.

Reviewers give us direction and insight that shape our manuscripts and bring them up to the latest standards. Every manuscript is quality tested. Students whose backgrounds match the intended audience work through every keystroke, carefully checking for clarity and pointing out errors in logic and sequence. Together with our own technical reviewers, these testers help us ensure that everything that carries our name is as error-free and easy to use as possible.

The Products

We show both *how* and *why* technology is critical to solving problems in the classroom and in whatever field you choose to teach or pursue. Our time-tested, step-by-step instructions provide unparalleled clarity. Examples and applications are chosen and crafted to motivate students.

The Illustrated Series Team

The Illustrated Series Team is committed to providing you with a quick, visual introduction to computer skills. No other series of books will get you up to speed faster in today's changing software environment. This book will suit your needs because it was delivered quickly, efficiently, and affordably. In every aspect of business, we rely on a commitment to quality and the use of technology. Each member of the Illustrated Team contributes to this process. The names of our team members are listed below.

Cynthia Anderson
Chia-Ling Barker
Donald Barker
Laura Bergs
David Beskeen
Ann Marie Buconjic
Rachel Bunin
Joan Carey
Patrick Carey
Sheralyn Carroll
Pam Conrad
Mary Therese Cozzola
Carol Cram
Kim Crowley
Linda Ericksen
Lisa Friedrichsen
Michael Halvorson
Meta Hirschl
Jane Hosie-Bounar
Marjorie Hunt
Steven Johnson
Nancy Ludlow
Tara O'Keefe
Harry Phillips
Nicole Jones Pinard
Katherine Pinard
Kevin Proot
Elizabeth Eisner Reding
Neil Salkind
Gregory Schultz
Ann Shaffer
Roger Skilling
Patty Stephan
Dan Swanson
Marie Swanson
Jennifer Thompson
Mark Vodnik
Jan Weingarten
Christie Williams
Janet Wilson

Preface

Welcome to this new and Enhanced Edition of *Microsoft Office Professional for Windows 3.1 Illustrated*. This Enhanced Edition contains the exact content from the First Edition, plus a bonus section at the end. The bonus section includes a unit on Microsoft Mail plus reference material and homework to supplement all the units in the book. If you would like additional coverage of Microsoft Office, we are proud to offer *Microsoft Office Professional for Windows 3.1: A Second Course Illustrated*, which is a continuation of this book.

Organization and Coverage

Microsoft Office Professional for Windows 3.1 — Illustrated Enhanced Edition is divided into six parts: Windows, Word 6, Excel 5, Access 2, PowerPoint 4, and Mail. Additionally, three integration units provide hands-on instructions on how to use these programs together productively. At the end of this book you'll also find a section containing additional exercises and task references.

Approach

This text provides new users of Microsoft Office with a highly visual and interactive learning experience. This hands-on approach makes it ideal for both self-paced or instructor-led classes.

Lessons: Information Displays

The basic lesson format of this text is the "information display," a two-page lesson that is sharply focused on a specific task. This sharp focus and the precise beginning and end of a lesson make it easy for students to study specific material. Modular lessons are less overwhelming for students, and they provide instructors with more flexibility in planning classes and assigning specific work. The units are modular as well and can be presented in any order.

Each lesson, or "information display," contains the following elements:

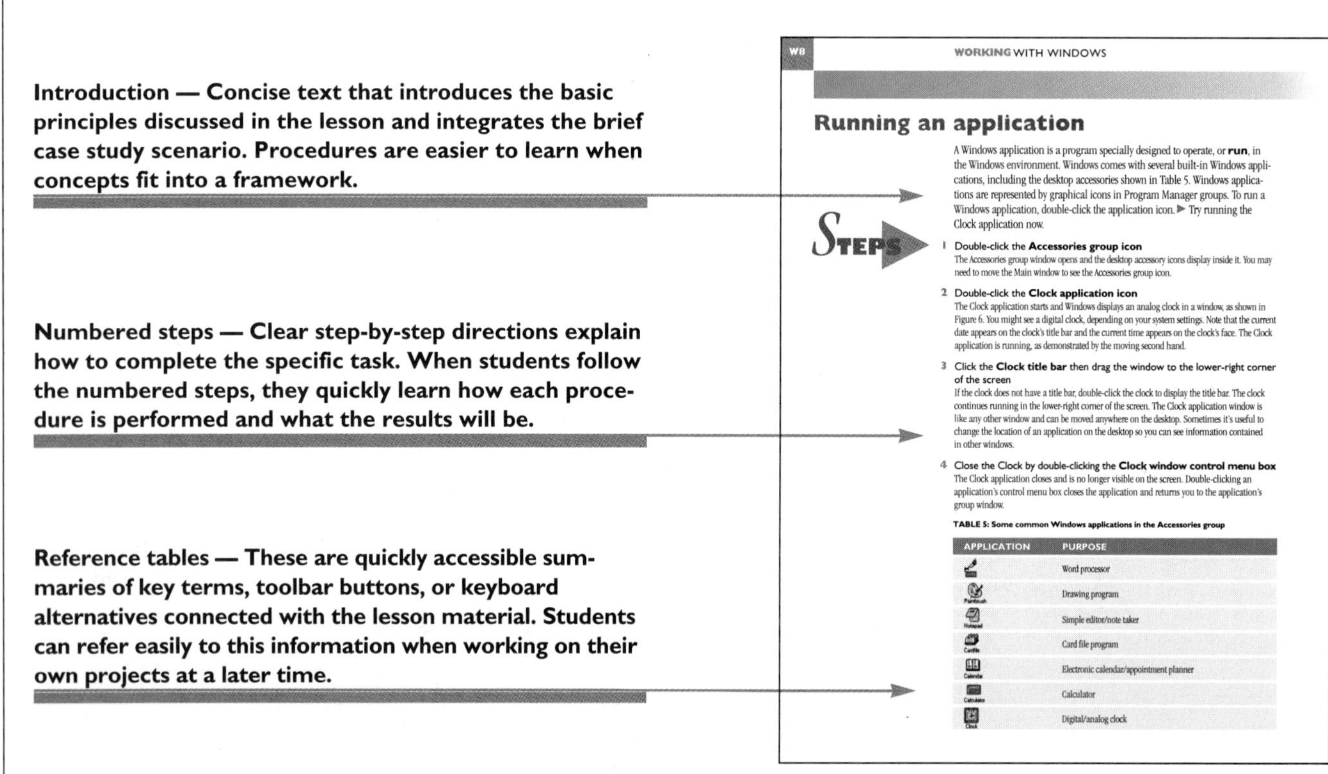

W8 WORKING WITH WINDOWS

Running an application

A Windows application is a program specially designed to operate, or **run**, in the Windows environment. Windows comes with several built-in Windows applications, including the desktop accessories shown in Table 5. Windows applications are represented by graphical icons in Program Manager groups. To run a Windows application, double-click the application icon. ▶ Try running the Clock application now.

1 Double-click the **Accessories group icon**
The Accessories group window opens and the desktop accessory icons display inside it. You may need to move the Main window to see the Accessories group icon.

2 Double-click the **Clock application icon**
The Clock application starts and Windows displays an analog clock in a window, as shown in Figure 6. You might see a digital clock, depending on your system settings. Note that the current date appears on the clock's title bar and the current time appears on the clock's face. The Clock application is running, as demonstrated by the moving second hand.

3 Click the **Clock title bar** then drag the window to the lower-right corner of the screen
If the clock does not have a title bar, double-click the clock to display the title bar. The clock continues running in the lower-right corner of the screen. The Clock application window is like any other window and can be moved anywhere on the desktop. Sometimes it's useful to change the location of an application on the desktop so you can see information contained in other windows.

4 Close the Clock by double-clicking the **Clock window control menu box**
The Clock application closes and is no longer visible on the screen. Double-clicking an application's control menu box closes the application and returns you to the application's group window.

TABLE 5: Some common Windows applications in the Accessories group

APPLICATION	PURPOSE
	Word processor
Paintbrush	Drawing program
Notepad	Simple editor/note taker
Cardfile	Card file program
Calendar	Electronic calendar/appointment planner
Calculator	Calculator
Clock	Digital/analog clock

About this Enhanced Edition

This special Enhanced Edition contains the exact content from the First Edition plus additional material and tools to give your students the best learning experience possible. The enhancements we've added since the First Edition are as follows:

- **Unit on Microsoft Mail and similuation program:** At the end of this book, you'll find a new unit on Microsoft Mail. This unit was designed to be used with Learning Mail, a special simulation program that mimics the experience of working with Microsoft Mail. The Learning Mail program lets you teach Microsoft Mail in a controlled environment without having to install the actual Microsoft Mail program. The Learning Mail program disk is contained in your Instructor's Resource Kit and can be installed on standalone computers.
- **Additional homework and reference material:** We've also added an entire new section of assessment material at the end of the book. This bonus section includes problems and exercises to supplement the units in the book, as well as task references for the skills learned in every unit.
- **CourseHelp:** CourseHelp is a student reinforcement tool offering computer-based annotated tutorials. These on-screen "slide shows" help students understand the most difficult concepts in a specific application. To see a CourseHelp "movie clip" refer to the back cover of this book. This book features CourseHelps on the following topics:
    - Moving and Copying Data
    - Creating and Formatting Sections
    - Moving and Copying Text
    - Relative versus Absolute Cell Referencing
    - Choosing a Chart Type
    - Planning a Database
    - Sorting Records
    - Filtering Records
    - Aligning, Grouping, and Stacking Objects
    - Screen Show Effects
    - Using Object Linking and Embedding

Camera icons in the Table of Contents indicate that CourseHelps are available for particular lessons.

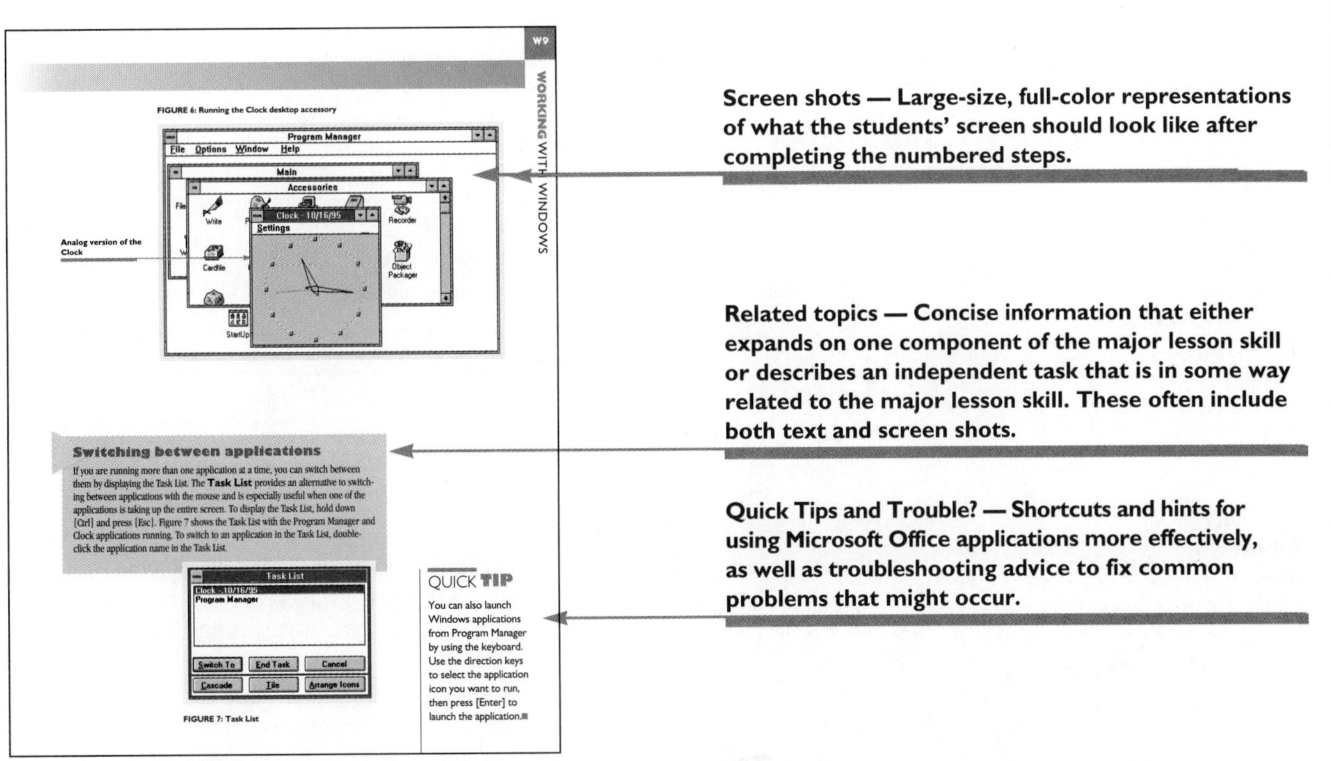

CourseTools

CourseTools are Course Technology's way of putting the resources and information needed to teach and learn effectively into your hands. With an integrated array of teaching and learning tools that offer you and your students a broad range of technology-based instructional options, we believe that CourseTools represents the highest quality and most cutting-edge resources available to instructors today. Briefly, the CourseTools available with this text are:

CourseHelp

CourseHelp is a student reinforcement tool offering computer-based annotated tutorials. These on-screen "slide shows" help students understand the most difficult concepts in a specific application. A picture of a movie camera in the table of contents indicates that a CourseHelp is available for a given lesson.

Learning Mail program

Learning Mail is a simulation program designed to mimic the experience of using Microsoft Mail. Using Learning Mail, your students will learn to send, receive, forward and reply to messages, and manage an inbox. To complete the Microsoft Mail unit, your students must use a computer that has the Learning Mail program installed. The Learning Mail program disk is contained in the Instructors Resource Kit and installs on standalone machines. Adopters of this text are granted the right to install Learning Mail on any standalone computer or network.

Student Disk

To use this book students must have the Student Disks. See the inside front or inside back cover for more information on the Student Disks. Adopters of this text are granted the right to post the Student Disks on any standalone computer or network used by students who have purchased this product.

Course Online Faculty Companion

This new World Wide Web site offers Course Technology customers a password-protected Faculty Lounge where you can find everything you need to prepare for class. This new site is an ongoing project and will continue to evolve throughout the semester.

Course Online Student Companion

Our second Web site is a place where students can access challenging, engaging, and relevant exercises. Student sites can be found at http://coursetools.com. These new sites are also ongoing projects and will continue to evolve throughout the semester.

Instructor's Resource Kit

This is quality assurance tested and includes:

- Solutions to all lessons and end-of-unit material
- Disk containing solutions to all lessons and end-of-unit material
- Unit notes which contain teaching tips from the author
- Extra Independent Challenges
- Transparency Masters of key concepts
- Student Disks
- CourseHelp Disks
- Learning Mail program disk

Course Test Manager

Designed by Course Technology, this cutting-edge Windows-based testing software helps instructors design and administer tests and pre-tests. This full-featured program also has an online testing component that allows students to take tests at the computer and have their exams automatically graded.

Brief Contents

Contents

TABLES

Microsoft Office

UNIT

TABLES

Microsoft Word 6.0 for Windows

TABLES

Microsoft Excel 5.0 for Windows

TABLES

Integration

Microsoft Access 2.0 for Windows

TABLES

Integration

Microsoft PowerPoint 4.0 for Windows

TABLES

Integration

UNIT 3 Integrating Word, Excel, Access, and PowerPoint *I-17*

TABLES

Microsoft Mail for Windows

UNIT 1 Getting Started with Microsoft Mail *MM 1*

TABLES

Additional Exercises

Task References

Microsoft® Windows™ 3.1

UNIT 1 **Getting Started with Microsoft Windows 3.1**

UNIT 2 **Creating and Managing Files**

Read This Before You Begin Microsoft Windows 3.1

To the Student

To complete some of the step-by-step lessons, Applications Reviews, and Independent Challenges in this book, you must have a Student Disk. You can use a blank, formatted disk or, if you are using another Illustrated book from Course Technology, Inc., *use the Student Disk that accompanies that book*. If you use a Student Disk from another Illustrated book, your instructor will do one of the following: 1) provide you with your own copy of the disk; 2) have you copy it from the network onto your own floppy disk; or 3) have you copy the lesson files from a network into your own subdirectory on the network. Always use your own copies of the lesson and exercise files. See your instructor or technical support person for further information.

Using Your Own Computer

If you are going to work through this book using your own computer, you need a computer system running Microsoft Windows 3.1 and a blank, formatted disk or a Student Disk. If you are using another Illustrated book, use the Student Disk that accompanies that book. If you are not using another Illustrated book, you can simply use a blank, formatted disk to work through these units. This blank, formatted disk becomes your Student Disk.

To the Instructor

This book does not come with a Student Disk. Students do not need any files to work through these units. However, students are asked to create a MY_FILES directory on their Student Disk that they will use to store the files they create and save.

If you have adopted another Illustrated book, instruct your students to use the Student Disk that accompanies that book as they work through these units. If you have adopted more than one Illustrated book, or if another Illustrated book has more than one Student Disk, instruct your students to create a MY_FILES directory on each Student Disk. If you are not using another Illustrated book, you can instruct your students to use a blank, formatted disk to work through these units. This blank, formatted disk becomes their Student Disk.

The instructions in this book assume that the students know which drive and directory contain the Student Disk, so it's important that you provide disk location information before the students start working through the units.

UNIT 1

OBJECTIVES

- Start Windows
- Use the mouse
- Use Program Manager groups
- Resize a window
- Use scroll bars
- Run an application
- Use menus
- Use dialog boxes
- Arrange windows and icons
- Exit Windows

Getting Started WITH MICROSOFT WINDOWS 3.1

Microsoft Windows 3.1 is the **graphical user interface** (GUI) that works hand in hand with MS-DOS to control the basic operation of your computer and the programs you run on it. Windows is a comprehensive control program that helps you run useful, task-oriented programs known as **applications**. ▶ This unit will introduce you to basic skills that you can use in all Windows applications. First you'll learn how to start Windows and how to use the mouse in the Windows environment. Next you'll get some hands-on experience with Program Manager, and you'll learn how to work with groups, resize a window, scroll a window, run an application, use menus and dialog boxes, and arrange windows and icons. Then you'll learn how to exit a Windows application and exit Windows itself. ▶

Starting Windows

Windows is started, or **launched**, from MS-DOS with the WIN command. Once started, Windows takes over most of the duties of MS-DOS and provides a graphical environment in which you run your applications. Windows has several advantages over MS-DOS. As a graphical interface, it uses meaningful pictures and symbols known as **icons** to replace hard-to-remember commands. Also, each application is represented in a rectangular space called a **window**. ▶ Once you launch Windows, you see the Windows desktop. The **desktop** is an electronic version of a desk that provides workspace for different computing tasks. Use Table 1-1 to identify the key elements of the desktop, referring to Figure 1-1 for their locations. Because the Windows desktop can be customized, your desktop might look slightly different. ▶ Try starting Windows now.

1. **If your computer is not on, turn it on**
   The computer displays some technical information as it starts up and tests its circuitry. MS-DOS starts automatically, then displays the **command prompt** (usually C:\>). The command prompt gives you access to MS-DOS commands and applications. If your computer is set up so that it automatically runs Windows when it starts, the command prompt will not appear. You can then skip Step 2.

2. **Type win then press [Enter]**
   This command starts Windows. The screen momentarily goes blank while the computer starts Windows. An hourglass appears, indicating Windows is busy processing a command. Then the Program Manager appears on your screen, as shown in Figure 1. Your screen might look slightly different depending on which applications are installed on your computer.

FIGURE 1-1: Program Manager window

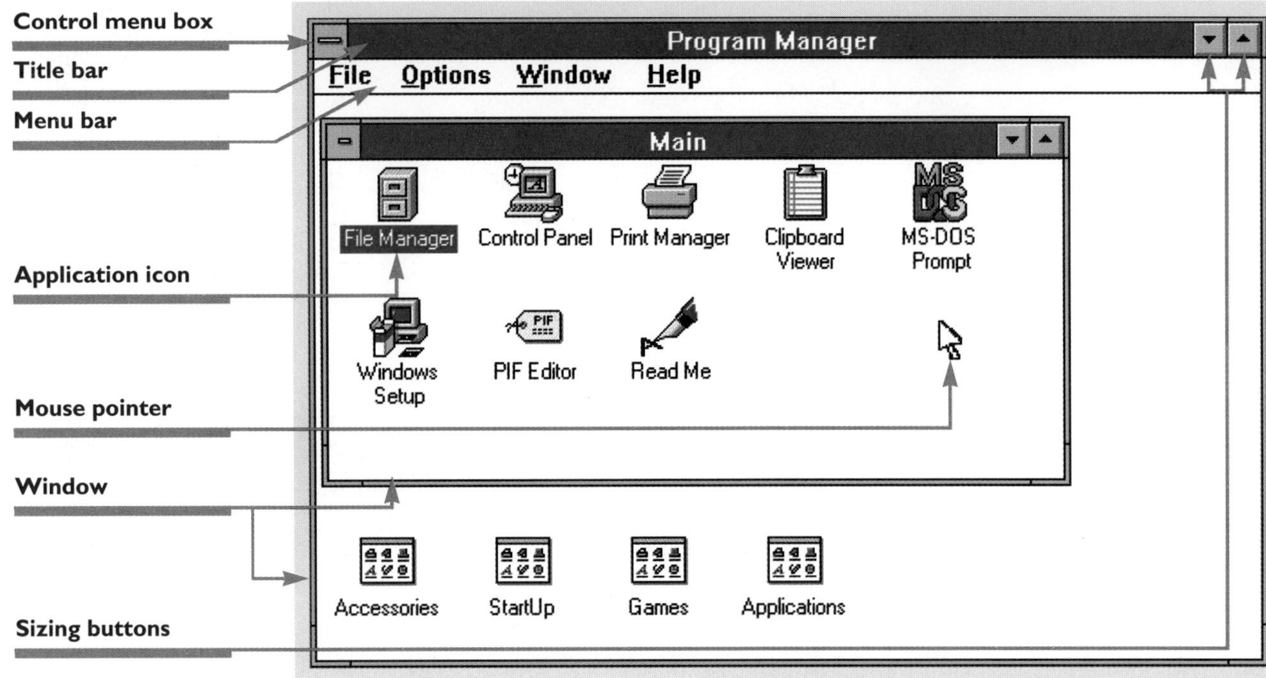

TABLE 1-1:
Elements of the Windows desktop

DESKTOP ELEMENT	DESCRIPTION
Program Manager	The main control program of Windows; all Windows applications are started from Program Manager
Window	A rectangular space framed by a double border on the screen; Program Manager is framed in a window
Application icon	The graphic representation of a Windows application
Title bar	The area directly below a window's top border that displays the name of a window or an application
Sizing buttons	Buttons in the upper-right corner of a window that you can use to minimize, maximize, or restore a window
Menu bar	The area under the title bar on a window that provides access to an application's commands
Control menu box	A box in the upper-left corner of each window that provides a menu used to resize, move, maximize, minimize, or close a window; double-clicking this box closes a window or an application
Mouse pointer	An arrow indicating the current location of the mouse on the desktop

Using the mouse

The **mouse** is a handheld input device that you roll on your desk to position the mouse pointer on the Windows desktop. When you move the mouse on your desk, the **mouse pointer** on the screen moves in the same direction. The buttons on the mouse, as shown in Figure 1-2, are used to select icons and commands, and to indicate the work to be done in applications. Table 1-2 lists the four basic mouse techniques. Table 1-3 shows some common mouse pointer shapes. ▶ Try using the mouse now.

1. **Locate the mouse pointer on the Windows desktop and move the mouse across your desk**
   Watch how the mouse pointer moves on the Windows desktop in response to your movements. Try moving the mouse pointer in circles, then back and forth in straight lines.

2. **Position the mouse pointer over the Control Panel application icon in the Main group window**
   Positioning the mouse pointer over an icon is called **pointing**. The Control Panel icon is a graphical representation of the Control Panel application, a special program that controls the operation of the Windows environment. If the Control Panel application icon is not visible in the Main group window, point to any other icon. The Program Manager is customizable so the Control Panel could be hidden from view or in a different window.

3. **Press and release the left mouse button**
   Unless otherwise indicated, you will use the left mouse button to perform all mouse operations. Pressing and releasing the mouse button is called **clicking**. When you position the mouse pointer on an icon in Program Manager then click, you **select** the icon. When the Control Panel icon is selected, its title is highlighted, as shown in Figure 1-3. If you clicked an icon that caused a menu to open, click the icon again to close the menu. You'll learn about menus later. Now practice a mouse skill called **dragging**.

4. **With the icon selected, press and hold the left mouse button, then move the mouse down and to the right and release the mouse button**
   The icon changes from color to black and white and moves with the mouse pointer. When you release the mouse button, the icon relocates in the group window.

5. **Drag the Control Panel application icon back to its original position**

TABLE 1-2: Basic mouse techniques

TECHNIQUE	HOW TO DO IT
Pointing	Move the mouse pointer to position it over an item on the desktop
Clicking	Press and release the mouse button
Double-clicking	Press and release the mouse button twice quickly
Dragging	Point at an item, press and hold the mouse button, move the mouse to a new location, then release the mouse button

FIGURE 1-2: The mouse

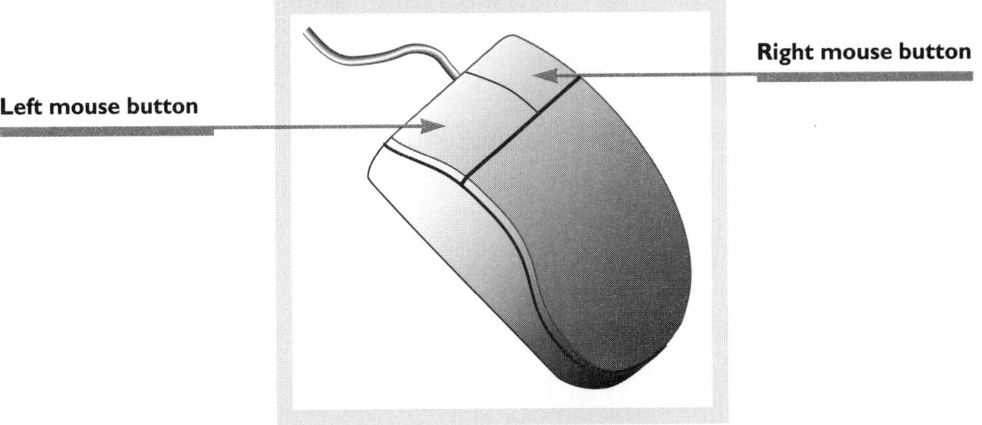

FIGURE 1-3: Selecting an icon

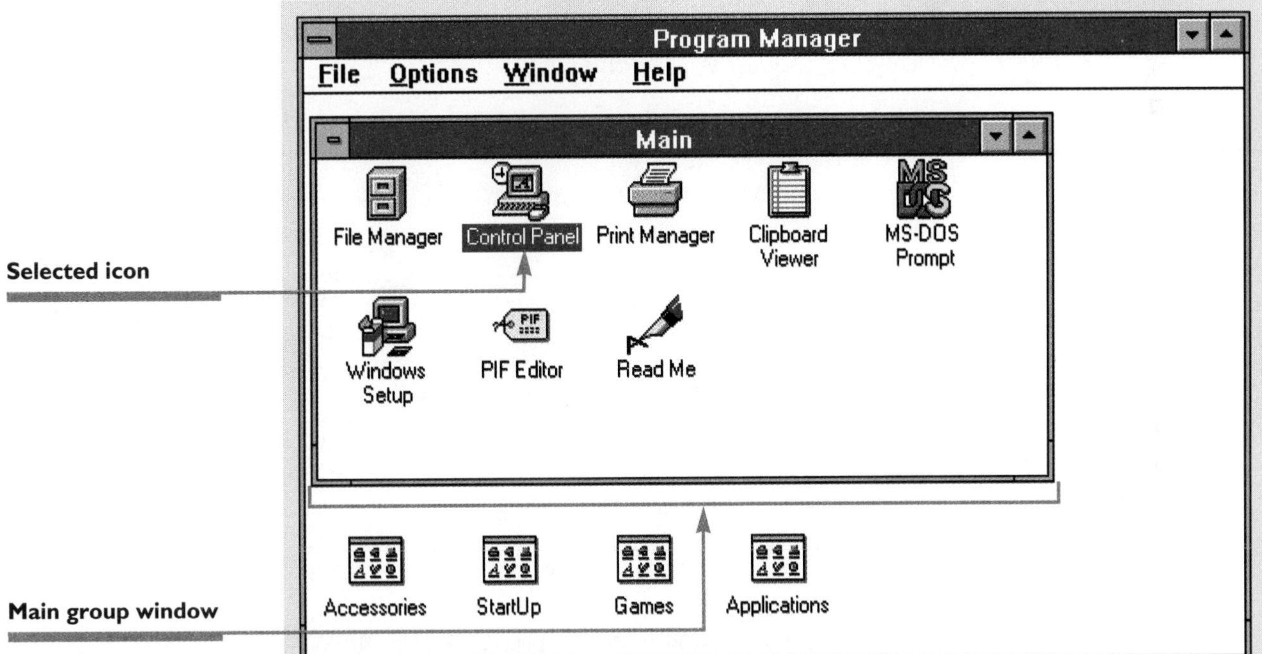

TABLE 1-3: Common mouse pointer shapes

SHAPE	USED TO
↖ (arrow)	Select items, choose commands, start applications, and work in applications
I	Position mouse pointer for editing or inserting text; called the insertion point or cursor
⧗ (hourglass)	Indicate Windows is busy processing a command
⇔	Change the size of a window; appears when mouse pointer is on the border of a window

QUICK TIP

Windows comes with a short tutorial about using the mouse and improving your hand-eye coordination. Press [Alt][H], then [W] and follow the instructions on the screen to run the tutorial.

Using Program Manager groups

In Program Manager, you start applications and organize your applications into windows called **groups**. A group can appear as an open window or as an icon in the Program Manager window. Each group has a name related to its contents, and you can reorganize the groups to suit your needs. The standard Windows groups are described in Table 1-4, but each can be customized to include additional applications. ▶ Try working with groups now.

1. **If necessary, double-click the Main group icon to open the Main group window**
   The Main group icon is usually located at the bottom of the Program Manager window.

2. **Double-click the Accessories group icon**
   When you double-click the Accessories group icon, it expands into the Accessories group window, as shown in Figure 1-4. Your group window might contain different icons. Now move the Accessories group window to the right.

3. **Click the Accessories group window title bar, then drag the window to the right**
   An outline of the window moves to the right with the mouse. When you release the mouse button, the Accessories group window moves to the location you've indicated. Moving a window lets you see what is beneath it. Any window in the Windows environment can be moved with this technique.

4. **Click the title bar of the Main group window**
   The Main group window becomes the **active window**, the one you are currently working in. Other windows, including the Accessories group window, are considered background windows. Note that the active window has a highlighted title bar. Program Manager has a highlighted title bar because it is the **active application**.

5. **Activate the Accessories group window by clicking anywhere in that window**
   The Accessories group window becomes the active window again. Now try closing the Accessories group window.

6. **Double-click the control menu box in the Accessories group window**
   When you double-click this box, the Accessories group window shrinks to an icon and the Main group window becomes the active window, as shown in Figure 1-5. Double-clicking the control menu box is the easiest way to close a window or an application.

FIGURE 1-4: Accessories group expanded into a window

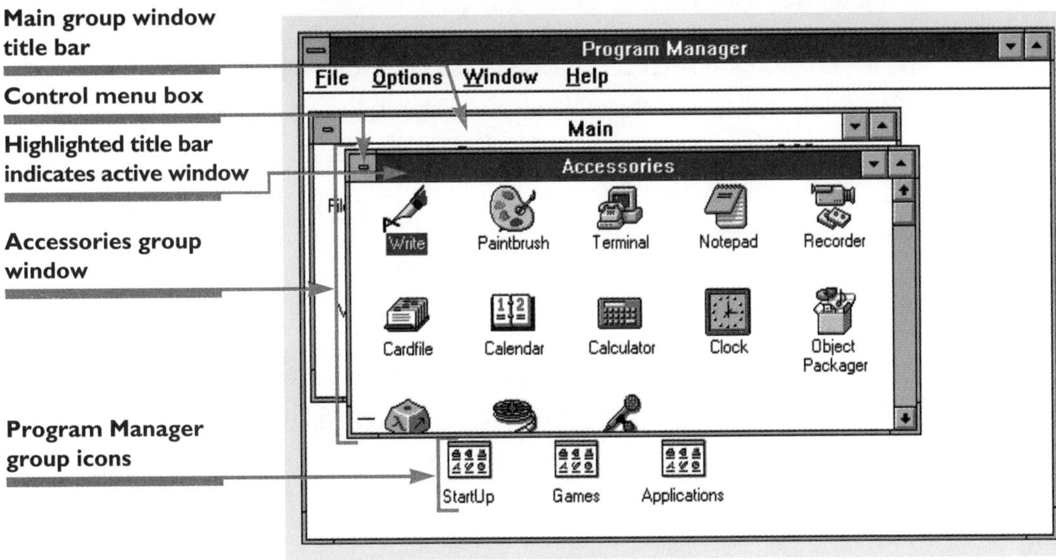

FIGURE 1-5: Closing the Accessories group window

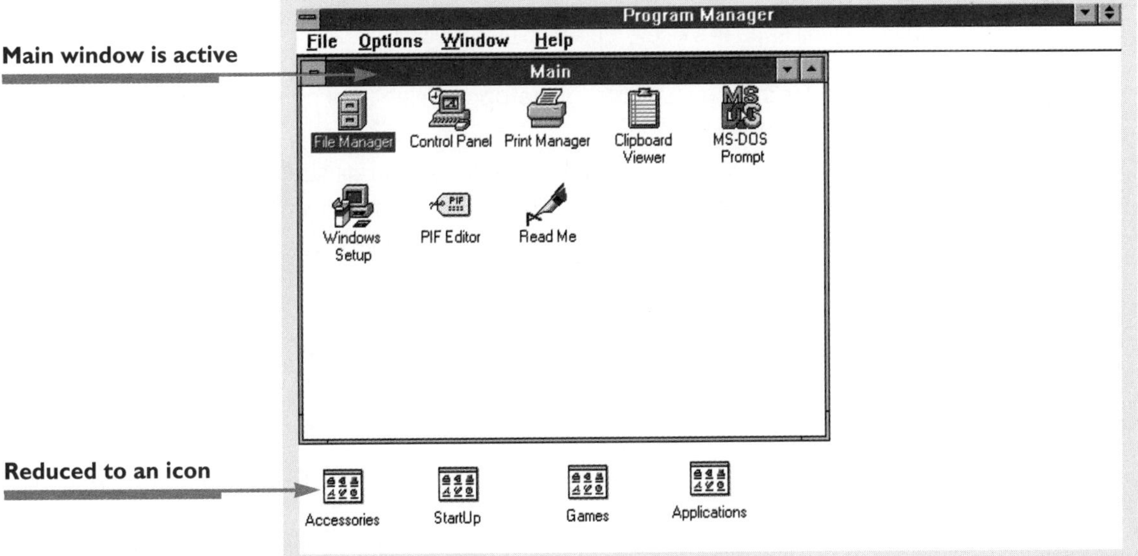

TABLE 1-4:
Standard Windows groups

GROUP NAME	CONTENTS
Main	Applications that control how Windows works; the primary Windows group
Accessories	Useful desktop accessories for day-to-day tasks
StartUp	Applications that run automatically when Windows is started
Games	Game applications for Windows
Applications	Applications found on your hard disk

QUICK **TIP**

To switch between active windows using the keyboard, press [Ctrl][F6].■

Resizing a window

The Windows desktop can get cluttered with icons and windows if you are working with several applications. Each window is surrounded by a standard border and sizing buttons that allow you to minimize, maximize, and restore windows as needed. The sizing buttons are shown in Table 1-5. They help you keep the desktop organized. ▶ Try sizing the Program Manager and Accessories group windows now.

1 Click the **Minimize button** in the upper-right corner of the Program Manager window
When you minimize a window, it shrinks to an icon at the bottom of the screen, as shown in Figure 1-6. Windows applications continue to run after you minimize them.

2 Restore the Program Manager window to its previous size by double-clicking the Program Manager icon
The Program manager window returns to its previous size.

3 Click the **Maximize button** in the upper-right corner of the Program Manager window
When you maximize a window, it takes up the whole screen, as shown in Figure 1-7.

4 Click the **Restore button** in the upper-right corner of the Program Manager window
The Restore button, shown in Figure 1-7, appears *after* an application has been maximized. The Restore button returns an application to its original size. In addition to minimizing, maximizing, and restoring windows, you can also change the dimensions of any window. Open the Accessories group and change the dimensions of its window.

5 Double-click the **Accessories group icon**, then position the mouse pointer on the right edge of the Accessories group window until the pointer changes to ⇔

6 Drag the Accessories window border to the right to increase the window's width
You can increase or decrease the size of a window, but its shape will always be a rectangle. Finally, decrease the width of the Accessories group window before proceeding to the next lesson.

7 Drag the Accessories group window border to the left until it is the same size as in Figure 1-8
Continue with the next lesson.

TABLE 1-5:
Buttons for managing windows

BUTTON	PURPOSE
▼	Minimizes an application to an icon on the bottom of the screen
▲	Maximizes an application to its largest possible size
⬍	Restores an application, returning it to its original size

FIGURE 1-6: Program Manager minimized

FIGURE 1-7: Program Manager maximized

Restore button

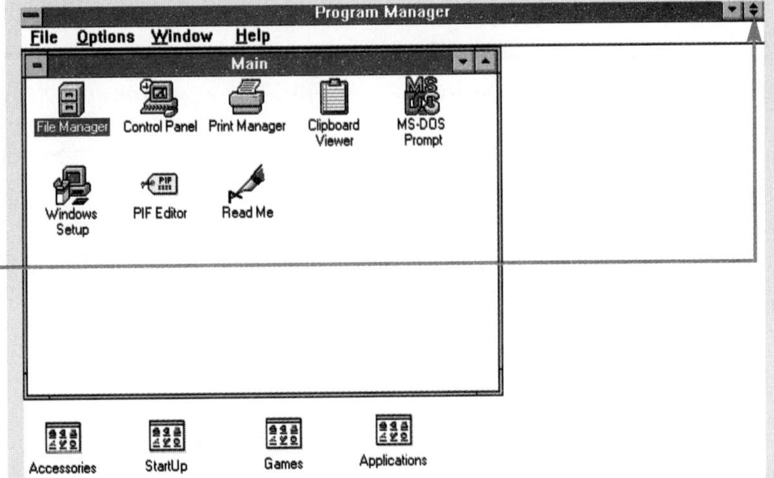

FIGURE 1-8: Accessories group window resized

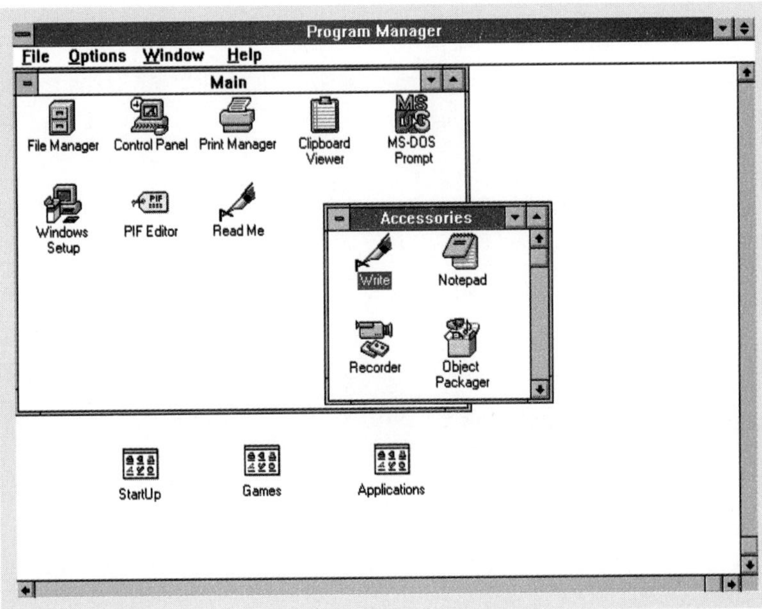

Using scroll bars

If a window contains more information than can be displayed at one time, **scroll bars** appear on the right and/or bottom edges of the window to give you access to that information. For example, when you resized the Accessories group window, scroll bars appeared on the right, as shown in Figure 1-9. Both the horizontal and vertical scroll bars have **scroll arrows** and **scroll boxes** that help you to move around the window. To move around the window, you click the vertical or horizontal arrows that point in the direction in which you want to move, or you can drag the scroll box along the scroll bar. ▶ Scroll through the Accessories group window to view the available applications.

1. **Make sure your Accessories group window is open with the vertical scroll bar visible**
2. **Click the down scroll arrow on the vertical scroll bar once**
   Notice that the contents of the window and the vertical scroll box scroll up a small increment, as shown in Figure 1-9. This technique is useful when you only need to scroll a short distance. You can click the scroll arrows several times to move a greater distance or you can use the scroll box.
3. **Drag the scroll box down to the bottom of the vertical scroll bar**
   Use the scroll box if you want to move quickly from one end of a window to another. You can also click in the scroll bar, above or below the scroll box to scroll a window in larger increments. The horizontal scroll bar and scroll box works in the same way as the vertical scroll bar and scroll box, except the horizontal scroll bar moves the contents of a window left to right or right to left.
4. **Scroll the Accessories group window until the Clock application is visible**
   See Figure 1-10. In the next lesson, you will learn how to run the Clock application.

FIGURE 1-9: Window with vertical scroll bar

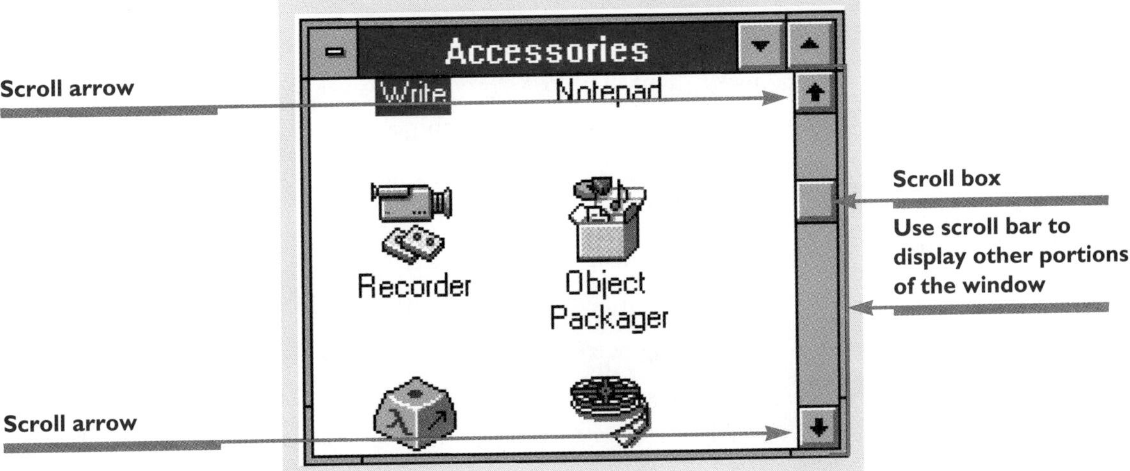

FIGURE 1-10: Scrolling the Accessories group window

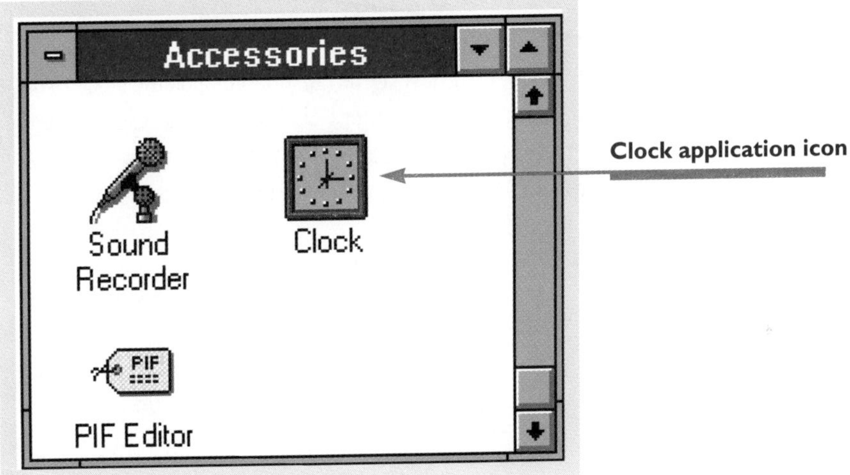

QUICK TIP

You can use direction keys on the keyboard to scroll the contents of an active window. (Remember that an active window is the window with the highlighted title bar.) To scroll vertically, press [↑] or [↓]. To scroll horizontally, press [←] or [→].■

Running an application

A Windows application is a program specially designed to operate, or **run**, in the Windows environment. Windows comes with several built-in Windows applications, including the desktop accessories shown in Table 1-6. Windows applications are represented by icons in Program Manager groups. To run a Windows application, double-click the application icon. In Windows, you can run more than one application at a time. See the related topic "Switching between applications" for more information. ▶ Try running the Clock application now.

1 Double-click the **Clock application icon** in the Accessories group window
The Clock application starts and displays an analog clock in a window, as shown in Figure 1-11. You might see a digital clock, depending on your system settings. Note that the current date appears on the clock's title bar and the current time appears on the clock's face. The Clock application is running, as demonstrated by the moving second hand.

2 Click the **Clock window title bar**, then drag the window to the lower-right corner of the screen
If the clock does not have a title bar, double-click the clock to display the title bar. The clock continues running in the lower-right corner of the screen. The Clock application window is like any other window and can be moved anywhere on the desktop. Sometimes it's useful to change the location of an application on the desktop so you can see information contained in other windows.

3 Double-click the **control menu box** on the Clock application window to close it
The Clock application closes and is no longer visible on the screen. Double-clicking an application's control menu box closes the application and returns you to the application's group window.

TABLE 1-6: Some common Windows applications in the Accessories group

APPLICATION	PURPOSE
Write	Word processor
Paintbrush	Drawing program
Notepad	Simple editor/note taker
Cardfile	Card file program
Calendar	Calendar/appointment planner
Calculator	Calculator
Clock	Digital/analog clock

FIGURE 1-11: Running the Clock desktop accessory

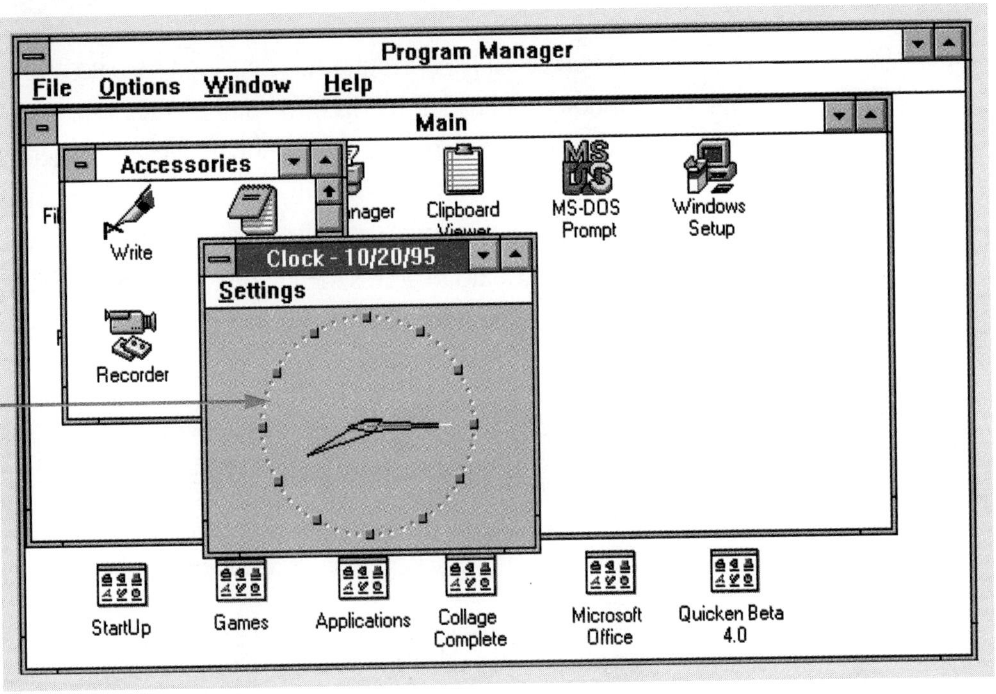

Analog version of the clock

Switching between applications

Running more than one application at a time is called **multitasking**. This is useful if you want to share information between applications. When you have more than one application running, you can use the **Task List** to switch between applications. To display the Task List, press [Ctrl] [Esc]. Figure 1-12 shows the Task List with the Program Manager and Clock applications running. To switch to an application in the Task List, double-click the application name in the Task List.

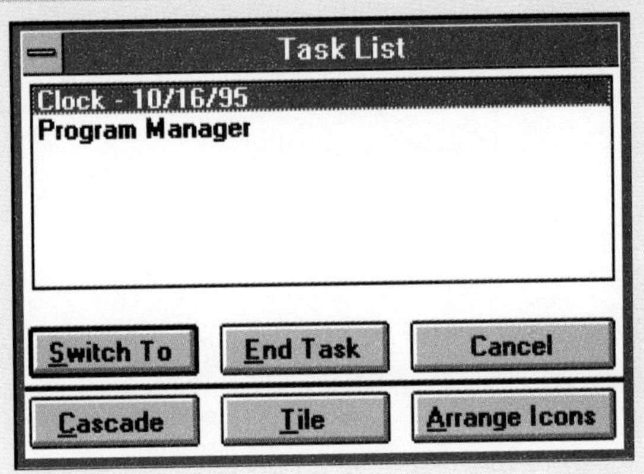

FIGURE 1-12: Task List

QUICK TIP

To switch quickly between several applications, press [Alt][Tab] until you see the application you want. Release [Alt] to switch to that application.

Using menus

A **menu** is a list of commands that you use to accomplish certain tasks. Each Windows application has its own set of menus, which are located on the **menu bar** along the top of the application window. The menus organize commands into groups of related operations. For example, the Help menu contains commands for accessing Windows' extensive on-line Help system. You can use both the mouse and the keyboard to access menu commands. See Table 1-7 for examples of what you might see on a typical menu. ▶ Use the Help menu to open Windows on-line Help.

1 Click **Help** on the Program Manager menu bar
The Help menu opens, as shown in Figure 1-13.

2 Click **Contents** on the Help menu
The Program Manager Help window appears and displays its contents page.

3 Position the pointer over the green underlined text **Switch Between Applications** until the pointer changes to 👆
If you are using a monochrome monitor, this text is in black.

4 Click the topic **Switch Between Applications**
Another Help window opens, giving you information on how to switch between applications. Read this information, using the scroll bars as necessary. It should reinforce what you learned in the "Running an application" lesson. You can use Program Manager Help to answer any questions that arise as you are working with Windows.

5 Click **Back** to return to the contents page
You can also open menus by pressing the Alt key and then the underlined letter on the menu bar. Now use the keyboard, instead of the mouse, to exit Help.

6 Press **[Alt]**
The File menu is selected as shown in Figure 1-14.

7 Press **[F]** to open the File menu
You could also press [↓] or [Enter] to open the menu. The File menu opens. Notice that a letter in each command is underlined. You can access these commands by pressing the underlined letter. Notice also that the Open and Print Setup commands are followed by an ellipsis (...). An **ellipsis** indicates that a dialog box will open when you choose this command. You will learn about dialog boxes in the next lesson.

Now you can exit Help.

8 Press **[X]** to exit Help

FIGURE 1-13: Help menu on Program Manager menu bar

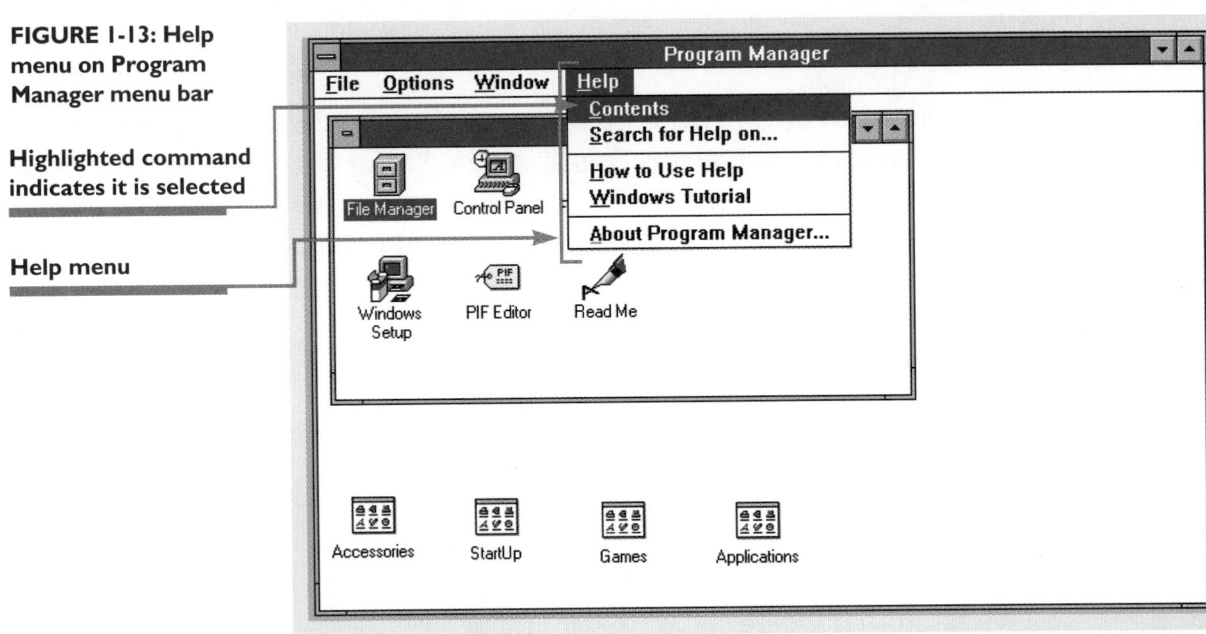

FIGURE 1-14: File highlighted on Help window menu bar

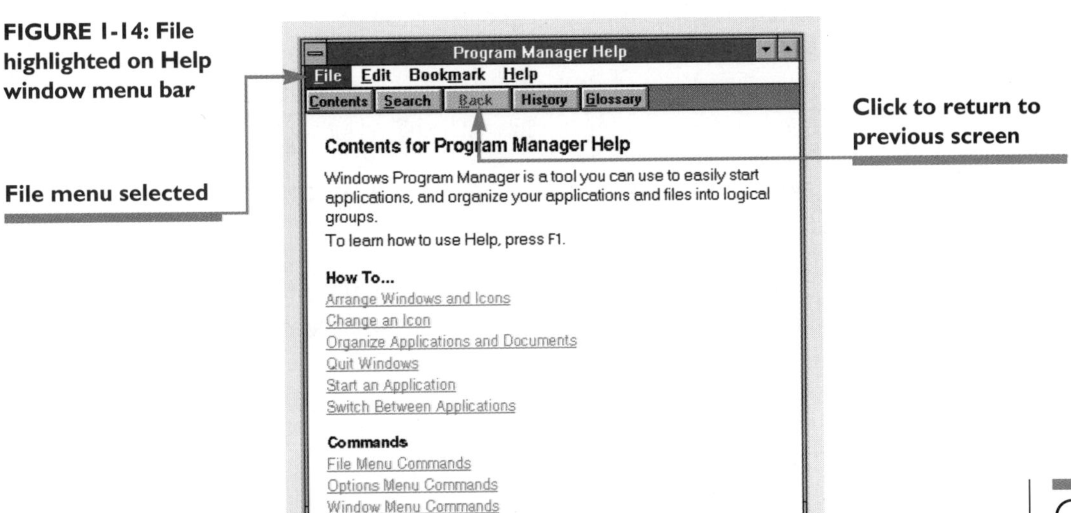

QUICK TIP

To learn how to use Help, press [F1].

TABLE 1-7: Typical items on a menu

ITEM	DESCRIPTION	EXAMPLE
Dimmed command	A menu command that is not currently available	Undo
Ellipsis	Choosing this menu command opens a dialog box that asks for further information	Paste Special...
Triangle	Clicking this button opens a cascading menu containing an additional list of menu commands	Axis ▸
Keyboard shortcut	A keyboard alternative for executing a menu command	Cut Ctrl+X
Underlined letter	Pressing the underlined letter executes this menu command	Copy Right

Using dialog boxes

Sometimes when you select a command from a menu, the command needs more information before it can complete its task. A **dialog box** opens requesting more information. See Table 1-8 for some of the typical elements of a dialog box. ▶ Try using the Control Panel, which lets you customize your Windows desktop, to practice using dialog boxes.

1 Click the **Main group window** to make it active, then double-click the **Control Panel application icon**
Drag other windows out of the way, if necessary. If the Control Panel application icon is not in the main group window, ask your technical support person for assistance. The Control Panel group window opens.

2 Click **Settings** on the menu bar
A menu appears listing all the commands that let you adjust different aspects of your desktop.

3 Click **Desktop** to display the Desktop dialog box
This dialog box provides options to customize your desktop. See Figure 1-15. Next, locate the Screen Saver section in the middle of the dialog box. A **screen saver** is a moving pattern that fills your screen after your computer has not been used for a specified amount of time.

4 Click the **Name list arrow** in the Screen Saver section
A list of available screen saver patterns appears.

5 Click the screen saver pattern of your choice, then click **Test**
The screen saver pattern you chose appears. It will remain on the screen until you move the mouse or press a key.

The Test button is a **command button**. The two most common command buttons are OK and Cancel, which you'll see in almost every dialog box.

6 Move the mouse to exit the screen saver
Next, you'll adjust the cursor blink rate in the Cursor Blink Rate section of the dialog box. The **cursor**, or in some applications called the insertion point, is the blinking vertical line that shows you where you are on the screen. See Figure 1-15.

7 Drag the scroll box all the way to the right of the scroll bar, then click the **left arrow** in the scroll bar a few times
By moving the scroll box between Slow and Fast on the scroll bar, you can adjust the cursor blink rate to suit your needs.

8 Click **OK** to save your changes and close the dialog box
Clicking OK accepts your changes; clicking Cancel rejects your changes. Now you can exit the Control Panel.

9 Double-click the **control menu box** on the Control Panel window to close it

FIGURE 1-15: Desktop dialog box

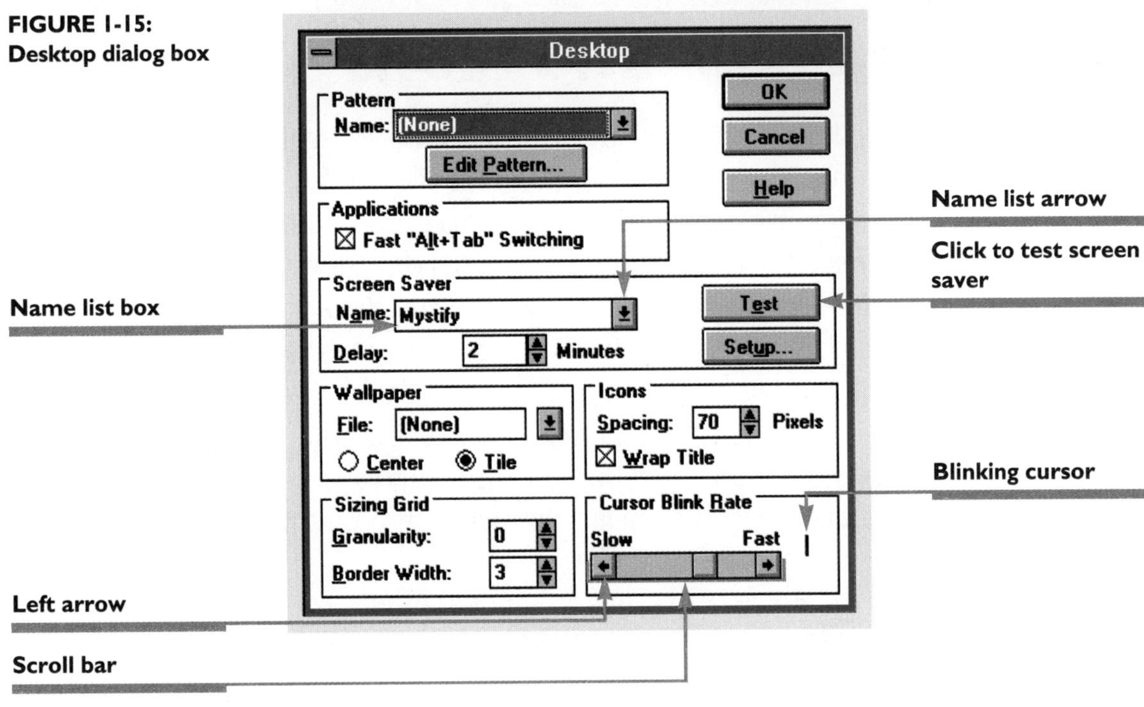

If you are in a computer lab, you should return the desktop settings you changed to their original state.

TABLE 1-8: Typical items in a dialog box

ITEM	DESCRIPTION	EXAMPLE
Check box	Clicking this square box turns a dialog box option on or off	☒ Wrap Title
Text box	A box in which you type text	tours.wk4
Radio button	Clicking this small circle selects a single dialog box option	◉ Tile
Command button	Clicking this button executes the dialog box command	OK
List box	A box containing a list of items; to choose an item, click the list arrow, then click the desired item	c: ms-dos_5

Arranging windows and icons

If your desktop contains many groups that you open regularly, you might find that the open windows clutter your desktop. The Tile and Cascade commands on the Window menu let you view all your open group windows at once in an organized arrangement. You can also use the Window menu to open all the program groups installed on your computer. ▶ Once you are comfortable working with Windows, you might decide to reorganize the icon in your group windows. You can easily move an icon from one group window to another by dragging it with the mouse. In the following steps, you'll drag the Clock application icon from the Accessories group window to the StartUp group window. The StartUp group window contains programs that automatically start running when you launch Windows.

1 **Click the Program Manager window Maximize button to maximize this window, then click Window on the menu bar**

The Window menu opens, as shown in Figure 1-16, displaying the commands Cascade, Tile, and Arrange Icons, followed by a numbered list of the program groups installed on your computer. You might see a check mark next to one of the items, indicating that this program group is the active one. Locate StartUp on the numbered list. If you don't see StartUp, see your instructor or technical support person for assistance.

2 **Click StartUp**

The StartUp group window opens. Depending on how your computer is set up, you might see some program icons already in this window. At this point, your screen is getting cluttered with three program group windows open (Main, Accessories, and StartUp). Use the Cascade command to arrange them in an orderly way.

3 **Click Window on the menu bar, then click Cascade**

The windows appear in a layered arrangement, with the title bars of each showing. This formation is neatly organized and shows all your open group windows, but it doesn't allow you to easily drag the Clock application icon from the Accessories group window to the StartUp group window. The Tile command arranges the windows so that the contents of all the open windows are visible.

4 **Click Window on the menu bar, then click Tile**

The windows are now positioned in an ideal way to drag an icon from one window to another. Before continuing to Step 5, locate the Clock application icon in the Accessories group window. If you don't see the icon, use the scroll bar to bring it into view.

5 **Drag the Clock application icon from the Accessories group window to the StartUp group window**

Your screen now looks like Figure 1-17. The Clock application will automatically start the next time Windows is launched. If you are working on your own computer and want to leave the Clock in the StartUp group, skip Step 6 and continue to the next lesson, "Exiting Windows." If you are working in a computer lab, move the Clock application icon back to its original location in the Accessories group window.

6 **Drag the Clock application icon from the StartUp group window to the Accessories group window**

The Clock icon is now back in the Accessories group.

FIGURE 1-16: Window menu

Check mark indicates the active program group

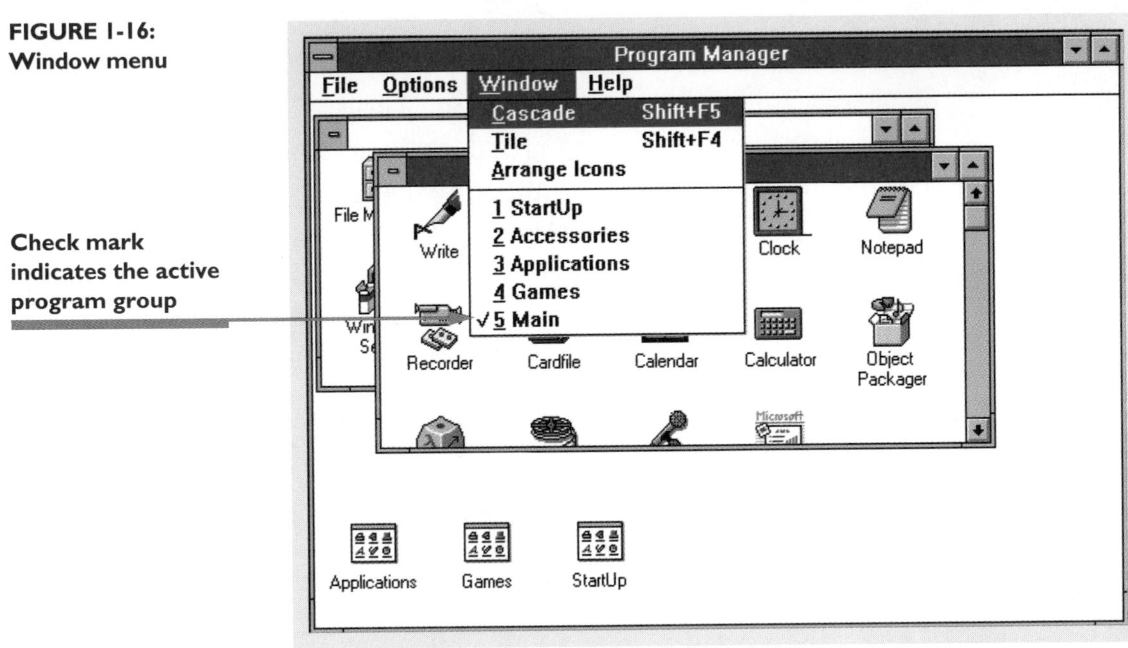

FIGURE 1-17: Tiled group windows

StartUp group window with Clock application icon

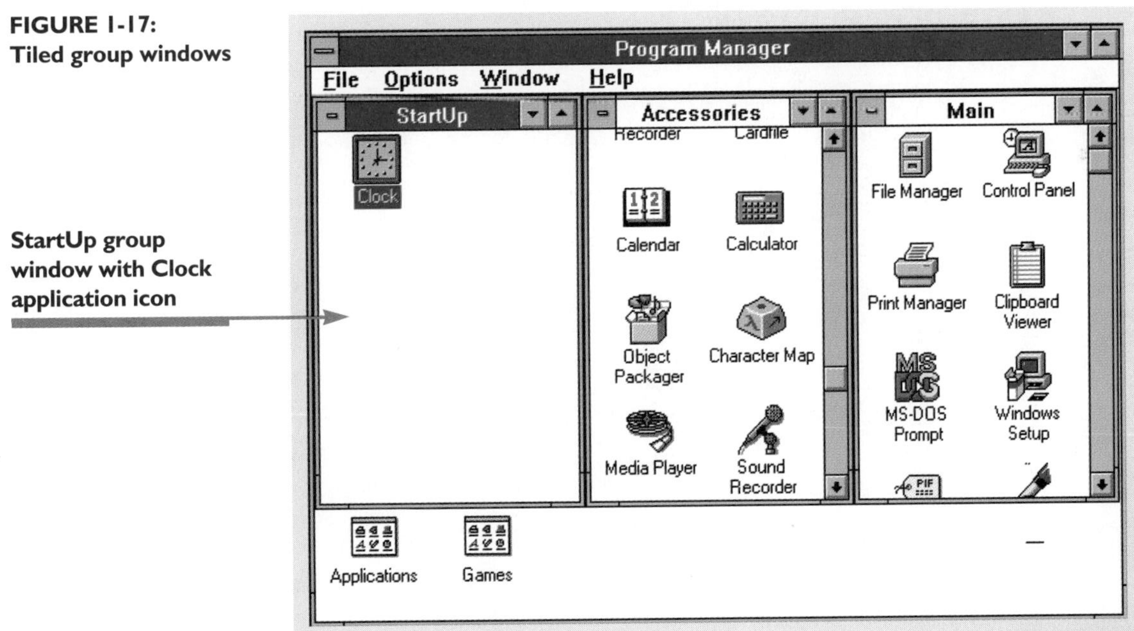

QUICK TIP

To move a copy of an icon from one group window to another, press and hold [Ctrl] as you drag the icon.

Exiting Windows

When you are finished working with Windows, close all the applications you are running and exit Windows from the Program Manager. Do not turn off the computer while Windows is running; you could lose important data if you turn off your computer too soon. For more information, see the related topic "Exiting Windows with the Program Manager control menu box." ▶ Now try closing all your active applications and exiting Windows.

1 **Close any active applications or group windows by double-clicking the control menu boxes on the open windows, one at a time**
The windows close. If you have any unsaved changes in your application, a dialog box opens, asking if you want to save them.

2 Click **File** on the Program Manager menu bar
The File menu opens, as shown in Figure 1-18.

3 Click **Exit Windows**
Program Manager displays the Exit Windows dialog box, as shown in Figure 1-19. You have two options at this point: click OK to exit Windows, or click Cancel to abort the Exit Windows command and return to the Program Manager.

4 Click **OK** to exit Windows
Windows closes and the MS-DOS command prompt appears. You can now safely turn off the computer.

FIGURE 1-18: Exiting Windows using the File menu

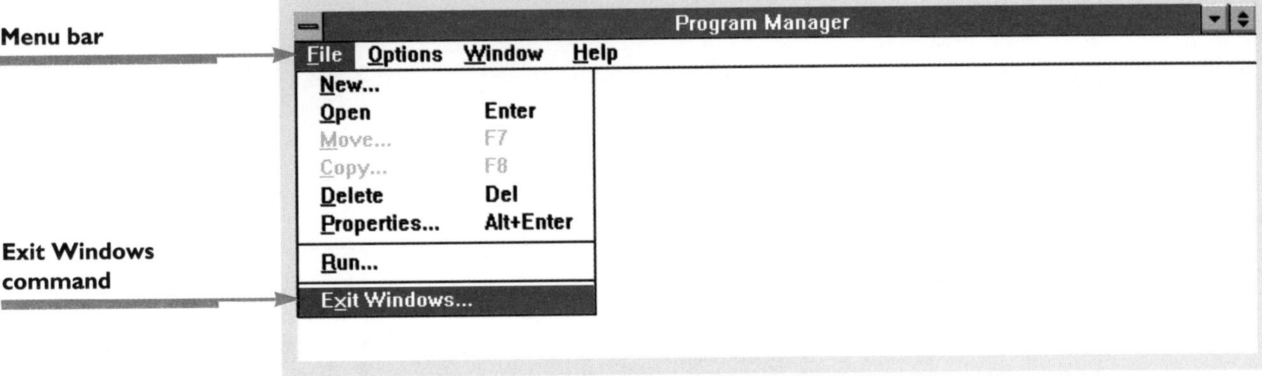

FIGURE 1-19: Exit Windows dialog box

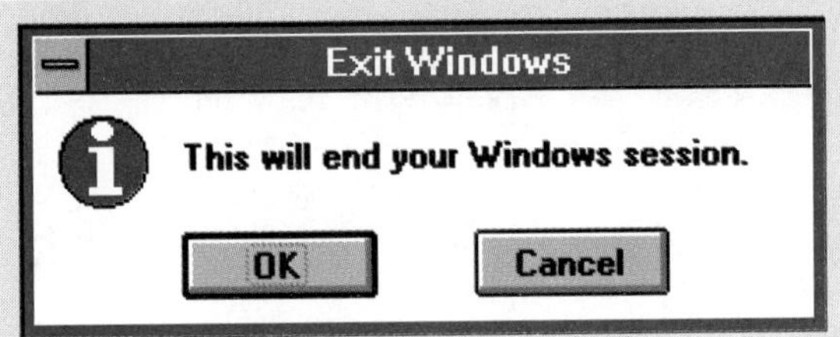

Exiting Windows with the Program Manager control menu box

You can also exit Windows by double-clicking the control menu box in the upper-left corner of the Program Manager window, as shown in Figure 1-20. After you double-click the control menu box, you see the Exit Windows dialog box. Click OK to exit Windows.

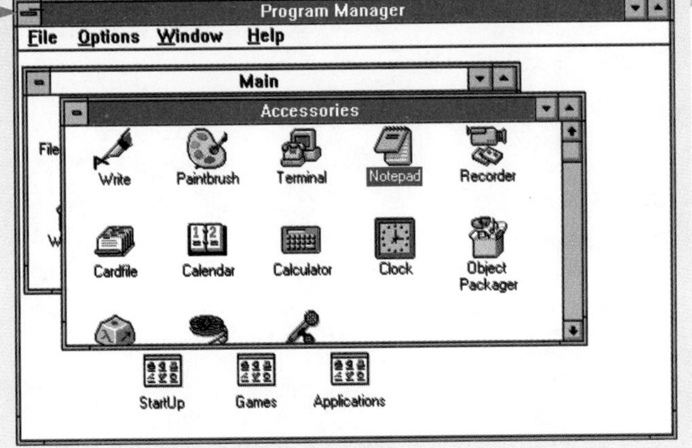

FIGURE 1-20: Exiting Windows with the Program Manager control menu box

TROUBLE?

If you do not exit from Windows before turning off the computer, you might lose data from the applications you used while you were running Windows. Always close your applications and exit from Windows before turning off your computer. Do not turn off the computer if you are in a computer lab.■

CONCEPTSREVIEW

Label each of the elements of the Windows screen shown in Figure 1-21.

1 ____

2 ____

3 ____

4 ____

5 ____

6 ____

7 ____

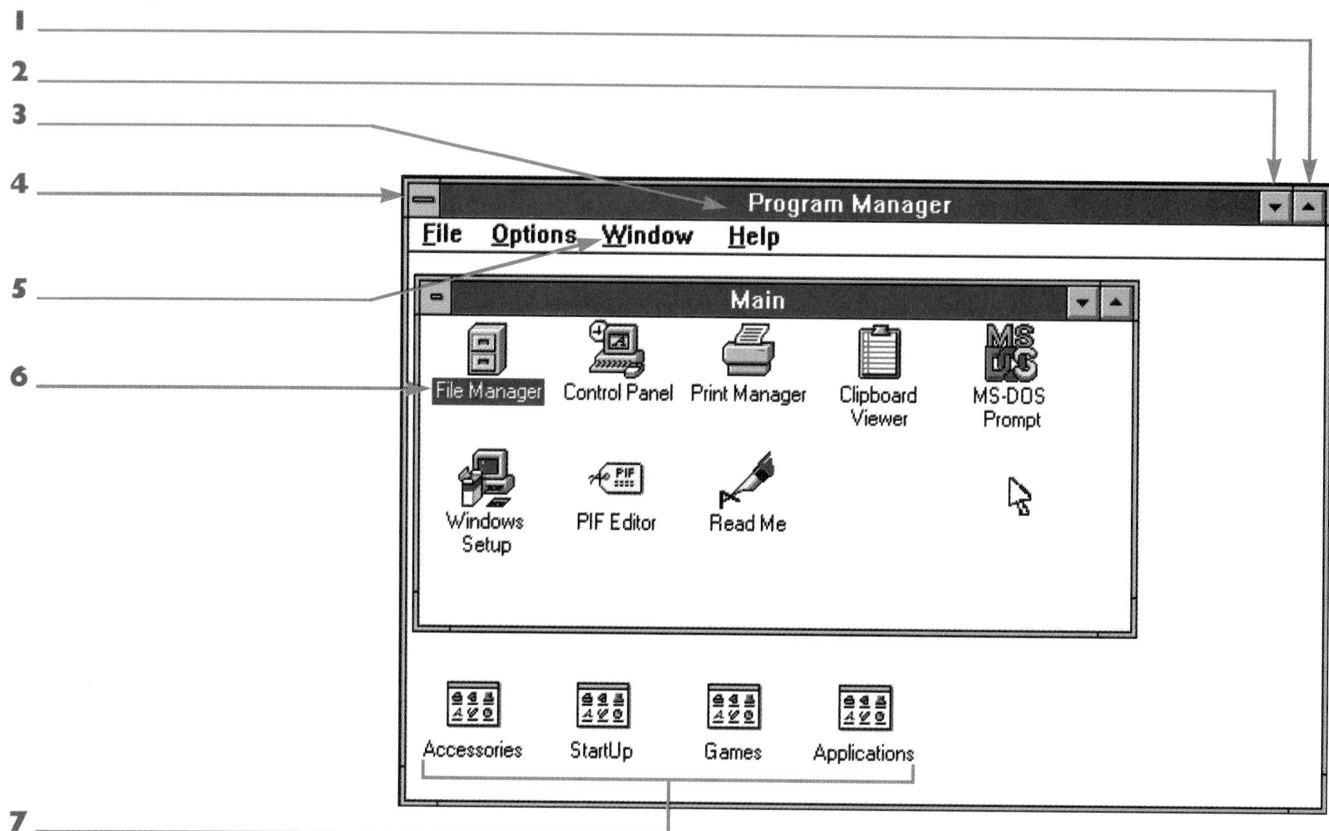

FIGURE 1-21

Match each of the statements with the term it describes.

8 Shrinks an application window to an icon

9 Displays the name of the window or application

10 Serves as a launching pad for all applications

11 Requests more information that you supply before executing command

12 Lets the user point at screen menus and icons

a. Program Manager
b. Dialog box
c. Mouse
d. Title bar
e. Minimize button

Select the best answer from the list of choices.

13 The acronym GUI means
a. Grayed user information
b. Group user icons
c. Graphical user interface
d. Group user interconnect

14 The term for starting Windows is
a. Prompting
b. Launching
c. Applying
d. Processing

15 The small pictures that represent items such as applications are called

a. Icons

b. Windows

c. Buttons

d. Pointers

16 All of the following are examples of using a mouse, EXCEPT:

a. Clicking the Maximize button

b. Pressing [Enter]

c. Pointing at the control menu box

d. Dragging the Games group icon

17 When Windows is busy performing a task, the mouse pointer changes to a(n)

a. Hand

b. Arrow

c Clock

d. Hourglass

18 The term for moving an item to a new location on the desktop is

a. Pointing

b. Clicking

c. Dragging

d. Restoring

19 The Clock, Notepad, and Calendar applications in Windows are known as

a. Menu commands

b. Control panels

c. Sizing buttons

d. Desktop accessories

20 The Maximize button is used to

a. Return a window to its original size

b. Expand a window to fill the computer screen

c. Scroll slowly through a window

d. Run programs from the main menu

21 What appears if a window contains more information than can be displayed in the window?

a. Program icon

b. Cascading menu

c. Scroll bars

d. Check box

22 A window is active when its title bar is

a. Highlighted

b. Dimmed

c. Checked

d. Underlined

23 What is the term for changing the dimensions of a window?

a. Selecting

b. Resizing

c. Navigating

d. Scrolling

24 The menu bar provides access to an application's functions through

a. Icons

b. Scroll bars

c. Commands

d. Control menu box

25 When your desktop is too cluttered, you can organize it by all the following methods, EXCEPT:

a. Double-clicking the control menu box to close unneeded windows

b. Using the Tile command to view all open group windows

c. Using the Cascade command to open group window title bars

d. Clicking File, clicking Exit Windows, then clicking OK

26 You can exit Windows by double-clicking the

a. Accessories group icon

b. Program Manager control menu box

c. Main window menu bar

d. Control Panel application

APPLICATIONS REVIEW

1 Start Windows and identify items on the screen.

a. Turn on the computer, if necessary.

b. At the command prompt, Launch Windows. After Windows loads and the Program Manager appears, try to identify as many items on the desktop as you can, without referring to the lesson material. Then compare your results with Figure 1-1.

2 Minimize and restore the Program Manager window.

a. Click the Minimize button. Notice that the Program Manager window shrinks to an icon at the bottom of the screen. Now try restoring the window.

b. Double-click the Program Manager icon. The Program Manager window opens.

c. Practice minimizing and restoring other windows on the desktop.

3 Resize and move the Program Manager window.

a. Activate the Program Manager window.

b. Resize the Program Manager window up and to the right until the Program Manager takes up the top third of your screen.

c. Drag the Program Manager title bar to reposition the window at the bottom of the screen.

4 Practice working with menus and dialog boxes.

a. Open the Accessories group.

b. Start the Calculator application.

c. Click numbers and operators as you would on a handheld calculator to perform some simple arithmetic operations.

d. Close the Calculator window when you are finished.

e. Start the Clock application.

f. Using the Settings menu on the Clock menu bar, change the display from digital to analog or analog to digital.

g. Change the settings back, then exit the Clock application.

5 Exit Windows.

a. Close any open applications.

b. Using the control menu box of the Program Manager window, exit Windows. The Exit Windows dialog box appears.

c. Click OK. Windows closes and the MS-DOS command prompt appears.

INDEPENDENT CHALLENGE

Microsoft Windows 3.1 provides an on-line tutorial that can help you master essential Windows controls and concepts. The tutorial features interactive lessons that teach you how to use Windows elements such as the mouse, Program Manager, menus, and icons. The tutorial also covers how to use Help.

The tutorial material you should use depends on your level of experience with Windows. Some users might want to review the basics of Windows. Others might want to explore additional and advanced Windows topics, such as managing files and customizing windows.

Ask your instructor or technical support person about how to use the Windows tutorial.

To complete this challenge:

1 Turn on the computer and start Windows if necessary.

2 Click Help on the Program Manager menu bar.

3 Click Windows Tutorial.

4 After the introductory screen, read the instructions that appear on the screen.

5 Continue through the tutorial.

6 You can press [Esc] at any time during the tutorial if you want to exit it.

7 Exit Windows when you complete the on-line tutorial.

UNIT 2

OBJECTIVES

- Create and save a Paintbrush file
- Start and view File Manager
- Create a directory
- Move, copy, and rename files
- Format and copy disks

Creating AND MANAGING FILES

Now that you have learned the basics of Microsoft Windows 3.1, you can explore its file management features. In this unit, you will create a file using **Paintbrush**, a drawing program that comes with Windows, then learn how File Manager can help you organize the files you create. Finally, you will learn how to copy and format disks. To complete this unit you will need a Student Disk. For more information on your Student Disk, refer to the page entitled "Read This Before You Begin Microsoft Windows 3.1" at the beginning of this book. ▶

Creating and saving a Paintbrush file

Much of your work with Windows will involve creating and saving different types of files. The files you create using a computer are stored in the computer's random access memory (RAM). **RAM** is a temporary storage space that is erased when the computer is turned off. To store a file permanently, you need to save it to a disk. You can save your work to either a 3.5-inch or 5.25-inch disk, also known as a **floppy disk**, which you insert into the drive of your computer (i.e., drive A or drive B), or a hard disk, which is built into your computer (usually drive C). ▶ In this lesson you will create a file using Paintbrush, then you will save the Paintbrush file to your Student Disk.

1. Make sure your Student Disk is in the disk drive
2. In Program Manager double-click the Accessories group icon, then double-click the **Paintbrush application icon** to start Paintbrush
   The Paintbrush window opens on your screen. Notice the title and menu bars across the top. Along the left side of the window is the Toolbox and Linesize box. The white rectangular area, called the **drawing area**, is where you draw. The **color palette**, which contains the colors you can use to paint with, are at the bottom of the window.
3. Click the maximize button, if necessary, to maximize the window, then click the Brush tool
   The Brush tool is a freehand drawing tool that you will control with your mouse. See Table 2-1 for a description of each of the Paintbrush tools.
4. In the Linesize box, click the **thickest line width**
   The selection arrow moves down to the left of the thickest line. Make sure the black colored box appears in the color selection area. See Figure 2-1. Now you are ready to create a simple picture.
5. Move the mouse pointer onto the drawing area of the Paintbrush window, press and hold the **left mouse button**, drag the mouse in a large circle, then release the mouse button
6. Add eyes and a mouth inside the circle to create a smiling face
   Next, you will add color to the image.
7. Click the **Paint Roller tool** in the Toolbox, click the **yellow box** (top row, fourth from left), then point inside the smiling face and click
   The Paint Roller fills the area with the currently selected color.

Turn to page W30 to compare your screen to Figure 2-2 and save this file to your Student Disk.

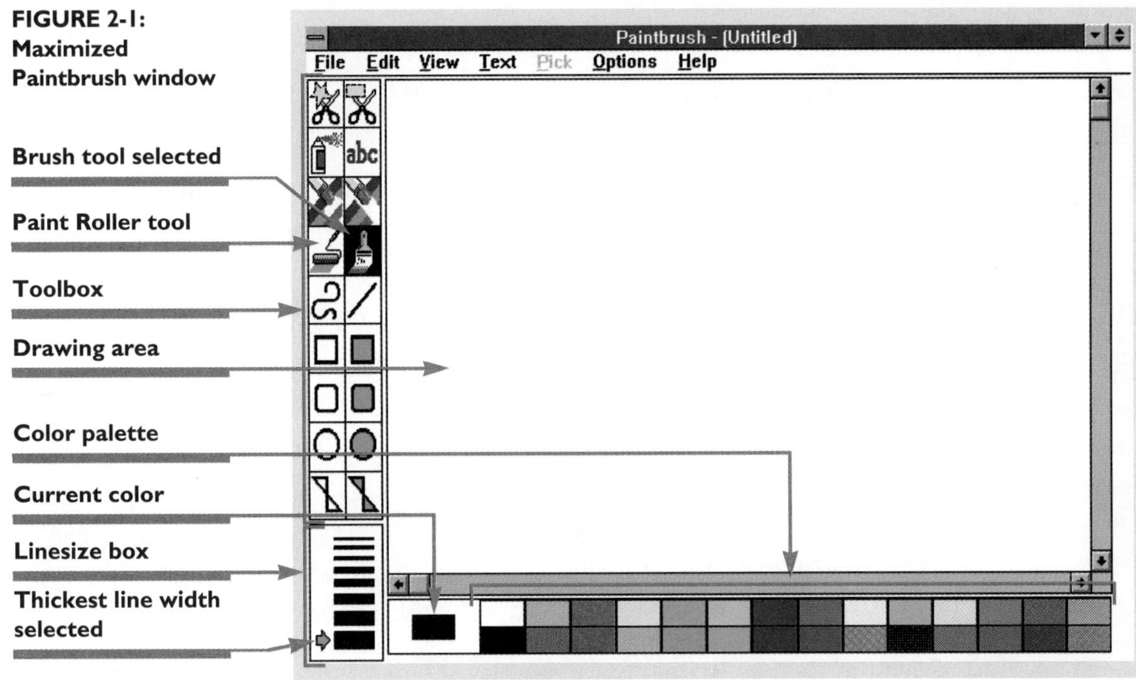

FIGURE 2-1: Maximized Paintbrush window

TABLE 2-1: Paintbrush Tools

TOOL	DESCRIPTION	TOOL	DESCRIPTION
	Use to define a free-form cutout		Use to define a rectangular cutout
	Use to produce a circular spray of dots	abc	Use to add text to your drawings
	Use to change the selected foreground color under the cursor to the selected background color or use to change every occurrence of one color in the drawing area to another color		Use to change all the foreground colors that it touches to the selected background color
	Use to fill any closed shape or area with the selected foreground color		Use to draw freehand shapes and lines in the selected foreground color and drawing width
	Use to draw curved lines in the selected foreground color and drawing width		Use to draw straight lines in the selected foreground color and drawing width
	Use to draw hollow squares or rectangles in the selected foreground color and drawing width		Use to draw squares or rectangles that are filled with the selected foreground color and bordered with the selected background color
	Use the same way as the box tool above; the difference is these boxes have rounded corners		Use the same way as the filled box tool above; the difference is these boxes have rounded corners
	Use to draw hollow circles or ellipses in the selected foreground color and drawing width		Use to draw circles or ellipses that are filled with the selected foreground color and bordered with the selected background color
	Use to draw polygons from connected straight-line segments in the selected foreground color and drawing width		Use to draw polygons that are filled with the selected foreground color and bordered by the selected background color

Creating and saving a Paintbrush file, continued

Compare the file you just created to Figure 2-2. Don't worry if your file looks slightly different from Figure 2-2. If you want to start over, see the TROUBLE? on the next page. Now, you need to save the Paintbrush file to your Student Disk. You will find the Save and Save As commands on the File menu in most Windows applications.

8 Click **File** on the menu bar, then click **Save As**
The Save As dialog box opens, as shown in Figure 2-3. This dialog box allows you to choose a disk drive, directory, filename, and file type for your image.

9 Type **smile** in the File Name text box
Your entry replaces the highlighted (selected) *.bmp, which is the **file extension** that identifies the type of file you created. Paintbrush will automatically add this file extension when you click OK. Now you need to specify the drive where your Student Disk is located.

10 Click the **Drives list arrow** to display the drives on your computer, click **a:** or **b:** depending on which drive contains your Student Disk, then click **OK**
The Save As dialog box closes and SMILE.BMP is now saved to your Student Disk. Next, you'll exit Paintbrush.

11 Click **File** on the menu bar, then click **Exit**
The Paintbrush application window closes.

FIGURE 2-2: The Paintbrush window with smiling face

FIGURE 2-3: Save As dialog box

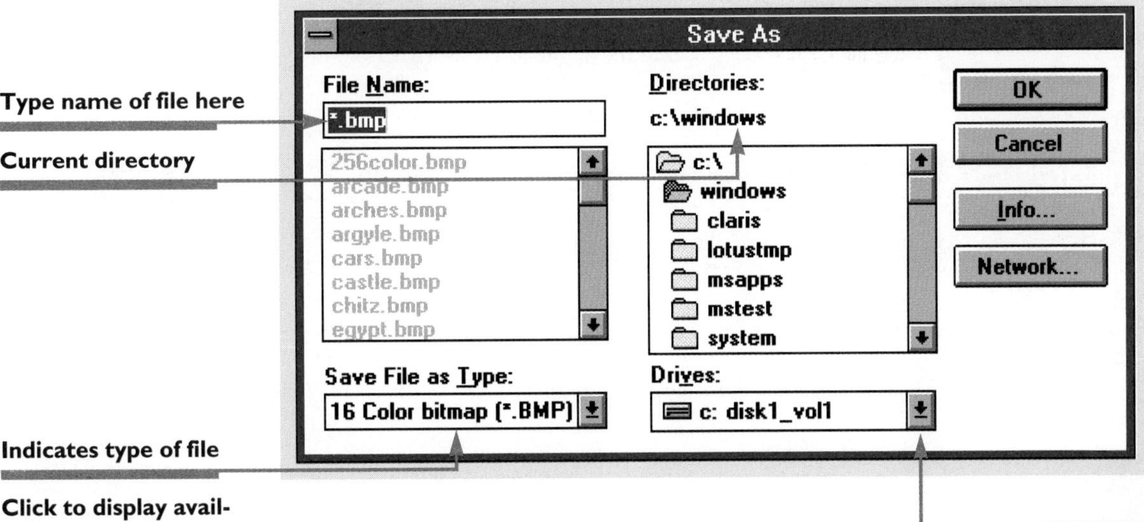

TROUBLE?

If you made a mistake while painting and want to start over, click File on the menu bar, click New, then click No when asked to save the previous image.

Starting and viewing File Manager

Windows comes with an application called **File Manager** that you can use to organize your files. Moving, copying, deleting, renaming, and searching for specific files are just some of the many tasks you can accomplish using File Manager. ▶ Use File Manager to view the contents of your Student Disk and become familiar with the various parts of the File Manager window.

1 In the Program Manager window, double-click the **Main group icon**, or if the window is already open, click the **Main group window** to activate it, then double-click the **File Manager application icon**
The File Manager window opens, as shown in Figure 2-4. Your File Manager will contain different drives and directories. The **directory window** is divided by the **split bar**. The left side of the directory window displays the structure of the current drive, which is drive C, or the **directory tree**. The right side of the directory window displays a list of files and subdirectories in the selected directory. See Table 2-2 for a description of the various icons used in the directory window. The status bar displays the information about the current drive and directory and other information to help you with file management tasks.

2 Click the **drive icon** that corresponds to the drive containing your Student Disk
An hourglass icon appears as File Manager reads the drive containing your Student Disk. After a moment, File Manager displays the contents of your Student Disk. See Table 2-3 for a description of the various drive icons.

3 Scroll, if necessary, to find SMILE.BMP, the file you created in the previous lesson
With File Manager open, continue to the next lesson where you'll create a directory on your Student Disk.

TABLE 2-2: Directory window icons

ICON	DESCRIPTION
↑..	Displays the contents of a directory one level up in the directory tree
	Represents a directory
+	Represents a directory that contains additional directories not displayed in the directory tree
−	Represents a directory that contains additional directories that are displayed in the directory tree
	Represents an open directory; the files in this directory are listed in the right side of the directory window
	Represents an application file; these files start applications or start programs
	Represents a document file associated with an application; when you double-click this icon, the application that you used to create it starts
	Represents other document files
!	Represents hidden, system, read-only files

FIGURE 2-4: File Manager window

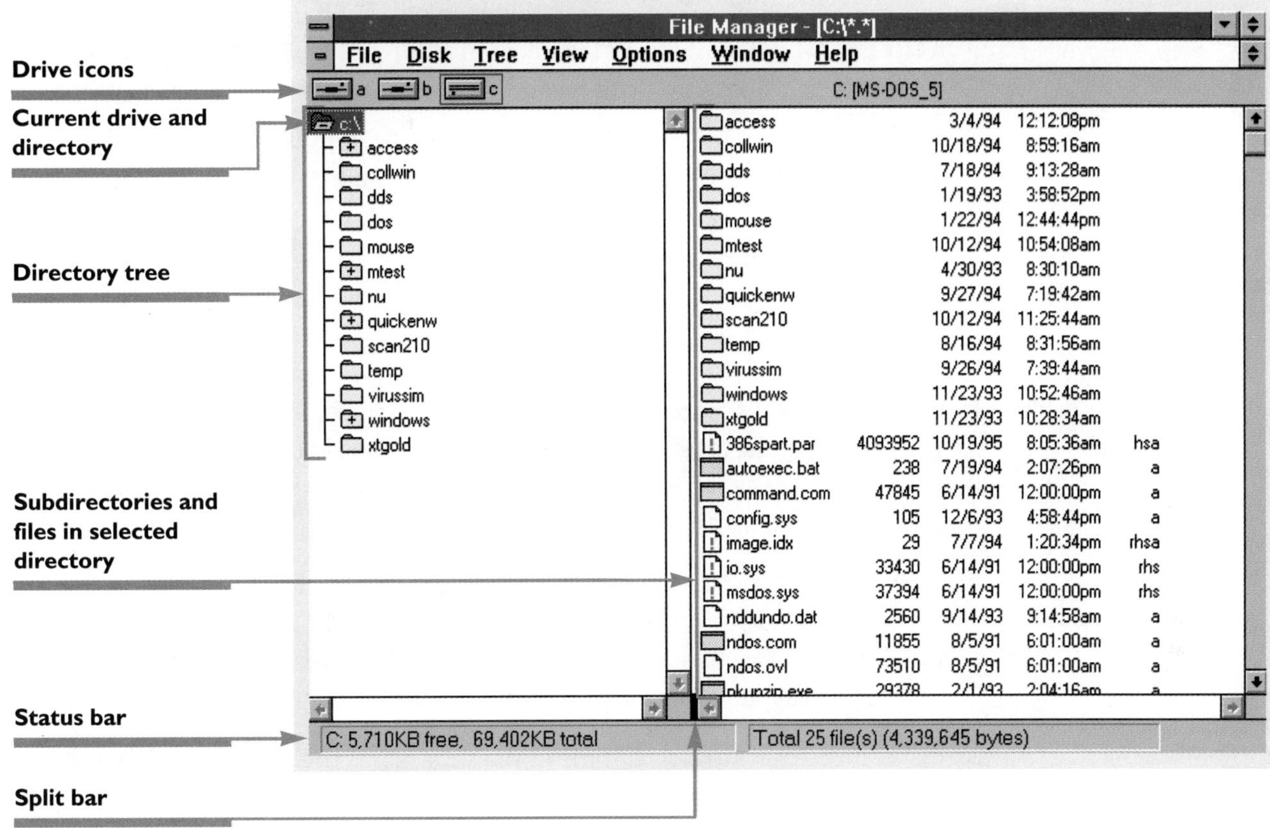

TABLE 2-3: Drive Icons

DRIVE ICON	TYPE OF DRIVE
	Floppy drive
	Hard drive
	Network drive
	CD ROM drive

TROUBLE?

Click the maximize button in the File Manager window to maximize this window.

Creating a directory

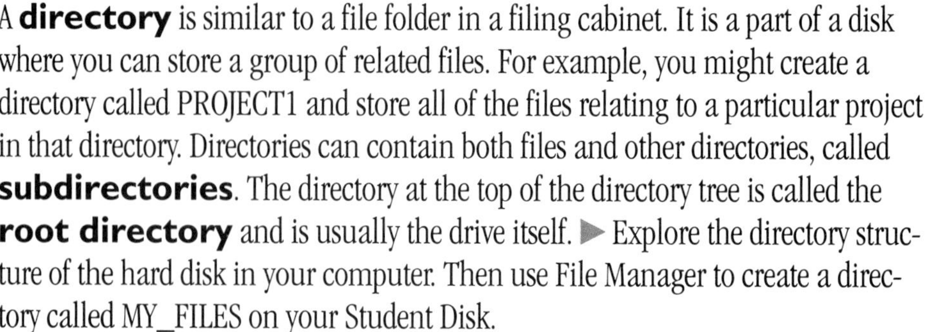

A **directory** is similar to a file folder in a filing cabinet. It is a part of a disk where you can store a group of related files. For example, you might create a directory called PROJECT1 and store all of the files relating to a particular project in that directory. Directories can contain both files and other directories, called **subdirectories**. The directory at the top of the directory tree is called the **root directory** and is usually the drive itself. ▶ Explore the directory structure of the hard disk in your computer. Then use File Manager to create a directory called MY_FILES on your Student Disk.

1 **Click the drive C icon to display the contents of this drive**
The directories appear in the left side of the directory window and a list of the files and directories in the selected directory appear in the right side of the window. You can use the Tree menu to see all of the branches of the directory tree.

2 **Click Tree on the menu bar, then click Expand All**
You can now view the entire tree structure of drive C, or the root directory, as shown in Figure 2-5. You might have to scroll up and down to view all the subdirectories. Now that you can navigate through a directory tree you are ready to create a directory on your Student Disk.

3 **Make sure your Student Disk is in the disk drive, then click the drive A icon (or the drive B icon if your Student Disk is in drive B)**
File Manager pauses while your computer reads the contents of your Student Disk. You want to create the directory below the root directory.

4 **Click File on the menu bar, then click Create Directory**
The Create Directory dialog box opens. The Current Directory line should read A:\. You will name the new directory MY_FILES. Directory names can have up to 11 characters but cannot include spaces, commas, or backslashes.

5 **Type my_files in the Name text box, then click OK**
Be sure to type the underscore. This new directory appears on your Student Disk, as shown in Figure 2-6. You can use this directory to store all of the files you create and save. In the next lesson, you will move the SMILE.BMP file into this directory.

FIGURE 2-5: Directory tree

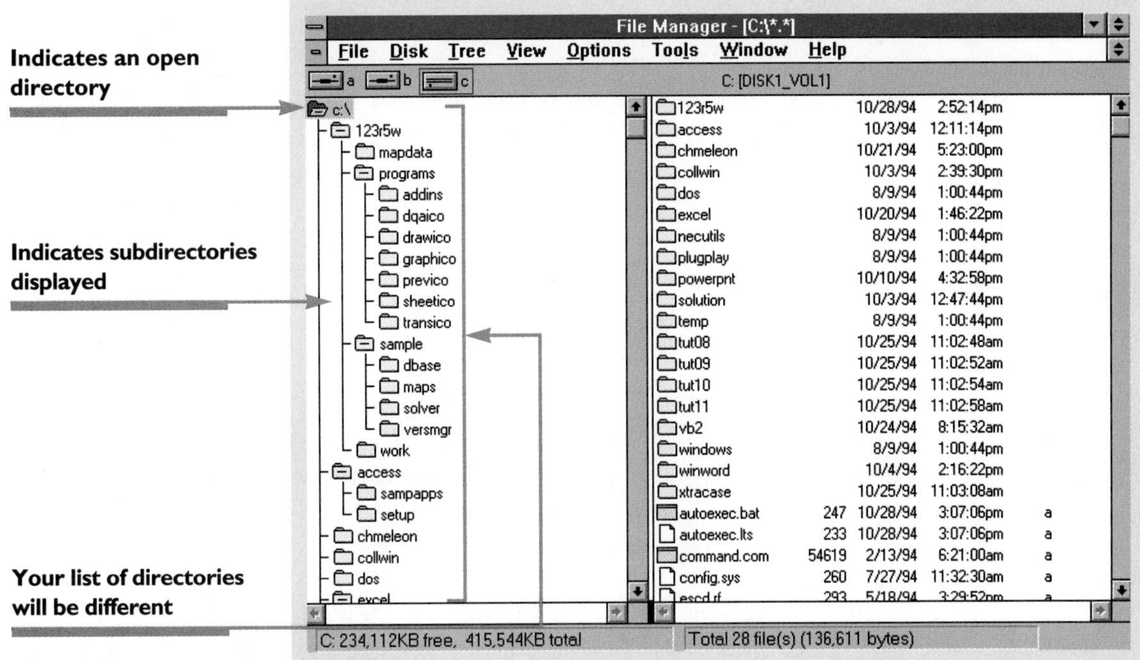

FIGURE 2-6: MY_FILES directory on your Student Disk

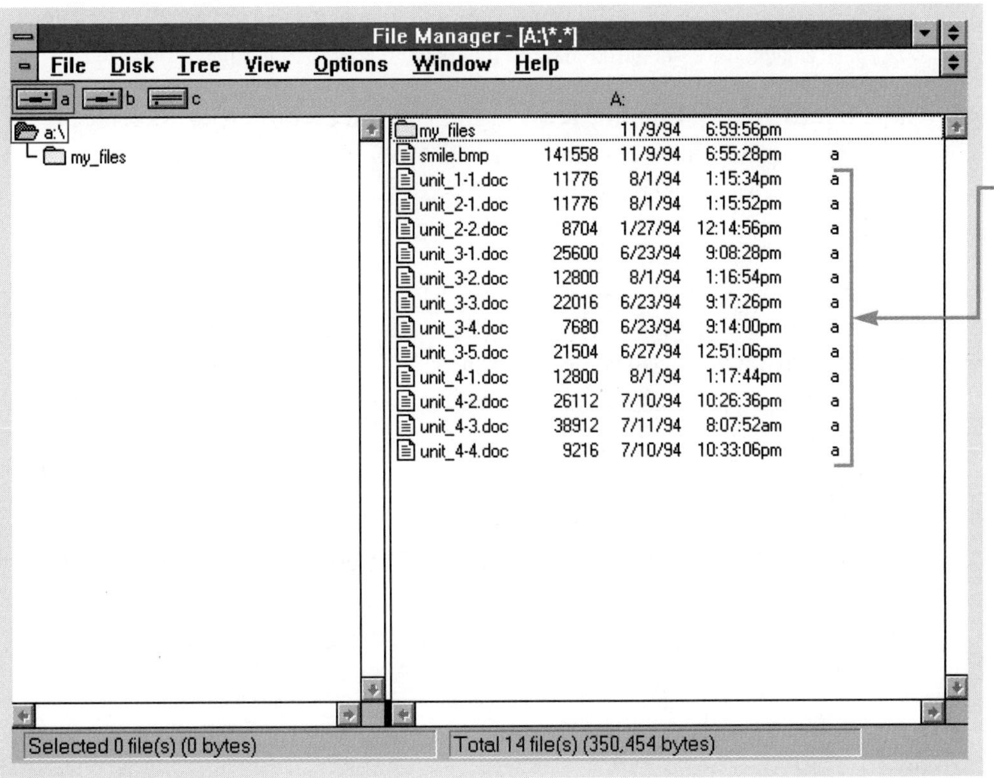

TROUBLE?

If you create the directory in the wrong place, select it then press [Delete]. Two confirmation dialog boxes will appear. They will ask you if you are sure you want to delete the directory. Make *absolutely sure* that you selected the MY_FILES directory. Click YES in both dialog boxes, then create the directory again.■

Moving, copying, and renaming files

File Manager allows you to move, copy, and rename files and directories. These commands appear on the File menu. Often you will need to move files from one drive or directory to another. At other times you might want to copy a file to create an identical file in a new location. ▶ Use File Manager to move the SMILE.BMP file to the MY_FILES directory on your Student Disk. Then, make a copy of this file and rename it.

1 Make sure that File Manager displays the root directory on your Student Disk

2 Click the **SMILE.BMP file icon**, then drag it slowly to the left
The mouse pointer changes to [icon], as shown in Figure 2-7. The new pointer shape indicates that you are performing a drag-and-drop operation. **Drag-and-drop** is one method for moving and copying files. You can also move files by clicking Move on the File menu, then typing the filenames of the files you wish to move.

3 Drag the SMILE.BMP file icon over the MY_FILES directory on your Student Disk until the MY_FILES directory is selected, then release the mouse button and click Yes to confirm
The file does not appear in the root directory anymore—it appears in the MY_FILES directory. Don't worry if you move a file to the wrong place; simply drag it again to the correct location. Now, make a backup copy of SMILE.BMP in the root directory of your Student Disk.

4 Click the **SMILE.BMP file icon** in the MY_FILES directory to select it, click **File** on the menu bar, then click **Copy**
The Copy Dialog box opens, as shown in Figure 2-8. It shows the current directory and the currently selected files. You need to type the new location in the To text box.

5 Type **a:** in the To text box, then click **OK**
File Manager creates a copy of SMILE.BMP on the root directory of your Student Disk. Note that you can also copy files using the Drag-and-Drop method. Simply press [Ctrl] as you drag the file. The mouse pointer changes to [icon].

Now you can rename the file using a backup extension, .BAK. See Table 2-4 for a description of some other file extensions.

6 Click the **SMILE.BMP file icon** on the root directory, click **File** on the menu bar, then click **Rename**
The Rename dialog box opens with SMILE.BMP in the From text box. You will type the new name in the To text box.

7 Click in the To text box to place the insertion point if necessary, type **smile.bak**, then click **OK**
You should now have two copies of the Paintbrush file on your Student Disk: one in the MY_FILES directory, and a backup in the root directory.

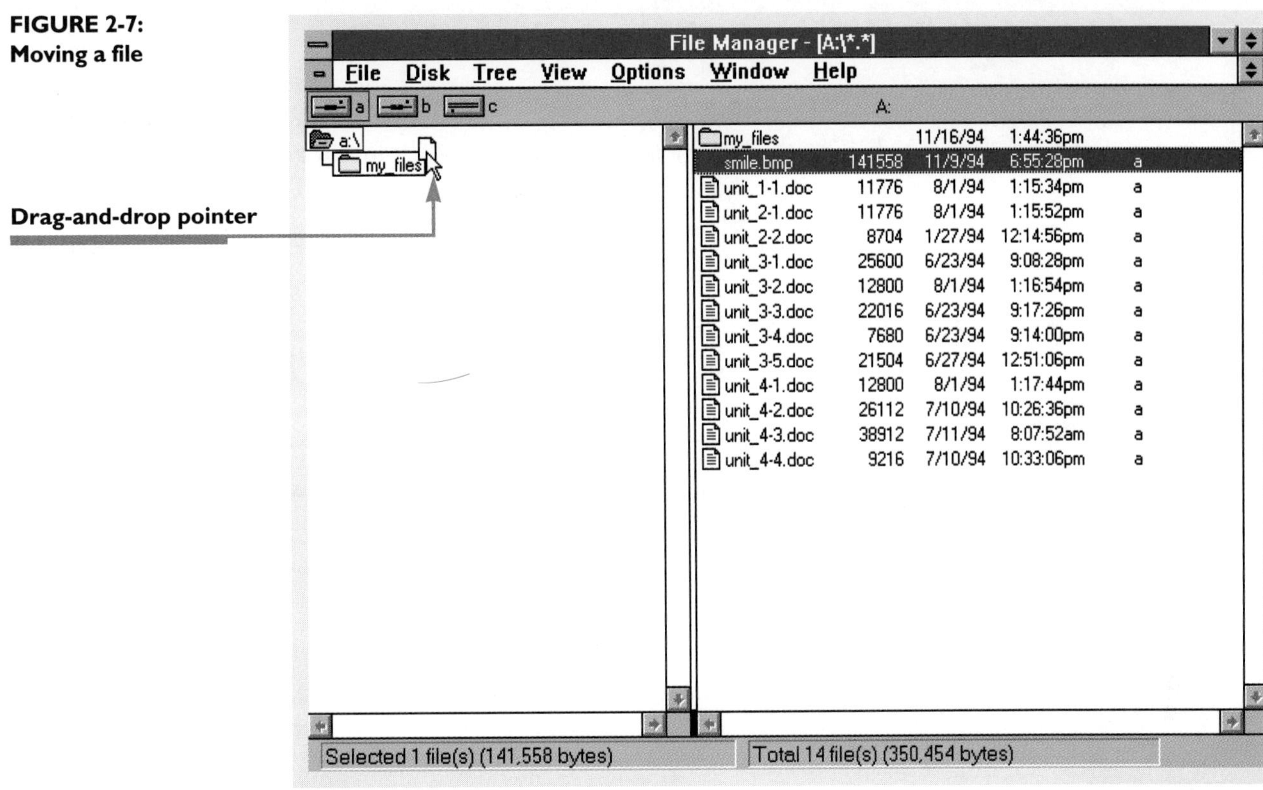

FIGURE 2-7: Moving a file

FIGURE 2-8: Copy dialog box

Copy
Current Directory: A:\MY_FILES
From: SMILE.BMP
To:
Copy to Clipboard
OK
Cancel
Help

QUICK TIP

To select several files for moving or copying, press and hold [Ctrl] while clicking each file icon. Your mouse pointer will change to when you drag them to another location.

TABLE 2-4: Common file extensions

EXTENSION	FILE TYPE	EXTENSION	FILE TYPE
.txt	Text file	.exe	Executable files
.doc	MS Word document file	.com	Executable files
.bmp	Windows bitmap file	.bat	Batch files
.xls	MS Excel spreadsheet file	.wri	Windows Write file
.tmp	Temporary file	.drv	Windows driver file
.wmf	Windows metafile	.hlp	Help file
.wk4	Lotus 1-2-3 worksheet file	.bak	Backup file

Formatting and copying disks

You must format disks before using them. **Formatting** a disk erases any data on it and allows a computer to read it. You use File Manager to format disks and to copy the entire contents of one disk to another disk. You should make backup copies of your most important disks (for example, program disks). ▶ ***Do not complete these steps until your instructor tells you to.*** Read these steps now to become familiar with the process of formatting and copying disks.

1. **Place an unformatted, 3.5-inch disk in drive A or drive B**
2. **Click Disk on the File Manager menu bar, then click Format Disk**
   The Format Disk dialog box opens. This dialog box contains a list box to select both the drive and the capacity of the disk you want to format. **Capacity** indicates whether the disk is double density or high density. See Table 2-5 for a description of each command on the Disk menu.
3. **Select the appropriate drive and capacity, then click OK**
   Figure 2-9 shows an example of how your dialog box might look if you want to format a 1.44 MB high density disk in drive A. Another dialog box opens, warning you that all data will be erased from your disk.
4. **Click Yes**
   A dialog box opens, indicating that the disk is being initialized. When the operation is complete, File Manager displays a dialog box, showing the amount of space on your newly formatted disk. The dialog box also asks if you want to format another disk.
5. **Click No**
   Remove the formatted disk from the drive and attach a disk label that identifies the contents of the disk. Now you are ready to copy information to this disk.
6. **Click Disk on the menu bar, click Copy, then specify the source and destination drives**
   The Copy dialog box opens with two list boxes. Use these boxes to specify the source and destination drives. When copying a disk, File Manager takes all the information from one disk, called the **source**, and copies it onto a new disk, called the **destination**. Be careful what you use for a destination disk because all of its original information will be lost. Also, the Copy command will only work if both disks are of the same type, for example, both 3.5-inch high-density disks. Figure 2-10 shows an example of this completed dialog box.
7. **Place your source disk in the appropriate drive, then click OK**
   A dialog box appears to warn you that all data will be lost on the destination disk.
8. **Click Yes then press [Enter] when you are prompted to insert the source disk**
   Copy shows its progress as a percentage as it copies the source disk into memory. At some point, Copy will stop reading from the source disk and ask you to insert the destination disk.
9. **Remove your source disk and insert your destination disk, then click OK**
   File Manager now places all the information from the source disk onto the destination disk.
10. **Double-click the control menu box in the File Manager window to exit File Manager**

FIGURE 2-9: Format dialog box

Check the drive and capacity before clicking OK

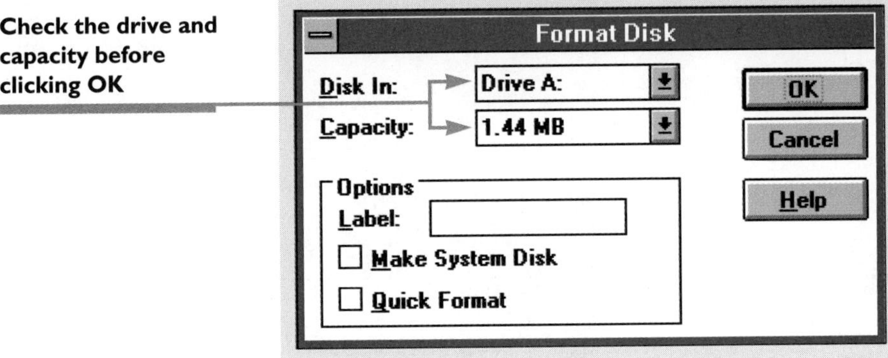

FIGURE 2-10: Completed Copy Disk dialog box

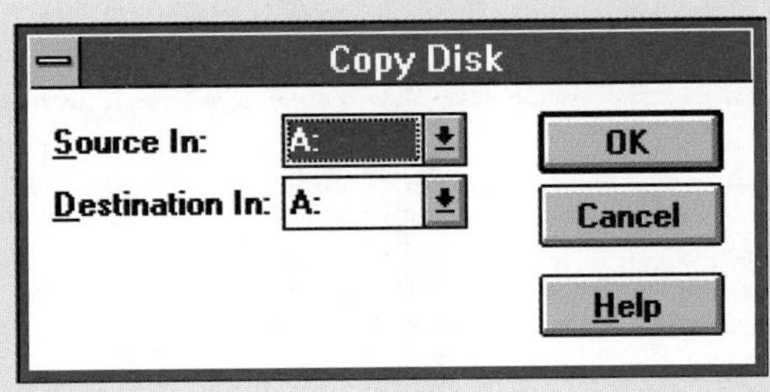

TABLE 2-5: Disk menu commands

COMMAND	DESCRIPTION
Copy Disk	Copies a floppy disk
Label Disk	Assigns an electronic label to a disk
Format Disk	Makes a floppy disk usable to your computer
Make System Disk	Copies special system files to a disk
Select Drive	Chooses a drive to view

TROUBLE?

If you're not sure if your disk is formatted, place it in the drive and click the corresponding drive icon. If File Manager can read the disk, it is already formatted.

CONCEPTS REVIEW

Label each of the elements of the File Manager window shown in Figure 2-11.

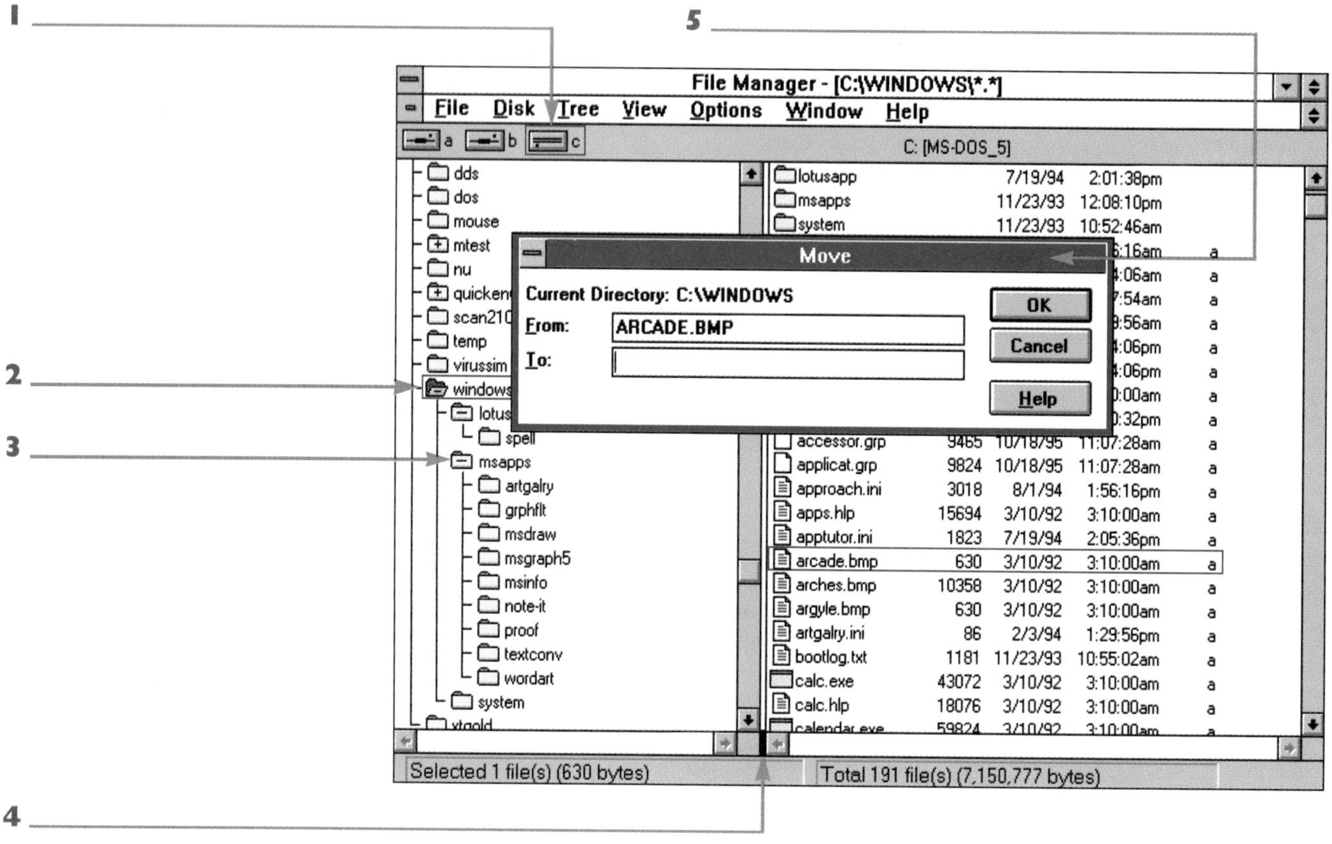

1 ______

2 ______

3 ______

4 ______

5 ______

FIGURE 2-11

Match each of the descriptions with the appropriate icon.

6 
7
8
9
10

a. Directory that contains other undisplayed directories

b. Document or File associated with an application

c. Application File

d. Up one directory

e. Directory

11 Which extension is associated with Paintbrush files?

a. .txt

b. .bmp

c. .tmp

d. .wk4

Select the best answer from the list of choices.

12 Which tool would you use to add text to your Paintbrush drawing?

a. 

b.

c. abc

d.

13 File Manager is a Windows application that lets you

a. Select different desktop wallpaper

b. Move a file from one location to another

c. Type entries into a text file

d. Determine what programs begin automatically when you start Windows

14 In which program group can you usually find the File Manager application icon?

a. Accessories

b. File Manager

c. Startup

d. Main

15 The temporary storage space used by your computer when you work is called

a. A hard disk

b. RAM

c. A monitor

d. A file

16 For most Windows applications, the Save command is usually located on which menu?

a. File

b. Edit

c. Help

d. Save

17 The icon that File Manager uses to represent a floppy drive is

a.

b.

c.

d.

18 C:\ means

a. The root directory on drive C

b. It is a subdirectory

c. Not on drive C

d. All of the above

19 A directory tree is

a. A listing of file contents

b. A list of drives

c. The way File Manager organizes your directories

d. None of the above

20 If you want to backup a file on your disk

a. Copy the file and rename the original file using the .BAK extension

b. Click Backup on the File menu

c. Rename the file using the .BAK extension

d. Move the file to a backup directory

21 When you copy a disk, the source disk

a. Is the location where files will be placed

b. Contains the information that will be placed on the second disk

c. Is the same as the destination disk

d. Will be erased

22 Before a computer can read or write to a disk, you must __________ it.

a. Copy

b. Format

c. Erase

d. Open

APPLICATIONS REVIEW

1 Create and save a Paintbrush file.

a. Start Windows, then start Paintbrush.

b. Create your own unique, colorful design using several colors with several of Paintbrush's tools.

c. Insert your Student Disk in the appropriate disk drive, then save the picture as ART.BMP to the MY_FILES directory.

d. Exit Paintbrush.

2 Start and view File Manager.

a. Open File Manager.

b. Be sure your Student Disk is in either drive A or drive B, then double-click the drive icon containing your Student Disk.

c. Double-click the drive C icon.

d. Double-click the c:\ directory icon on the left side of the drive C window, then scroll down the left side of the drive window to see the available directories. When you see the Windows directory icon, double-click it to see the directories and files available in the Windows directory.

3 Create a Directory.

a. Create a subdirectory under the MY_FILES directory on your Student Disk.

b. Click the drive A icon to display the contents of your Student Disk. The new subdirectory will go below the MY_FILES directory.

c. Click the MY_FILES directory icon on the left side of the window. This tells File manager that the new subdirectory will go below the MY_FILES directory.

d. Click File on the menu bar, then click Create Directory. The Create Directory dialog box opens and prompts you to name the new directory. Type "unit2" in the Name text box, then click OK.

e. If you don't want to keep this directory on your disk, click the UNIT2 directory, then press [del] to delete this directory.

4 Move, copy, and rename files.

a. Copy the ART.BMP file into the root directory on your Student Disk.

b. Rename the ART.BMP file in the root directory ART.BAK.

c. Move the ART.BAK file into the MY_FILES directory on your Student Disk.

5 Format and copy a disk.

a. Format a new blank disk using the Format Disk command on the Disk menu. Check that the drive and capacity is correct.

b. Make a copy of your Student Disk using the Copy Disk command on the Disk menu. In the Copy dialog box, make sure that drive A (or drive B) is both the source and the destination drive, then click OK. Your Student Disk is the source disk.

c. When File Manager prompts you, remove your Student Disk and insert the newly formatted disk. This is the destination disk.

d. Close File Manager, then exit Windows.

INDEPENDENT CHALLENGE

It is important to develop a sound, organized plan when you manage files and directories. Practice your skills by organizing the following list of names into a coherent and logical directory tree. Rewrite the following list of directories as it might appear in File Manager. Pay special attention to the contents of each directory and use as many or few subdirectories as you feel are necessary. Feel free to use the directory tree on your computer as a model for your work. Also, you might want to create a directory to hold related subdirectories.

C:\	
\wrdprcsr	(Word Processor)
\sprdshet	(Spreadsheet)
\graphs	
\sheets	
\resumes	
\report92	
\report93	
\docs	
\pong	(Game)
\blaster	(Game)
\report94	
\windows	
\system	
\games	

Glossary

Active application The software program you are currently working in, indicated by a highlighted title bar.

Active window The window you are currently working in, indicated by a highlighted title bar.

Applications Useful, task-oriented software programs.

Check box The box you click that turns a dialog box option on or off.

Click To press and release the mouse button one time. You click to select items, choose commands, and work in applications.

Command button The button you click that executes the dialog box command.

Command prompt Usually represented as C:\>, it gives you access to MS-DOS commands and applications.

Copy To create a duplicate item. You can choose to place this duplicate item in a new location.

Cursor The blinking vertical line that indicates where you are on the screen. Also known as the insertion point.

Dialog box A box that opens giving you more options for executing a command.

Dimmed command A menu command that is not currently available.

Directory tree A graphical structure of a directory that shows the root directory, files, and subdirectories.

Double-click To press the mouse button twice quickly. You double-click to start and exit applications.

Drag To point at an item, press and hold the mouse button, move the mouse to a new location, then release the mouse button.

Drag-and-drop A method used to move items with the mouse instead of the keyboard.

Ellipsis Portion of a menu command that indicates that choosing this command will open a dialog box that asks for further information.

File Manager An application that comes with Windows that helps you to organize your files and work with disks.

List box A box containing a list of items. To choose an item, click the list arrow, then click the desired item.

Maximize button Enlarges an application window to its largest possible size.

Menu A list of commands that you can use to accomplish certain tasks.

Menu bar A set of menus that appear at the top of an application window.

Minimize button Reduces an application window to an icon at the bottom of the screen.

Mouse A handheld input device.

Mouse pointer A graphical representation showing where the mouse is positioned on the desktop. The shape changes, depending on where it is positioned.

Move To place an item in a new location.

Multitasking The ability for more than one application to run at the same time.

Point To position the mouse pointer on an item on the desktop.

Radio button The small circle you click to select or deselect a single dialog box option.

Random Access Memory (RAM) Temporary storage space that is erased when the computer is turned off.

Restore button Restores an application to its previous size.

Root directory The directory at the top of the directory tree, usually the drive itself.

Run Operate.

Scroll arrows (left and right) The arrows in scroll bars that you click to move along the scroll bar in small increments.

Scroll bars (horizontal and vertical) Appear when a window contains more information than can be displayed at one time and allow you to navigate the window. Scroll bars contain scroll boxes and scroll arrows.

Screen saver A moving pattern that fills your screen after your computer has not been used for a specified amount of time.

Scroll boxes (horizontal and vertical) Located in scroll bars and used to move along the scroll bar in larger increments.

Select Click an item to select it. When you select an item, it becomes highlighted, or active.

Source disk The original disk when copying disks.

Split bar The bar that divides the directory window in the File Manager.

Subdirectory A directory within another directory.

Target disk The disk that the source disk copies to when you are copying disks.

Task List A window that displays a list of applications you are currently running and allows you to switch between applications. Double-click anywhere on the desktop or press [Ctrl] [Esc] to display.

Text box A box in which you type text.

Index

L

M

N

P

R

S

UNIT

OBJECTIVES

- Define Office components
- Learn about Office applications

Introducing MICROSOFT OFFICE

Microsoft Office is a collection of software programs, or **applications**, designed to take advantage of the Windows interface and improve your computer efficiency. When applications are grouped together as in Microsoft Office, the grouping of applications is called a **suite**, and all the programs have similar icons, functions, and commands. ▶ This unit introduces you to Nomad Ltd, an outdoor sporting gear and adventure travel company with five regional offices. Nomad Ltd organizes guided outdoor tours for activities like hiking, rafting, and biking. The company also sells the equipment needed to do these activities. By exploring how Nomad Ltd uses Microsoft Office's components, you will learn how each application can be used in a business environment. ▶

Defining Office components

Microsoft Office contains all the applications commonly used in businesses. The Microsoft Office Manager (MOM) is a special toolbar that allows you to switch between applications simply by clicking the appropriate button on the toolbar. It is an optional add-on application and might not be loaded on your machine. If you have MOM, look for Quick Tips in the three integration units that tell you which buttons to click. The applications included in Office are listed in Table 1. Office is available in two editions: Professional and Standard. Office Professional contains Access, the database application; Office Standard does not. ▶ Nomad Ltd employees began using Office Professional when the five regional offices switched from manual functions to networked personal computers using Windows. Figure 1 is Nomad's organizational chart.

Below are some of the ways the company uses Office to create its Annual Report:

- **Create text documents using Word**
  Word is the word processor component of Office. You use a **word processor** to create documents, such as descriptions of Nomad's financial condition and projected expansion reports. Employees edit and format the documents, then use the software to check the spelling before the documents are printed and distributed.
- **Analyze sales figures using Excel**
  Excel is the spreadsheet in Office. You use a **spreadsheet** to analyze data, perform calculations, and create charts. Employees at Nomad's headquarters gather sales data for all of Nomad's regional offices, then compare each region's data for areas of strength and weakness.
- **Track product inventory using Access**
  Access is the database management system in Office. A **database** is a collection of related information, such as a list of employees and their social security numbers, salaries, and vacation time. A **database management system** organizes databases and allows you to cross check information in them. Employees at Nomad created an inventory database that allows the buyers to see which products sell best by region, on a daily basis.
- **Create presentation graphics using PowerPoint**
  PowerPoint is the presentation graphics application in Office. You use **presentation graphics** to develop graphics to enhance written reports and slides for visual presentations. Figure 1 was created using PowerPoint.
- **Link information among applications to increase accuracy**
  Information in one application in Office can be **dynamically linked** to another application. A **dynamic link** means that if the data in the first application changes, the information in the second application will be automatically updated. For example, data in an Excel spreadsheet can be linked to a chart in a PowerPoint slide. This means that the chart in PowerPoint will be automatically updated if a value in the Excel worksheet is changed. Prior to the installation of Office, Nomad employees had to make corrections manually, leading to incorrect, inconsistent, or outdated information in reports.
- **Share graphics**
  All Office components have **embedding** capabilities. For example, the company logo can be made available to all regional offices and can be placed in Word, Excel, Access, and PowerPoint files.

FIGURE 1: Nomad Ltd organization chart

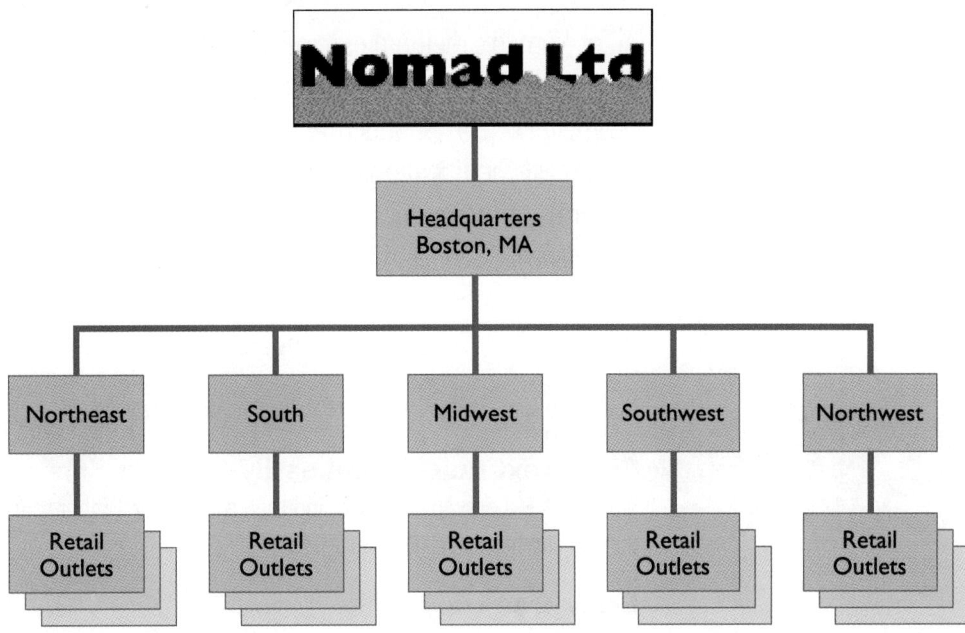

TABLE 1: Microsoft Office

BUTTON	APPLICATION	FUNCTION
	Word 6.0	Word processing
	Excel 5.0	Spreadsheet
	Access 2.0	Database
	PowerPoint 4.0	Presentation graphics
	Mail	Electronic mail

Learning about Office applications

All of Nomad's regional offices use Word and Excel while gathering data for the Annual Report. Word allows you to create and edit text documents, such as a newsletter or correspondence. Using Word, you can compose a document and then make easy modifications. The result is a professional-looking document. Excel performs numeric calculations rapidly and accurately. Like traditional paper-based spreadsheets, an electronic spreadsheet contains a **worksheet** area that is divided into columns and rows that form individual **cells**. Cells can contain text, numbers, formulas, or a combination of all three. ▶

Below are some of the benefits of using Word and Excel:

- **Enter text quickly and easily**
  Word makes it easy to enter text and then edit it later. Rather than having to retype a document, the text can be rearranged or revised.

- **Error-free copy**
  You use Word's spell checker after you finish typing. It compares each word in a document to a built-in dictionary and notifies you if it does not recognize a word. Word's AutoCorrect feature automatically corrects words as you type them. Word provides several entries for commonly misspelled words, but you can add your own.

- **Combining text and graphics**
  Using Word, you can combine text and graphics easily. Figure 2 shows a sample memo containing text and graphics.

- **Special effects**
  The ability to create columnar documents, drop caps (capital letters that take up two or three lines), and word art (text you customize by changing its appearance to become three-dimensional or shadowed) adds a professional quality to your documents.

- **Calculate results quickly and accurately**
  Using Excel, you enter only data and formulas. Excel calculates the results.

- **Recalculate easily**
  Excel recalculates any results based on a changed entry automatically.

- **Create charts**
  Excel makes it easy to create charts based on information in a worksheet. With Excel, charts are automatically updated as data changes. The worksheet in Figure 3 shows a column chart that graphically shows the distribution of sales for each of Nomad's regional offices.

FIGURE 2: Memo created in Word

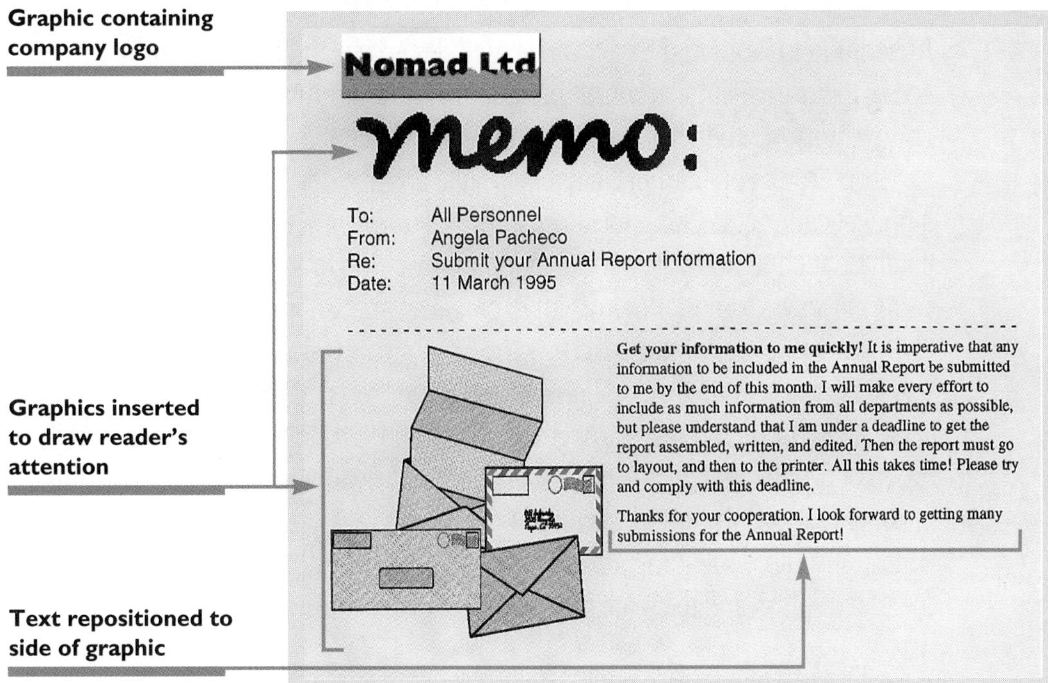

Graphic containing company logo

Graphics inserted to draw reader's attention

Text repositioned to side of graphic

FIGURE 3: Sales summary and chart created in Excel

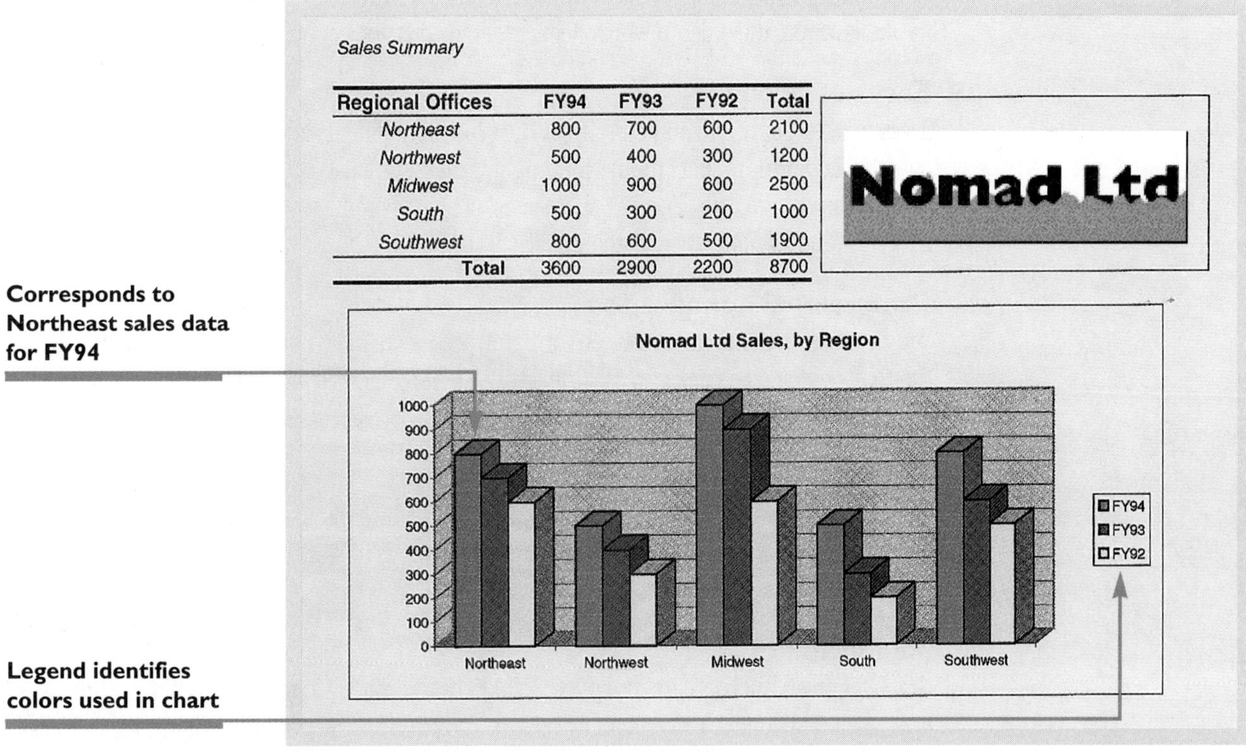

Regional Offices	FY94	FY93	FY92	Total
Northeast	800	700	600	2100
Northwest	500	400	300	1200
Midwest	1000	900	600	2500
South	500	300	200	1000
Southwest	800	600	500	1900
Total	3600	2900	2200	8700

Corresponds to Northeast sales data for FY94

Legend identifies colors used in chart

Learning about Office applications, continued

In addition to Word and Excel, Office includes Access and PowerPoint. You use Access to arrange large amounts of data in various groups or databases, such as an inventory of products. The information in the databases can be retrieved in a variety of ways. For example, a database like an inventory list might be arranged alphabetically, by stocking location, or by the number of units on order. A powerful database such as Access lets you look up information quickly, easily, and in a wide variety of ways. You use PowerPoint to create a variety of presentation materials on slides. In PowerPoint, a **slide** is the work area in which handouts, outlines, speakers' notes, and 35-mm slides are produced. You can also create an on-line slide show in which flowing images appear on a PC monitor and are viewed by a group of people. Usually the computer is hooked up to a projector so a roomful of people can see the demonstration. ▶ Nomad's regional offices use Access to control inventory spending and PowerPoint to create attractive materials for in-store displays and to create presentations for the Annual Meeting.

Below are some of the benefits of using Access and PowerPoint:

- **Easy entry**
  Employees enter inventory items in whatever order they are received. Because Access organizes the data for you, the order in which items are entered is not a concern.
- **Easy retrieval**
  Access makes it easy for you to specify **criteria**, or conditions, and then produce a list of all data that conforms to that criteria. You might want to see a list of products by supplier or a list of discontinued products. Figure 4 shows a list of bicycle products sold at Nomad's retail stores sorted by product name then by the supplier ID number.
- **Professional appearance**
  You can enter data into an on-screen form that you create in Access. This makes entering data more efficient and less prone to making errors. Figure 5 shows a screen form that can be used for data entry and can be printed.
- **Create and edit easily on a slide**
  Text can be written directly on a PowerPoint slide, enabling you to see if your slide looks cluttered. Editing is accomplished using the same methods as in Word. Text can be cut, copied, pasted, and moved simply and easily.
- **Add graphics**
  Graphic images, such as clip art, an Excel chart, or a corporate logo, further enhance any presentation materials. PowerPoint accepts the most commonly available graphic file formats and comes with more than 1,000 clip art images. PowerPoint also allows you to create your own shapes and design your own text. Figure 6 shows a slide containing an Excel chart.

FIGURE 4: List of bicycle inventory items in Access

Items first sorted alphabetically by product name

Consecutive entry numbers rearranged by sort orders

Items then sorted in descending order by supplier ID

Products 9/1

Entry #	Product ID	Product Name	Supplier ID	Units In Stock	Units On Order	Unit Price	Reorder Level	ReorderAmount	Units
121	11162	Look PP166 pedals	94	45	0	$45.00	10	36	Pair
87	11162	Look PP166 pedals	91	45	0	$45.00	10	36	Pair
70	11162	Look PP166 pedals	63	45	0	$45.00	10	36	Pair
138	11162	Look PP166 pedals	63	45	0	$45.00	10	36	Pair
19	11162	Look PP166 pedals	63	45	0	$45.75	10	36	Pair
2	11162	Look PP166 pedals	63	45	0	$45.00	10	36	Pair
104	11162	Look PP166 pedals	63	45	0	$45.00	10	36	Pair
36	11162	Look PP166 pedals - adv	63	45	0	$45.00	10	36	Pair
53	11162	Look PP168 pedals	63	45	0	$45.00	10	36	Pair
67	76662	Nomad Aerospoke Wheels	56	30	0	$200.00	15	30	Each
16	76662	Nomad Aerospoke Wheels	56	30	0	$200.00	15	30	Each
152	76662	Nomad Aerospoke Wheels	56	30	0	$200.00	15	30	Each
33	76662	Nomad Aerospoke Wheels	56	30	0	$200.00	15	30	Each
84	76662	Nomad Aerospoke Wheels	56	30	0	$200.00	15	30	Each
101	76662	Nomad Aerospoke Wheels	52	30	0	$200.00	15	30	Each
118	76662	Nomad Aerospoke Wheels	51	30	0	$200.00	15	30	Each
135	76662	Nomad Aerospoke Wheels	51	30	0	$200.00	15	30	Each
50	76662	Nomad Aerospoke Wheels - Pr	56	30	0	$200.00	15	30	Each
133	32323	Nomad Beauty Handlebar tap	10	27	40	$2.00	30	40	Each
116	32323	Nomad Beauty Handlebar tap	10	27	40	$2.00	30	40	Each

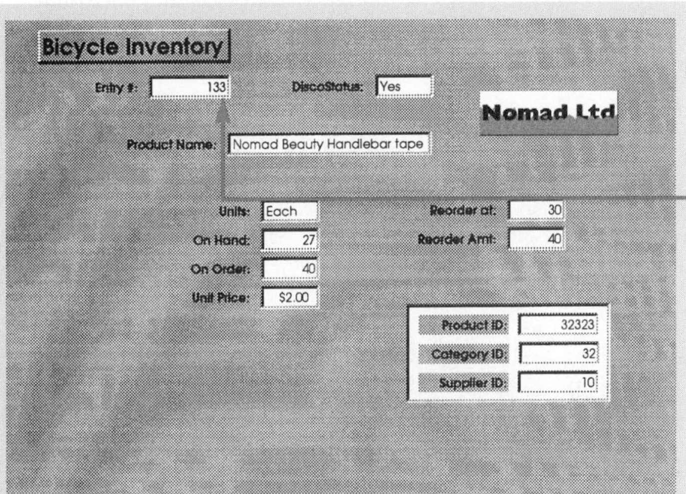

FIGURE 5: Inventory screen form in Access

Field number automatically advances to the next number with each new entry

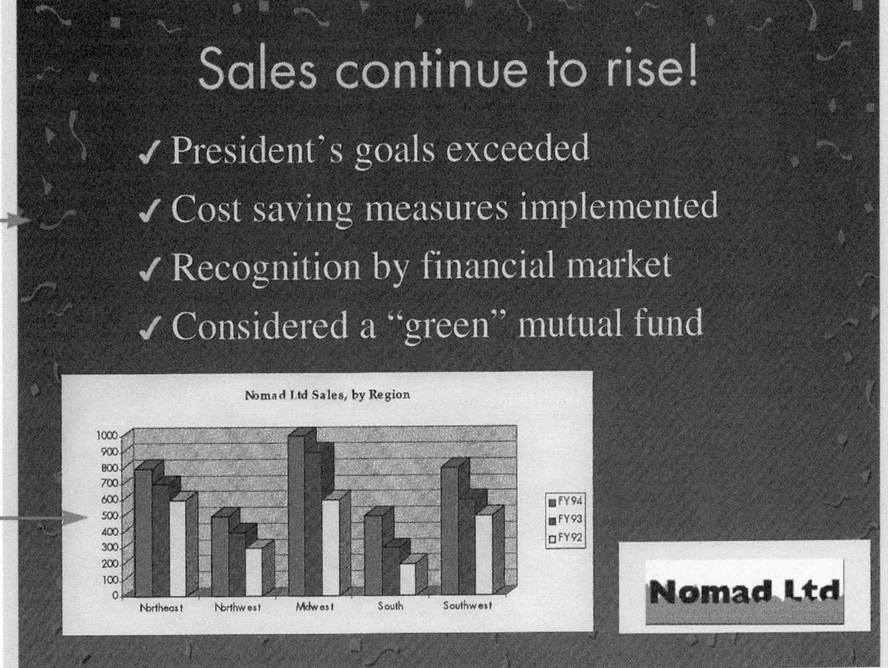

FIGURE 6: PowerPoint slide with Excel chart

Background layout created using PowerPoint template

Excel chart as a graphic image

CONCEPTS REVIEW

Match each application with the correct icon.

1 Microsoft PowerPoint
2 Microsoft Excel
3 Microsoft Word
4 Microsoft Access

a.
b.
c.
d.

Select the best answer from the list of choices.

5 Excel can be used for all of the following tasks, EXCEPT:
   a. Entering columns or rows of numbers
   b. Creating charts
   c. Creating columnar text
   d. Recalculating numeric data

6 Which of the following is *not* a feature found in Word?
   a. AutoCorrect
   b. Drop cap
   c. Slide
   d. On-screen form

7 Word documents can
   a. Be easily modified and rearranged
   b. Contain graphics
   c. Bc in a columnar format
   d. Contain all these effects

8 You can create an on-screen slide show containing graphics and text using
   a. Word
   b. PowerPoint
   c. Excel
   d. Access

9 Access forms can be made easy to use through the use of
   a. Levers
   b. Check boxes
   c. Controls
   d. Switches

10 PowerPoint can create all of the following, EXCEPT:
   a. Handouts
   b. Slides
   c. Outlines
   d. Data entry screen forms

Microsoft® Word 6.0

for Windows™

Read This Before You Begin Microsoft Word 6.0

Word 6.0 Screen Check

At the beginning of each unit, verify that:

- The document window is maximized, and the document is displayed in Normal View.
- Only the Standard and Formatting toolbars are displayed.
- The scroll bars and the ruler are displayed.
- The Show/Hide button is selected, and magnification is set to 100%.
- The default font is Times New Roman, and the default point size is 10.

To the Student

The exercises and examples in this book feature sample Word document files stored on the Student Disk provided to your instructor. To complete the step-by-step exercises in this book, you must have a Student Disk. Your instructor will either provide you with your own copy of the Student Disk or will make the Student Disk files available to you over a network in your school's computer lab. See your instructor or technical support person for further information.

Using Your Own Computer

If you are going to work through this book using your own computer, you need a computer system running Microsoft Windows 3.1, Microsoft Word 6.0 for Windows, and a Student Disk. *You will not be able to complete the step-by-step exercises in this book using your own computer until you have your own Student Disk.* This book assumes the default settings under a Complete installation of Microsoft Word 6.0 for Windows. Do not install "Help for WordPerfect users."

To the Instructor

Bundled with the instructor's copy of this book is the Student Disk, which contains all the files your students need to complete the step-by-step exercises in this book. Adopters of this text are granted the right to distribute the files on the Student Disk to any student who has purchased a copy of this text. You are free to post all of these files to a network or standalone workstations, or simply provide copies of the disk to your students. The instructions in this book assume that the students know which drive and directory contain the Student Disk files, so it's important that you provide disk location information before the students start working through the units. This book also assumes that Word 6.0 is set up using the Complete installation procedure.

Using the Student Disk Files

To keep the original files on the Student Disk intact, the instructions in this book for opening files require two important steps: (1) open the existing file and (2) save it as a new file with a new name. This procedure ensures that the original file will remain unmodified in case the student wants to redo the exercise.

To organize their files, students are instructed to save their files to the MY_FILES directory on their Student Disk that they created in *Microsoft Windows 3.1*. In case your students did not complete this lesson, it is included in the Instructor's Manual that accompanies this book. You can circulate this to your students, or you can instruct them to simply save to drive A or drive B.

UNIT 1

OBJECTIVES

- Define word processing software
- Start Word 6.0 for Windows
- View the Word application window
- Work with dialog boxes, toolbars, and buttons
- Open a document and move through it
- Get Help
- Close a document and exit Word

Getting Started WITH MICROSOFT WORD 6.0

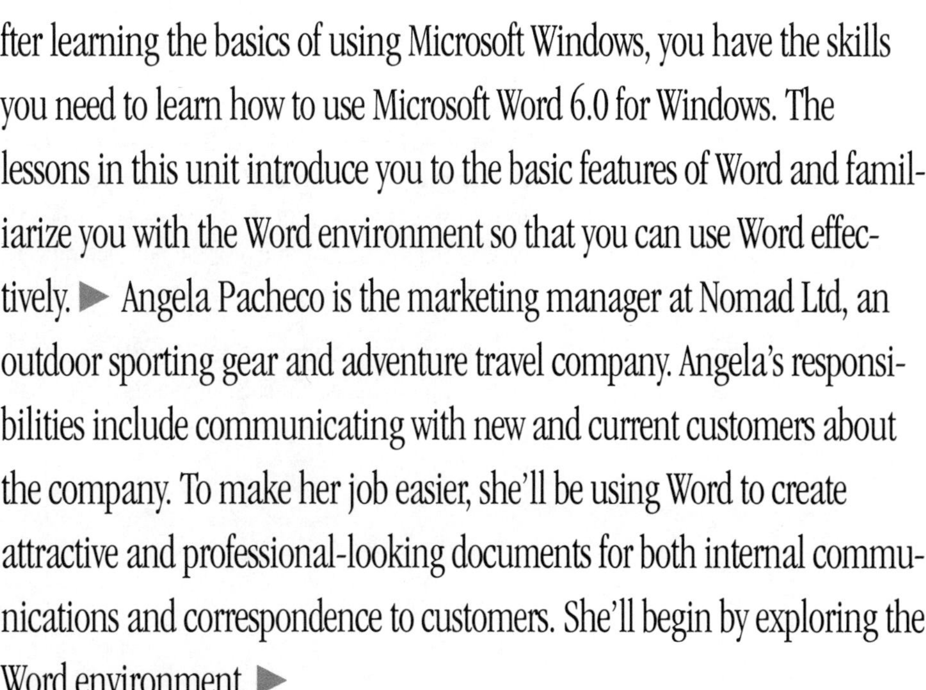

After learning the basics of using Microsoft Windows, you have the skills you need to learn how to use Microsoft Word 6.0 for Windows. The lessons in this unit introduce you to the basic features of Word and familiarize you with the Word environment so that you can use Word effectively. ▶ Angela Pacheco is the marketing manager at Nomad Ltd, an outdoor sporting gear and adventure travel company. Angela's responsibilities include communicating with new and current customers about the company. To make her job easier, she'll be using Word to create attractive and professional-looking documents for both internal communications and correspondence to customers. She'll begin by exploring the Word environment. ▶

Defining word processing software

Microsoft Word 6.0 is a full-featured **word processing** application that allows you to create attractive and professional-looking documents quickly and easily. Word processing offers many advantages compared to typing. Because the information you enter in a word processing document is stored electronically by your computer, it is easy to revise and reuse text in documents you have already created. In addition, you can enhance your documents by giving text a special appearance and adding lines, shading, and even pictures (called **graphics**). Figure 1-1 illustrates the kinds of features you can use in your documents.

With word processing software, Angela will be able to perform the following tasks:

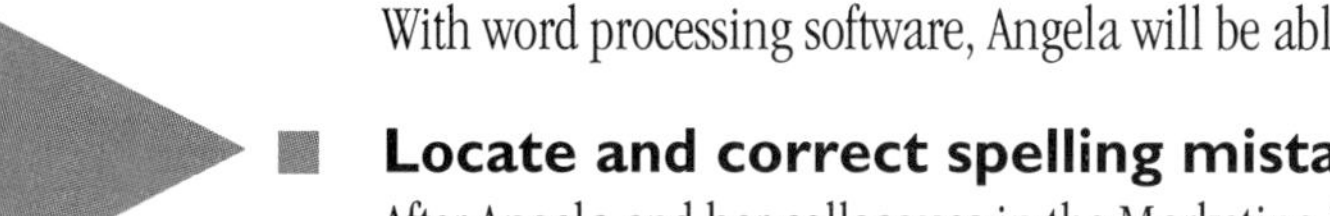

- **Locate and correct spelling mistakes and grammatical errors**
  After Angela and her colleagues in the Marketing Department use Word to create documents for the Annual Report, they use Word's proofreading tools to identify errors and correct them.
- **Copy and move text and graphics without retyping**
  Angela can save time by copying text found in other documents, and using it again in the material for the Annual Report. Within the same document, she can reorganize text and graphics.
- **Enhance the appearance of documents by adding formatting**
  By applying different types of formatting to important parts of documents, Angela can create documents that convey their message quickly and effectively to their readers. Word features, such as the Formatting toolbar and AutoFormat, help Angela do this quickly.
- **Align text in rows and columns using tables**
  Although Nomad uses a spreadsheet application, Microsoft Excel, for complex financial analysis, Angela can use tables in Word to present small amounts of financial information in an easy-to-read format.
- **Add visual interest to documents by inserting graphics and arranging text in different ways**
  Before using Word, Angela often used expensive desktop publishing resources outside the company to create attractive and professional-looking newsletters and other marketing materials. Now she can use Word to create the professional documents she needs, without the extra cost.
- **Preview a document as it will look when printed**
  Before printing her documents, Angela can preview all the pages of her work at one time. By getting the "big picture" of the document, she can catch mistakes and make final adjustments before printing.

FIGURE 1-1: Features in a Word document

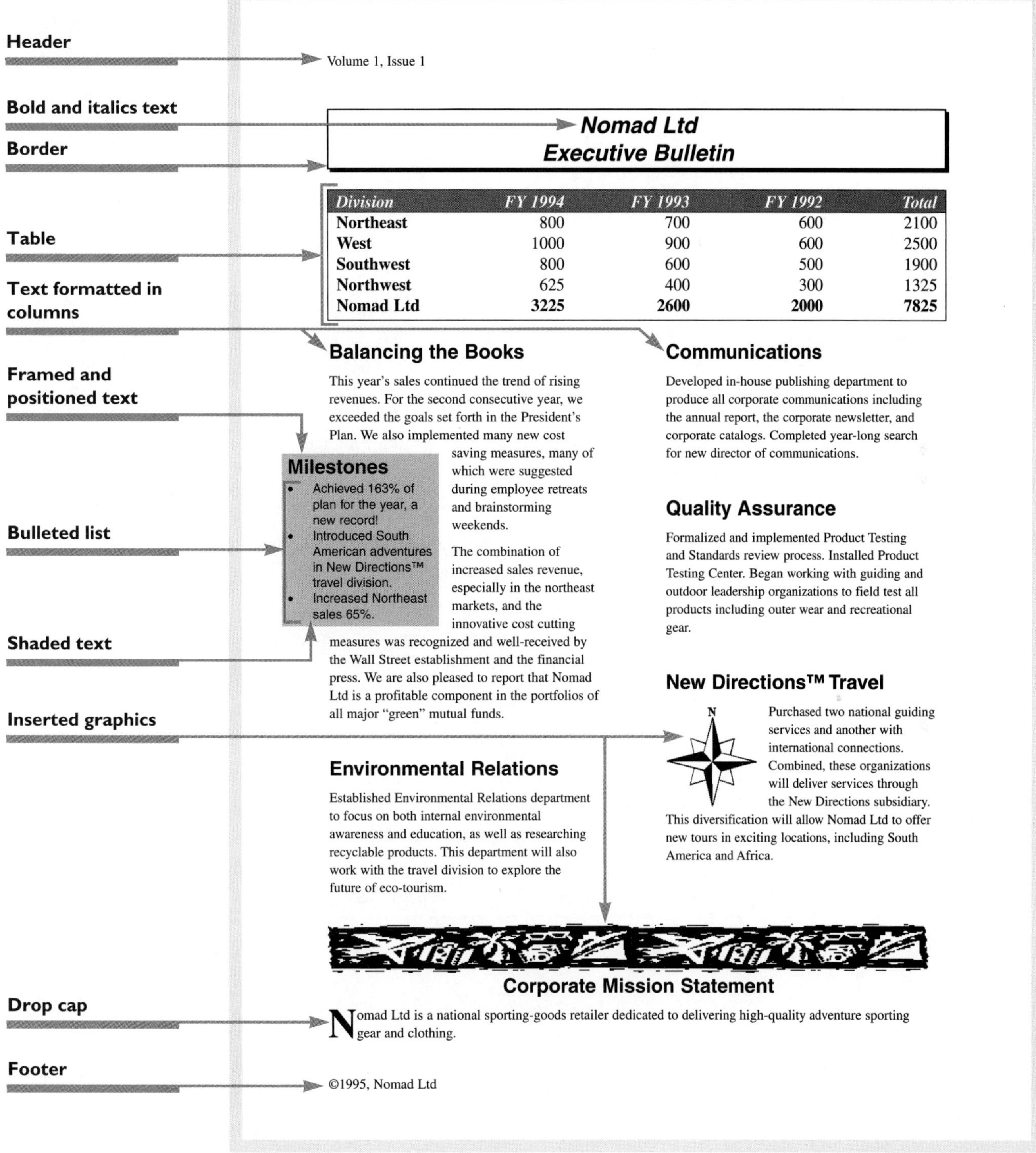

Volume 1, Issue 1

Nomad Ltd
Executive Bulletin

Division	*FY 1994*	*FY 1993*	*FY 1992*	*Total*
Northeast	800	700	600	2100
West	1000	900	600	2500
Southwest	800	600	500	1900
Northwest	625	400	300	1325
Nomad Ltd	**3225**	**2600**	**2000**	**7825**

Balancing the Books

This year's sales continued the trend of rising revenues. For the second consecutive year, we exceeded the goals set forth in the President's Plan. We also implemented many new cost saving measures, many of which were suggested during employee retreats and brainstorming weekends.

Milestones
- Achieved 163% of plan for the year, a new record!
- Introduced South American adventures in New Directions™ travel division.
- Increased Northeast sales 65%.

The combination of increased sales revenue, especially in the northeast markets, and the innovative cost cutting measures was recognized and well-received by the Wall Street establishment and the financial press. We are also pleased to report that Nomad Ltd is a profitable component in the portfolios of all major "green" mutual funds.

Environmental Relations

Established Environmental Relations department to focus on both internal environmental awareness and education, as well as researching recyclable products. This department will also work with the travel division to explore the future of eco-tourism.

Communications

Developed in-house publishing department to produce all corporate communications including the annual report, the corporate newsletter, and corporate catalogs. Completed year-long search for new director of communications.

Quality Assurance

Formalized and implemented Product Testing and Standards review process. Installed Product Testing Center. Began working with guiding and outdoor leadership organizations to field test all products including outer wear and recreational gear.

New Directions™ Travel

N

Purchased two national guiding services and another with international connections. Combined, these organizations will deliver services through the New Directions subsidiary. This diversification will allow Nomad Ltd to offer new tours in exciting locations, including South America and Africa.

Corporate Mission Statement

Nomad Ltd is a national sporting-goods retailer dedicated to delivering high-quality adventure sporting gear and clothing.

©1995, Nomad Ltd

Starting Word 6.0 for Windows

To start Word, you first start Windows, as described in "Microsoft Windows 3.1." Then, you open the program group window that contains the Word application icon—usually the Microsoft Office program group. If you are using a computer on a network, your procedure for starting Word might be different. Ask your technical support person or instructor if there are any special procedures for starting Word on your computer. ▶ Angela's first step in learning to use Word is to start the application.

1 Make sure the Program Manager window is open
The Program Manager icon might appear at the bottom of your screen. Double-click it to open it, if necessary.

2 Double-click the **Microsoft Office program group icon**
The Microsoft Word icon appears inside the Microsoft Office program group, as shown in Figure 1-2. Depending on the applications installed on your computer, the icons shown in this program group might be different. If you cannot locate the Microsoft Office program group, click Window on the Program Manager menu bar, then click Microsoft Office.

3 Double-click the **Microsoft Word application icon**
Word opens and displays the Tip of the Day dialog box, which provides a brief note describing a Word feature or command. (If the Tip of the Day dialog box does not open, this feature has been **disabled** (turned off) by someone else using the computer you're working on; skip Step 4 and continue with the next lesson.) Later in this unit, you will learn about dialog boxes. For now, you'll simply close the dialog box.

4 Click **OK**
The Tip of the Day dialog box closes, and the application window appears, as shown in Figure 1-3. The blinking vertical line, called the **insertion point**, in the application window indicates where text will appear when you begin typing. When you first start the Word application, you can begin creating a new document right away. You will learn how to type in a new document in the next unit. For now Angela continues to explore basic Word features.

FIGURE 1-2: Microsoft Office program group

Microsoft Word application icon

Your available applications might vary

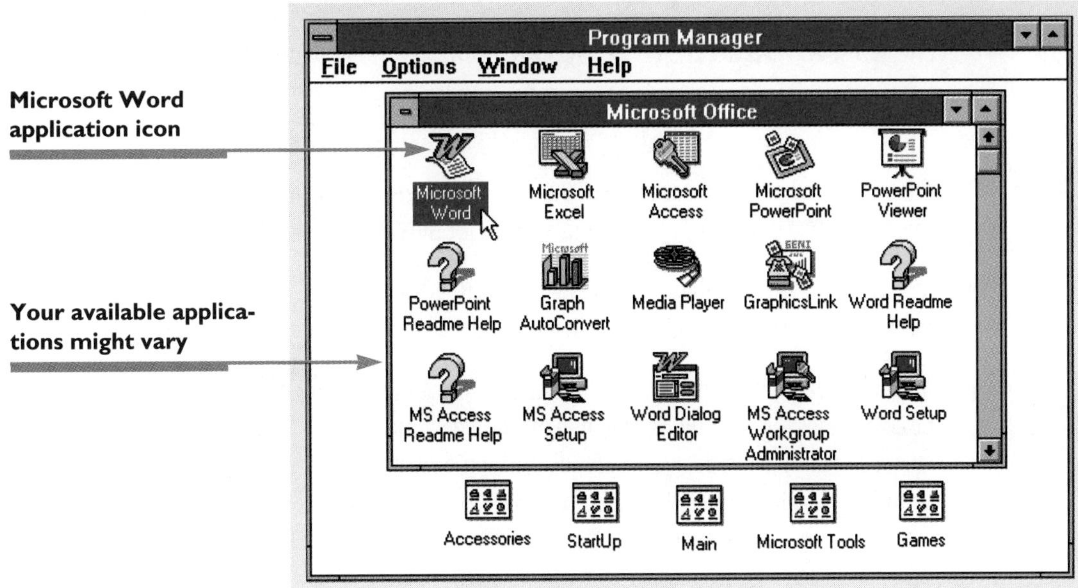

FIGURE 1-3: Word application window

Insertion point

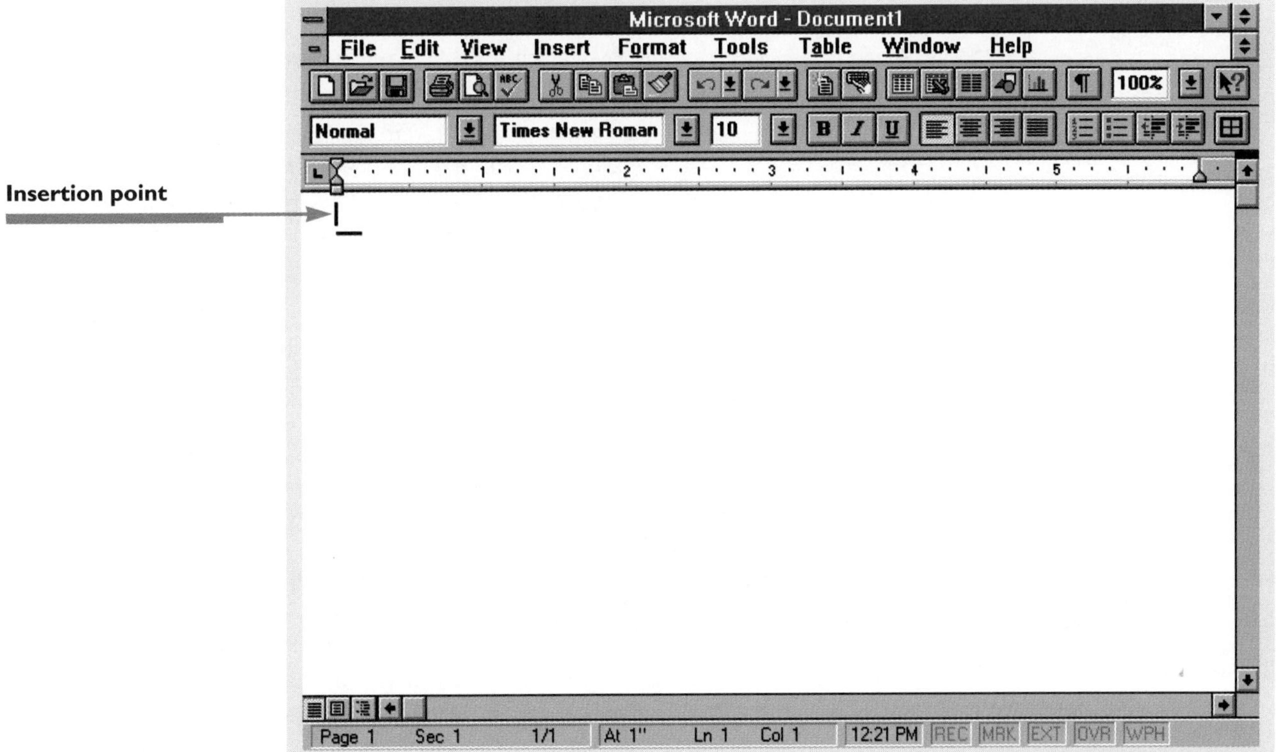

Viewing the Word application window

The Word **application window** contains the features described below. On your computer, locate each of the elements using Figure 1-4 for reference.

- The **title bar** displays the name of the application and the document. Until you save the document and give it a name, the temporary name for the document is DOCUMENT1.
- The **menu bar** lists the names of the menus that contain Word commands. Clicking a menu name on the menu bar displays a list of commands from which you can choose.
- The **Standard toolbar** contains buttons for the most frequently used commands, such as the commands for opening, saving, and printing documents. Clicking buttons on a toolbar is often faster than using the menu. However, in some cases, using the menu offers additional options not available by clicking a button. You can find out what a button does by displaying its ToolTip. See the related topic "ToolTips" for more information. This toolbar is one of the two default toolbars.
- The **Formatting toolbar** contains buttons for the most frequently used formatting commands, such as the commands for applying bold to text or aligning text. This toolbar is one of the two default toolbars. Other toolbars related to other features are also available, as you will see in later units.
- The **horizontal ruler** displays tab settings, left and right paragraph and document margins, and column widths (only in page layout view). In page layout view, a **vertical ruler** is also displayed. You'll learn more about the different Word views later in this book.
- The **document window** displays the work area for typing text and working with your document. When the mouse pointer is in the document window, the pointer changes to an **I-beam**, I. You can have as many document windows open as you want. Each window can be minimized, maximized, and sized. When you are working in only one document at a time, it is a good idea to maximize the document window.
- The **vertical and horizontal scroll bars** display the relative position of the currently displayed text in the document. You use the scroll bars and scroll boxes to view different parts of your document.
- The **view buttons**, which appear in the horizontal scroll bar, allow you to display the document in one of three views. Each view offers features that are useful in the different phases of working with a document. You'll learn more about the three views later in this book.
- The **status bar** displays the current page number and section number, the total number of pages in the document, and the vertical position of the insertion point (in inches and in lines from the upper-left corner of the document). You also see the status of commands in effect and the current time. The status bar also displays descriptions of commands and buttons as you move around the window.

FIGURE 1-4: Elements of the Word application window

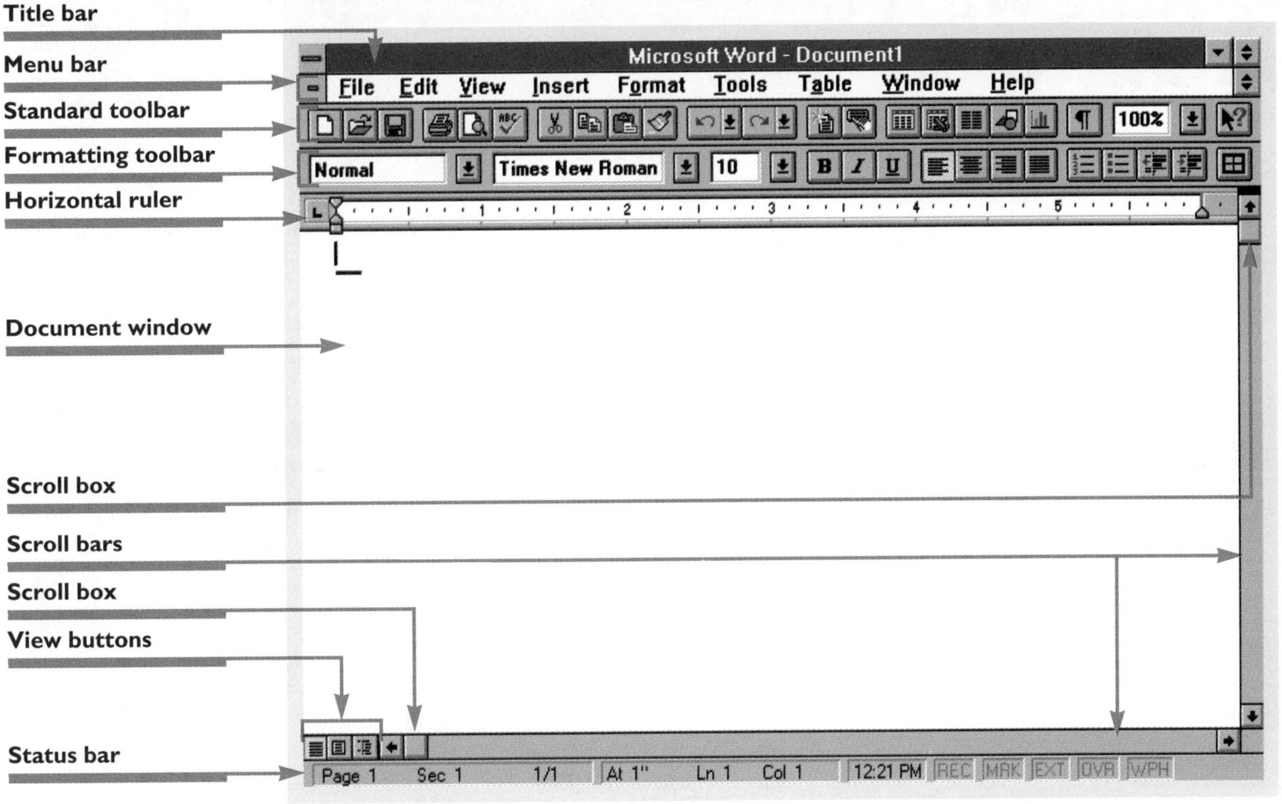

ToolTips

As you move the mouse pointer over a button on a toolbar, the name of the button—called a **ToolTip**—appears below or above the button. A brief description of the button also appears in the status bar.

TROUBLE?

If your document window is not maximized, click the document window Maximize button. If the Page Layout View button in the horizontal scroll bar appears "depressed," indicating it is selected, the document is in page layout view. To display the document in normal view, click the Normal View button in the horizontal scroll bar.

Working with dialog boxes, toolbars, and buttons

Word often provides several ways to complete the same task—using menus, toolbars, or keyboard shortcuts. After you become familiar with the different techniques, use the one you prefer. Before you can begin using Word to create and edit documents, you need to become familiar with using dialog boxes, toolbars, and buttons to perform tasks. ▶ Angela decides to turn off the option for displaying the Tip of the Day dialog box when she starts Word and to display special characters that represent how text is formatted.

1 **Click Help on the menu bar, then click Tip of the Day**
The Tip of the Day dialog box opens, as shown in Figure 1-5. Note that the text in your dialog box might be different. Clicking a command that has an ellipsis (...) displays a dialog box in which you can specify the options you want for the command. In the Tip of the Day dialog box, you can view helpful hints for using Word, and specify whether this dialog box opens when you start Word. The "x" in the Show Tips at Startup check box indicates that the feature is activated. If the check box on your screen does not contain an "x," click OK and skip to Step 3.

2 Click the **Show Tips at Startup check box** to remove the "x," then click **OK** or press **[Enter]**
Clearing this check box disables the Show Tips at Startup option so that this dialog box will not open automatically when you start Word. You can click OK or press [Enter] to carry out a command; otherwise, click Cancel or press [Esc] to close a dialog box without making a change.

3 Click the **Show/Hide ¶ button** ¶ on the Standard toolbar, as shown in Figure 1-6
This button displays nonprinting characters that represent spaces, paragraphs, and tabs, as shown in Table 1-1. Displaying these characters helps you recognize the format of a document as you work in it. These characters appear only on the screen, not in your printed documents. Note that when you click ¶, it appears "depressed," indicating it is selected. If you click the button again, the nonprinting characters are not displayed. In this book, you will usually work with nonprinting characters displayed.

Figure 1-6 also identifies buttons you will use later in this unit.

TABLE 1-1: Nonprinting characters

NONPRINTING CHARACTER	REPRESENTS
¶	Paragraph mark
·	Space
→	Tab character

FIGURE 1-5: Tip of the Day dialog box

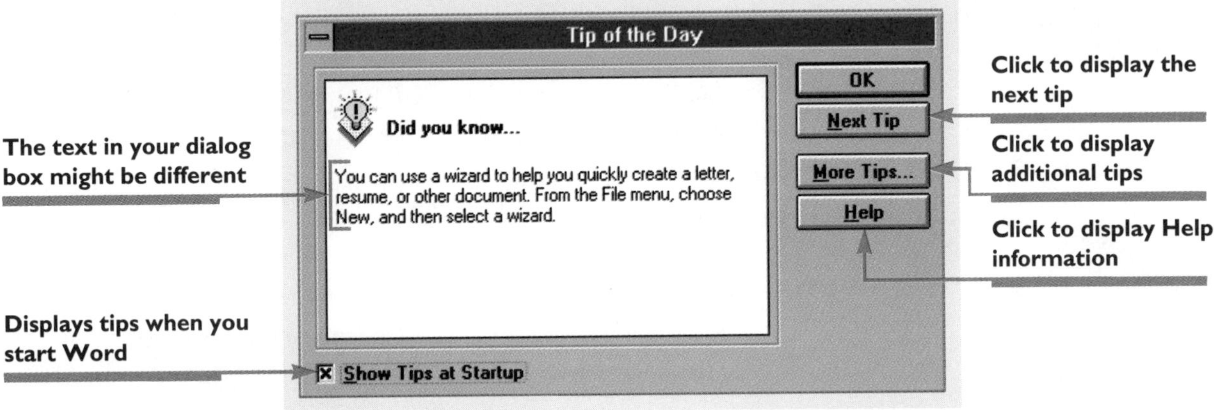

FIGURE 1-6: Standard and Formatting toolbars

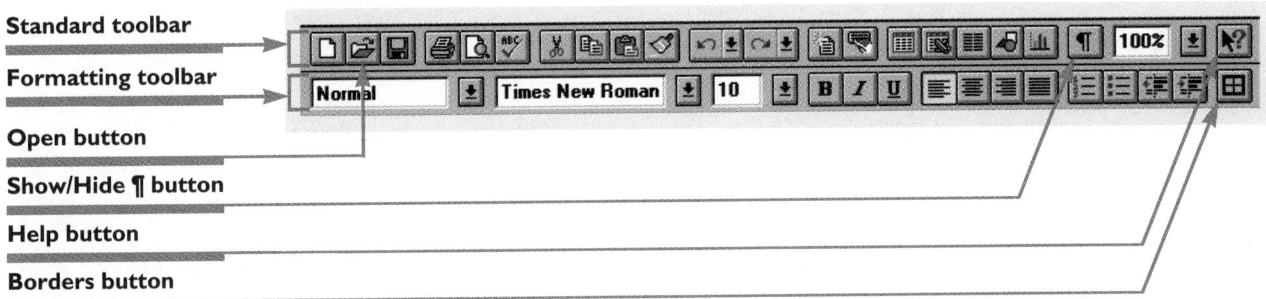

TROUBLE?

The Standard and Formatting toolbars appear by default in the Word application window. If you cannot see the Standard or Formatting toolbar, click View on the menu bar then click Toolbars. In the Toolbars dialog box, you can click the check boxes for the toolbars you want to display. Verify that only the Standard and Formatting check boxes are checked.■

Working with dialog boxes, toolbars, and buttons, continued

In addition to the menus on the menu bar, Word has shortcut menus. These offer another method for performing tasks quickly. See the related topic "Using shortcut menus" for more information. ▶ Angela wants to explore the Word environment further by viewing another toolbar and dialog box.

4 **Click the Borders button on the Formatting toolbar**
Clicking this button displays the Borders toolbar below the Formatting toolbar. Later in this book, you will learn to use the Borders toolbar to add lines and shading to text.

5 **Click again**
The Borders button is no longer selected, and the Borders toolbar is no longer displayed. Next, Angela wants to view the features available on the Options dialog box.

6 **Click Tools on the menu bar, then click Options**
The Options dialog box opens, as shown in Figure 1-7. Note that the dialog box is divided into **tabs**, or different sections. Each tab in this dialog box contains options you can specify for different Word features. For example, you can choose to display only some of the nonprinting characters when you click the Show/Hide ¶ button. However, Angela wants to be sure that *all* of the nonprinting characters appear when she clicks this button.

7 **Click the View tab (if it is not already the frontmost tab) and make sure the All check box in the Nonprinting Characters section is checked**
If the All check box does not contain an "x," click the check box. You can display and choose options for other Word features by clicking the appropriate tab. For now, Angela closes the dialog box, so she can continue exploring Word.

8 **Click Cancel to close the dialog box (or click OK if you selected the All option in Step 7)**

FIGURE 1-7: Options dialog box

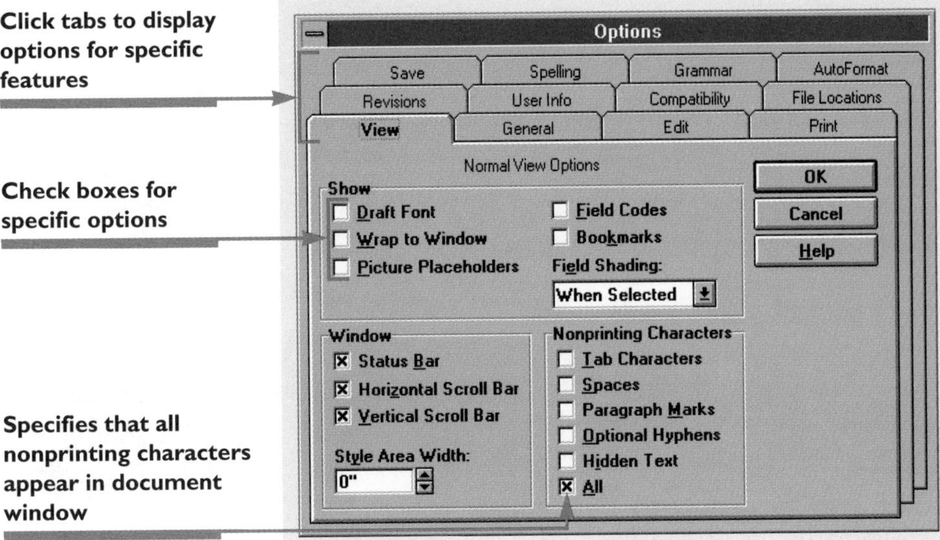

Using shortcut menus

Shortcut menus contain commands you are likely to use in specific situations. You display a shortcut menu by clicking the right mouse button. For example, when you click text with the right mouse button, you see a menu of commands that are useful when editing text, as shown in Figure 1-8. You close a shortcut menu by clicking anywhere outside the menu.

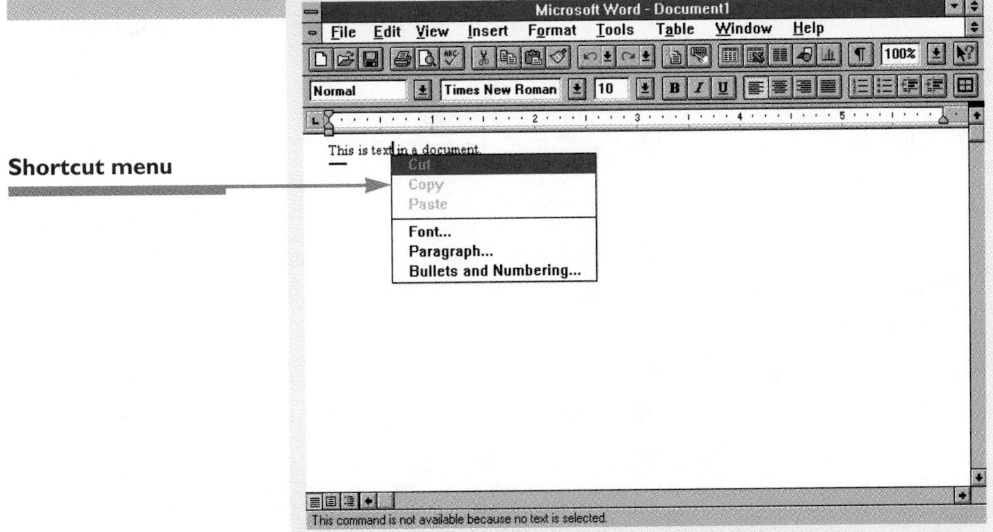

FIGURE 1-8: Shortcut menu in the document window

TROUBLE?

If you choose a command by mistake, click Edit on the menu bar, then click Undo. The Undo command reverses the results of your last action.■

Opening a document and moving through it

To view or work in a Word document, you first need to open the document. You can use either the Open command on the File menu or the Open button on the Standard toolbar to open a document. ▶ Angela wants to view a document created by one of her colleagues in the Marketing Department.

1 Place your Student Disk in drive A
To complete the units in this book, you need a Student Disk. See your instructor for a copy of the Student Disk, if you do not already have one. Also, these lessons assume your Student Disk is in drive A. If you are using a different drive or if your practice files are stored on a network, ask your technical support person or instructor where to find your practice files.

2 Click the **Open button** on the Standard toolbar
Word displays the Open dialog box, as shown in Figure 1-9. In this dialog box, you select the document you want to open. The files, directories, and drive names on your computer might be different from those shown in the figure.

3 Click the **Drives list arrow**, then click **a:**
The list of files stored on drive A appears in the File Name list box. In this case, the list shows the documents you will use to learn about Word.

4 In the File Name list box, click **UNIT_1-1.DOC**, then click **OK**
The document UNIT_1-1.DOC opens in the document window. Table 1-2 describes the different ways in which you can move around in a document. To review the document, Angela uses a variety of techniques to display different parts of the document.

5 Click the **down scroll arrow** at the bottom of the vertical scroll bar, then click the **up scroll arrow** at the top of the vertical scroll bar
When you click the down scroll arrow, the first line in the document scrolls off the top of the screen and a new line of text appears at the bottom. When you click the up scroll arrow, the window scrolls up one line.

6 Click below the scroll box in the vertical scroll bar, then click above the scroll box
The window scrolls down then up one window of text. When you use the scroll arrows and bars to move around in a document, you are simply displaying other parts of the document; the insertion point does *not* move. To move the insertion point, you must either click the left mouse button at the location you want, or use one of the techniques described in Table 1-2.

7 Drag the scroll box to the bottom of the vertical scroll bar, then click the **left mouse button** to place the insertion point at the end of the document

8 Press and hold **[Ctrl]** and press **[Home]**
The first part of the document appears in the document window, and the insertion point is located in front of the first character in the document.

If a dialog box opens when you press [Ctrl][Home], the Help for WordPerfect Users option has been activated on your computer. You need to deactivate this option so that the navigation keys will work as noted in this book. To turn the option off, double-click WPH in the status bar, click Options to display the Help Options dialog box, clear the Help for WordPerfect Users check box and the Navigation Keys for WordPerfect Users check box, click OK, then click Close.

FIGURE 1-9: Open dialog box

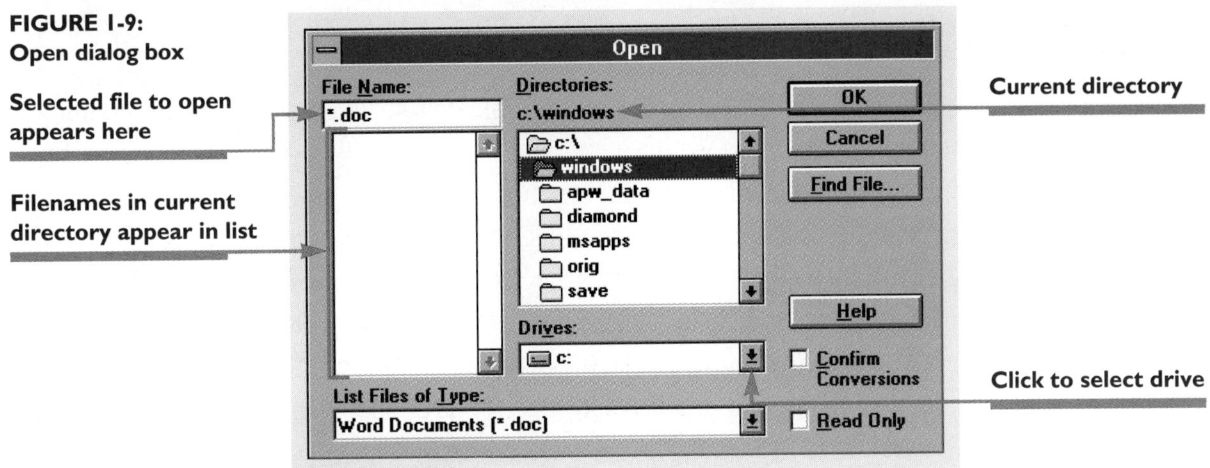

TABLE 1-2: Keyboard navigation techniques

TO MOVE	PRESS
Left one character	The Left Arrow key [←]
Right one character	The Right Arrow key [→]
Left one word	[Ctrl][←]
Right one word	[Ctrl][→]
To the start of a line	[Home]
To the end of a line	[End]
Up one line	The Up Arrow key [↑]
Down one line	The Down Arrow key [↓]
Up one paragraph	[Ctrl][↑]
Down one paragraph	[Ctrl][↓]
Up one screen	[Page Up]
Down one screen	[Page Down]
To the first character on the first page	[Ctrl][Home]
To the last character on the last page	[Ctrl][End]

QUICK TIP

To go to a specific page in a document, double-click the page number in the status bar. In the Go To dialog box, type the number of the page you want to go to, then press [Enter].■

TROUBLE?

The [Home], [End], [Page Up], and [Page Down] keys are located above the arrow keys on your keyboard.■

Getting Help

The Word application includes an on-line Help system that provides information and instructions on Word features and commands while you are using Word. You can get as little or as much information as you want, from quick definitions to detailed procedures. See the related topic "More about using Help" for additional information. Table 1-3 describes the Help commands available on the Help menu. You can also get help by clicking the Help button that is available in most dialog boxes. ▶ In her role as marketing manager for Nomad Ltd, Angela expects to create documents that contain many pages. She decides to use Word's on-line Help to learn how to move quickly to a specific page.

1. **Click Help on the menu bar**
   The Help menu displays the Help commands, which are described in Table 1-3.
2. **Click Search for Help on**
   The Search dialog box opens, as shown in Figure 1-10. In this dialog box, you can type a topic and view the entries that provide more information. Notice that the insertion point is in the search text box, ready for you to type the topic for which you want to search. Angela wants more information on navigating through a document.
3. **In the search text box, type navigating then click Show Topics**
   Notice that as you type each character, topics that match your typing appear in the search topics list. After you click Show Topics, a list of related topics appears in the bottom of the Search dialog box. Next, Angela selects the specific topic that will provide the information she needs.
4. **Click the text Going to a page, bookmark, footnote, table, annotation, graphic, (if it is not already selected), then click Go To**
   Information about moving around in a document appears in the How To window. Read this information to learn more about moving to a specific location in a document.
5. **Scroll the How To window, then click the underlined text Go To command**
   The Help window displays information about the Go To command. Clicking underlined text displays a Help window about the underlined topic. You can return to the previous topic by clicking Back. Angela wants to clarify her understanding of the insertion point.
6. **Click the dotted underlined text insertion point**
   A pop-up window defining the insertion point appears. Clicking text underlined with a dotted line displays a definition.
7. **Read the information then click anywhere in the pop-up window to close it**
8. **Double-click the control menu box on the current Help window to close it**
   The Help window about the Go To command closes, but the How To window remains open.
9. **Double-click the control menu box on the How To window to close it**
   The How To window closes, and you return to the document.

FIGURE 1-10: Search dialog box

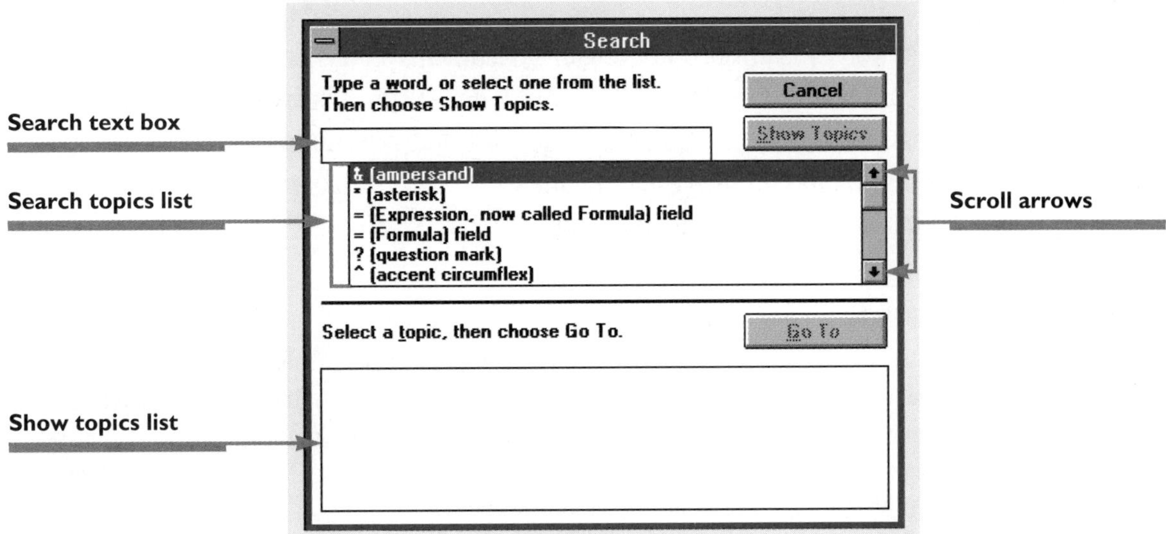

More about using Help

By clicking Contents on the Help menu, then clicking Using Word, you can display general word processing categories. By clicking the underlined text, you can jump to a specific topic. You can move and size the Help window if it blocks your view of the document. To work in the document and display the Help window at the same time, choose Always on Top from the Help menu in the Word Help window.

TABLE 1-3: Help commands

HELP COMMAND	DESCRIPTION
Contents	Displays Help topic categories
Search for Help on	Displays Search dialog box in which you can search for a specific topic
Index	Displays alphabetical list of Help topics
Quick Preview	Displays demonstrations about Getting Started, What's New?, Tips for WordPerfect Users
Examples and Demos	Displays a demonstration of a selected Word feature
Tip of the Day	Displays Tip of the Day dialog box for viewing helpful hints
WordPerfect Help	Shows the Word equivalent for a WordPerfect command
Technical Support	Displays information about support services
About Microsoft Word	Displays licensing and system information

QUICK TIP

Use the Help pointer to get Help information about any part of the window. Click the Help button on the Standard toolbar, then with the Help pointer click an item to display information about it.

Closing a document and exiting Word

After you have finished working in a document, you generally save your work and then close the document. When you are done using Word, you need to exit the application. For a comparison of the Close and Exit commands, refer to Table 1-4. ▶ Angela has finished exploring the Word document for now, so she closes the document and exits the application.

1. **Click File on the menu bar, then click Close**
   When you close a document after making changes that you have not saved, Word asks whether you want to save your changes. You also see this same message when you exit the application before saving changes in the document. Because Angela did not make any changes to the document (she was just reviewing it to explore Word features and to see what her colleague had written), she will close the document without saving it.

2. **If the message appears asking if you want to save changes, click No**
   The document closes, and Word displays the application window with only the File and Help menus available, as shown in Figure 1-11.

3. **Click File on the menu bar, then click Exit**
   The Exit command closes the Word application and returns you to the Program Manager.

TABLE 1-4: Close vs. Exit

CLOSING A DOCUMENT	EXITING WORD
Puts away the document file	Puts away all files
Leaves Word running so that you can choose to open another document or use on-line Help	Returns you to the Program Manager where you can choose to run another application

FIGURE 1-11: Word window with no open documents

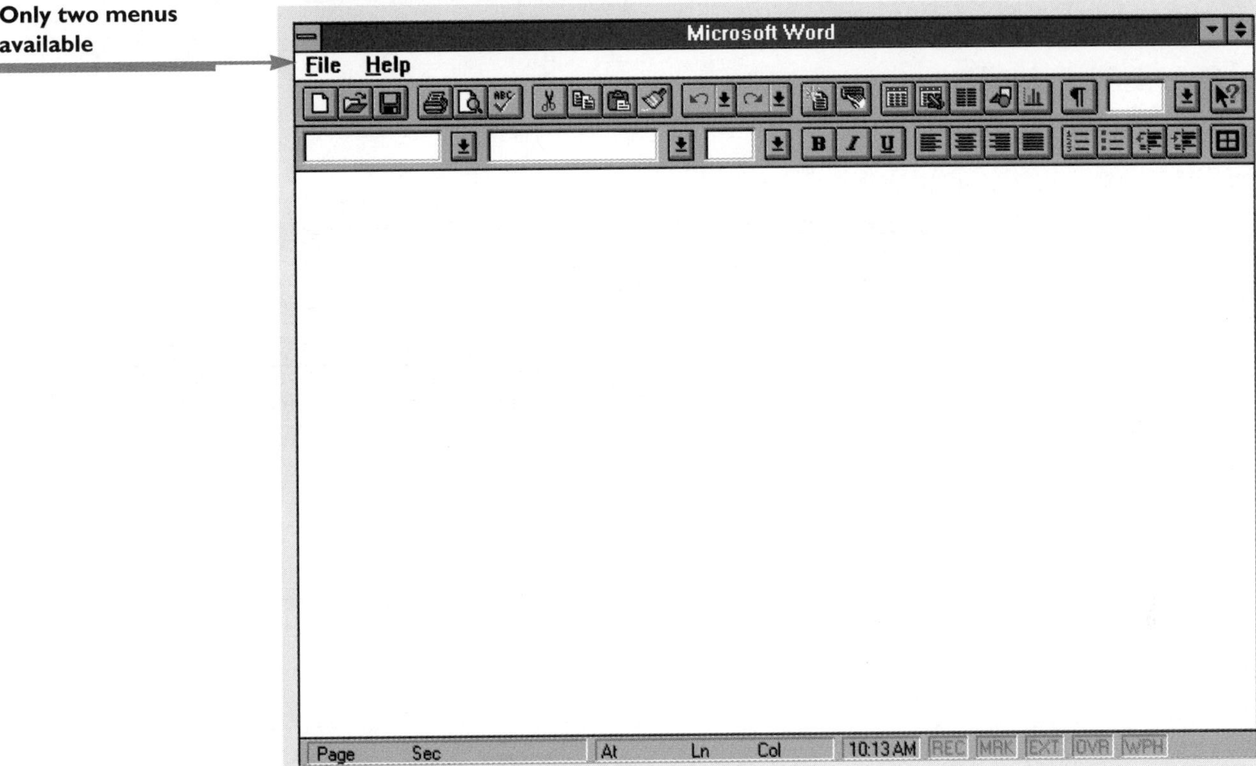

QUICK TIP

Double-clicking the control menu box next to the menu bar closes the document. Double-clicking the control menu box in the title bar exits the application.

CONCEPTSREVIEW

Label each of the elements of the Word application window in Figure 1-12.

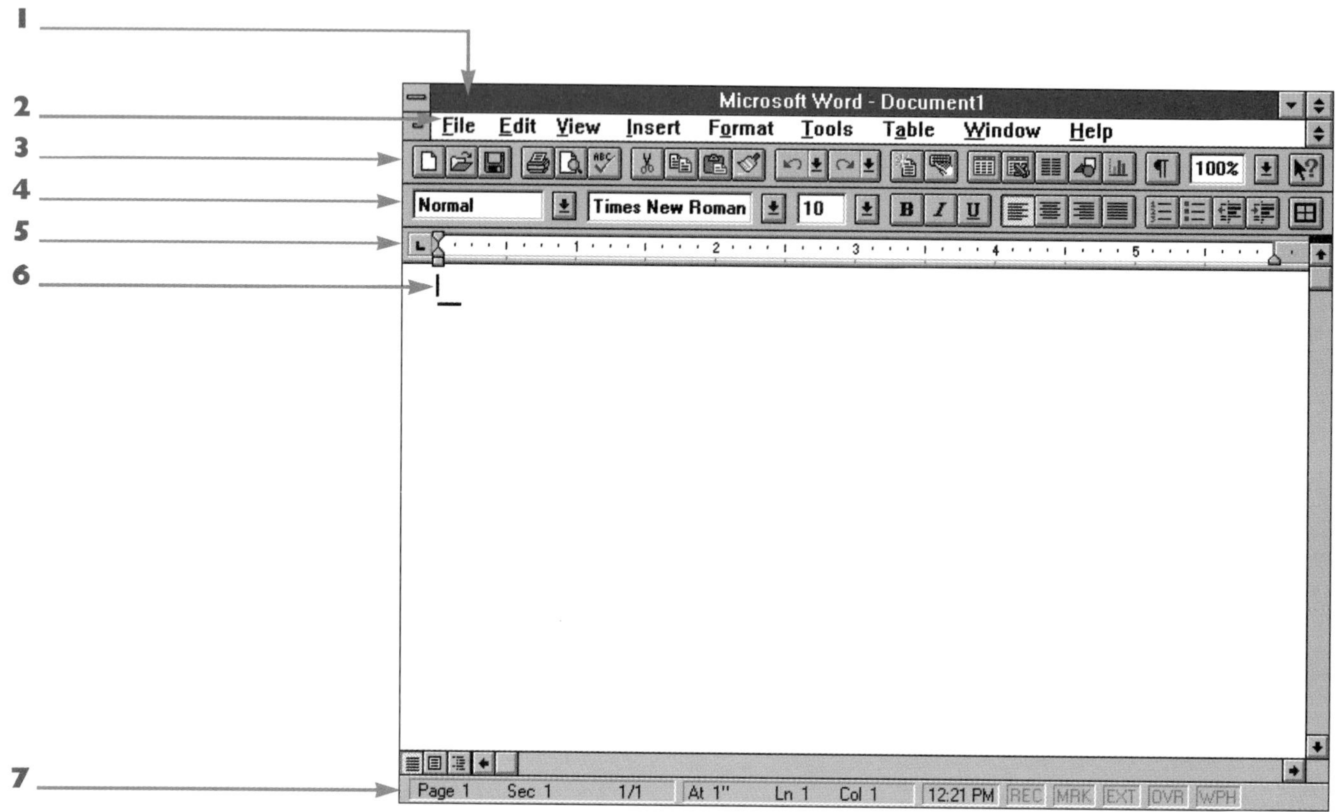

FIGURE 1-12

Match each of the following terms with the statement that best describes its function.

8 Toolbar

9 Document window

10 Ruler

11 Status bar

12 Right mouse button

a. Displays area in which you enter text

b. Identifies location of insertion point, command status, button descriptions

c. Contains buttons for easy access to commands

d. Displays shortcut menus

e. Displays tab settings, paragraph and document margins, and column width

Select the best answer from the list of choices.

13 Word processing is similar to

a. Performing financial analysis

b. Filling in forms

c. Typing

d. Forecasting mortgage payments

14 To display another part of a document, you

a. Click in the Moving toolbar

b. Scroll with a scroll bar

c. Drag the ruler

d. Select the control menu box

15 Commands followed by an ellipsis (...)
- a. Are unavailable
- b. Are available on the Formatting toolbar
- c. Display Help information when you choose them
- d. Display a dialog box when you choose them

16 You can get Help in any of the following ways, EXCEPT:
- a. Clicking Help in a dialog box
- b. Double-clicking anywhere in the document window
- c. Clicking the Help button on the Standard toolbar
- d. Clicking Help on the menu bar

17 To search for a topic in Help, you
- a. Click Help on the menu bar, then click Search for Help on
- b. Select the command then click the Help button on the Standard toolbar
- c. Click the Help button on the Standard toolbar
- d. Click the Help button on the Formatting toolbar

18 The Close command on the File menu
- a. Closes Word without saving any changes
- b. Closes the current document and, if you have made any changes, asks if you want to save them
- c. Closes all currently open Word documents
- d. Closes the current document without saving changes

APPLICATIONS REVIEW

1 Start Word then identify the parts of the window.
- a. Double-click the Microsoft Office program group icon in the Program Manager window.
- b. Double-click the Microsoft Word application icon.
- c. Read the Tip of the Day, if it appears. Clear the Show Tips at Startup check box, then click OK.
- d. Identify as many elements of the Word window as you can without referring to the unit material.

2 Explore the Word document window.
- a. Click each of the menus and drag the mouse button through all the commands on each menu. Read the command descriptions that appear in the status bar. To close a menu without making a selection, drag the mouse away from the menu, then release the mouse button.
- b. Point to each of the buttons on the toolbars, and read the ToolTips and descriptions.
- c. Click Tools then click Options. In the Options dialog box, click the Edit tab and make sure that the first three options are selected.
- d. Click OK to close the dialog box.

3 Explore Word Help.
- a. Click Help and view the Help commands.
- b. Click Search for Help on.
- c. Scroll through several topics and review them.
- d. In the search text box, type a topic about which you want more information.
- e. Click Show Topics to display related topics.
- f. Click a topic then click Go To. Read the information that appears in the How To window.
- g. Double-click the control menu box on the How To window to close it.
- h. Double-click the Help window control menu box to exit Help.

4 Close the document window and exit Word.
- a. Click File on the menu bar, then click Close.
- b. Click No if you see a message asking if you want to save your changes.
- c. Click File on the menu bar, then click Exit.

INDEPENDENT CHALLENGE 1

The Quick Preview command on the Help menu provides an on-line, animated tour of Word features, including many of the features you learned about in this unit. This tour also gives you an overview of the many different ways you can use Word to create documents of all types. To start the demonstration, click Help on the menu bar then click Quick Preview. Then select Getting Started and follow the instructions on the screen.

INDEPENDENT CHALLENGE 2

You can use the keyboard or the mouse to move around in a document and to choose a command. Use on-line Help to learn about the keyboard shortcuts for opening a document and navigating in Word. Search for the Open command and display the topic for shortcut keys. Then use the shortcut keys to open the document you used earlier in this lesson, UNIT_1-1.DOC. Search for keyboard shortcuts and display the topic for using shortcut keys to move around in a Word document. After moving through the document, use a shortcut key to close the document *without saving it*.

UNIT 2

OBJECTIVES

- Plan a document
- Enter text and save a document
- Insert and delete text
- Select and replace text
- Open a document and save it with a new name
- Copy and move text
- Correct spelling errors
- Preview a document
- Print a document

Creating AND EDITING A DOCUMENT

Now that you are familiar with the basics of the Word environment, you are ready to create a new document. After entering text in a new document, you can easily insert, delete, and replace text. You can also rearrange text by copying and moving selected text. ▶ At Nomad Ltd, Angela needs to create a letter to Nomad's shareholders. Her letter will include text that she will copy from another document, which was already prepared by a colleague in the Marketing Department. Before printing the document, Angela needs to check the document's spelling and preview the document to see how it will look when printed. ▶

Planning a document

Although Word makes it easy to modify documents after you have created them, it is always a good idea to plan the document before you begin typing it. Planning a document helps you work more effectively by helping you focus on the features you will need to use. Planning a document involves four areas: content, organization, tone, and format. Begin by determining what you want to say: in other words, identify the content of the document. Next, organize the ideas into a logical order in which they should be presented. With the content and organization clarified, you can begin writing using a tone that matches the content, purpose, and audience of the document. For example, the words you use in an announcement to a company picnic will be different in tone from a business letter requesting payment for an overdue invoice. Finally, you can make the document visually appealing, using formatting that emphasizes the ideas presented in the document and that is consistent with the content, tone, and organization. ▶ Angela wants to inform shareholders of an upcoming Annual Meeting and provide an overview of the year's highlights.

1. **Choose the information and important points you want to cover in the document**
   Angela writes down her ideas for the document, as shown in Figure 2-1.
2. **Decide how the information will be organized**
   Because the information about the meeting is most important, Angela decides to present it first. The company highlights are included next. Later, if Angela decides to rearrange the structure of the document, she can use Word's editing features to move, copy, and cut text as needed.
3. **Choose the tone of the document**
   Because the document is being sent to corporate shareholders, Angela will use a business-like tone. In addition, it has been a good year at Nomad Ltd, so Angela will also use a positive, enthusiastic tone intended to encourage shareholders to feel good about their investments in the company. Angela can edit the document as needed until she achieves exactly the tone she wants.
4. **Think about how you want the document to look**
   To best communicate this information to her readers, Angela plans to use a straightforward business letter format for her document. The letter will include lists, directions, and a signature block. Each will require special formatting to distinguish these parts from the rest of the letter. If Angela changes her mind about the format of the document, she can make adjustments later.

FIGURE 2-1: Angela's document plan

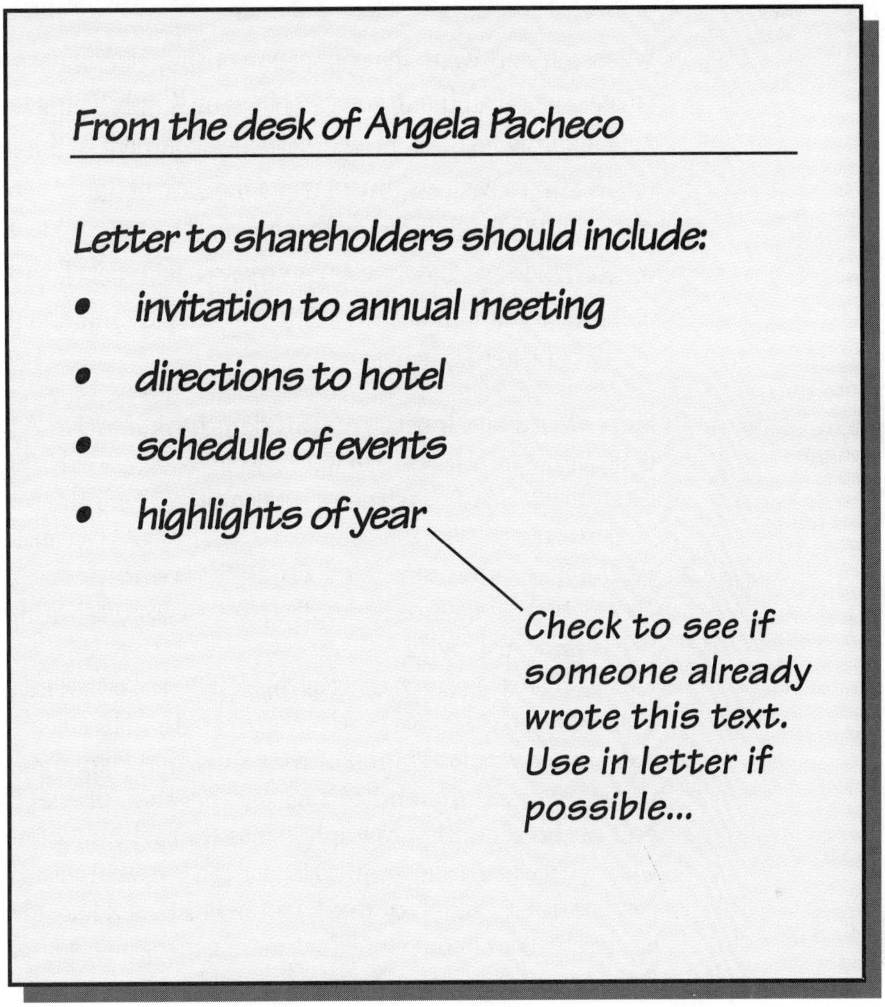

From the desk of Angela Pacheco

Letter to shareholders should include:

- invitation to annual meeting
- directions to hotel
- schedule of events
- highlights of year

Check to see if someone already wrote this text. Use in letter if possible...

Entering text and saving a document

When you start Word, the application opens a document window in which you can create a new document. You can begin by simply typing text at the insertion point. After entering text, you need to save the document so that it is stored permanently on disk. You save a document using the Save or Save As command on the File menu, or the Save button on the Standard toolbar. Table 2-1 shows the difference between the Save and Save As commands. ▶ Angela begins by typing the greeting and two paragraphs of her letter to Nomad Ltd's shareholders. After she types the text of her letter, she can save it.

1. **Start Word and insert your Student Disk in drive A**
   If you are unsure of how to start Word, refer to "Starting Word 6.0 for Windows" in Unit 1. Also, refer to the "Word 6.0 Screen Check" section on the "Read This Before You Begin Microsoft Word 6.0" page to make sure your Word screen is set up appropriately.
2. At the insertion point, type **Dear Shareholder:**
   The text appears to the left of the insertion point. The paragraph mark moves to the right as you type.
3. Press **[Enter]** twice
   Pressing [Enter] displays a paragraph mark at the end of the line, and moves the insertion point to the next line. The second paragraph mark creates a blank line.
4. Type the two paragraphs of text shown in Figure 2-2; do not press [Enter] until you reach the end of a paragraph, then press **[Enter]** twice (at the end of the second paragraph, press [Enter] only once)
   When you are typing and you reach the end of a line, Word automatically moves the text to the next line. This is called **word-wrap**. Pressing [Enter] twice inserts a blank line between paragraphs. Don't be concerned about making typing mistakes. Later in this unit, you will learn how to make revisions. Also, don't be concerned if your text wraps differently from the text shown in the figure. Exactly how text wraps can depend on the kind of monitor you are using or the type of printer you have selected. Next, Angela saves her letter.
5. Click **File** on the menu bar then click **Save As**
   The Save As dialog box opens. In this dialog box, you need to assign a name to the document you are creating, replacing the default filename supplied by Word.
6. In the File Name text box, type **SHRHOLDR**
   Your document name can contain up to eight characters. Word automatically adds the file extension .DOC to the filename. Also, note that it doesn't matter whether you enter the filename in uppercase or lowercase. Next, you need to instruct Word to save the file to your Student Disk.
7. Click the **Drives list arrow**, then click **a:**
   These lessons assume your Student Disk is in drive A. If you are using a different drive or storing your practice files on a network, click the appropriate drive. If you are not saving files to the MY_FILES directory of your Student Disk, or if you did not complete the exercises in "Microsoft Windows 3.1," you can skip Step 8.
8. In the Directories list box, make sure the **MY_FILES** directory is selected
   To select a directory, double-click the directory name. Compare the completed dialog box to Figure 2-3.
9. Click **OK**
   The document is saved with the name SHRHOLDR.

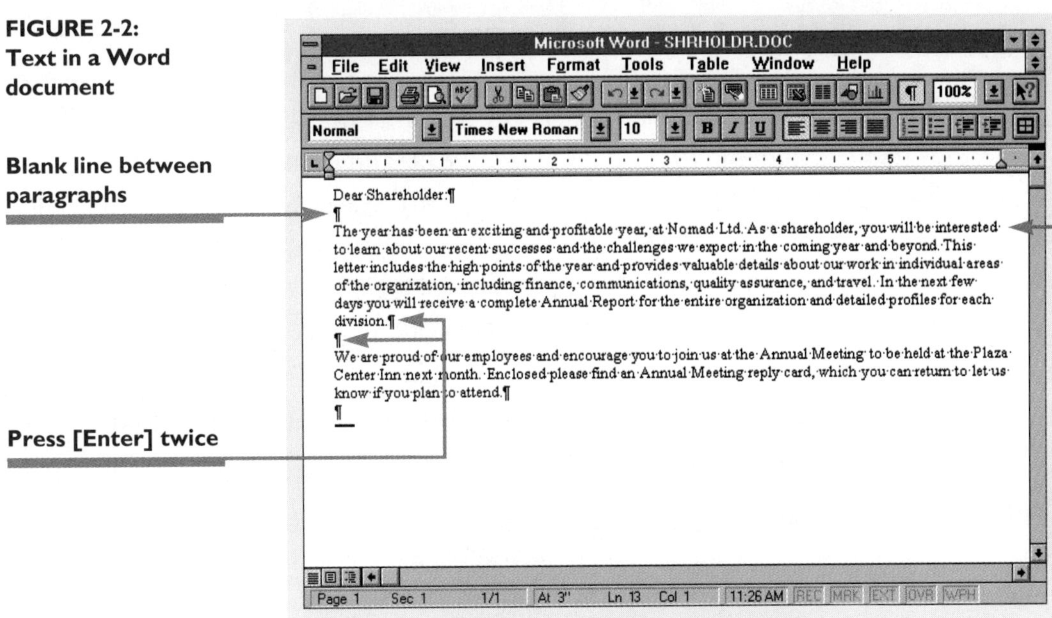

FIGURE 2-2: Text in a Word document

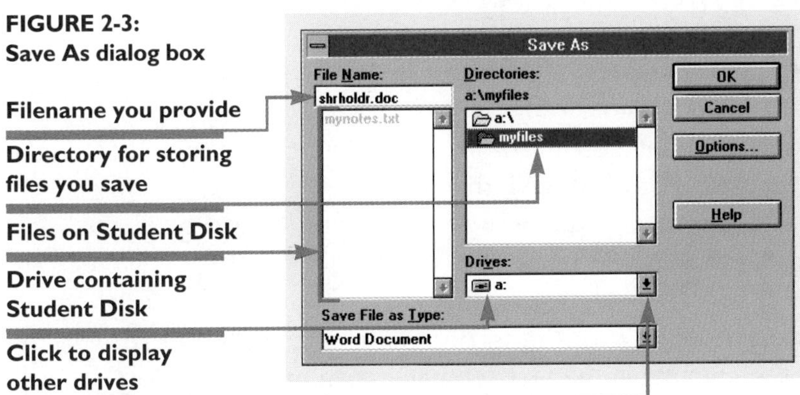

FIGURE 2-3: Save As dialog box

Inserting spaces between sentences

When you first learned how to type, you might have been instructed to insert two spaces after a period between sentences. Because of advances in typography and the size and shape of text used in word processing applications, you need to type only one space between sentences.

TABLE 2-1: The difference between the Save and Save As commands

COMMAND	DESCRIPTION	PURPOSE
Save As	Saves file, requires input name	To save a file the first time, to change the filename, or to save the file for use in a different application. Useful for backups.
Save	Saves named file	To save any changes to the original file. Fast and easy—do this often to protect your work.

TROUBLE?

If you cannot see the nonprinting characters (spaces, tabs, and paragraph marks), click the Show/Hide ¶ button ¶ on the Standard toolbar. If not all of the nonprinting characters appear, choose Options from the Tools menu. Click the View tab, then in the Nonprinting Characters section, click All.■

QUICK TIP

The keyboard shortcut for saving a document is [Ctrl][S].■

Inserting and deleting text

After typing text, you'll often need to edit it by inserting new text or deleting text you want to remove. To insert text, place the insertion point where you want the new text to appear, then simply start typing. To delete text, place the insertion point next to the text you want to delete, then press [Backspace] to remove characters to the left of the insertion point, or press [Delete] to remove characters to the right of the insertion point. Whenever you insert or delete text, the existing text is automatically reformatted. ▶ First, Angela wants to add the inside address to her letter, then she'll make a few corrections to the letter using [Delete] and [Backspace] to remove individual characters of text.

1. Place the insertion point in front of the word "Dear" and type the following address, pressing [Enter] after each line:
   Ms. Mary Ruiz [Enter]
   321 Orange Way [Enter]
   Green Valley, CA 90272 [Enter]
2. Press **[Enter]** again to insert a blank line above the greeting
   Next, Angela wants to change the word "The" in the first sentence to "This."
3. Place the insertion point after the word "The" (but before the space) in the first sentence, press **[Backspace]**, then type **is**
   The "e" to the left of the insertion point is removed, and the letters "is" are inserted. Next, Angela notices that the comma after the second occurrence of the word "year" is unnecessary, so she will delete this character as well.
4. Place the insertion point after the second occurrence of the word "year" (but before the comma) in the first sentence, then press **[Delete]**
   The comma is removed. Next, Angela decides to add today's date to the beginning of the letter. She needs to move to the beginning of the document before she can insert it.
5. Press **[Ctrl][Home]** to place the insertion point at the beginning of the document
   Notice that the status bar displays the position of the insertion point as you move around in the document. With the insertion point at the beginning of the document, Angela can quickly insert the date using the Date and Time command.
6. Click **Insert** on the menu bar, then click **Date and Time**
   The Date and Time dialog box opens, as shown in Figure 2-4. In this dialog box, you can select the format in which the date and/or time will appear in your document. Word automatically displays the date based on your computer's system clock, so the dates you see in the dialog box might be different from those shown in the figure. For letters and other business correspondence, Angela prefers the fourth option in the list.
7. In the dialog box, click the **fourth option** in the list, then click **OK**
   Today's date automatically appears in the document.
8. Press **[Enter]** twice
   Compare your document to Figure 2-5; however, the date you see might be different.
9. Click **File** on the menu bar, then click **Save**
   Your changes to the letter are saved in the document file. Because you already saved and named the document, the Save As dialog box does not open when you choose Save.

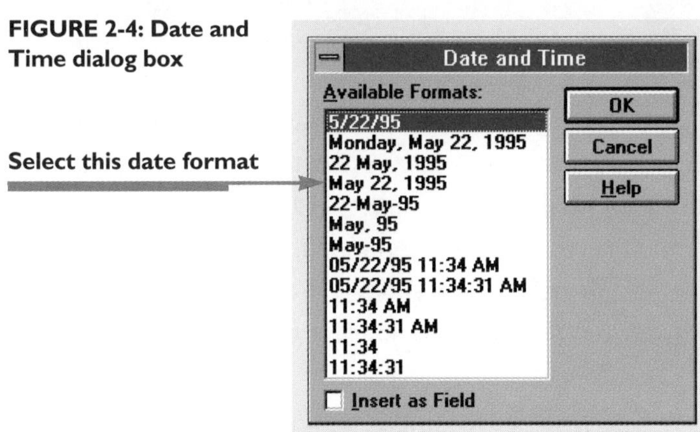

FIGURE 2-4: Date and Time dialog box

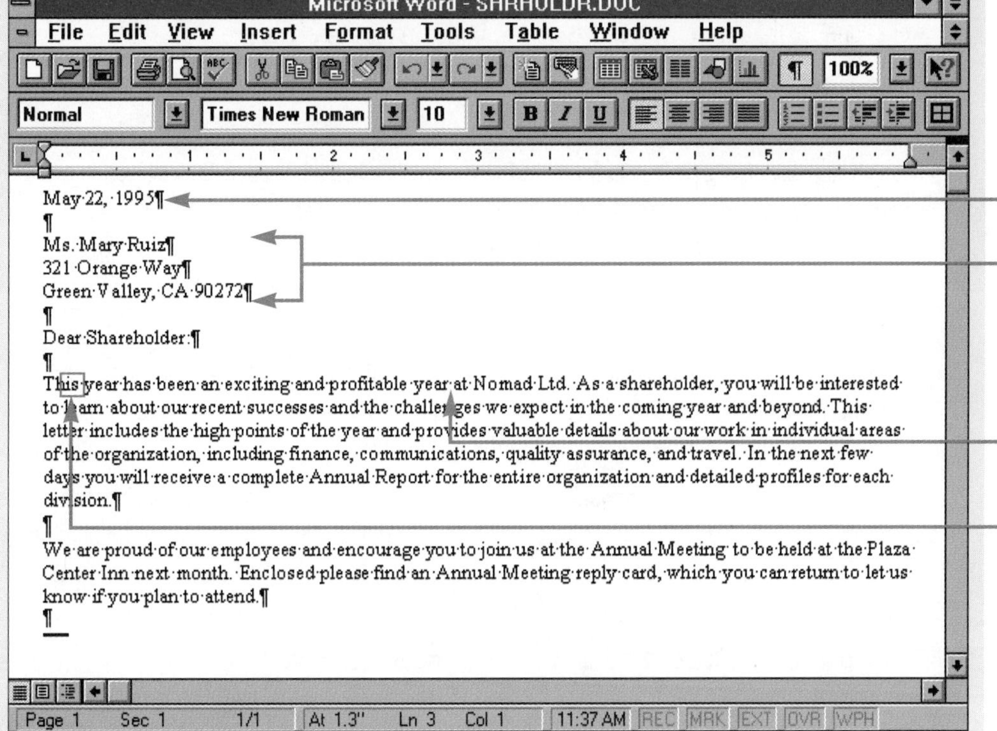

FIGURE 2-5: Letter after inserting and deleting text

Inserting date and time codes

When you use the Date and Time command, Word inserts a special code that displays the system date on your computer. Whenever you use the Print Preview or Print command, the date is automatically updated. When the insertion point is inside a code, the entire code appears shaded. This indicates that the text displayed is actually the result of a code.

TROUBLE?

If your typing overwrites existing text, check to see if the indicator "OVR" appears in the status bar. If it does, this means that Word is in Overtype mode. You need to switch back to Insert mode by pressing [Insert] or double-clicking OVR in the status bar, so that text you type does not overwrite existing text.

Selecting and replacing text

In addition to editing characters one at a time, you can also edit multiple characters, words, paragraphs, or the entire document. Most Word editing techniques require first selecting the text you want to edit. For example, to delete existing text and replace it with new text, you first select the text you want to remove then type the new text. This feature is called **Typing Replaces Selection**. Table 2-2 describes the different ways to select text. ▶ Next, Angela will use various techniques to select and replace text.

1. **Place the insertion point in front of the second occurrence of the word year in the first sentence and drag across the word**
   The word is highlighted, indicating it is selected. Angela wants to replace the selection with the word "one" so that the word "year" is not used twice in the same sentence.
2. **Type one**
   The word "one" replaces the selected word. Now Angela replaces several words with one word.
3. **Place the insertion point in front of the word please in the last sentence and drag across it and the next word, find, then release the mouse button**
   Both words and the spaces are selected. The next operation you perform will affect the selected text. If you drag across too many words, drag back over the text to deselect it.
4. **Type is**
   The word "is" replaces the selected text. Word automatically inserts the correct spacing and reformats the text after the insertion point. Angela decides that the word "summarizes" would be more accurate than the word "includes" in the third sentence.
5. **Double-click the word includes in the third sentence, then type summarizes**
   The word "summarizes" replaces the selected text, along with the correct spacing. If you change your mind after making an editing change, you can reverse it with the Undo button on the Standard toolbar. Angela decides to use the Undo button to reinsert the word "includes."
6. **Click the Undo button on the Standard toolbar**
   Your editing action is reversed, and the word "includes" replaces the word "summarizes." Clicking the Undo button reverses the most recent action. The arrow next to the Undo button displays a list of all changes you've made since opening the document, so you can undo one or more changes. The Redo button reverses an action you've undone.
7. **Click the Redo button on the Standard toolbar**
   The word "summarizes" reappears. As with the Undo feature, the arrow next to the Redo button displays a list of changes you can redo.
8. **Position the pointer to the far left of the first line of the body of the letter until the pointer changes to then click**
   The first line of text is selected when you click next to the line in the selection bar. The **selection bar** is the area to the left of the text in your document, as shown in Figure 2-6.
9. **Click anywhere in the document to deselect the text, then click the Save button on the Standard toolbar**
   The first line is no longer selected. Whenever you want to deselect text, simply click in the document window. Clicking the Save button is the same as choosing Save from the File menu.

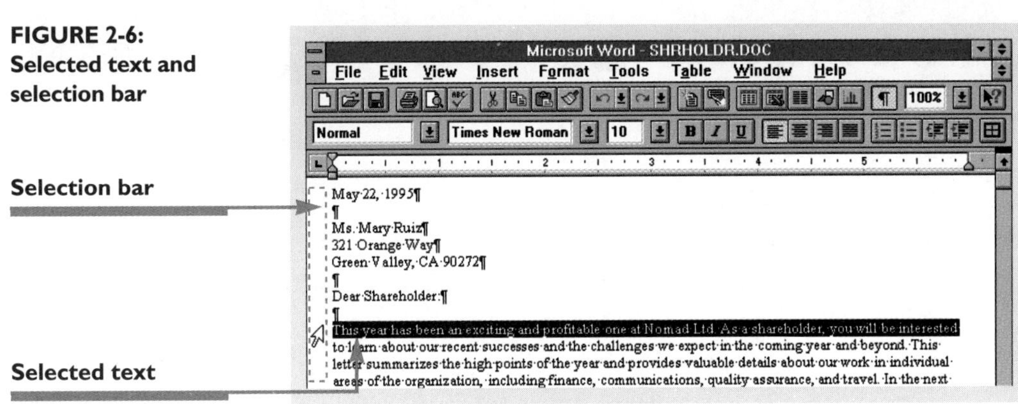

FIGURE 2-6: Selected text and selection bar

TROUBLE?

If text you type does not replace selected text, click Tools, click Options, click the Edit tab, then click to select the Typing Replaces Selection check box. Click OK to return to the document.■

TABLE 2-2: Mouse and keyboard selection techniques

SELECTING TEXT WITH THE MOUSE	DO THIS
A word	Double-click the word
A sentence	Press and hold [Ctrl] and click in the sentence
A paragraph	Triple-click in the paragraph, or double-click in the selection bar next to the paragraph
A line of text	Click in the selection bar next to the line
An entire document	Press and hold [Ctrl] and click anywhere in the selection bar, or triple-click in the selection bar
A vertical block of text	Press and hold [Alt] and drag through the text
A large amount of text	Place the insertion point at the beginning of the text, move to the end of the desired selection, then press and hold [Shift] and click

SELECTING TEXT WITH THE KEYBOARD	AT THE START OF THE SELECTION, PRESS	AT THE END OF THE SELECTION, PRESS
A character	[Shift][→]	[Shift][←]
A word	[Ctrl][Shift][→]	[Ctrl][Shift][←]
A paragraph	[Ctrl][Shift][↓]	[Ctrl][Shift][↑]
To the end/start of a line	[Shift][End]	[Shift][Home]
To the end/start of a document	[Ctrl][Shift][End]	[Ctrl][Shift][Home]
An entire document	[Ctrl][A]	
A vertical block of text	[Ctrl][Shift][F8] and select with the arrow keys	

Opening a document and saving it with a new name

In Unit 1, you opened an existing document, then closed it without saving changes. When you open a document and you want to work with it, but you want to make sure that no changes are made to it, you can save the document with a new name. This creates a copy of the document, leaving the original intact. ▶ Earlier Angela reviewed a document created by a colleague at Nomad Ltd. This document contains additional text Angela wants to use in her letter. So that she does not alter the original file for this other document, Angela opens the document and saves it with a new name. Then she can use the text in her saved copy of the document to add to her letter.

1. **Click the Open button on the Standard toolbar**
   Word displays the Open dialog box, as shown in Figure 2-7. The MY_FILES directory is the current directory because this was the last directory you accessed (when you saved a file earlier in this unit). If you are not saving files to the MY_FILES directory, skip Step 2. Drive A should be the current directory.

2. **Double-click the a:\ directory in the Directories list box to display the list of practice files stored on your Student Disk**
   When you double-click a new directory to make it the current directory, the files in the directory appear in the File Name list box.

3. **Click the document named UNIT_2-1.DOC in the File Name list box, then click OK**
   The document UNIT_2-1.DOC appears in the document window, as shown in Figure 2-8. To keep this original file intact, Angela will save it with a new name, SUMMARY. Then she'll continue working with this copy of the original file.

4. **Click File on the menu bar, then click Save As**
   The Save As dialog box opens, in which you can enter a new name for the document.

5. **Make sure the Drives list box displays the drive containing your Student Disk**
   If you are not saving files to the MY_FILES directory, skip Step 6 and continue with Step 7.

6. **Double-click the MY_FILES directory to make it the current directory**

7. **In the File Name text box, type SUMMARY then click OK**
   The document is saved with the new name, and the original document is closed.

FIGURE 2-7: Open dialog box

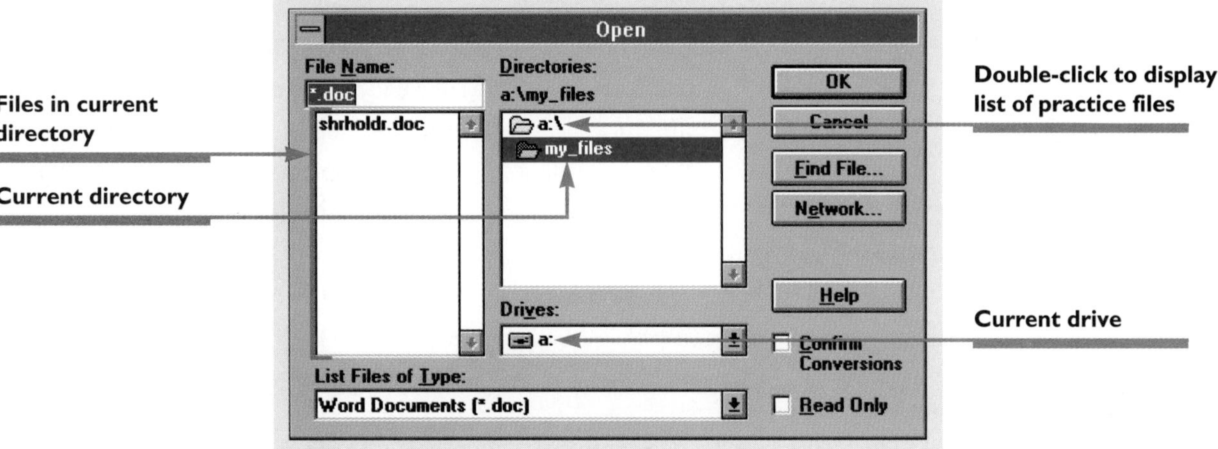

FIGURE 2-8: Open Word document

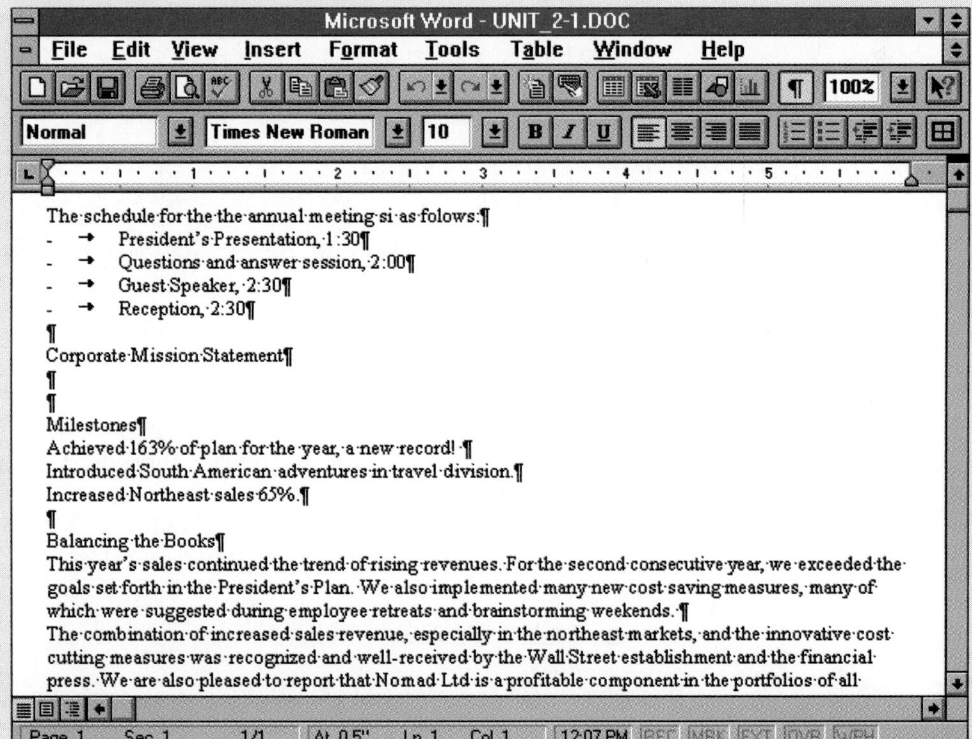

QUICK TIP

You can double-click a filename in the Open dialog box to open the document. This is faster than clicking the filename then clicking OK.

Copying and moving text

Moving and Copying Data

You can copy existing text that you want to reuse in a document, and you can remove text from its current location and place it elsewhere in a document. There are two ways to copy and move text: you can drag the text to a new location using the mouse, or you can use the Clipboard. The **Clipboard** is a temporary storage area for text and is available in any Windows application. Table 2-3 summarizes the techniques you can use to move and copy text using the Clipboard. ▶ Now that Angela has opened and reviewed the document created by her colleague, she can copy text from it to her letter. Angela displays both documents at once, in separate windows, so that she can work in both documents at the same time.

1. **Click Window on the menu bar, then click Arrange All**
   Both documents appear in the application window, as shown in Figure 2-9. Each appears in its own document window, with its own scroll bars, rulers, and Minimize and Maximize buttons (these buttons only appear in the currently active document window). Angela wants to copy all the text from her colleague's document to her letter.
2. **With the pointer in the selection bar of the SUMMARY document, triple-click the left mouse button**
   Triple-clicking in the selection bar selects the entire document.
3. **Click the Copy button on the Standard toolbar**
   The selected text is copied to the Clipboard. By placing text on the Clipboard (with either the Cut or Copy command), you can insert the text anywhere in the document as many times as you want. Angela wants to place this text before the last sentence in her letter.
4. **Click in the SHRHOLDR document window to make it active, then place the insertion point in front of the last sentence, as shown in Figure 2-10**
5. **Click the Paste button on the Standard toolbar**
   The copied text is inserted, but remains on the Clipboard until you copy or cut new text. Angela now wants to copy and move selected text in her letter. To make it easier to work in her document, Angela maximizes the SHRHOLDR document window.
6. **Click anywhere in the SHRHOLDR document window, then click the Maximize button**
   With this document window maximized, Angela can see more of the document at once.

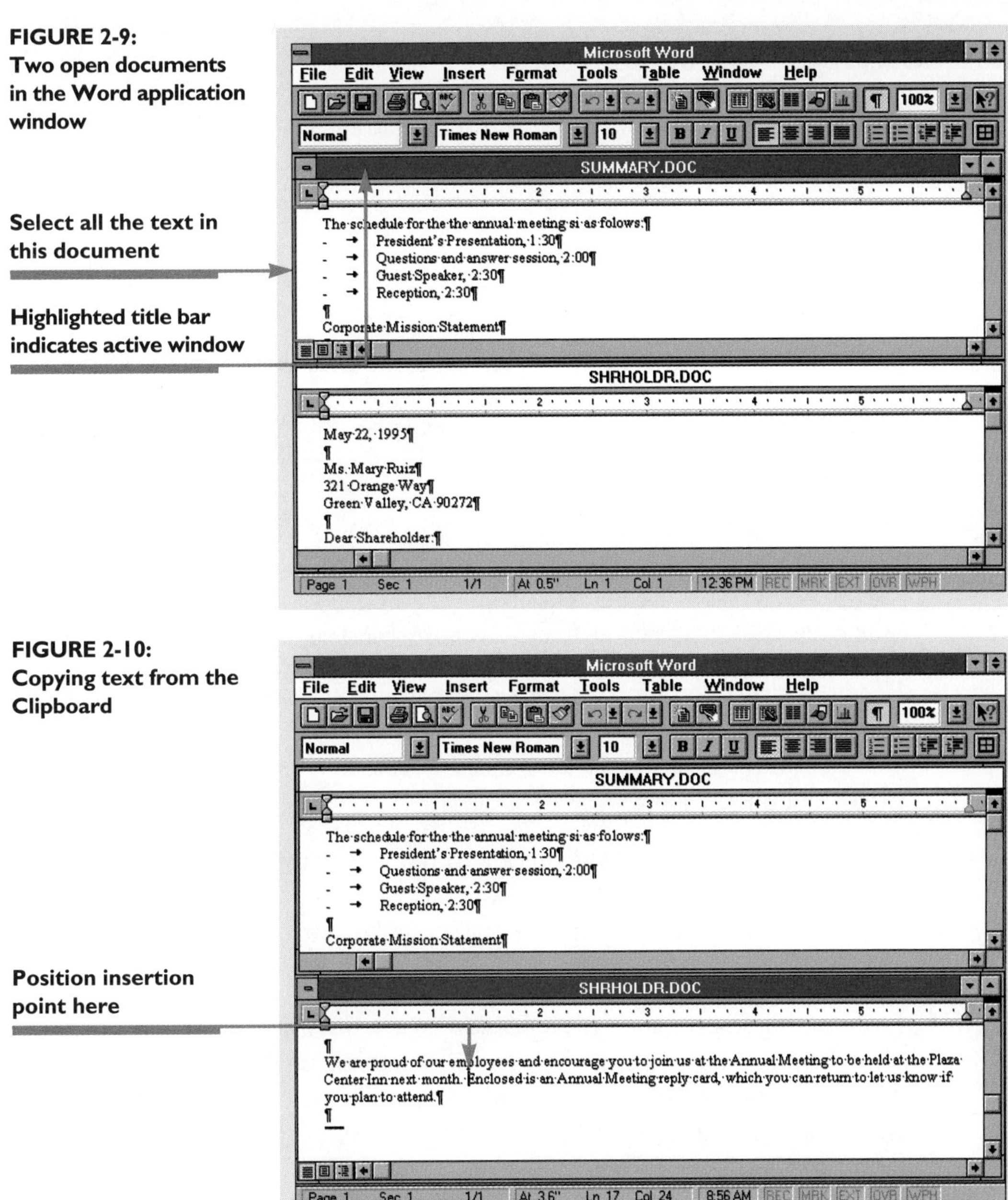

FIGURE 2-9: Two open documents in the Word application window

FIGURE 2-10: Copying text from the Clipboard

TABLE 2-3: Menu commands, buttons, and keyboard shortcuts for copying and moving text

ACTION	MENU COMMAND	WITH A BUTTON	WITH THE KEYBOARD
Cut selected text	Click Edit then click Cut to place the text on the Clipboard and remove the selection from the document	[Cut button]	[Ctrl][X]
Copy selected text	Click Edit then click Copy to place the text on the Clipboard and retain the selection in the document	[Copy button]	[Ctrl][C]
Paste	Click Edit then click Paste to paste the contents of the Clipboard at the insertion point	[Paste button]	[Ctrl][V]

Copying and moving text, continued

First, Angela wants to copy the company name, Nomad Ltd, to other locations in the document.

7 Select the text **Nomad Ltd** in the first paragraph, then click the **Copy button** on the Standard toolbar
The selected text is copied to the Clipboard. Angela wants to place this text in front of the word "shareholder" in the next sentence.

8 Place the insertion point after the space in front of the word **shareholder**, then click the **Paste button** on the Standard toolbar
The text "Nomad Ltd" is inserted, as shown in Figure 2-11. Angela wants to insert the company name again, this time after the word "our" in the next paragraph.

9 Place the insertion point after the space after the word **our** in the next paragraph, then click on the Standard toolbar
The text Nomad Ltd is inserted. Angela now wants to move the last sentence to follow the schedule of events.

10 Press **[Ctrl][End]** to move quickly to the end of the document, then select the last sentence in the document
With the sentence selected, Angela uses the dragging method to move the text to the new location in the document.

11 Position the pointer over the selection, press and hold the mouse button until the pointer changes from I to ; *do not release the mouse button yet*
When you select only part of a document and hold down the mouse button, the text remains highlighted as you drag the mouse to move the text. If you want to copy selected text rather than move it, press and hold [Ctrl] first.

12 Drag the mouse up, scrolling through the document until you see the schedule of events, place the vertical bar of the pointer in the first line below the last event, then release the mouse button
The sentence is inserted. Compare your document to Figure 2-12. Angela decides this is a good time to save her work.

13 In the letter document, click the **Save button** on the Standard toolbar
The changes you made to the SHRHOLDR letter are saved.

FIGURE 2-11: Document with inserted text

Inserted text

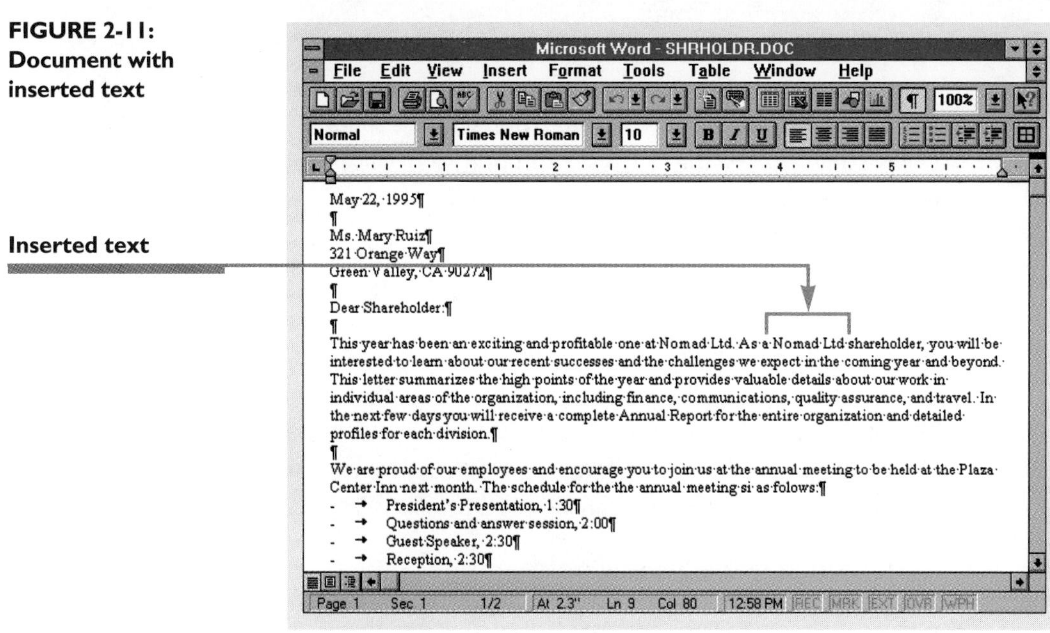

FIGURE 2-12: Completed document

Copied text

Moved text

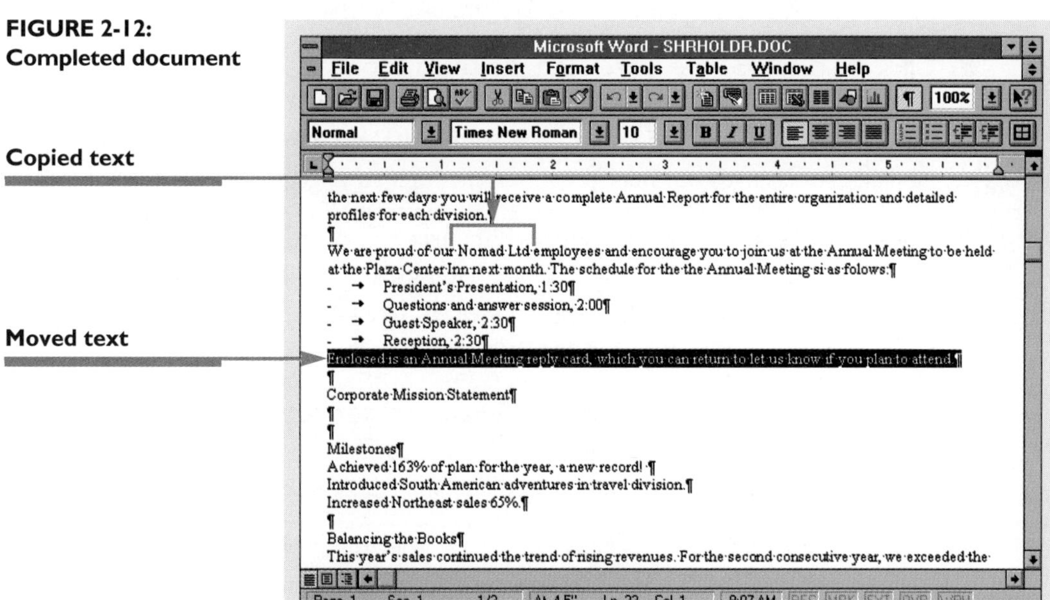

TROUBLE?

If the selected text does not move when you try to drag, click Tools, click Options, click the Edit tab, then click to select the Drag-and-Drop Text Editing check box.■

The Delete key vs. the Cut command

Pressing [Delete] is not the same as using the Cut command. The Cut command places the selected text on the Clipboard after removing it from the document. Pressing [Delete] only removes the text; the text is not on the Clipboard and is not available for pasting.

Correcting spelling errors

Word's Spelling command identifies and corrects spelling errors and repeated words (such as "the the"). This command identifies as misspelled any words not found in the Word dictionary, including proper nouns. From a list of suggested spellings, you can choose the spelling you want to use. ▶ Before Angela prints her letter, she checks that it contains no spelling errors.

1 Press **[Ctrl][Home]** to place the insertion point at the beginning of the document, then click the **Spelling button** on the Standard toolbar
The Spelling dialog box opens, showing the first error located in the document—the word "Ruiz," as shown in Figure 2-13. Figure 2-13 also describes the options in the Spelling dialog box. The identified word is a proper noun and is not misspelled so Angela ignores this error.

2 Click **Ignore** in the Spelling dialog box
Word identifies "Ltd" as the next misspelled word. Suggested spellings are displayed in the Suggestions list box. Because this is part of the company name and appears often in company correspondence, Angela decides to add this word to the Word dictionary.

3 Click **Add** to add the word "Ltd" to the dictionary
The next time the Spelling command encounters this word, it will not be identified as misspelled. Next, the Spelling dialog box indicates that the word "the" is repeated. The options available in the dialog box change when Word identifies a repeated word. Angela deletes the repeated word.

4 Click **Delete** to delete the second occurrence of the word
The Spelling command identifies "si" as the next misspelled word. Because this is a typing mistake Angela makes frequently, she creates an **AutoCorrect entry** for this word so that this misspelling will be corrected automatically as she types it.

5 Click **AutoCorrect** to create an AutoCorrect entry
If someone has already created an AutoCorrect entry for "si," you will see a message asking if you want to replace the existing entry. Click OK to continue.

The next time Angela types "si" followed by a space, Word will supply the corrected word "is." See the related topic "More about AutoCorrect" for additional information. The word "folows" is identified as misspelled and a suggested correction appears in the Change To text box.

6 Click **Change** in the Spelling dialog box to replace "folows"
A message box opens, indicating that the spell check process is now complete.

7 Click **OK** to close the dialog box and return to the document
Angela decides to add one more paragraph of text and to test her AutoCorrect entry.

8 Place the insertion point in front of the paragraph mark below "Corporate Mission Statement," then type the following text (make sure you type the incorrect word "si" and watch how AutoCorrect corrects it:
Nomad Ltd si a national sporting-goods retailer dedicated to delivering high-quality adventure sporting gear and clothing.

9 Click the **Save button** on the Standard toolbar

FIGURE 2-13: Spelling dialog box

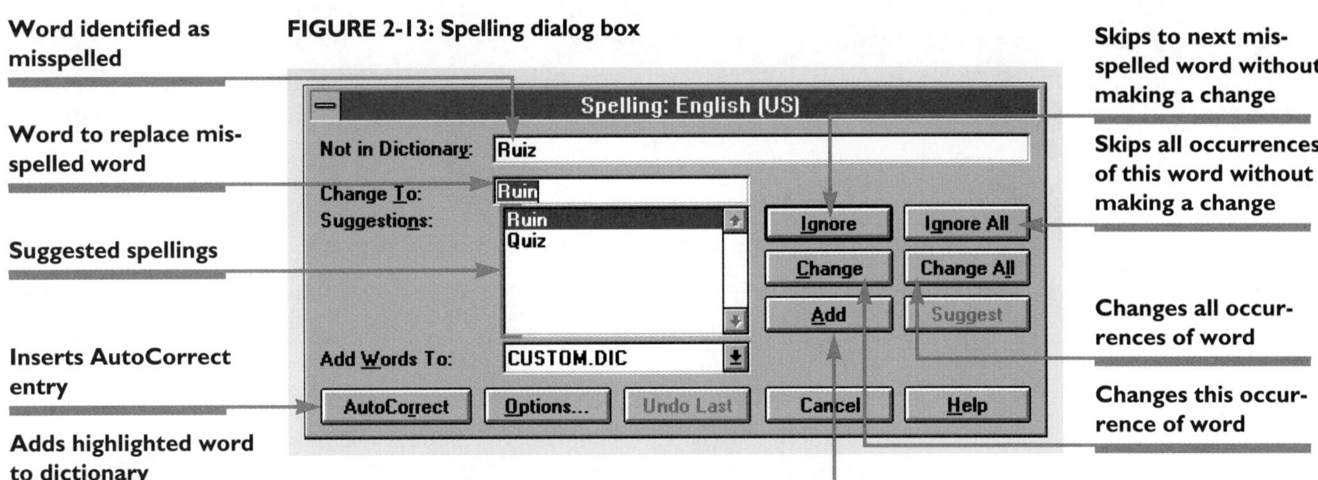

More about AutoCorrect

Word provides several AutoCorrect entries for correcting some common typing errors. It also provides the correct capitalization if you type two capital letters at the beginning of a word, and corrects the capitalization when you type the names of days. With the AutoCorrect feature, you can specify the kind of quotation marks to use in the document, and that the first character in a sentence should be capitalized. You can add AutoCorrect entries when Word locates a misspelled word in the Spelling dialog box, or you can click Tools then click AutoCorrect to display the AutoCorrect dialog box, as shown in Figure 2-14. In this dialog box, you can select or deselect the AutoCorrect features, and add entries at any time.

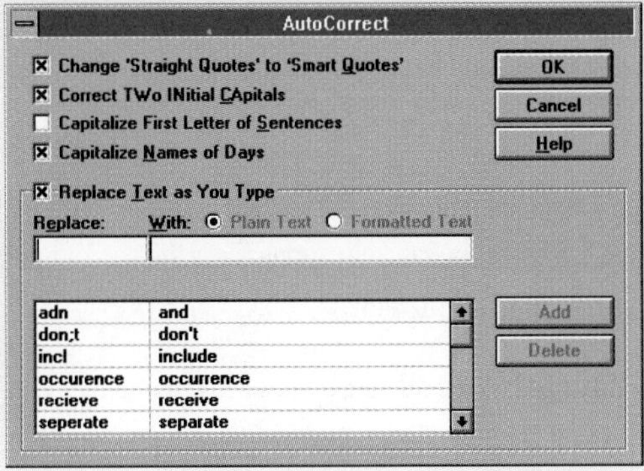

FIGURE 2-14: AutoCorrect dialog box

TROUBLE?

If the Spelling command does not identify the same misspelled words as described in this lesson, it means that someone else has already added words to the dictionary on this computer or that you made additional typing mistakes when you typed the letter. Correct any other errors identified in the spell check, as appropriate.■

Previewing a document

After proofreading and correcting your document, you are almost ready to print it. Before you do, it is a good idea to display the document using the Print Preview command. In print preview, you can easily check your page margins and the overall appearance of your document. If you notice additional changes you would like to make, you can get a close-up view of the page and make final changes before printing. ▶ Angela is now ready to preview her letter to see how it will look before printing it.

1 **Click the Print Preview button on the Standard toolbar**
The document appears in the Preview window, as shown in Figure 2-15. The size of the page you see depends on the number and size of pages displayed the last time someone used the Print Preview command. If you see more than one page, click the One Page button on the Print Preview toolbar. As she views the document, Angela realizes she needs to get a close-up view of the schedule of events to examine it more closely.

2 **Click the page near the schedule of events**
Notice that the pointer changes to when you position it in the document. The document is magnified, as shown in Figure 2-16. In print preview you can make quick changes without returning to the document window first. Angela decides to add extra space between the schedule of events and the next line of text.

3 **Click the Magnifier button on the Print Preview toolbar**
The Magnifier pointer changes to the insertion point when it is in text. Now you can edit the text.

4 **Place the insertion point in front of the word Enclosed after the schedule, then press [Enter]**
A blank line is inserted. Next, Angela decides to break the document into two parts. The part on the first page is the letter, and the part on the second page is the summary of the year's highlights. She decides to insert a page break between the two parts of the document.

5 **Place the insertion point in front of the word Corporate, click Insert on the menu bar, then click Break**
The Break dialog box opens. See the related topic "About page breaks" for more information.

6 **Make sure the Page Break button is selected, then click OK**
All the text after the insertion point now appears on the second page. Angela wants to view both pages of the document in print preview.

7 **Click the Multiple Pages button on the Print Preview toolbar, then drag to select two pages**
You see both pages of the document.

8 **Click the Close button on the Print Preview toolbar**
The Preview window closes and you return to the document in the normal view.

9 **Click the Save button on the Standard toolbar**

FIGURE 2-15: Document in print preview

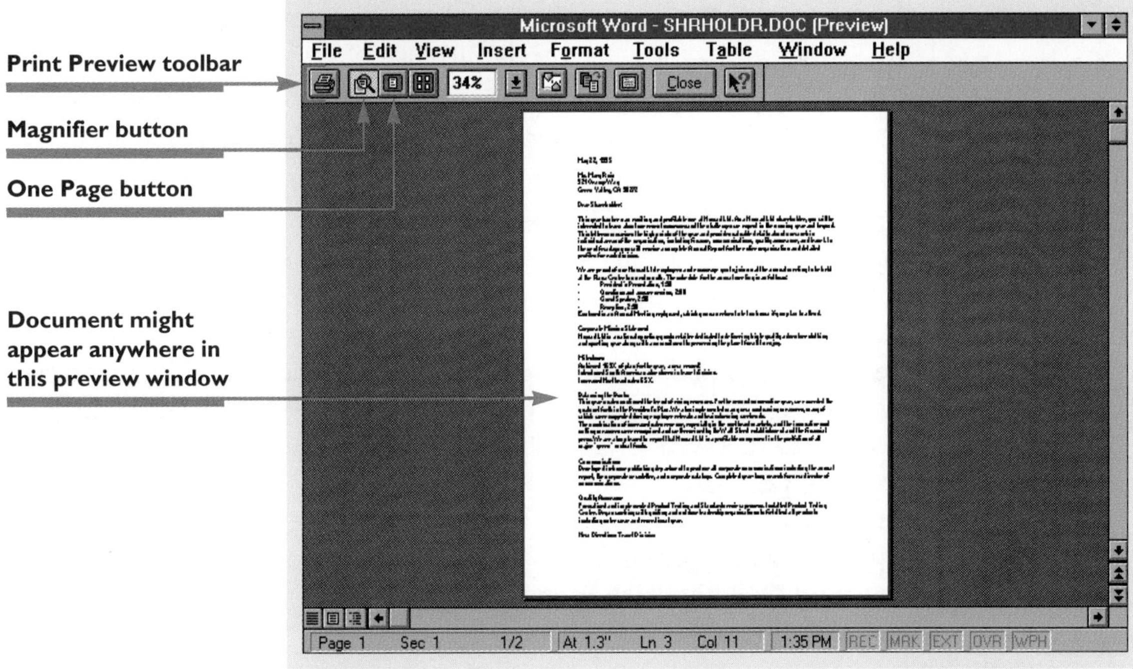

FIGURE 2-16: Close-up view of document

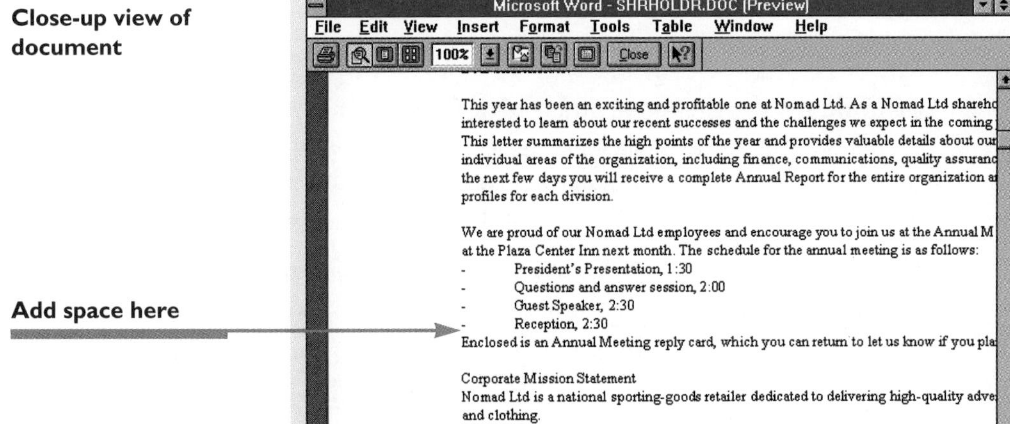

About page breaks

When the amount of text requires more than one page, Word automatically inserts a **soft page break** and formats the text onto a new page. A light dotted line appears between pages to represent a soft page break in your document. If you want to specify where a page break should occur, you can insert a **hard**, or **manual, page break**. A hard page break is represented by a darker dotted line between pages with the words "Page Break" in the center of the dotted line. You cannot delete a soft page break, but you can delete a hard page break by selecting the dotted line and pressing [Delete].

QUICK TIP

A quick way to display the document in print preview is to press [Ctrl][F2].■

Printing a document

Printing a document is as simple as clicking the Print button on the Standard toolbar (or the Print Preview toolbar). However, to take advantage of many printing options, use the Print command on the File menu. This command displays the Print dialog box in which you can select the print options you want to use, depending on your needs and the size of the document you want to print. See Table 2-4 to learn more about printing options.▶ Now that Angela has proofread and corrected her document, she will add a closing and then print the document.

1 Place the insertion point in the paragraph mark at the end of the first page, above the page break line, press **[Enter]**, then type the following text (be sure to press [Enter] after each line)
Sincerely, [Enter]
[Enter]
Angela Pacheco [Enter]
Marketing Division Manager [Enter]
Nomad Ltd [Enter]

2 Click the **Save button** on the Standard toolbar
The changes are saved in the document. Now Angela is ready to print, so she makes sure the printer is on and contains paper.

3 Click **File** on the menu bar, then click **Print**
The Print dialog box opens, as shown in Figure 2-17. In this dialog box, you can specify the print options you want to use when you print your document. The name of the printer and the options you have available might be different, depending on the kind of printer you have set up on your computer.

4 In the Copies text box, type **2**
The entry "2" replaces the default entry of "1." You will print a copy of this document for yourself and for your instructor.

5 Click **OK**
The Print dialog box closes, and your document is printed.

6 Click **File** on the menu bar, then click **Close**
The SHRHOLDR document closes. The SUMMARY document appears in the document window. This document was open while you worked on the letter. You can close this document as well.

7 Click **File** on the menu bar, then click **Close**
A dialog box might open asking if you want to save changes to the SUMMARY document.

8 Click **Yes** to save changes to the document

9 Click **File** on the menu bar, then click **Exit** to close the Word application

FIGURE 2-17: Print dialog box

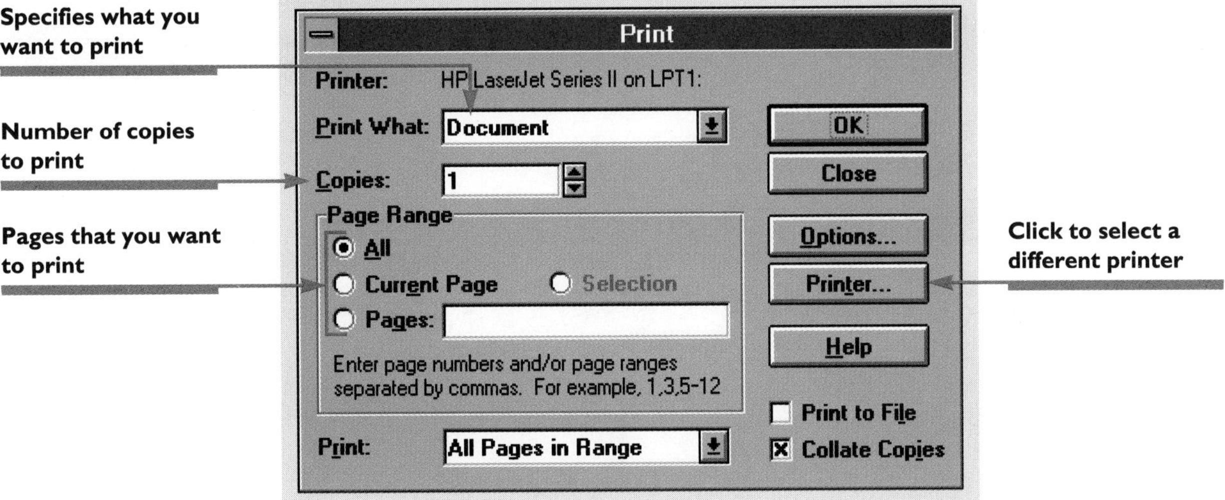

TABLE 2-4: Printing options

PRINT OPTIONS	DESCRIPTION
Printer	Displays the name of the selected printer and print connection
Print What	Prints the document (default), or only the summary information, annotations, styles, or other text associated with the document
Copies	Specifies the number of copies to print
Page Range	Specifies the pages to print: • *All*: prints the complete document • *Current Page*: prints the page with the insertion point or the selected page • *Selection*: prints selected text only • *Pages*: prints user-specified pages (separate single pages with a comma, a range of pages with a hyphen)
Print	Specifies the print order for the page range: All Pages in Range, Odd Pages, Even Pages
Print to File	Print a document to a new file instead of a printer
Collate Copies	Prints all pages of the first copy before printing subsequent copies, when multiple copies are selected (not available on all printers)

QUICK TIP

The shortcut key for the Print command is [Ctrl][P].

TROUBLE?

If you are not connected to a printer, ask your technical support person or instructor for assistance.

CONCEPTSREVIEW

Describe each of the parts of the Spelling dialog box in Figure 2-18.

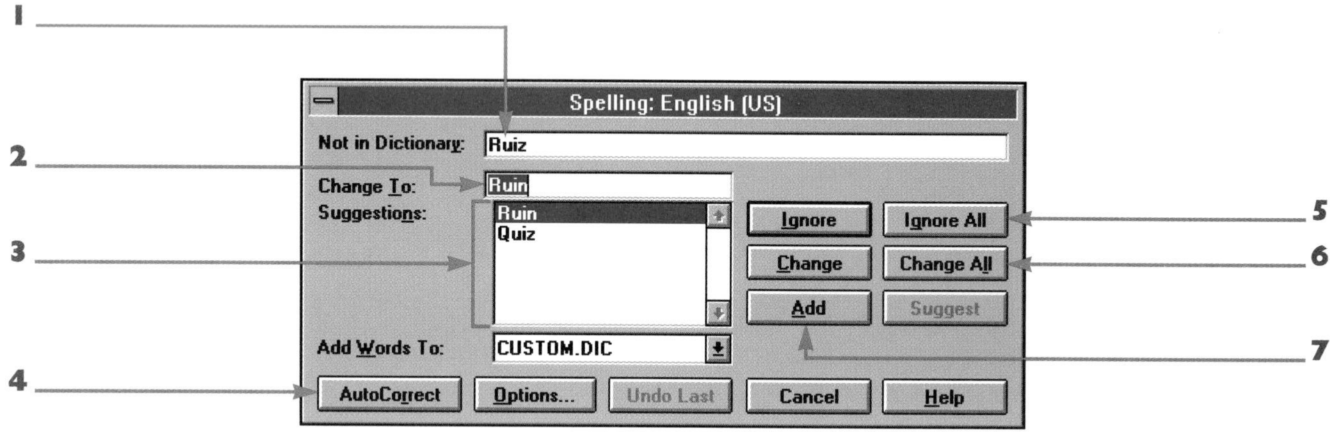

FIGURE 2-18

Match each of the following terms with the statement that best describes its function.

8 Selecting text and typing text in its place

9 Typing text between existing text

10 Removing text to the right or left of the insertion point

11 Temporary holding area for text to be pasted

12 Duplicating text in multiple locations

13 Removing text to be inserted in another location

14 Inserting the contents of the Clipboard

a. Deleting
b. Clipboard
c. Replacing
d. Copying
e. Inserting
f. Pasting
g. Cutting

Select the best answer from the list of choices.

15 Which of the following methods is NOT a way to select text?

a. Clicking in the selection bar
b. Dragging across text
c. Double-clicking a word with the left mouse button
d. Dragging text to the selection bar

16 Which of the following statements about the selection bar is NOT true?

a. You can select the entire document from the selection bar.
b. You can select part of a line from the selection bar.
c. You can select a line from the selection bar.
d. You must always use the mouse to select text from the selection bar.

17 Which key do you press to remove text to the left of the insertion point?

a. [Backspace]
b. [Delete]
c. [Cut]
d. [Overtype]

18 To place text on the Clipboard, you must first

a. Click the Copy button
b. Click the Cut button
c. Click the Paste button
d. Select the text

19 How many times can you use the Paste button to insert the contents of the Clipboard?

a. Twice

b. Once

c. Depends on the memory of the computer

d. Unlimited number of times

20 How many previous actions can you undo?

a. Two

b. One

c. All actions since the last time you saved the document

d. All actions since you opened the document

21 To display two open documents at once, you use which menu and command?

a. Click Window on the menu bar, then click Arrange All

b. Click Window on the menu bar, then click Split

c. Click Window on the menu bar, then click New Window

d. Click File on the menu bar, click Print Preview, then click Multiple Pages

22 What keys do you press to move the insertion point to the first character in a document?

a. [Ctrl][Home]

b. [Home]

c. [Alt][Page Up]

d. [Shift][Tab]

23 For most efficient document creation, when is the best time to proofread your document?

a. Just before printing

b. As soon as you have finished typing it

c. Before rearranging text

d. As you type, so you don't make any mistakes

24 What option is NOT available in the Spelling dialog box when a spelling error is identified?

a. Add the word to the dictionary

b. Add an AutoCorrect entry

c. Delete the incorrect word

d. Choose a suggested spelling

25 When does AutoCorrect correct your typing mistake?

a. When you press [Spacebar] after typing the word incorrectly

b. When you type a misspelled word

c. When you click the AutoCorrect button in the Spelling dialog box

d. When you click the AutoCorrect button on the Formatting toolbar

26 Which statement best describes the AutoCorrect feature?

a. Word comes with hundreds of AutoCorrect entries.

b. There must be an AutoCorrect entry for each typing mistake you want corrected automatically.

c. AutoCorrect "knows" what you want to type and types it for you.

d. AutoCorrect corrects grammatical errors as you make them.

27 In print preview, how do you get a close-up view of a page?

a. Click the Print Preview button

b. Click the Close button

c. Click the page with the Magnifier pointer

d. Click the One Page button

APPLICATIONS REVIEW

1 Create a new document and save it.

a. Start Word and complete the Word screen check procedure described on the "Read This Before You Begin Microsoft Word 6.0" page. Make sure you insert your Student Disk in the disk drive.

b. At the insertion point, type a short letter to a local business describing your interest in learning more about the company and requesting a copy of their annual report. Don't type the inside address or a closing yet. For a greeting, type "To Whom It May Concern:".

c. For a closing type "Sincerly," then press [Enter] twice. Be sure to misspell the word so that you can correct it later.

d. Click File on the menu bar, then click Save As.

e. Make the MY_FILES directory active on your Student Disk.

f. In the File Name text box, type NEWLTTR then click OK.

2 Insert and delete text.

a. Place the insertion point at the beginning of the document. Now type the inside address. Use whatever contact name, title, company name, and address that you want.

b. Press [Enter] twice, then type your name and press [Enter]. Then type your street address and press [Enter]. Type your city, state and zip code and press [Enter] again. Then type your phone number.

c. Use [Backspace] to delete your phone number. Press [Enter] once more.

3 Select and replace text.

a. Select the text "To Whom It May Concern," then type "Dear" followed by the name of the recipient of the letter; for example, Mr. Martin.

b. Select the last word of the document, then press [Delete] to delete the entire word.

c. Click the Undo button to restore the original text.

d. Use selecting and replacing techniques to correct any mistakes in your letter.

4 Copy and move text.

a. Use the two different copying techniques (using the Clipboard, and using the mouse and [Ctrl] to drag text) to copy the first sentence to the end of the document. Use the Undo button to reverse each action.

b. Use the two different moving techniques (using the Clipboard, and using the mouse to drag text) to move the first sentence to the end of the document. Use the Undo button to reverse each action.

c. Select your name and address at the beginning of the document (include the paragraph mark before your name) and move this text to the end of the document using either the mouse method or the Clipboard method.

d. Click the Save button on the Standard toolbar to save your document.

5 Correct spelling in a document.

a. Click the Spelling button on the Standard toolbar and correct any spelling errors.

b. Add your name to the custom dictionary, if Word identifies it as misspelled.

c. Add "Sincerly" as an AutoCorrect entry so that Word will provide the correct spelling "Sincerely" automatically. (If this AutoCorrect entry already exists, add an AutoCorrect entry of your choice after completing the spell check, using the AutoCorrect dialog box.)

d. Click OK to close the Spelling dialog box and return to the document.

e. Save your changes.

6 Preview a document.

a. Click the Print Preview button on the Standard toolbar.

b. Click the page near the signature.

c. Click the Magnifier button on the Print Preview toolbar.

d. Select the text under your name then type "Public Relations."

e. Click the One Page button on the Print Preview toolbar.

f. Click the Close button on the Print Preview toolbar.

g. Save your changes.

7 Print a document.

a. Click File on the menu bar, then click Print.

b. In the Copies box, type 2.

c. Click OK.

d. Click File on the menu bar, then click Close.

e. Click File on the menu bar, then click Exit.

INDEPENDENT CHALLENGE 1

Suppose you are the fundraising coordinator for a local theater company, called Lightwell Players. In response to a request for information from a potential corporate sponsor, create a new document that is a short letter describing the benefits of being a sponsor. To end your letter, open one of the documents you used in this unit. Then copy the last paragraph and the closing with your signature to the end of your letter. Edit this copied text to include your name, the appropriate title (fundraising coordinator), and company name (Lightwell Players). Save the document with the name LGHTWELL.DOC to the MY_FILES directory on your Student Disk. Preview and print the document, then close it.

INDEPENDENT CHALLENGE 2

As an account representative for At Your Service Temps, a temporary office services company, you drafted a letter describing the corporate discount program to a current customer. Open the document named UNIT_2-2.DOC from your Student Disk, then save it as TEMPS.DOC to your MY_FILES directory. Check the spelling in the document. Add the name of the newsletter to the dictionary. Create AutoCorrect entries for typographical errors, such as "haev." Save your changes to the document. Preview the document, then print it. Close the document and exit Word.

UNIT 3

OBJECTIVES

- Format text
- Align text with tabs
- Format paragraphs
- Create bulleted and numbered lists
- Format a document with AutoFormat and the Style Gallery
- Modify styles
- Apply borders and shading
- Format a paragraph with a drop cap
- Adjust document margins

Formatting A DOCUMENT

So far you've used Word to enter, edit, and rearrange text in a document. In this unit, you'll use Word's formatting capabilities to change the appearance of text on the page. Because Word is a **WYSIWYG** application (pronounced wizzy-wig, it stands for **W**hat **Y**ou **S**ee **I**s **W**hat **Y**ou **G**et), your document will print with the same formatting that you see displayed in the document window. ▶ Angela needs to format her letter to Nomad Ltd's shareholders to emphasize important topics. She's also been asked to improve the appearance of the summary of highlights, which is now a separate document. ▶

Formatting text

Formatting text means changing the appearance of the letters and words in your document. The text format settings you can change are summarized in Table 3-1. Basic formatting options (such as bold, italics, font, and font size) are available on the Formatting toolbar, shown in Figure 3-1. Additional formatting options are available with the Font command on the Format menu, which displays the Font dialog box shown in Figure 3-2. ▶ Angela begins formatting her letter to Nomad's shareholders by emphasizing selected text.

1. **Start Word and insert your Student Disk in drive A**
   See the instructions in Unit 1 if you are unsure of how to start Word. Also, refer to the "Word 6.0 Screen Check" section on the "Read This Before You Begin Microsoft Word 6.0" page to make sure your Word screen is set up appropriately.
2. **Open the document named UNIT_3-1.DOC from your Student Disk and save it as COVER.DOC to your MY_FILES directory**
   This document contains Angela's letter. Angela made additional revisions to the letter by adding two lists and removing the schedule because it has not been finalized yet. To draw attention to the location of the Annual Meeting, Angela decides to format this text in italics.
3. **Select the first occurrence of the text Plaza Center Inn in the third paragraph, then click the Italic button on the Formatting toolbar**
   The text now appears in italics. Next, Angela decides to bold the company name.
4. **Select the first occurrence of the text Nomad Ltd in the first paragraph, then click the Bold button on the Formatting toolbar**
   Deselect the text to see that it now appears in bold. Angela decides to emphasize this text even more by changing the font.
5. **Select the text again, click the Font list arrow on the Formatting toolbar, then click Arial**
   The text appears in the Arial font. The fonts available in the Font list box depend on the fonts installed on your computer. Arial is one of the Windows TrueType fonts, designated by a double "T" in the Font list. **TrueType fonts** display text as it will appear when printed. Angela thinks that the characters in the company name are too large, so she decides to reduce the font size of this text.
6. **With the same text still selected, click the Font Size list arrow on the Formatting toolbar, then click 9**
   The selected text appears in 9 point type. Because Angela wants all occurrences of the company name to be formatted this way, she uses the Format Painter to copy the formatting to the other occurrences.
7. **With the same words still selected, double-click the Format Painter button on the Standard toolbar**
   Word's **Format Painter** copies the formatting of selected text to the next text you select. By double-clicking the button instead of simply clicking, this feature remains in effect so that you can select and change multiple occurrences of text. Notice that the pointer changes to .
8. **Drag across each occurrence of Nomad Ltd in the document, except in the signature block at the end of the letter**
   The formatting of the selected text is copied to the text you drag across. Scroll to the top of the screen and compare your document to Figure 3-3.
9. **Click to deactivate the Format Painter feature, then click the Save button on the Standard toolbar to save your changes**

FIGURE 3-1: Text formatting buttons on Formatting toolbar

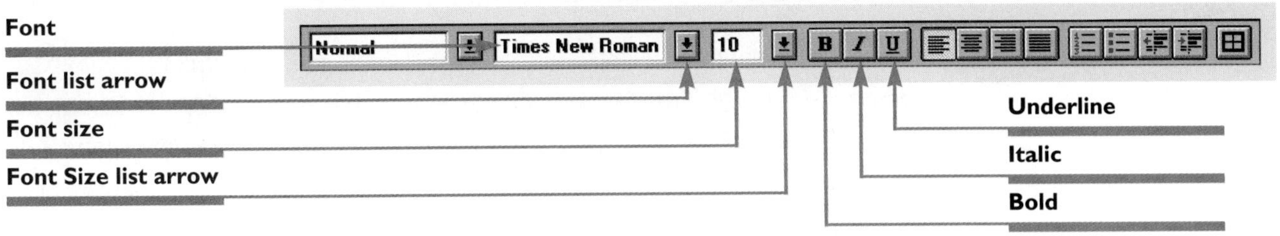

Font

Font list arrow

Font size

Font Size list arrow

Underline

Italic

Bold

FIGURE 3-2: Font dialog box

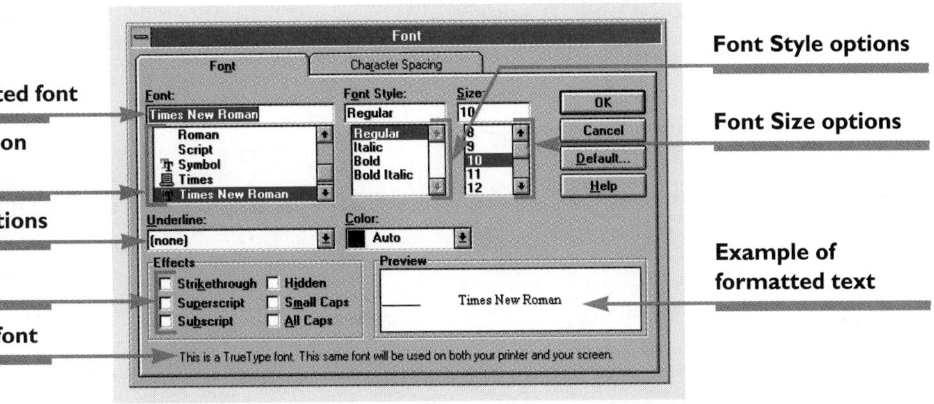

Currently selected font

Fonts available on your computer

Underlining options

Effects options

Description of font

Font Style options

Font Size options

Example of formatted text

FIGURE 3-3: Formatted letter

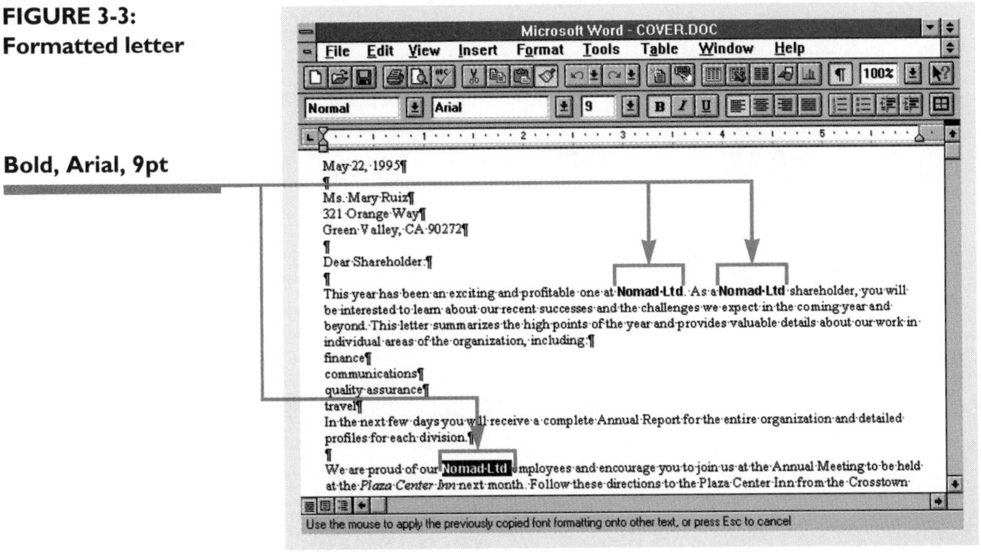

Bold, Arial, 9pt

TABLE 3-1: Text formatting options

SETTING	DESCRIPTION
Font	The name given to a collection of characters (letters, numerals, symbols, and punctuation marks) with a specific design. This text appears in a font named Arial. This text appears in a font named Times New Roman.
Font Size	The physical size of text, measured in points (pts). A point is 1/72". The bigger the number of points, the larger the font size.
Font Style	The appearance of text as **bold**, *italicized*, or underlined, or any combination of these formats.
Effects	The appearance of text as SMALL CAPS, ALL CAPS, hidden text, ~~strikethrough~~, subscript ($_{\text{subscript}}$), or superscript (^{superscript}).

Aligning text with tabs

Another way to change the appearance of text is to use tabs to align or indent text. When you press [Tab], the insertion point moves to the next tab stop. By default, tab stops are located at every half inch, but you can use the horizontal ruler (Figure 3-4) to position and create new tab stops. Table 3-2 describes the four different types of tabs and their corresponding tab markers as they appear on the ruler. ▶ Angela has received the final schedule of events for the Annual Meeting and would like to include it in the letter. To make the schedule easier to read, she uses tabs to align the events and the corresponding start times. First, she sets the tab stops on the ruler for the first line of the schedule.

1. **Make sure the tab alignment selector at the left end of the ruler displays the left-aligned tab marker (see Figure 3-4)**
   If the left-aligned tab marker is not displayed, click the tab alignment selector until the left-aligned tab marker appears (see Table 3-2). The left-aligned tab is the default alignment for tab stops.
2. **Place the insertion point in front of the paragraph mark above the last sentence of the letter, then in the horizontal ruler click the ¾" mark**
   A left-aligned tab marker appears where you clicked in the ruler. Next Angela wants to align the start times so the right edges are aligned evenly under each other. To do this, she selects the right-aligned tab marker from the tab alignment selector before placing another tab stop.
3. Click the **tab alignment selector** until you see the **right-aligned tab marker**
   Each time you click the tab alignment selector, the tab marker changes to represent a new alignment for the next tab stop you place. With the right-aligned tab marker selected, Angela places a new tab stop on the ruler.
4. In the horizontal ruler, click the **3"** mark
   A right-aligned tab marker appears where you clicked in the ruler, as shown in Figure 3-5. This means that the right edge of text that appears after a tab character in this line will be aligned with this tab stop. With the tab stops set in the ruler, Angela is ready to enter the schedule of events.
5. Press **[Tab]** then type **Board of Directors meeting**
   The left edge of the text is positioned under the tab stop at the ¾" mark. Next, type the time this event is scheduled.
6. Press **[Tab]** then type **11:30**
   The right edge of the time is positioned under the next tab stop.
7. Press **[Enter]** and continue typing the remaining events and times shown in Figure 3-6
   The new line retains the tab settings you created in the previous line. Be sure to press [Tab] before each event and before each time and press [Enter] at the end of each line. Notice that a nonprinting character appears each time you pressed [Tab] or [Enter].
8. Click the **Save button** on the Standard toolbar

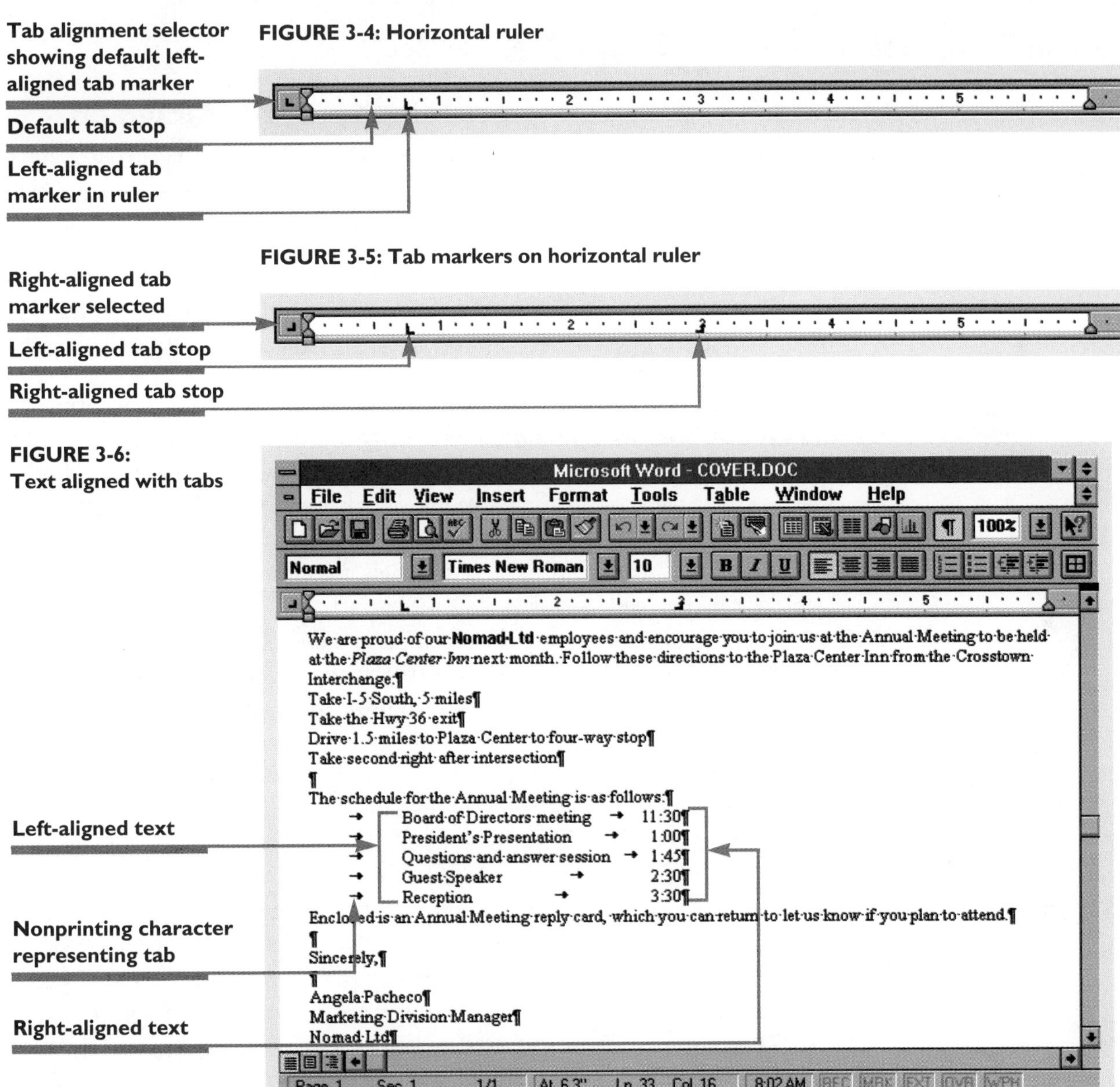

FIGURE 3-4: Horizontal ruler

FIGURE 3-5: Tab markers on horizontal ruler

FIGURE 3-6: Text aligned with tabs

TABLE 3-2: Different types of tabs

ALIGNMENT	DESCRIPTION	BUTTON
Left	Text aligns at the left and extends to the right of the tab stop	L
Center	Text aligns at the middle of the tab stop, extending an equal distance to the left and right of the stop	⊥
Right	Text aligns at the right and extends to the left of the tab stop	┘
Decimal	Text aligns at the decimal point; text before the decimal extends to the left, and text after extends to the right	⊥.

TROUBLE?

If you have difficulty getting the tab marker to appear, try clicking below the hash marks (small lines) or numbers on the ruler.■

Formatting paragraphs

In addition to formatting text, you can also format paragraphs. **Paragraph formatting** refers to the spacing, alignment, and indentation of text in paragraphs, as summarized in Table 3-3. Common paragraph formatting commands are available on the Formatting toolbar, as shown in Figure 3-7; however, additional formatting options are available when you choose the Paragraph command from the Format menu. ▶Angela wants to improve the appearance of her letter by changing the formatting of certain paragraphs. First, she decides to align the date with the right margin.

1. **Place the insertion point in the line that contains the date, then click the Align Right button on the Formatting toolbar**
   The date is aligned at the right margin of the page. You do not need to select the entire line or paragraph to apply paragraph formatting because paragraph formatting affects the entire current paragraph—that is, the one containing the insertion point. Angela realizes that the signature block at the end of the letter should be closer to the right margin, so that its right edge appears aligned under the right edge of the date.
2. **Select the lines beginning with "Sincerely" and ending with the company name, then drag the left indent marker (the rectangle below the triangles on the left edge of the horizontal ruler) to the 4¼" mark, as shown in Figure 3-8**
   The text moves to align under the 4¼" mark. Next, Angela wants to make the schedule of events easier to read by increasing the spacing before and after each paragraph that makes up the schedule.
3. **Select all the paragraphs for the schedule of events**
   Select these lines quickly by clicking in the selection bar to the left of the first line, then drag to select the remaining lines.
4. **Click Format on the menu bar, then click Paragraph**
   The Paragraph dialog box opens, as shown in Figure 3-9. Make sure the Indents and Spacing tab is selected. The Preview box displays an example of text in the current settings. Because Spacing options provide more precise spacing between paragraphs than using extra paragraph marks, Angela will use the Spacing options to increase the spacing before and after each selected paragraph to 3 pts.
5. **In the Spacing section, select the 0 in the Before text box, then type 3**
   You can type a specific number of points in the Before and After text boxes, or you can click the arrows to increase or decrease spacing in increments of 6 pts.
6. **Select the 0 in the After text box, type 3, then click OK**
   The letter now shows the increased spacing before and after the paragraphs in the schedule of events. Compare your document to Figure 3-10.
7. **Click the Save button on the Standard toolbar**

TABLE 3-3: Paragraph formatting options

SETTING	DESCRIPTION
Line Spacing	The amount of space between lines within a paragraph
Spacing Before and After	The amount of space before the first line and after the last line of a paragraph
Indentation	The beginning and/or end of lines of text in a paragraph in relation to the left and right margins
Alignment	The distribution of text within a paragraph between the left and right margins

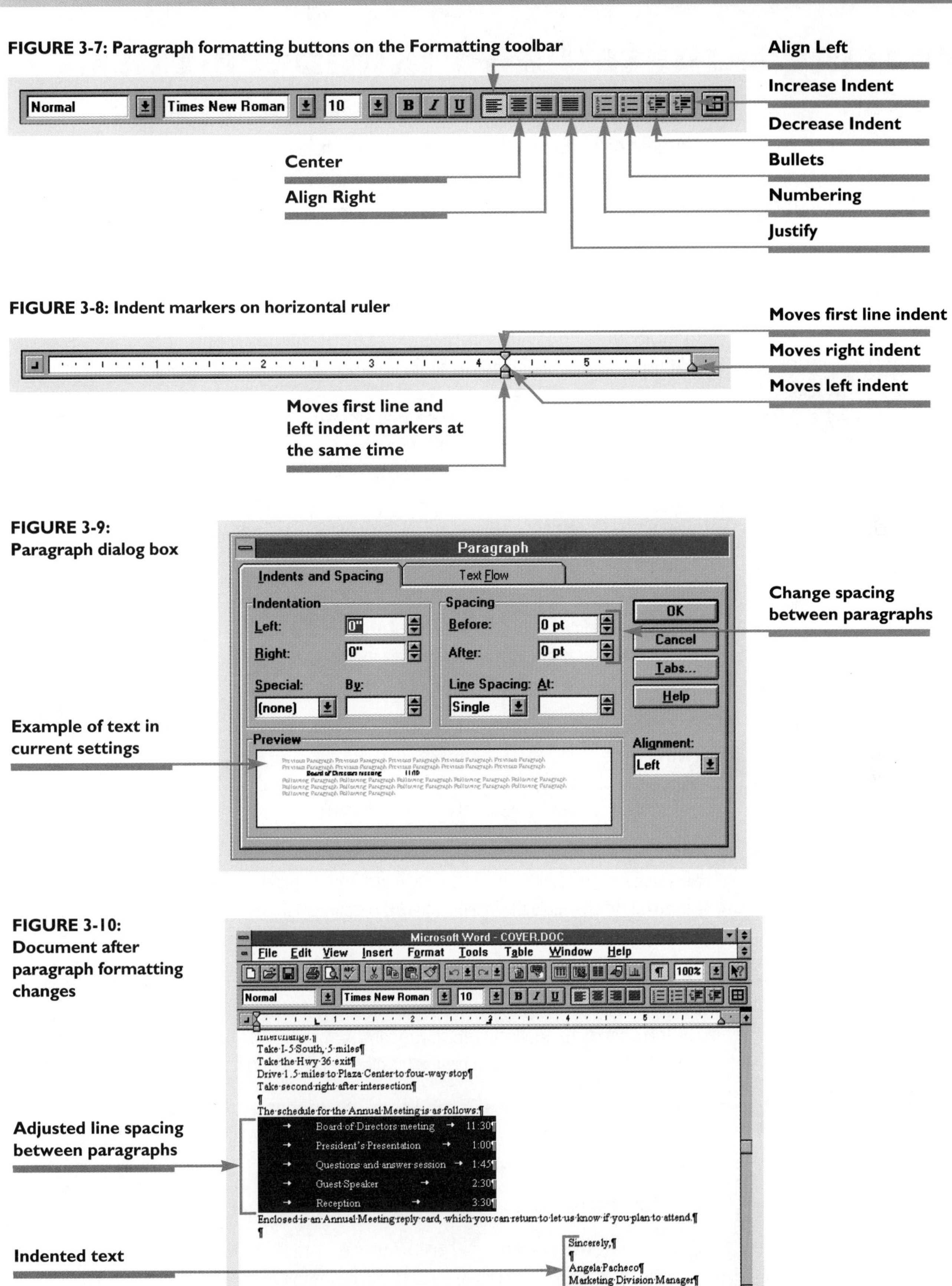

FIGURE 3-7: Paragraph formatting buttons on the Formatting toolbar

FIGURE 3-8: Indent markers on horizontal ruler

FIGURE 3-9: Paragraph dialog box

FIGURE 3-10: Document after paragraph formatting changes

Creating bulleted and numbered lists

With Word you can create bulleted and numbered lists easily and quickly. The Numbering button on the Formatting toolbar lets you number selected paragraphs, starting with 1. With the Bullets button, you can insert a bullet in front of each item in a list. A **bullet** is a small symbol, such as a solid circle or some other shape, that marks each item. Adding bullets or numbers to a list makes it easier to identify each item. Generally, you use numbered lists to show a sequence, and bulleted lists to identify nonsequential items in a list. ► Angela decides to draw attention to the list of departments by formatting it with bullets; then she'll add numbers to the directions to the Annual Meeting to clarify the sequence.

1 Select the list of department names starting with "finance," then click the **Bullets button** on the Formatting toolbar
Bullet characters appear in front of each item in the list, as shown in Figure 3-11. You can change the bullet characters if you'd like. See the related topic "Bullets and numbers" for more information. To clarify the sequence of the steps in the directions, Angela decides to number the list of directions.

2 Select the four items starting with "Take I-5 ..." at the end of the second paragraph, then click the **Numbering button** on the Formatting toolbar
The list of directions is now a numbered list. Angela realizes that she forgot to include a step in her directions, so she inserts the step in the list.

3 Place the insertion point after step 2 in the list of directions, then press **[Enter]**
When you press [Enter], the remaining items are renumbered to reflect a new item in the middle of the list. Now Angela can type the additional step.

4 After the number, type **Turn left at lights**
Next Angela wants the list of directions to match the alignment of the schedule of events. She can do this by changing the indentation of these paragraphs using the Increase Indent button on the Formatting toolbar.

5 Select all the paragraphs in the list of directions, then click the **Increase Indent button** on the Formatting toolbar
The list of directions is indented at the ½" mark. Angela decides that the list of departments should also have the same alignment as the other lists in the document.

6 Select all the paragraphs in the list of departments, then click
The list is aligned with the other lists in the document. This completes the formatting for the cover letter. Angela is now ready to save and print her letter.

7 Click the **Save button** on the Standard toolbar

8 Click the **Print button** to print the entire document
Compare your document to Figure 3-12. Angela now wants to close the letter then begin formatting the document containing the summary of highlights.

9 Click **File** on the menu bar, then click **Close**

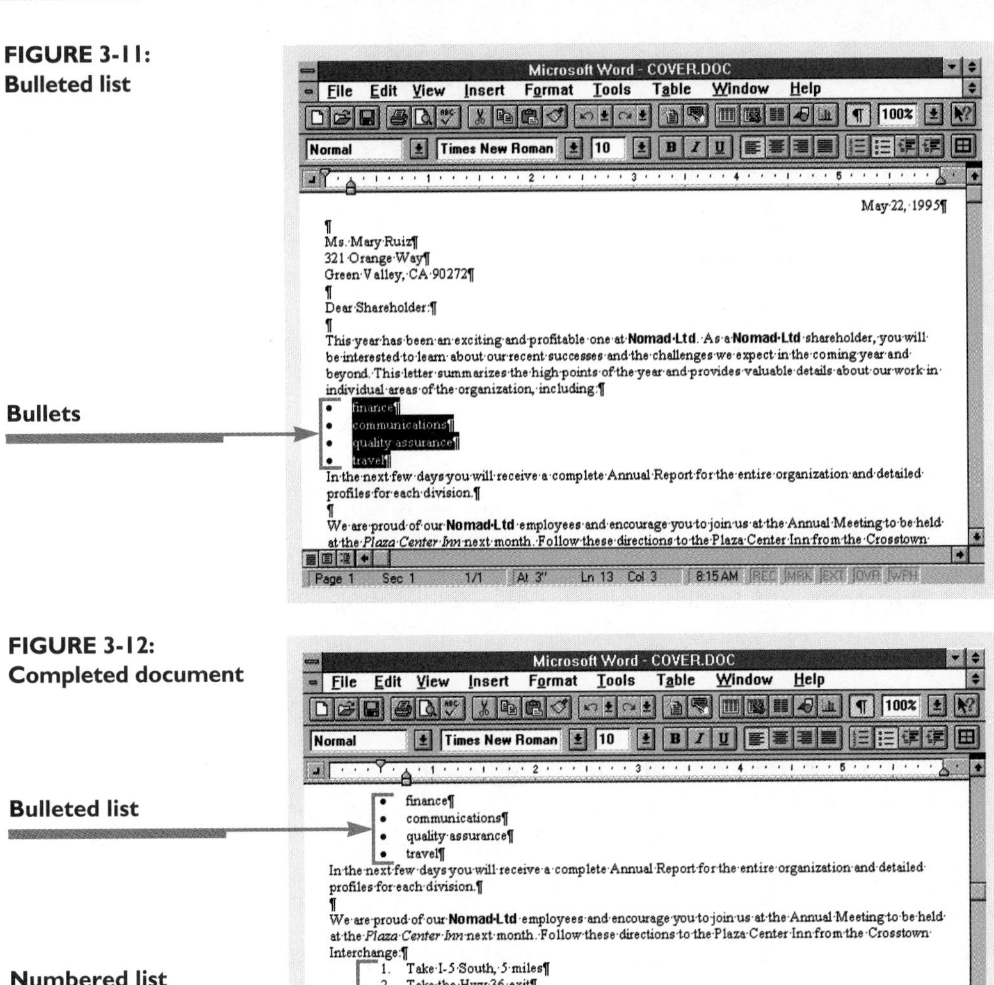

FIGURE 3-11: Bulleted list

FIGURE 3-12: Completed document

Bullets and numbering options

You can select other number formats or bullet styles by using the Bullets and Numbering command on the Format menu, which displays the Bullets and Numbering dialog box shown in Figure 3-13.

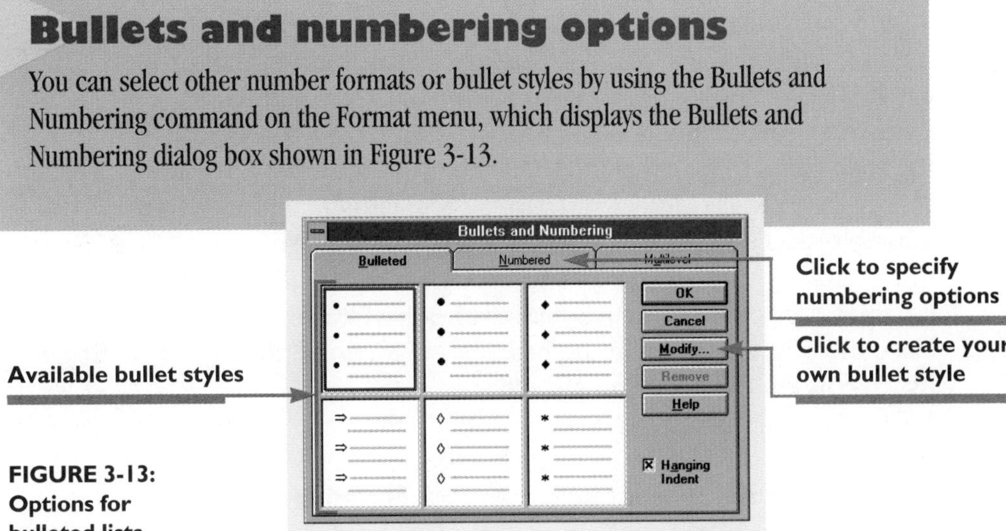

FIGURE 3-13: Options for bulleted lists

Formatting a document with AutoFormat and the Style Gallery

You can have Word automatically format your document with AutoFormat. With this feature, Word makes a number of changes, described in Table 3-4, that improve the appearance of a document. Word also applies a set of styles stored in a template. A **style** is a named set of format settings that you can apply to text. For example, a heading style determines how a title is formatted. A **template** is a special document containing styles and other options you want to use in a specific document. You can also use the Style Gallery to format your document in styles from different templates provided by Word. ▶ Angela wants to add attractive formatting to the summary document. First she'll use the AutoFormat button to apply formatting from the current (and default) template, NORMAL.DOT.

1. Open the document named UNIT_3-2.DOC from your Student Disk and save it as EXECSUMM.DOC to your MY_FILES directory
   This document is the summary of the year's highlights at Nomad Ltd.
2. Click the **AutoFormat button** on the Standard toolbar
   AutoFormat enhances the appearance of the document, as shown in Figure 3-14. Headings now appear in a larger, bold Arial font. Bullets replace hyphens in the list, and the ™ symbol replaces (tm). The document looks much better, but Angela decides to give it a more contemporary "feel" by choosing a different template from the Style Gallery.
3. Click **Format** on the menu bar, then click **Style Gallery**
   The Style Gallery dialog box opens, as shown in Figure 3-15. In this dialog box, you can choose from the list of templates that Word provides, and preview your document as it would appear formatted with styles from the selected template. Angela selects a contemporary template and previews the document.
4. In the Template list box, scroll the list of templates, then click **REPORT2**
   In the Preview of box, the document appears as it would if formatted with the styles in the REPORT2 template. Angela decides to format the document using the styles in this template.
5. Click **OK**
   Word applies the styles defined in the template to your document. Compare your document to Figure 3-16. Note that the text in the body of the document changes to Arial, the headings for each topic appear in all uppercase, and a line appears under each heading. To see which style was applied to the headings, Angela places the insertion point in a heading.
6. Place the insertion point in the heading **Balancing the Books** and notice the style name that appears in the Style list box on the Formatting toolbar
   The style name Heading 1 in the Style list box indicates this is the style applied to the current paragraph. Because of its location under the large bold title, the text "Milestones" was not correctly analyzed as a heading during the AutoFormat process. It should be formatted the same as the other headings. Angela can quickly apply the Heading 1 style to this text.
7. Place the insertion point in the heading **Milestones**, then click the **Style list arrow** on the Formatting toolbar
   The Style list box displays the styles available in the REPORT2 template. Angela selects Heading 1 because this is the style that AutoFormat applied to the other headings in the document.
8. Scroll through the Style list box, then click **Heading 1**
9. Click the **Save button** on the Standard toolbar

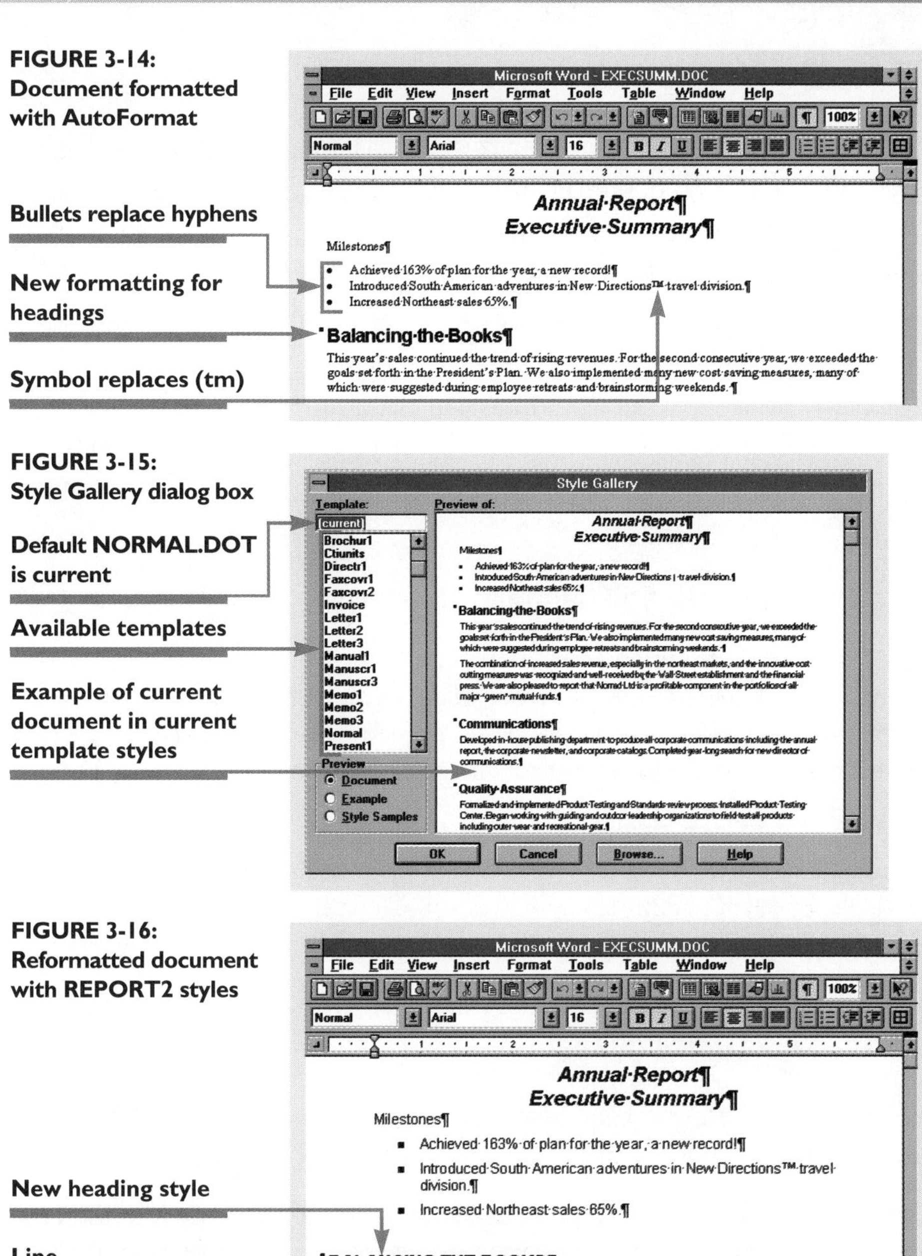

FIGURE 3-14: Document formatted with AutoFormat

FIGURE 3-15: Style Gallery dialog box

FIGURE 3-16: Reformatted document with REPORT2 styles

TABLE 3-4: Changes made by AutoFormat

CHANGE	DESCRIPTION
Applies styles	Applies paragraph styles to all paragraphs in a document, including headings, lists, body text, salutations, addresses, etc.
Adjusts spacing	Adds and removes extra paragraph marks as needed; replaces spaces and tabs with proper indentation
Replaces symbols and characters	Replaces hyphens and other symbols used to denote a list with bullets; replaces "straight" quotes with “Smart” (curly) quotes; inserts the trademark, registered trademark, and copyright symbols where indicated

QUICK TIP

To review the changes made with AutoFormat, use the AutoFormat command on the Format menu (instead of the AutoFormat button). Then in the AutoFormat dialog box, click Review Changes to examine and then reject or accept individual changes.

Modifying styles

When you use styles to format text, you can change format settings quickly and consistently for every occurrence of the style in the document. By modifying a style, the appearance of all text formatted in that style also changes. You save time and make fewer mistakes because you don't need to search for each occurrence of text that has formatting you want to change. See the related topic "More about styles and templates" for more information. ▶ After reviewing the new formatting, Angela decides that the headings formatted in all uppercase look too big in the document. After modifying the case format (with the Change Case command) for the first heading, she'll update the Heading 1 style to change all the text formatted with this style.

1. Select the heading **MILESTONES** at the beginning of the document
2. Click **Format** on the menu bar, then click **Change Case**
   The Change Case dialog box opens. In this dialog box, you can specify the case—uppercase or lowercase—for selected text. Angela wants the text to appear with only the first character of each word in uppercase, so she decides to use the format called Title Case.
3. Click the **Title Case radio button**, then click **OK**
   The selected text appears with the first character of each word capitalized. Now that this heading contains the formatting she prefers, Angela needs to modify the Heading 1 style based on the modified "Milestones" heading to format all the headings in the document in the same way.
4. With the text still selected, click the **Style list arrow** on the Formatting toolbar, then click **Heading 1**
   The Reapply Style dialog box opens, as shown in Figure 3-17. You can either redefine the style based on the selected text, or reformat the selected text with the original attributes of the style. In this case, Angela wants to modify the style based on the currently selected text.
5. Click **OK** to redefine the Heading 1 style based on the currently selected text
   All text formatted with the Heading 1 style now appears in the Title Case format throughout the document.
6. Click the **Save button** 💾 on the Standard toolbar
   Compare your document to Figure 3-18.

FIGURE 3-17: Reapply Style dialog box

Redefines style based on selection default

Reapplies previous style formatting to selection

Reapply Style

Style: Heading 1

Do you want to:

Redefine the style using the selection as an example?

Return the formatting of the selection to the style?

OK

Cancel

Help

FIGURE 3-18: Updated style

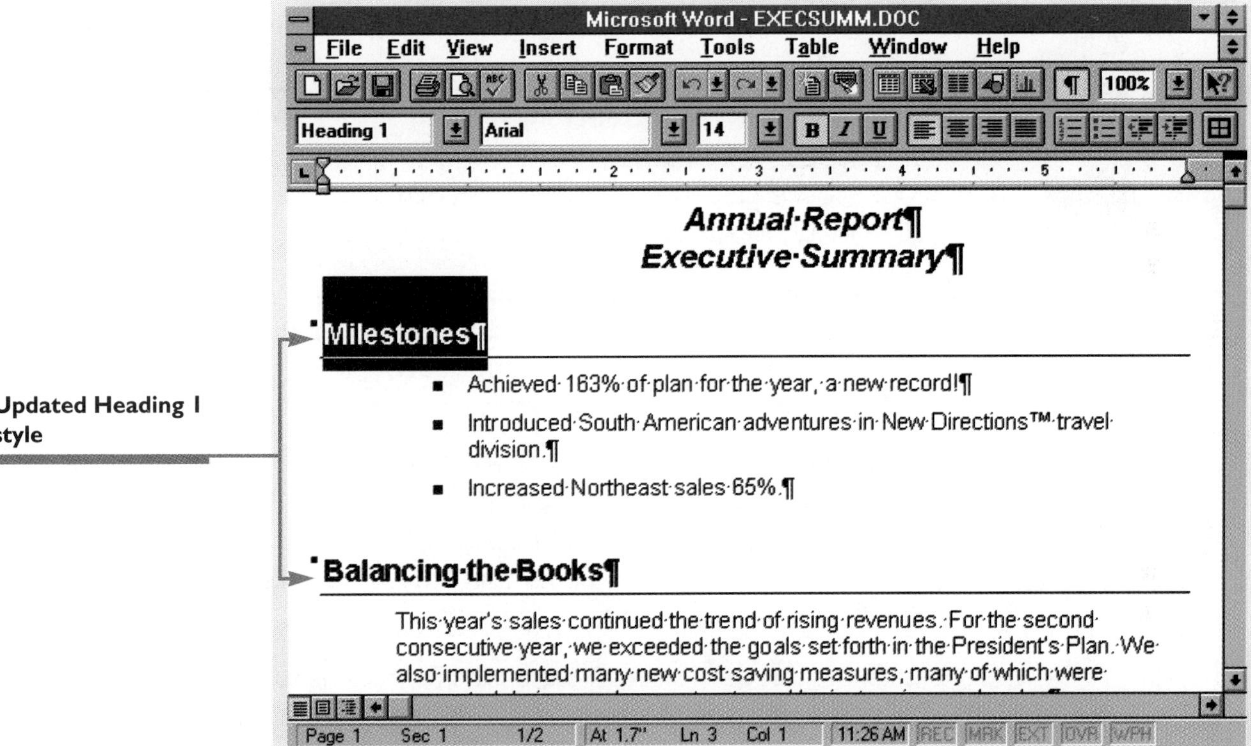

More about styles and templates

A **paragraph style** is a collection of paragraph format settings that affect an entire paragraph (like the styles you used in this lesson). **Character styles** affect only selected text, not entire paragraphs. Character styles are not created with the AutoFormat command, so you must use the Style command on the Format menu to create them. The format settings of a style are determined by a template. For example, in the template called REPORT1, the Body Text style formats text in Times New Roman, whereas in the REPORT2 template, the same style formats text in the Arial font. Word comes with many different templates, each containing collections of styles with a variety of format settings that are appropriate for the kind of document you want to create.

QUICK TIP

You can quickly apply a style by pressing [Ctrl][Shift][S], typing the name of the style, then pressing [Enter].

Applying borders and shading

Borders and shading add visual interest to paragraphs of text. **Borders** are lines you can add to the top, bottom, or sides of paragraphs. Preset border settings make it easy to create a box around a paragraph. You can also select lines of varying thickness, including double lines. **Shading** is a background color or pattern you add behind the text of a paragraph. You can apply both borders and shading to emphasize areas of your document. ▶ Angela wants to use borders and shading to emphasize certain areas in the document. First, she'll add a shadow box around the text in the title to set it off from the rest of the document.

1 Select the first two lines of the document, click **Format** on the menu bar, then click **Borders and Shading**
The Paragraph Borders and Shading dialog box opens, as shown in Figure 3-19. Make sure the Borders tab is selected. The Border section of the dialog box gives you a preview of the border settings you make for your document.

2 In the Presets section, click the **Shadow icon**
This selection creates a shadow box around the selected paragraphs. A shadow box has thicker lines on the right and bottom, creating a shadow effect for the box. Angela decides to specify a thicker line for the box. Note that like fonts, line thickness is measured in points (pts).

3 In the Style section, click **1½ pt** then click **OK**
The dialog box closes and the text you selected is formatted with a shadow box border with a 1½ pt line. Note that the border extends to the left and right margins. Next, Angela wants to add shading behind the three lines of text describing Nomad's milestones. This time she'll use the Borders toolbar to format the text.

4 Click the **Borders button** on the Formatting toolbar
The Borders toolbar appears at the top of the document window, as shown in Figure 3-20. The Borders toolbar contains many of the same settings available in the Paragraph Borders and Shading dialog box.

5 Select the three lines of text below the **Milestones** heading, then click the **Shading list arrow**
Angela wants to emphasize this text by applying a light gray background to it.

6 Click **10%**
The text appears with a shaded background.

7 Click on the Formatting toolbar, then deselect the text
The Borders toolbar is no longer displayed. Compare your document to Figure 3-21.

8 Click the **Save button** on the Standard toolbar

FIGURE 3-19: Paragraph Borders and Shading dialog box

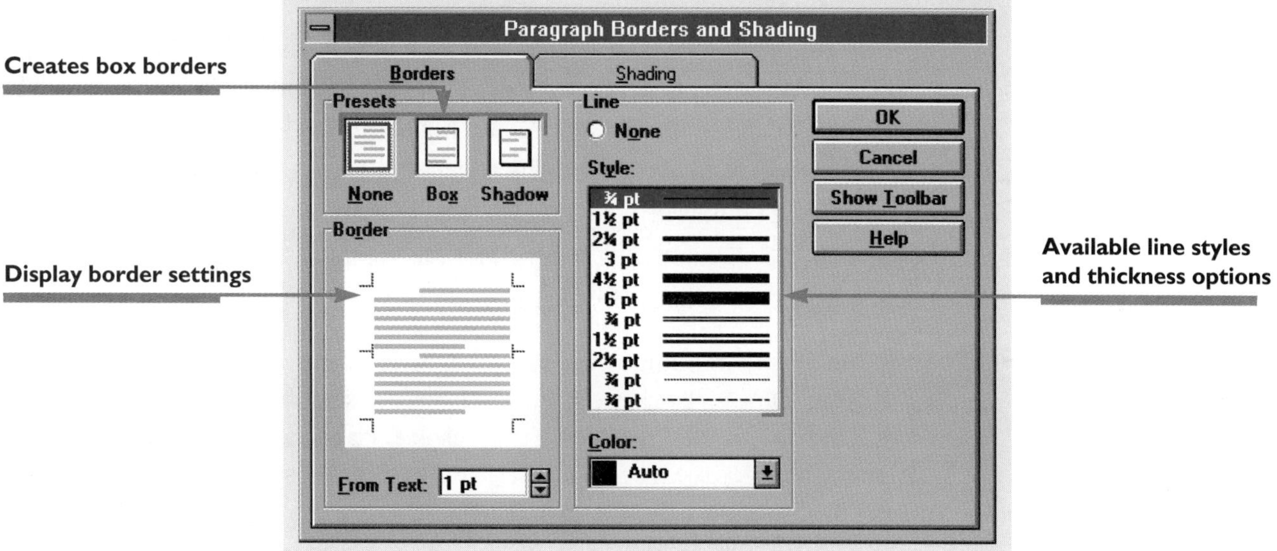

FIGURE 3-20: Borders toolbar

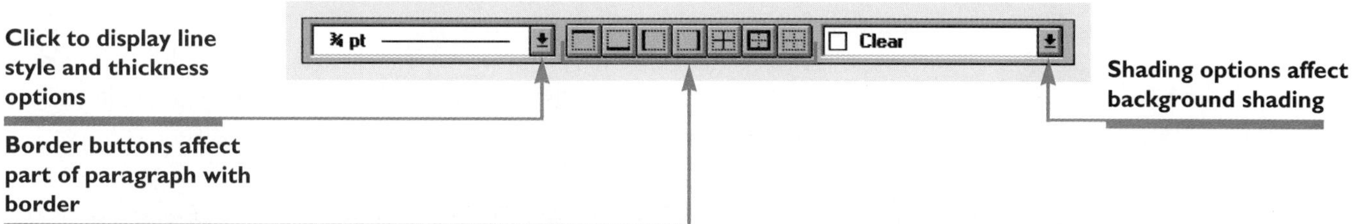

FIGURE 3-21: Borders and shading in the document

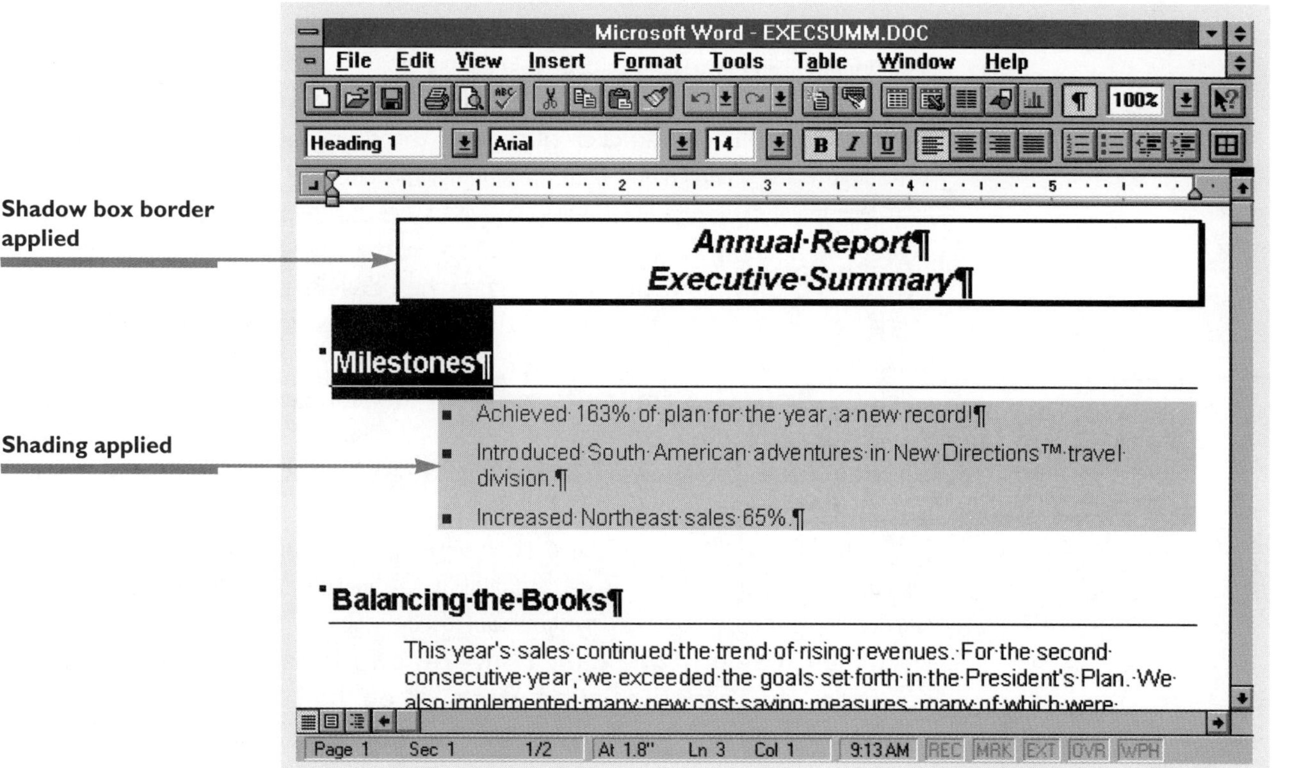

Formatting a paragraph with a drop cap

Another way to draw attention to a specific part of a document is to use a drop cap. A **drop cap** is the first letter of a paragraph that is formatted to be dramatically larger than the rest of the text in the paragraph. This kind of formatting is often used in newsletters, magazines, and newspapers. In Word, you can use the Drop Cap command on the Format menu to create this visually interesting effect in your own documents. ▶ To highlight the importance of the last paragraph in the document, Angela decides to use a drop cap.

1. **Place the insertion point in the last paragraph of the document**
   You do not need to select the character you want formatted as a drop cap.
2. **Click Format on the menu bar, then click Drop Cap**
   The Drop Cap dialog box opens, as shown in Figure 3-22. In this dialog box, you can specify how you want the drop cap formatted. For example, using the custom options you can specify a different font for the drop cap, the number of lines to drop the letter, and the distance from the drop cap to the rest of the paragraph. Angela wants to use the Dropped format and extend the drop cap to two lines.
3. **In the Position section, click the Dropped icon, type 2 in the Lines to Drop text box, then click OK**
   A message box appears informing you that using drop caps formats the text with a frame and that to see the text formatted with a frame, you need to display the document in page layout view. See Table 3-5 for a summary of the different document views, and read the related topics "Displaying document views" for more information.
4. **Click Yes in the message box to display the document in page layout view**
   The first character of the paragraph is now two times larger than the surrounding text, as shown in Figure 3-23. Note that a frame appears around the drop cap and the text of the paragraph is formatted around the drop cap. You will learn about using frames in the next unit. For now, Angela wants to add even greater emphasis to this paragraph, so she formats the drop cap in bold.
5. **Select the letter N inside the frame, click the Bold button on the Formatting toolbar, then click outside of the drop cap to deselect the text**
   To distinguish the general nature of the mission statement from the specific information about each department in the document, Angela centers the heading for the mission statement.
6. **Select the heading Corporate Mission Statement, click the Center button on the Formatting toolbar, then deselect the text**
   Angela has completed formatting the text for now, so she previews the document to see how it will look when she prints it.
7. **Click the Print Preview button on the Standard toolbar to display the document in print preview**
8. **Click the Multiple Pages button to display both pages of the document, if necessary**
   The Multiple Pages button allows you to specify the number of pages of your document you want to display in print preview. To select multiple pages, hold down the Multiple Pages button and drag to select the number of pages you want to see.
9. **Click the Close button on the Print Preview toolbar to return to your document, then click the Save button on the Standard toolbar**
   You'll continue working in page layout view to make final changes, then print the document.

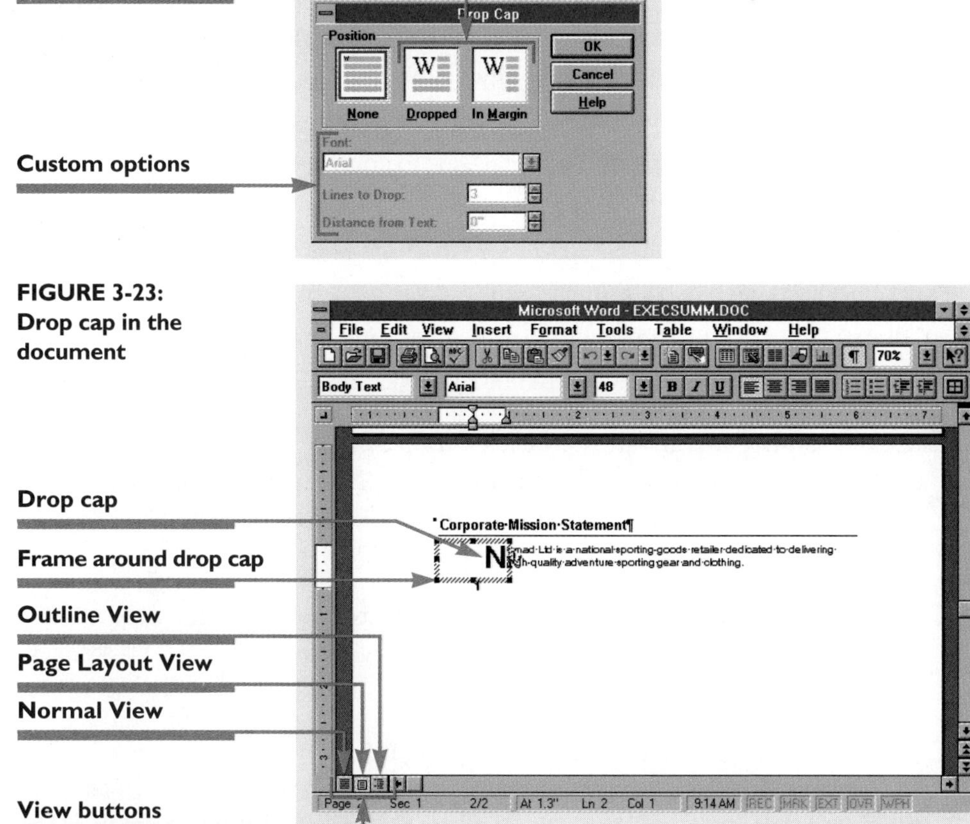

FIGURE 3-22: Drop Cap dialog box

FIGURE 3-23: Drop cap in the document

Displaying document views

The different document views allow you to focus on different aspects of word processing. For example, to see the arrangement of text in columns or frames and still be able to edit the document, you need to display the document in page layout view. You can quickly switch views by clicking the view buttons on the left of the horizontal scroll bar, as shown in Figure 3-23. Additional views (described in Table 3-5) are available on the View menu, the File menu, and the Standard toolbar.

TABLE 3-5: Document views

VIEW	DESCRIPTION	USE TO
Normal	Displays the default document view	Type, format, and edit text. You cannot see text arranged with special formatting such as drop caps, frames, or columns in normal view.
Page layout	Displays the document as it will appear when printed	Edit and view placement of text and graphics on the page as it will appear when printed. You see the edges of the page, as well as headers and footers in the document.
Outline	Displays selected level of headings and body text	View major headings to easily reorganize a large document. Your documents need to have Heading styles applied before you can use outline view effectively.
Print preview	Displays entire page(s) on one screen	Review page breaks, all pages, and formatting, and make minor changes to text before printing.

Adjusting document margins

A **margin** is the distance between the text of a document and the top, bottom, or side edges of the page. With the Page Setup command, you can change the amount of space that surrounds the text. You can individually adjust the top, bottom, left, and right margins. You might decide to change the margins to fit more (or less) text on a page, add extra space next to text for notes, or simply create an interesting effect by using white space. **White space** is the part of a page that contains no text. ▶ When she previewed the document, Angela noticed that a small part of the document appears on a page by itself. She decides to adjust the margins so that the document will fit on one page.

1. **Click File on the menu bar, then click Page Setup**
   The Page Setup dialog box opens, as shown in Figure 3-24. In the dialog box, you have a variety of options that affect the appearance of the overall pages of text. Angela wants to adjust the page margins, so she will use the options on the Margins tab.
2. **Click the Margins tab, if it is not already selected in the dialog box**
   To change the margin settings, you can either click the up and down arrows next to the appropriate box, or type the setting you want in the box. Angela wants to reduce the top margin to 0.5".
3. **Click the Top down arrow until it displays 0.5"**
   This setting will reduce the amount of space at the top of the page from 1" to ½". The Preview section shows the effect of this change in the document. Generally, the bottom margin should be the same size as the top margin, so Angela needs to adjust the bottom margin as well.
4. **Click the Bottom down arrow until it displays 0.5"**
   This setting will reduce the amount of space at the bottom of the page from 1" to ½". To allow even more room for text on the page, Angela decides to reduce the space at the left and right margins.
5. **Click the Left down arrow until it displays 1"**
   This setting will reduce the amount of space at the left of the page from 1.25" to 1". Angela needs to adjust the right margin to match the left margin.
6. **Click the Right down arrow until it displays 1" then click OK**
   Angela has finished adjusting the margins and is now ready to save and preview her document.
7. **Click the Save button on the Standard toolbar, then click the Print Preview button to display the document in print preview**
   The document appears on one page. Compare your document to Figure 3-25. Angela now wants to print the document then exit Word.
8. **Click the Print button on the Print Preview toolbar**
9. **Click File on the menu bar, then click Exit**
   If a dialog box appears asking if you want to save changes to NORMAL.DOT (the default template), click No. This prevents you from changing to the default styles in NORMAL.DOT. Changing NORMAL.DOT can affect format settings and styles for other Word users on your computer.

FIGURE 3-24: Page Setup dialog box

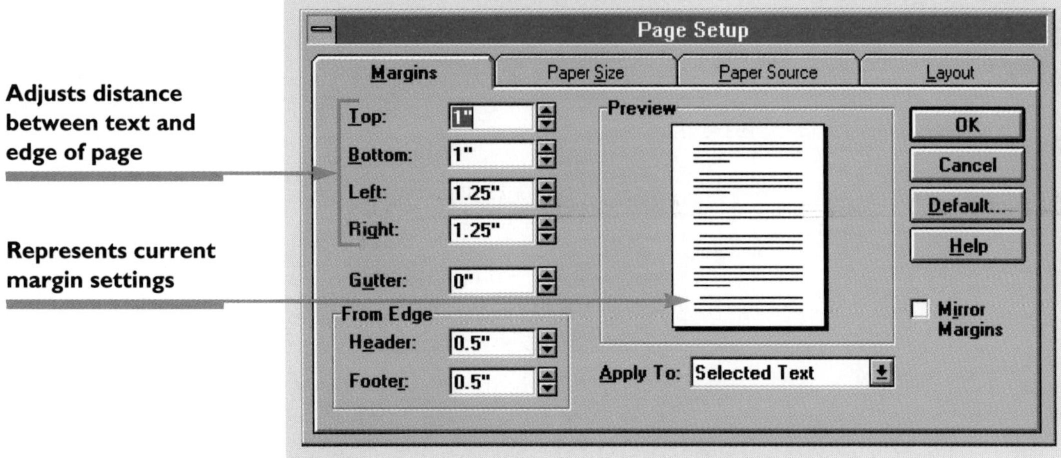

FIGURE 3-25: Document in print preview

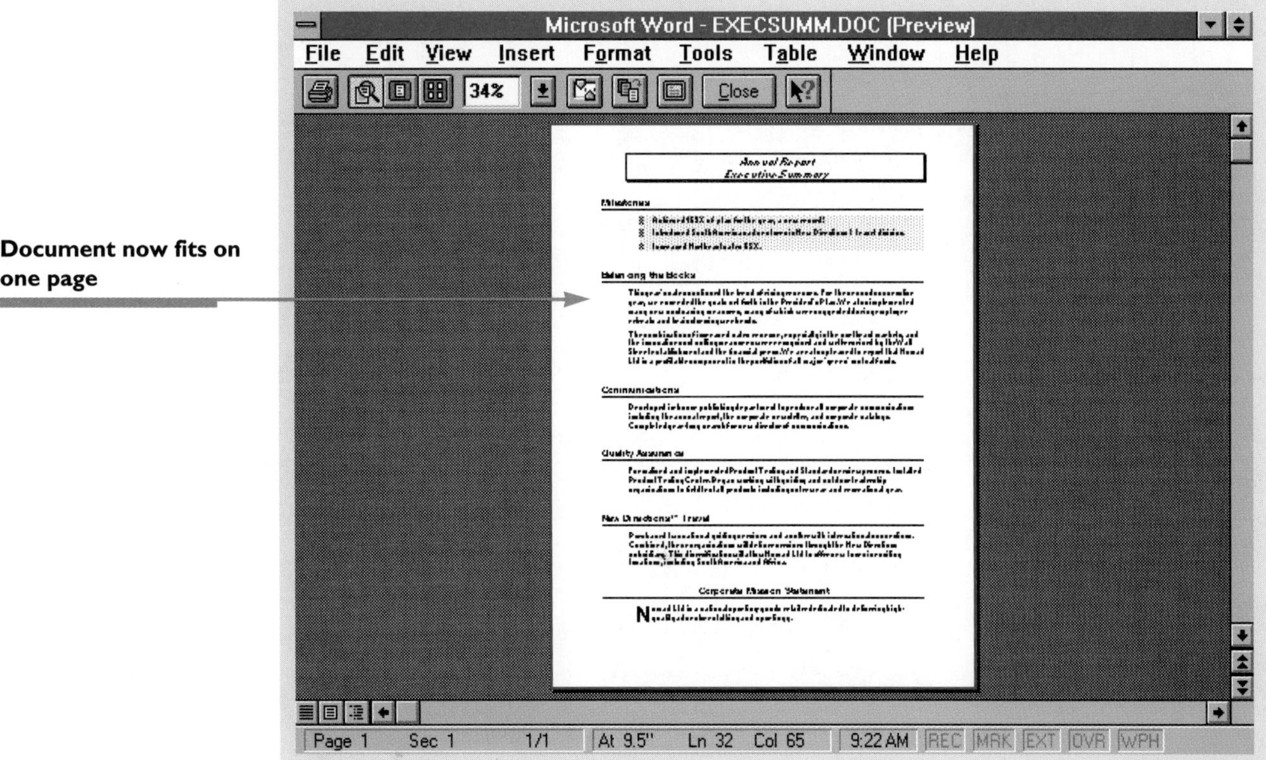

CONCEPTSREVIEW

Label each of the formatting elements used in the document shown in Figure 3-26.

1 ____________________

2 ____________________

3 ____________________

4 ____________________

5 ____________________

6 ____________________

7 ____________________

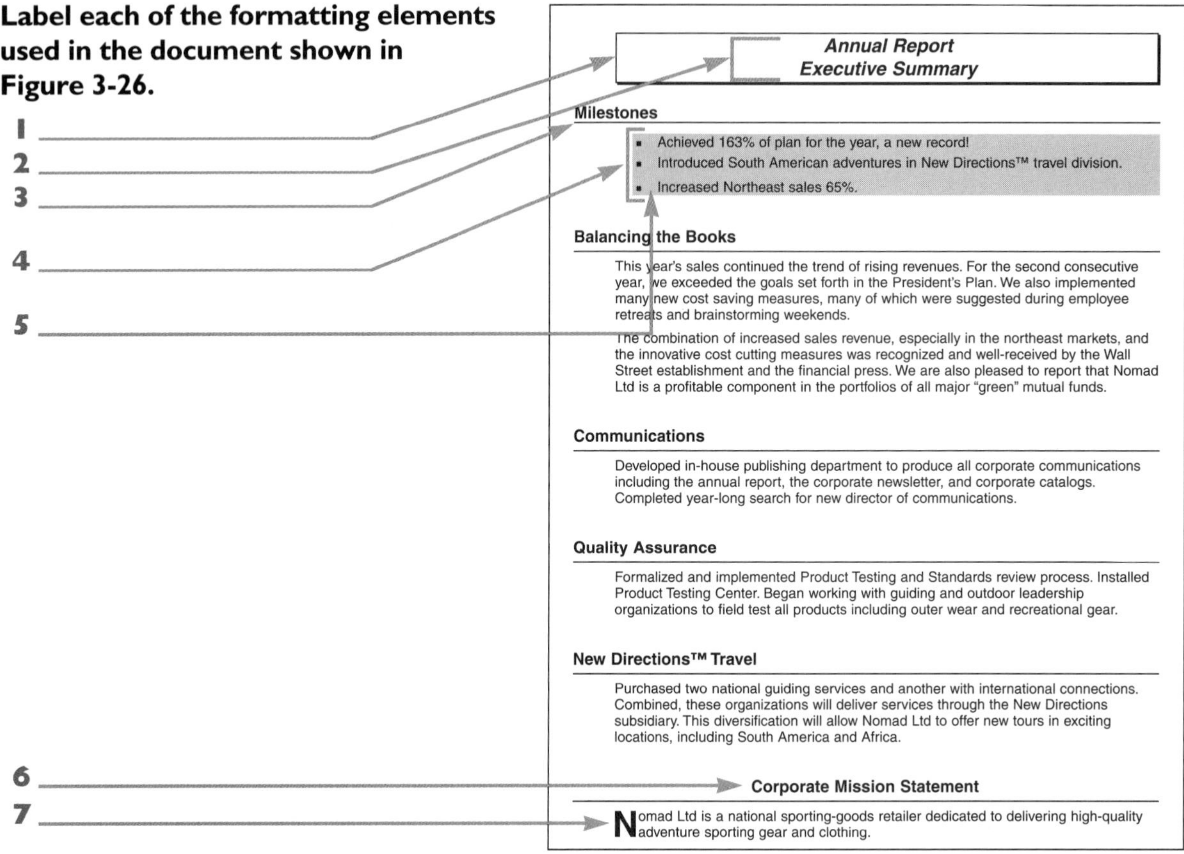

FIGURE 3-26

Match each of the following terms with the statement that best describes its function.

8 Changes the appearance of letters, numbers, and punctuation

9 A named set of paragraph format settings

10 Symbols or graphics preceding items in a list

11 Lines added to paragraphs of text

12 Changes the line spacing, alignment, and space between paragraphs

13 Displays documents in alternative collections of styles

14 Collections of styles

15 Changes the first character of a paragraph to be significantly larger than the surrounding text

a. Bullets

b. Borders

c. Paragraph styles

d. Text formatting

e. Templates

f. Style Gallery

g. Paragraph formatting

h. Drop cap

Select the best answer from the list of choices:

16 Which text formatting feature is NOT available on the Formatting toolbar?

a. Bold

b. Italics

c. Double-underline

d. Character styles

17 Which paragraph formatting feature is NOT available on the Formatting toolbar?

a. Paragraph alignment

b. Line spacing

c. Paragraph styles

d. Indentation

18 To add a specific amount of space between paragraphs, the best solution is to

a. Press [Enter] until you get the amount of space you want

b. Use the Spacing Before and After options in the Paragraph dialog box

c. Adjust the top margin for each paragraph

d. Use the Line Spacing options in the Paragraph dialog box

19 Which command automatically formats the first character of a paragraph to be significantly larger than the rest of the text in the paragraph?

a. The Change Case command on the Format menu

b. The Font command on the Format menu

c. The Drop Cap command on the Format menu

d. The Drop Cap button on the Formatting toolbar

20 Which of the following is the fastest way to change from all uppercase to all lowercase?

a. The Change Case command on the Format menu

b. The Font command on the Format menu

c. The Drop Cap command on the Format menu

d. The Font Size button on the Formatting toolbar

APPLICATIONSREVIEW

1 Format text.

a. Start Word and open the document named UNIT_3-3.DOC from your Student Disk. Save the document as OPENROAD.DOC to your MY_FILES directory.

b. Select the first occurrence of "OpenRoads(tm), Inc." then click the Bold button on the Formatting toolbar. With the text still selected, click the Italic button.

c. Use the Format Painter to apply this formatting to the second occurrence of this name in the document.

d. Save your changes.

2 Create bulleted lists.

a. Select the list of items starting with "tracks the location..." and ending with "generates pre-printed..."

b. Click the Bullets button on the Formatting toolbar, then click to deselect the text.

c. Select the two items "1-5 lb. shipment" and "5-10 lb. shipment" and make these bulleted items also.

3 Use AutoFormat.

a. Click the AutoFormat button to apply standard styles and formatting to your document.

b. Review the changes in your document.

4 Use the Style Gallery.

a. Click Format on the menu bar, then click Style Gallery.

b. Select several different templates and examine your document as it would appear formatted in these templates.

c. Click Letter2 in the list of templates, then click OK.

d. Save your changes.

5 Apply paragraph formatting and styles.

a. With the insertion point in the first paragraph in the body of the letter, click the Justify button on the Formatting toolbar.

b. Select the Body Text style from the Style list box.

c. Make sure the option for redefining the style is selected in the Reapply Style dialog box, then click OK.

d. Save your changes.

6 Adjust page margins.

a. Click File on the menu bar, then click Page Setup. Make sure the Margins tab is displayed in the Page Setup dialog box.

b. In the Top text box, specify a 2" margin.

c. In the Bottom text box, specify a 2" margin.

d. In the Left text box, specify a 1.5" margin.

e. In the Right text box, specify a 1.5" margin.

f. Save your changes.

g. Be sure to select the placeholder [your name] at the bottom of the letter and replace it with your name.

h. Preview then print your document. Your completed document should look like Figure 3-27. Exit Word.

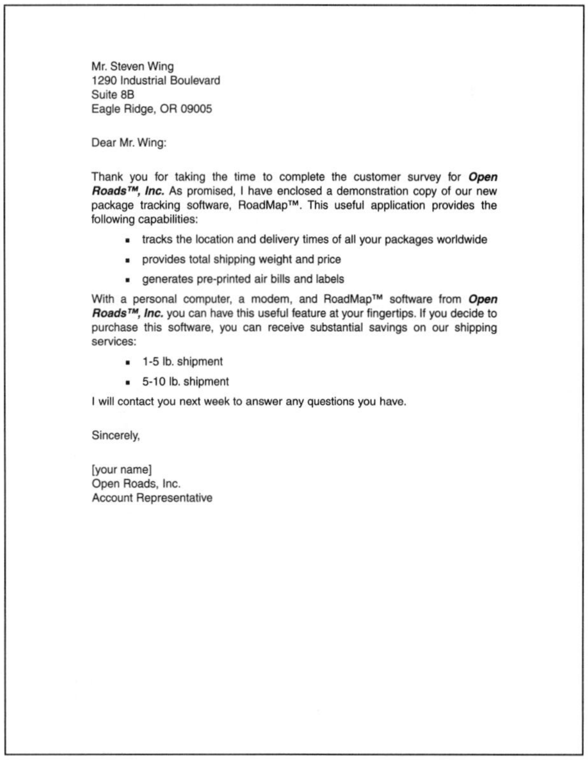

Mr. Steven Wing
1290 Industrial Boulevard
Suite 8B
Eagle Ridge, OR 09005

Dear Mr. Wing:

Thank you for taking the time to complete the customer survey for ***Open Roads™, Inc.*** As promised, I have enclosed a demonstration copy of our new package tracking software, RoadMap™. This useful application provides the following capabilities:

- tracks the location and delivery times of all your packages worldwide
- provides total shipping weight and price
- generates pre-printed air bills and labels

With a personal computer, a modem, and RoadMap™ software from ***Open Roads™, Inc.*** you can have this useful feature at your fingertips. If you decide to purchase this software, you can receive substantial savings on our shipping services:

- 1-5 lb. shipment
- 5-10 lb. shipment

I will contact you next week to answer any questions you have.

Sincerely,

[your name]
Open Roads, Inc.
Account Representative

FIGURE 3-27

INDEPENDENT CHALLENGE 1

Suppose you are in charge of marketing for a community orchestra. As part of your responsibilities, you must prepare a poster for an upcoming concert series. Your assistant has already prepared a draft for you, and you need to format it to improve its appearance. Open the document named UNIT_3-4.DOC from your Student Disk and save it as MUSCNITE.DOC to your MY_FILES directory. Start your formatting by using the AutoFormat button. Then use Figure 3-28 as a guide for further enhancing the document's appearance. When finished formatting, preview then print your document.

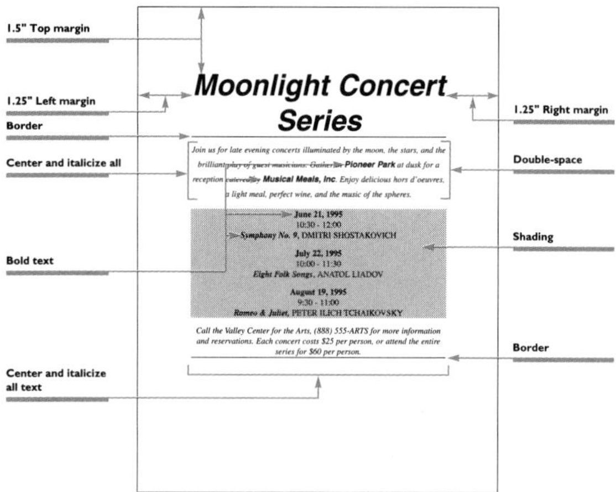

FIGURE 3-28

INDEPENDENT CHALLENGE 2

You are the director of communications for a small software company, MySoft International. Your task is to prepare for the release of a new multimedia educational game called "CrazyBugz." This package, designed for children 8 to 14 years old, allows the creative assembly of a variety of eight-legged creatures, real and imaginary, using computer software. Open the document named UNIT_3-5.DOC from your Student Disk and save it as CRZYBUGZ.DOC to your MY_FILES directory. First improve the appearance of the document using AutoFormat, then create a press release based on the PRESREL2 template in the Style Gallery. Apply the Title style to the centered text. Then use Figure 3-29 as a guide for further enhancing the document's appearance. Be sure to replace the placeholder [Your Name] with your name. When finished formatting, preview then print your document. Close the document then exit Word.

MYSOFT INTERNATIONAL
111 Center Avenue
Eden Valley, MN 55382
(888)555-BUGZ

New Product!

Press Release

For Immediate Release
Thursday, June 23, 1995

Contact: [Your Name]
MySoft International
(888)555-BUGZ

Eden Valley, MN — MySoft International is excited to announce the immediate release of a new multimedia educational game called "CrazyBugz." This package, designed for children 8 to 14 years old, allows the creative assembly of a variety of eight-legged creatures, real and imaginary, using computer software. Like all MySoft software, CrazyBugz offers these great benefits:

- stimulates young imaginations
- increases eye-to-hand coordination
- provides non-gender specific play

Watch for this product to appear in the retail chains for children's toys, as well as software retailers. List price is $29.99.

FIGURE 3-29

UNIT 4

OBJECTIVES

- Create a table
- Add rows and columns in a table
- Calculate data in a table
- Format a table
- Arrange text in columns
- Position text using frames
- Insert and position graphics
- Create headers and footers

Arranging TEXT AND GRAPHICS

By formatting text and paragraphs, you can make your document easier to read. Word provides additional formatting techniques for arranging text and graphics on the page to give your document a polished, professional appearance. For example, by formatting text in a table you can quickly add or delete text without reformatting all the rows and columns, and you can use the Table AutoFormat command to make a table easier to read with preset borders and shading combinations. By adding and positioning graphics in a document, you can achieve dramatic effects. ▶ Angela used different formatting techniques to produce a simple report summarizing the year's highlights; now she wants to use the same text in a newsletter format for the Nomad Ltd senior management newsletter, the *Executive Bulletin*. ▶

Creating a table

A **table** is text arranged in a grid of rows and columns. You can use the Insert Table button on the Standard toolbar or the Insert Table command on the Table menu to create a blank table wherever you place the insertion point. The Insert Table button displays a grid (as shown in Figure 4-1) in which you drag to select the number of rows and columns you want; with the Insert Table command you can specify the number of rows and columns and choose different table formatting options. ▶ Angela wants the *Executive Bulletin* newsletter to display financial information about company profits in a table.

1 **Start Word and insert your Student Disk in drive A**
Refer to the "Word 6.0 Screen Check" section on the "Read This Before You Begin Microsoft Word 6.0" page to make sure your Word screen is set up appropriately.

2 **Open the document named UNIT_4-1.DOC from your Student Disk and save it as BULLETIN.DOC to your MY_FILES directory**
This document is similar to the one you used in the previous unit; however, it contains additional text about a new department and additional formatting.

3 **Place the insertion point in front of the second paragraph mark below the last item in the list of Milestones, then click the Insert Table button on the Standard toolbar**
Angela's table requires four columns (one for each of the years, plus one for the divisions) and five rows (one for each of the divisions, plus one for the columns headings).

4 **Drag in the grid until it indicates a 5 x 4 Table, then release the mouse button**
A grid of cells appears, as shown in Figure 4-2. A **cell** is the intersection of a row and a column, and contains a **cell marker** identifying the end of the contents in the cell. The **end-of-row marker** outside the table identifies the end of a row. **Gridlines** surround each cell so that you can see the structure of the table. Neither the markers nor gridlines appear when you print the document. Now that Angela has created the structure for her table, she can enter the column headings.

5 **With the insertion point in the first cell, type Division then press [Tab]**
To move to the next cell in a table, press [Tab]. To move to the previous cell, press [Shift][Tab]. Angela can now enter the headings for the three remaining columns. To show company profits for the past three *fiscal years*, she uses the designation "FY."

6 **Type the following text in the remaining cells in the first row; be sure to press [Tab] to move to the next cell:**
FY 1994 FY 1993 FY 1992 [Tab]

7 **Type the remaining information, as shown in Figure 4-3, pressing [Tab] to move to the next cell; do *not* press [Tab] at the end of the last row**

8 **Click the Save button on the Standard toolbar**
Your changes are saved in the document. Compare your document to Figure 4-3.

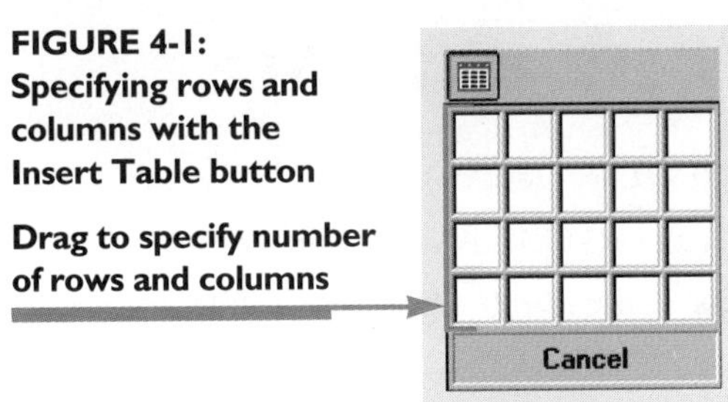

FIGURE 4-1: Specifying rows and columns with the Insert Table button

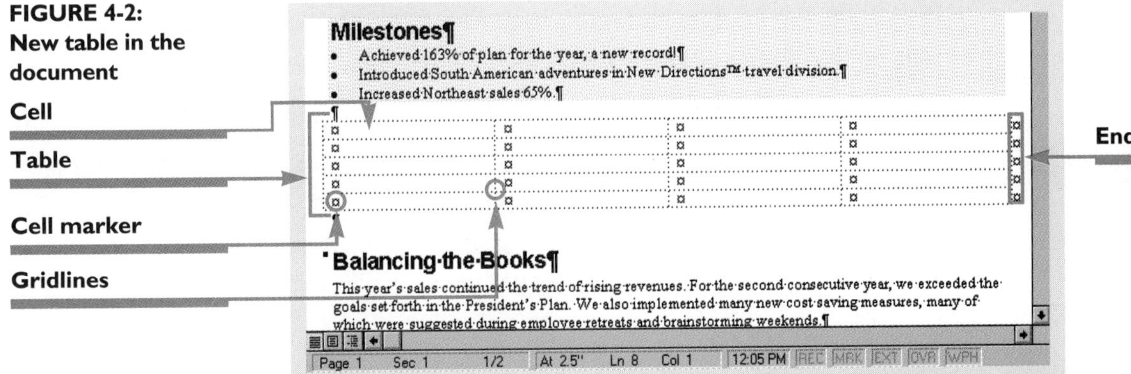

FIGURE 4-2: New table in the document

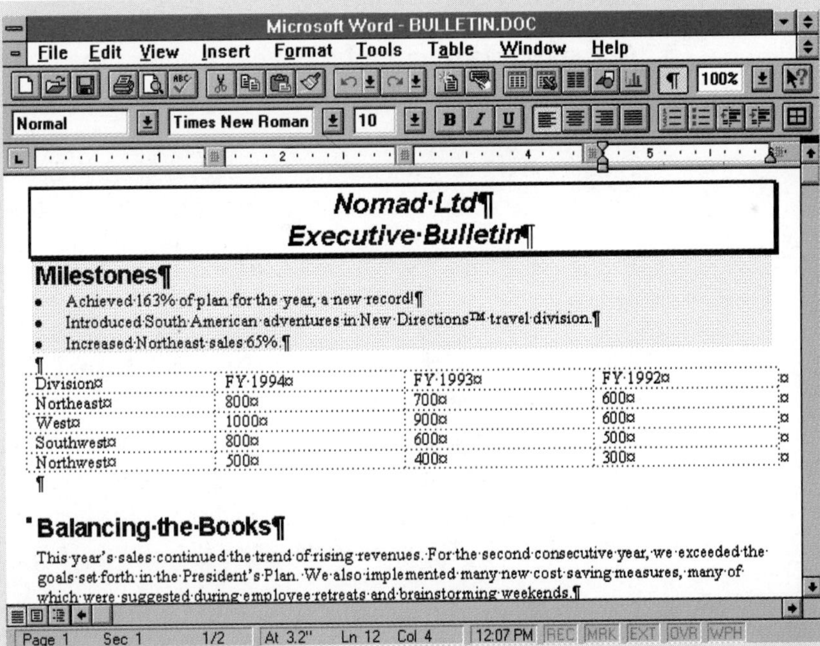

FIGURE 4-3: Text in the table

TROUBLE?

By default, Word displays gridlines in a table. If the gridlines do not appear in your table, click Table on the menu bar, then click Gridlines.

Converting text to a table

You can convert existing text that is already formatted with tabs, commas, or paragraph marks into a table by selecting the text and then using the Insert Table button on the Standard toolbar, or the Insert Table command or the Convert Text to Table command on the Table menu.

Adding rows and columns in a table

When working with tables, you often need to change the number of rows or columns to add or remove information. You can quickly add or delete rows and columns without having to rearrange text in the table. To work with tables you use different navigation keys. Table 4-1 summarizes how to move around and select text in a table. ▶ Angela would like to include total figures for each division for the last three years. She also wants to provide totals for the entire company in each year. So that she can include these calculations, Angela needs to add one row and one column to the table.

1 **Place the insertion point in the last cell of the last row of the table (if it is not already there), then press [Tab]**
Pressing [Tab] in the last cell of the last row creates a new row of cells at the bottom of the table. The insertion point is in the first cell of the new row, so Angela can type a label.

2 **Type Nomad Ltd**
Next, Angela will add a new column to the end of the table. To do so, she must first select the end-of-row markers at the right edge of the table.

3 **At the top-right edge of the table, position the pointer above the end-of-row marker, and when the pointer changes to ↓, as shown in Figure 4-4, click the left mouse button**
The column of end-of-row markers is selected, as shown in Figure 4-4. With the end-of-row markers selected, Angela can now add another column to the table.

See the related topic "Using the selection bar in tables" for more information on selection techniques.

4 **Click Table on the menu bar, then click Insert Columns**
A new blank column is inserted at the right end of the table, beyond the document margins. You might need to scroll your window to the right to see the new column. (You will learn to adjust column widths later in this unit.) You can also click the Insert Columns/Rows button on the Standard toolbar to insert a new column or row. This button is the same as the Insert Table button, but the ToolTip name for the button changes based on what is currently selected.

5 **Click to place the insertion point in the first cell of the new column, then type Total**
The column is no longer selected, and the text appears at the top of the column.

6 **Place the insertion point in the first cell under the Total column heading to prepare for the next lesson**

7 **Click the Save button on the Standard toolbar to save your changes**

FIGURE 4-4: Selecting a column

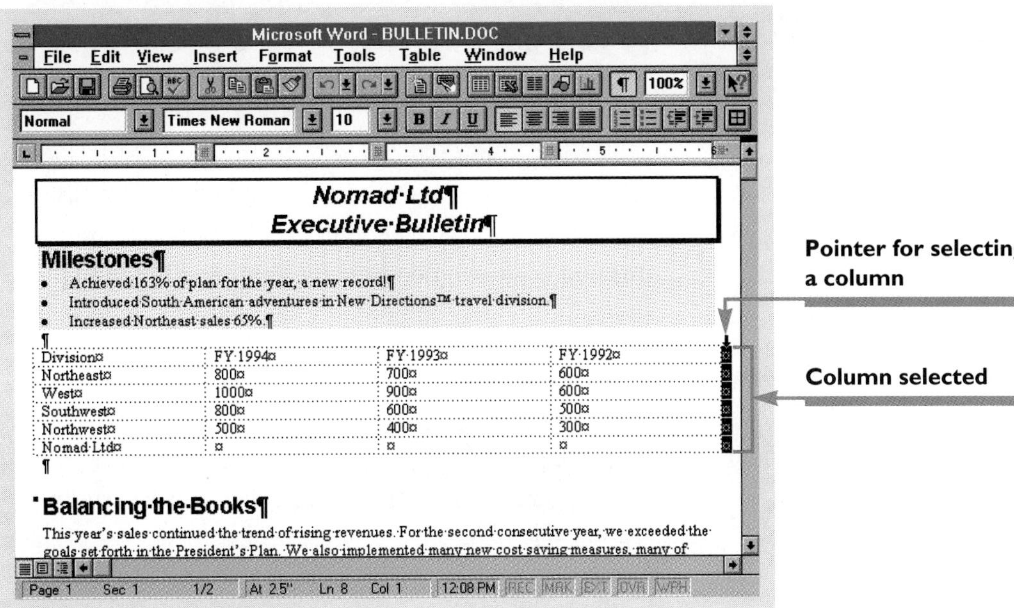

Using the selection bar in tables

The area to the left of each row in a table contains the selection bar. Clicking in the selection bar to the left of a row selects that row in the same way clicking in the selection bar to the left of a line of text selects the entire line. In addition, each cell in the table contains its own selection bar. You can click the selection bar to the left of text in a cell to select an individual cell.

TABLE 4-1: Table navigation and selection techniques

TO	PRESS
Move to and select the contents of the next cell in a table	[Tab]
Move to and select the contents of the previous cell in a table	[Shift][Tab]
Move to the first cell in a row	[Alt][Home]
Move to the last cell in a row	[Alt][End]
Move to the top cell in a column	[Alt][Page Up]
Move to the bottom cell in a column	[Alt][Page Down]
Select a column	[Alt] and click the left mouse button
Select the entire table	[Alt][5] on the numeric keypad ([Num Lock] must be turned off)

QUICK TIP

To quickly delete a row or column using the keyboard, select the row or column then press [Shift][Delete] or [Ctrl][X]. To remove only the text from a selected row or column, press [Delete].

Calculating data in a table

With the Formula command, you can perform calculations on the data in a table. Built-in formulas make it easy to quickly perform standard calculations (such as totals or averages), or you can enter your own formulas. See the related topic "Creating your own calculations" for more information. ▶ In the new column and row Angela added, she'll use the Formula command to calculate the totals she needs.

1 **Click Table on the menu bar, then click Formula**
The Formula dialog box opens, as shown in Figure 4-5. In this dialog box, you can select a built-in formula or specify your own. Based on the location of the insertion point in the table, Word suggests a formula in the Formula box—in this case, the built-in SUM formula—and suggests which cells to use in the calculation. In this case, the values in the cells to the *left* of the insertion point will be added and displayed as the total. This is the formula that Angela wants.

2 **Click OK**
The dialog box closes and the sum of the values in the row appears in the current cell. To repeat this calculation for the other totals, Angela presses [F4] in each row. The F4 key repeats your last action.

3 **Press [↓] to move the insertion point to the next cell in the Total column, press [F4], then repeat this step in each of the next two cells in this column**
The sum of the values in each row appears in each cell in the Total column. Now Angela wants to add the values in each column to determine totals for each year.

4 **Place the insertion point in the last cell of the second column, click Table on the menu bar, then click Formula**
The Formula dialog box opens and displays the suggested formula, =SUM(ABOVE). Because this is the formula she wants to use, Angela accepts the default calculation.

5 **Click OK**
The dialog box closes and the sum of the values in the column appears in the current cell. To repeat this calculation for the other totals, Angela presses [F4] in each column.

6 **Press [Tab] to move to the next column, press [F4], then repeat this step for the two remaining columns**
The total amounts appear in the cells for each column. Angela realizes that the number for the Northwest division for 1994 should be 625, not 500. After revising this figure, Angela needs to update the calculations in the table.

7 **Select the contents of the second cell in the fifth row (500), then type 625**
The new value appears in the cell. However, Word does not automatically update the totals to reflect the new value. Angela needs to recalculate the totals in the table using [F9].

8 **With the insertion point somewhere in the table, click Table on the menu bar, click Select Table, then press [F9]**
Click anywhere outside of the table to deselect it. Note that the totals in the table are updated to reflect the new value. Scroll your window to the right and compare your table to Figure 4-6.

9 **Click the Save button on the Standard toolbar to save your changes**

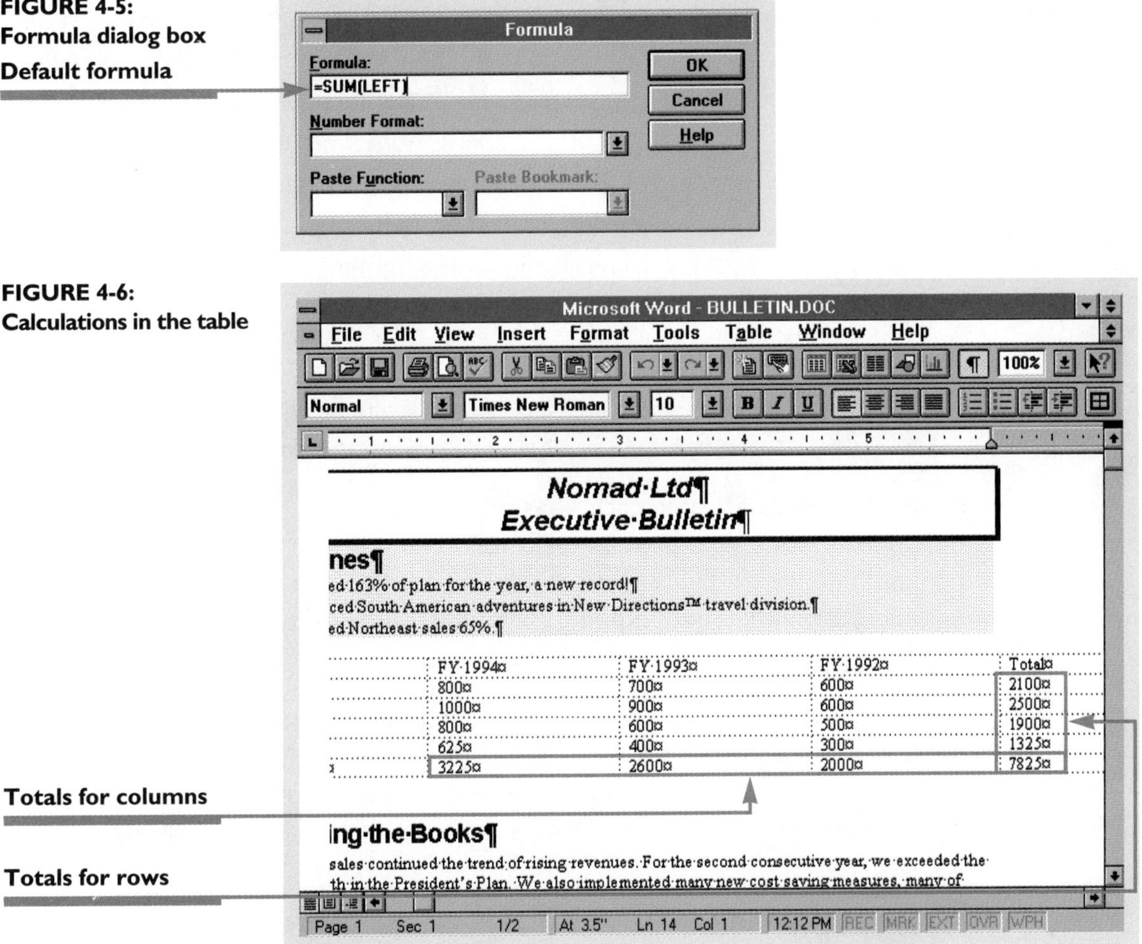

Creating your own calculations

To enter your own calculation in the Formula dialog box, you must refer to other cells in the table using cell references. A **cell reference** identifies a cell's position in the table. Each cell reference contains a letter to identify its column (A, B, C and so on) and a number (1, 2, 3 and so on) to identify its row. For example, the first cell in the first row is A1; the second cell in the first row is B1, and so on. See Figure 4-7. The formula to determine the difference between 1994 and 1993 results for the Northeast division would be =B2–C2. Multiplication is represented by an asterisk (*); division is represented by a slash (/).

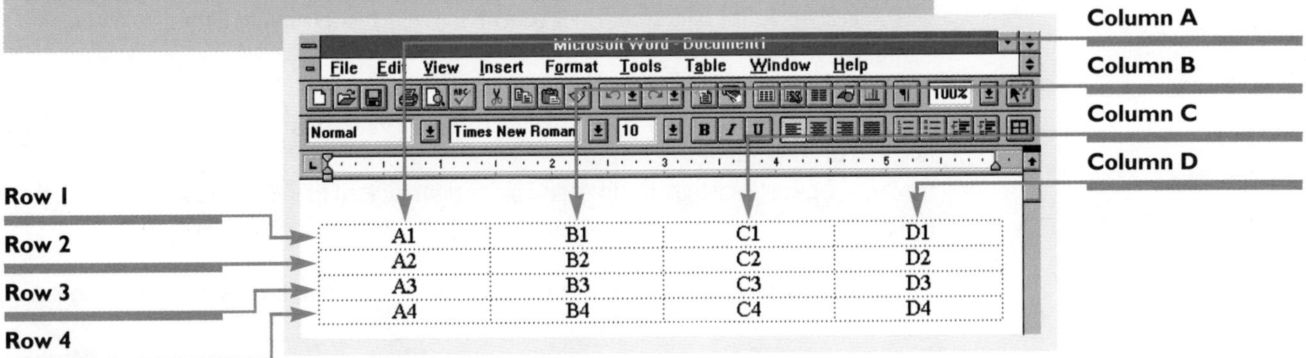

FIGURE 4-7: Cell references

Formatting a table

You can improve the appearance of a table by adding lines and shading. With the Table AutoFormat command you can choose from a variety of preset table formats. ▶ Now that she has entered the financial results in a table and calculated the necessary total amounts, Angela decides to improve the appearance of the table by applying attractive borders and shading using the Table AutoFormat command.

1. **With the insertion point inside the table, click Table on the menu bar, then click Table AutoFormat**
   The Table AutoFormat dialog box opens, as shown in Figure 4-8. In this dialog box, you can preview different preset table formats. Angela decides to use a classic preset format.
2. **In the Formats list box, click Classic 4**
   The Preview section shows how Classic 4 formats a table. Also, notice that in the Apply Special Format To section, the Heading Rows and First Column options are already selected. This means that special formatting (such as bold text or shading) will be applied to these areas of the table.
3. **Click OK**
   Word applies the Classic 4 format to the table. The column headings appear in a white, italicized font on a gray background, and the text in the first column is bold. Because Angela wants the table to span the width of the page, she needs to increase the width of the columns in the table. She can change the size of all the columns with the Cell Height and Width command.
4. **Select the entire table, click Table on the menu bar, then click Cell Height and Width**
   The Cell Height and Width dialog box opens. In this dialog box, you can specify the height and width of selected rows and columns.
5. **Click the Column tab**
   On the Column tab you can specify the width of selected columns. The width of the document between the left and right margins is approximately 6"; therefore, each column must be 1.2" wide to span the width of the text. With the entire table selected, Angela can change the width of all the columns at once.
6. **Click the Width of Columns up arrow until 1.2" is displayed, then click OK**
   The dialog box closes and the table is formatted with columns that span the width of the margins. Angela thinks the table would look better if the contents of columns 2 through 5 were right-aligned.
7. **Select columns 2 through 5 then click the Align Right button on the Formatting toolbar**
   Deselect the table to see that the numbers appear right-aligned in the columns, as shown in Figure 4-9.
8. **Click the Save button on the Standard toolbar to save your changes**

FIGURE 4-8: Table AutoFormat dialog box

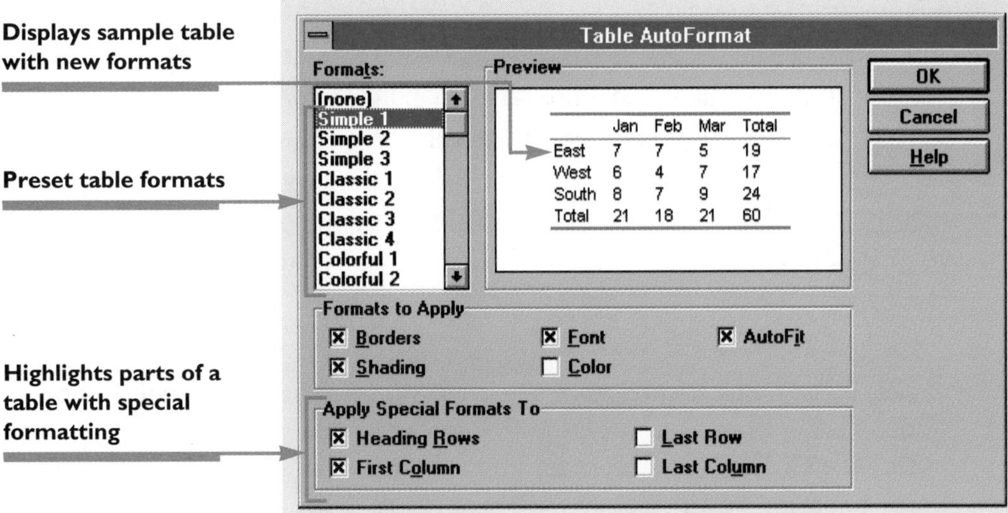

FIGURE 4-9: Completed table

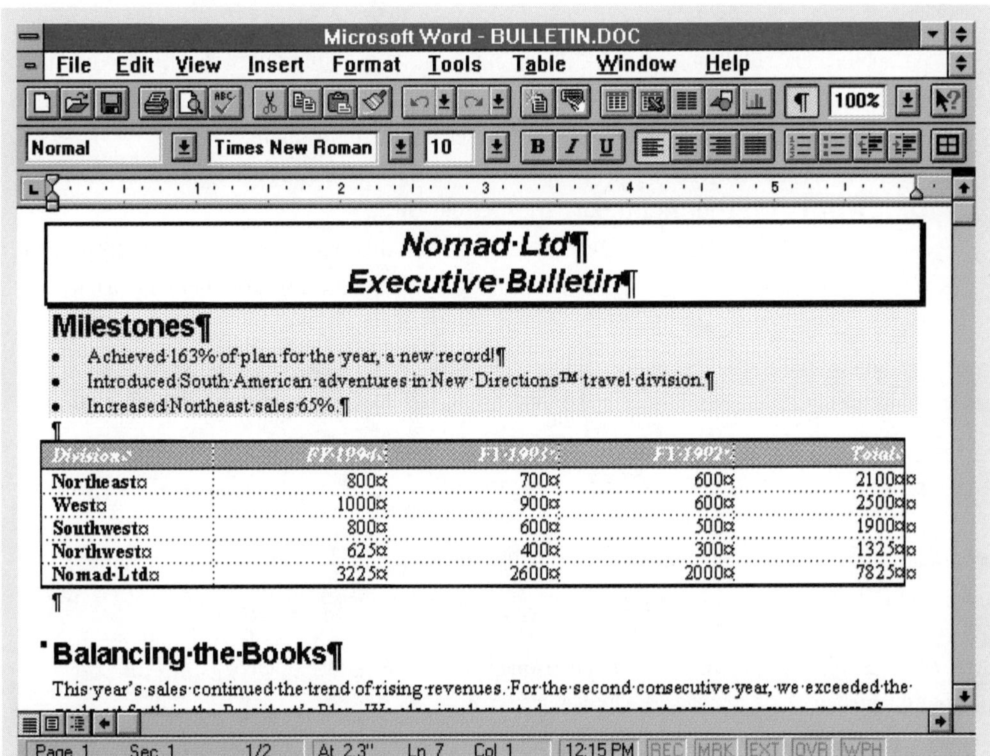

QUICK TIP

You can also adjust column width by dragging the gridlines between columns.

Arranging text in columns

Creating and Formatting Sections

In newsletters, magazines, and other forms of mass communication, it is common to format text in multiple columns rather than in one column as you usually see in letters, reports, and memos. ▶ Angela will explore formatting the document in multiple columns to give the *Executive Bulletin* the appearance of a newsletter. She begins by formatting the document into two columns. She can do this quickly with the Columns button.

1. Press **[Ctrl][Home]** to place the insertion point at the beginning of the document
2. Click the **Columns button** on the Standard toolbar, then click and drag to select **2 columns**, as shown in Figure 4-10
   Word formats your document into two columns; however, when a document is displayed in normal view, you see only one column. You need to switch to page layout view to display the two columns.
3. Click the **Page Layout View button** on the horizontal scroll bar
   The document is formatted into two columns, as shown in Figure 4-11. Note that you see only part of the table. To display all of the table, Angela needs to format this part of the document in one column. She can format different parts of the document with different numbers of columns by creating **sections**. She can then format each section individually.
4. With the insertion point in front of the heading **Balancing the Books**, click **Insert** on the menu bar, then click **Break**
   The Break dialog box opens, as shown in Figure 4-12. In this dialog box, you can specify the kind of break you want to insert. Table 4-2 summarizes the types of breaks you can insert in a document.

TABLE 4-2: Types of breaks in a document

BREAK	DESCRIPTION
Page break	Places the text after the insertion point on a new page; use this break when you want the following text to start on a new page
Column break	Places text after the insertion point in the next column; use this kind of break when you want to redistribute the amount of text that appears in each column
Section break	Creates a new section in the document; use this break when you want to format different parts of the document with different column and page setup settings
Next page section break	Creates a new section on a new page; use this break when you want the next section to start on a new page
Continuous section break	Creates a new section on the same page; use this break when you want the next section to start on the same page
Even page section break	Creates a new section that appears on the next even-numbered page; use this break when you want the next section to start on an even-numbered page
Odd page section break	Creates a new section that appears on the next odd-numbered page; use this break when you want the next section to start on an odd-numbered page

FIGURE 4-10: Specifying columns with the Columns button

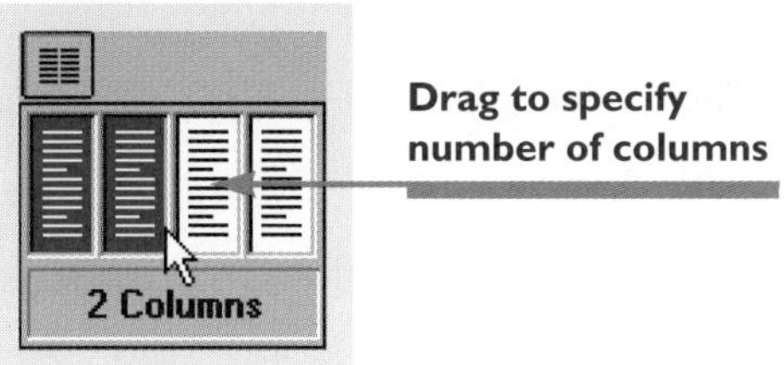

FIGURE 4-11: Columns in page layout view

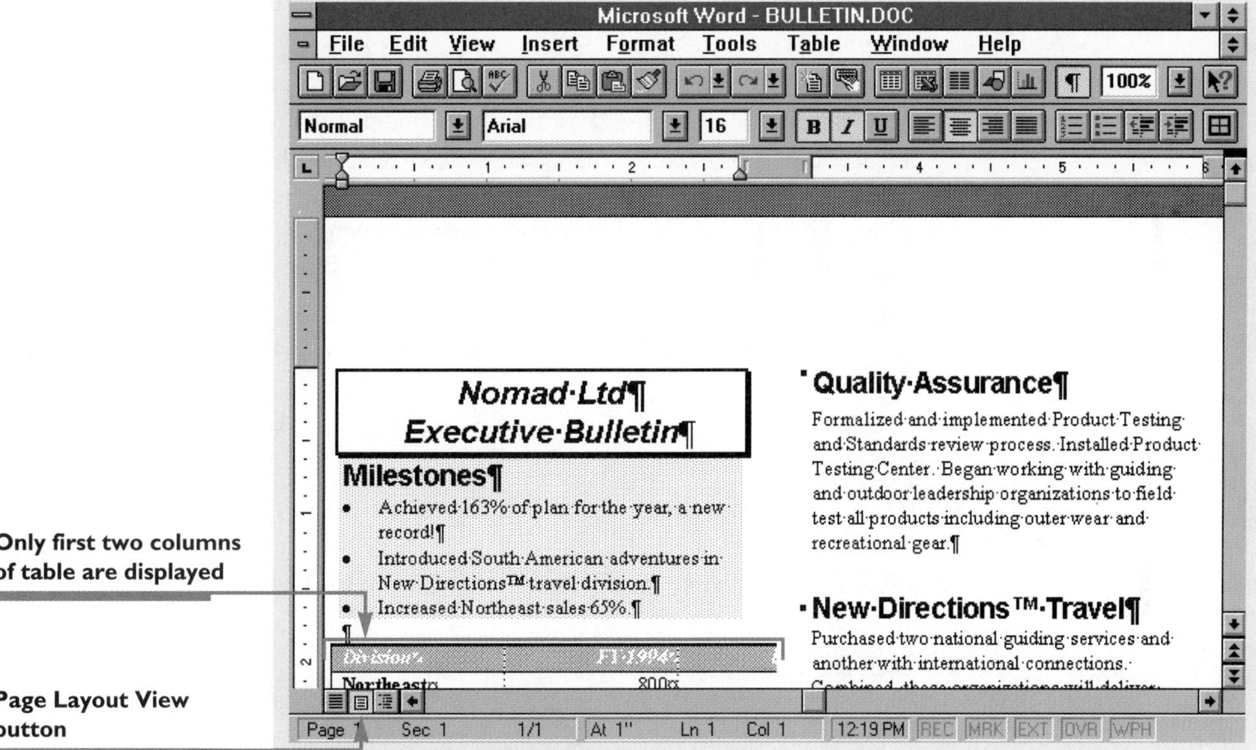

FIGURE 4-12: Break dialog box

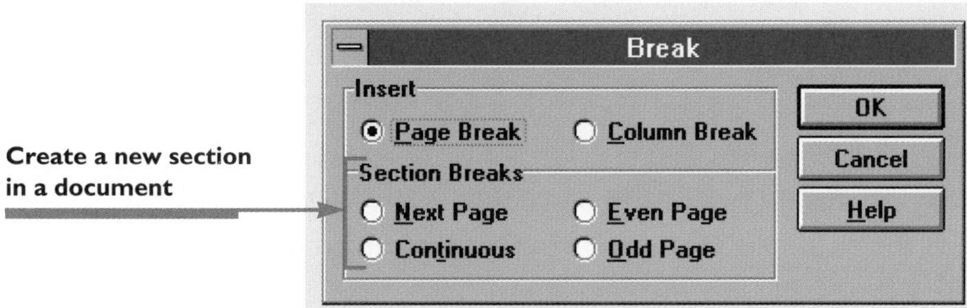

Arranging text in columns, continued

Because she wants the next section to appear on the same page, Angela selects a continuous section break.

5 In the Section Breaks section, click the **Continuous radio button**, then click **OK**
Word creates a new section that appears on the same page as the previous section. A section break appears as a double-dotted line labeled "End of Section," as shown in Figure 4-13. The status bar now indicates that the insertion point is in section 2. With two sections in her document, Angela can now format the first section as one column, so that the entire width of the table will be visible.

6 Place the insertion point anywhere in section 1 (refer to the status bar for the location), then click and drag to select **1 column**
The first section, which contains the Milestones information and the table, now appears in one column. To visually balance the formatting at the bottom of the page with the one-column formatting at the top, Angela decides to create another section that will contain the mission statement topic, and format it as one column.

7 Place the insertion point in front of the paragraph mark above the heading **Corporate Mission Statement**, click **Insert** on the menu bar, then click **Break**
In the Break dialog box, Angela again specifies a continuous section break so that the new section appears on the same page.

8 In the Section Breaks section, click the **Continuous radio button**, then click **OK**
With a new section break inserted in the document, Angela can now format the new section in one column.

9 Click then drag to select **1 Column**
The third section of the document is formatted in one column, as shown in Figure 4-14. To see the results of her changes better, Angela adjusts the magnification of the text.

10 Click the **Zoom Control list arrow** on the right end of the Standard toolbar
The Zoom Control box displays a list of preset magnifications you can use to display your document. With the Zoom Control settings you can increase the magnification to get a close-up view of the text, or you can decrease the magnification to see the overall appearance of a page.

11 Click **Page Width**
The document appears reduced so that you can see three sides (bottom, right, and left) of the page. This setting provides a better view of the text, but Angela prefers to see more of the document, so she can rearrange text on the page more easily. She reduces the magnification to 60%.

12 Select the percentage in the **Zoom Control box**, type **60**, then press **[Enter]**
Now you can see more of the page, as shown in Figure 4-15. Notice that the magnification settings you use depend on the type of monitor you are using and your personal preferences. If the magnification setting is too small for you to work with, consider using a larger setting.

13 Click the **Save button** on the Standard toolbar to save your changes

FIGURE 4-13: New section

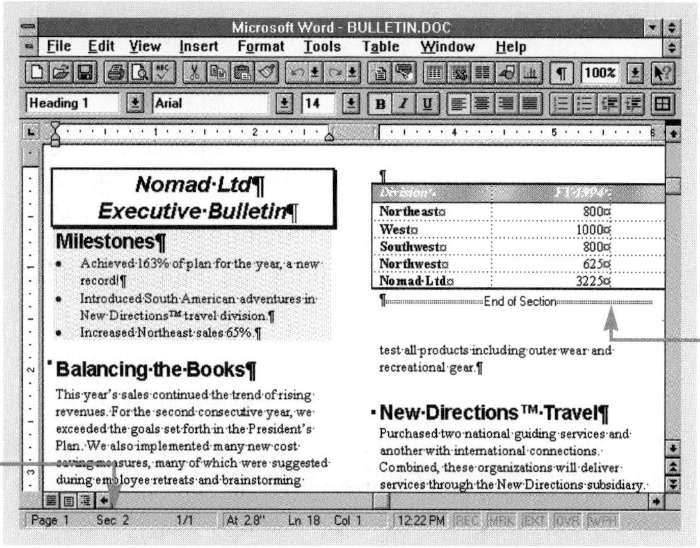

Insertion point is now in section 2

Section break

FIGURE 4-14: Multiple column formatting

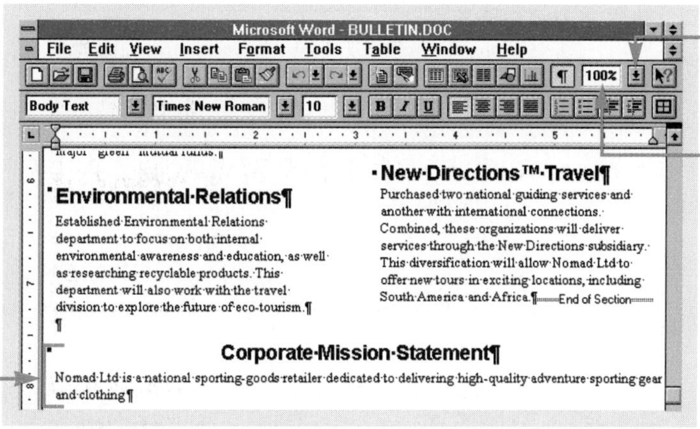

Zoom Control list arrow

Zoom Control box

Section 3 formatted in one column

FIGURE 4-15: Document in 60% magnification

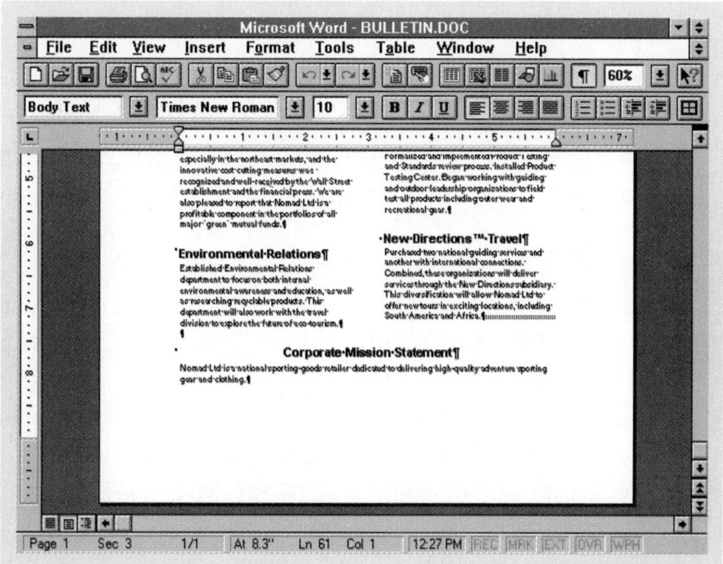

TROUBLE?

Word inserts a break at the current location of the insertion point when you choose the Break command. If your formatting is not what you expected, you can always click the Undo button on the Standard toolbar, then verify that the insertion point is in the correct location before you choose Break.

Positioning text using frames

Important information can make a greater impact if you adjust the size or position of the area in which the text appears. For example, the shaded text in the first part of the *Executive Bulletin* could be presented attractively as a **sidebar**, which is a smaller boxed section of text positioned vertically next to a main article. To create a sidebar, you need to insert a frame around the appropriate text. As you saw in Unit 3 when creating a drop cap, a **frame** is a border that surrounds text or a graphic so that you can move and format the framed object without affecting the formatting of the surrounding text. With frames you can position text (or graphics) exactly where you want on the page. ▶ Angela decides to position the milestone topics in the left margin to give readers an overview of the topics in the bulletin at a glance.

1. Select the heading **Milestones** and the **three bulleted items** in the list below the heading
   With the text selected, Angela can insert a frame around it.
2. Click **Insert** on the menu bar, then click **Frame**
   A gray hashed border representing the frame appears around the paragraph. Notice that the frame has **handles**—small black boxes— around it; the handles allow you to resize the frame. See the related topic "Dragging sizing handles" for more information. Now Angela can change the size and shape of the area containing the text.
3. Place the pointer over the **right center sizing handle** until the pointer changes to ↔, drag the handle to the left until the frame is about 1.5" wide, then release the mouse button
   The text appears in a long rectangle at the left edge of the page. Framing text gives you a great deal of flexibility in placing the text anywhere you want, even outside the page margins. Notice that an anchor icon appears next to the paragraph containing the framed text. The **anchor icon** indicates the paragraph with which the frame is associated. If you move the paragraph, the framed text moves with it. Next, Angela creates a sidebar by dragging the framed text beyond the left margin.
4. Position the pointer over a border of the frame until the pointer changes to ✥, then drag the framed text about ½" to the left and about 2½" down so that the anchor icon appears near the Balancing the Books heading
   The sidebar appears outside the left margin as a long box of text. Angela would like the sidebar to be evenly spaced between the beginning and end of the first article.
5. Position the pointer over a border of the frame until the pointer changes to ✥, and drag the framed text until it is similar to the text shown in Figure 4-16
   Next, Angela makes the text in the sidebar easier to read by using the Arial font.
6. Click the **Font list arrow** on the Formatting toolbar, then click **Arial**
   The text inside the frame appears in the Arial font. Notice that the formatting of the surrounding text is not changed and the right margin has not changed. To improve the appearance of the document, Angela reduces the font size of the items in the bulleted list, which reduces the size of the sidebar.
7. Select the **three bulleted items**, click the **Font Size list arrow** on the Formatting toolbar, then click **9**
   The font size of the bulleted items is reduced without changing the font size of the surrounding text outside the frame. Deselect the text and compare your document to Figure 4-17.
8. Click the **Save button** 💾 on the Standard toolbar to save your changes

FIGURE 4-16: Framed and positioned text

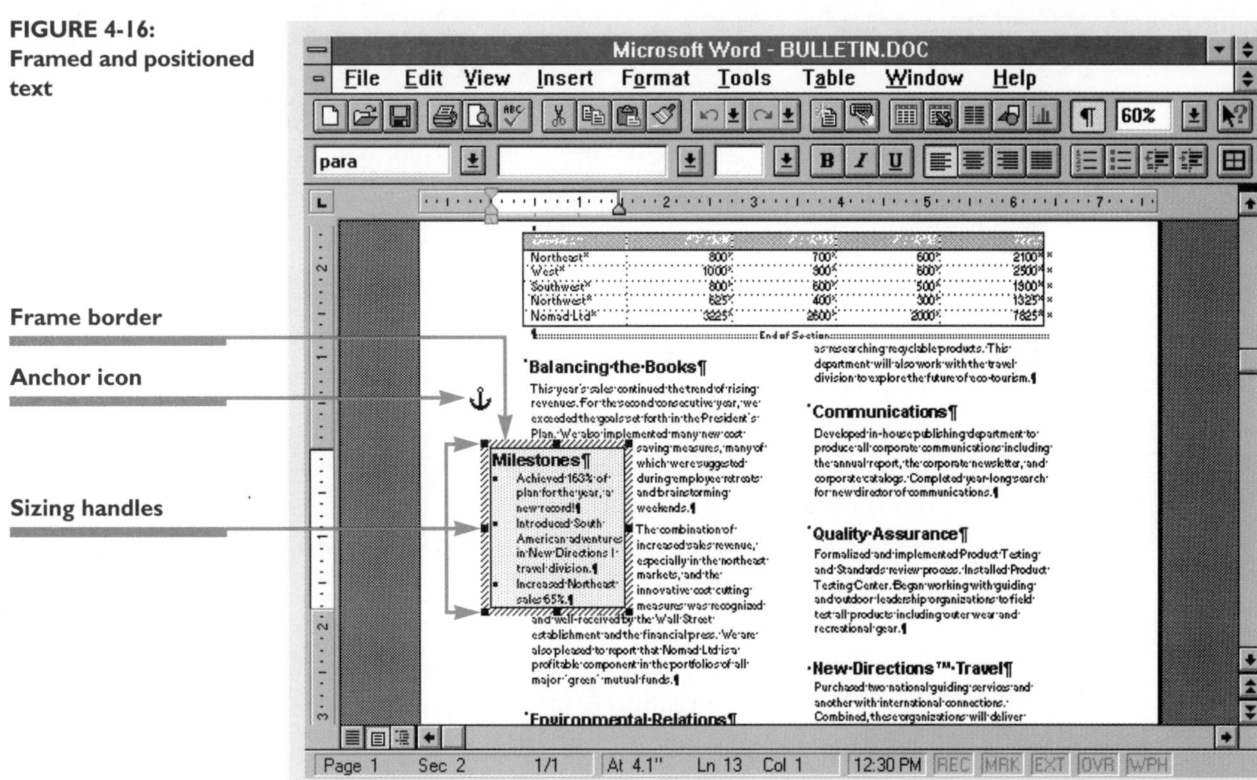

FIGURE 4-17: Formatted and framed text

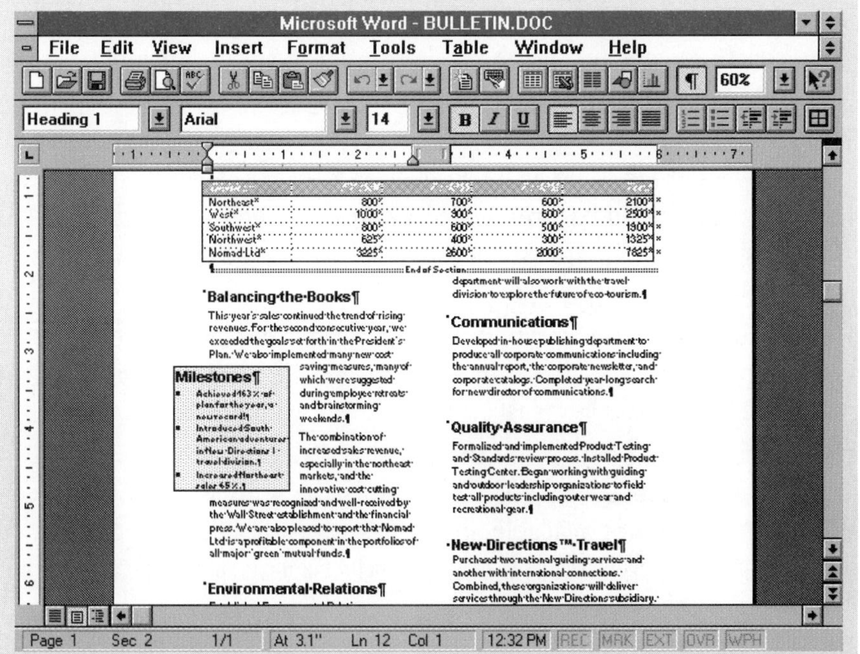

Dragging sizing handles

Dragging a top, bottom, or side handle allows you to size the object in one direction. Dragging a corner handle allows you to size the object in two directions at once, retaining the same proportions.

TROUBLE?

As you move a framed object, the anchor icon might "jump" from line to line. This is normal. After you position the object, you can move it a small amount without changing the position of the anchor icon. This allows you to place the object exactly where you want. Continue moving the object until it appears where you want. Or click the Undo button on the Standard toolbar and place the object again.

Inserting and positioning graphics

In Word you can insert pictures (in the form of graphic files, many of which are provided with Word) to better illustrate ideas and enhance your document. You can also use graphic files created in other applications. After you insert a graphic, you can size and frame it to fit where you want. ▶ In the *Executive Bulletin*, Angela wants to insert a logo in the article about the new division.

1 Place the insertion point in front of the heading **New Directions™ Travel**, click **Insert** on the menu bar, then click **Picture**
The Insert Picture dialog box opens, as shown in Figure 4-18. In this dialog box, you can select and preview a picture you want to insert in a document. The dialog box displays the default CLIPART directory in the Word directory.

2 In the File Name list box, scroll to and click **COMPASS.WMF**, then click the **Preview Picture check box** (if it is not already selected)
This is the correct graphic the new division is using, so Angela inserts it in the document.

3 Click **OK**
The graphic is inserted in the document at the insertion point. Depending on the type of computer you are using, the graphic might require a moment or two to appear. After inserting a graphic, you often need to resize it using the sizing handles. As you drag a sizing handle, the status bar displays the percentage of change in size. Because the graphic is too large to appear next to the text in the column, Angela drags a corner sizing handle to make the graphic smaller.

4 Select the graphic (if it is not already selected), then drag the sizing handle in the lower-right corner up and to the left until the status bar indicates the graphic is **50%** of its original height and width
The graphic is now smaller, as shown in Figure 4-19. Angela inserts a frame around the graphic to position it below the heading, so that the text in the article surrounds the graphic.

5 Click **Insert** on the menu bar, then click **Frame**

6 Position the graphic down and to the right so that it appears below the New Directions™ Travel heading
The text in the article surrounds the graphic, as shown in Figure 4-20. If the graphic does not look like the one in Figure 4-20, keep positioning it until it does. Next, Angela decides to add a graphic that will serve as a border between the second and third sections in the document.

7 With the insertion point in front of the heading **Corporate Mission Statement**, repeat Steps 1 through 3 to insert the graphic named **TRAVEL.WMF** or if not available, insert any other border-like picture
After inserting the graphic, Angela decides to reduce the height of the graphic by 50% so that it creates a narrower divider between sections.

8 Select the graphic (if necessary) then drag the bottom center sizing handle up until the graphic is **50%** of its original height
The image is distorted a little from the original because it was sized in only one direction. Nevertheless, this is still a pleasing visual effect. Compare your document to Figure 4-21. Note that if you didn't use TRAVEL.WMF, your document will look different.

9 Click the **Save button** on the Standard toolbar to save your changes

FIGURE 4-18: Insert Picture dialog box

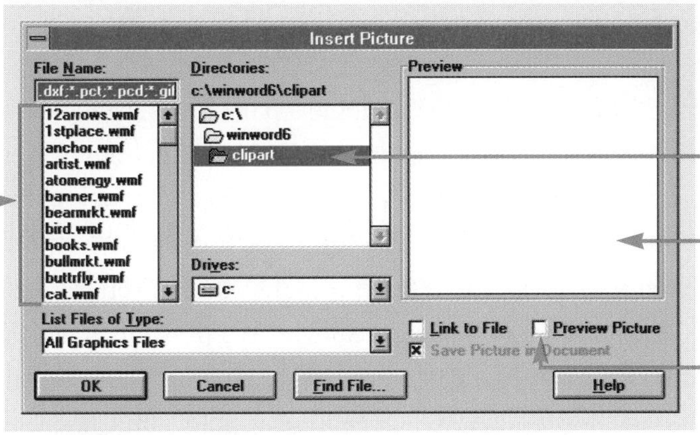

Picture files

Default graphics directory

Displays preview of selected graphic

Click to display preview of graphic

FIGURE 4-19: Sized graphic

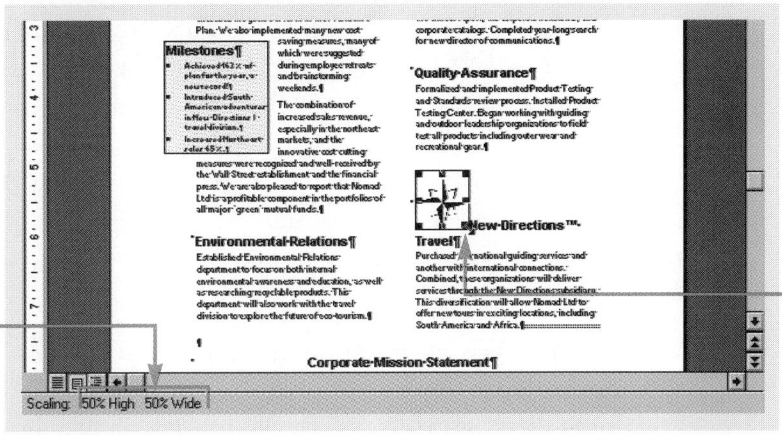

Dimensions displayed in status bar

Sizing pointer

FIGURE 4-20: Positioned graphic

Article text surrounds graphic

Graphic is below heading

FIGURE 4-21: Completed document

Inserted graphics

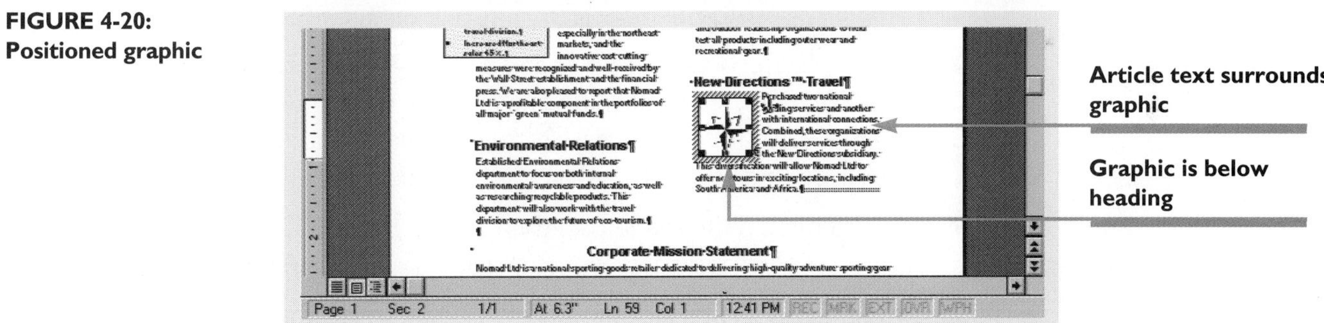

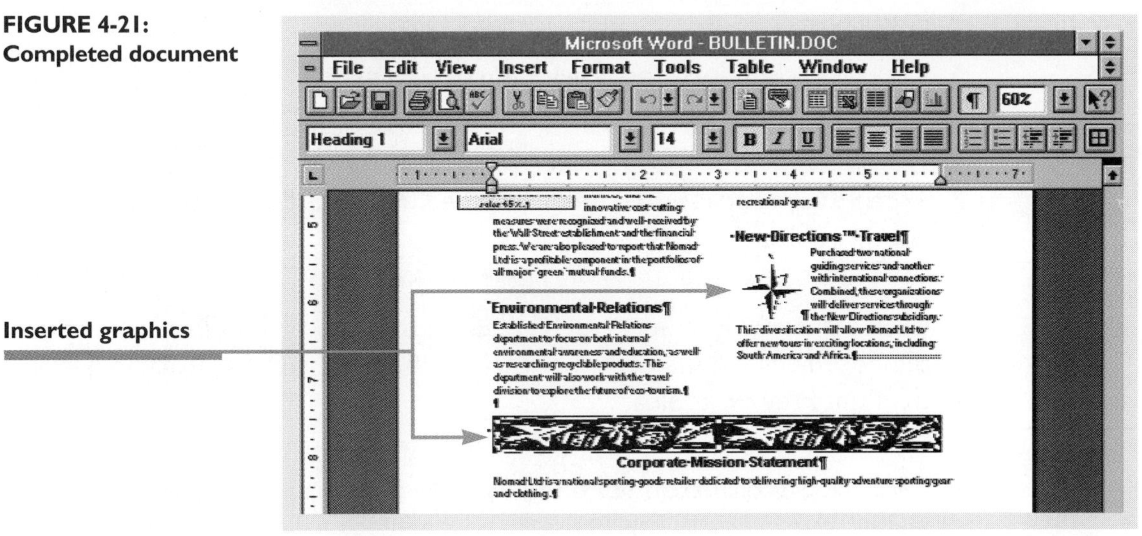

Creating headers and footers

Information that appears at the top of every page in a document is called a **header**; information that appears at the bottom of every page in a document is called a **footer**. Headers and footers usually contain basic information such as the page number, the date, or the document name. In Word you can type the text you want to appear in headers and footers, or you can insert fields to supply specific information automatically. ▶ As a finishing touch to the *Executive Bulletin*, Angela wants to include the date and the volume and issue number in the header. In the footer, she will include the company name and a copyright symbol.

1 Click **View** on the menu bar, then click **Header and Footer**
The Header and Footer toolbar appears, as shown in Figure 4-22. The text in the body of the document appears grayed out; you cannot edit the text of the document when you display the Header and Footer toolbar. The header area of the document is outlined with a dashed rectangle, which does not appear when you print the document. In the header area, Angela types the volume and issue number of the bulletin.

2 With the insertion point in the Header-Section 1 area, type **Volume 1, Issue 1**
The text appears in the header. Next, Angela includes the date at the right margin.

3 Press **[Tab]** twice then click the **Date button** on the Header and Footer toolbar
Your computer's system date appears at the right margin. Now, Angela wants to add a footer at the bottom of the page.

4 Click the **Switch Between Header and Footer button** on the Header and Footer toolbar to move to the footer area
The Footer-Section 1 area appears in the document window. Angela can now enter the copyright information she wants to include as part of the bulletin. First, she inserts the copyright symbol.

5 Click **Insert** on the menu bar, then click **Symbol**
The Symbol dialog box opens, as shown in Figure 4-23. Depending on the fonts available on your computer, your Symbol dialog box might look different. Make sure that either the Symbol or [normal text] font appears in the Font list box (click the Font list arrow to select one of these fonts, if necessary). Angela locates the copyright symbol (©) and inserts it in the footer.

6 Click ©, click **Insert**, then click **Close**
The copyright symbol appears in the footer. Angela can continue typing the rest of the text for the copyright notice.

7 Type **1995, Nomad Ltd** then click the **Close button** on the Header and Footer toolbar
The document now contains text in the header and footer.

8 Click the **Print Preview button** on the Standard toolbar to see how the document will look when printed, then click the **Print button** on the Print Preview toolbar
Compare your printed document to Figure 4-24.

9 Click the **Save button** on the Standard toolbar, click **File** on the menu bar, then click **Exit**

FIGURE 4-22: Viewing the header

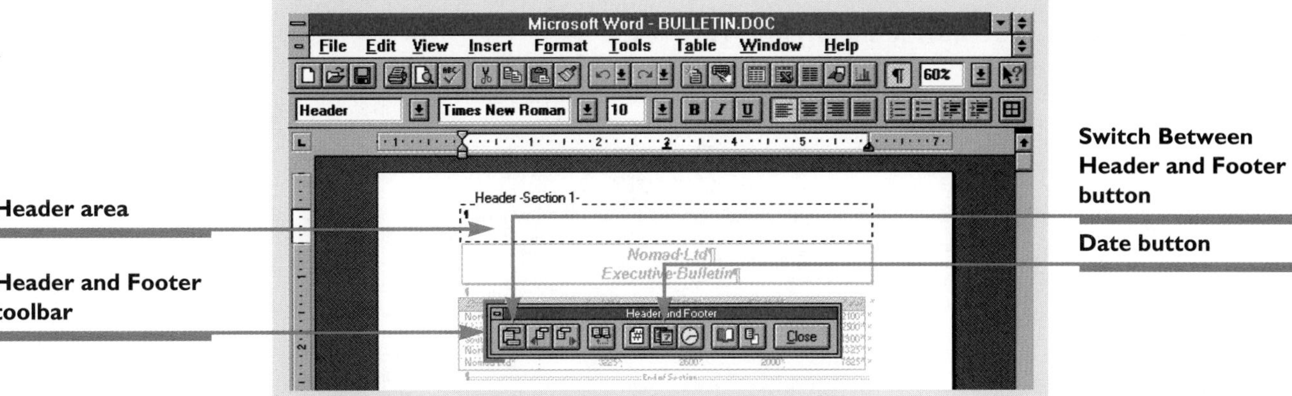

FIGURE 4-23: Symbol dialog box

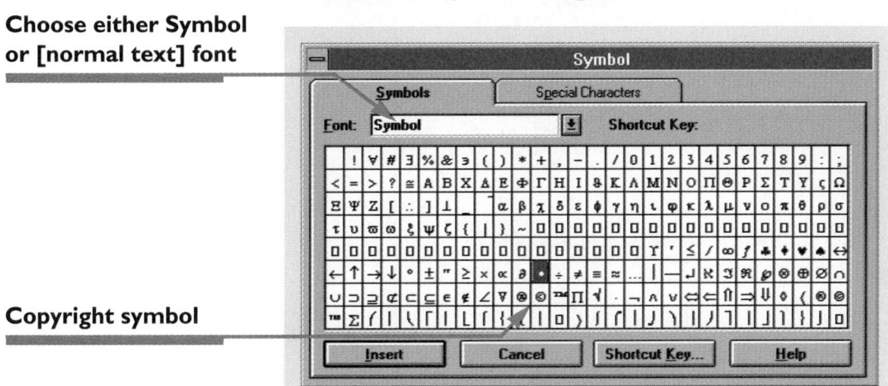

FIGURE 4-24: Completed document

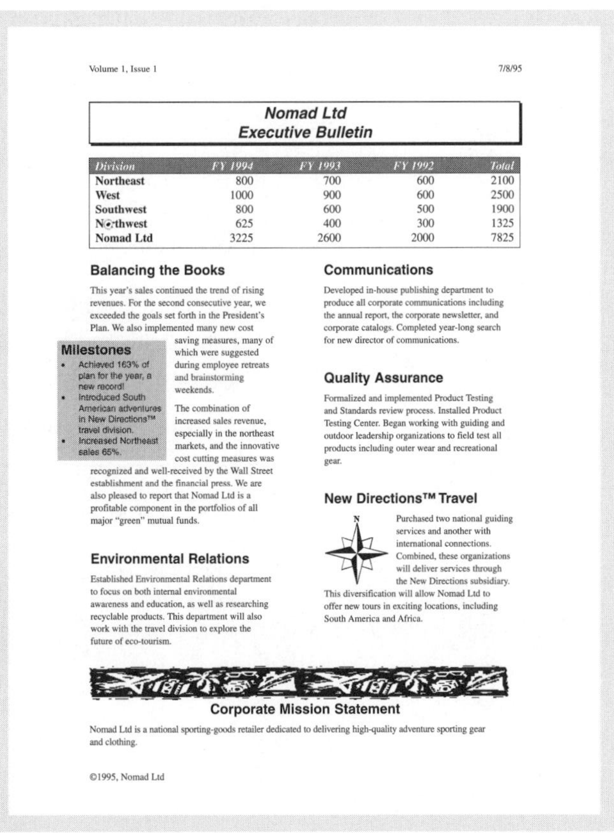

Volume 1, Issue 1 7/8/95

Nomad Ltd
Executive Bulletin

Division	FY 1994	FY 1993	FY 1992	Total
Northeast	800	700	600	2100
West	1000	900	600	2500
Southwest	800	600	500	1900
N◉rthwest	625	400	300	1325
Nomad Ltd	3225	2600	2000	7825

Balancing the Books

This year's sales continued the trend of rising revenues. For the second consecutive year, we exceeded the goals set forth in the President's Plan. We also implemented many new cost saving measures, many of which were suggested during employee retreats and brainstorming weekends.

The combination of increased sales revenue, especially in the northeast markets, and the innovative cost cutting measures was recognized and well-received by the Wall Street establishment and the financial press. We are also pleased to report that Nomad Ltd is a profitable component in the portfolios of all major "green" mutual funds.

Milestones

- Achieved 163% of plan for the year, a new record!
- Introduced South American adventures in New Directions™ travel division.
- Increased Northeast sales 65%.

Environmental Relations

Established Environmental Relations department to focus on both internal environmental awareness and education, as well as researching recyclable products. This department will also work with the travel division to explore the future of eco-tourism.

Communications

Developed in-house publishing department to produce all corporate communications including the annual report, the corporate newsletter, and corporate catalogs. Completed year-long search for new director of communications.

Quality Assurance

Formalized and implemented Product Testing and Standards review process. Installed Product Testing Center. Began working with guiding and outdoor leadership organizations to field test all products including outer wear and recreational gear.

New Directions™ Travel

Purchased two national guiding services and another with international connections. Combined, these organizations will deliver services through the New Directions subsidiary. This diversification will allow Nomad Ltd to offer new tours in exciting locations, including South America and Africa.

Corporate Mission Statement

Nomad Ltd is a national sporting-goods retailer dedicated to delivering high-quality adventure sporting gear and clothing.

©1995, Nomad Ltd

CONCEPTS REVIEW

Label each item of the newsletter shown in Figure 4-25.

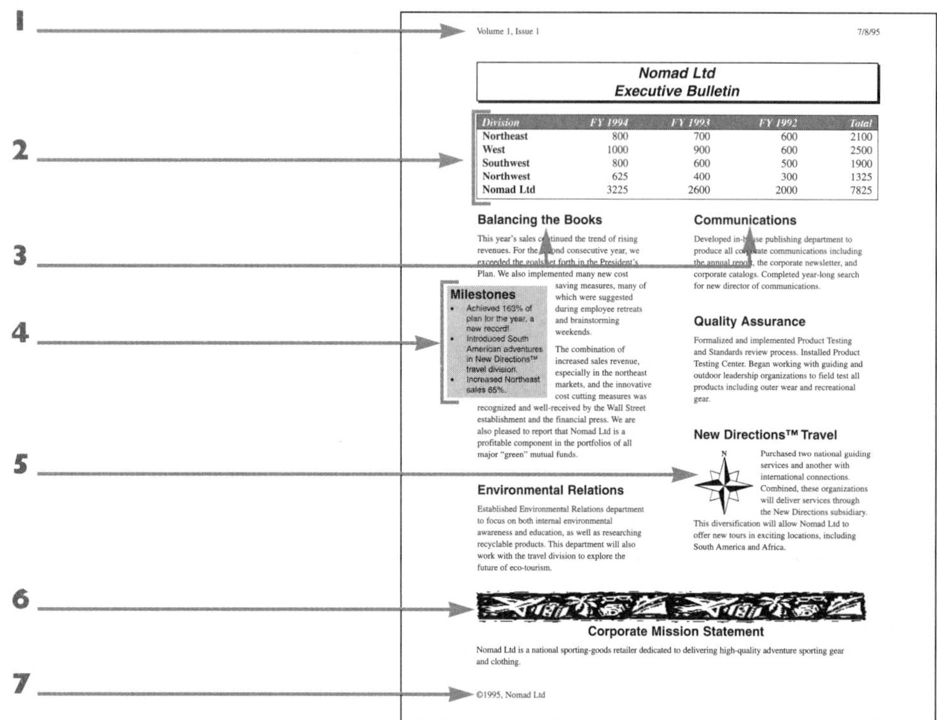

Volume 1, Issue 1 — 7/8/95

Nomad Ltd
Executive Bulletin

Division	FY 1994	FY 1993	FY 1992	Total
Northeast	800	700	600	2100
West	1000	900	600	2500
Southwest	800	600	500	1900
Northwest	625	400	300	1325
Nomad Ltd	3225	2600	2000	7825

Balancing the Books

This year's sales continued the trend of rising revenues. For the second consecutive year, we exceeded the goals set forth in the President's Plan. We also implemented many new cost saving measures, many of which were suggested during employee retreats and brainstorming weekends.

The combination of increased sales revenue, especially in the northeast markets, and the innovative cost cutting measures was recognized and well-received by the Wall Street establishment and the financial press. We are also pleased to report that Nomad Ltd is a profitable component in the portfolios of all major "green" mutual funds.

Milestones

- Achieved 163% of plan for the year, a new record!
- Introduced South American adventures in New Directions™ travel division.
- Increased Northeast sales 65%.

Environmental Relations

Established Environmental Relations department to focus on both internal environmental awareness and education, as well as researching recyclable products. This department will also work with the travel division to explore the future of eco-tourism.

Communications

Developed in-house publishing department to produce all corporate communications including the annual report, the corporate newsletter, and corporate catalogs. Completed year-long search for new director of communications.

Quality Assurance

Formalized and implemented Product Testing and Standards review process. Installed Product Testing Center. Began working with guiding and outdoor leadership organizations to field test all products including outer wear and recreational gear.

New Directions™ Travel

N

Purchased two national guiding services and another with international connections. Combined, these organizations will deliver services through the New Directions subsidiary. This diversification will allow Nomad Ltd to offer new tours in exciting locations, including South America and Africa.

Corporate Mission Statement

Nomad Ltd is a national sporting-goods retailer dedicated to delivering high-quality adventure sporting gear and clothing.

©1995, Nomad Ltd

FIGURE 4-25

Match each of the following terms with the statement that best describes its function.

8 Table
9 Gridlines
10 Cell
11 SUM
12 Frame
13 Section
14 Sizing handles
15 Column break
16 Header
17 Columns button

a. Allow you to size an object
b. Arranges text in rows and columns
c. Separates each intersection of rows and columns in a table
d. Allows you to position text or graphics anywhere on the page
e. The intersection of a row and column in a table
f. Allows you to format individual parts of a document with different settings
g. The default calculation with the Formula command
h. Moves text from one column to the next
i. Formats text into columns using default settings
j. Text at the top of every page

Select the best answer from the list of choices.

18 To insert a column at the end of a table, you must first
a. Select the last column
b. Place the insertion point in the last column
c. Select the last cell in the table
d. Select the end-of-row markers at the right edge of the table

19 Before positioning text or a graphic without changing the formatting of surrounding text, you must first
a. Select the object and size it
b. Select the object and insert a frame
c. Select the object and move it
d. Select the object then click the Frame button

20 To insert a header you click View, click Header and Footer, and then
a. Click the Header check box, and type the text of the header
b. Click the Go to Top button, and type the text of the header
c. Type the text of the header
d. Enter your header preferences and text in the Insert Header dialog box

APPLICATIONS REVIEW

1 Create a table.

a. Start Word.

b. Open the document named UNIT_4-2.DOC from your Student Disk and save it as SQUARPEG.DOC to your MY_FILES directory.

c. With the insertion point in front of the paragraph mark above the heading Othello, click the Insert Table button on the Standard toolbar and drag to select a grid that is four columns wide and five rows long.

d. Enter price information in the table, using Figure 4-26:

2 Format the table.

a. With the insertion point inside the table, click Table then click Table AutoFormat.

b. Be sure the AutoFit and Last Column check boxes are cleared, and that the Last Row check box is checked.

c. Choose the Simple 1 format and click OK.

d. Select the first row of the table.

e. Click the Borders button on the Formatting toolbar, then click the Shading list arrow on the Borders toolbar and choose 5% shading.

f. Click the Borders button on the Formatting toolbar to hide the Borders toolbar.

3 Use columns to format text.

a. Click outside of the table, click the Columns button on the Standard toolbar, then drag to select three columns.

b. Click the Page Layout View button on the horizontal scroll bar.

c. Place the insertion point in front of the heading Macbeth. Click Insert, click Break, click the Column Break radio button, then click OK.

d. Place the insertion point in front of the heading Hamlet, then press [F4] and save your work.

4 Create and format sections.

a. Place the insertion point in front of the heading Othello. Click Insert, click Break, click the Continuous radio button, then click OK.

b. Place the insertion point in section 1, click the Columns button on the Standard toolbar, then click one column.

c. Place the insertion point before the paragraph mark above the heading Still Can't Decide?, click Insert, click Break, click the Continuous radio button, then click OK.

d. Click the Columns button on the Standard toolbar, then click one column and save your work.

5 Position text and graphics using frames.

a. Select the chart object near the end of the document.

b. Drag the bottom-left corner sizing handle up and to the right until the chart is 90% of its original height and 90% of its original width.

c. Click Insert then click Frame.

d. Drag the chart to the left of the last paragraph on the previous page, aligning the anchor icon with the first bullet item and the left edge of the chart with the left margin.

e. Select the entire shaded paragraph near the beginning of the document, click Insert, then click Frame.

f. Drag the right center sizing handle to the left until the frame is about 1" wide.

g. Position the pointer over a border of the frame until the pointer changes to the frame pointer, then drag the framed text 1½" to the left and ½" down.

h. Click the Center button on the Formatting toolbar, then save your work.

6 Insert graphics.

a. Place the insertion point before the paragraph mark above the heading Still Can't Decide?, click Insert, then click Picture.

b. In the File Name list box click DIVIDER3.WMF, then click the Preview Picture check box (if it is not already selected) and click OK.

c. Select the graphic (if it is not already selected), then drag the right center sizing handle to the right margin.

d. Drag the bottom center sizing handle down about ½" then save your work.

7 Insert headers and footers.

a. Click View then click Header and Footer.

b. Type "Winter 1995" in the header area.

c. Click the Switch Between Header and Footer button on the Header and Footer toolbar.

d. Click Insert then click Symbol.

e. Click ©, click Insert, then click Close.

f. Type "1995, Square Peg Theatre."

g. Click the Close button on the Header and Footer toolbar.

h. Preview, then print the document and compare it to Figure 4-26.

i. Close the file, then exit Word.

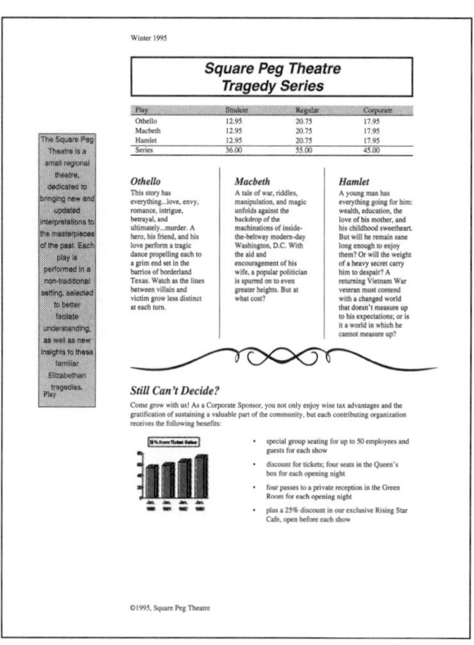

Winter 1995

Square Peg Theatre
Tragedy Series

Play	Student	Regular	Corporate
Othello	12.95	20.75	17.95
Macbeth	12.95	20.75	17.95
Hamlet	12.95	20.75	17.95
Series	36.00	55.00	45.00

The Square Peg Theatre is a small regional theatre, dedicated to bringing new and updated interpretations to the masterpieces of the past. Each play is performed in a non-traditional setting, selected to better facilate understanding, as well as new insights to these familiar Elizabethan tragedies.
Play

Othello
This story has everything...love, envy, romance, intrigue, betrayal, and ultimately...murder. A hero, his friend, and his love perform a tragic dance propelling each to a grim end set in the barrios of borderland Texas. Watch as the lines between villain and victim grow less distinct at each turn.

Macbeth
A tale of war, riddles, manipulation, and magic unfolds against the backdrop of the machinations of inside-the-beltway modern-day Washington, D.C. With the aid and encouragement of his wife, a popular politician is spurred on to even greater heights. But at what cost?

Hamlet
A young man has everything going for him: wealth, education, the love of his mother, and his childhood sweetheart. But will he remain sane long enough to enjoy them? Or will the weight of a heavy secret carry him to despair? A returning Vietnam War veteran must contend with a changed world that doesn't measure up to his expectations; or is it a world in which he cannot measure up?

Still Can't Decide?
Come grow with us! As a Corporate Sponsor, you not only enjoy wise tax advantages and the gratification of sustaining a valuable part of the community, but each contributing organization receives the following benefits:

- special group seating for up to 50 employees and guests for each show
- discount for tickets; four seats in the Queen's box for each opening night
- four passes to a private reception in the Green Room for each opening night
- plus a 25% discount in our exclusive Rising Star Cafe, open before each show

©1995, Square Peg Theatre

FIGURE 4-26

INDEPENDENT CHALLENGE 1

As the marketing manager of a large computer company, you are responsible for producing an executive summary to the corporate report. Using the document in Figure 4-27 as a guide, create a document that identifies the highlights of the past year. To save time, you can start with a draft named UNIT_4-3.DOC from your Student Disk and save it as BIGSYS.DOC to your MY_FILES directory.

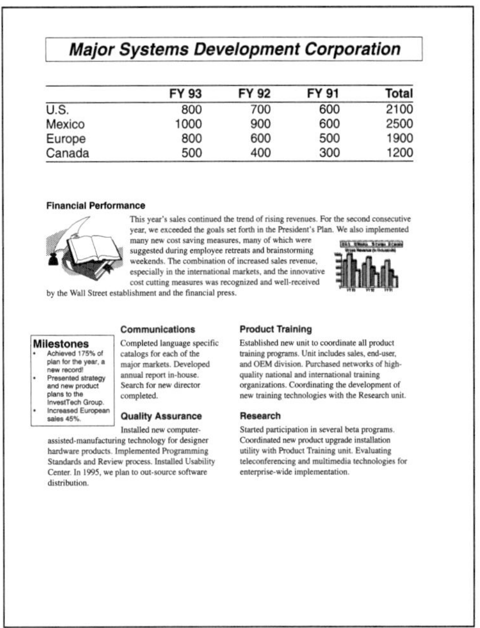

Major Systems Development Corporation

	FY 93	FY 92	FY 91	Total
U.S.	800	700	600	2100
Mexico	1000	900	600	2500
Europe	800	600	500	1900
Canada	500	400	300	1200

Financial Performance

This year's sales continued the trend of rising revenues. For the second consecutive year, we exceeded the goals set forth in the President's Plan. We also implemented many new cost saving measures, many of which were suggested during employee retreats and brainstorming weekends. The combination of increased sales revenue, especially in the international markets, and the innovative cost cutting measures was recognized and well-received by the Wall Street establishment and the financial press.

Milestones
- Achieved 175% of plan for the year, a new record!
- Presented strategy and new product plans to the InvestTech Group.
- Increased European sales 45%.

Communications

Completed language specific catalogs for each of the major markets. Developed annual report in-house. Search for new director completed.

Quality Assurance

Installed new computer-assisted-manufacturing technology for designer hardware products. Implemented Programming Standards and Review process. Installed Usability Center. In 1995, we plan to out-source software distribution.

Product Training

Established new unit to coordinate all product training programs. Unit includes sales, end-user, and OEM division. Purchased networks of high-quality national and international training organizations. Coordinating the development of new training technologies with the Research unit.

Research

Started participation in several beta programs. Coordinated new product upgrade installation utility with Product Training unit. Evaluating teleconferencing and multimedia technologies for enterprise-wide implementation.

FIGURE 4-27

INDEPENDENT CHALLENGE 2

Nomad Ltd would like its shareholders who want to attend the Annual Meeting to complete a short registration form. Format the table, and use frames and the CLIPART file called PARTY.WMF to create a registration form that looks like the one shown in Figure 4-28. Start by opening the draft document named UNIT_4-4.DOC from your Student Disk and save it as INVITE.DOC to your MY_FILES directory.

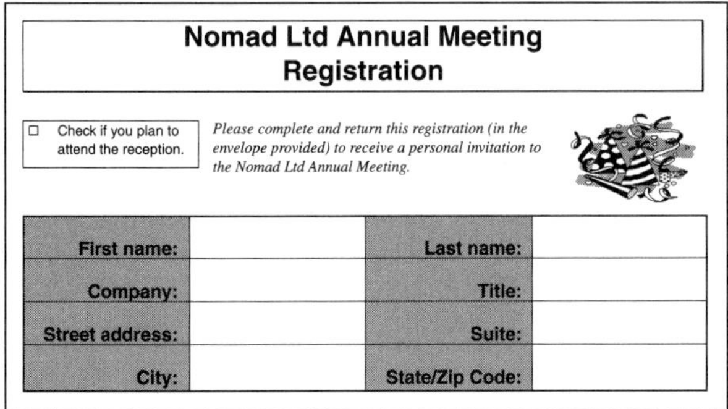

Nomad Ltd Annual Meeting Registration

☐ Check if you plan to attend the reception.

Please complete and return this registration (in the envelope provided) to receive a personal invitation to the Nomad Ltd Annual Meeting.

First name:		Last name:	
Company:		Title:	
Street address:		Suite:	
City:		State/Zip Code:	

FIGURE 4-28

Glossary

Alignment The horizontal position of text within the width of a line or between tab stops.

Application A software program, such as Microsoft Word.

Application window A window that contains the running application. It displays the menus and provides the workspace for any document used within the application.

Arrow keys The [↑], [↓], [←], and [→] keys. Used to move the insertion point or to select menu commands or options.

Automatic save A feature that automatically saves document changes in a temporary file at specified intervals.

AutoCorrect A feature that automatically corrects a misspelled word that you type. Word provides several entries for commonly misspelled words, but you can add your own.

AutoFormat A feature that improves the appearance of a document by applying consistent formatting and styles based on a default document template or a document template you select.

AutoText entry A stored text or graphic you want to use again.

Border A straight vertical or horizontal line between columns in a section, next to or around paragraphs and graphics, or in a table. *See also* Rule.

Bullet A small graphic, usually a round or square dot, often used to identify items in a list.

Cell The intersection of a row and a column.

Cell reference The address or name of a specific cell. Each cell reference contains a letter (A, B, C, and so on) to identify its column and a number (1, 2, 3, and so on) to identify its row.

Character style A stored set of text format settings.

Click To press and release a mouse button in one motion.

Clipboard A temporary storage area for cut or copied text or graphics. You can paste the contents of the Clipboard into any Word document. The Clipboard holds the information until you cut or copy another piece of text or a graphic.

Control menu A menu that includes commands with which you can control the size and position of the Word window and switch to another application.

Crop To cut away the parts of a graphic you don't want to appear.

Cut A command that removes selected text or a graphic from a document and places it on the Clipboard so you can paste it to another place in the document or to another document.

Default template A template with the file name NORMAL.DOT that contains default menus, AutoCorrect entries, styles, and page setup settings. Documents use the global template unless you specify a custom template. *See also* Template.

Defaults Predefined settings such as page margins, tab spacing, and shortcut key assignments. The default template when you create documents is NORMAL.DOT.

Dialog box A windows that appears when you choose a command whose name is followed by an ellipsis (...). A dialog box allows you to make selections that determine how the command affects the selected area.

Directories Subdivisions of a disk that work like a filing system to help you organize files.

Document window A rectangular portion of the screen in which you view and edit a document. You can have up to nine document windows open in the Word application window.

Drag To hold down the mouse button while moving the mouse.

Drive A mechanism in a computer or an area on a network used to retrieve and store information. Personal computers often have one hard disk drive labeled C and two drives labeled A and B that read removable floppy disks.

Edit To add, delete, or change text and graphics.

Effects Refers to whether text appears in small caps, all caps, hidden text, struckthrough, subscripted, or superscripted.

Extend selection To lengthen a selection. When you extend a selection, it grows progressively larger each time you press [F8]. To shrink the selection, press [Shift] + [F8].

File A document that has been created, then saved, under a unique file name.

Font A name given to a collection of characters (letters, numerals, symbols, and punctuation marks) with a specific design. Arial and Times New Roman are examples of font names.

Font size Refers to the physical size of text, measured in points (pts). One inch equals 72 points.

Font style Refers to whether text appears as bold, italicized, or underlined, or any combination of these formats.

Format The way text appears on a page. In Word, a format comes from direct formatting and the application of styles. The four types of formats are character, paragraph, section, and document.

Formatting toolbar A bar that contains buttons and options for the most frequently used Word formatting commands.

Frame A box you add to mark an area of text or graphic in a document so that you can easily position it on a page. Once you insert an object into a frame, you can drag it to the position you want in page layout view.

Graphics A picture, chart, or drawing in a document.

Graphic object An element in a document that can be moved, sized, and modified without leaving Word.

Hanging indent A paragraph format in which the first line of a paragraph starts farther left than the subsequent lines.

Header and footer A header is text or graphics that appear at the top of every page in a section. A footer appears at the bottom of every page. Headers and footers often contain page numbers, chapter titles, dates, and author names. Headers and footers appear in the header or footer pane for editing.

Hidden text A character format that allows you to show or hide designated text. Word indicates hidden text by underlining it with a dotted line.

Horizontal ruler A graphical bar displayed across the top of the document window in all views. You can use the ruler to indent paragraphs, set tab stops, adjust left and right paragraph margins, and change column widths in a table.

Indent The distance between text boundaries and page margins.

Insertion point Blinking vertical line on the Word screen that shows your current location and where text and graphics are inserted.

Landscape A term used to refer to horizontal page orientation; opposite of portrait, or vertical, orientation.

Line break Mark inserted where you want to end one line and start another without starting a new paragraph.

Line spacing The height of a line of text, including extra spacing. Line spacing is often measured in lines or points.

Margin The distance between the edge of the text in the document and the top, bottom, or side edges of the page.

Menu bar The horizontal bar under the title bar that lists the names of the menus that contain Word commands.

Nonprinting characters Marks displayed on the screen to indicate characters that do not print, such as tab characters or paragraph marks.

Normal view The view you see when you start Word. Normal view is used for most editing and formatting tasks.

Object A table, chart, graphic, equation, or other form of information you create and edit with an application other than Word, but whose data you insert and store in a Word document.

Overtype An option for replacing existing characters one by one as you type. When you select the Overtype option, the letters "OVR" appear in the status bar.

Page break The point at which one page ends and another begins. A break you insert (created by pressing [Ctrl] + [Enter]) is called a hard break; a break determined by the page layout is called a soft break.

Page layout view A view of a document as it will appear when you print it.

Paragraph style A stored set of paragraph format settings.

Paste To insert cut or copied text into a document from the temporary storage area called the Clipboard.

Point size A measurement used for the size of text characters. There are 72 points per inch.

Portrait A term used to refer to vertical page orientation; opposite of "landscape," or horizontal, orientation.

Record The entire collection of fields related to an item or individual, contained in the data source.

Repaginate To calculate and insert page breaks at the correct point in a document.

Repetitive text Text that you use often in documents.

Rule A straight vertical or horizontal line between columns in a section, next to paragraphs, or in a table. You can assign a variety of widths to a rule. *See also* Border.

Sans serif font A font whose characters do not include serifs, the small strokes at the ends of the characters. Arial is a sans serif font.

Scale To change the height and/or width of a graphic by a percentage. You can choose to preserve or change the relative proportions of elements within the graphic.

Scroll bars Bars that appear on the right and bottom borders of a window that allow you to scroll the window vertically and horizontally to view portions of the document not currently visible.

Selection bar An unmarked column at the left edge of a document window used to select text with the mouse.

Serif font A font that has small strokes at the ends of the characters. Times New Roman and Palatino are serif fonts.

Shading The color or pattern behind text or graphics.

Soft return A line break created by pressing [Shift] + [Enter]. This creates a new line without creating a new paragraph.

Standard toolbar The topmost bar of buttons that provides access to frequently used Word commands.

Status bar The horizontal bar located at the bottom of the Word window. It displays the current page number and section number, the total number of pages in the document, and the vertical position (in inches) of the insertion point. You also see the status of commands in effect, and the current time, as well as descriptions of commands and buttons as you move around the window.

Style A group of formatting instructions that you name and store and are able to modify. When you apply a style to selected characters and paragraphs, all the formatting instructions of that style are applied at once.

Style area An area to the left of the selection in which the names of applied styles are displayed.

Style Gallery A feature that allows you to examine the overall formatting and styles used in a document template. With the Style Gallery you can also preview your document formatted in the styles from a selected template.

Tab stop A measured position for placing and aligning text at a specific place on a line. Word has four kinds of tab stops, left-aligned (the default), centered, right-aligned, and decimal.

Table One or more rows of cells commonly used to display numbers and other items for quick reference and analysis. Items in a table are organized into rows and columns. You can convert text into a table with the Insert Table command on the Table menu.

Template A special kind of document that provides basic tools and text for creating a document. Templates can contain the following elements: styles, AutoText items, macros, customized menu and key assignments, and text or graphics that are the same in different types of documents.

Title bar The horizontal bar at the top of a window that displays the name of the document or application that appears in that window. Until you save the document and give it a name, the temporary name for the document is DOCUMENT1.

Toolbar A horizontal bar with buttons that provide access to the most commonly used commands in Word, such as opening, copying, and printing files.

ToolTip When you move the pointer over a button, the name of the button appears below the button and a brief description of its function appears in the status bar.

Vertical alignment The placement of text on a page in relation to the top, bottom, or center of the page.

Vertical ruler A graphical bar displayed at the left edge of the document window in the page layout and print preview views. You can use this ruler to adjust the top and bottom page margins, and change row height in a table.

View A display that shows certain aspects of the document. Word has six views: normal, draft, outline, page layout, full screen, and print preview.

View buttons Appear in the horizontal scroll bar. Allow you to display the document in one of three views: Normal, Page Layout, and Outline.

Wizard A feature that provides a series of dialog boxes that guide you through the process of creating a specific document.

Word processing application An application used for creating documents efficiently. Usually includes features beyond simple editing, such as formatting and arranging text and graphics to create attractive documents, as well as the ability to merge documents for form letters and envelopes.

Word-wrap Automatic placement of a word on the next line. When you type text and reach the right margin or indent, Word checks to see if the entire word you type fits on the current line. If not, Word automatically places the entire word on the next line.

WYSIWYG (What You See Is What You Get) An application that indicates a document will print with the same formatting that is displayed in the document window.

Index

Microsoft® Excel 5.0

for Windows™

UNIT 1 **Getting Started with Microsoft Excel 5.0**

UNIT 2 **Creating a Worksheet**

UNIT 3 **Modifying a Worksheet**

UNIT 4 **Working with Charts**

Read This Before You Begin Microsoft Excel 5.0

To the Student

The lessons and exercises in this book feature several Excel workbook files provided to your instructor. To complete the step-by-step lessons, Applications Reviews, and Independent Challenges in this book, you must have a Student Disk. Your instructor will do one of the following: 1) provide you with your own copy of the disk; 2) have you copy it from the network onto your own floppy disk; or 3) have you copy the lesson files from a network into your own subdirectory on the network. Always use your own copies of the lesson and exercise files. See your instructor or technical support person for further information.

Using Your Own Computer

If you are going to work through this book using your own computer, you need a computer system running Microsoft Windows 3.1, Microsoft Excel 5.0 for Windows, and a Student Disk. *You will not be able to complete the step-by-step lessons in this book using your own computer until you have your own Student Disk.* This book assumes the default settings under a Standard installation of Microsoft Excel 5.0 for Windows.

To the Instructor

Bundled with the instructor's copy of this book is a Student Disk. The Student Disk contains all the files your students need to complete the step-by-step lessons in the units, Applications Reviews, and Independent Challenges. As an adopter of this text, you are granted the right to distribute the files on the Student Disk to any student who has purchased a copy of the text. You are free to post all of these files to a network or standalone workstations, or simply provide copies of the disk to your students. The instructions in this book assume that the students know which drive and directory contain the Student Disk, so it's important that you provide disk location information before the students start working through the units. This book also assumes that Excel 5.0 is set up using the Standard installation procedure.

Using the Student Disk Files

To keep the original files on the Student Disk intact, the instructions in this book for opening files require two important steps: (1) open the existing file and (2) save it as a new file with a new name. This procedure ensures that the original file will remain unmodified in case the student wants to redo any lesson or exercise.

To organize their files, students are instructed to save their files to the MY_FILES directory on their Student Disk that they created in *Microsoft Windows 3.1*. In case your students did not complete this lesson, it is included in the Instructor's Manual that accompanies this book. You can circulate this to your students, or you can instruct them to simply save to drive A or drive B.

UNIT 1

OBJECTIVES

- Define spreadsheet software
- Start Excel 5.0 for Windows
- View the Excel window
- Work with Excel menus and dialog boxes
- Work with buttons
- Get Help
- Move around the worksheet
- Name a sheet
- Close a workbook and exit Excel

Getting Started WITH MICROSOFT EXCEL 5.0

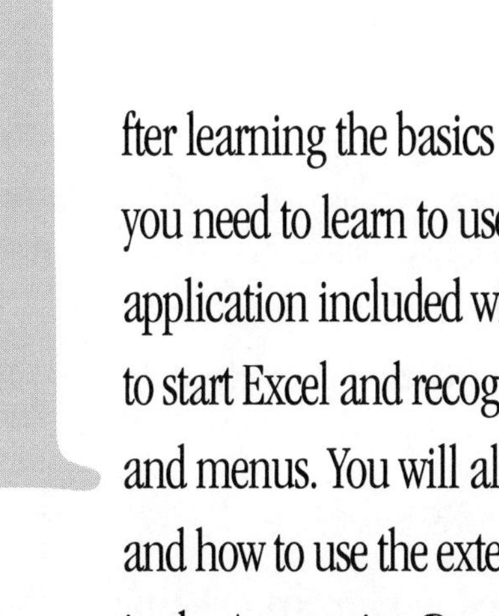

After learning the basics of using Microsoft Windows, you have the skills you need to learn to use Microsoft Excel 5.0 for Windows, the spreadsheet application included with Microsoft Office. In this unit, you will learn how to start Excel and recognize and use different elements of the Excel window and menus. You will also learn the best ways to move around a worksheet and how to use the extensive on-line Help system. ▶ Evan Brillstein works in the Accounting Department at Nomad Ltd, an outdoor sporting gear and adventure travel company. Evan will use Excel to track tour sales. ▶

Defining spreadsheet software

Excel is an electronic spreadsheet that runs on Windows computers. An **electronic spreadsheet** uses a computer to perform numeric calculations rapidly and accurately. See Table 1-1 for common ways spreadsheets are used in business. An electronic spreadsheet is also referred to as a **worksheet**, which is the document that you produce when you use Excel. A worksheet created with Excel allows Evan to work quickly and efficiently, and the result produced will be accurate and easily updated. He will be able to produce more professional-looking documents. Figure 1-1 shows a budget worksheet that Evan created using pencil and paper. Figure 1-2 shows the same worksheet that Evan can create using Excel.

Excel is better than the paper system for the following reasons:

- **Enter data quickly and accurately**
  With Excel, Evan can enter information faster and more accurately than he could using the pencil and paper method. He needs to enter only data and formulas, and Excel calculates the results.

- **Recalculate easily**
  Fixing errors using Excel is easy, and any results based on a changed entry are recalculated automatically.

- **Perform What-if Analysis**
  One of the most powerful decision-making features of Excel is the ability to change data and then quickly recalculate changed results. Anytime you use a worksheet to answer the question "what if," you are performing a what-if analysis. For instance, if the advertising budget for May were increased to $3,000, Evan could enter the new figure into the spreadsheet and immediately find out the impact on the overall budget.

- **Change the appearance of information**
  Excel provides powerful features for enhancing a spreadsheet so that information is visually appealing and easy to understand.

- **Create charts**
  Excel makes it easy to create charts based on information in a worksheet. With Excel, charts are automatically updated as data changes. The worksheet in Figure 1-2 includes a pie chart that graphically shows the distribution of expenses for the second quarter.

- **Share information with other users**
  Because everyone at Nomad is now using Microsoft Office, it's easy for Evan to share information with his colleagues. If Evan wants to use the data from someone else's worksheet, he accesses their files through the network or by disk.

- **Create new worksheets from existing ones quickly**
  It's easy for Evan to take an existing Excel worksheet and quickly modify it to create a new one.

FIGURE 1-1: Traditional paper worksheet

Nomad Ltd

	Qtr 1	Qtr 2	Qtr 3	Qtr 4	Total
Net Sales	48,000	76,000	64,000	80,000	268,000
Expenses:					
Salary	8,000	8,000	8,000	8,000	32,000
Interest	4,800	5,600	6,400	7,200	24,000
Rent	2,400	2,400	2,400	2,400	9,600
Ads	3,600	8,000	16,000	20,000	47,600
COG	16,000	16,800	20,000	20,400	73,200
Total Exp	34,800	40,800	52,800	58,000	186,400
Net Income	13,200	35,200	11,200	22,000	81,600

FIGURE 1-2: Excel worksheet

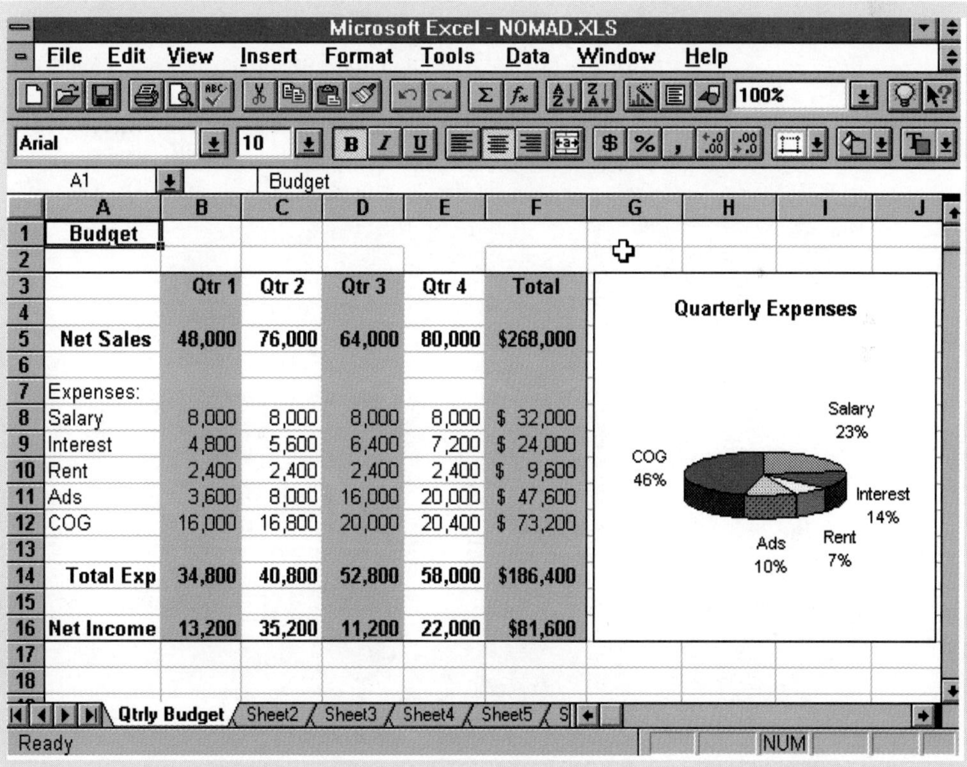

TABLE 1-1: Common business spreadsheet uses

USE	SOLUTION
Maintenance of values	Calculation of figures
Visual representation of values	Chart based on worksheet figures

Starting Excel 5.0 for Windows

To start Excel, you first start Windows, as described in "Microsoft Windows 3.1." Then you open the Microsoft Office program group window that contains the Microsoft Excel application icon. A slightly different procedure might be required for computers on a network and those that use utility programs to enhance Windows. If you need assistance, ask your instructor or technical support person for help. ▶ Evan starts Excel now.

1 Make sure the Program Manager window is open
The Program Manager icon might appear at the bottom of your screen. Double-click it to open it, if necessary.

2 Double-click the **Microsoft Office program group icon**
The Microsoft Office group window opens, displaying the Microsoft Excel icon and other Microsoft applications as shown in Figure 1-3. Your desktop might look different depending on the applications installed on your computer. The Microsoft Office group icon on your screen might already be maximized. If you cannot locate the Microsoft Office program icon, click Window on the Program Manager menu bar, then click Microsoft Office.

3 Double-click the **Microsoft Excel application icon**
Excel opens and a blank worksheet appears. In the next lesson, you will familiarize yourself with the elements of the Excel worksheet window.

FIGURE 1-3: Microsoft Office program icon group

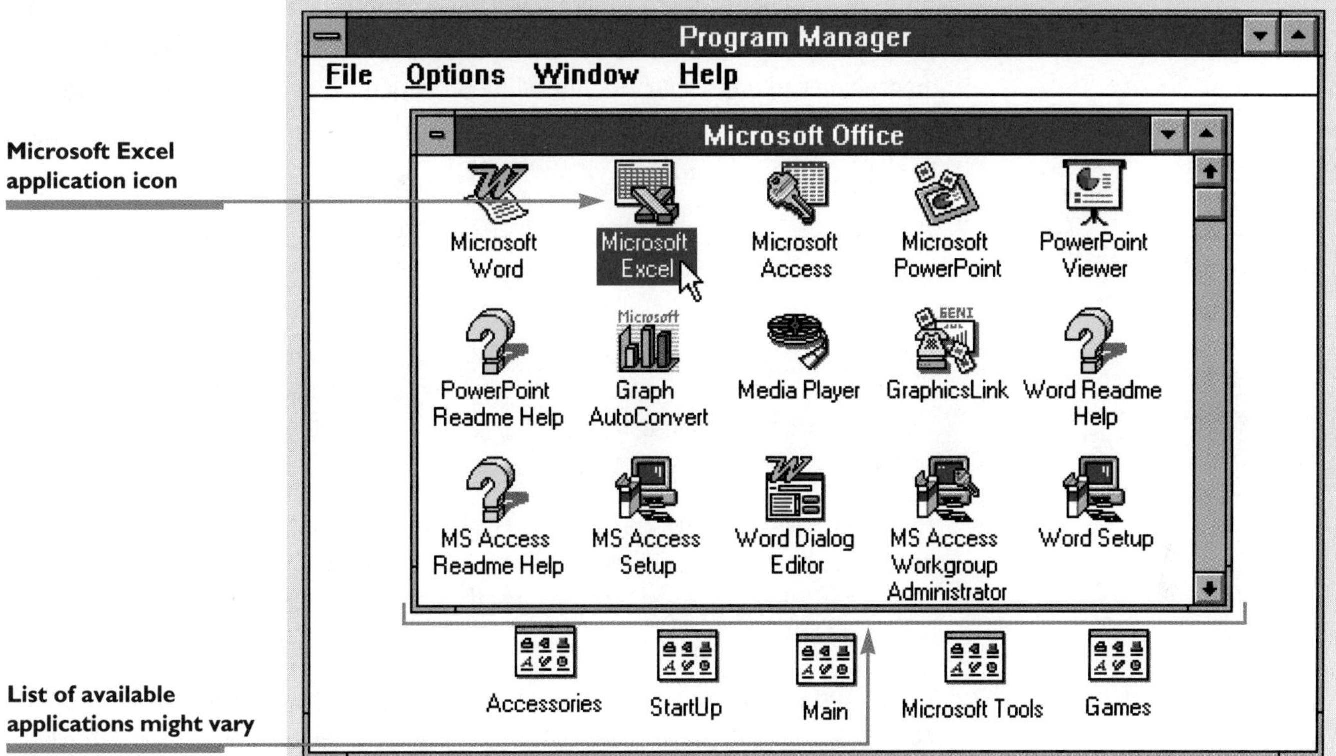

TROUBLE?

If you don't have a Microsoft Office program group icon, look for one called Microsoft Excel.

Viewing the Excel window

When you start Excel, the computer displays the **worksheet window**, the area where you enter data, and the window elements that enable you to create and work with worksheets. Familiarize yourself with the Excel worksheet window and its elements by comparing the descriptions below to Figure 1-4.

- The **worksheet window** contains a grid of columns and rows. Columns are labeled alphabetically (A, B, C, etc.) and rows are labeled numerically (1, 2, 3 etc.). The worksheet window displays only a tiny fraction of the whole worksheet, which has a total of 256 columns and 16,384 rows. The intersection of a column and a row is a **cell**. Cells can contain text, numbers, formulas, or a combination of all three. Every cell has its own unique location or **cell address**, which is identified by the coordinates of the intersecting column and row. For example, the cell address of the cell in the upper-left corner of a worksheet is A1.
- The **cell pointer** is a dark rectangle that highlights the cell you are working in, or the **active cell**. In Figure 1-4, the cell pointer is located at A1, so A1 is the active cell. To make another cell active, click any other cell or press the arrow keys on your keyboard to move the cell pointer.
- The **title bar** displays the application name (Microsoft Excel) and the filename of the open worksheet (in this case, Book1). The title bar also contains a control menu box and resizing buttons, which you learned about in "Microsoft Windows 3.1."
- The **menu bar** contains menus from which you choose Excel commands. As with all Windows applications, you can choose a menu command by clicking it with the mouse or by pressing [Alt] plus the underlined letter in the menu name.
- The **name box** displays the active cell address. In Figure 1-4, "A1" appears in the name box, which means that A1 is the active cell.
- The **formula bar** allows you to enter or edit data in the worksheet.
- The **toolbars** contain buttons for the most frequently used Excel commands. To choose a button, simply click it with the left mouse button. The face of any button has a graphic representation of its function; for instance, the printing button has a printer on its face.
- **Sheet tabs** below the worksheet grid enable you to keep your work in collections called **workbooks**. Each workbook contains 16 worksheets by default and can contain a maximum of 255 sheets. Sheet tabs can be given meaningful names. **Sheet tab scrolling buttons** help you move from one sheet to another.
- The **status bar** is located at the bottom of the Excel window. The left side of the status bar provides a brief description of the active command or task in progress. The right side of the status bar shows the status of important keys, such as the Caps Lock key and the Num Lock key.

FIGURE 1-4: Excel worksheet window elements

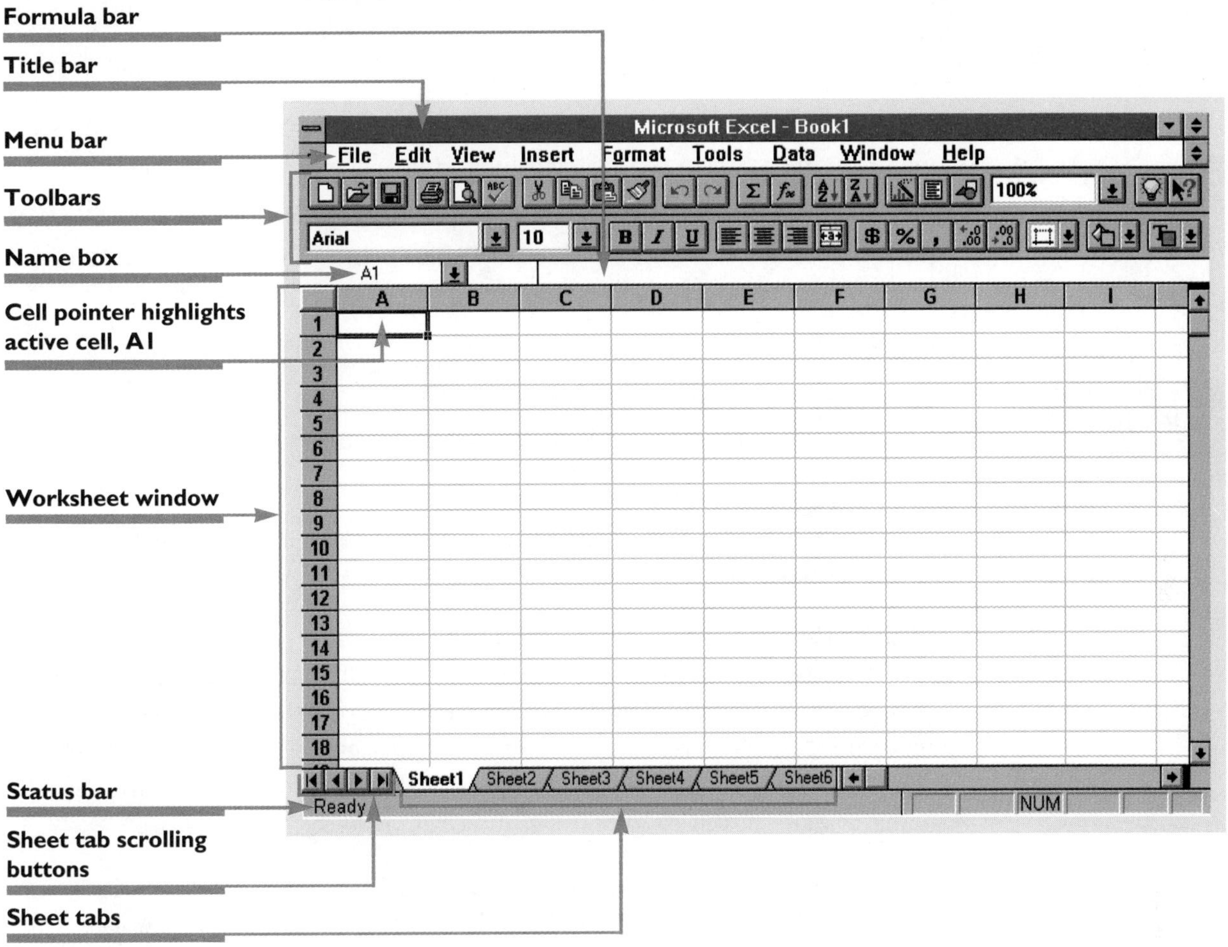

TROUBLE?

If your worksheet does not fill the screen as shown in Figure 1-4, click the Maximize button in the worksheet window.■

Working with Excel menus and dialog boxes

Like many other Windows applications, Excel provides many commands on its menu bar that you can use to create and format a worksheet. When you choose a menu command that is followed by an ellipsis (...), a dialog box opens. A **dialog box** is a window in which you can specify the options you want for the command. ▶ Evan uses the Format Cells dialog box to enter and format the title for his budget worksheet.

1 **Click cell A1 to make it the active cell**
The cell pointer surrounds A1, and A1 appears in the name box.

2 **Type Budget then press [Enter]**
The word "Budget" appears in cell A1, aligned on the left side of the cell. To center this text in the cell, you will use a command from the Format menu.

3 **Click cell A1 then click Format on the menu bar**
The Format menu opens, displaying a list of commands relating to the appearance of the worksheet. See Figure 1-5. You also could have pressed [Alt][O] to open the Format menu. See the related topic "Using keyboard shortcuts" for more information. Notice that a description of the highlighted menu command displays in the status line. The Cells command has an ellipsis after it, which means that a dialog box will display when Evan chooses this command.

4 **Click Cells**
The Format Cells dialog box opens. See Figure 1-6. Many dialog boxes in Excel have tabs like the workbook tabs. The **tabs** separate the various formatting options for the selected command into sub-dialog boxes. The last tab used appears on top. Your screen might display a different tab than the one shown in Figure 1-6.

5 **Click the Alignment tab**
The Alignment tab moves to the front of the dialog box, providing options for changing the alignment of the text in the active cell. Notice the check box next to the Wrap Text option. **Check boxes** toggle an option on or off.

6 **In the Horizontal section, click the round circle next to the word "Center"**
The round circle is called a **radio button**. Radio buttons display when only one option can be chosen in a section of a dialog box.

7 **Click OK or press [Enter]**
If a command button in a dialog box has a dark border around it, you can press [Enter] to choose that button. The dialog box closes and the word "Budget" is centered in cell A1.

FIGURE 1-5: Format menu

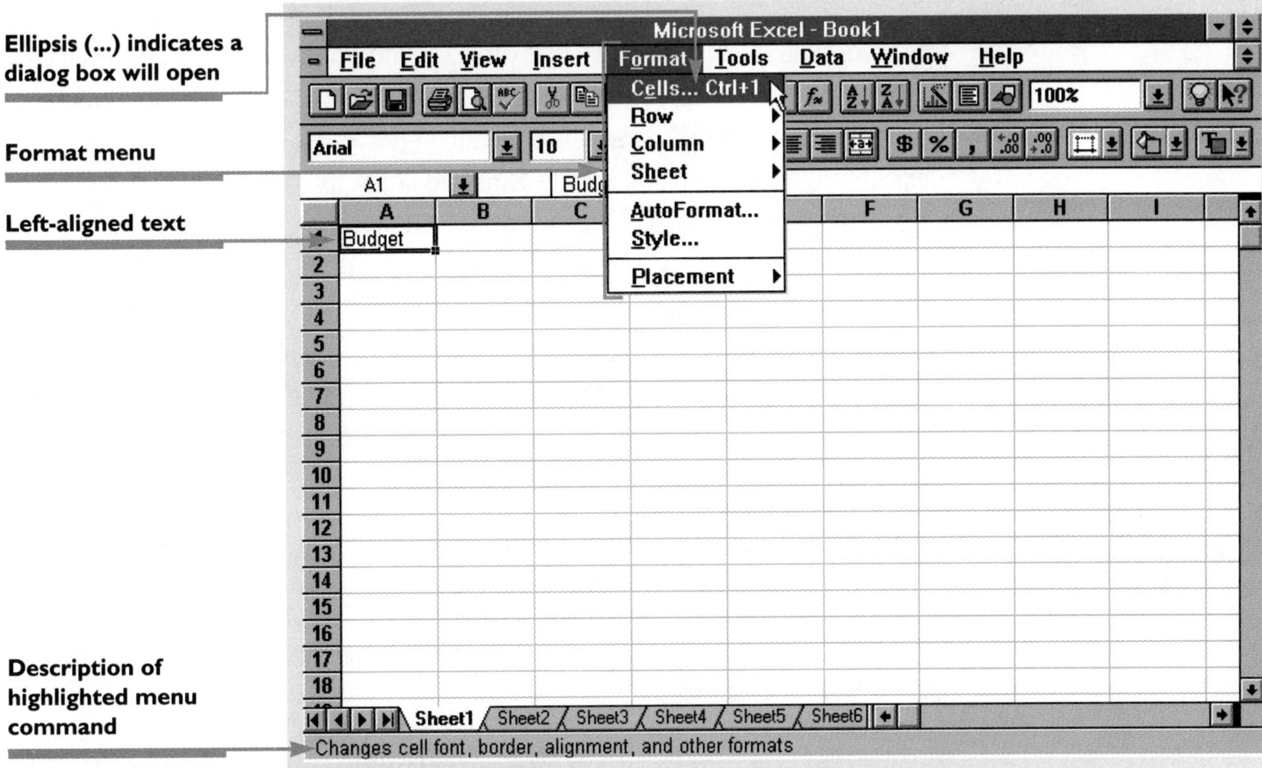

FIGURE 1-6: Format Cells dialog box

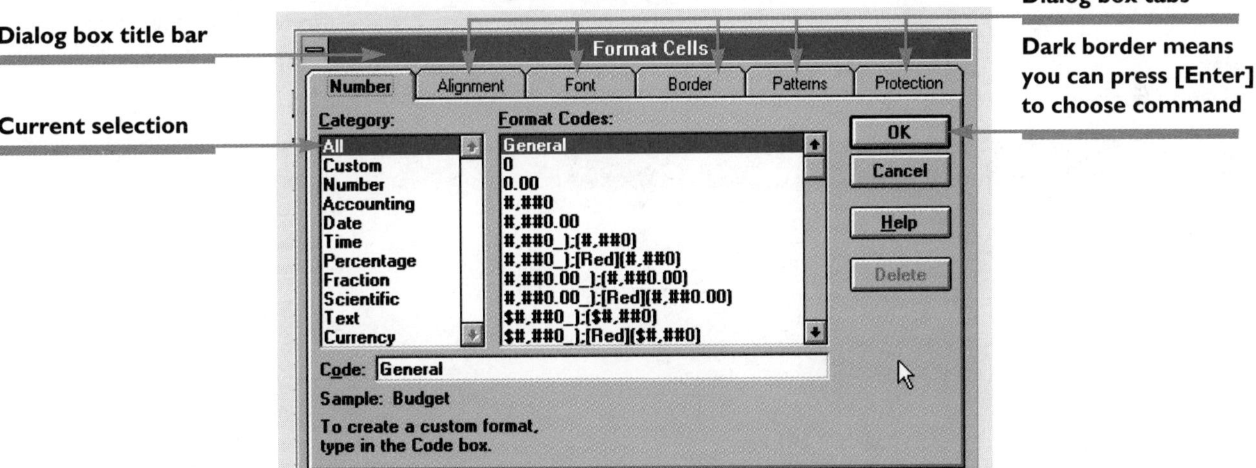

Using keyboard shortcuts

Pointer-movement keys can be used to make choices within a dialog box or menu. To choose a menu from the keyboard, press [Alt] and the underlined letter in the menu you want to select. To choose a command from a menu, press [↑] or [↓], then press [Enter] or press the underlined letter of the command you want to select. To open a new menu, press [→] or [←]. To move within a dialog box, press the underlined letter of the command you want to execute.

QUICK TIP

To close a menu without choosing a command, click anywhere outside the menu, or press [Esc].

Working with buttons

Buttons give you easy access to a variety of commonly used Excel commands. Clicking a button to execute a command is faster than using the menu. Buttons are organized in **toolbars**. The Standard and Formatting toolbars, which appear below the menu bar, are the default toolbars, as shown in Figure 1-7. In addition to these toolbars, Excel provides toolbars that contain buttons for specific purposes such as charting; these will be discussed in future units. You can also customize the toolbars so they contain the buttons for the commands you use most often or reposition them on the screen. See the related topic "Repositioning toolbars" for more information. See Table 1-2 for a description of most frequently used buttons. ▶ Evan uses the Bold button to format his worksheet title, then explores some of the other buttons.

1 **Move the mouse pointer over the Bold button [B] on the Formatting toolbar, *but do not click the mouse button***
When you move the pointer over a button, the ToolTip associated with that button appears. The **ToolTip** displays the name of the button, and a description of the button appears in the status bar. See Figure 1-8.

2 **Click cell A1 to make it the active cell, then click [B]**
The word Budget becomes bold. The Bold button is a **toggle button**, which means that if you clicked the Bold button again, you would remove the bold formatting. Notice that the Center and Bold buttons appear "depressed," indicating that the cell contents are centered and bold.

3 **Move the mouse pointer over the other buttons in the Standard and Formatting toolbars to display the names of these buttons**
Notice how much can be accomplished using buttons.

TABLE 1-2: Frequently used buttons

ICON	NAME	DESCRIPTION
	Open	Opens a file
	Save	Saves a file
	Print	Opens the Print dialog box
	Print Preview	Shows the worksheet as it will appear when it is printed
	Spelling	Checks the spelling in the current workbook
	Cut	Cuts the selected range to the Clipboard
	Copy	Copies the selected range to the Clipboard
	Paste	Pastes Clipboard contents into the current workbook at the cell pointer
B	Bold	Adds/removes bold formatting

FIGURE 1-7: Standard and Formatting toolbars

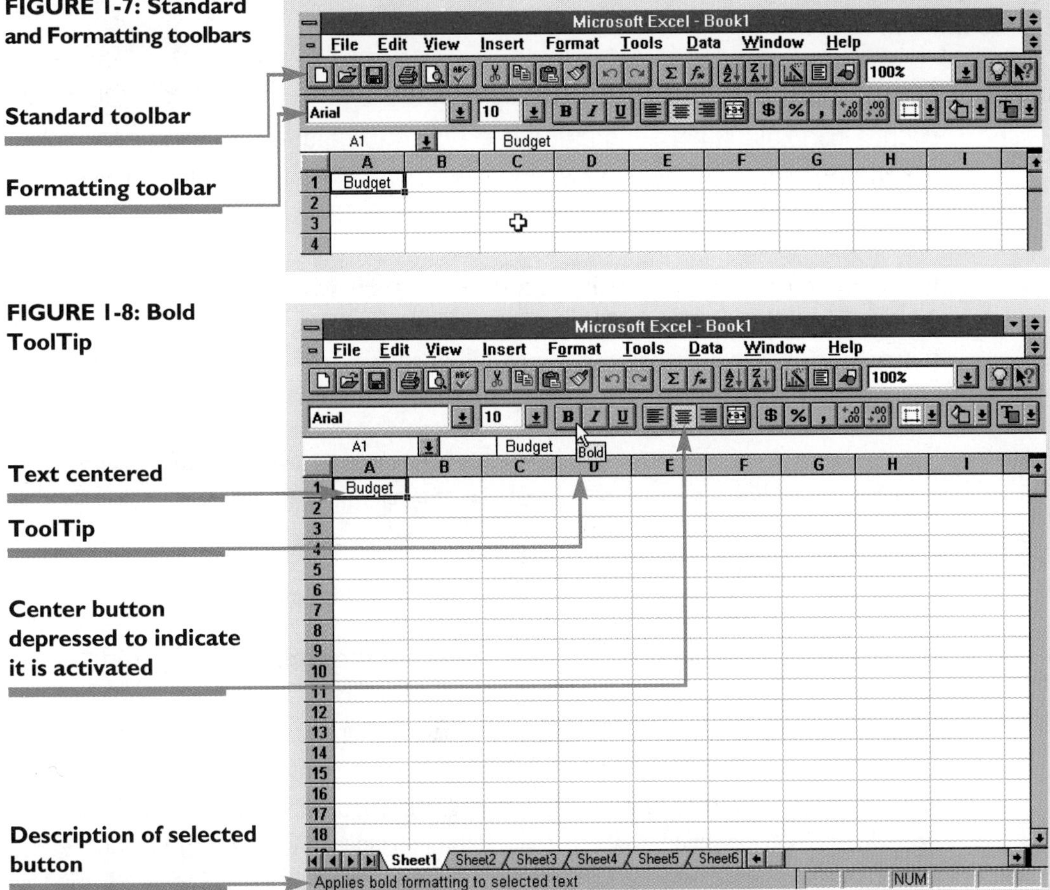

FIGURE 1-8: Bold ToolTip

Repositioning toolbars

To allow you to make the best use of your work area, toolbars can be moved and resized. Each toolbar can be positioned along the top of the window, as shown in Figure 1-7, or it can "float" within its own window. To change a toolbar's location, click and hold the pointer in the gray area around the edge of the toolbar, then drag the toolbar away from its current location. To resize a floating toolbar, position the pointer over the edge of the toolbar window until it becomes ⇔, then drag the edge until the window is the size you want. In Figure 1-9, the Standard toolbar is floating. Compare Figure 1-9 with Figure 1-8.

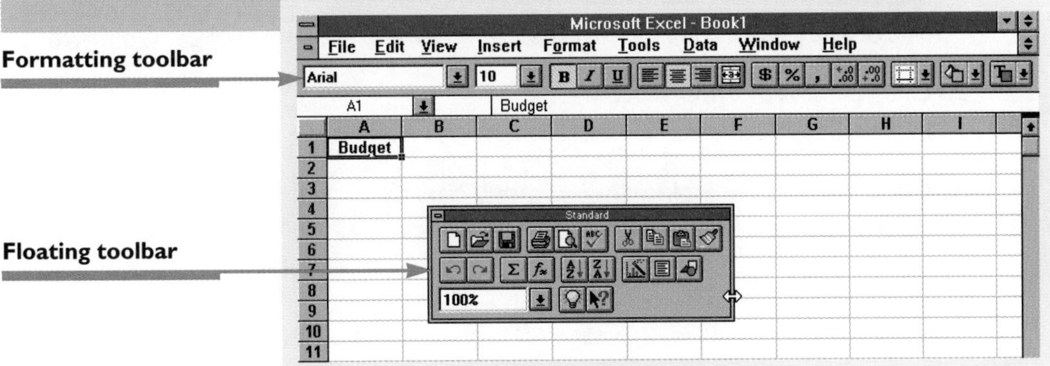

FIGURE 1-9: Standard toolbar floating

Getting Help

Excel features an extensive on-line Help system that gives you immediate access to definitions, explanations, and useful tips. Help information appears in a separate window that you can resize and refer to as you work. ▶ Evan decides to use Excel's on-line Help to learn more about toolbars.

1 **Click Help on the menu bar, then click Search for Help on**
The Search dialog box opens. See Figure 1-10. In this dialog box, you can type a specific topic or feature and view the entries that provide more information.

2 **In the search text box, type too**
Notice as you type each character, the alphabetically arranged topics scroll in the search topics list below the text box. After you type the second o, "toolbars" appears in the list.

3 **Click toolbars then click Show Topics**
A list of related topics displays in the box at the bottom of the dialog box.

4 **Scroll down the show topics list until you see the topic "Moving and resizing toolbars," click to select it, then click Go To**
Two windows open: Help and How To. If the How To window appears under the Help window, click within its border to make the How To window active. See Figure 1-11. Depending on the type and size of your monitor, the two windows might appear on different sides of the screen. The Help window contains buttons that will lead you through different sets of instructions for Excel. Help buttons appearing under the Help menu bar are described in Table 1-3. The How To window displays information about moving and resizing toolbars, the topic you selected. You can click the words with the green dotted underline (or black dotted underline, depending on your monitor) to open a pop-up window with more information about that topic.

5 **Move the pointer to the dotted-underline text floating toolbar until the pointer changes to 👆, then click**
Depending on your monitor, this text could have a black dotted underline or a green dotted underline. A pop-up window containing a definition of a floating toolbar opens.

6 **After reading the information, click anywhere outside the pop-up window or press [Esc] to close the pop-up window**
Clicking the Overview button will display general information about customizing toolbars in the Help window. You can use the Example and Practice button to see examples of the topic you've selected or to practice performing a task.

7 **Click the Overview button**
Evan reads this information and then decides to close the Help window.

8 **Click File on the Help window menu bar, then click Exit**
The Help window closes and you return to your worksheet.

FIGURE 1-10: Search dialog box

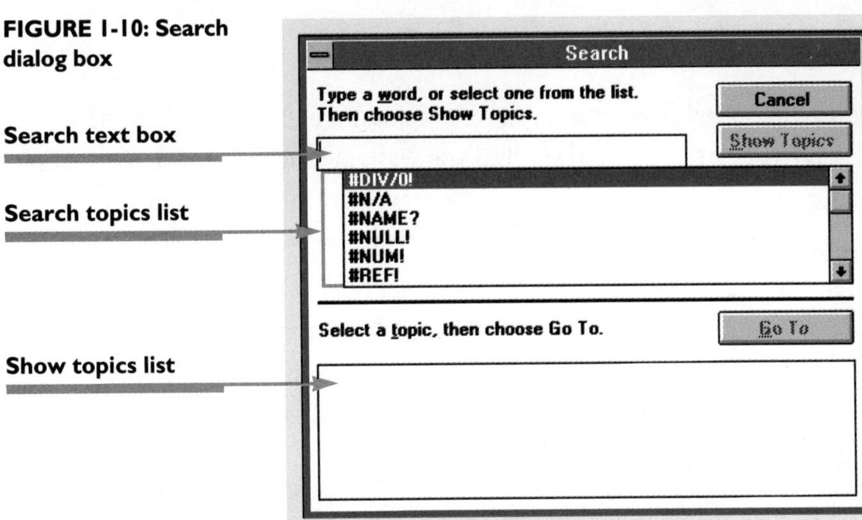

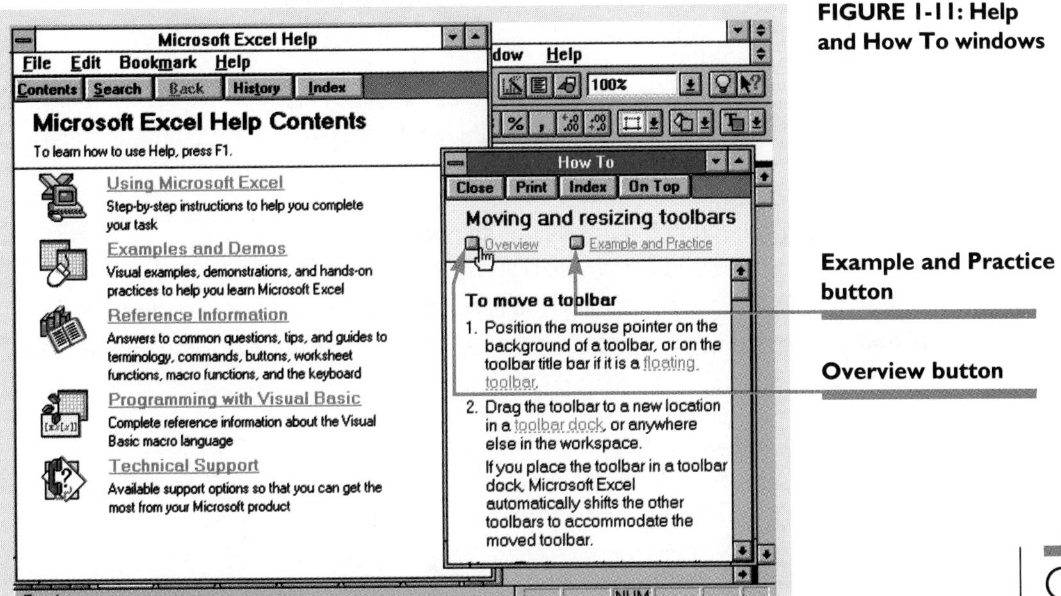

FIGURE 1-11: Help and How To windows

TABLE 1-3: The Help buttons

BUTTON	DESCRIPTION
Contents	Displays Help topic categories
Search	Displays search dialog box in which you can search for a specific topic
Back	Returns you to the previous topic
History	Displays a list of Help topics to which you have recently referred
Index	Displays an alphabetical listing of topics

QUICK TIP

If you need help while you are working on a particular topic, click the Help button on the Standard toolbar. The mouse pointer changes to **?**. Point to a part of the worksheet or a command on a menu, and then click. Excel's Help system displays context-sensitive information about your current location.

Moving around the worksheet

With over a billion cells available to you, it's important to know how to move around, or **navigate**, the worksheet. If you want to move up, down, or over one or two cells, you can simply press the pointer-movement keys ([↑] [↓] [←] [→]). To move longer distances within the worksheet window, you might prefer to use the mouse and click the desired cell address. If the desired cell address is not visible within the worksheet window, you can use the scroll bars or the Go To command to move the location into view. Table 1-4 lists helpful techniques for moving around the worksheet. Evan uses a combination of methods to practice navigating the worksheet.

1 Click cell **I18**

The cell pointer highlights cell I18 in the lower-right corner of your worksheet window.

2 Press **[→]**

The cell pointer moves over one cell to J18, moving the entire worksheet over one column. Notice that cell A1, which contains the word "Budget," is no longer visible in the worksheet window.

3 On the vertical scroll bar, click the **down arrow** once

The worksheet window scrolls down one row, so that row 1 scrolls off the top of the window. You can move a window's contents one row or column at a time by clicking on the vertical or horizontal scroll bar arrows. You can move a screenful at a time by clicking on either side of a scroll box.

4 Click to the right of the horizontal scroll box

Columns K through S should appear in your worksheet window. If you need to travel a great distance across a worksheet, you can use the Go To command.

5 Click **Edit** on the menu bar, then click **Go To**

The Go To dialog box opens. See Figure 1-12. You could also press [F5] to display the Go To dialog box.

6 Type **Z1000** in the Reference text box, then click **OK**

The cell pointer highlights cell Z1000 in the lower-right corner of the worksheet window. You could use the Go To command or the scroll bars to move the cell pointer back to the beginning of the worksheet, but there is a faster way to move the cell pointer directly to cell A1.

7 Press **[Ctrl][Home]**

The cell pointer highlights cell A1.

FIGURE 1-12: Go To dialog box

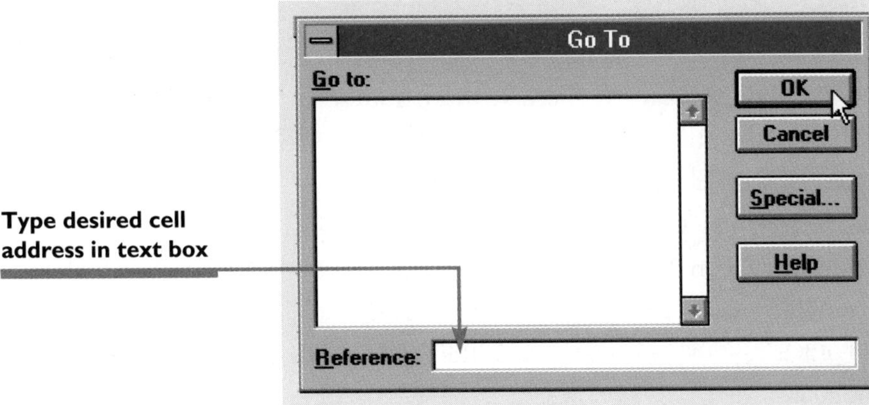

TABLE 1-4: Worksheet navigation techniques

TO MOVE	DO THIS
Up one row	Press [↑]
Down one row	Press [↓]
Left one cell	Press [←]
Right one cell	Press[→]
Up one screenful	Press [PgUp]
Down one screenful	Press [PgDn]
Left one screenful	Press [Alt][PgUp]
Right one screenful	Press [Alt][PgDn]
Left one column	Click the left arrow on the horizontal scroll bar
Right one column	Click the right arrow on the horizontal scroll bar
Cell A1	Press [Ctrl][Home]
Column A in current row	Press [Home]
Last active column in current row	Press [End]

Naming a sheet

Each workbook initially contains 16 worksheets. When the workbook is first open, the first worksheet is the active sheet. To move from sheet to sheet, click the desired sheet tab located at the bottom of the worksheet window. Sheet tab scrolling buttons, located to the left of the sheet tabs, allow rapid movement among the sheets. To make it easier to identify the sheets in a workbook, you can name each sheet. The name appears on the sheet tab. For instance, sheets within a single workbook could be named for individual sales people to better track performance goals. ▶ Evan practices moving from sheet to sheet and decides to name two sheets in his workbook.

1. **Click the Sheet2 tab**
   Sheet2 becomes active. Its tab moves to the front, and the tab for Sheet1 moves to the background. The word "Budget" disappears from view because it is in cell A1 of Sheet1.
2. **Click the Sheet5 tab**
   Sheet5 becomes active. Now Evan will rename Sheet1 so it has a name that he can easily remember.
3. **Double-click the Sheet1 tab**
   The Rename Sheet dialog box opens with the default sheet name (Sheet1) selected in the Name text box. You could also click Format in the menu bar, click Sheet, then click Rename to display the Rename Sheet dialog box.
4. **Type Qtrly Budget in the Name text box**
   See Figure 1-13. The new name automatically replaced the default name in the Name text box. Worksheet names can have up to 31 characters, including spaces and punctuation.
5. **Click OK**
   Notice that the tab of the first sheet says "Qtrly Budget." See Figure 1-14.
6. **Double-click Sheet2 then rename this sheet Additional Info**
   You can also rearrange sheets if necessary. See the related topic "Moving sheets" for additional information.

FIGURE 1-13: Rename Sheet dialog box

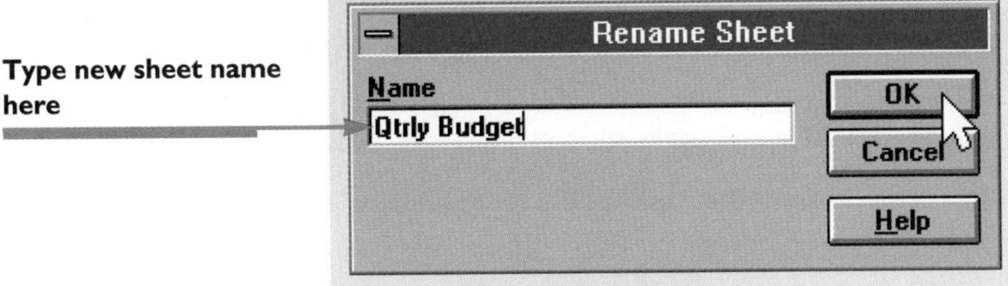

FIGURE 1-14: Renamed sheet in workbook

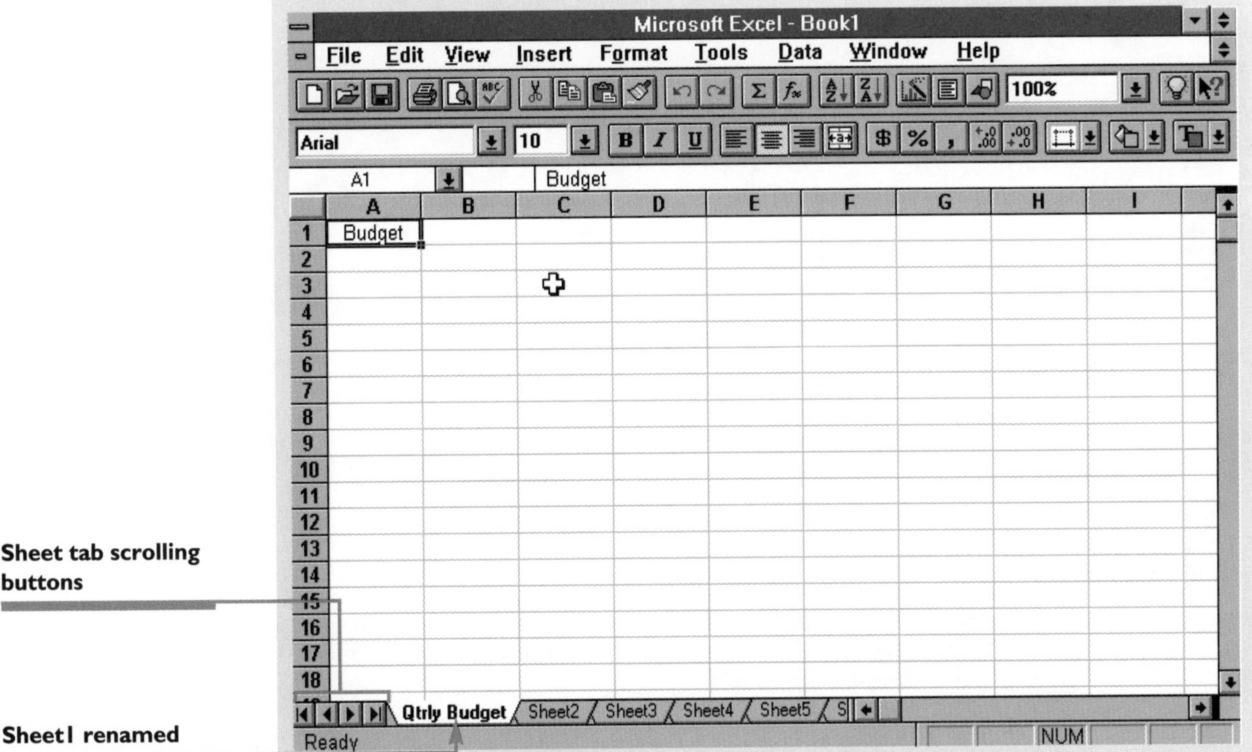

Moving sheets

You can easily rearrange worksheets in a workbook. To move a sheet, position the mouse pointer on the sheet tab, click and hold the left mouse button, then drag the sheet tab to its new location. A small arrow and an icon of a document just above the sheet tabs indicates the new location of the worksheet, as shown in Figure 1-15.

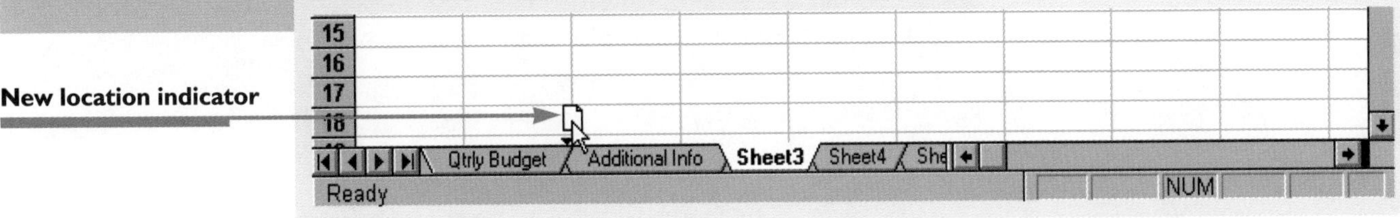

FIGURE 1-15: Moving Sheet3 after Qtrly Budget sheet

Closing a workbook and exiting Excel

When you have finished working on a workbook, you need to save the file and close it. To close a file, click Close on the File menu. When you have completed all your work in Excel, you need to exit the application. To exit Excel, click Exit on the File menu. For a comparison of the Close and Exit commands, refer to Table 1-5. ▶ Evan needs to gather more information before creating his worksheet, so he closes the workbook and then exits Excel.

1. **Click File on the menu bar**
   See Figure 1-16.
2. **Click Close**
   You could also double-click the workbook control menu box instead of choosing File Close. A dialog box opens, asking if you want to save changes in "Book1" before closing. See Figure 1-17. Because he was only practicing, Evan does not want to save the workbook.
3. **Click No**
   Excel closes the workbook and displays a blank worksheet window. Notice that the menu bar contains only the File and Help menu choices.
4. **Click File then click Exit**
   You could also double-click the application control menu box to exit the application. Excel closes and computer memory is freed up for other computing tasks.

TABLE 1-5: Excel's Close and Exit commands

CLOSING A FILE	EXITING EXCEL
Puts away a workbook file	Puts away all workbook files
Leaves Excel running if you choose to open another file	Returns you to the Program Manager where you can choose to run another application

FIGURE 1-16: Closing a workbook using the File menu

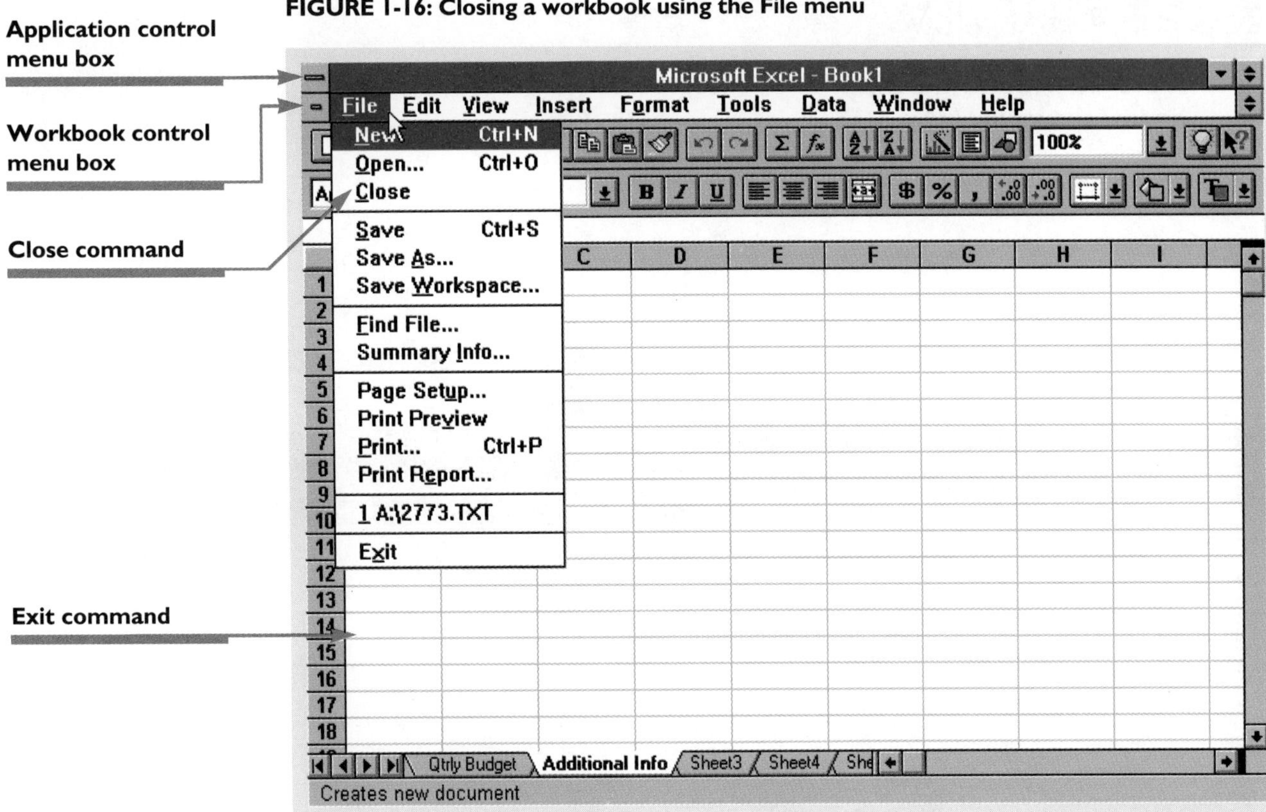

FIGURE 1-17: Microsoft Excel save changes dialog box

QUICK TIP

To exit Excel and close several files at once, choose Exit from the File menu. Excel will prompt you to save changes to each workbook before exiting.

CONCEPTS REVIEW

Label each of the elements of the Excel worksheet window shown in Figure 1-18.

1 ____

2 ____

3 ____

4 ____

5 ____

6 ____

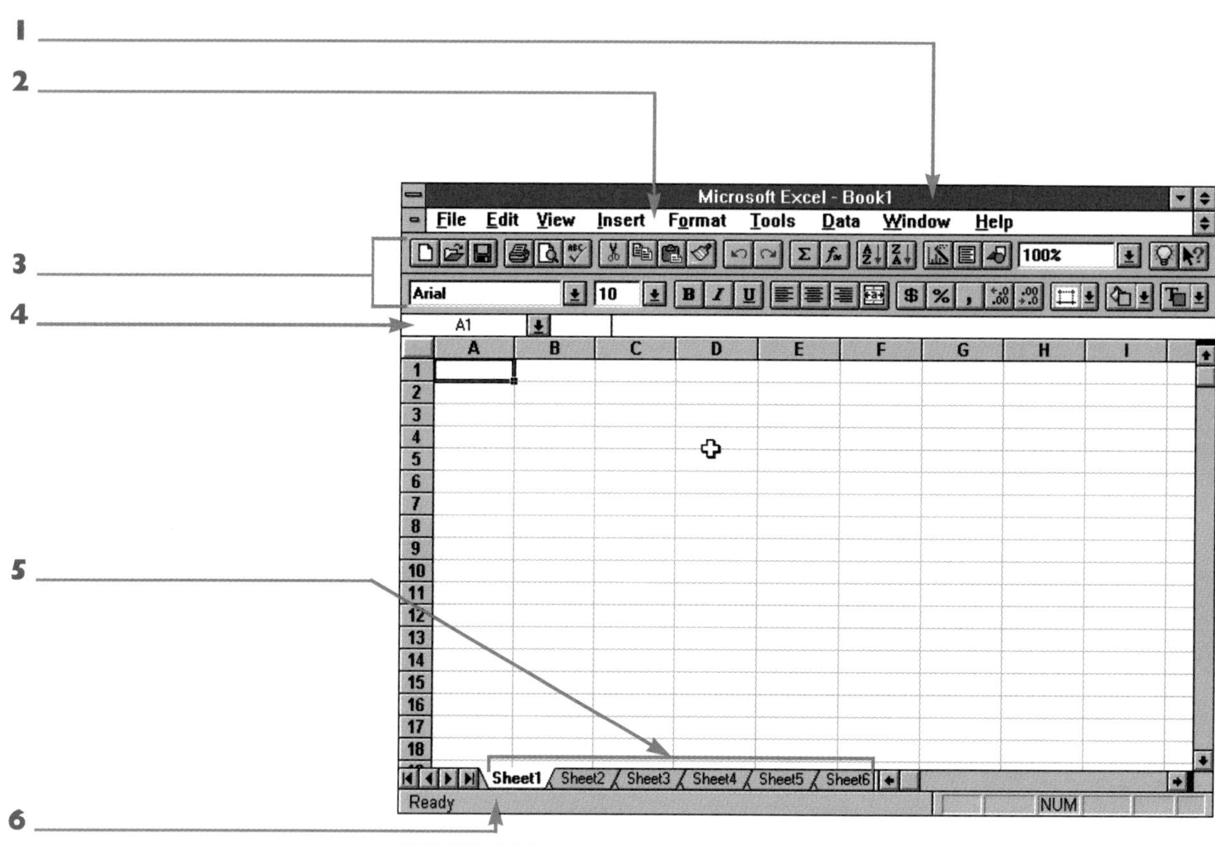

FIGURE 1-18

Match each of the terms with the statement that describes its function.

7 Area that contains a grid of columns and rows

8 The intersection of a column and row

9 Graphic symbol that depicts a task or function

10 Collection of worksheets

11 Rectangle that indicates the cell you are currently working in

12 Displays the active cell address

a. Cell pointer
b. Button
c. Worksheet window
d. Name box
e. Cell
f. Workbook

Select the best answer from the list of choices.

13 An electronic spreadsheet can perform all of the following tasks, EXCEPT:

a. Display information visually
b. Calculate data accurately
c. Plan worksheet objectives
d. Recalculate updated information

14 You can move a screen at a time all of the following ways, EXCEPT:

a. Press [PgUp]
b. Press [Alt][PgDn]
c. Press [Alt][PgUp]
d. Press [↑]

15 Which key(s) do you press to move quickly to cell A1?

a. [Ctrl][Home]

b. [Alt]

c. [Esc][Home]

d. [Enter]

16 A menu command that is followed by an ellipsis means

a. The command is not currently available

b. Clicking the command will display a dialog box

c. Clicking the command will display a submenu

d. The command has no keyboard shortcut

17 You can get Excel Help any of the following ways, EXCEPT:

a. Clicking Help on the menu bar

b. Pressing [F1]

c. Clicking the Help button on the Standard toolbar

d. Minimizing the application window

18 Which key(s) do you press to move the active cell to the right one column?

a. [Enter]

b. [Right Arrow]

c. [Esc]

d. [Alt][R]

19 How do you open the Rename Sheet dialog box?

a. Double-click any sheet tab scrolling button

b. Click the name box list arrow with the right mouse button

c. Click the Name Sheet Tab button

d. Double-click the sheet tab

20 Which key(s) move the cell pointer quickly to the last active column in the current row?

a. [Ctrl][End]

b. [Alt]

c. [End]

d. [Enter]

21 Which of the following statements about buttons is *NOT* true?

a. You choose a button by clicking it.

b. You can move a button by dragging it.

c. A ToolTip, which describes the button, displays when you position the mouse pointer over the button.

d. Buttons appear depressed when selected.

APPLICATIONS REVIEW

1 Start Excel and identify the elements in the worksheet window.

a. Double-click the Microsoft Office group icon in the Program Manager window.

b. Double-click the Microsoft Excel application icon.

c. Try to identify as many elements in the Excel worksheet window as you can without referring to the unit material.

2 Explore Excel menus.

a. Click Edit on the menu bar. Notice that a description of the highlighted Undo command displays in the status bar.

b. Drag through the commands on the Edit menu so that you can review the brief descriptions in the status bar. Press [Esc] if necessary.

c. Click Format on the menu bar.

d. Move through the commands using [↓], and review the descriptions in the status bar.

e. Click Cells on the Format menu to display the Format Cells dialog box. Click each of the tabs and review the options for each tab. Press [Esc] or click cancel.

f. Review other commands on the Excel menu bar in the same fashion.

3 Explore buttons.

a. Position the mouse pointer over each button on the Standard and Formatting toolbars.

b. Write down each button's function.

c. Start a list of buttons that duplicate menu commands. Add to this list as you come across more buttons that duplicate menu commands.

4 Explore Excel Help.

a. Click Help on the menu bar.

b. Click Search for Help on. The Search dialog box displays.

c. Identify all of the buttons that appear in the Search dialog box.

d. Click the down scroll arrow on the search topics list box to view available topics.

e. Select a topic from the list box, then click Show Topics.

f. Select a topic to read, then click Go To.

g. Click File on the Help menu bar, then click Exit.

5 Move around the worksheet.

a. Press [Ctrl][Home] to move the cell pointer to cell A1.

b. Press [→] once to move the cell pointer right one column.

c. Press [↓] twice to move the cell pointer down two rows to cell B3.

d. Click the right arrow on the horizontal scroll bar to move the screen to the right by one column.

e. Click the left arrow on the horizontal scroll bar to move the screen back to its original column display.

6 Name a sheet.

a. Double-click the Sheet3 tab.

b. Type "March" in the Rename Sheet dialog box, then click OK.

c. Click the Sheet4 tab.

d. Click the Sheet2 tab.

e. Double-click the Sheet1 tab.

f. Type "January" in the Rename Sheet dialog box, then click OK.

7 Close the workbook and exit Excel.

a. Click File on the menu bar, then click Close.

b. Click No when asked if you want to save the worksheet.

c. If necessary, close any other worksheets you might have opened.

d. Click File on the menu bar, then click Exit.

INDEPENDENT CHALLENGE 1

Excel's on-line Help provides definitions, explanations, procedures, and other helpful information. It also provides examples and demonstrations to show you how Excel features work. Topics include elements such as the active cell, status bar, buttons, and dialog boxes, as well as detailed information about Excel commands and options. To explore Help, click Examples and Demos from the Help menu, then read all the information on the "Using Toolbars" and "Selecting Cells, Choosing Commands" topics. Use the Search for Help on command to find information about dialog boxes, the active cell, and the status bar. Return to your workbook when you are finished reading about these Excel features.

INDEPENDENT CHALLENGE 2

Spreadsheet software has many uses that can affect the way work is done. Some examples of how Excel can be used are discussed in the beginning of this unit. Use your own personal or business experiences to come up with five examples of how Excel could be used in a business setting.

To complete this independent challenge:

1 Think of five business tasks that you could complete more efficiently using an Excel worksheet.

2 Sketch a sample of each worksheet. See Figure 1-19, which is an example of a payroll worksheet.

3 Submit your sketches.

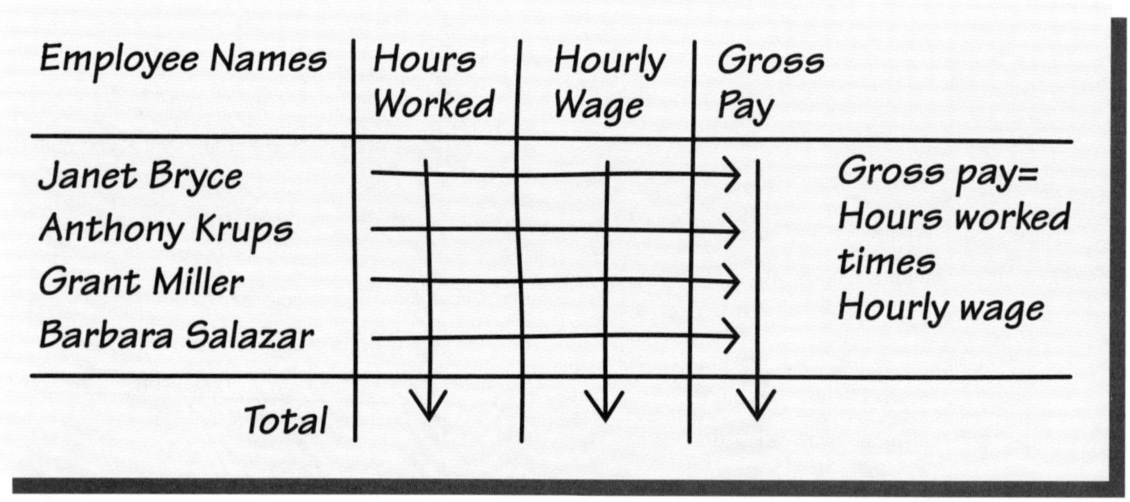

Employee Names	Hours Worked	Hourly Wage	Gross Pay
Janet Bryce			
Anthony Krups			
Grant Miller			
Barbara Salazar			
Total			

Gross pay= Hours worked times Hourly wage

FIGURE 1-19

UNIT 2

OBJECTIVES

- Plan and design a worksheet
- Enter labels
- Enter values
- Edit cell entries
- Work with ranges
- Enter formulas
- Use Excel functions
- Save a workbook
- Preview and print a worksheet

Creating A WORKSHEET

Now that you are familiar with Excel menus, dialog boxes, tools, and online Help system and you know how to navigate within an Excel workbook, you are ready to plan and build your own worksheets. When you build a worksheet, you enter text, values, and formulas into worksheet cells. Once you create a worksheet, you can save the workbook containing the worksheet and print it. Helping managers plan for the future is one of the many ways Excel is useful for businesses. ▶ Evan Brillstein has received a request from the Marketing Department for a forecast of this year's anticipated summer tour business. Marketing hopes that the tour business will increase 20% over last year's figures. ▶

Planning and designing a worksheet

Before you start entering data into a worksheet, you need to know the purpose and approximate layout of the worksheet. Evan wants to forecast Nomad's 1995 summer tour sales. The sales goal, identified by the Marketing Department, for the summer of 1995 is to increase the 1994 summer sales totals by 20%. ▶ Using Figure 2-1 and the planning guidelines below, follow Evan as he plans his worksheet.

- Determine the purpose of the worksheet and give it a meaningful title.
  Evan needs to forecast summer tour sales for 1995. Evan titles the worksheet "1995 Summer Tour Sales Forecast."

- Determine your worksheet's desired results, sometimes called **output**.
  Evan needs to determine what the 1995 sales totals will be if sales increase by 20% over the 1994 sales totals.

- Collect all the information, sometimes called **input**, that will produce the results you want to see.
  Evan gathers together the sales data for the 1994 summer tour season. The season ran from June through August. The types of tours sold in these months included Bike, Raft, Horse, and Bus.

- Determine the calculations, or **formulas**, necessary to achieve the desired results.
  First, Evan needs to total the number of tours sold for each month of the 1994 summer season. Then he needs to add these totals together to determine the grand total of summer tour sales. Finally, the 1994 monthly totals and grand total must be multiplied by 1.2 to calculate a 20% increase for the 1995 summer tour season.

- Sketch on paper how you want the worksheet to look; that is, identify where the labels and values will go. **Labels** are text entries that describe and help you understand the data in a worksheet. **Values** are the numbers used in calculations.
  Evan decides to put tour types in rows and the months in columns. He enters the tour sales data in his sketch and indicates where the monthly sales totals and the grand total should go. Below the totals, he writes out the formula for determining a 20% increase in sales for 1995. Evan's sketch of his worksheet is shown in Figure 2-1.

FIGURE 2-1: Worksheet sketch showing labels, values, and calculations

1995 Summer Tours Sales Forecast

	June	July	August	Totals
Bike	14	10	6	3 month total
Raft	7	8	12	↓
Horse	12	7	6	↓
Bus	1	2	9	↓
Totals	June Total	July Total	August Total	Grand Total for 1994
1995 Sales	Total x 1.2	→	→	→

Entering labels

Labels are used to identify the data in the rows and columns of a worksheet. They are also used to make your worksheet readable and understandable. For these reasons, you should enter all labels in your worksheet first. Labels can contain text and numerical information not used in calculations such as dates, times, or address numbers. Labels are left-aligned by default. ▶ Using his sketch as a guide, Evan begins building his worksheet by entering the labels.

1. Start Excel and make sure you have an empty workbook in the Excel worksheet window
   If you need help starting Excel, refer to the lesson "Starting Excel 5.0 for Windows" in Unit 1.
2. Click cell **B4** to make it the active cell
   Notice that the cell address B4 appears in the name box. Now Evan enters the worksheet title.
3. Type **1995 Summer Tours Sales Forecast**, as shown in Figure 2-2, then click the **Enter button** on the formula bar
   You must click or use one of the other methods listed in Table 2-1 to confirm your entry. Notice that the title does not fit in cell B4 and spreads across several columns. If a label does not fit in a cell, Excel displays the remaining characters in the next cell as long as it is empty. Otherwise, the label is truncated, or cut off. The contents of B4, the active cell, displays in the formula bar. When a cell contains both text and numbers, Excel recognizes the entry as a label. If you want to enter a number as a label, you would type an apostrophe (') before the first number.
4. Click cell **A6**, type **Bike**, then press **[Enter]** to complete the entry and move the cell pointer to cell A7; type **Raft** in cell A7, then press **[Enter]**; type **Horse** in cell A8, then press **[Enter]**; then type **Bus** in cell A9, then press **[Enter]**
   Now Evan enters the labels for the rows containing the totals and the 1995 sales forecast.
5. Click cell **A11**, type **Total**, then press **[Enter]**; click cell **A13**, type **1995 Sales**, then press **[Enter]**
   Next he enters the labels for the summer months.
6. Click cell **B5**, type **June**, then click ; click cell **C5**, type **July**, then click ; click cell **D5**, type **August**, then click
7. Click cell **E5**, type **Total**, then click
   All the labels for Evan's worksheet are now entered. See Figure 2-3.

FIGURE 2-2: Worksheet with title entered

Enter button

Formula bar

Title spreads across columns

FIGURE 2-3: Worksheet with labels entered

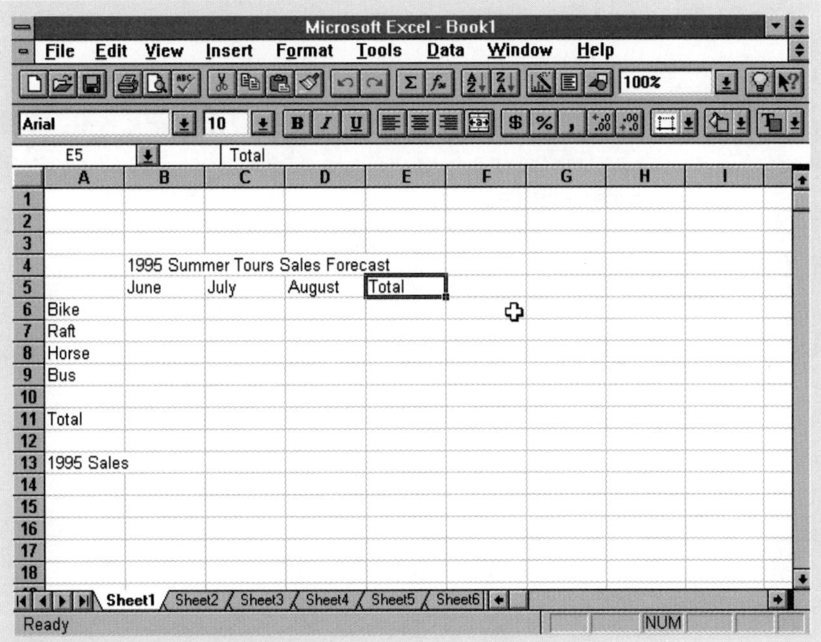

TABLE 2-1: Confirming cell entries

ACTION	CONFIRMS ENTRY THEN
Click ✓	Cell pointer stays in current cell
Press [Enter]	Moves the cell pointer one row down
Press [Shift][Enter]	Moves the cell pointer one row up
Press [Tab]	Moves the cell pointer one column to the right
Press [Shift][Tab]	Moves the cell pointer one column to the left
Click in another cell	Moves the cell pointer to the cell that is clicked

TROUBLE?

If you notice a mistake in a cell entry after it has been confirmed, select the cell you want to edit and press [F2]. Use [Backspace] and [Delete] to make any corrections, then click the Enter button ✓ or press [Enter] to confirm the corrected entry.■

Entering values

Values, which include numbers, formulas, and functions, are used in calculations. Excel recognizes an entry as a value when it is a number or begins with one of these symbols: +, -, =, @, #, or $. All values are right-aligned by default. ▶ Evan enters the sales data from the 1994 summer season into his worksheet.

1. Click cell **B6**, type **14**, then press **[Enter]**; type **7** in cell B7, then press **[Enter]**; type **12** in cell B8, then press **[Enter]**; type **1** in cell B9, then press **[Enter]**

   All the tour sales for the month of June are now entered. Now Evan enters the sales for the month of July.

2. Click cell **C6**, type **10**, then press **[Enter]**; type **8** in cell C7, then press **[Enter]**; type **7** in cell C8, then press **[Enter]**; type **2** in cell C9, then press **[Enter]**

   Next he enters the tour sales for August.

3. Click cell **D6**, type **6**, then press **[Enter]**; type **12** in cell D7, then press **[Enter]**; type **6** in cell D8, then press **[Enter]**; type **9** in cell D9, then press **[Enter]**

   Evan has entered all the labels and data he needs for his worksheet. Compare your worksheet to Figure 2-4.

FIGURE 2-4 Worksheet with labels and values entered

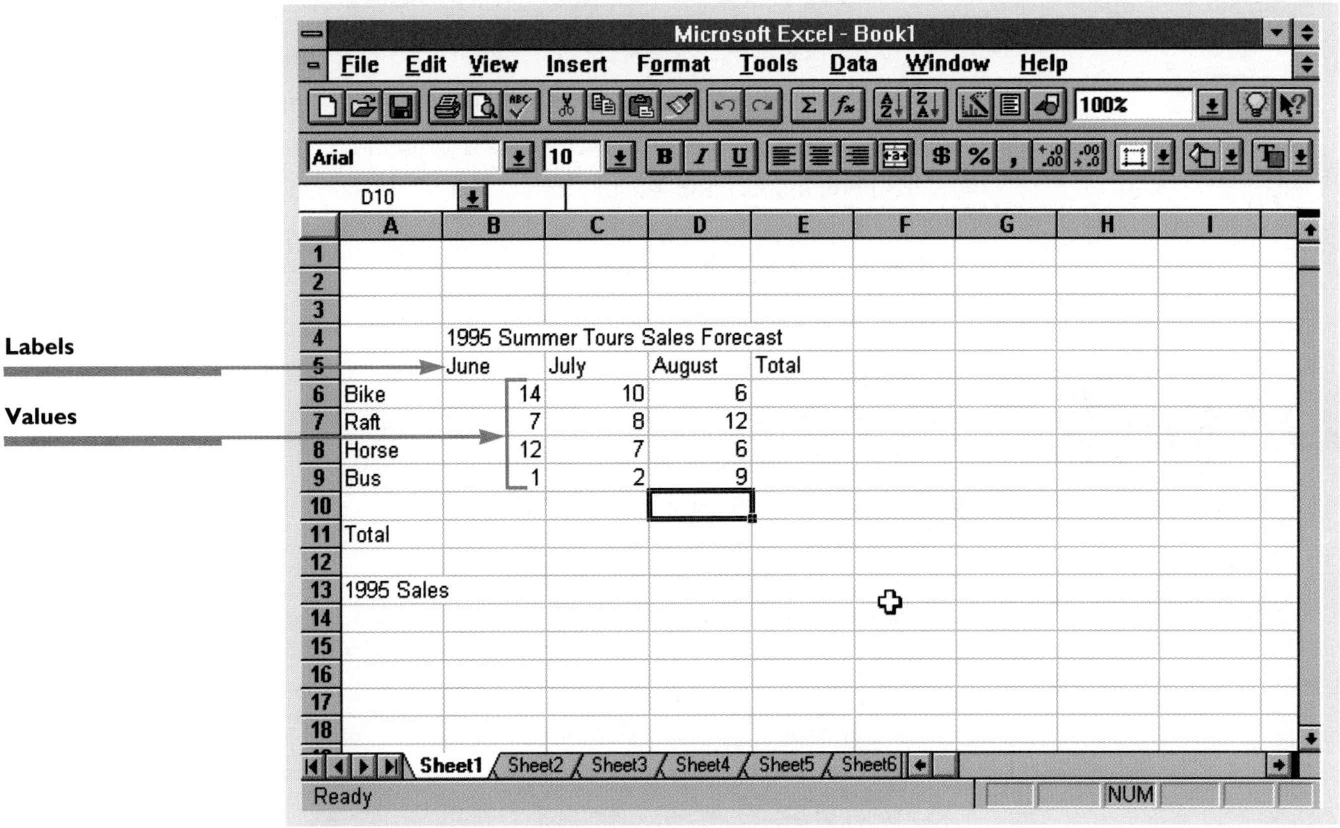

Labels

Values

Microsoft Excel - Book1

File Edit View Insert Format Tools Data Window Help

D10

	A	B	C	D	E
1					
2					
3					
4		1995 Summer Tours Sales Forecast			
5		June	July	August	Total
6	Bike	14	10	6	
7	Raft	7	8	12	
8	Horse	12	7	6	
9	Bus	1	2	9	
10					
11	Total				
12					
13	1995 Sales				

Sheet1 Sheet2 Sheet3 Sheet4 Sheet5 Sheet6

Ready NUM

To enter a number, such as the year 1994, as a label so it will not be included in a calculation, type an apostrophe (') before the number. ■

Editing cell entries

You can change the contents of any cells at any time. To edit the contents of a cell, you first select the cell you want to edit, then click the formula bar, double-click the selected cell, or press [F2]. This puts Excel into Edit mode. To make sure you are in Edit mode, check the mode indicator on the far left of the status bar. Refer to Table 2-2 for more information on the mode indicator. ▶ After checking his worksheet, Evan notices that he entered the wrong value for the June bus tours and forgot to include the canoe tours. He fixes the bus tours figure, and he decides to add the canoe sales data to the raft sales figures.

1. Click cell **B9**
   This cell contains June bus tours, which Evan needs to change to 2.
2. Click anywhere in the formula bar
   Excel goes into Edit mode, and the mode indicator displays "Edit." A blinking vertical line, called the **insertion point**, appears in the formula bar, and if you move the mouse pointer to the formula bar, the pointer changes to I. See Figure 2-5.
3. Press **[Backspace]**, type **2**, then press **[Enter]** or click the **Enter button** on the formula bar
   Evan now needs to add "/Canoe" to the Raft label.
4. Click cell **A7** then press **[F2]**
   Excel is in Edit mode again, but the insertion point is in the cell.
5. Type /**Canoe** then press **[Enter]**
   The label changes to Raft/Canoe, which is a little too long to fit in the cell. Don't worry about this. You will learn how to change the width of a column later.
6. Double-click cell **B7**
   Double-clicking a cell also puts Excel into Edit mode with the insertion point in the cell.
7. Press **[Delete]** then type **9**
   See Figure 2-6.
8. Click to confirm the entry
   You can also cancel the entry if you notice a mistake. See the related topic "Using the Cancel button" for more information.

TABLE 2-2: Understanding the mode indicator

MODE	DESCRIPTION
Edit	You are editing a cell entry.
Enter	You are entering data.
Error	You have made an entry Excel cannot understand; click the Help tool on the Standard toolbar or click OK.
Point	You have specified a range without a formula.
Ready	Excel is ready for you to enter data or choose a command.
Wait	Excel is completing a task.

FIGURE 2-5: Worksheet in Edit mode

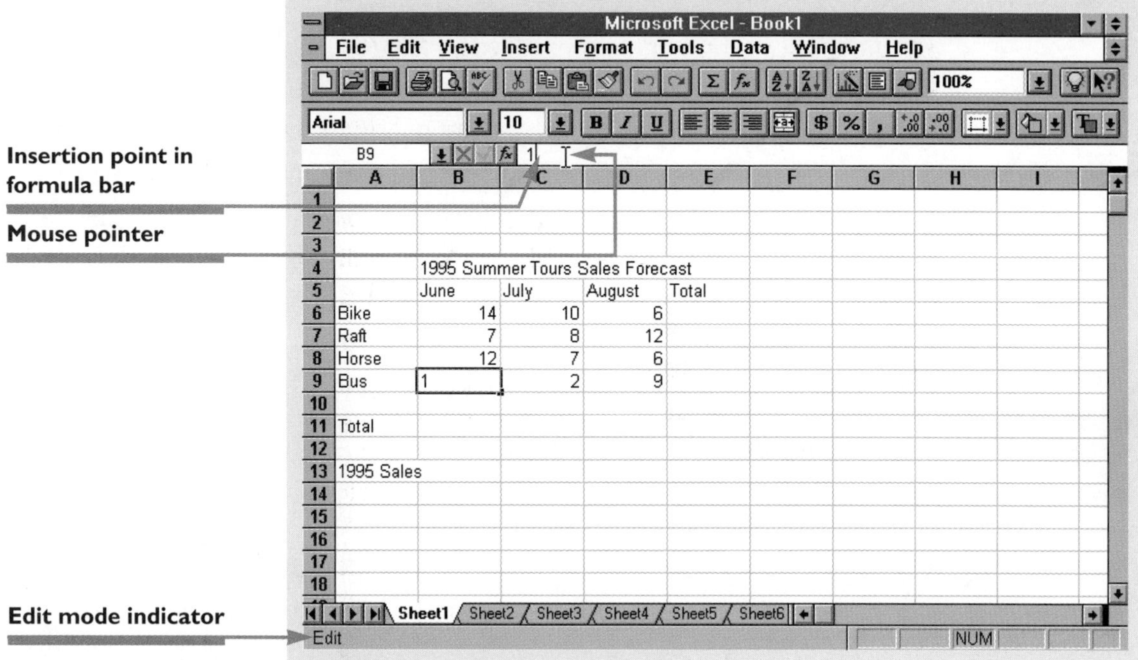

FIGURE 2-6: Worksheet with edits completed

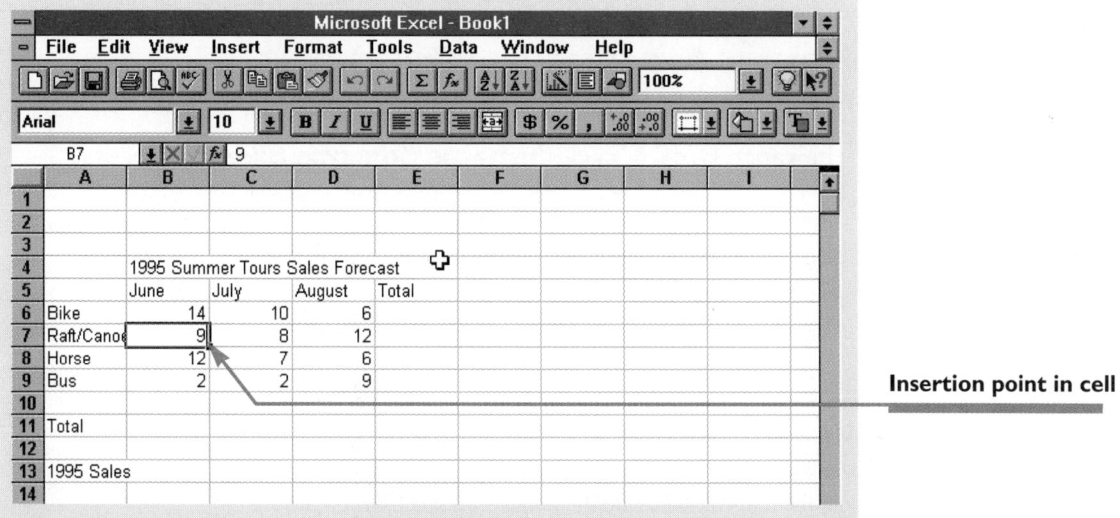

Using the Cancel button

When you enter data into a cell, the Cancel button appears immediately to the left of the Enter button on the formula bar. If you make a mistake entering data or editing a cell entry, you can click the Cancel button instead of confirming the entry. This removes the data entered, and the cell reverts to its original contents.

QUICK TIP

If you make a mistake, click the Undo button on the Standard toolbar or choose Undo from the Edit menu before doing anything else.

Working with ranges

Any group of cells (two or more) is called a **range**. To select a range, click the first cell and drag to the last cell you want included in the range. The range address is defined by noting the first and last cells in the range. Figure 2-7 shows a selected range whose address is B6:C9. You can give a meaningful name to a range, and then use the range name in formulas. Named ranges are usually easier to remember than cell addresses and they also help you move around the workbook quickly. See the related topic "Using range names to move around the workbook" for more information. ▶ To make his forecasting worksheet easier to understand, Evan decides to use named ranges in the worksheet.

1. Click cell **B6** then drag to cell **B9** to select the range B6:B9
2. Click the **name box** to select the cell address B6
3. Type **June** then press **[Enter]**
   Now whenever cells B6:B9 are selected, the range name "June" will appear in the name box.
4. Click cell **C6** then drag to cell **C9** to select the range C6:C9; click the **name box**, type **July**, then press **[Enter]**
5. Click cell **D6** then drag to cell **D9** to select the range D6:D9; click the **name box**, type **August**, then press **[Enter]**
   Next, Evan names the four ranges containing the data for each type of tour.
6. Select the range **B6:D6**, click the **name box**, type **Bike**, then press **[Enter]**
7. Name the range B7:D7 **RaftCanoe**, range B8:D8 **Horse**, and range B9:D9 **Bus**
   Note that there is no slash separating the words Raft and Canoe in the range name for the range B7:D7.
8. Click the **name box list arrow** to see the list of range names in this worksheet
   Notice that the named ranges are in alphabetical order. See Figure 2-8.
9. Click anywhere outside the range name list to close it

FIGURE 2-7: Worksheet showing selected range of cells

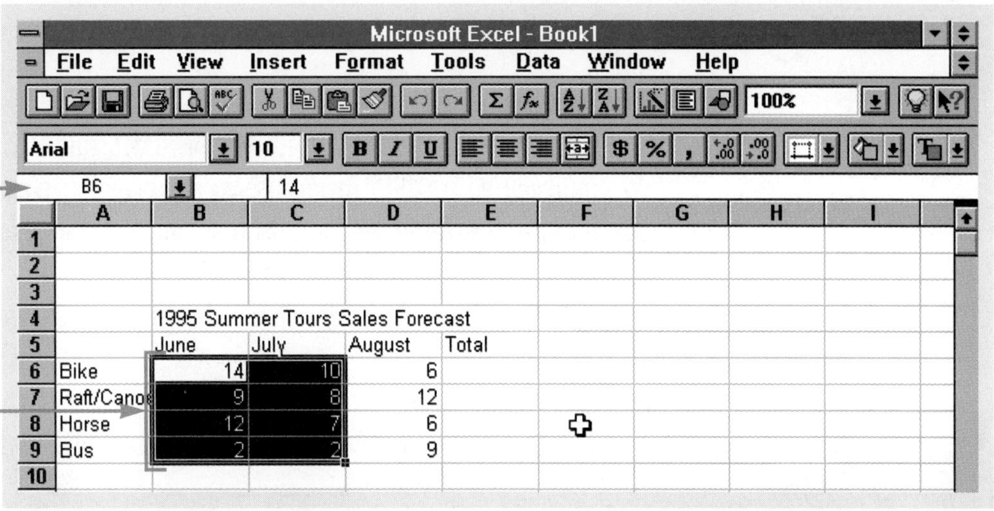

Name box

Selected range

FIGURE 2-8: List of range names

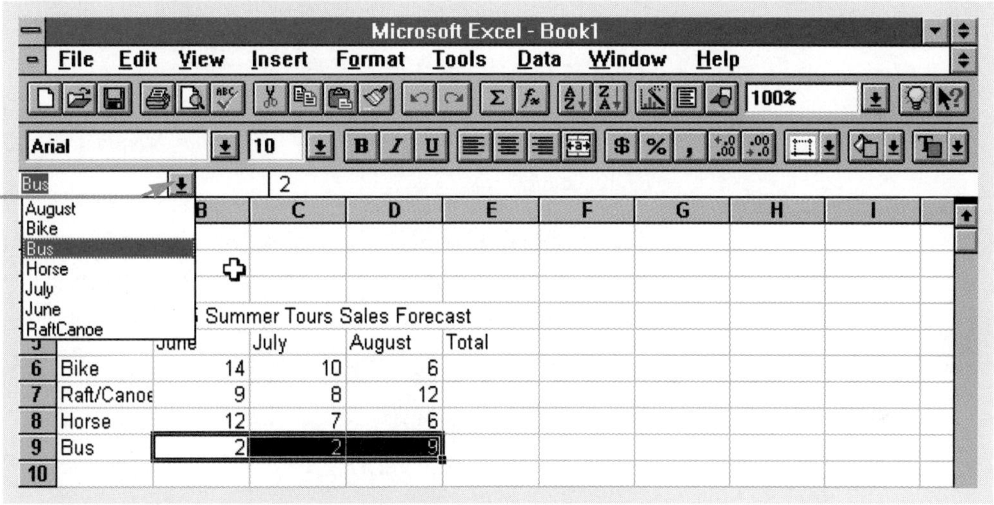

Click to display range names

Using range names to move around a workbook

You can use range names to move around a workbook quickly. Click the name box list arrow, then click the name of the range you want to go to, as shown in Figure 2-9. The cell pointer moves immediately to that range in the workbook.

August range selected

Cell pointer moves to selected range

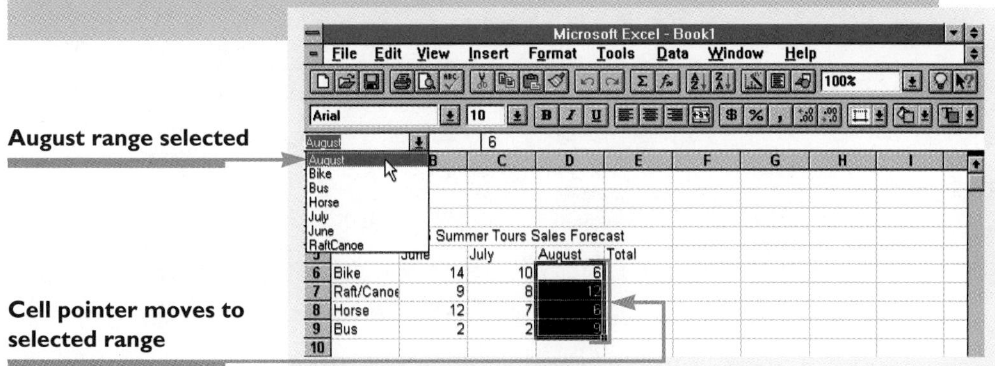

FIGURE 2-9: Moving the cell pointer using range names

TROUBLE?

If you make a mistake selecting and naming a range, click Insert on the menu bar, click Name, then click Define. In the Define Name dialog box, highlight the range name you need to redefine, click Delete, then click Close. Select and name the range again.

Entering formulas

Formulas are used to perform numeric calculations such as adding, multiplying and averaging. Formulas in an Excel worksheet start with the formula prefix—the equal sign (=). All formulas use **arithmetic operators** to perform calculations. See Table 2-3 for a list of Excel operators. Formulas often contain cell addresses and range names. Using a cell address or range name in a formula is called **cell referencing**. Using cell references keeps your worksheet up-to-date and accurate. If you change a value in a cell, any formula containing that cell reference will be automatically recalculated using the new value. ▶ Evan uses formulas to add the monthly tour totals for June, July, and August.

1 Click cell **B11**
This is the cell where Evan wants to put the calculation that will total the June sales.

2 Type = (equal sign)
The equal sign at the beginning of an entry tells Excel that a formula is about to be entered rather than a label or a value. The total June sales is equal to the sum of the values in cells B6, B7, B8, and B9.

3 Type **b6+b7+b8+b9** then click the **Enter button** on the formula bar
The result of 37 appears in cell B11, and the formula appears in the formula bar. See Figure 2-10. Next, Evan adds the number of tours in July.

4 Click cell **C11**, type **=c6+c7+c8+c9**, then click
The result of 27 appears in C11. Finally, Evan enters the formula to calculate the August tour sales.

5 Click cell **D11**, type **=d6+d7+d8+d9**, then click
The total tour sales for August appears in cell D11. Compare your results with Figure 2-11.

TABLE 2-3: Excel arithmetic operators

OPERATOR	PURPOSE	EXAMPLE
+	Performs addition	=A5+A7
-	Performs subtraction	=A5-10
*	Performs multiplication	=A5*A7
/	Performs division	=A5/A7

FIGURE 2-10: Worksheet showing formula and result

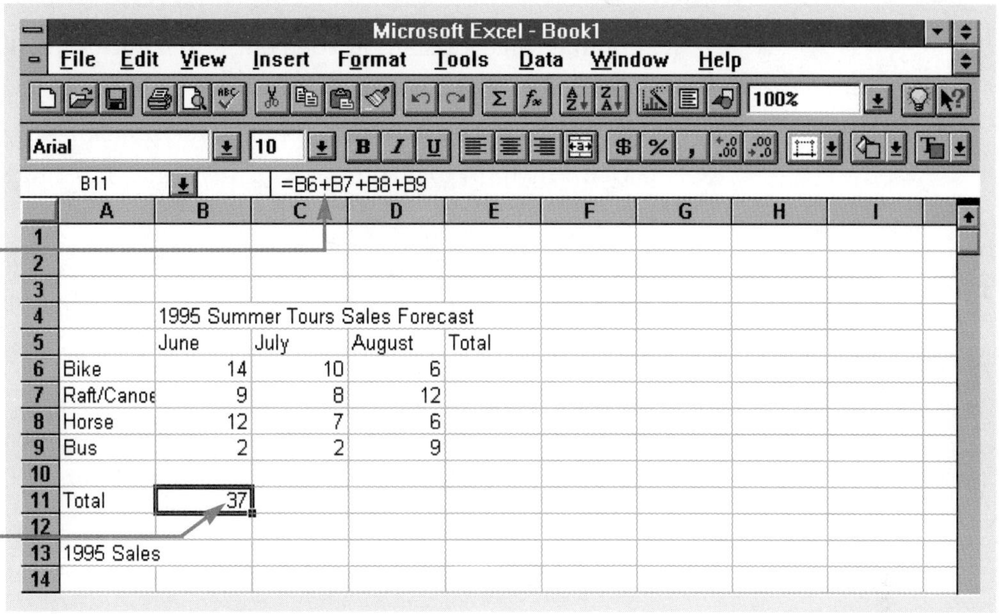

Formula in formula bar

Calculated result in cell

FIGURE 2-11: Worksheet with formulas for monthly totals entered

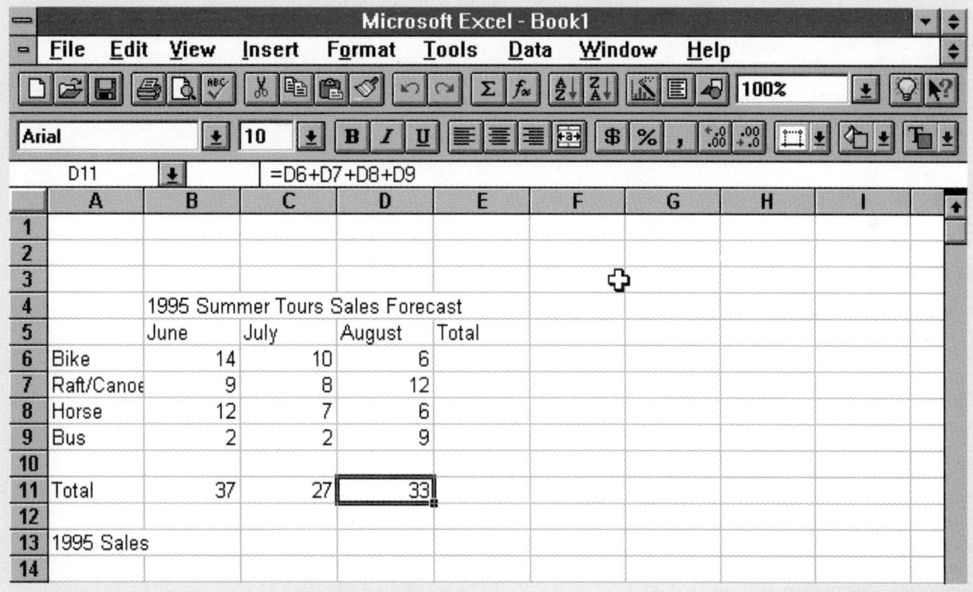

TROUBLE?

If the formula instead of the result appears in the cell after you click the Enter button, make sure you began the formula with = (equal sign).

Entering formulas, continued

Formulas can contain more than one arithmetic operator. In these situations, Excel decides which operation to perform first. See the related topic "Order of precedence in Excel formulas" for more information. ▶ Now that Evan has calculated the monthly total tour sales for 1994, he can use these figures to calculate the forecast for 1995. He will use the multiplication symbol, * (the asterisk), to write the formula calculating a 20% increase of 1994 sales. This time he will click the cell address to be included in the formula rather than typing it.

6 **Click cell B13, type =, click cell B11, type *1.2, then click the Enter button ☑ on the formula bar**

To calculate the 20% increase you multiply the total by 1.2. This formula calculates the result of multiplying the total monthly tour sales for June, cell B11, by 1.2. The result of 44.4 appears in cell B13.

Now Evan calculates the 20% increase for July and August.

7 **Click cell C13, type =, click cell C11, type *1.2, then click ☑**

8 **Click cell D13, type =, click cell D11, type *1.2, then click ☑**

Compare your results with Figure 2-12.

FIGURE 2-12: Calculated results for 20% increase

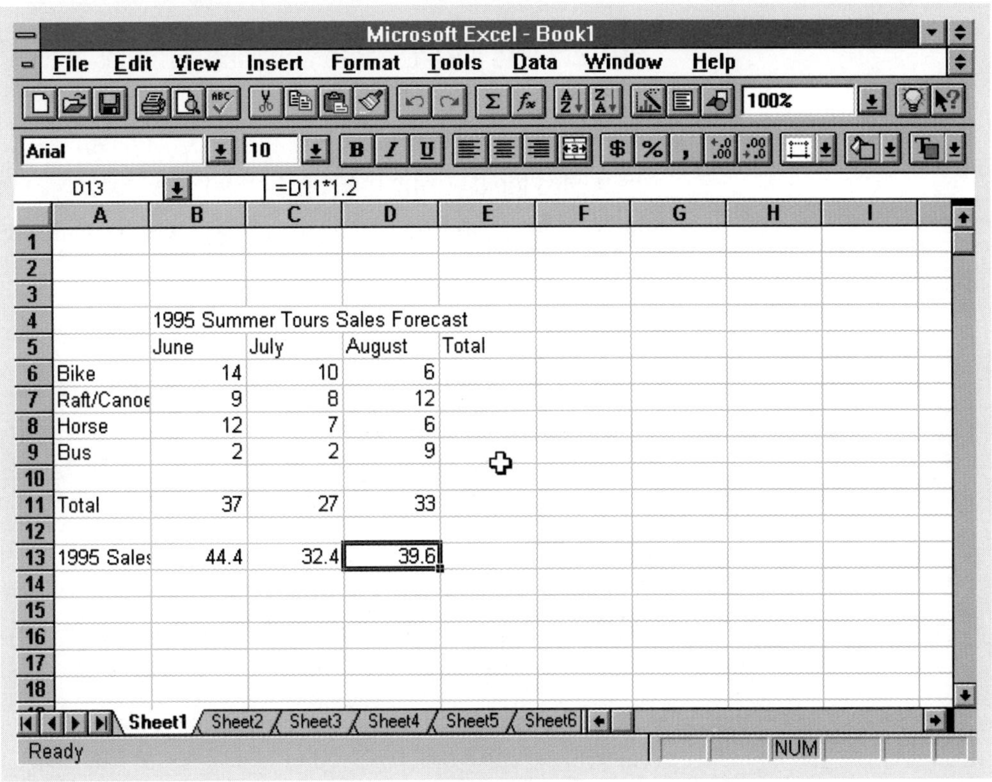

Microsoft Excel - Book1

D13 =D11*1.2

	A	B	C	D	E
4		1995 Summer Tours Sales Forecast			
5		June	July	August	Total
6	Bike	14	10	6	
7	Raft/Canoe	9	8	12	
8	Horse	12	7	6	
9	Bus	2	2	9	
10					
11	Total	37	27	33	
12					
13	1995 Sales	44.4	32.4	39.6	

Order of precedence in Excel formulas

Each of the formulas for Evan's calculations involves only one arithmetic operator, but a formula can include several operations. When you work with formulas that have more than one operator, the **order of precedence** is very important. If a formula contains two or more operators, such as 4 + .55/4000 * 25, the computer performs the calculations in a particular sequence based on these rules:

Calculated 1st	Calculation of exponents
Calculated 2nd	Multiplication and division, left to right
Calculated 3rd	Addition and subtraction, left to right

In the example 4 + .55/4000 * 25, Excel performs the arithmetic operations in the following order. First, 4000 is divided into .55. Next Excel multiplies the result of .55/4000 by 25, then adds 4 to the result. You can change the order of calculations by using parentheses. Operations inside parentheses are calculated before any other operations.

Using Excel functions

Functions are predefined worksheet formulas that enable you to do complex calculations easily. Functions always begin with the formula prefix = (the equal sign). You can enter functions manually or you can use the Function Wizard. See the related topic "Using the Function Wizard" for more information. ▶ Evan uses the SUM function to calculate the grand totals in his worksheet.

1 Click cell **E6**
This is the cell where Evan wants to display the total of all bike tours for June, July, and August.

2 Position the pointer over the **AutoSum tool** [Σ] on the Standard toolbar
See the Figure 2-13. AutoSum sets up the SUM function to add the values in the cells above the cell pointer. If there are no values in the cells above the cell pointer, it adds the values in the cells to the left of the cell pointer—in this case, the values in cells B6, C6, and D6.

3 Click [Σ]
The formula =SUM(B6:D6) appears in the formula bar. The information inside the parentheses is the argument. An **argument** can be a value, a range of cells, text, or another function. After verifying that Excel has selected the correct range, Evan confirms the entry.

4 Click the **Enter button** on the formula bar
The result appears in cell E6. Next Evan calculates the total of raft and canoe tours.

5 Click cell **E7**, click [Σ], then click
Now he calculates the three-month total of the horse tours.

6 Click cell **E8** then click [Σ]
AutoSum sets up a function to sum the two values in the cells above the active cell. Evan needs to change the argument.

7 Click cell **B8** then drag to select the range **B8:D8**
As you drag, the argument in the SUM function changes to reflect the range being chosen.

8 Click to confirm the entry

9 Enter the SUM function in cells E9, E11 and E13
Make sure you add the values to the left of the active cell, not the values above it. See Figure 2-14.

TABLE 2-4: Frequently used functions

FUNCTION	DESCRIPTION
SUM(*argument*)	Calculates the sum of the arguments
AVERAGE(*argument*)	Calculates the average of the arguments
MAX(*argument*)	Displays the largest value among the arguments
MIN(*argument*)	Displays the smallest value among the arguments
COUNT(*argument*)	Calculates the number of values in the arguments

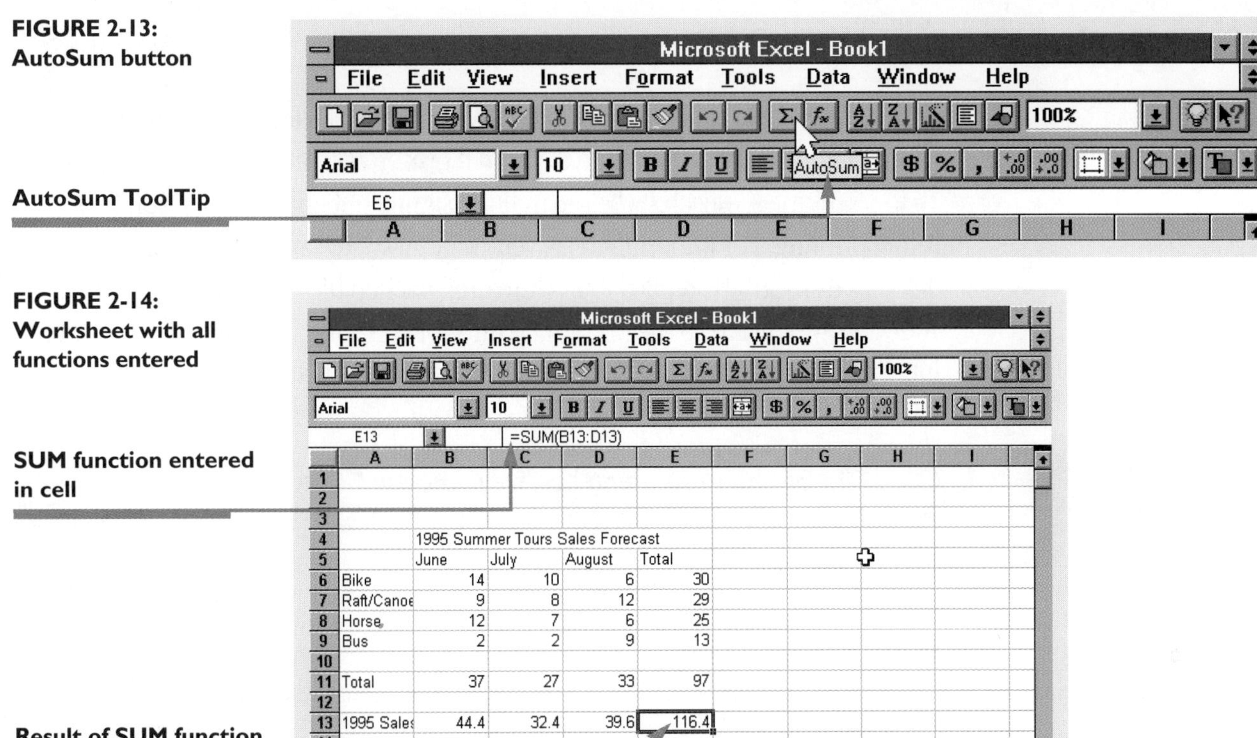

Using the Function Wizard

The Function Wizard button is located to the right of the AutoSum button on the Standard toolbar. To use the Function Wizard, click . In the Function Wizard - Step 1 of 2 dialog box, shown in Figure 2-15, click the category containing the function you want, then click the desired function. The function appears in the formula bar. Click Next to display the Function Wizard - Step 2 of 2 dialog box, fill in values or cell addresses for the arguments, then click Finish.

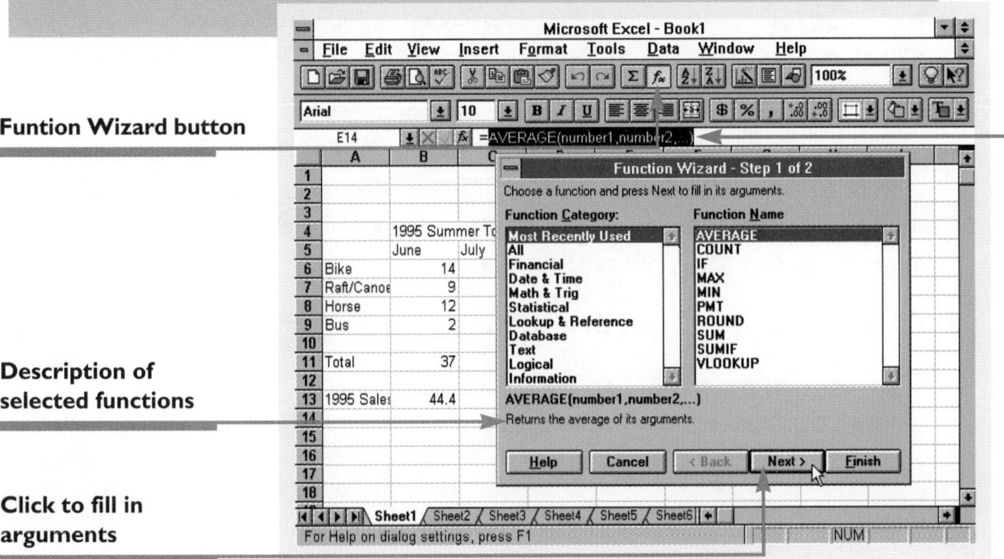

FIGURE 2-15: First Function Wizard dialog box

QUICK TIP

If you are not sure what a specific function does, use the Function Wizard to see a description of its function.

Saving a workbook

As you might have learned in "Microsoft Windows 3.1" to store the workbook permanently, you must save it to a file on a disk. You should save your work every 10 to 15 minutes, especially before making significant changes in a workbook and before printing. For important files, you might want to save a copy of the file on a different disk. See the related topic "Creating backup files" for more information. You will save this file to the MY_FILES directory on your Student Disk. For more information about your Student Disk, refer to "Read This Before You Begin Microsoft Excel 5.0" on page 2 of this application. ▶ Evan wants to save his work.

1. **Click File on the main menu bar, then choose Save As**
   The Save As dialog box opens. See Figure 2-16. The text in the File Name text box is already selected.
2. **Type tours to replace the default filename**
   Filenames can contain up to eight characters. These characters can be lower- or uppercase letters, numbers, or any symbols except for spaces, commas, or the following symbols: . \ / [ ] " ^ : * ?.
   Excel automatically adds the .XLS extension to the filename.
3. **Insert your Student Disk in the appropriate drive**
4. **Click the Drives list arrow, then click a:**
   These lessons assume that your Student Disk is in drive A. If you are using a different drive or storing your practice files on a network, click the appropriate drive.
5. **In the Directories list box, double-click the MY_FILES directory, then click OK**
   If you don't have a MY_FILES directory, simply click OK. The Save As dialog box closes, and the Summary Info dialog box opens. As you create more files with Excel, you can use the Summary Info boxes to help you organize your files. For now, just click OK to close this dialog box.
6. **Click OK**
   The Summary Info dialog box closes, and the filename appears in the title bar at the top of the workbook. The workbook is saved to the MY_FILES directory on your Student Disk as a file named TOURS.XLS. Next, Evan enters his name at the top of the worksheet, so if others who use this worksheet have questions about it, they can ask him.
7. **Click cell A2, type Evan Brillstein, then press [Enter]**
8. **Click File on the menu bar, then click Save**
   This saves the changes made to a file that has already been named. Save a file frequently while working on it to protect all data. Table 2-5 shows the difference between the Save and the Save As commands.

FIGURE 2-16: Save As dialog box

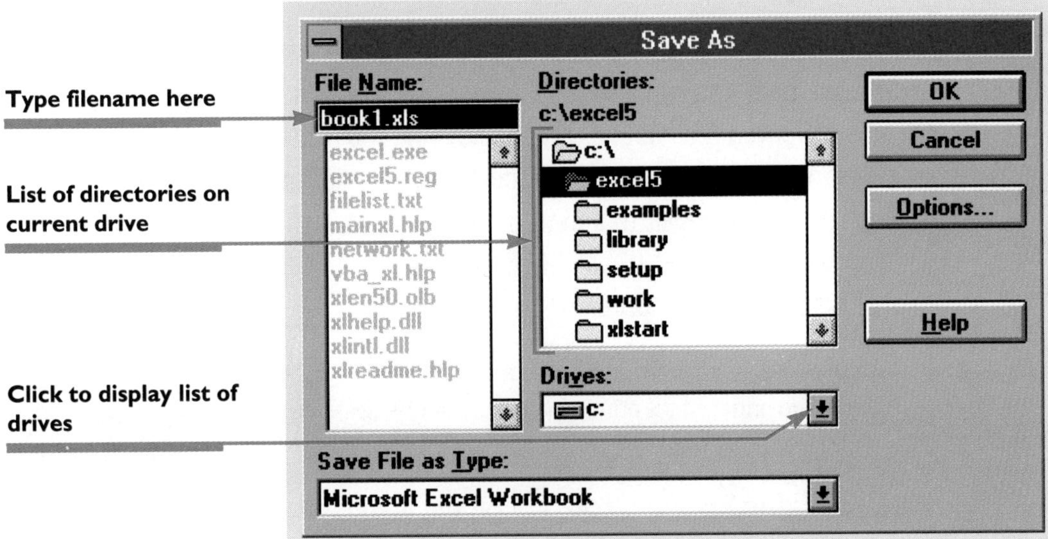

Creating backup files

It's good practice to back up your files in case something happens to your disk. To create a backup copy of a file, save the file again to a second disk or with another file extension such as .BAK.

QUICK TIP

You can click the Save button on the Standard toolbar or use the shortcut key [Ctrl][S] to save a file.

TABLE 2-5:
The difference between the Save and Save As commands

COMMAND	DESCRIPTION	PURPOSE
Save As	Saves file, requires input name	To save a file the first time, to change the filename, or to save the file for use in a different application. Useful for backups.
Save	Saves named file	To save any changes to the original file. Fast and easy—do this often to protect your work.

Previewing and printing a worksheet

You print a worksheet when it is completed to have a paper copy to reference, file, or send to others. You can also print a worksheet that is not complete to review or work on when you are not at a computer. Before you print a worksheet, you should preview it. When you preview a worksheet, you see a copy of the worksheet exactly as it will appear on paper. You preview the worksheet to make sure that it will fit on a page before you print it. Table 2-6 provides printing tips. ▶ Evan previews and then prints a copy of the tours worksheet.

1. **Make sure the printer is on and contains paper**
   If a file is sent to print and the printer is off, an error message appears. Evan previews the worksheet to check its overall appearance.
2. Click the **Print Preview tool** on the Standard toolbar
   You could also click File on the menu bar, then click Print Preview. A miniature version of the worksheet appears on the screen, as shown in Figure 2-17. If there were more than one page, you could click Next and Previous to move between pages. You can also enlarge the image by clicking the Zoom button. See the related topic "Using Zoom in Print Preview" for more information. After verifying that the preview image is correct, Evan prints the worksheet.
3. Click **Print**
   The Print dialog box opens, as shown in Figure 2-18.
4. Make sure that the **Selected Sheet(s) radio button** is selected and that **1** appears in the Copies text box
   Now Evan is ready to print the worksheet.
5. Click **OK**
   The Printing dialog box appears while the file is sent to the printer. Note that the dialog box contains a Cancel button that you can use to cancel the print job.
6. Click **File** on the menu bar, then click **Close** to close the workbook
7. Click **File** on the menu bar, then click **Exit**
   Excel closes and you are returned to the Program Manager window.

TABLE 2-6:
Worksheet printing guidelines

BEFORE YOU PRINT	RECOMMENDATION
Check the printer	Make sure the printer is on and on-line, that it has paper, and there are no error messages or warning signals.
Check the printer selection	Use the Printer Setup command in the Print dialog box to verify that the correct printer is selected.
Preview the worksheet	Check the formatted image for page breaks, page setup (vertical or horizontal), and overall appearance of the worksheet.

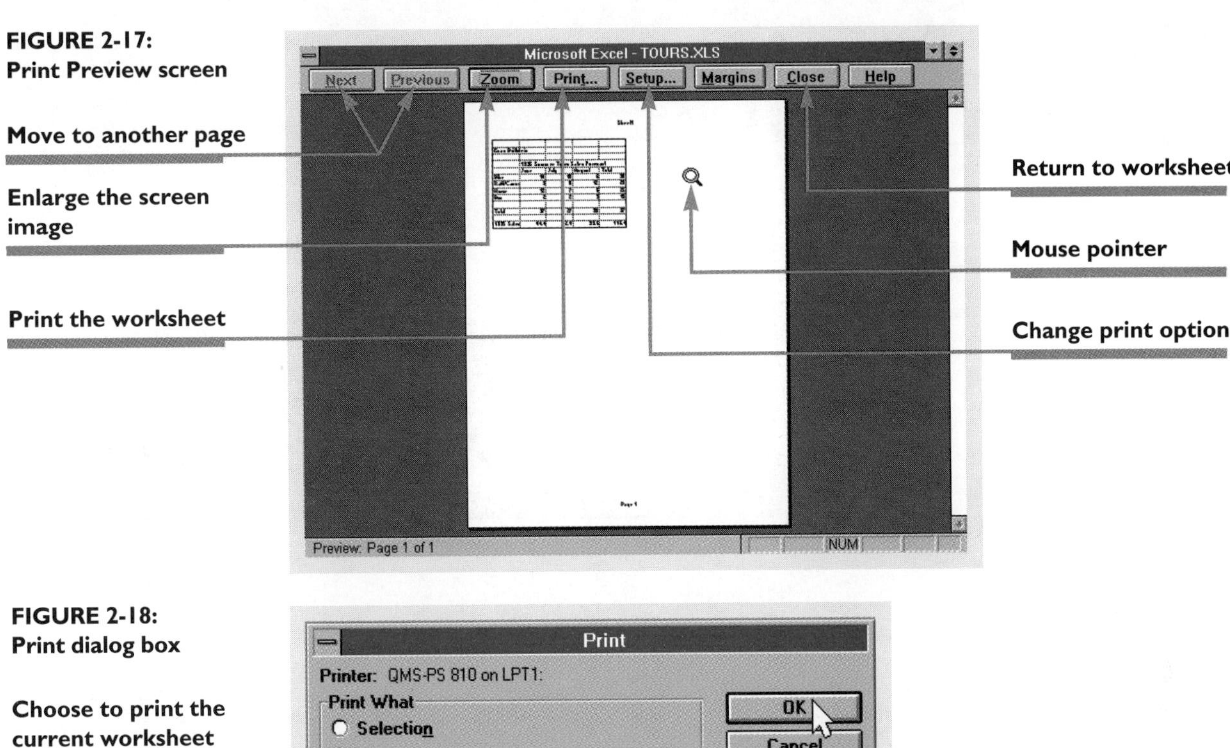

FIGURE 2-17: Print Preview screen

FIGURE 2-18: Print dialog box

Using Zoom in Print Preview

When you are in the Print Preview window, you can make the image of the page larger by clicking the Zoom button. You can also position the mouse pointer over a specific part of the worksheet page, then click it to view that section of the page. While the image is zoomed in, use the scroll bars to view different sections of the page. See Figure 2-19.

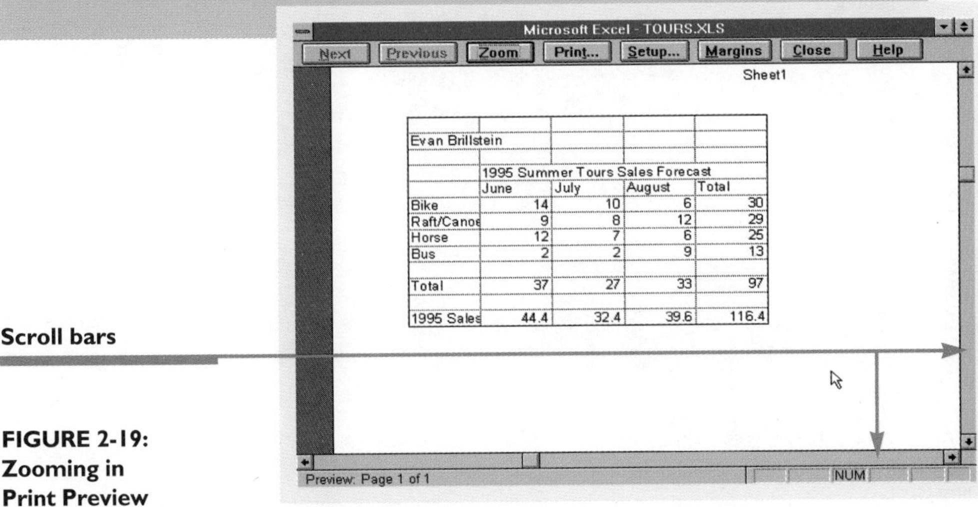

FIGURE 2-19: Zooming in Print Preview

QUICK TIP

You should save your worksheet prior to printing, so if anything happens to the file as it is being sent to the printer, you will have a clean copy saved to your disk.■

CONCEPTS REVIEW

Label each of the elements of the Excel worksheet window shown in Figure 2-20.

1 ______
2 ______
3 ______
4 ______
5 ______
6 ______
7 ______

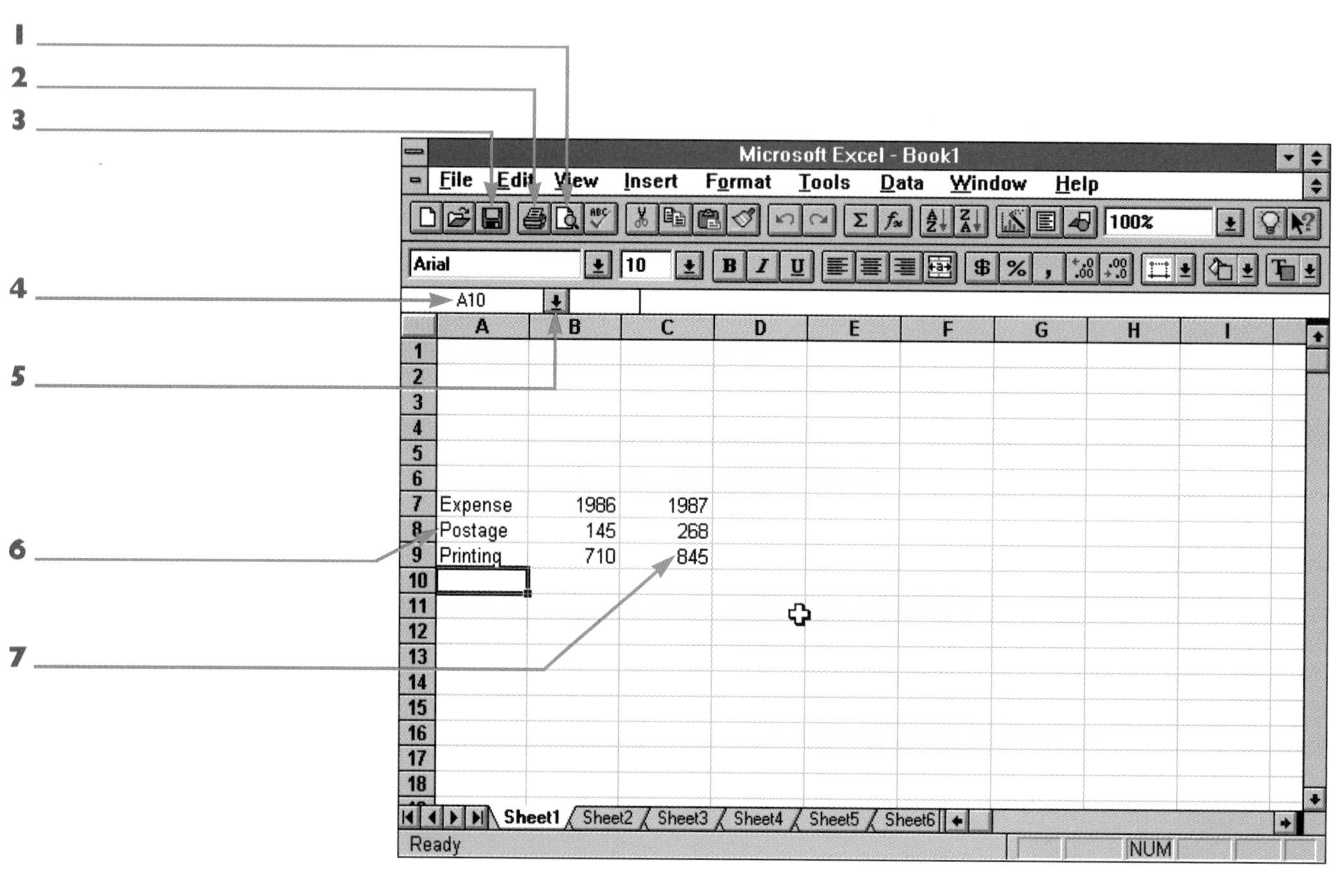

FIGURE 2-20

Match each of the terms with the statement that describes its function.

8 A predefined formula that provides a shortcut for commonly used calculations

9 A cell entry that performs a calculation in an Excel worksheet

10 A specified group of cells, which can include the entire worksheet

11 The location of a particular cell in a worksheet, identified by a column letter and row number

12 The character that identifies a value as a label

a. Range
b. Function
c. Cell address
d. Apostrophe
e. Formula

Select the best answer from the list of choices.

13 All of the following confirm an entry in a cell, EXCEPT:
a. Clicking the Cancel button
b. Clicking the Enter button
c. Pressing [Enter]
d. Pressing [↓]

14 The first character in any Excel formula is
a. *
b. /
c. =
d. @

APPLICATIONS REVIEW

1 Enter labels and save a workbook.

a. Start Excel and make sure you have an empty workbook in the Excel worksheet window.

b. Name Sheet1 tab Funds.

c. Save the workbook as FUNDS.XLS to the MY_FILES directory on your Student Disk.

d. Type "Total" in cell A6, then press [Enter].

e. Click cell B1 then type "SHARES."

f. Click the Enter button on the formula bar to enter Shares in cell B1.

g. Press [→] to move to C1, then type "PRICE."

h. Press [Tab] to move to cell D1.

i. Type "Sold" then press [Esc]. Note that the entry disappears from the cell. Leave cell D1 blank.

j. Save your work.

2 Enter values and name ranges.

a. Enter the four mutual funds labels and values from Table 2-7 into the range A1:C5 in the Funds worksheet.

TABLE 2-7

	SHARES	PRICE
Arch	210	10.01
RST	50	18.45
United	100	34.50
Vista	65	11.15

b. Name range B2:B5 Shares.

c. Name range C2:C5 Price.

d. Save, then preview and print the worksheet.

3 Enter formulas, then preview and print the worksheet.

a. Click cell B6.

b. Enter the formula B2+B3+B4+B5.

c. Save your work, then preview and print the data in the Funds worksheet.

4 Use Excel functions.

a. Click cell C7.

b. Enter the function AVERAGE(C2..C5).

c. Type the label "Average Price" in cell A7.

d. Save your work.

e. Preview and print this worksheet.

f. Close the workbook.

5 Build a simple check register to balance a checkbook. Set up the worksheet using the data from Table 2-8 in a new workbook.

TABLE 2-8

CHECK NO.	DATE	DESC	AMOUNT
1601	June 17	Cleaning	12.65
1602	June 29	Tickets	38.02
1603	July 18	Cable	14.50
1604	July 25	Food	47.98

a. Click the New Workbook button to open a new workbook.

b. Name Sheet1 tab Checkbook.

c. Enter the label "Check Register" in cell A1.

d. Enter the column labels in the range A3:D3.

e. Enter all four check numbers, with the corresponding dates, descriptions, and amounts in the range A4:D7. Don't worry if the format of the date entries changes.

f. Generate a total of the check amounts you have entered. Enter the function SUM(D4..D7) in cell D8. Enter the label "Total" in cell A8.

g. Save the workbook as CHECK.XLS, then preview and print the worksheet.

6 Edit cell entries and preview the worksheet.

a. Change the description for check 1601 to Laundry.

b. Click cell D5, click in the formula bar, then edit the amount for check 1602 to 43.62.

c. Click cell D6, press [F2], then edit the amount for check 1603 to 23.22.

d. Save your work, preview and print the worksheet, then close the workbook.

7 Develop a worksheet that calculates the weekly payroll for Suncoast Security Systems. Open a new workbook and set up the worksheet using the data from Table 2-9.

TABLE 2-9

EMPLOYEE	HOURS WORKED	HOURLY WAGE	GROSS PAY
D. Hillman	32	9	
S. Lipski	25	12	
L. Skillings	40	7	

a. Click the New Workbook button to open a new workbook.

b. Enter the column labels, beginning in cell A2. Use two rows for the labels.

c. Enter the employee names, hours worked, and wage information using Table 2-9.

d. Enter the formula B4+B5+B6 in cell B7 to calculate the total hours worked.

e. Name Sheet1 tab Suncoast.

f. Save your workbook as SUNSEC.XLS to your MY_FILES directory, then preview and print the worksheet.

INDEPENDENT CHALLENGE 1

You are the box office manager for Lightwell Players, a regional theater company. Your responsibilities include tracking seasonal ticket sales for the company's main stage productions and anticipating ticket sales for the next season. Lightwell Players sell four types of tickets: reserved seating, general admission, senior citizen tickets, and student tickets.

The 1993-94 season included productions of *Hamlet, The Cherry Orchard, Fires in the Mirror, The Shadow Box,* and *Heartbreak House.*

Open a new workbook and save it as THEATER.XLS to the MY_FILES directory on your Student Disk. Plan and build a worksheet that tracks the sales of each of the four ticket types for all five of the plays. Calculate the total ticket sales for each play, the total sales for each of the four ticket types, and the total sales for all ticket types.

Enter your own sales data, but assume the following: the Lightwell Players sold 800 tickets during the season; reserved seating was the most popular ticket type for all of the shows except for *The Shadow Box*; no play sold more than 10 student tickets. Plan and build a second worksheet in the workbook that reflects a 5% increase in all ticket types.

To complete this independent challenge:

1 Think about the results you want to see, the information you need to build these worksheets, and what types of calculations must be performed.

2 Sketch sample worksheets on a piece of paper indicating how the information should be laid out. What information should go in the columns? In the rows?

3 Build the worksheets by entering a title, row labels, column headings, and formulas. Use named ranges to make the worksheet easier to read, and rename the sheet tabs to easily identify the contents of each sheet. (*Hint:* If your columns are too narrow, position the cell pointer in the column you want to widen. To widen the column, click Format on the menu bar, click Column, click Width, choose a new column width, then click OK.)

4 Use separate worksheets for the ticket sales and projected sales showing the 5% increase.

5 Save your work, then preview and print the worksheets.

6 Submit your sketches and printed worksheets.

INDEPENDENT CHALLENGE 2

You have been promoted to Computer Lab Manager at your school, and it is your responsibility to make sure there are enough computers for students during scheduled classes. Currently, you have four classrooms: three with IBM PC's and one with Macintoshes. Classes are scheduled Monday, Wednesday, and Friday in two-hour increments from 9AM to 5PM (the lab closes at 7PM) and each room can currently accommodate 20 computers.

Open a new workbook and save it as LABMNGR.XLS. Plan and build a worksheet that tracks the number of students who can currently use available computers per two-hour class. Create your enrollment data, but assume that current enrollment averages at 85% of each room's daily capacity. Using an additional worksheet, show the impact of an enrollment increase of 25%. To complete this independent challenge:

1 Think about how to construct these worksheets to create the desired output.

2 Sketch sample worksheets on a piece of paper, indicating how the information should be laid out.

3 Build the worksheets by entering a title, row labels, column headings, and formulas. Use named ranges to make the worksheet easier to read, and rename the sheets to easily identify their contents.

4 Use separate sheets for actual enrollment and projected changes.

5 Save your work, then preview and print the worksheets.

6 Submit your sketches and printed worksheets.

UNIT 3

OBJECTIVES

- Open an existing workbook
- Insert and delete rows and columns
- Copy and move cell entries
- Copy and move formulas
- Copy formulas with absolute references
- Adjust column widths
- Format values
- Format cell data with fonts and point sizes
- Format cell data with attributes and alignment

Modifying A WORKSHEET

Building on your ability to create a worksheet and enter data into it, you will now learn how to insert and delete columns and rows, move, copy, paste and format cell contents, and resize columns. ▶ The marketing managers at Nomad Ltd told Evan Brillstein that it would be helpful to have forecasts for the entire year, so Evan prepared a worksheet containing the forecast for the Spring and Fall Tours Sales and another worksheet with the forecast for the Winter Tours Sales. He created these new worksheets as Sheet2 and Sheet3 in the workbook containing the 1995 Summer Tours Sales Forecast. Having three related worksheets in one workbook makes it easier for Evan to compare them. ▶

Opening an existing workbook

Sometimes it's useful to create a new worksheet by modifying one that already exists. This saves you from having to retype information. Throughout this book, you will be instructed to open a file from your Student Disk, use the Save As command to create a copy of the file with a new name, and then modify the new file by following the lesson steps. Saving the files with new names keeps your original Student Disk files intact in case you have to start the lesson over again or you wish to repeat an exercise. ▶ Follow as Evan opens his 1995 Tours Forecast workbook, then uses the Save As command to create a copy with a new name.

1 **Start Excel then click the Open button on the Standard toolbar**
The Open File dialog box opens. See Figure 3-1. Notice that it is very similar to the Save As dialog box you saw in Unit 2.

2 Click the **Drives list arrow**
A list of the available drives appears. Locate the drive that contains your Student Disk. In these lessons we assume your Student Disk is in drive A.

3 Click **a:**
A list of the files on your Student Disk appears in the File Name list box, with the default filename placeholder in the File Name text box already selected.

4 In the File Name list box, click **UNIT_3-1.XLS**, then click **OK**
The file UNIT_3-1.XLS opens. You could also double-click the filename in the File Name list to open the file. To create and save a copy of this file with a new name, Evan uses the Save As command.

5 Click **File** on the menu bar, then click **Save As**
The Save As dialog box opens.

6 Make sure the Drives list box displays the drive containing your Student Disk, then double-click MY_FILES in the list of directories
You should save all your files to your Student Disk in the MY_FILES directory, unless instructed otherwise. If you do not have a MY_FILES directory, simply save the file to your Student Disk.

7 In the File Name text box, select the current filename (if necessary), then type **TOURINFO**
See Figure 3-2.

8 Click **OK** to close the Save As dialog box and save the file, then click **OK** again to close the Summary Info dialog box if necessary
The file UNIT_3-1.XLS closes, and a duplicate file named TOURINFO.XLS is now open.

FIGURE 3-1: Open File dialog box

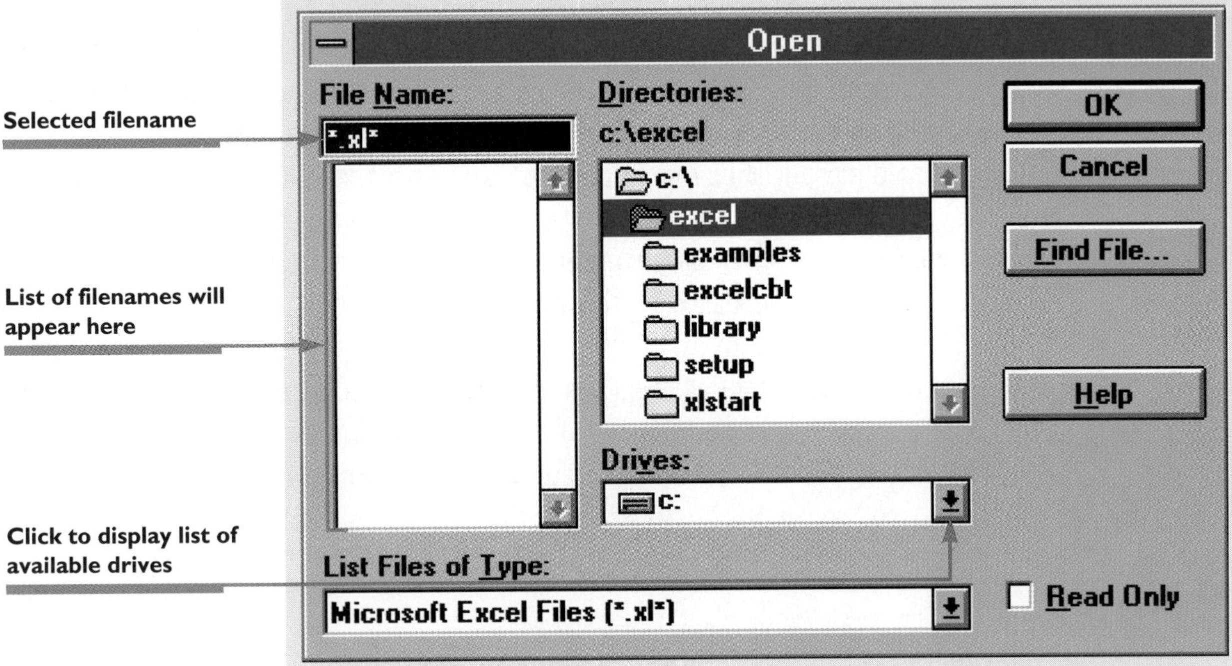

FIGURE 3-2: Save As dialog box

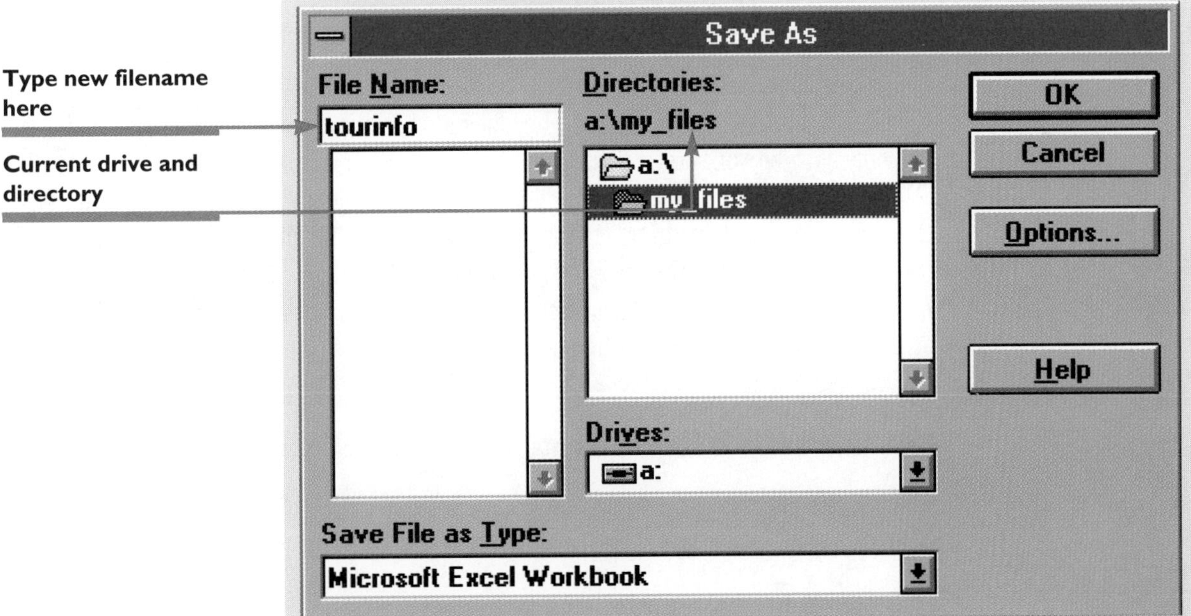

TROUBLE?

All lessons from this point on assume you have Excel running. If you need help starting Excel, refer to Unit 1.■

Inserting and deleting rows and columns

As you modify a worksheet, you might find it necessary to insert or delete rows and columns. For example, you might need to insert rows to accommodate new inventory products or remove a column of yearly totals that are no longer current. Inserting or deleting rows or columns can help to make your worksheet more attractive and readable. Inserting or deleting rows or columns can also cause problems with formulas that reference cells in that area. For information on how to avoid these problems, see the related topic "Using dummy columns and rows." ▶ Evan has already improved the appearance of his worksheet by using the Bold button to format the column headings. Now, he decides to insert a row between the worksheet title and the column labels. Evan also decides to discontinue bus tours for the 1995 summer season because of slow sales in 1994, so he needs to delete the row containing bus tour information.

1. Double-click the **Sheet1 tab**, then name it **Summer**

   This will identify this sheet of the workbook.

2. Click cell **A5**, click **Insert** on the menu bar, then click **Cells**

   The Insert dialog box opens. See Figure 3-3. You can choose to insert a column or a row, or you can shift the data in the cells in the active column right or in the active row down. Evan wants to insert a row to add some space between the title and column headings.

3. Click the **Entire Row radio button**, then click **OK**

   A blank row is inserted between the title and the month labels. When you insert a new row, the contents of the worksheet shifts down from the newly inserted row. When you insert a new column, the contents of the worksheet shifts to the right from the point of the new column. Now Evan deletes the row containing information about bus sales. Because the formulas in row 12 use ranges whose **anchors** (cells used in the range address) are in row 10 (the bus sales row), he can't delete row 10 without having to change the formulas. To get around this problem, he clears the data from row 10, then he deletes the blank row 11 so the worksheet doesn't have two blank rows together.

4. Select the range **A10:E10**, containing the bus tour information

5. Click **Edit** on the menu bar, click **Clear**, then click **All**

   The data in the range A10:E10 disappears. Notice that the formula results in rows 12 and 14 are adjusted because of the deletion of bus tour sales. Now delete a blank row.

6. Click the **row 11 selector button** (the gray box containing the row number to the left of the worksheet)

   All of row 11 is selected as shown in Figure 3-4.

7. Click **Edit** in the menu bar, then click **Delete**

   Excel deletes row 11, and all rows below this shift up one row. Evan is satisfied with the appearance of his worksheet and decides to save the changes.

8. Click the **Save button** on the Standard toolbar

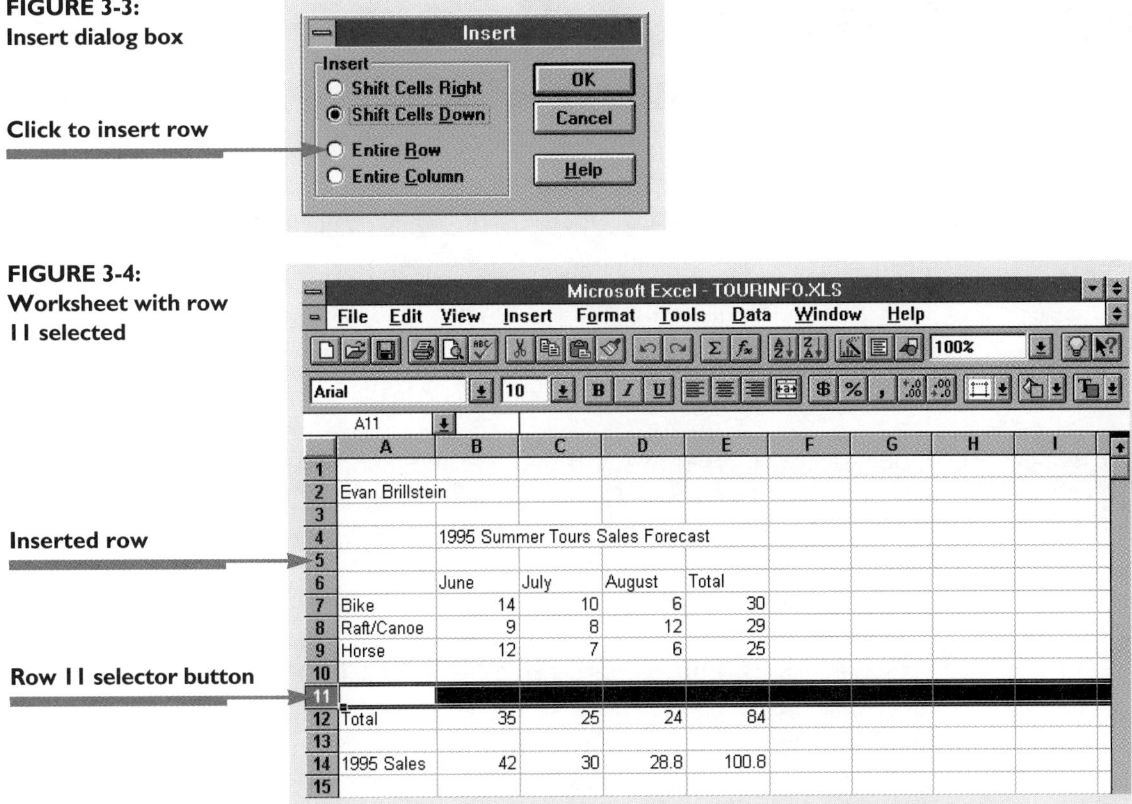

FIGURE 3-3: Insert dialog box

FIGURE 3-4: Worksheet with row 11 selected

Using dummy columns and rows

You use cell references and ranges in formulas. When you add or delete a column or row *within* a range used in a formula, Excel automatically adjusts the formula to reflect the change. However, when you add a column or row at the *end* of a range used in a formula, you must modify the formula to reflect the additional column or row. To eliminate having to edit the formula, you can include a dummy column and dummy row in the range you need to use in the formula. A **dummy column** or **dummy row** is a blank column or row included at the end of a range, as shown in Figure 3-5. Then if you add another column or row to the end of the range, the formula will automatically be modified to include the new data.

FIGURE 3-5: Formula with dummy row

Microsoft Excel - TOURINFO.XLS

E11 =SUM(E7:E10)

	A	B	C	D	E
1					
2	Evan Brillstein				
3					
4		1995 Summer Tours Sales Forecast			
5					
6		June	July	August	Total
7	Bike	14	10	6	30
8	Raft/Canoe	9	8	12	29
9	Horse	12	7	6	25
10					
11	Total	35	25	24	84
12					
13	1995 Sales	42	30	28.8	100.8
14					

Formula with dummy row

Dummy row

Rows included in formula

Copying and moving cell entries

Moving and Copying Text

Using the Cut, Copy, and Paste buttons or Excel's drag-and-drop feature, you can copy or move information from one cell or range in your worksheet to another. You can also cut, copy, and paste data from one worksheet to another. For information on adding and deleting worksheets, see the related topic on the next page. ▶ Evan included the 1995 forecast for Spring and Fall Tours Sales in his TOURINFO workbook. He already entered the spring report in Sheet2 and will finish entering the labels and data for the fall report. Using the Copy and Paste buttons and drag-and-drop, Evan copies information from the spring report to the fall report.

1 Double-click the **Sheet2 tab** then rename it **Spring-Fall**
Don't worry if you can't see all of the labels. You will fix this later. First, Evan copies the labels identifying the types of tours from the spring report to the fall report.

2 Select the range **A4:A9**, then click the **Copy button** on the Standard toolbar
The selected range (A4:A9) is copied to the Clipboard. The **Clipboard** is a temporary storage file that holds all the selected information you copy or cut. The Cut button would remove the selected information and place it on the Clipboard. To copy the contents of the Clipboard to a new location, you click a new cell, then use the Paste command.

3 Click cell **A13** then click the **Paste button** on the Standard toolbar
The contents of the Clipboard is copied into the range A13:A18. When pasting the contents of the Clipboard into the worksheet, you need to specify only the first cell of the range where you want the copied selection to go. Evan decides to use drag-and-drop to copy the Total label.

4 Click cell **E3** then position the pointer on any edge of the cell until the pointer changes to

5 While the pointer is , press and hold down **[Ctrl]**
The pointer changes to .

6 While still pressing **[Ctrl]**, press and hold the **left mouse button** then drag the cell contents to cell **E12**
As you drag, an outline of the cell moves with the pointer, as shown in Figure 3-6. When you release the mouse button, the Total label appears in cell E12. Evan now decides to move the worksheet title over to the left. To use drag-and-drop to move, rather than copy, data to a new cell, do not press [Ctrl].

7 Click cell **C1**, then position the mouse on the edge of the cell until it changes to , then drag the cell contents to **A1**
Evan enters fall sales data into the range B13:D16, as shown in Figure 3-7.

8 Using the information shown in Figure 3-7, enter the sales data for the fall tours into the range B13:D16
Compare your worksheet to Figure 3-7, then continue to the next lesson.

FIGURE 3-6: Using drag-and-drop to copy information

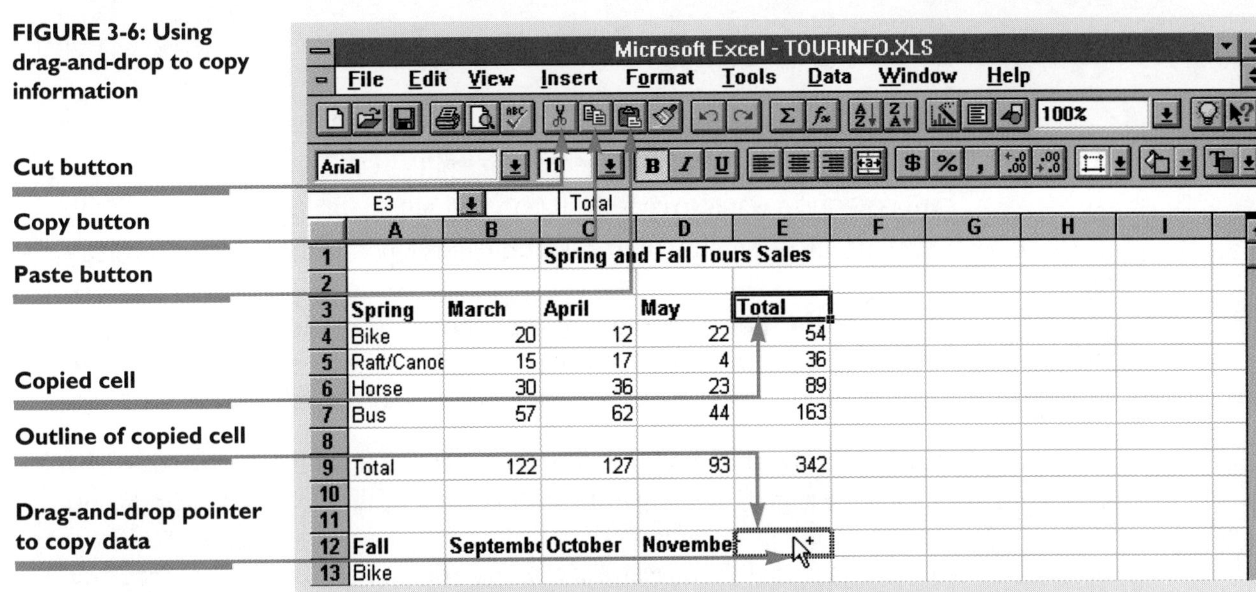

FIGURE 3-7: Worksheet with fall tours data entered

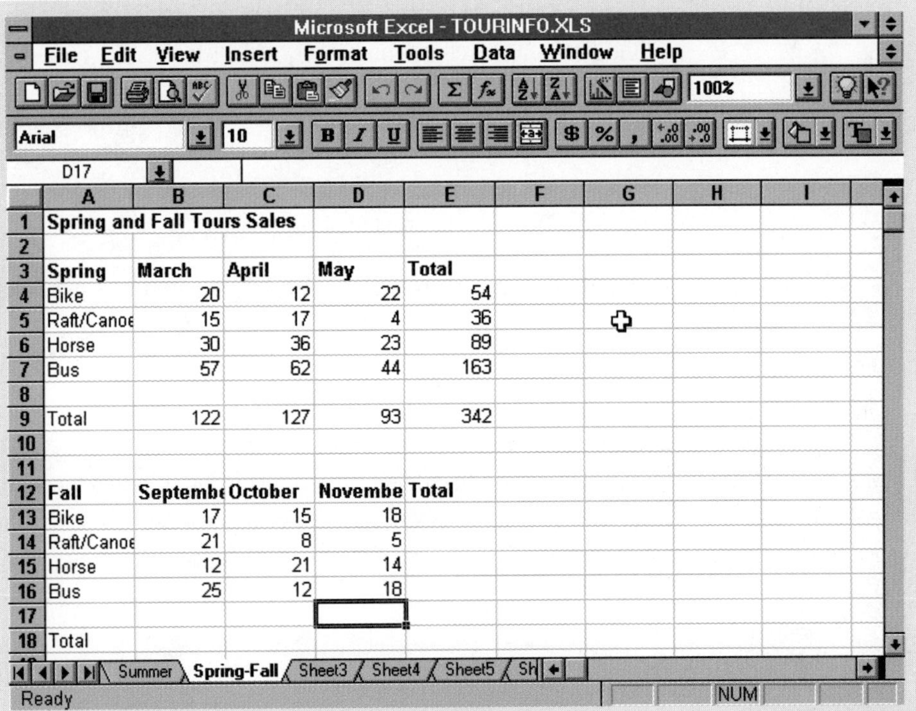

Adding and deleting worksheets

You can add or delete worksheets as necessary. To add a worksheet, click Insert on the menu bar, then click Worksheet. A new worksheet is added immediately *before* the active worksheet. To delete a worksheet, click Edit on the menu bar, then click Delete Sheet. The active worksheet is deleted, and the worksheet immediately *after* becomes the active worksheet.

TROUBLE?

When you drag-and-drop into occupied cells, you will be asked if you want to replace the existing cells. Click OK to replace the contents with the cell you are moving.■

Copying and moving formulas

Copying and moving formulas allows you to reuse formulas you've already created. Copying formulas, rather than retyping them, helps prevent new typing errors. ▶ Evan wants to copy the formulas that total the types of tours and that add the tours per month from the spring tours report to the fall tours report.

1. **Click cell E4 then click the Copy button on the Standard toolbar**
   The formula for calculating the total number of spring bike tours is copied to the Clipboard. Notice that the formula in the formula bar appears as =SUM(B4:D4).

2. **Click cell E13 then click the Paste button on the Standard toolbar**
   The formula from cell E4 is copied into cell E13. A new result of 50 appears in E13. Notice in the formula bar that the cell references have changed, so that the range B13:D13 appears in the formula. Formulas in Excel contain relative cell references. A **relative cell reference** tells Excel to copy the formula to a new cell, but to substitute new cell references that are in the same relative position to the new formula location. In this case, Excel inserted cells D13, C13 and B13, the three cell references immediately to the left of E13.

   Notice that the bottom right corner of the active cell contains a small square, called the **fill handle**. Evan uses the fill handle to copy the formula in cell E13 to cells E14, E15, and E16. You can also use the fill handle to copy labels. See the related topic "Filling ranges with a series of labels" for more information.

3. **Position the pointer over the fill handle until it changes to +**

4. **Drag the fill handle to select the range E13: E16**
   See Figure 3-8.

5. **Release the mouse button**
   Once you release the mouse button, the fill handle copies the formula from the active cell (E13) and pastes it into each cell of the selected range. Again, because the formula uses relative cell references, cells E14 through E16 correctly display the totals for raft and canoe, horse, and bus tours.

FIGURE 3-8: Selected range using the fill handle

Microsoft Excel - TOURINFO.XLS

=SUM(B13:D13)

	A	B	C	D	E
1	Spring and Fall Tours Sales				
2					
3	Spring	March	April	May	Total
4	Bike	20	12	22	54
5	Raft/Canoe	15	17	4	36
6	Horse	30	36	23	89
7	Bus	57	62	44	163
8					
9	Total	122	127	93	342
10					
11					
12	Fall	Septembe	October	Novembe	Total
13	Bike	17	15	18	50
14	Raft/Canoe	21	8	5	
15	Horse	12	21	14	
16	Bus	25	12	18	
17					
18	Total				

Summer | Spring-Fall | Sheet3 | Sheet4 | Sheet5

Drag outside selection to extend series or fill; drag inside to clear

Mouse pointer

Formula in E13 will be copied to E14:E16

Filling ranges with a series of labels

You can fill cells with a series of labels using the fill handle. You can fill cells with sequential months, days of the week, years, and text plus a number (Quarter 1, Quarter 2,...). Figure 3-9 shows a series of months being created with the fill handle. As you drag the fill handle, the contents of the last filled cell appears in the name box. You can also use the Fill Series command on the Edit menu.

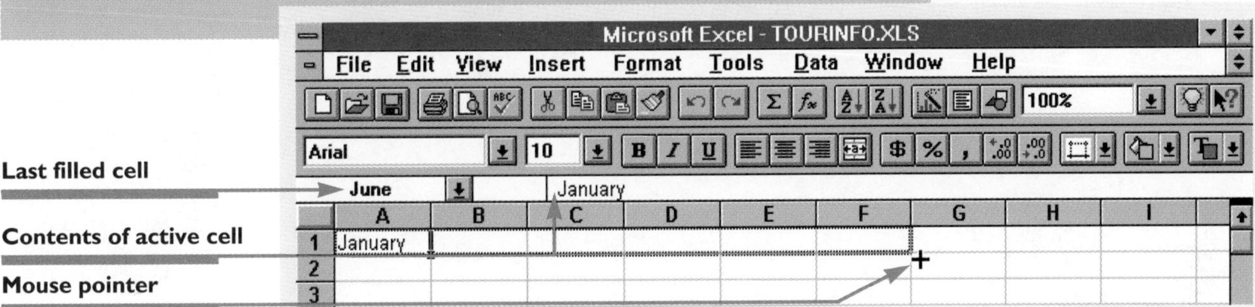

FIGURE 3-9: Using the fill handle to create a label series

QUICK TIP

Use the Fill Series command on the Edit menu to examine all of Excel's available fill series options.

Copying and moving formulas, continued

To complete the fall tours section of his worksheet, Evan now must copy the formulas from the range B9:E9 to the range B18:E18. To do this, he'll use the Copy and Paste commands and the Fill Right command.

6 **Click cell B9, click Edit on the menu bar, then click Copy**
The Copy command on the Edit menu has the same effect as clicking the Copy button on the Standard toolbar. See Table 3-1 for Cut, Copy, Paste, and Undo shortcuts.

7 **Click cell B18, click Edit on the menu bar, then click Paste**
See Figure 3-10. The formula for calculating the September tours sales appears in the formula bar. You can also cut, copy, and paste among sheets in a workbook. Now Evan uses the Fill Right command to copy the formula from cell B18 to cells C18, D18, and E18.

8 **Select the range B18:E18**

9 **Click Edit on the menu bar, click Fill, then click Right**
The rest of the totals are filled in correctly. Compare your worksheet to Figure 3-11.

10 **Click the Save button on the Standard toolbar**

TABLE 3-1: Cut, Copy, Paste, and Undo shortcuts

TOOL	KEYBOARD	MENU COMMAND	DESCRIPTION
	[Ctrl][X]	Edit Cut	Deletes the selection from the cell or range and places it on the Clipboard
	[Ctrl][C]	Edit Copy	Copies the selection to the Clipboard
	[Ctrl][V]	Edit Paste	Pastes the contents of the Clipboard in the current cell or range
	[Ctrl][Z]	Edit Undo	Undoes the last editing action

FIGURE 3-10: Worksheet with copied formula

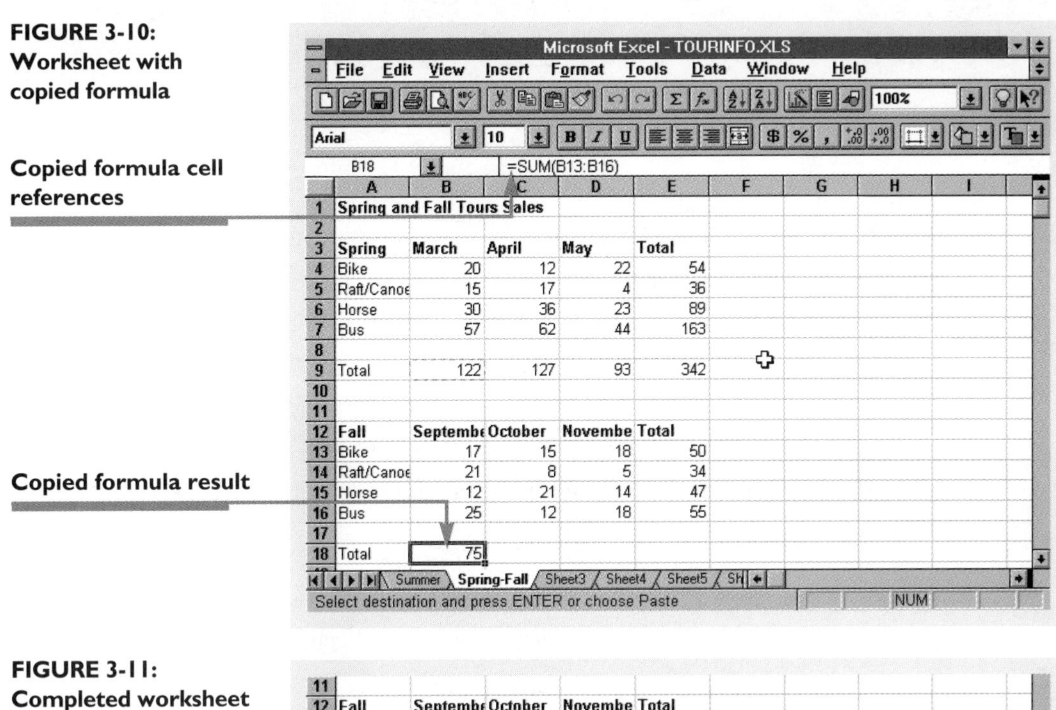

	A	B	C	D	E
1	Spring and Fall Tours Sales				
2					
3	Spring	March	April	May	Total
4	Bike	20	12	22	54
5	Raft/Canoe	15	17	4	36
6	Horse	30	36	23	89
7	Bus	57	62	44	163
8					
9	Total	122	127	93	342
10					
11					
12	Fall	Septembe	October	Novembe	Total
13	Bike	17	15	18	50
14	Raft/Canoe	21	8	5	34
15	Horse	12	21	14	47
16	Bus	25	12	18	55
17					
18	Total	75			

FIGURE 3-11: Completed worksheet with all formulas copied

	A	B	C	D	E
11					
12	Fall	Septembe	October	Novembe	Total
13	Bike	17	15	18	50
14	Raft/Canoe	21	8	5	34
15	Horse	12	21	14	47
16	Bus	25	12	18	55
17					
18	Total	75	56	55	186

Summer | Spring-Fall | Sheet3 | Sheet4 | Sheet5

Ready NUM

Using Find & Replace to edit a worksheet

If the worksheet is large and you need to make repeated changes to a worksheet's labels or formulas, use the Replace command on the Edit menu to locate the data you want to change and change it. The Replace dialog box is shown in Figure 3-12. Enter the text, values, or formulas you want to change, called the **search criteria**, in the Find What text box. In the Replace with text box, enter the text, values, or formulas you want to replace the search criteria. Click Find Next to find the next occurrence of the search criteria, then click Replace to replace it with the replacement data, or click Replace All to replace all the instances of the search criteria in the workbook with the replacement data.

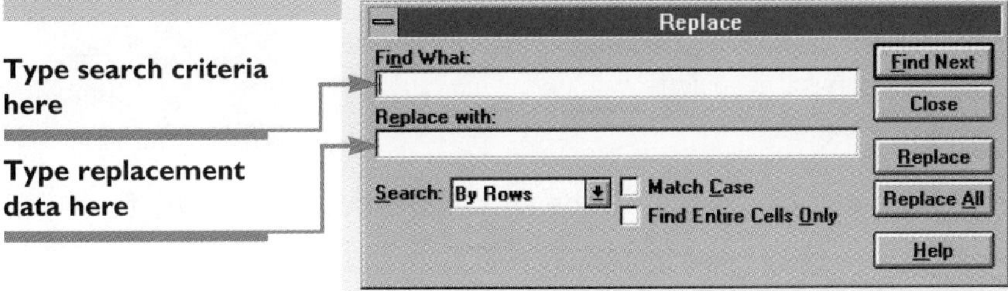

FIGURE 3-12: Replace dialog box

Copying formulas with absolute references

Relative versus Absolute Cell Referencing

Sometimes you might want a cell reference to always refer to a particular cell address. In such an instance, you would use an absolute cell reference. An **absolute cell reference** always refers to a specific cell address, even if you move the formula to a new location. You identify an absolute reference by placing a dollar sign ($) before the row letter and column number of the address (for example $A$1). ▶ Evan decides to add a column that calculates a possible increase in the number of spring tours in 1996. He wants to do a what-if analysis and recalculate the spreadsheet several times, changing the percentage that the tours might increase each time.

1. **Click cell G1, type Change, then press [→]**
   Evan stores the increase factor that will be used in the what-if analysis in cell H1.
2. **Type 1.1 in cell H1, then press [Enter]**
   This represents a 10% increase in sales.
3. **Click cell F3, type 1996?, then press [Enter]**
   Now, he creates a formula that uses an absolute reference to cell H1.
4. **In cell F4, type =E4*H1, then click the Enter button on the formula bar**
   The result of 59.4 appears in cell F4. Evan now uses the fill handle to copy the formula in cell F4 to F5:F7.
5. **Drag the fill handle to select the range F4:F7**
   The resulting values in the range F5:F7 are all zeros. When Evan looks at the formula in cell F5, which is =E5*H2, he realizes he needs to use an absolute reference to cell H1. Evan can correct this error by editing cell F4 using [F4], a shortcut key, to change the relative cell reference to an absolute cell reference.
6. **Click cell F4, press [F2] to change to Edit mode, then press [F4]**
   Dollar signs appear, changing the H1 cell reference to absolute. See Figure 3-13.
7. **Click the Enter button on the formula toolbar**
   Now that the formula correctly contains an absolute cell reference, Evan uses the fill handle to copy the formula in cell F4 to F5:F7.
8. **Drag the fill handle to select the range F4:F7**
   Now Evan completes his what-if analysis by changing the value in cell H1 from 1.1 to 1.25 to indicate a 25% increase in sales.
9. **Click cell H1, type 1.25, then click the Enter button on the formula bar**
   The values in the range F4:F7 change. Compare your worksheet to Figure 3-14.

FIGURE 3-13: Absolute cell reference in cell F4

Microsoft Excel - TOURINFO.XLS

F4 =E4*$H$1

	A	B	C	D	E	F	G	H	I
1	Spring and Fall Tours Sales						Change	1.1	
2									
3	Spring	March	April	May	Total	1996?			
4	Bike	20	12	22	54	=E4*$H$1			
5	Raft/Canoe	15	17	4	36	0			
6	Horse	30	36	23	89	0			
7	Bus	57	62	44	163	0			
8									
9	Total	122	127	93	342				
10									
11									
12	Fall	Septembe	October	Novembe	Total				
13	Bike	17	15	18	50				
14	Raft/Canoe	21	8	5	34				
15	Horse	12	21	14	47				
16	Bus	25	12	18	55				
17									
18	Total	75	56	55	186				

Summer / Spring-Fall / Sheet3 / Sheet4 / Sheet5 / Sh

Edit NUM

Absolute cell reference in formula

Incorrect values due to relative reference

FIGURE 3-14: Worksheet with What-if value

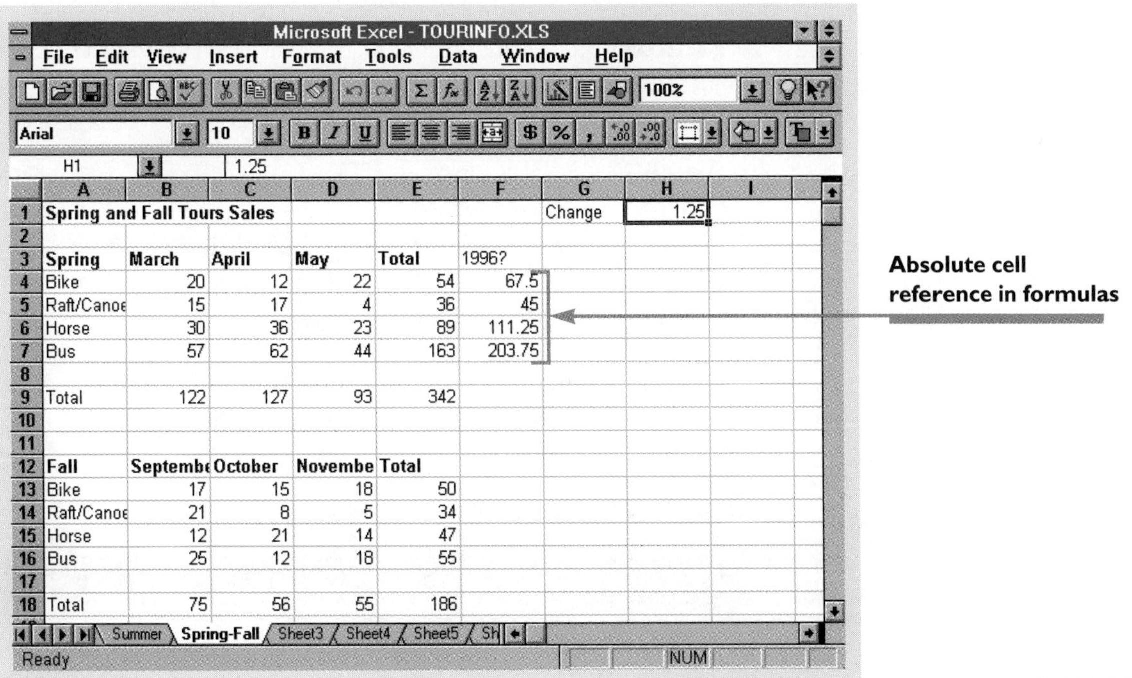

Microsoft Excel - TOURINFO.XLS

H1 1.25

	A	B	C	D	E	F	G	H	I
1	Spring and Fall Tours Sales						Change	1.25	
2									
3	Spring	March	April	May	Total	1996?			
4	Bike	20	12	22	54	67.5			
5	Raft/Canoe	15	17	4	36	45			
6	Horse	30	36	23	89	111.25			
7	Bus	57	62	44	163	203.75			
8									
9	Total	122	127	93	342				
10									
11									
12	Fall	Septembe	October	Novembe	Total				
13	Bike	17	15	18	50				
14	Raft/Canoe	21	8	5	34				
15	Horse	12	21	14	47				
16	Bus	25	12	18	55				
17									
18	Total	75	56	55	186				

Summer / Spring-Fall / Sheet3 / Sheet4 / Sheet5 / Sh

Ready NUM

Absolute cell reference in formulas

QUICK TIP

Before you copy or move a formula, check to see if you need to use an absolute cell reference.

Adjusting column widths

As you work with a worksheet, you might need to adjust the width of the columns to make your worksheet more usable. The default column width is 8.43 characters wide, a little less than one inch. With Excel, you can adjust the column width for one or more columns using the mouse or the Column command on the Format menu. Table 3-2 describes the commands available on the Format Column menu. You can also adjust the height of rows. See the related topic "Specifying row height" for more information. ▶ Evan notices that some of the labels in column A and the fall month names don't fit in the cells. He decides to adjust the widths of columns A, B, C, and D so that the labels fit in the cells.

1. **Position the pointer on the column line between the columns A and B**
   The pointer changes to ↔, as shown in Figure 3-15. Evan makes the column wider.
2. **Drag the line to the right until column A is wide enough to accommodate all of the Raft/Canoe label**
   Evan resizes the columns so they automatically accommodate the widest entry in a cell.
3. **Position the pointer on the column line between columns B and C until it changes to ↔, then double-click the left mouse button**
   The width of column B is automatically resized to fit the widest entry, in this case, September. This feature is called **AutoFit**. You use the Column Width command on the Format menu to adjust several columns to the same width.
4. **Select the C, D, and E column selector buttons (the gray boxes containing the column letters just above the worksheet)**
5. **Click Format on the menu bar, click Column, then click Width**
   The Column Width dialog box appears. See Figure 3-16. Move the dialog box, if necessary, by dragging it by its title bar so you can see the contents of the worksheet.
6. **Type 10 in the Column Width text box, then click OK**
   The column widths change to reflect the new settings. Evan is satisfied and decides to save his worksheet.
7. **Click the Save button on the Standard toolbar**

TABLE 3-2: Format Column commands

COMMAND	DESCRIPTION
Width	Sets the width to a specific number of characters
AutoFit Selection	Fits the widest entry
Hide	Hides column(s)
Unhide	Unhides column(s)
Standard Width	Resets to default widths

FIGURE 3-15: Preparing to change the column width

Mouse pointer between columns A and B

Microsoft Excel - TOURINFO.XLS

H1 | 1.25

	A	B	C	D	E	F	G	H	I
1	Spring and Fall Tours Sales						Change	1.25	
2									
3	Spring	March	April	May	Total	1996?			
4	Bike	20	12	22	54	67.5			
5	Raft/Canoe	15	17	4	36	45			
6	Horse	30	36	23	89	111.25			
7	Bus	57	62	44	163	203.75			
8									

FIGURE 3-16: Worksheet with Column Width dialog box

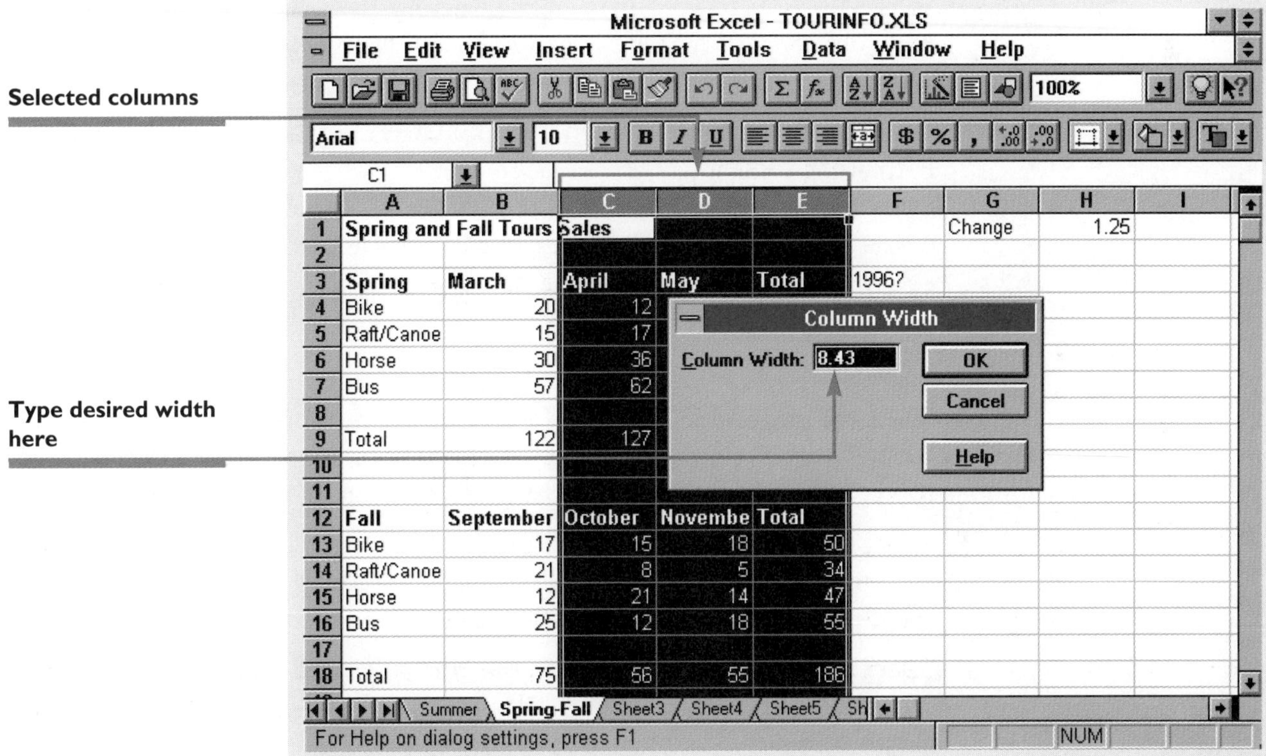

Specifying row height

The Row Height command on the Format menu allows you to customize row height to improve readability. Row height is calculated in **points**, units of measure also used for fonts—one inch equals 72 points. The row height must exceed the size of the font you are using. For example, if you are using a 12 point font, the row height must be more than 12 points. Normally, you don't need to adjust row heights manually. If you format something in a row to be a larger point size, Excel will adjust the row to fit the largest point size in the row.

QUICK TIP

To reset columns to the default width, select the range of cells, then use the Column Standard Width command on the Format menu. Click OK in the dialog box to accept the default width.

Formatting values

Formatting is how information appears in cells; it does not alter the data in any way. To format a cell, you select it, then apply the formatting you want. You can also format a range of cells. Cells and ranges can be formatted before or after data is entered. If you enter a value in a cell, and the cell appears to display the data incorrectly, you need to format the cell to display the value correctly. You might also want more than one cell to have the same format. For more information on how to do this, see the related topic, "Using the Format Painter." ▶ The Marketing Department has also requested that Evan track tour advertising expenses. Evan developed a worksheet that tracks invoices for tour advertising. He formatted some of the values in the worksheet, and now he needs to finish.

1. Open the worksheet UNIT_3-2.XLS from your Student Disk, then save it as TOUR_ADS to your MY_FILES directory
   Refer to the lesson "Opening an existing worksheet" in this unit if you need help. First, Evan wants to format the data in the Cost ea. column so it displays with a dollar sign.
2. Select the range **E4:E32**, then click the **Currency button** [$] on the Formatting toolbar
   Excel adds dollar signs and 2 decimal places to the Cost ea. column data. Columns G, H, and I contain dollar values also, but Evan doesn't want to repeat the dollar sign.
3. Select the range **G4:I32**, then click the **Comma button** [,] on the Formatting toolbar
   Column J contains percentages.
4. Select the range **J4:J32**, click the **Percentage button** [%] on the Formatting toolbar, then click the **Increase Decimal tool** [+.0 .00] to show 1 decimal place
   Data in the % of Total column is changed. Now Evan reformats the invoice dates.
5. Select the range **B4:B31**, click **Format** on the menu bar, then click **Cells**
   The Format Cells dialog box appears with the Number tab in front. See Figure 3-17. You can also use this dialog box to format ranges with currency, comma, and percentages.
6. Select the format **d-mmm-yy** in the Format Codes list box, then click **OK**
   The selected dates change in appearance, but they no longer fit in the cells. Evan also notices that the totals in row 32 of columns E and G are too wide for their cells. He needs to use AutoFit to widen these columns.
7. Position the pointer between columns B and C until it changes to ✛, then double-click the **left mouse button**; then double-click the **left mouse button** when ✛ is between columns E and F and between columns G and H
   Evan doesn't need the year to appear in the Inv Due column.
8. Select the range **C4:C31**, click **Format** on the menu bar, click **Cells**, click **d-mmm** in the Format Codes list box, then click **OK**
   Compare your worksheet to Figure 3-18. Now save the workbook.
9. Click the **Save button** [💾] on the Standard toolbar

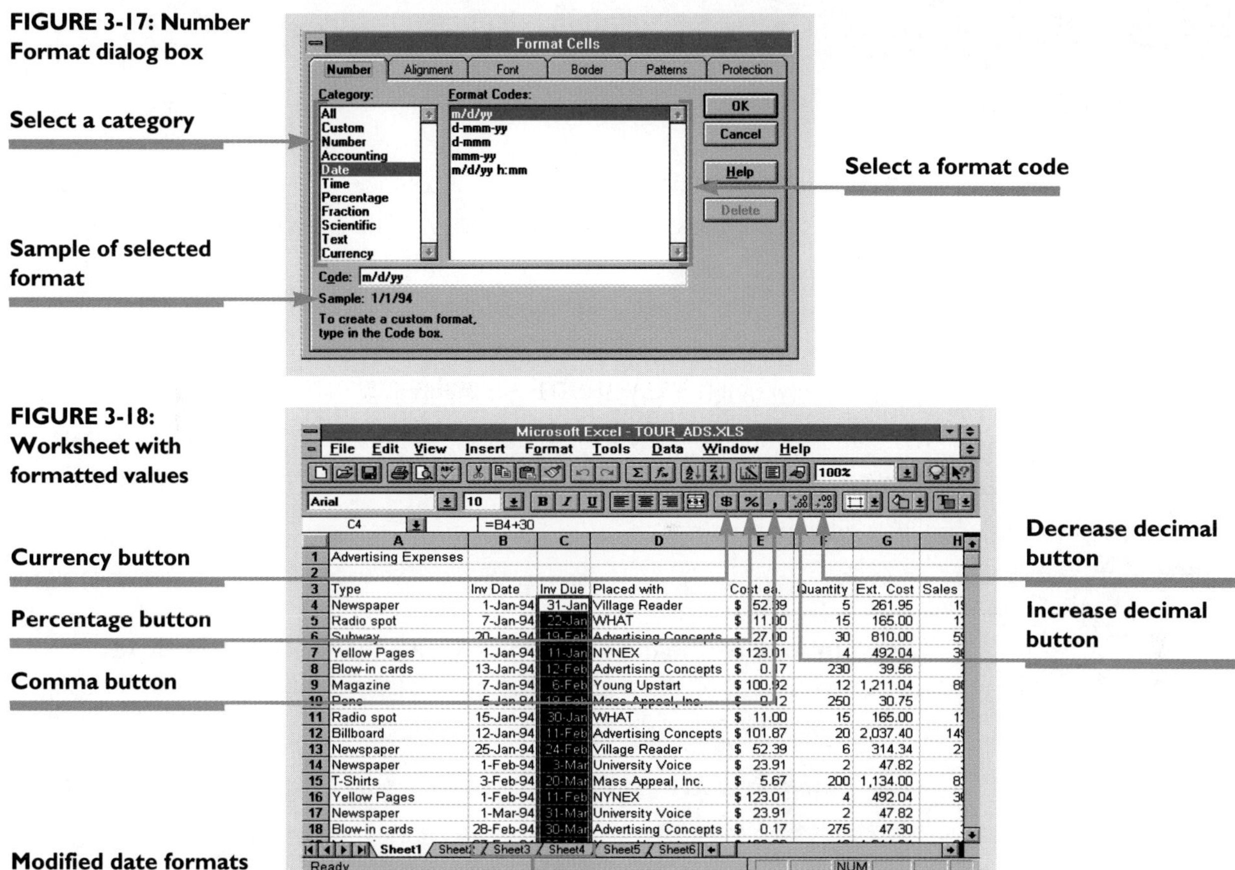

FIGURE 3-17: Number Format dialog box

FIGURE 3-18: Worksheet with formatted values

Using the Format Painter

A cell's format can be "painted" into other cells using the Format Painter button on the Formatting toolbar. This is similar to using drag-and-drop to copy information, but instead of copying cell contents, you copy only the cell format. Select the cell containing the desired format, then click . The pointer changes to , as shown in Figure 3-19. Use this pointer to select the cell or range you want to contain the painted format.

FIGURE 3-19: Using the Format Painter

Mouse pointer

Cell to be painted

Destination of painted format

TROUBLE?

If you don't see UNIT_3-2.XLS in the File Name list box in the Open dialog box, double-click the letter of the drive containing your Student Disk (probably drive A) in the Directories list box.

Formatting cell data with fonts and point sizes

A **font** is the name given to a collection of characters (letters, numerals, symbols, and punctuation marks) with a specific design. The **point size** is the physical size of the text, measured in points. The default font in Excel is 10 point Arial. You can change the font, the size, or both of any entry or section in a worksheet by using the Format command on the menu bar or by using the Formatting toolbar. See the related topic, "Using the Formatting toolbar to change fonts and sizes" for more information on that method. Table 3-3 shows several fonts in different sizes. ▶ Evan wants to change the font and size of these labels to make the title and labels stand out.

1. **Press [Ctrl][Home] to move to cell A1**
2. **Click Format on the menu bar, click Cells, then click the Font tab**
   See Figure 3-20. Evan decides to change the font of the title from Arial to Times New Roman, and he will increase the font size to 24.
3. **Click Times New Roman in the Font list box, then click 24 in the Size list box, then click OK**
   If you don't have Times New Roman in your list of fonts, choose another font. The title font appears in 24 point Times New Roman, and the Formatting toolbar displays the new font and size information. Next, Evan makes the labels larger.
4. **Select the range A3:J3, then click Format on the menu bar, then click Cells**
   The Font tab should still be the front-most tab.
5. **Click Times New Roman in the Font list box, click 14 in the Size list box, then click OK**
6. **Resize the column widths in columns A through J so the larger labels fit in their cells**
   Compare your worksheet to Figure 3-21.
7. **Click the Save button on the Standard toolbar to save your formatting changes**

TABLE 3-3: Types of fonts

FONT	12 POINT	24 POINT
Arial	Excel	Excel
Helvetica	Excel	Excel
Palatino	Excel	Excel
Times	Excel	Excel

FIGURE 3-20: Font tab of the Format Cells dialog box

Currently selected font

Available fonts on your computer

Sample of selected font

Effects options

Type a custom size or select a size from the list

Formatting attribute options

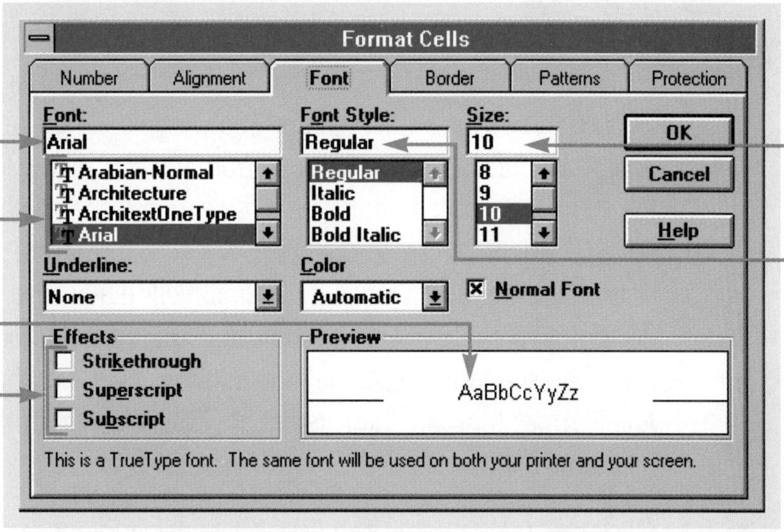

FIGURE 3-21: Worksheet with enlarged title and labels

Title after changing to 24 point Times New Roman

Column headings now 14 point Times New Roman

Font and size of active cell

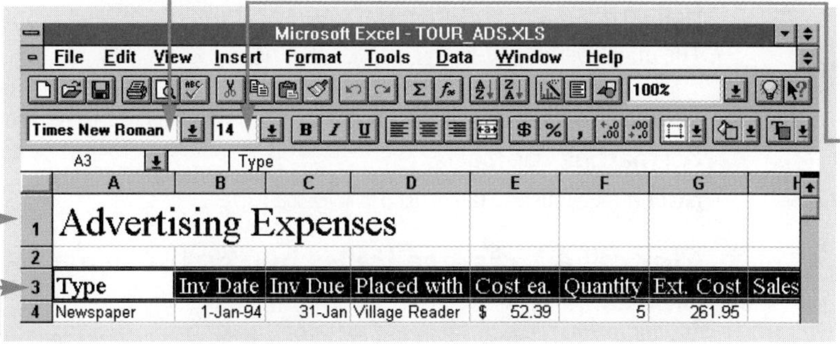

Using the Formatting toolbar to change fonts and sizes

The font and size of the active cell appear on the Formatting toolbar. Click the Font list arrow, as shown in Figure 3-22, to see a list of available fonts. If you want to change the font, first select the text, click the Font list arrow, then choose the font you want. You can change the size of selected text in the same way, but click the Size list arrow to display a list of available point sizes.

Font list arrow

Size list arrow

Available fonts installed on your computer

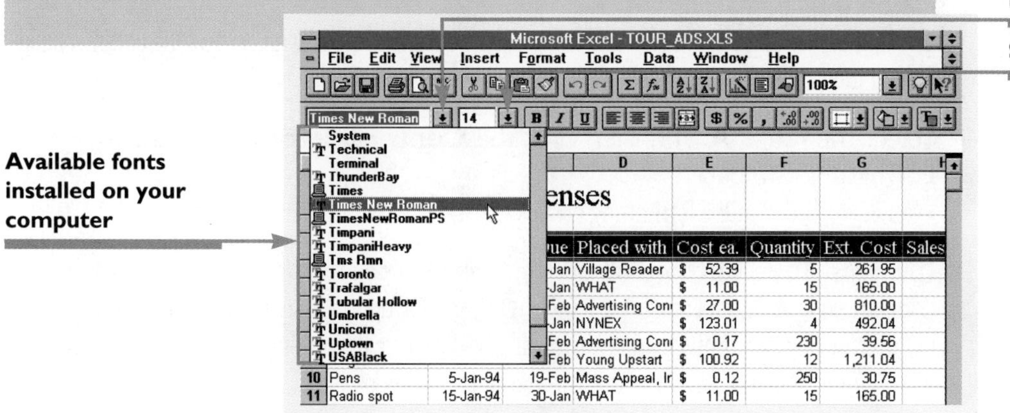

FIGURE 3-22: Available fonts on the Formatting toolbar

QUICK TIP

The Format cells dialog box displays a sample of the selected font. Use the Format Cells command if you're unsure of a font's appearance.

Formatting cell data with attributes and alignment

Attributes are styling features such as bold, italics, and underlining. You can apply bold, italics, and underlining from the Formatting toolbar or from the Font tab of the Format Cells dialog box. You can also change the alignment of text in cells. Left, right, or center alignment can be applied from the Formatting toolbar, or from the Alignment tab of the Format Cells dialog box. See Table 3-4 for a description of the available attribute and alignment buttons. Excel also has predefined worksheet formats to make formatting easier; See the related topic "Using AutoFormat" for more information. ▶ Evan wants to further refine his worksheet by adding bold and underline formatting and centering some of the labels.

1. **Click cell A1 to select the title Advertising Expenses, then click the Bold button on the Formatting toolbar**
   The title Advertising Expenses appears in bold.
2. **Select the range A3:J3, then click the Underline button on the Formatting toolbar**
   Excel underlines the labels in the selected range.
3. **Click cell A3, click the Italics button on the Formatting toolbar, then click**
   The word "Type" appears in boldface italic type. Notice that the Bold, Italics, and Underline buttons are depressed. Evan decides he doesn't like the italic formatting. He removes it by clicking again.
4. **Click**
   Excel removes italics from cell A3.
5. **Add bold formatting to the rest of the labels in the range B3:J3**
   Evan wants to center the title over the data.
6. **Select the range A1:F1, then click the Center Across Columns button on the Formatting toolbar**
   The title Advertising Expenses is centered across 6 columns. Now Evan centers the column headings in their cells.
7. **Select the range A3:J3, then click the Center button on the Formatting toolbar**
   Evan is satisfied with the formatting on this worksheet so he saves his changes.
8. **Click the Save button on the Standard toolbar**
   Compare your screen to Figure 3-23. Highlighting information on a worksheet can be useful, but overuse of any attribute can be distracting and make a document less readable. Be consistent, adding emphasis the same way throughout a workbook.
9. **Close the workbook then exit Excel**

FIGURE 3-23: Worksheet with formatting attributes applied

Center button

Tools depressed

Column headings centered, bold, and underlined

Title centered across columns

Using AutoFormat

Excel provides 16 preset formats called **AutoFormats**, which allow instant formatting of large amounts of data. AutoFormats are designed for worksheets with labels in the left column and top rows and totals in the bottom row or right column. To use AutoFormatting, select the data to be formatted, click Format on the menu bar, click AutoFormat, then select a format from the Table Format list box, as shown in Figure 3-24.

List of AutoFormats

Sample of selected AutoFormat

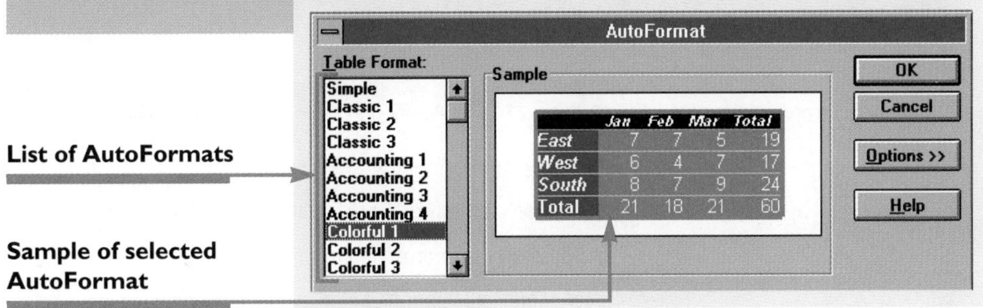

FIGURE 3-24: AutoFormat dialog box

TABLE 3-4: Formatting buttons

ICON	DESCRIPTION	ICON	DESCRIPTION
B	Adds boldface		Aligns left
I	Italicizes		Aligns center
U	Underlines		Aligns right
	Adds lines or borders		Centers across columns

QUICK TIP

When selecting a large, unnamed range, select the upper left-most cell in the range, press and hold [Shift], then click the lower right-most cell in the range.

CONCEPTSREVIEW

Label each of the elements of the Excel worksheet window shown in Figure 3-25.

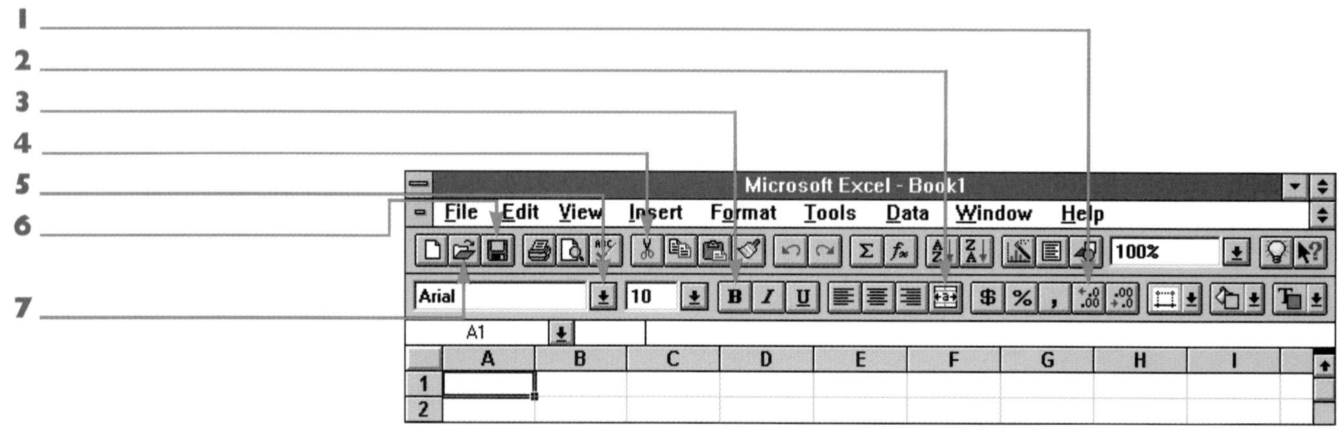

FIGURE 3-25

Match each of the statements to the command or button it describes.

8 Adds a new row or column

9 Erases the contents of a cell

10 Duplicates the contents of a cell

11 Changes the point size of selected cells

12 Pastes the contents of the Clipboard in the current cell

13 Changes the format to Currency

a. Format Cells

b. Edit Delete

c. Insert Row/Column

d.

e. $

f.

Select the best answer from the list of choices.

14 When you copy data using the Copy button, Excel puts the selected data on the

a. Border

b. Menu

c. Clipboard

d. Range

15 A cell address that changes when copied into a new location is called a(n)

a. Absolute reference

b. Relative reference

c. Mixed reference

d. Combined reference

16 Cell D4 contains the formula =A4+B4+C4. If you copy this formula to cell D5, what will the formula be in cell D5?

a. =$A$4+$B$4+$C$4

b. =A4+B4+C4-D4

c. =D5-D4

d. =A5+B5+C5

APPLICATIONSREVIEW

1 Adjust column widths.

a. Open a new workbook.

b. Enter the information from Table 3-5 in your worksheet.

c. Adjust all columns widths using the AutoFit feature.

d. Save this workbook as CHAIRS.XLS to the MY_FILES directory on your Student Disk.

TABLE 3-5

Country Oak Chairs, Inc.

Quarterly Sales Sheet

Description	Price	Sold	TOTALS
Rocker	1299	1104	
Recliner	800	1805	
Bar stool	159	1098	
Dinette	369	1254	

2 Format cell data with new fonts and point sizes.
   a. Select the range of cells containing the column titles.
   b. Change the font of the column titles to Times New Roman.
   c. Increase the point size of the column titles to 14 point.
   d. Resize columns as necessary.
   e. Select the range of values in the Price column.
   f. Click the Currency button.
   g. Save your workbook changes.

3 Copy and move formulas.
   a. Enter the formula B4*C4 in cell D4. Adjust the number formatting, as needed.
   b. Copy the formula in cell D4 to cells D5, D6, D7, and D8.
   c. Adjust column widths as necessary.
   d. Save your workbook changes.

4 Format cell data with attributes and alignment.
   a. Select the worksheet title Country Oak Chairs, Inc.
   b. Click the Bold button to apply boldface to the title.
   c. Select the label Quarterly Sales Sheet.
   d. Click the Underline button to apply underlining to the label.
   e. Select the range of cells containing the column titles.
   f. Click the Align Center button to center the column titles.
   g. Resize the column widths as necessary to fit the data.
   h. Save your changes, then preview, and print the workbook.

5 Insert a row.
   a. Insert a new row between rows 4 and 5.
   b. Add Country Oak Chairs' newest product—a Shaker bench in the newly inserted row. Enter 239 for the price and 360 for the number sold.
   c. Use the fill handle to copy the formula in cell D4 to D5.
   d. Save your changes, then preview and print the workbook.

6 Format values.
   a. Open a new workbook.
   b. Enter the information from Table 3-6 in your worksheet. Type "National Public Radio" contributions in cell A1, then type the values in the range A2:C7.
   c. Use the Currency format to format the numbers in the Pledged column.
   d. Use the Percent format with no decimal places for the numbers in the % Received column.
   e. Change the width of the City column to 14 characters.
   f. Make the worksheet title bold.
   g. Save your workbook as NPR.XLS to the MY_FILES directory on your Student Disk, then preview and print it.

TABLE 3-6
National Public Radio contributions

City	Pledged	% Received
Honolulu	63000	.75
New York	42000	.63
San Francisco	45750	.54
Boston	52950	.52
Seattle	60000	.81

7 Open an existing workbook.
   a. Open the file UNIT_3-3.XLS from your Student Disk.
   b. Save it as RECAP.XLS to the MY_FILES directory on your Student Disk.
   c. Use the Bold button and Center button to format the column heads and row titles.
   d. Increase the point size of the column headings in row 3 to 12 point.
   e. Save your changes.

8 Copy formulas with absolute references.
   a. Type "5.7%" in cell H3, then format this cell as a percentage with one decimal place.
   b. Enter the formula F4*$H$3 in cell G4.
   c. Copy the formula in cell G4 to G5:G9 using any method.
   d. Save your changes, then preview and print the workbook.
   e. Close the workbook then exit Excel.

INDEPENDENT CHALLENGE 1

Write Brothers is a Houston-based company that manufactures high-quality pens and markers. As the finance manager, one of your responsibilities is to analyze the monthly reports from your five district sales offices. Your boss, Joanne Parker, has just told you to prepare a quarterly sales report for an upcoming meeting. Since several top executives will be attending this meeting, Joanne reminds you that the report must look professional. In particular, she asks you to emphasize the company's surge in profits during the last month and to highlight the fact that the Northeastern district continues to outpace the other districts.

Plan and build a worksheet that shows the company's sales during the last three months. Make sure you include:

- The number of pens sold (units sold) and the associated revenues (total sales) for each of the five district sales offices. The five Write Brothers sales districts include: Northeastern, Midwestern, Southeastern, Southern, and Western.
- Calculations that show month-by-month totals and a three-month cumulative total.
- Calculations that show each district's share of sales (percent of units sold).
- Formatting enhancements to emphasize the recent month's sales surge and the Northeast district's sales leadership.

To complete this independent challenge:

1 Prepare a worksheet plan that states your goal, lists the worksheet data you'll need, and identifies the formulas for the different calculations.

2 Sketch a sample worksheet on a piece of paper, indicating how the information should be organized and formatted. How will you calculate the totals? What formulas can you copy to save time and keystrokes? Do any of these formulas need to use an absolute reference? How will you show dollar amounts? What information should be shown in bold? Do you need to use more than one font? More than one point size?

3 Build the worksheet with your own sales data. Enter the titles and labels first, then enter the numbers and formulas. Save the workbook as WRITE.XLS to the MY_FILES directory on your Student Disk.

4 Make enhancements to the worksheet. Adjust the column widths as necessary. Format labels and values, and change attributes and alignment.

5 Add a column that calculates a 10% increase in sales. Use an absolute cell reference in this calculation.

6 Before printing, preview the file so you know what the worksheet will look like. Adjust any items as needed, and print a copy. Save your work before closing the file.

7 Submit your worksheet plan, preliminary sketches, and the final printout.

INDEPENDENT CHALLENGE 2

As the new computer lab manager of your class, you are responsible for all the computer equipment used in your classroom. In addition to knowing the current hardware and software capabilities and approximate capital costs, you must also be concerned with the number of hours the equipment is used, whether you would like to make any upgrades prior to the next semester, and those approximate costs. Plan and build a workbook that details the hardware and software used in your classroom. Make sure you include:

- The number of units and number of hours used
- Calculations that show the approximate value of hardware by unit and within the room
- The installed software and its total calculated value
- A "wish list" of hardware and software upgrades and their respective costs
- Formatting enhancements that emphasize the items or highest priority

To complete this independent challenge:

1 Prepare a worksheet plan that states your goal, lists the worksheet data you'll need, and identifies the formulas for the different calculations.

2 Sketch a sample worksheet on a piece of paper, indicating how the information should be formatted. What calculations are required? Can any of the formulas be copied? Do any of the formulas require an absolute reference? How will you make the numbers easy to read? What information should be shown in bold? Do you need to use more than one font? More than one point size?

3 Build the worksheet with the data you have gathered. Estimate the costs of hardware and software if you are unsure. Enter the titles and labels first, then enter the numbers and formulas. Save the workbook as LABCOSTS.XLS to the MY_FILES directory on your Student Disk.

4 Make enhancements to the worksheet. Format labels and values, and change attributes and alignment.

5 Before printing, preview the file so you know what the worksheet will look like. Adjust any items as needed, and print a copy. Save your work before closing the file.

6 Submit your worksheet plan, preliminary sketches, and the final printout.

UNIT 4

OBJECTIVES

- Plan and design a chart
- Create a chart
- Edit a chart
- Move and resize a chart and its objects
- Change the appearance of a chart
- Enhance a chart
- Add text annotations and arrows to a chart
- Preview and print a chart

Working WITH CHARTS

Worksheets provide an effective way to organize information, but they are not always the best format for presenting data to others. Information in a selected range or worksheet can be easily converted to the visual format of a chart. Charts quickly communicate the relationships of data in a worksheet. In this unit, you will learn how to create a chart, edit a chart and change the chart type, add text annotations and arrows to a chart, then preview and print it. ▶ Evan Brillstein needs to create a chart showing the six-month sales history at Nomad Ltd for the Annual Meeting. He wants to illustrate the impact of an advertising campaign that started in June. ▶

Planning and designing a chart

Choosing a Chart Type

Before creating a chart, you need to plan what you want your chart to show and how you want it to look. ▶ Evan wants to create a chart to be used at the Annual Meeting. The chart will show the spring and summer sales throughout the Nomad Ltd regions. In early June, the Marketing Department launched a national advertising campaign. The results of the campaign were increased sales for the summer months. Evan wants his chart to illustrate this dramatic sales increase.

Evan uses the worksheet shown in Figure 4-1 and the following guidelines to plan the chart:

1 **Determine the purpose of the chart, and identify the data relationships you want to communicate visually**
Evan wants to create a chart that shows sales throughout Nomad's regions in the spring and summer months (March through August). He particularly wants to highlight the increase in sales that occurred in the summer months as a result of the advertising campaign.

2 **Determine the results you want to see and decide which chart type is most appropriate to use; Table 4-1 describes several different types of charts**
Because he wants to compare related data (sales in each of the regions) over a time period (the months March through August), Evan decides to use a column chart.

3 **Identify the worksheet data you want the chart to illustrate**
Evan is using data from his worksheet titled "Nomad Ltd Regions, Spring and Summer Sales," as shown in Figure 4-1. This worksheet contains the sales data for the five regions from March through August.

4 **Sketch the chart then use this sketch to decide where the chart elements should be placed**
Evan sketches his chart as shown in Figure 4-2. He puts the months on the horizontal axis (the **x-axis**) and the monthly sales figures on the vertical axis (the **y-axis**). The **tick marks** on the y-axis create a scale of measure for each value. Each value in a cell he selects for his chart is a **data point**. In any chart, each data point is visually represented by a **data marker**, which in this case is a column. A collection of related data points is a **data series**. In Evan's chart, there are five data series (Midwest, Northeast, Northwest, South, and Southwest) so he has included a **legend** to identify them.

FIGURE 4-1: Worksheet containing sales data

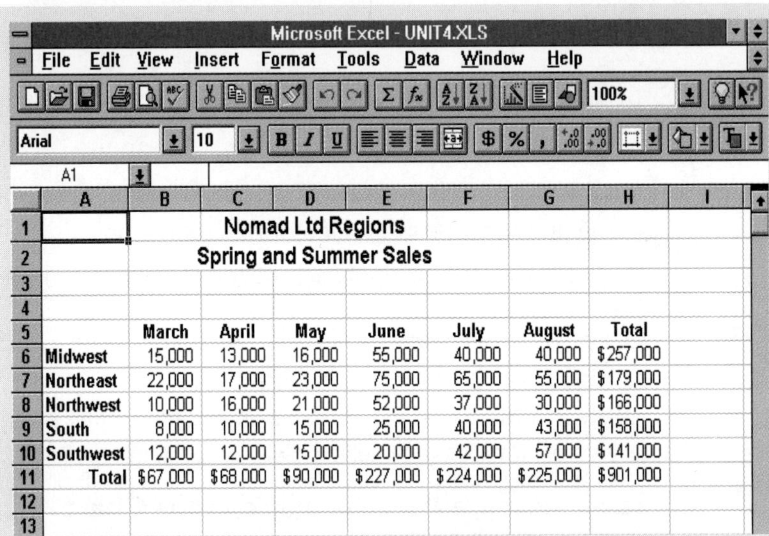

Microsoft Excel - UNIT4.XLS

File Edit View Insert Format Tools Data Window Help

	A	B	C	D	E	F	G	H
1			Nomad Ltd Regions					
2			Spring and Summer Sales					
3								
4								
5		March	April	May	June	July	August	Total
6	Midwest	15,000	13,000	16,000	55,000	40,000	40,000	$257,000
7	Northeast	22,000	17,000	23,000	75,000	65,000	55,000	$179,000
8	Northwest	10,000	16,000	21,000	52,000	37,000	30,000	$166,000
9	South	8,000	10,000	15,000	25,000	40,000	43,000	$158,000
10	Southwest	12,000	12,000	15,000	20,000	42,000	57,000	$141,000
11	Total	$67,000	$68,000	$90,000	$227,000	$224,000	$225,000	$901,000
12								
13								

FIGURE 4-2: Evan's sketch of the column chart

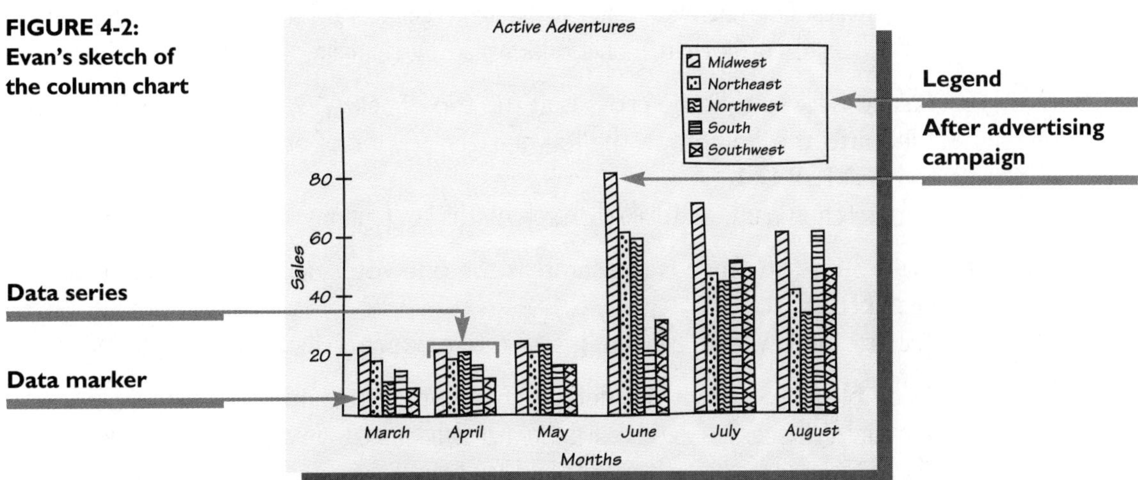

TABLE 4-1: Commonly used chart types

TYPE	BUTTON	DESCRIPTION
Area		Shows how volume changes over time
Bar		Compares distinct, unrelated objects over time using a horizontal format; sometimes referred to as a horizontal bar chart in other spreadsheet programs
Column		Compares distinct, unrelated objects over time using a vertical format; the Excel default; sometimes referred to as a bar chart in other spreadsheet programs
Line		Compares trends over even time intervals; similar to an area chart
Pie		Compares sizes of pieces as part of a whole; can have slices pulled away from the pie, or "exploded"
XY (scatter)		Compares trends over uneven time or measurement intervals; used in scientific and engineering disciplines for trend spotting and extrapolation
Combination	no button	Combines a column and line chart to compare data requiring different scales of measure

Creating a chart

To create a chart in Excel, you first select the range containing the data you want to chart. Once you've selected a range, you can use Excel's ChartWizard to lead you through the chart creation process. ▶ Using the worksheet containing the spring and summer sales data for the five regions, Evan will create a chart that shows the monthly sales of each region from March through August.

1 **Open the workbook UNIT_4-1.XLS from your Student Disk, then save it as REGIONS.XLS to the MY_FILES directory**
First, Evan needs to select the cells he wants to chart. He wants to include the monthly sales figures for each of the regions, but not the totals. He also wants to include the month and region labels.

2 **Select the range A5:G10, then click the ChartWizard button on the Standard toolbar**
When you click the ChartWizard button, the pointer changes to +. See Figure 4-3. This pointer draws the border of the chart. Evan decides to place the chart directly below the worksheet.

3 **Position + so that the cross is at the top of cell A13, as shown in Figure 4-3, then drag the pointer to the lower-right corner of cell H24 to select the range A13:H24**
The first of five ChartWizard dialog boxes opens. This box confirms the range of data to be charted.

4 **Make sure the range is the same as the one you selected in Step 2, then click Next**
The second ChartWizard dialog box lets you choose the type of chart you want to create.

5 **Click Next to accept the default chart type of column**
The third dialog box lets you choose the format of the chart. Evan wants each region to have a different color bar, so he again accepts the default choice.

6 **Click Next**
The fourth ChartWizard dialog box shows a sample chart using the data you selected. Notice that the regions (the *rows* in the selected range) are plotted according to the months (the *columns* in the selected range), and that the months were added as labels for each data series. You could switch this by clicking the Columns radio button below Data Series on the right side of the dialog box. Notice also that there is a legend showing each region and its corresponding color on the chart.

7 **Click Next**
In the last ChartWizard dialog box, you can choose to keep the legend, add a chart title, and add axis titles. Evan adds a title.

8 **Click in the Chart Title text box, then type Nomad Ltd Regional Sales**
After a moment, the title appears in the Sample Chart box. See Figure 4-4.

9 **Click Finish**
The column chart appears in the defined plot area, as shown in Figure 4-5. Your chart might look slightly different. Just as Evan had hoped, the chart shows the dramatic increase in sales between May and June. The **selection handles**, the small black squares at the corners and sides of the chart's border, indicate that the chart is selected. Anytime a chart is selected (as it is now), the Chart toolbar appears. It might be floating, as shown in Figure 4-5, or it might be fixed at the top of the worksheet window.

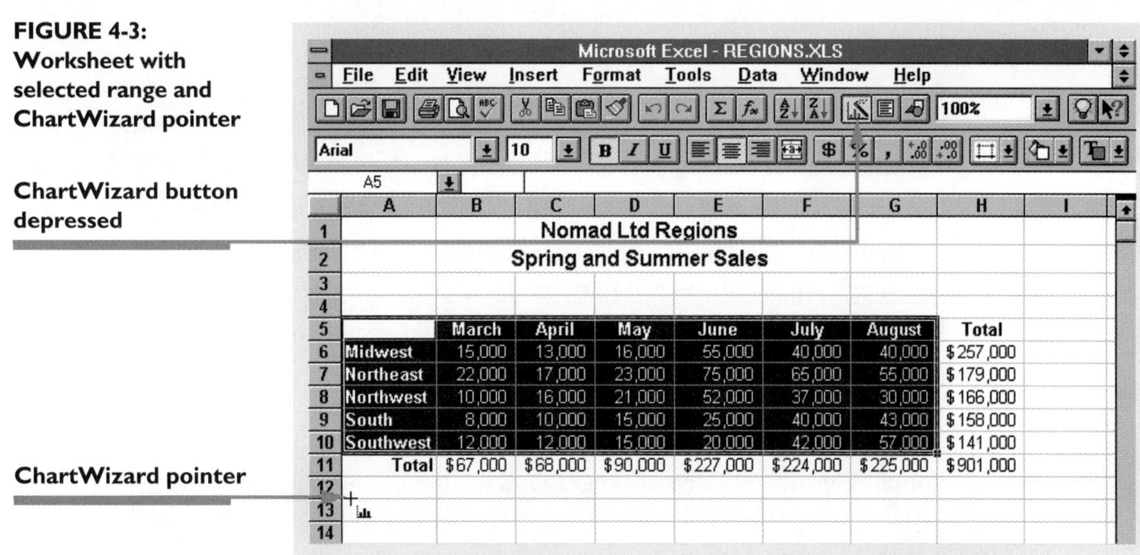

FIGURE 4-3: Worksheet with selected range and ChartWizard pointer

ChartWizard button depressed

ChartWizard pointer

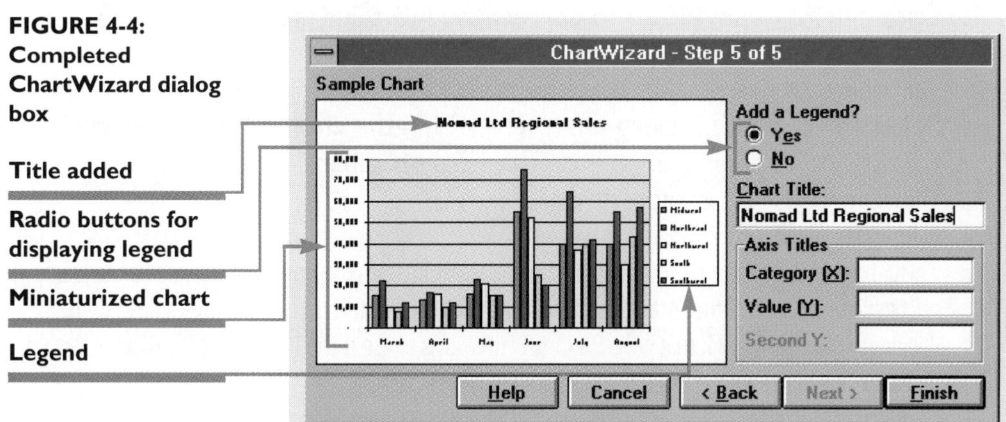

FIGURE 4-4: Completed ChartWizard dialog box

Title added

Radio buttons for displaying legend

Miniaturized chart

Legend

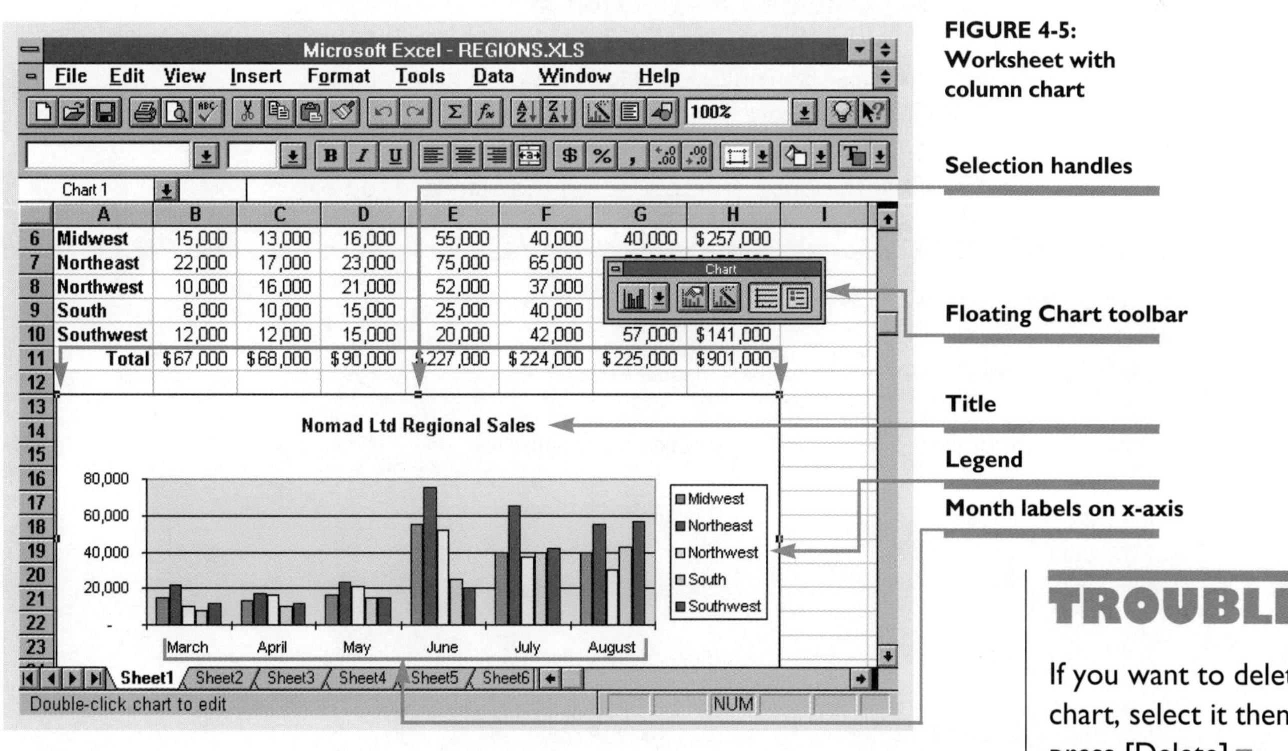

FIGURE 4-5: Worksheet with column chart

Selection handles

Floating Chart toolbar

Title

Legend

Month labels on x-axis

TROUBLE?

If you want to delete a chart, select it then press [Delete].

Editing a chart

Once you've created a chart, it's easy to modify it. You can change data values in the worksheet, and the chart will automatically be updated to reflect the new data. You can also easily change chart types using the buttons on the Chart toolbar. Table 4-2 shows and describes the Chart toolbar buttons. ▶ Evan looks over his worksheet and realizes he entered the wrong data for the Northwest region in July and August. After he corrects this data, he wants to find out what percentage of total sales the month of June represents. He will convert the column chart to a pie chart to find this out.

1. **Scroll the worksheet so that you can see both the chart and row 8, containing the Northwest region's sales figures, at the same time**
   As you enter the correct values, watch the columns for July and August in the chart change to reflect the new data values.
2. **Click cell F8, type 49000 to correct the July sales figure, press [→], type 45000 in cell G8, then press [Enter]**
   The Northwest columns for July and August reflect the increased sales figures. See Figure 4-6.
3. **Select the chart by clicking anywhere within the chart border, then click the Chart Type list arrow on the Chart toolbar**
   The chart type buttons appear, as shown in Figure 4-7.
4. **Click the 2-D Pie Chart button**
   The column chart changes to a pie chart showing total sales by month (the *columns* in the selected range). See Figure 4-8. Evan looks at the pie chart and takes some notes, and then decides to convert it back to a column chart. He wants to see if the large increase in sales would be better presented with a three-dimensional column chart.
5. **Click the Chart Type list arrow on the Chart toolbar, then click the 3-D Column Chart button**
   A three-dimensional column chart appears. The three-dimensional column format is too crowded, so Evan switches back to the two-dimensional format.
6. **Click the Chart Type list arrow on the Chart toolbar, then click the 2-D Column Chart button**
7. **Click the Save button on the Standard toolbar**

TABLE 4-2: Chart type buttons

BUTTON	DESCRIPTION	BUTTON	DESCRIPTION
	Displays 2-D area chart		Displays 3-D area chart
	Displays 2-D bar chart		Displays 3-D bar chart
	Displays 2-D column chart		Displays 3-D column chart
	Displays 2-D line chart		Displays 3-D line chart
	Displays 2-D pie chart		Displays 3-D pie chart
	Displays 2-D scatter chart		Displays 3-D surface chart
	Displays 2-D doughnut chart		Displays radar chart

FIGURE 4-6: Worksheet with new data entered for the Northwest region

New data

Adjusted data points

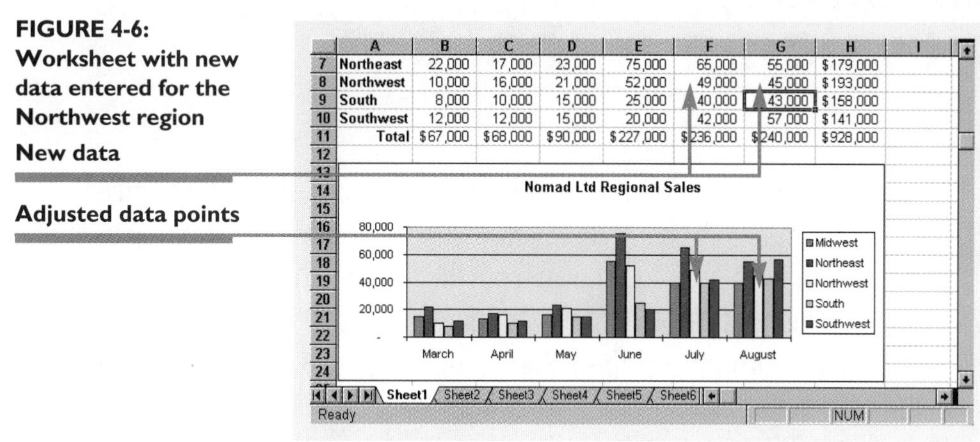

FIGURE 4-7: Chart Type list box

2-D Column Chart button

2-D Pie Chart button

3-D Column Chart button

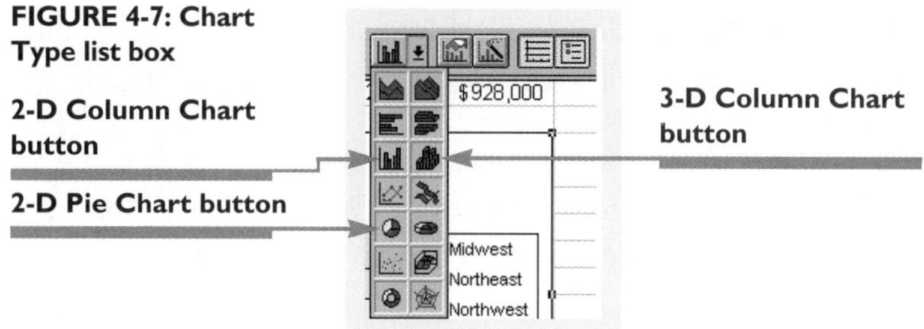

FIGURE 4-8: Pie chart

June sales pie slice

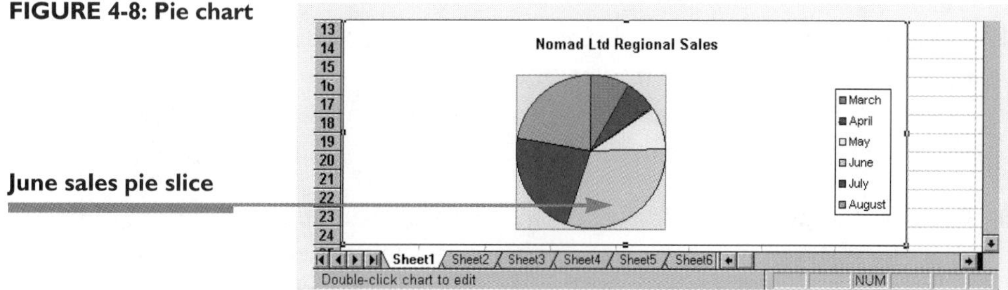

Rotating a chart

In a three-dimensional chart, columns or bars can sometimes be obscured by other data series within the same chart. You can rotate the chart until a better view is obtained. Double-click the chart, click the tip of one of its axes, then drag the handles until a more pleasing view of the data series appears. See Figure 4-9.

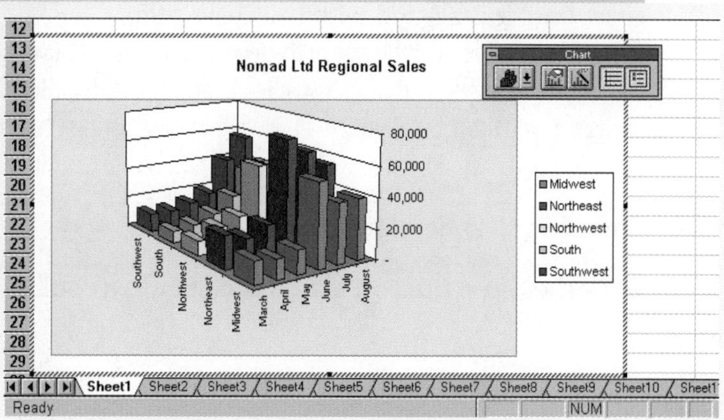

FIGURE 4-9: 3-D chart rotated with improved view of data series

Moving and resizing a chart and its objects

Charts are graphics, or drawn **objects**, and have no specific cell or range address. You can move charts anywhere on a worksheet without affecting formulas or data in the worksheet. You can even put them on another sheet. See the related topic "Viewing multiple worksheets" for more information. You can also easily resize a chart to improve its appearance by dragging the selection handles. Charts contain many elements—each is a separate object that you can move and resize. To move an object, select it then drag it or cut and copy it to a new location. To resize an object, use the selection handles. ▶ Evan wants to increase the size of the chart and center it on the worksheet. He also wants to move the legend up so that it is level with the title.

1. **Select the chart, scroll the worksheet until row 31 is visible, then position the pointer over the bottom center selection handle until the pointer changes to ↕**
   The pointer shape ↕ indicates that you can use a selection handle to resize the chart.
2. **Press and hold the mouse button, drag the lower edge of the chart to row 31, then release the mouse button**
   A dotted outline of the chart perimeter appears as the chart is being moved, and the pointer changes to +. The chart length is increased.
3. **Position the pointer over one of the selection handles on the right, then drag the chart about 1/2" to the right to the middle of column I**
   See Figure 4-10. Now, Evan moves the legend up so that it is level with the chart title.
4. **Double-click the chart**
   The chart is now in Edit mode. When the chart is in **Edit mode**, you can change elements within the chart border. When the chart is selected but not in Edit mode, you can move and resize the entire chart. In Edit mode, the border changes to a blue outline (shown in Figure 4-9) or the chart appears in its own window, and the menu bar changes to the Chart menu bar.
5. **Click the legend to select it, then drag it to the upper-right corner of the chart until it is aligned with the chart title**
   If the Chart toolbar is in the way of the legend, move it out of your way first. Selection handles appear around the legend when you click it, and a dotted outline of the legend perimeter appears as you drag. See Figure 4-11. Note that the floating Chart toolbar was moved to the other side of the window to move it out of the way of the repositioned legend.
6. **Press [Esc] to deselect the legend**
7. **Click the Save button on the Standard toolbar**

FIGURE 4-10: Worksheet with resized and centered chart

Lengthened to row 31

Widened to column I

FIGURE 4-11: Worksheet with repositioned legend

Chart menu bar

Repositioned legend

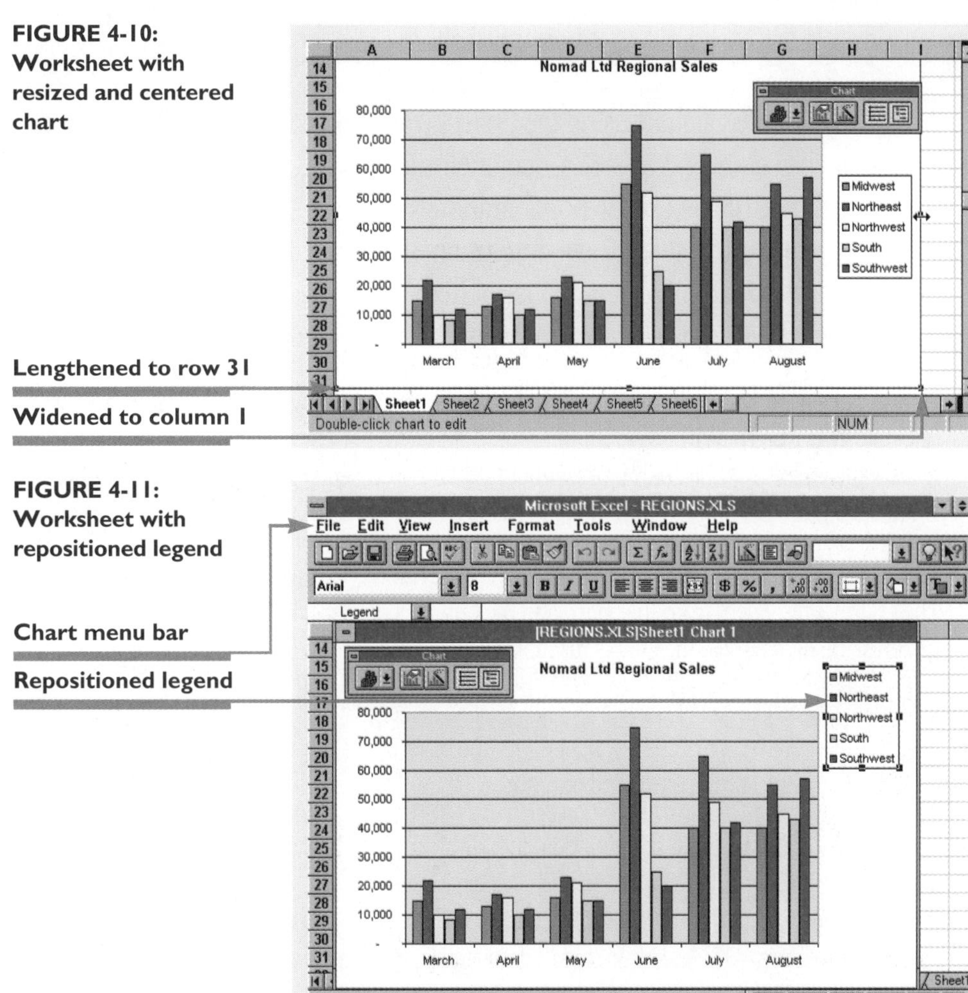

Viewing multiple worksheets

A workbook can be organized with a chart on one sheet and the data on another sheet. With this organization, you can still see the data next to the chart by opening multiple windows of the same workbook. This allows you to see portions of multiple sheets at the same time. Click Window on the menu bar, then click New Window. A new window containing the current workbook opens. To see the windows next to each other, click Window on the menu bar, click Arrange, then choose one of the options in the Arrange Windows dialog box. You can open one worksheet in one window and a different worksheet in the second window. See Figure 4-12. To close one window without closing the worksheet, double-click the control menu box on the window you want to close.

Individual window title bars

Active sheet tabs

FIGURE 4-12: Workbook with two windows open

Changing the appearance of a chart

After you've created a chart using the ChartWizard, you can use the Chart toolbar to change the colors of data series, add or eliminate a legend, and add or delete gridlines. **Gridlines** are the horizontal lines in the chart that enable the eye to follow the value on an axis. These buttons are listed in Table 4-3. ▶ Evan wants to make some changes in the appearance of his chart. He wants to see if the chart looks better without gridlines, and he wants to change the color of a data series.

1 Make sure the chart is still in Edit mode—that it has a blue border around it or is in its own window
Evan wants to see how the chart looks without gridlines. Currently gridlines appear and the Gridlines button on the Chart toolbar is depressed.

2 Click the **Gridlines button** on the Chart toolbar
The gridlines disappear from the chart, and the button is deselected. Evan decides that the gridlines are necessary to the chart's readability.

3 Click again
The gridlines reappear. Evan is not happy with the color of the columns for the South data series and would like the columns to stand out more.

4 With the chart in Edit mode, double-click any column in the South data series
Handles appear on all the columns in the series, and the Format Data Series dialog box opens, as shown in Figure 4-13. Make sure the Patterns tab is the front-most tab.

5 Click the **yellow box** (in the first row, third from the right), then click **OK**
All the columns in the series are yellow. Compare your finished chart to Figure 4-14. Evan is pleased with the change.

6 Click the **Save button** on the Standard toolbar

TABLE 4-3: Chart enhancement buttons

BUTTON	USE
	Adds or deletes gridlines
	Adds or deletes legend
	Returns you to the ChartWizard

FIGURE 4-13: Format Data Series dialog box

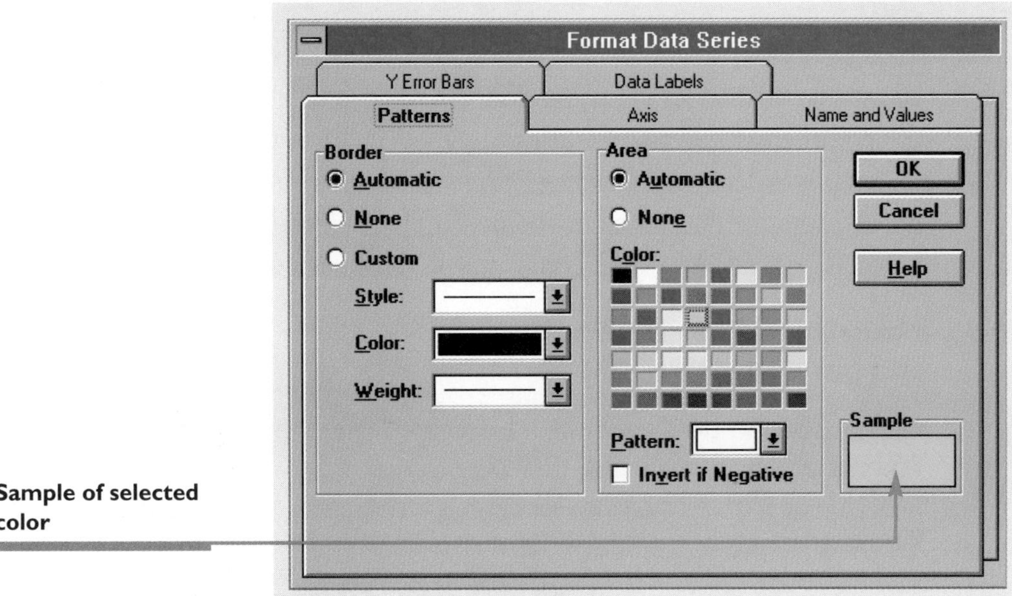

Sample of selected color

FIGURE 4-14: Chart with formatted data series

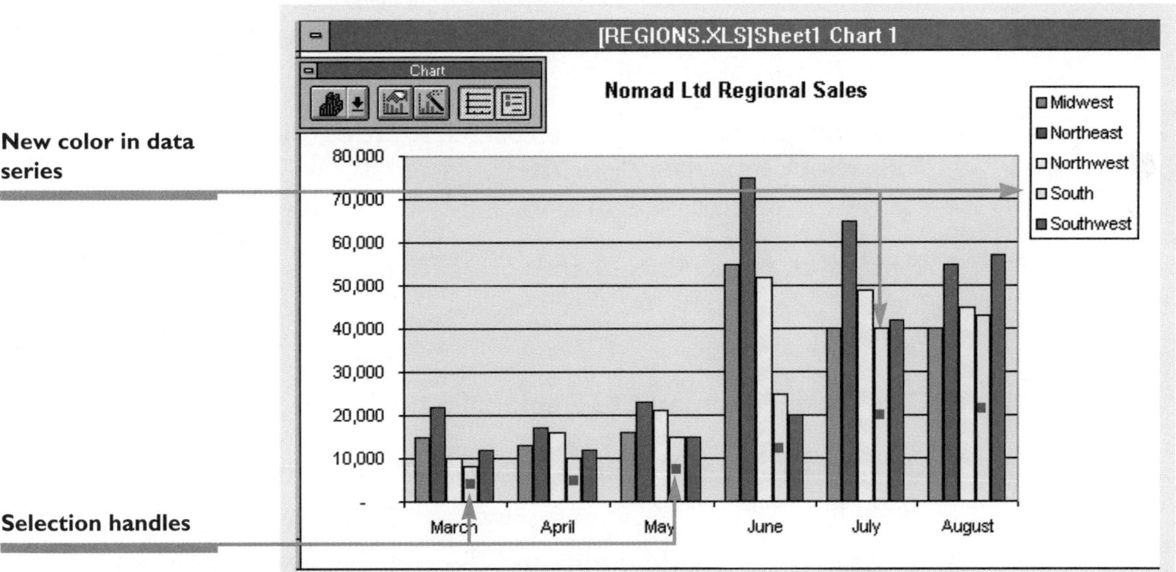

New color in data series

Selection handles

QUICK TIP

Experiment with different formats for your charts until you get just the right look.

Enhancing a chart

There are many ways to enhance a chart to make it easier to read and understand. You can create titles for the x-axis and y-axis, add graphics, or add background color. You can even format the text you use in a chart. See the related topic "Changing text font and alignment in charts" for more information. ▶ Evan wants to improve the appearance of his chart by creating titles for the x-axis and y-axis. He also decides to add a drop shadow to the title.

1 **Make sure the chart is in Edit mode**
Evan wants to add descriptive text to the x-axis.

2 Click **Insert** on the Chart menu bar, click **Titles**, click the **Category (X) Axis check box**, then click **OK**
A text box with selection handles around it and containing an "X" appears below the x-axis, as shown in Figure 4-15.

3 Type **Months** then click the **Enter button** on the formula bar
The word "Months" appears below the month labels. If you wanted to move the axis title to a new position, you could click on an edge of the selection and drag it. If you wanted to edit the axis title, position the pointer over the selected text box until it becomes I and click, then edit the text. Evan now adds text to the y-axis.

4 Click **Insert** on the Chart menu bar, click **Titles**, click the **Value (Y) Axis check box**, then click **OK**
A selected text box containing a "Y" appears to the left of the y-axis.

5 Type **Sales**, press **[Enter]**, then press **[Esc]** to deselect it
The word "Sales" appears to the left of the regions. Next Evan decides to add a drop shadow to the title.

6 Click the title **Nomad Ltd Regional Sales** to select it

7 Click the **Drawing button** on the Standard toolbar
The Drawing toolbar appears.

8 Click the **Drop Shadow button** on the Drawing toolbar, then press **[Esc]** to deselect the title
A drop shadow appears around the title. See Figure 4-16.

9 Click then click the **Save button** on the Standard toolbar
The Drawing toolbar no longer appears, and the chart is saved.

FIGURE 4-15: Chart with selected text box

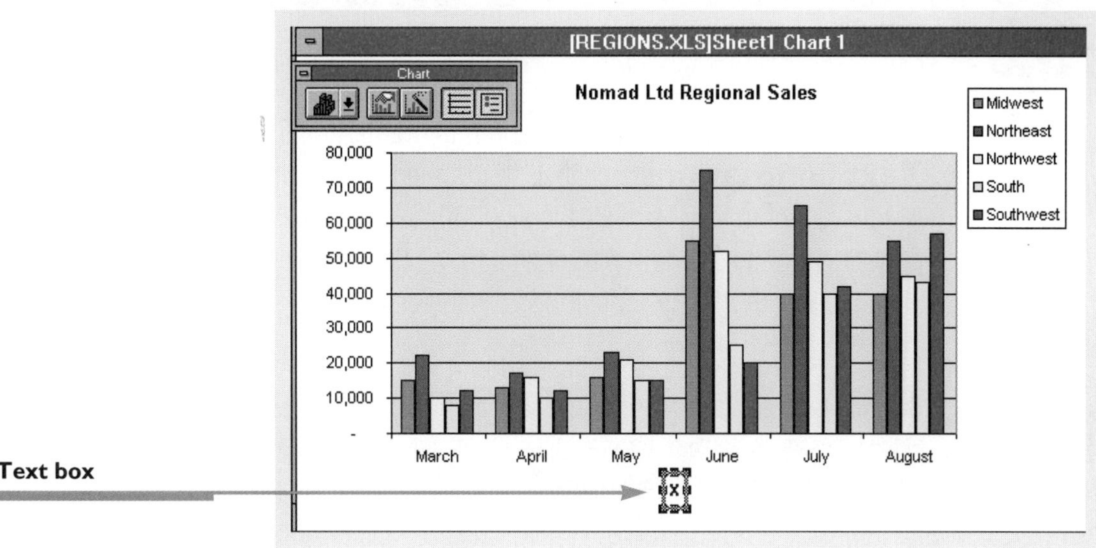

FIGURE 4-16: Enhanced chart

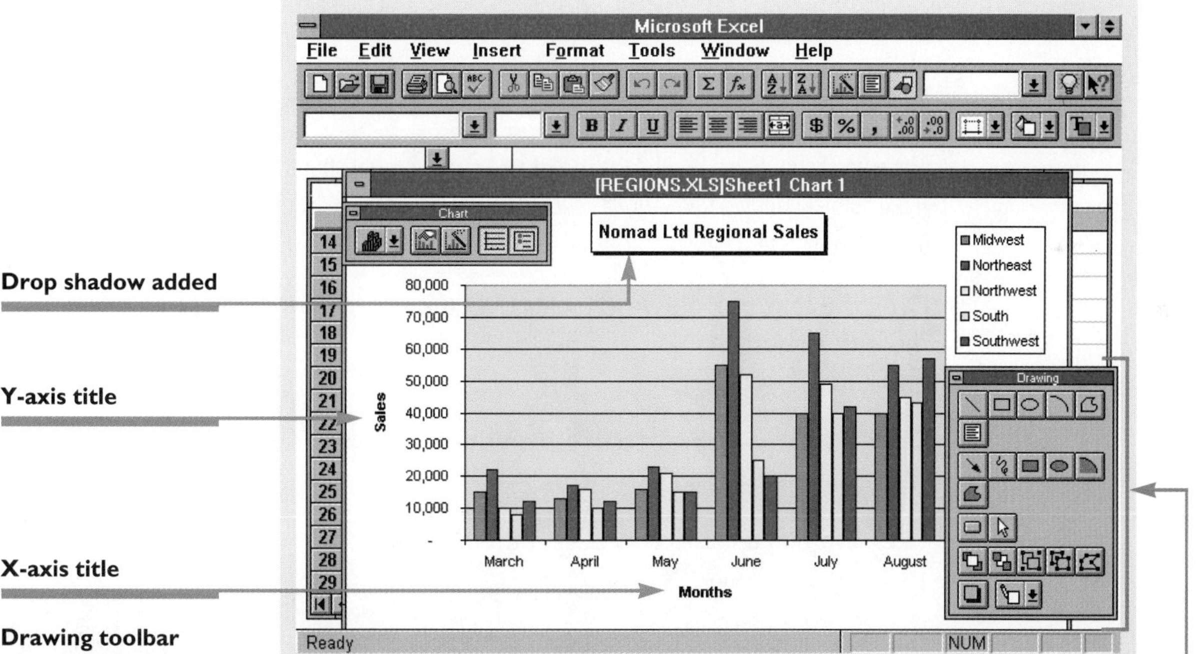

Changing text font and alignment in charts

The font and the alignment of axis text can be modified to make it more readable or to better fit within the plot area. With a chart in Edit mode, double-click the text to be modified. The Format Axis dialog box appears. Click the Font or the Alignment tab, make the desired changes, then click OK.

Adding text annotations and arrows to a chart

You can add arrows and text annotations to highlight information in your charts. **Text annotations** are labels that you add to a chart to draw attention to a certain part of it. See the related topic "Pulling out a pie slice" for another way to draw attention to a certain part of a chart. ▶ Evan wants to add a text annotation and an arrow to highlight the June sales increase.

1 Make sure the chart is in Edit mode

Evan wants to call attention to the June sales increase by drawing an arrow that points to the top of the June data series with the annotation, "After advertising campaign." To enter the text for an annotation, you simply start typing.

2 Type **After advertising campaign**, then click the **Enter button** on the formula bar

As you type, the text appears in the formula bar. After you confirm the entry, the text appears in a selected text box within the chart window. See Figure 4-17. Your text box might be in a different location on your screen.

3 Point to an edge of the text box, then press and hold the **left mouse button**

The pointer should be and the message in the status bar should say "Move selected objects." If the pointer changes to I or ↔, release the mouse button, click outside the text box area to deselect it, then select the text box and repeat Step 3.

4 Drag the text box above the chart, as shown in Figure 4-18, then release the mouse button

Evan is ready to add an arrow.

5 Click the **Drawing button** on the Standard toolbar

The Drawing toolbar appears.

6 Click the **Arrow button** on the Drawing toolbar

The pointer changes to +.

7 Position + under the word **campaign** in the text box, click the **left mouse button**, drag the line to the June sales, then release the mouse button

An arrowhead appears pointing to the June sales. Compare your finished chart to Figure 4-18.

8 Close the Drawing toolbar then click the **Save button** on the Standard toolbar

FIGURE 4-17: Chart with new text box

Drawing button

Move text box here

Selected floating text box

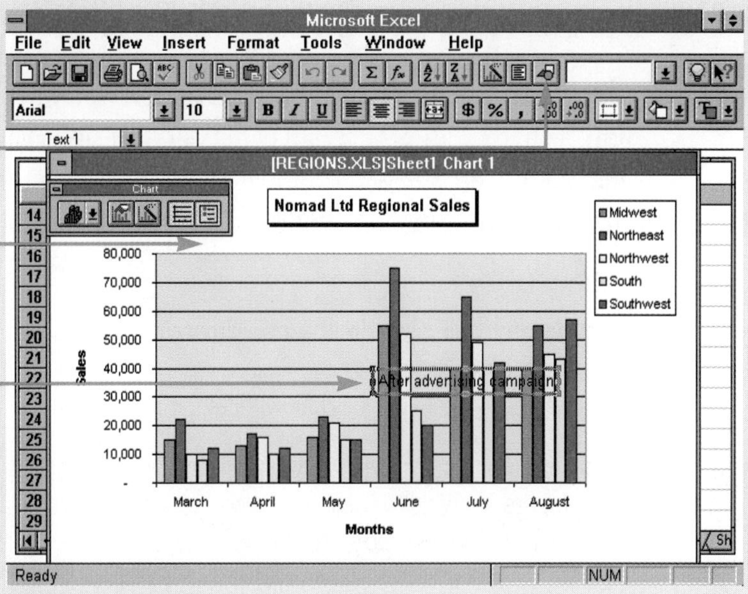

FIGURE 4-18: Completed chart with text annotation and arrow

Text annotation

Arrow

June sales

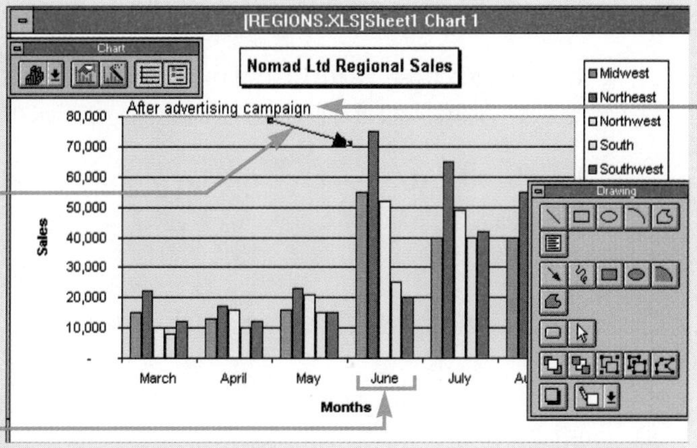

Pulling out a pie slice

Just as an arrow can call attention to a data series, you can emphasize a pie slice by **exploding** it, or pulling it away, from the pie chart. Once the chart is in Edit mode, click the pie to select it, click the desired slice to select only the slice, then drag the slice away from the pie, as shown in Figure 4-19.

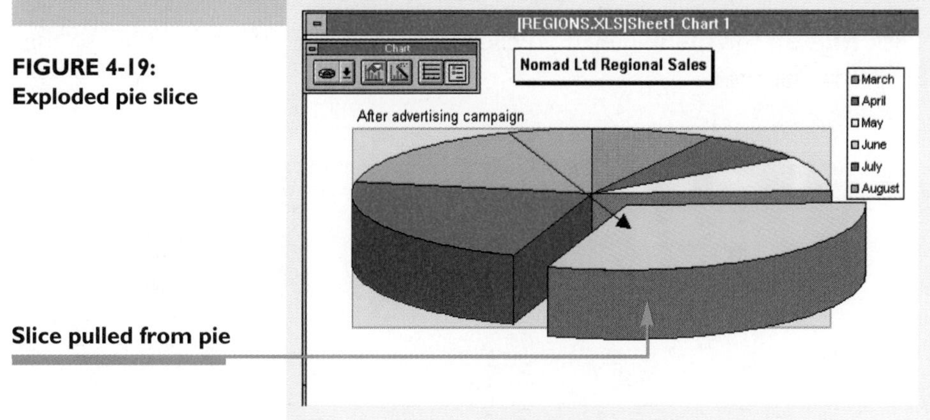

FIGURE 4-19: Exploded pie slice

Slice pulled from pie

QUICK TIP

You can insert text and an arrow in the data section of a worksheet by clicking the Text Box button on the Standard toolbar, drawing a text box, then typing the text and then adding the arrow.

Previewing and printing a chart

After you complete a chart to your satisfaction, you will need to print it. You can print a chart by itself, or as part of the worksheet. ▶ Evan is satisfied with the chart and wants to print it for the Annual Meeting. He will print the worksheet and the chart together, so that the shareholders can see the actual sales numbers for each tour type.

1 Click in any cell outside the chart to turn off Edit mode, then click outside the chart to deselect it
If you wanted to print only the chart without the data, you would leave the chart in Edit mode.

2 Click the **Print Preview button** on the Standard toolbar
The Print Preview window opens. Evan decides that the chart and data would look better if they were printed in **landscape** orientation—that is, with the page turned sideways. To change the orientation of the page, you must alter the page setup.

3 Click **Setup** to display the Page Setup dialog box, then click the **Page tab**

4 Click the **Landscape radio button** in the Orientation section
See Figure 4-20. Evan would also like to eliminate the gridlines that appear in the data.

5 Click the **Sheet tab** then click the **Gridlines check box** to deselect it
The chart and data will print too far over to the left of the page. Evan changes this using the Margins tab.

6 Click the **Margins tab**, double-click the **Left text box**, type **2.25**, then click **OK**
The print preview of the worksheet appears again. The data and chart are centered on the page that is turned sideways, and no gridlines appear. See Figure 4-21. Evan is satisfied with the way it looks and prints it.

7 Click **Print** to display the Print dialog box, then click **OK**
Your printed report should look like the image displayed in the Print Preview window.

8 Click the **Save button** on the Standard toolbar, click **File** on the menu bar, then click **Close**
Your workbook and chart close.

9 Click **File** on the menu bar, then click **Exit** to exit Excel and return to the Program Manager

FIGURE 4-20: Page tab of the Page Setup dialog box

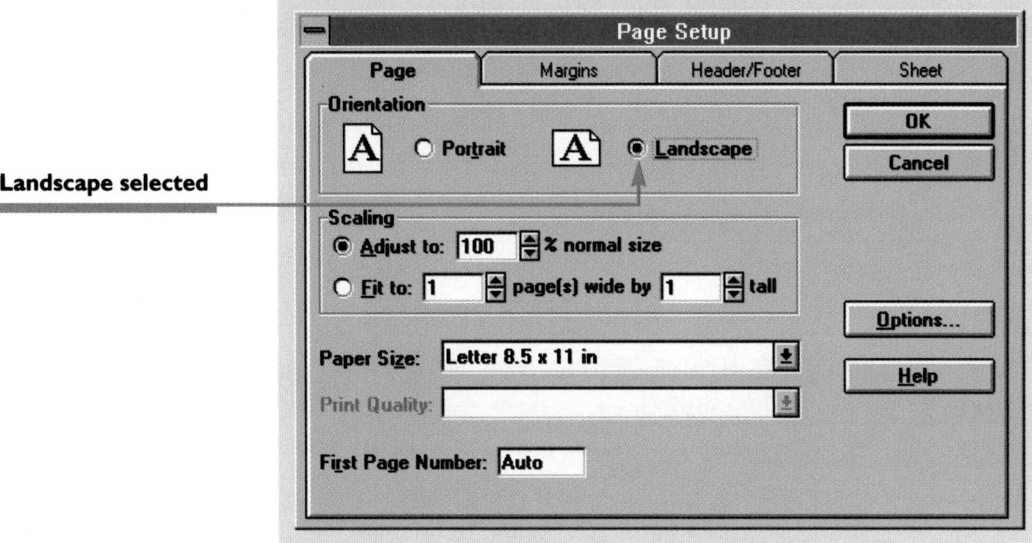

FIGURE 4-21: Chart and data ready to print

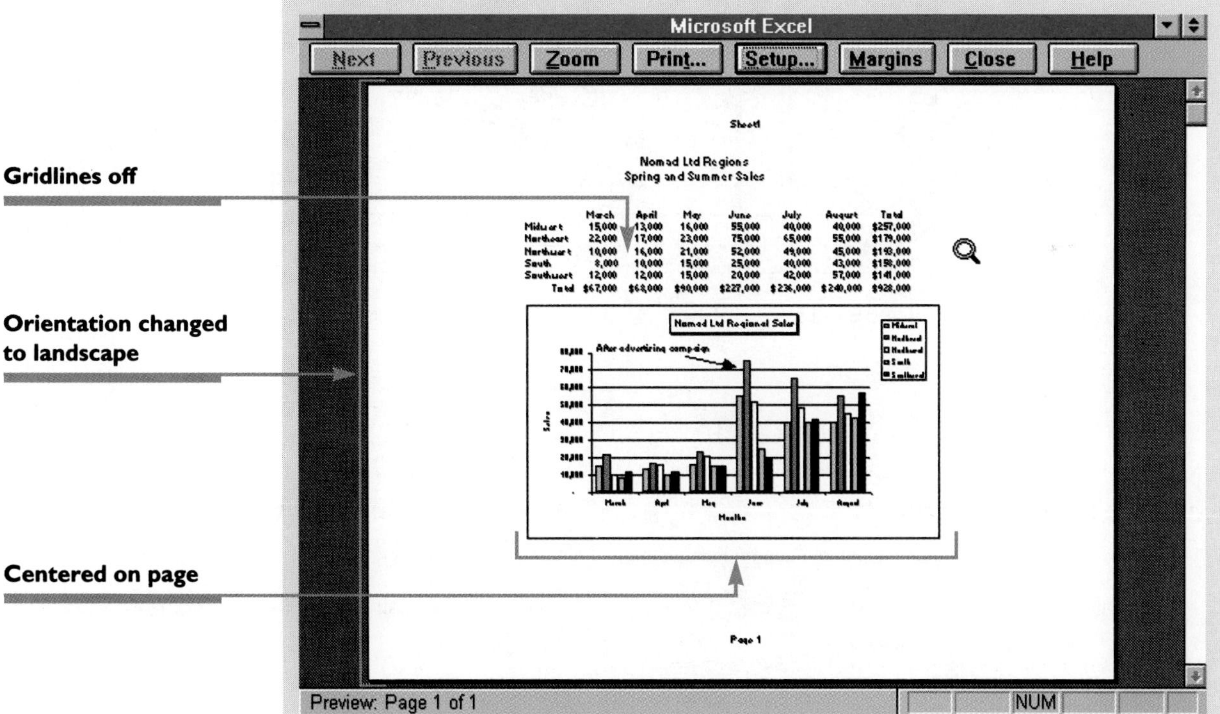

You can print charts and worksheets on transparencies for use on an overhead projector.

CONCEPTS REVIEW

Label each of the elements of the Excel chart shown in Figure 4-22.

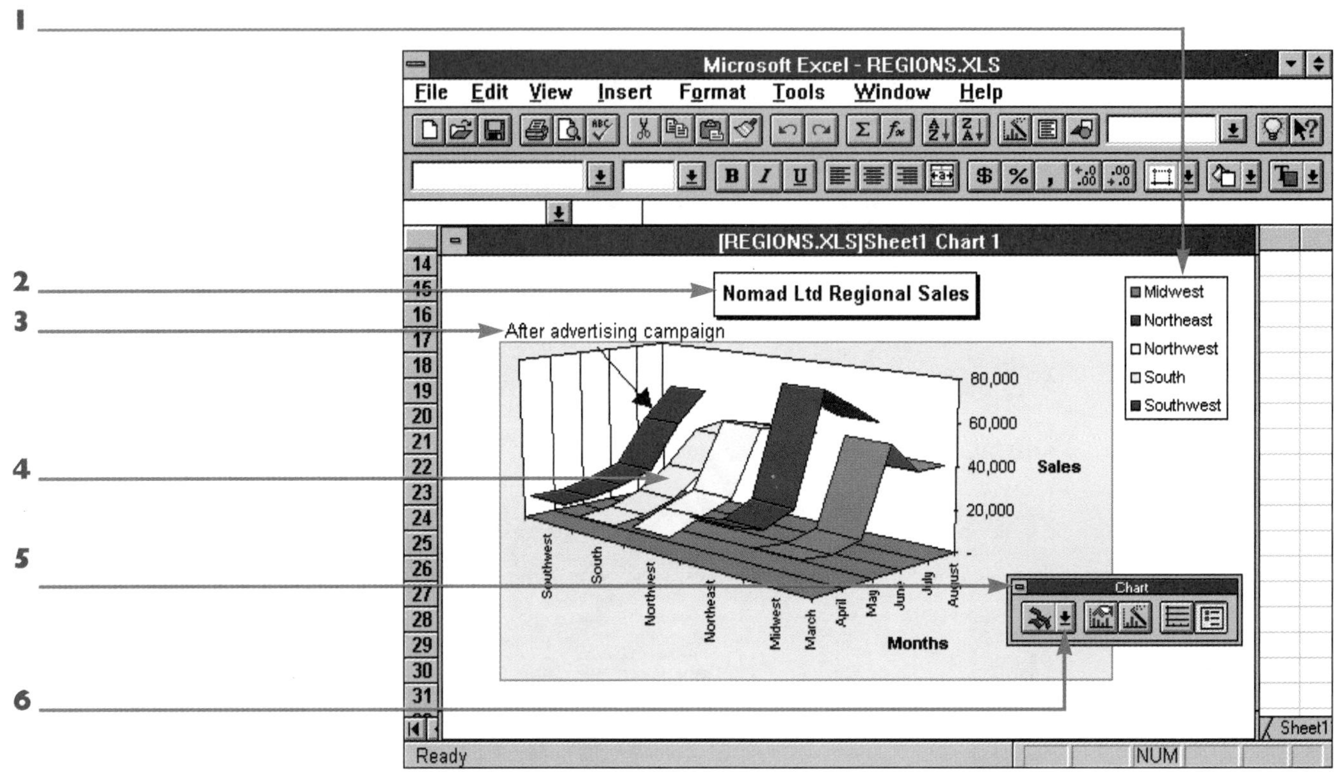

FIGURE 4-22

Match each of the statements with its chart type.

7 Shows how volume changes over time

8 Compares data as parts of a whole

9 Displays a column and line chart using different scales of measurement

10 Compares trends over even time intervals

11 Compares data over time—the Excel default

a. Column
b. Area
c. Pie
d. Combination
e. Line

Select the best answer from the list of choices.

12 The box that identifies patterns used for each data series is a
- a. Data point
- b. Plot
- c. Legend
- d. Range

13 What is the term for a row or column on a chart?
- a. Range address
- b. Axis titles
- c. Chart orientation
- d. Data series

14 The first step when creating a chart is to

a. Click Chart on the Insert menu

b. Select a cell

c. Select a range

d. Click the ChartWizard button on the Standard toolbar

15 The button used to add a drop shadow is

a. [button icon]

b. [button icon]

c. [button icon]

d. [button icon]

APPLICATIONSREVIEW

1 Create a distribution report worksheet, then create a column chart.

a. Start Excel, open a new workbook, then save it as SOFTWARE.XLS to the MY_FILES directory on your Student Disk.

b. Enter the information from Table 4-4 in your worksheet in range A1:E6. Resize columns and rows as necessary.

TABLE 4-4

	Excel	Word	WordPerfect	PageMaker
Accounting	10	1	9	0
Marketing	2	9	0	6
Engineering	12	5	7	1
Personnel	2	2	2	1
Production	6	3	4	0

c. Save your work.

d. Select all the entered information, then click the ChartWizard button.

e. Select the range in the worksheet where you want to insert the chart.

f. Complete the ChartWizard dialog boxes and build a two-dimensional column chart with a different color bar for each department and with the title "Software Distribution by Department."

g. Drag the selection handles of the chart so it fills your screen.

h. Save your work.

2 Edit a chart and change the chart type.

a. Change the value in cell B3 to 6 .

b. Select the chart by clicking on it.

c. Click the Chart Type list arrow on the Chart toolbar.

d. Click the 3-D Column Chart button in the list.

e. Save your work.

3 Add a text annotation and an arrow to the current chart.

a. Double-click the chart to put it in Edit mode.

b. Create the text annotation "Need More Computers."

c. Drag the text annotation about 1" above any of the Personnel bars.

d. Click the Arrow button on the Draw toolbar.

e. Click below the text annotation, drag down to the top of any one of the Personnel bars, then release the mouse button.

f. Add arrows from the text annotation to each of the remaining Personnel bars.

g. Save your work.

4 Enhance a chart.

a. Make sure the chart is still in Edit mode, then click Insert on the menu bar, click Titles, click the Category (X) Axis check box, then click OK.

b. Type "Department" in the selected text box below the x-axis, then click the Enter button on the formula bar.

c. Click Insert on the menu bar, click Titles, select Value (Y) Series check box, then click OK.

d. Type "Types of Software" in the selected text box to the left of the y-axis, then click the Enter button on the formula bar.

e. Save your work.

5 Change the appearance of a chart.

a. Make sure the chart is still in Edit mode.

b. Click the Gridlines button on the Chart toolbar.

c. Save your work.

6 Move and resize a chart object.

a. Make sure the chart is still in Edit mode.

b. Click the legend to select it.

c. Drag the selection handles to make the legend larger and wider by about 1/2".

d. Move the legend below the charted data.

e. Save your work.

7 Preview and print a chart.

a. Make sure the chart is still in Edit mode, then click the Print Preview button on the Standard toolbar.

b. Center the chart on the page and change the paper orientation to landscape.

c. Click Print in the Print Preview window.

d. Save your work, close the workbook, then exit Excel.

INDEPENDENT CHALLENGE 1

You are the operations manager for the Springfield Municipal Recycling Center. The Marketing Department wants you to create charts for a brochure that will advertise a new curbside recycling program. The data provided contains percentages of all collected recycled goods. Using this data, you need to create charts that show:

- How much of each type of recycled material Springfield collected in 1994 and what percentage of the whole each type represents. The center collects all types of paper, plastics, and glass from both business and residential customers.
- The yearly increases in the total amounts of recycled materials the center has collected since its inception three years ago. Springfield has experienced a 30% annual increase in collections.

To complete this independent challenge:

1. Prepare a worksheet plan that states your goal and identifies the formulas for any calculations.
2. Sketch a sample worksheet on a piece of paper describing how you will create the charts. Which type of chart is best suited for the information you need to display? What kind of chart enhancements will be necessary? Will a 3-D effect make your chart easier to understand?
3. Open the workbook UNIT_4-2.XLS on your Student Disk, then save it as RECYCLE.XLS to the MY_FILES directory.
4. Add a column that calculates the 30% increase in annual collections.
5. Create at least six different charts that show the distribution of recycled goods, as well as the distribution by customer type. Use the ChartWizard to switch the way data is plotted (columns vs. rows and vice versa) to come up with additional charts. Make sure your charts show the information requested above.
6. After creating the charts, make the appropriate enhancements. Include chart titles, legends, and axis titles.
7. Before printing, preview the file so you know what the charts will look like. Adjust any items as needed.
8. Print the charts without printing the data. Then print a copy of the entire worksheet. Save your work before closing the file.
9. Submit your worksheet plan, preliminary sketches, and the final worksheet printouts.

INDEPENDENT CHALLENGE 2

As an administrator with the US Census Bureau, you are concerned with the distribution of the population by age and gender. Using the statistical data provided below, you need to create charts that show:

- How the population is distributed, by age and gender
- How the population is distributed, by gender

AGE	MALE	FEMALE
65+	5%	7.5%
55-64	4%	4.5%
45-54	4.9%	5.2%
35-44	7.4%	7.6%
25-34	8.7%	8.7%
15-24	7.6%	7.3%
5-14	7.2%	6.9%
<5	3.9%	3.7%

To complete this independent challenge:

1. Prepare a worksheet plan that states your goal and identifies the formulas for any calculations.
2. Sketch a sample worksheet on a piece of paper describing how you will create the charts. Which type of charts are best suited for the information you need to display? What kind of chart enhancements will be necessary? Will a 3-D effect make your chart easier to understand?
3. Open a new workbook using the data above, and save it as CENSUS.XLS to the MY_FILES directory on your Student Disk.
4. Create at least six different charts that show the population in its entirety, by gender, by age, and by both gender and age. Use the ChartWizard to switch the way data is plotted (columns vs. rows and vice versa) to come up with additional charts. Make sure your charts show the information requested above.
5. Add annotated text and arrows highlighting any data you feel is particularly important. Change colors to emphasize significant data.
6. Before printing, preview the file so you know what the charts will look like. Adjust any items as needed.
7. Print the charts with the data. Save your work before closing the file.
8. Submit your worksheet plan, preliminary sketches, and the final worksheet printouts.

Glossary

Absolute reference A cell reference that contains a dollar sign before the column letter and/or row number to indicate the absolute, or fixed, contents of specific cells. For example, the formula $A$1+$B$1 calculates only the sum of these specific cells.

Active cell The cell in which you are working, indicated by the current location of the cell pointer.

Address The location of a specific cell or range expressed by the coordinates of column and row; for example, A1.

Alignment The horizontal placement of cell contents; for example, left, center, or right.

Anchors Cells listed in a range address. For example, in the formula =SUM(A1:A15), A1 and A15 are anchors.

Area chart A line chart in which each area is given a solid color or pattern to emphasize the relationships between the pieces of charted information.

Argument A value, range of cells, or text used in a macro or function. An argument is enclosed in parentheses; for example, =SUM(A1..B1).

Arithmetic operator A symbol used in formulas, such as + or –, to perform calculations.

Attributes The styling features such as bold, italics, and underlining that can be applied to cell contents.

AutoFormat A feature that provides preset schemes that can be applied to instantly format a range. Excel comes with sixteen AutoFormats, which include colors, fonts, and numeric formatting.

Bar chart The bar chart displays information as a series of (horizontal) bars.

Button A picture on a toolbar that represents a shortcut for performing a commonly used Excel command. For example, you can click the Save button to save a file.

Cancel button The button pictured with an "X" on it located on the formula bar. The Cancel button removes the changes made to the contents of the active cell and restores the previous cell contents.

Cell The intersection of a column and a row.

Cell address Unique location identified by intersecting column and row coordinates.

Cell pointer A highlighted rectangle around a cell that indicates the active cell.

Cell reference The address or name of a specific cell; cell references can be used in formulas and are relative or absolute.

Chart A graphic representation of selected worksheet information. Types include 2-D and 3-D column, bar, pie, area, and line charts.

Chart title The name assigned to a chart.

ChartWizard A feature that provides a series of dialog boxes that help create or modify a chart.

Check box A square box in a dialog box that you click to turn an option on or off.

Clear A command used to erase a cell's contents, formatting, or both.

Clipboard A temporary storage area for cut or copied data and graphics. You can paste the contents of the Clipboard into any Excel worksheet or open Excel workbook. The Clipboard holds the information until you cut or copy another piece of data or graphic.

Close A command that puts a file away but keeps Excel open so that you can continue to work on other workbooks.

Column chart The default chart type in Excel. The column chart displays information as a series of (vertical) columns.

Column selector button The gray box containing the column letter above the column.

Copy A command that copies the selected information and places it on the Clipboard.

Cut A command that removes the contents from a selected area of a worksheet and places them on the Clipboard, so you can paste the selected text in another worksheet or open workbook.

Data marker Visible representation of a data point, such as a column or pie slice.

Data point Individual piece of data plotted in a chart.

Data series The selected range in a worksheet that Excel converts into a graphic and displays as a chart.

Delete A command that removes cell contents from a worksheet.

Dialog box A window that displays when you choose a command whose name is followed by an ellipsis (. . .). A dialog box allows you to make selections that determine how the command affects the selected area.

Drag-and-drop A way of moving or copying cells, rows, and columns by dragging the data with the mouse to a new worksheet location.

Drive A mechanism in a computer or an area of a network used for retrieving and storing files. Personal computers usually have one hard disk drive labeled C and two drives labeled A and B that read removable floppy disks.

Dummy column/row Blank column or row included at the end of a range that enables a formula to adjust when columns or rows are added or deleted.

Edit Add, delete, or change the contents of a cell or worksheet.

Electronic spreadsheet A computer program that performs calculations on data and organizes information. A spreadsheet is divided into columns and rows that form individual cells.

Ellipsis A series of dots (...) following a command, indicating that more choices are available through a dialog box.

Enter button The button pictured with a checkmark on it located on the formula bar. The Enter button is used to confirm an entry to the active cell.

Exploding pie slice A slice of a pie chart that has been pulled away from a pie to add emphasis.

Fill Down A command that duplicates the contents of the selected cells in the range selected below the cell pointer.

Fill handle Small square in the lower-right corner of the active cell used to copy cell contents.

Fill right A command that duplicates the contents of the selected cells in the range selected to the right of the cell pointer.

Font The name given to a collection of characters (letters, numerals, symbols, and punctuation marks) with a specific design. Arial and Times New Roman are examples of font names.

Format The way text and numbers appear on a worksheet. *See also* Number format.

Formula A set of instructions that you enter in a cell to perform numeric calculations (adding, multiplying, averaging, etc.); for example, +A1+B1.

Formula bar The rectangular area, above the Excel worksheet window, that displays a cell's contents, including numbers, text, and formulas, when you click a cell. You can use the formula bar to enter and edit data in the active cell.

Function A special predefined worksheet formula that provides a shortcut for commonly used calculations; for example, AVERAGE. A function always begins with the formula prefix = (the equal sign).

Function Wizard A feature that provides a series of dialog boxes that list and describe all Excel functions and assists the user in function creation.

Gridlines Horizontal lines within a chart that make the chart easier to read.

Input Information that produces desired results in a worksheet.

Insertion point Blinking vertical line that appears in the formula bar during entry and editing.

Label Descriptive text or other information that identifies the rows and columns of a worksheet. Labels are not included in calculations.

Landscape Term used to refer to printing across the wider dimension of a page, generally 11" horizontally by 8 ½" vertically.

Legend A key explaining the information represented by colors or patterns in a chart.

Line chart A graph of data that is mapped by a series of lines. Line charts show changes in data or categories of data over time and can be used to document trends.

Menu bar The horizontal bar under the title bar on a window that lists the names of the menus that contain Excel commands. Click a menu name on the menu bar to display a list of commands.

Mode indicator A box located on the far left of the status bar that informs you of the program's status. For example, when Excel is performing a task, the word "Wait" appears in the mode indicator.

Mouse pointer An arrow that indicates the current location of the mouse on the desktop. The mouse pointer changes shapes at times depending on the application and task being executed or performed.

Name box The leftmost area on the formula bar that shows the name or address of the area currently selected. For example, "A1" refers to cell A1 of the current worksheet.

Number format A format applied to values to express numeric concepts, such as currency, date, and percent.

Object A chart or graphic image that can be moved and resized and contains handles when selected.

Open A command that retrieves a workbook from a disk and displays it on the screen.

Order of precedence The order in which Excel calculates parts of a formula: (1) exponents, (2) multiplication and division, and (3) addition and subtraction.

Output The end result of a worksheet.

Paste A command that moves information on the Clipboard to a new location. Excel pastes the formulas rather than the result unless the Paste Special command is used.

Paste Special A command that enables you to paste formulas as values, styles, or cell contents.

Pie chart A circular chart that displays data as slices of a pie. A pie chart is useful for showing the relationship of parts to a whole; pie slices can be pulled away, or exploded, from the pie for emphasis.

Point size Refers to the physical size of text, measured in points. One inch equals 72 points.

Print Preview A window that displays a reduced view of area to be printed.

Radio button Circle in a dialog box that allows you to choose one option from a list of options.

Range A selected group of adjacent cells.

Range format A format applied to a selected range in a worksheet.

Range name A name applied to a selected range in a worksheet.

Relative cell reference Used to indicate a relative position in the worksheet. This allows you to copy and move formulas from one area to another of the same dimensions. Excel automatically changes the column and row numbers to reflect the new position.

Row height The vertical dimension of a cell.

Row selector button Gray box containing the row number to the left of the row.

Save A command used to save incremental changes to a workbook.

Save As A command used to create a duplicate of the current workbook.

Scroll bars Bars that appear on the right and bottom borders of the window that allow you to scroll the window vertically and horizontally to view information not currently visible in the current worksheet.

Search criteria Text, values, or formulas you want to change using Find and Replace.

Selection handles Small black boxes at the corners and sides of charts and graphic images, indicating a chart is selected and can be moved or resized using the handles.

Sheet tab A description at the bottom of each worksheet that identifies the sheet in a workbook. In an open workbook, move to a worksheet by clicking its tab.

Sheet tab scrolling buttons Enable you to move among sheets within a workbook.

Status bar The horizontal bar at the bottom of the Excel window that provides information about the tasks Excel is performing or about current selections.

Text annotations Labels added to a chart to draw attention to a particular area.

Title bar The horizontal bar at the top of a window that displays the application name and workbook. Until you save the workbook and give it a name, the temporary name for the workbook is BOOK1.

Toggle button A choice that, when clicked, turns an option on. Clicking it again turns the option off.

Toolbar A horizontal bar within the Excel window that contains buttons for the most frequently used Excel commands. A toolbar can be positioned along the edge of the worksheet window or can float within its own window.

ToolTip Name and description of a button on the toolbar that appears when the mouse pointer is positioned over the button. The name appears under the button and the description in the status bar.

Values Numbers, formulas, or functions used in calculations.

"What-if" analysis Decision-making feature in which data is changed and automatically recalculated.

Workbook A collection of related worksheets contained within a single file.

Worksheet An electronic spreadsheet containing 256 columns by 16,384 rows.

Worksheet window A framed area of the Excel window containing a grid of columns and rows that is called a worksheet.

X-axis The horizontal line in a chart.

X-axis label A label describing the x-axis of a chart.

Y-axis The vertical line in a chart.

Y-axis label A label describing the y-axis of a chart.

Zoom A feature that enables you to focus on a larger or smaller part of the worksheet in Print Preview.

Index

C

D

E

F

M

N

O

S

T

U

V

W

X

Y

Z

UNIT 1

OBJECTIVES

- Open multiple applications
- Copy Word data into Excel
- Create a dynamic link (DDE) from Excel to Word

Integrating WORD AND EXCEL

Now that you have experienced the power of Word and Excel, it is time to learn how to integrate the applications. When you **integrate** applications, you combine information between them without retyping anything. ▶ Andrew Gillespie, the national sales manager for Nomad Ltd, collected the spring quarter sales data for clothing from the five sales regions. He compiled this information in a Word document, and now he wants to add an Excel column chart to his document. Andrew will use simple integration techniques to do this. He will then give the data back to the regional managers so each manager can see how his or his own region did compared to the other four regions. ▶

Opening multiple applications

When you are integrating information from one application to another, it is helpful to have both files open at the same time. The Windows environment gives you the ability to have more than one program open at a time. This is sometimes called **multitasking.** ▶ Before integrating the data, Andrew starts both Word and Excel. To make integrating the data easier, he aligns each application window side by side on the screen.

1 Double-click the **Microsoft Office program group icon** in the Program Manager window
The Microsoft Office group window opens. The application icons for both Word and Excel are in the Microsoft Office group. Application icons do not have to be in the same group to be opened at the same time.

2 Double-click the **Microsoft Word application icon**, then when the blank Word document appears, click **OK** to close the Tip of the Day dialog box if necessary
Andrew minimizes the application so he can prepare to open Excel.

3 Click the **Minimize button** in the application window
Word shrinks to an icon, as shown in Figure 1-1. Next, Andrew opens the Excel application.

4 Double-click the **Microsoft Excel application icon**
A blank Excel workbook appears.

Andrew uses a shortcut key combination to maximize the Word application and make it active.

5 Press **[Alt][Tab]**, but *do not release [Alt]*
A message box appears in the middle of the screen with the words "Program Manager" in it. Using the shortcut keys [Alt][Tab] causes the icons and names of open applications (whether or not they are minimized) to appear in the center of the screen. If more than one application is open, you can press [Tab] again while still holding down [Alt] to see the next icon in the center of the screen. When the application you want to make active appears, you release [Alt].

6 Press **[Tab]** again so that the Word application icon appears in the message box, as shown in Figure 1-2, then release [Alt]
Word maximizes and becomes the active application. Excel is still open and maximized, but it is not active. Now, Andrew needs to resize the Word window so it only occupies the left half of the screen.

7 Click the Word window upper **Restore button**, then drag the window borders so the window occupies the left half of the screen
Andrew activates Excel and resizes the worksheet window so it occupies the right half of the screen.

8 Click anywhere in the visible worksheet to activate Excel, then click the **Excel Window Restore button**

9 Drag the Excel window borders so this window occupies the right half of the screen
Compare your screen to Figure 1-3.

FIGURE 1-1: Word application minimized

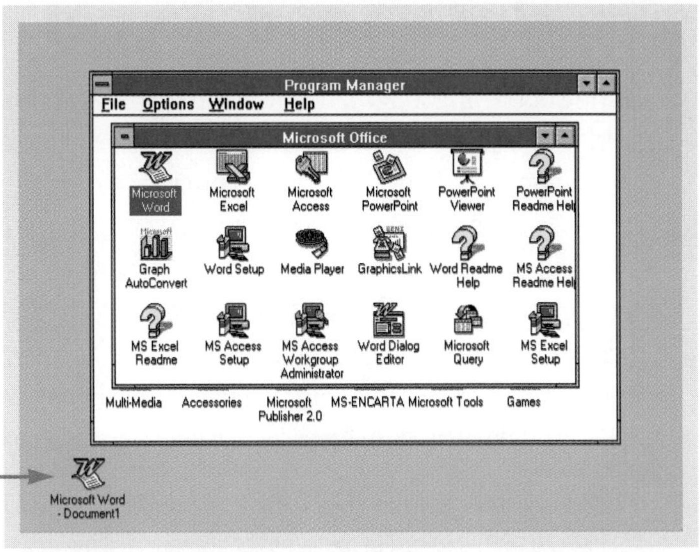

Minimized application icon

FIGURE 1-2: Word application icon in the center of the Excel worksheet

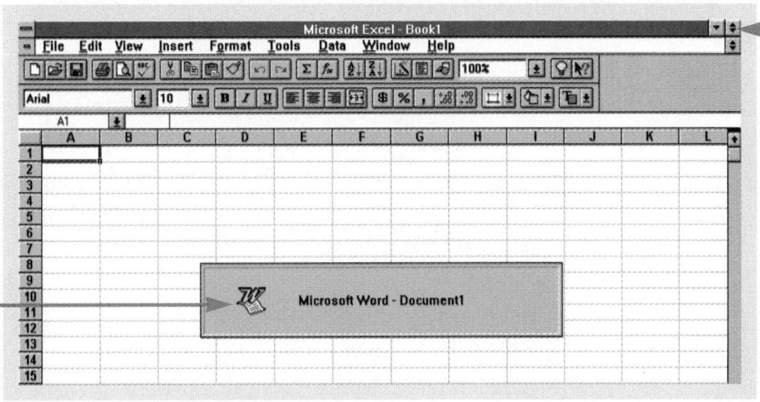

Restore button

Open application icons display in center when [Alt][Tab] is pressed

FIGURE 1-3: Word window and Excel window on the screen

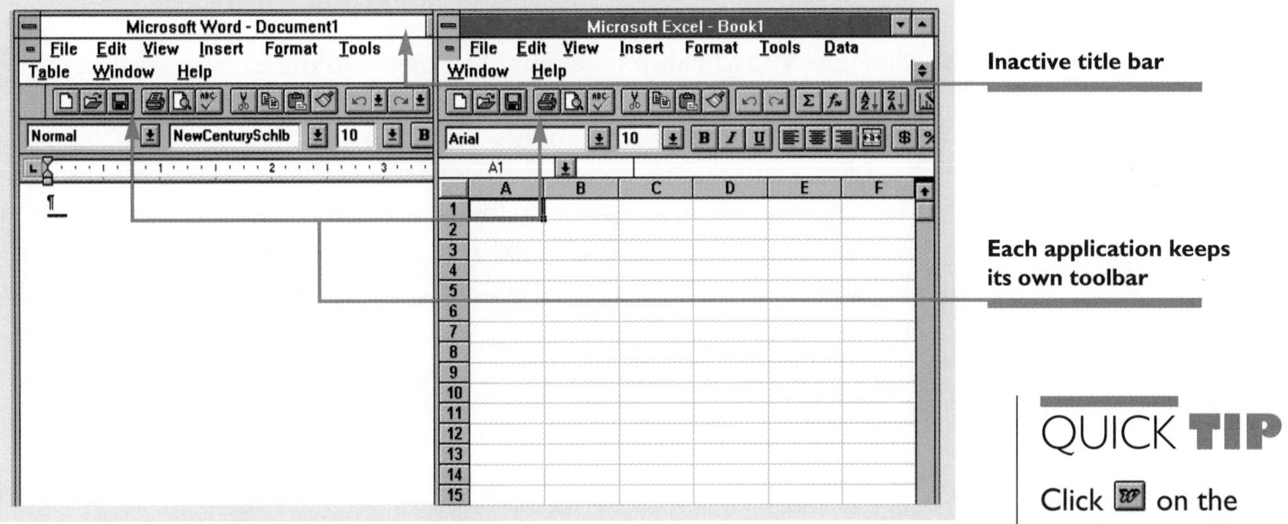

Inactive title bar

Each application keeps its own toolbar

QUICK TIP

Click on the Microsoft toolbar to start Word quickly. To start Excel quickly, click on the Microsoft toolbar.

Copying Word data into Excel

Moving or copying information from one application to another is just like moving or copying information within a single application. You can use the application's Cut, Copy, and Paste commands, toolbars if available, or in the case of Word, the drag-and-drop method. When you use drag-and-drop, the information is copied, not moved. Use drag-and-drop to copy information from one application to another. ▶ Andrew typed a memo to the regional managers that includes a Word table containing the spring quarter sales data from all five regions. He wants to add a column chart to the memo. To create the column chart in Excel, Andrew needs to first copy the data into an Excel workbook.

1 Click anywhere within the Word application window

Just like two windows open in the same application, clicking in a window makes that window active. Open Andrew's memo.

2 Open the file INT_I-1.DOC from your Student Disk, then save it as **REGIONS.DOC** to the MY_FILES directory

REGIONS.DOC appears in the Word application window, as shown in Figure 1-4. The Word document is the **source file**—the file from which the information is copied. The Excel workbook is the **target file**—the file that receives the copied information. Andrew will copy the table containing the spring quarter sales data.

3 Position the pointer in the selection bar next to the top row of the table until the pointer changes to

4 Press and hold the **mouse button** to select the top row of the table, then drag the pointer down until all of the rows are selected, then release the mouse button

5 Click the **Word table** then drag the pointer to the Excel worksheet so the destination of the table's outline is in range A1:D6, as shown in Figure 1-5, then release the mouse button

The information in the Word table is copied into the Excel worksheet, as shown in Figure 1-6. Using drag-and-drop is the easiest way to copy information from a source file to a target file. You could have also selected the Word table, clicked the Copy button on the Word Standard toolbar, then clicked the first destination cell in Excel and clicked the Paste button on the Excel Standard toolbar.

6 Click anywhere in the worksheet to make Excel active

7 Click the **Save button** on the Excel Standard toolbar, then save the workbook as REGIONS.XLS to the MY_FILES directory on your Student Disk

Now that the data is copied into the Excel worksheet, Andrew can easily create the column chart.

8 Close the REGIONS.XLS workbook file

Do not close the REGIONS.DOC Word file.

FIGURE 1-4: REGIONS.DOC open

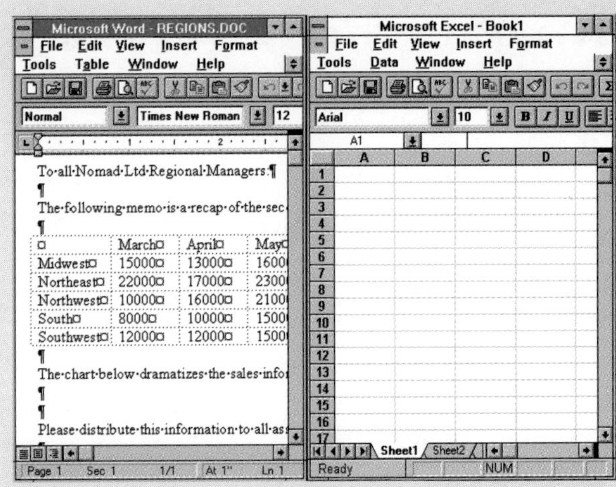

FIGURE 1-5: Drag-and-drop of Word text into an Excel worksheet

Drag-and-Drop pointer

Outline of destination

FIGURE 1-6: Word table copied into an Excel worksheet

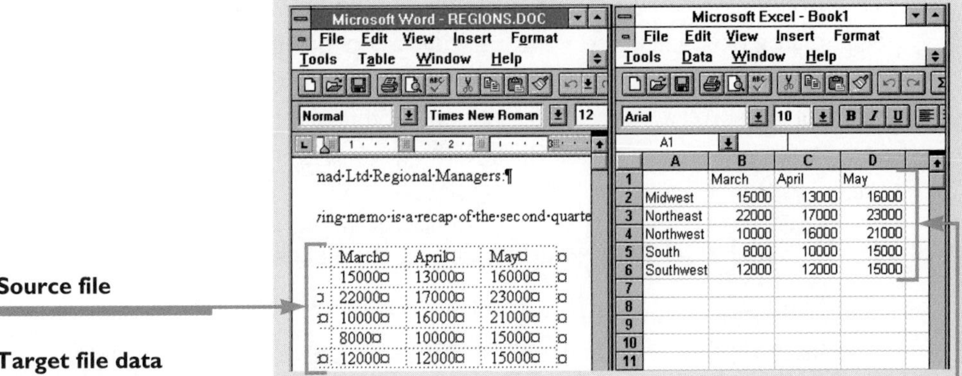

Creating a dynamic link (DDE) between Excel and Word

Sometimes you want the data in two applications to be dynamically linked, not just copied. A **dynamic link**—sometimes called **dynamic data exchange** or **DDE**—means that if the data in the source file is changed, the data in the target file will be automatically updated. ▶ Andrew created the column chart using the data that he had copied from the Word file. Now he wants to paste the chart into his memo. He decides to link it to the document rather than simply copy it, so that the Word memo will always reflect modifications made in the Excel worksheet.

1. Make the Excel window active, open the file INT_1-2.XLS from your Student Disk, then save it as REGSALES.XLS to your MY_FILES directory
   REGSALES.XLS appears in the Excel worksheet window. See Figure 1-7. This file contains the chart that Andrew created using the data he copied from the Word document. Andrew wants to copy the chart into the Word document using a dynamic link to the Excel worksheet.
2. Click **the chart** to select it, then click the **Copy button** on the Excel Standard toolbar
   The chart is copied to the Clipboard. Andrew positions the insertion point in the Word document where he wants the chart to appear.
3. Click anywhere in the Word application window to make it active, then click in the blank paragraph below the sentence that begins "The chart below dramatizes..."
4. Click **Edit** on the Word menu bar, click **Paste Special** to open the Paste Special dialog box, click the **Paste Link radio button**, then click **OK**
   The chart is copied into the Word document, and a dynamic link is created between the Word document and the Excel worksheet. Frank Jones, the Northwest regional manager, called Andrew to make a correction to one of the sales figures. The March sales for the Northeast were actually $12,000.
5. Make the Excel worksheet window active, then click cell **B3**
6. Type **12000** then press **[Enter]**
   Watch as the first column in the Northeast data series shrinks to reflect the new data. This change occurs in both the Excel worksheet and in the Word document, as shown in Figure 1-8.
7. Click the **Save button** on the Excel Standard toolbar to save the revised worksheet, then close the workbook
8. Make the Word window active, then click the **Save button** on the Word Standard toolbar to save the document
9. Click the **Print Preview button** on the Word Standard toolbar, then after examining your document, click the **Print button** on the Print Preview toolbar, then close the document

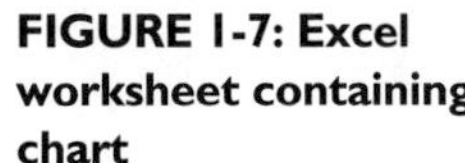

FIGURE 1-7: Excel worksheet containing chart

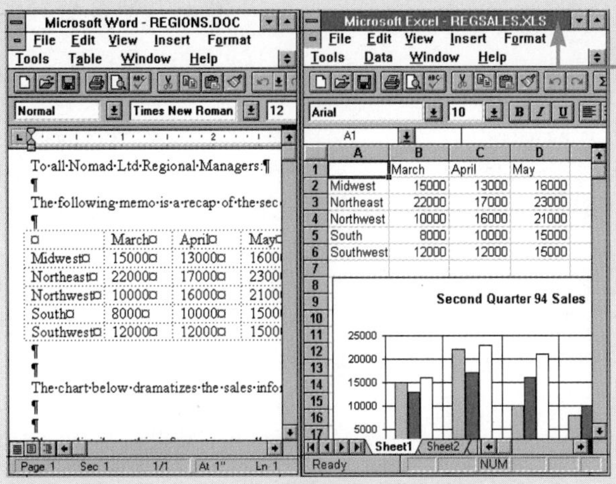

Title bar of source document

FIGURE 1-8: Excel chart linked to Word document

Modified data

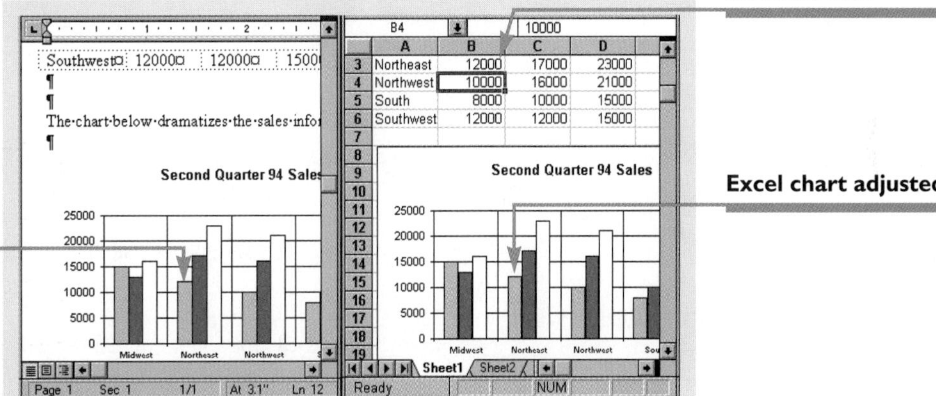

Dynamic link changes data here

Excel chart adjusted

Breaking links

If you are working with a file containing linked data and you decide that you don't want the linked object to change if the source file changes, you can break the link. In other words, you can change the object from a linked object to a pasted object. In the target file, click the object to select it, click Edit on the menu bar, then click Links to open the Links dialog box, shown in Figure 1-9. Click the name of the source file, click Break Link, then click OK. The object in the target file is no longer linked to the source file.

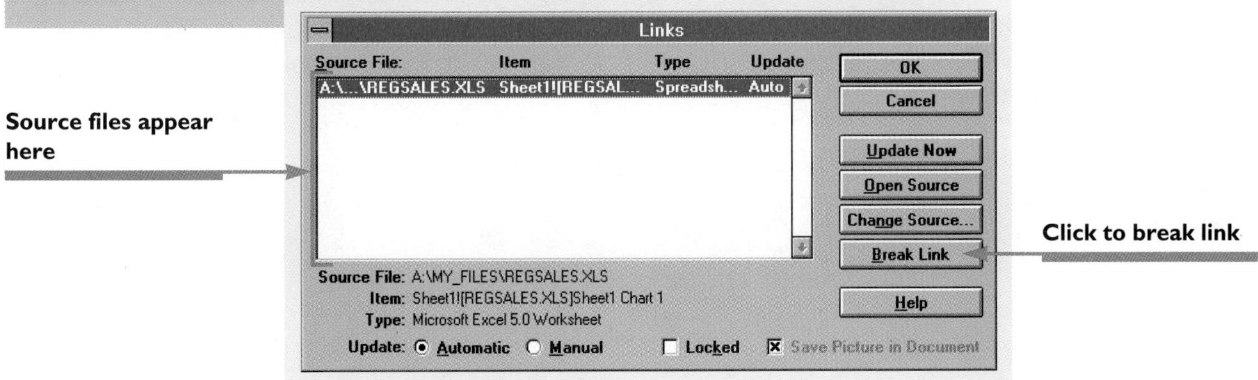

Source files appear here

Click to break link

FIGURE 1-9: Links dialog box

INDEPENDENT CHALLENGE I

You are the public relations manager for the Census Bureau for your geographic region. The census data is of interest to the people in your area, and you need to write descriptive text to interpret the data. It is your responsibility to condense and synthesize the data received from Census headquarters and create informative descriptions of information topical to your region. The finished product should be an attractive publication of no more than two pages in length. You can include text, spreadsheet data, and charts as you see fit.

Use the data found on the worksheet page called "Birth rates" in INT_1-3.XLS on your Student Disk. Save this file as CEN-DATA.XLS to the MY_FILES directory.

To complete this independent challenge:

1. Examine the data in CEN-DATA.XLS and write a short synopsis in a new Word document. Save the document as BRTHRATE.DOC to the MY_FILES directory on your Student Disk.
2. Decide how the information in CEN-DATA.XLS can best be used in the Word document. Should the actual data be shown in the document, or just a chart, or both?
3. Create a chart in the worksheet. Experiment with several types of charts until you find at least one which dramatizes the data.
4. Make sure your chart contains a legend and that each axis is labeled. Include a text annotation and arrow to emphasize a point of interest.
5. Create a new column on the worksheet that calculates a 5% increase in birth rates per month for 1993 through 1996.
6. Create a chart that shows the actual and projected growth.
7. Include a legend, labeled axes, a text annotation and arrow on this chart.
8. Include this speculative information in the Word document. Make sure you clearly label the data as projected.
9. Preview the document. Adjust any items as needed, then print it. Save the Word document and the Excel workbook. Submit your finished publication.

INDEPENDENT CHALLENGE 2

The Census Bureau has forwarded statistical data regarding marriage rates. Your office has received increasing pressure from area shops that rent formal wear, such as tuxedos and wedding gowns, to publicize these statistics. These business people want to examine trends and use this data to project sales. As a public servant, you are obligated to honor their request and pass along this information.

Open the Excel file INT_1-4.XLS from your Student Disk, then save it as MARRIAGE.XLS to the MY_FILES directory. You need to create a publication of no more than two pages in length that contains a synopsis of the national data, as well as a detailed breakdown of marriage statistics for your region. You can include text, spreadsheet data, and charts as you see fit.

To complete this independent challenge:

1. Create formulas in range B5:C13 that total the marriages by region.
2. Examine the national information, as well as the data for your region. How does your region compare to the nation?
3. Open a new Word document and save it as MARRIAGE.DOC to the MY_FILES directory on your Student Disk.
4. Begin writing your findings in this document.
5. Create a minimum of four charts—two for the national totals of marriage rates, and two for your region. Use different types of charts, as well as text annotations and arrows, to emphasize data within the charts.
6. Each chart should contain a legend and labeled axes.
7. Integrate data from the workbook into your document to create an attractive publication.
8. Preview your document. Adjust any items as needed, then print a copy. Save the Word document and the workbook. Submit your finished publication. Be prepared to make a short presentation on your findings.
9. Exit Word and Excel.

Microsoft® Access 2.0

for Windows™

UNIT 1	**Getting Started with Microsoft Access 2.0**
UNIT 2	**Creating a Database**
UNIT 3	**Modifying a Database**
UNIT 4	**Enhancing a Database**

Read This Before You Begin Microsoft Access 2.0

To the Student

The lessons and exercises in this book feature several Access database files provided to your instructor. To complete the step-by-step lessons, Applications Reviews, and Independent Challenges in this book, you must have a Student Disk. Your instructor will do one of the following: 1) provide you with your own copy of the disk; 2) have you copy it from the network onto your own floppy disk; or 3) have you copy the lesson files from a network into your own subdirectory on the network. Once you receive your own copy of the Student Disk, *make a copy of it* in case you want to redo any lesson in this book at a later time. See your instructor or technical support person for further information on how to copy a disk, if necessary.

Using Your Own Computer

If you are going to work through this book using your own computer, you need a computer system running Microsoft Windows 3.1, Microsoft Access 2.0 for Windows, and a Student Disk. *You will not be able to complete the step-by-step lessons in this book using your own computer until you have your own Student Disk.* Once you receive a Student Disk, *make a copy of it* in case you want to redo any lesson in this book at a later time. This book assumes the default settings under a Complete installation of Microsoft Access 2.0 for Windows.

To the Instructor

Bundled with the instructor's copy of this book is the Student Disk. The Student Disk contains all the files your students need to complete the step-by-step lessons in the units, Applications Reviews, and Independent Challenges. As an adopter of this text, you are granted the right to distribute the files on the Student Disk to any student who has purchased a copy of the text. You are free to post all of these files to a network or standalone workstations, or simply provide copies of the disk to your students. The instructions in this book assume that the students know which drive and directory contain the Student Disk, so it's important that you provide disk location information before the students start working through the units. This book also assumes that Access 2.0 is set up using the Complete installation procedure.

Using the Student Disk Files

To keep the original files on the Student Disk intact, instruct your students to *make a copy of their Student Disk before they begin working through the units*. Instructions on how to copy a disk can be found in the lesson entitled "Formatting and Copying Disks" in *Microsoft Windows 3.1*. These instructions are also provided in the Instructor's Manual that accompanies this book. This procedure ensures that the original database files will remain unmodified in case the students want to redo any lesson or exercise.

To organize their files, students are instructed to save their files to the MY_FILES directory on their Student Disk that they created in *Microsoft Windows 3.1*. In case your students did not complete this lesson, it is included in the Instructor's Manual that accompanies this book. You can circulate this to your students, or you can instruct them to simply save to drive A or drive B.

UNIT 1

OBJECTIVES

- Define database software
- Start Access 2.0 for Windows
- View the Access window
- Open a database table
- Use dialog boxes, toolbars, and buttons
- Get Help
- Move through a database table
- Close a database and exit Access

Getting Started WITH MICROSOFT ACCESS 2.0

Now that you're familiar with Microsoft Windows, you're ready to learn how to use Microsoft Access 2.0 for Windows. In this unit, you will learn the basic features of Access, a popular database program, and the various components of a database. You will also learn how to use different elements of the Access window, and how to use the extensive on-line Help system available in Access. ▶ Michael Belmont is the Travel Division manager at Nomad Ltd, an outdoor gear and adventure travel company. Recently, Nomad switched to Access from a paper-based system for storing and maintaining customer records. Michael will use Access to maintain customer information for Nomad. ▶

Defining database software

Access is a database program that runs in the Windows environment. A **database** is a collection of data related to a particular topic or purpose (for example, customer data). Information in a database is organized into **fields**, or categories, such as customer name. A group of related fields, such as all information on a particular customer, is called a **record**. A collection of related records is called a **table**. A database, specifically a **relational database**, is a collection of related tables that can share information. Figure 1-1 shows the structure of a database. Traditionally, businesses kept track of customer information using index cards, as illustrated in Figure 1-2. However, an electronic database, like Access, allows you to store, retrieve, and manipulate data more quickly and easily. See Table 1-1 for common ways in which databases are used in business.

With database software Michael can:

- **Enter data quickly and easily**
  With Access, Michael can enter information on Nomad's customers faster and more accurately than he could using the paper-based method. He can enter data using screen forms, which contain **controls** such as check boxes, list boxes, and option buttons, to facilitate data entry. Figure 1-3 shows customer information in an Access form.

- **Organize records in different ways**
  After Michael specifies a sort order, Access automatically keeps records organized, regardless of the order in which they are entered.

- **Locate specific records quickly**
  By creating a **query**, a definition of the records he wants to find, Michael can instruct Access to locate the record or records matching his query.

- **Eliminate duplicate data**
  Access ensures that each record is unique. Using the paper system, Michael could have duplicate customer records if he forgot that an index card already existed for a particular customer.

- **Create relationships among tables in a database**
  Access is a relational database, which allows information within its tables to be shared. This means that Michael needs to enter a customer name only once and it will be referenced in other tables in Nomad's database.

- **Create reports**
  Generating professional reports is easy with Access. Michael can produce reports to illustrate different relationships among the data and share these reports with other Nomad employees.

- **Change the appearance of information**
  Access provides powerful features for enhancing table data so that information is visually appealing and easy to understand.

FIGURE 1-1: Structure of a database

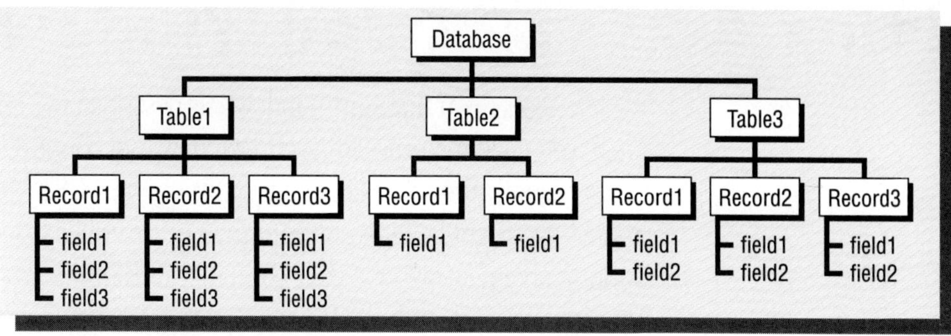

FIGURE 1-2: Customer information on an index card

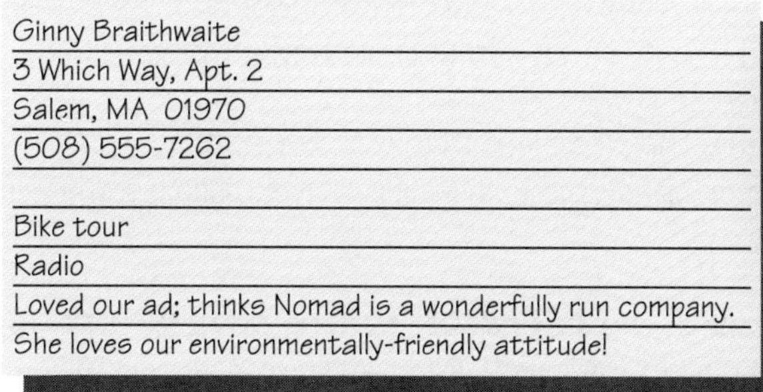

FIGURE 1-3: Customer information in an Access form

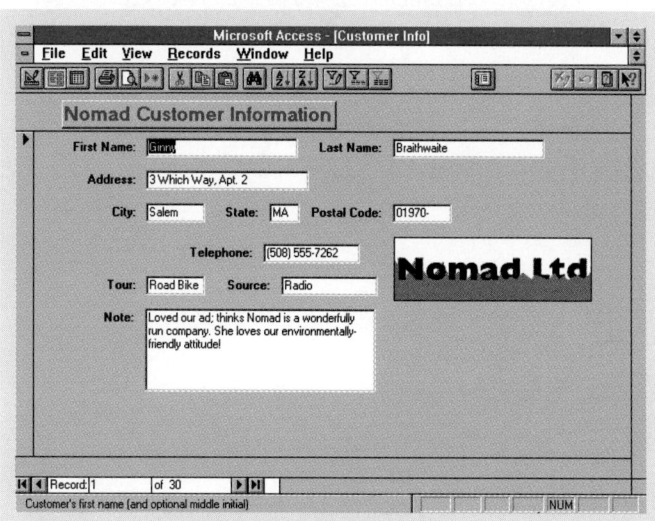

TABLE 1-1: Common business uses for a database

USE	SOLUTION
Storing data	On-screen forms
Maintaining data	Updated records
Representing data visually	Charts based on specified data
Manipulating data	Sorting, filtering, and analyzing data
Sharing information with others	Report generation
Locating specific records	Querying tables to find specific records

Starting Access 2.0 for Windows

To start Access, you first start Windows, as described in "Microsoft Windows 3.1." Then, you open the program group window that contains the Access application icon—usually the Microsoft Office program group. The procedure you follow to start Access might be different from the one described below, especially if you are working on a network or if your computer uses utility programs to enhance Windows. Ask your technical support person or instructor if there are any special procedures for starting Access on your computer. ▶ Michael first needs to start Access so that he can begin to learn how to use it.

1 Make sure the Program Manager is open
The Program Manager icon might appear at the bottom of your screen. Double-click it to open it, if necessary.

2 Double-click the **Microsoft Office program group icon**
The Microsoft Office group window opens and contains the Microsoft Access application icon, as shown in Figure 1-4. Your screen will probably look different depending on which applications are installed on your computer. If you cannot locate the Microsoft Office program icon, click Window on the Program Manager menu bar, then click Microsoft Office.

3 Double-click the **Microsoft Access application icon**
Access opens and displays the Access window. If a window named MS Access Cue Cards opens, double-click its control menu box to close it.

FIGURE 1-4: Microsoft Access application icon selected

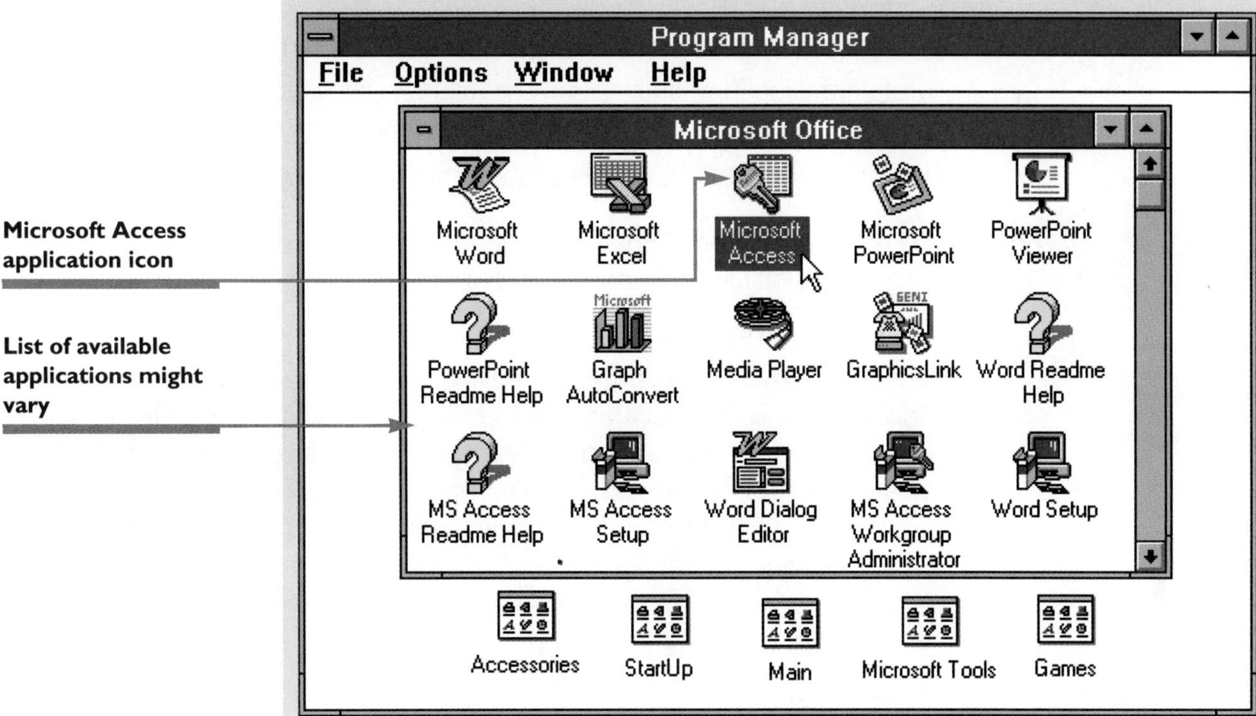

TROUBLE?

If you can't locate the Microsoft Office program group icon, then locate the Microsoft Access application icon and double-click it to start Access.■

Viewing the Access window

The Access window contains many elements that help you enter and manipulate the information in your database. Some of these elements, which are described in Table 1-2 and identified in Figure 1-5, are common to all Windows applications. ▶ Michael decides to explore the elements of the Access window.

1 Look at each of the elements shown in Figure 1-5
Michael browses through the commands in the File menu.

2 Click **File** on the menu bar
The File menu opens, as shown in Figure 1-6. Notice that the New Database command is highlighted and that the status bar displays the message, "Create a new database." When a menu is open, the status bar displays a descriptive message about the highlighted command. Some menu commands are **dimmed**, indicating they are unavailable at this time. Some commands include an **ellipsis** (...), which means that when you choose the command Access will display a dialog box in which you must specify the options you want for the command. Other commands contain keyboard shortcuts (on the right side of the menu). **Shortcut keys** are key combinations you can press instead of choosing the command from the menu.

3 Press **[Esc]** twice to close the File menu
Pressing [Esc] once closes the File menu, but File on the menu bar is still highlighted. Pressing [Esc] the second time deselects the menu name. Michael decides to open the File menu using the appropriate key combination. To use shortcut keys, you press and hold [Alt] then press the underlined letter of the menu or option you want to select.

4 Press and hold **[Alt]** then press **[F]**
The File menu opens again.

5 Move the mouse pointer off the menu, then click anywhere in the window (except on the menu) to close the menu without making a selection

TABLE 1-2: Elements of the Access window

ELEMENT	DESCRIPTION
Menu bar	Contains menus used in Access
Startup window	Area from which database operations take place
Status bar	Displays messages regarding operations and displays descriptions of toolbar buttons
Title bar	Contains application and filename of active database
Database toolbar	Contains buttons for commonly performed tasks

FIGURE 1-5: Access window

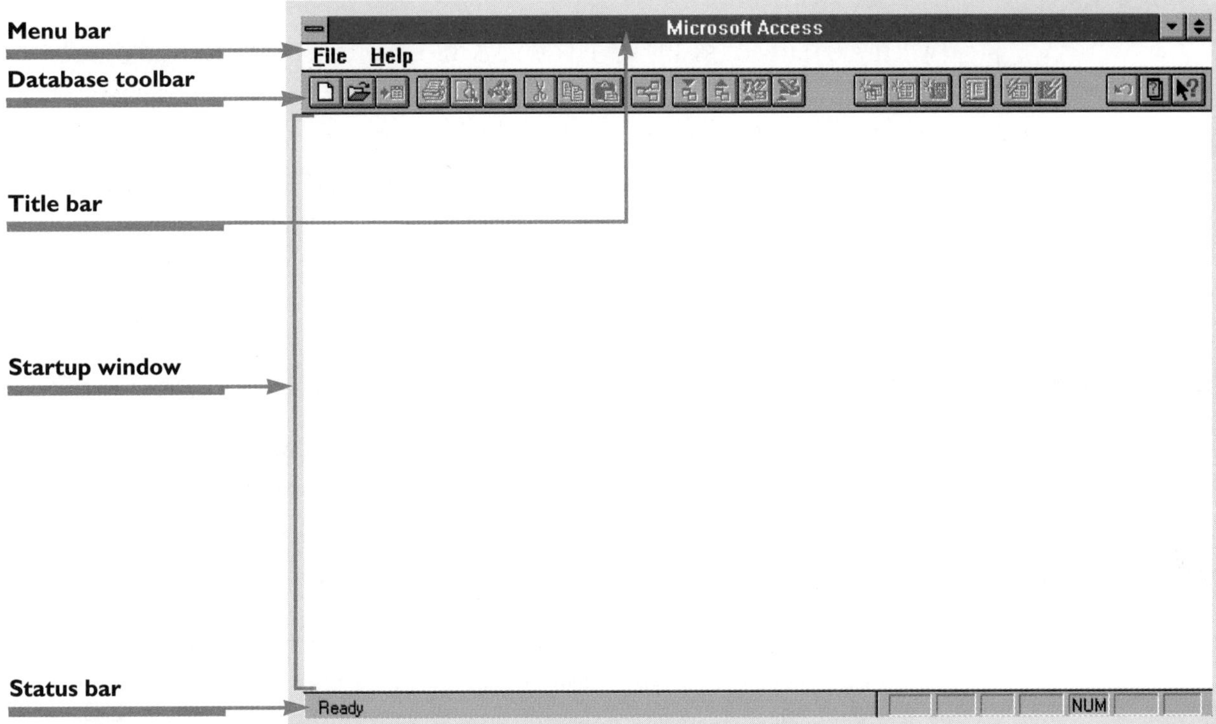

FIGURE 1-6: File menu in startup window

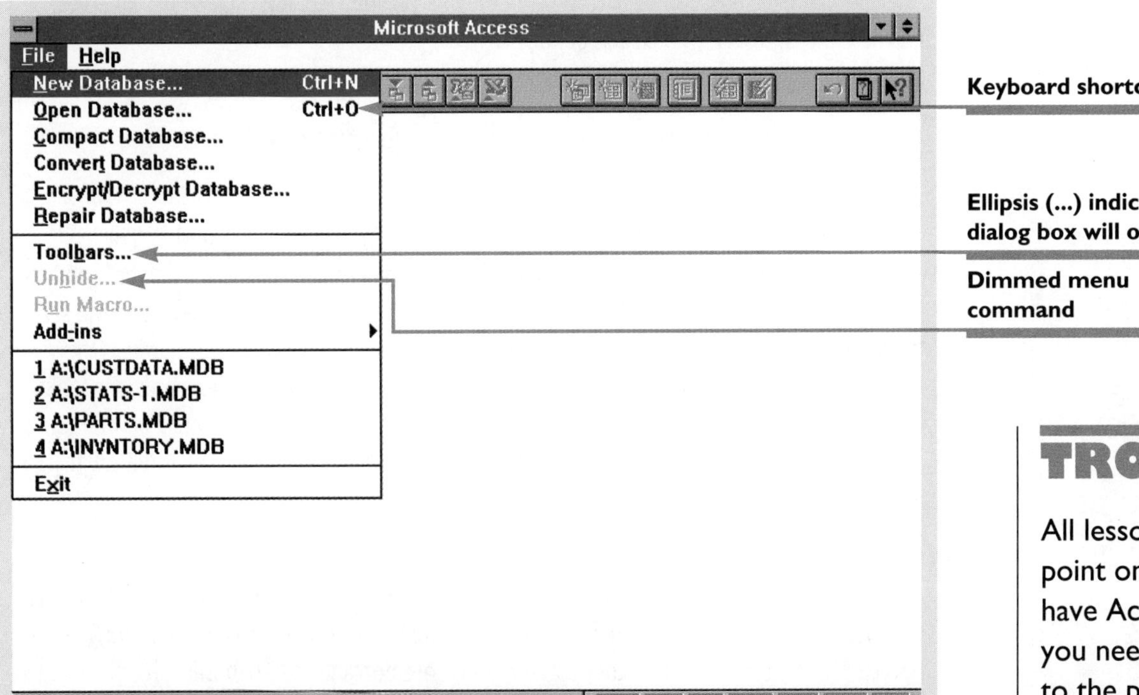

TROUBLE?

All lessons from this point on assume you have Access running. If you need help, refer to the previous lesson, "Starting Access 2.0 for Windows," or ask your technical support person or instructor for assistance.■

Opening a database table

When you start Access, the screen displays the **startup window**, the area from which you carry out all database operations. After you open a database, Access displays the Database window. The **Database window** provides access to all objects in the database. Table 1-3 describes the objects—such as tables, forms, and reports—that help you use the information in a database. ▶ Michael wants to open a database containing information about Nomad's products to see how it is structured.

1. **Place your Student Disk in drive A**

   To complete the units in this book, you need a Student Disk. See your instructor for a copy of the Student Disk, if you do not already have one. These lessons assume your Student Disk is in drive A. If you are using a different drive, substitute that drive for drive A in the lessons.

   Also, *make sure you have made a copy of your Student Disk*, as instructed on the "Read This Before You Begin Microsoft Access 2.0" page, before you use your Student Disk.

2. **Click the Open Database button on the Database toolbar**

   Access displays the Open Database dialog box, as shown in Figure 1-7. Your dialog box might look slightly different from the one shown.

3. **Click the Drives list arrow, then click a:**

   The File Name list box now displays a list of the files on your Student Disk. Note that Access database files have a file extension of .MDB.

4. **In the File Name list box, click INVNTORY.MDB**

   The selected filename replaces the default filename in the File Name text box.

5. **Click OK**

   The Database window for the file INVNTORY.MDB opens, as shown in Figure 1-8. The left side of the Database window contains the **object buttons** for the Access database objects (which are described in Table 1-3). Each object button appears on its own **tab**, and the Table tab is currently the front-most tab in the dialog box. The right side of the window lists the tables in the selected database (in this case, the INVNTORY database contains only one table, Products). The command buttons at the top of the window allow you to create a new table, open an existing table, or design your own table. Michael wants to open the Products table, which is already selected.

6. **Click Open**

   A window for the Products table opens. The table contains information about 17 Nomad products. The information is organized by fields (columns). Note that the first two columns are both named "Product ID"; however, they contain different information. When this table was created, Access assigned the field Product ID as the Counter field (the first column in the table). The **Counter field** counts the number of records in the table. The second Product ID column contains identification numbers for Nomad's products.

FIGURE 1-7: Open Database dialog box

Selected filename appears here

List of filenames

Click to display list of available drives

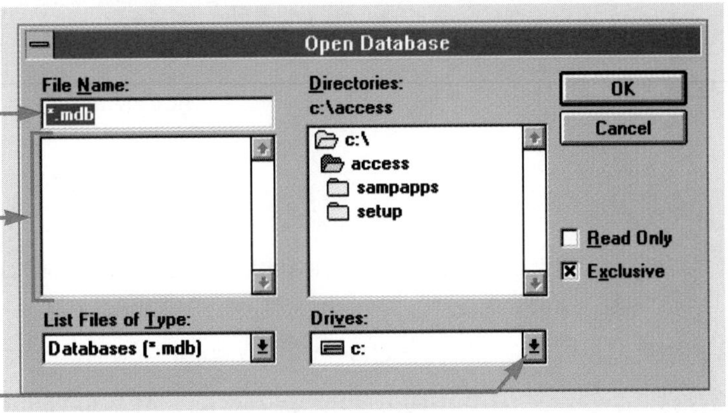

FIGURE 1-8: Database window

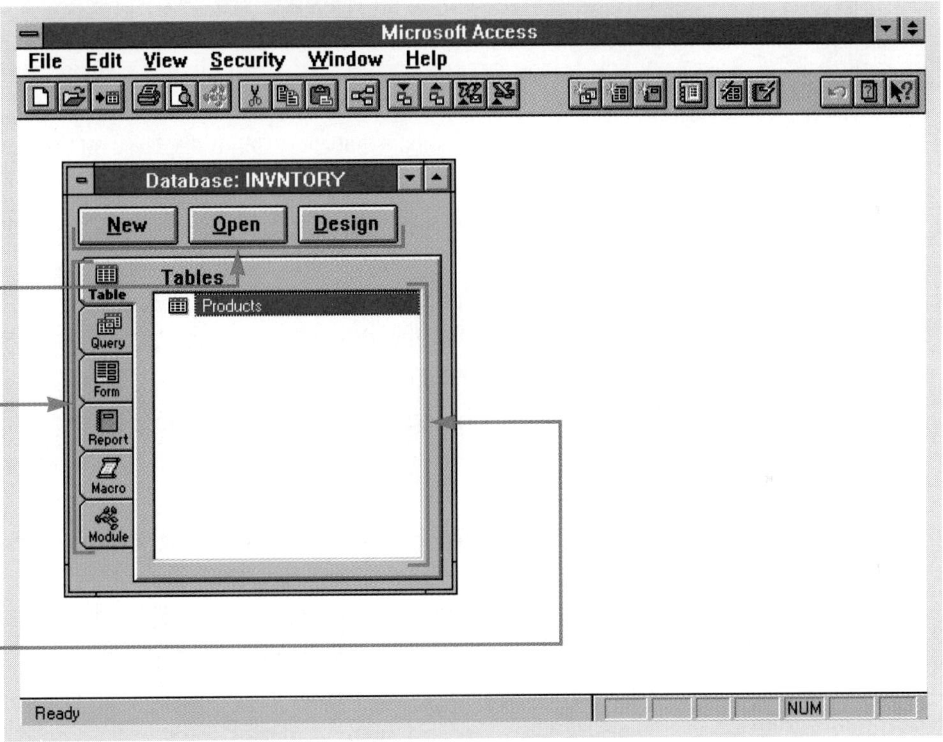

Command buttons allow you to create, open, or modify a table

Object buttons

Tables list box

TABLE 1-3: Database objects

OBJECT	DESCRIPTION
Table	Stores related data in rows (records) and columns (fields)
Query	Asks a question of data in a table; used to find qualifying records
Form	Displays table data in a layout of fields on the screen
Report	Provides printed information from a table, which can include calculations
Macro	Automates database tasks, which can be reduced to a single command
Module	Automates complex tasks using a built-in programming language

To open a database file quickly, you can double-click the filename in the File Name list box of the Open Database dialog box.

Using dialog boxes, toolbars, and buttons

As in many other Microsoft applications, you can choose commands and perform most tasks in Access using either the menus or the toolbars. For more information on choosing commands, see the related topic "Using shortcut keys." Table 1-4 contains a list of commonly used buttons on the Database toolbar. Access contains a variety of toolbars, which appear depending on your current task. ▶ Michael wants to explore how to work with dialog boxes and toolbar buttons. He begins by checking to see which toolbars are available in Access.

1. **Click View on the menu bar, then click Toolbars**
   The Toolbars dialog box opens, as shown in Figure 1-9. This dialog box displays all the toolbars available in Access. Toolbars that are currently displayed on the screen are identified with a check mark. Michael wants to display another toolbar.
2. **Click Table Design then click Show**
   The Table Design toolbar appears, and the Show button changes to Hide, which you can click to hide, or dismiss, a displayed toolbar. Notice that most of the buttons on the Table Design toolbar are dimmed, indicating that they are not available. Michael wants to hide the Table Design toolbar and close this dialog box.
3. **Click Hide to hide the Table Design toolbar, then click Close**
   Michael wants to see which buttons are available on the Database toolbar to become familiar with the types of tasks he can perform in Access.
4. **Move the mouse pointer over the Print Preview button on the Database toolbar, *but do not click the mouse button***
   When you move the pointer over a button, a **ToolTip** displays the name of the button, and a description of the button appears in the status bar. See Figure 1-10.
5. **Move the mouse pointer over each button on the Database toolbar and read its ToolTip and status bar description**

TABLE 1-4: Commonly used buttons on the Database toolbar

BUTTON	NAME	DESCRIPTION
	New Database	Creates a new database
	Open Database	Opens an existing database
	Print	Opens the Print dialog box for the current object
	Print Preview	Opens a Print Preview window for the current object
	Cut	Removes the selected item and places it in the Clipboard
	Copy	Copies the selected area to the Clipboard
	Paste	Pastes the contents of the Clipboard to the selected area

FIGURE 1-9: Toolbars dialog box

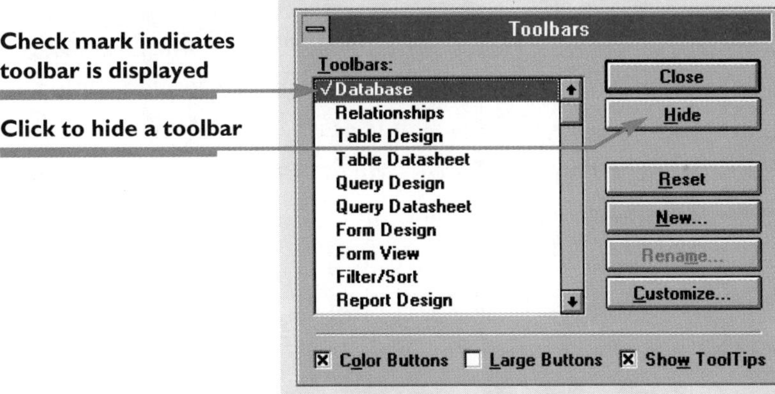

FIGURE 1-10: Print Preview ToolTip

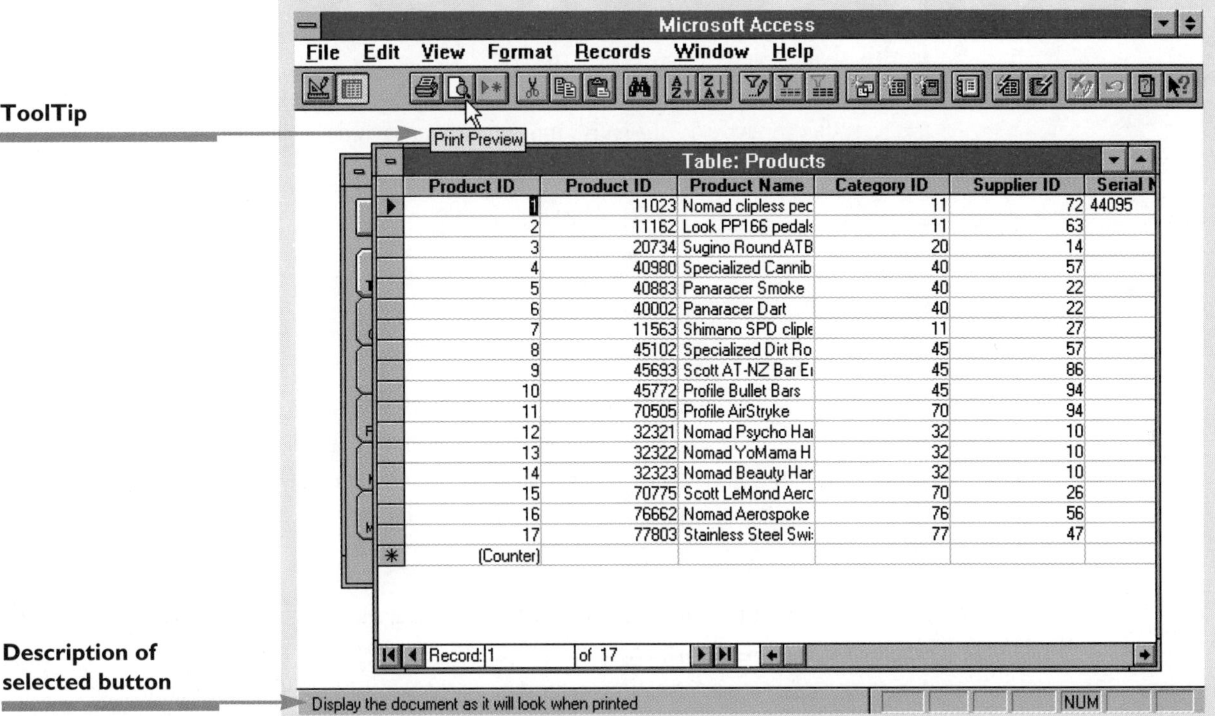

Using shortcut keys

You can use cursor or pointer-movement keys to make choices in a dialog box or menu. To open a menu from the keyboard, press [Alt] and the underlined letter in the name of the menu you want to select. To choose a command from a menu, use [↑] or [↓], then press [Enter] or press the underlined letter of the command you want to select. To open a different menu, use [→] or [←]. To move within a dialog box, press the underlined letter of the command you want to execute.

Getting Help

Access provides an extensive on-line Help system that gives you immediate access to definitions, explanations, and useful tips. Help information is displayed in a separate window, which you can resize and refer to as you work. The easiest way to get Help is to press [F1] at any time, and Access will display context-sensitive Help information for the task you are currently performing. The Help window contains buttons that lead you through different sets of instructions for Access, as described in Table 1-5. ▶ Michael wants to find information on moving through a database table, and he decides to use the Access on-line Help to do so.

1 **Click Help on the menu bar, then click Search**
The Search dialog box opens. See Figure 1-11. You use this dialog box to look up a specific topic or feature.

2 **In the search text box, type movi**
As you type each character, the alphabetically arranged topics scroll in the search list below the text box. After you type "i," the entry "moving between records" appears selected in the list below the text box.

3 **Click Show Topics**
A new list appears in the Show Topics list below the Search list. Michael wants to read the selected topic, "Moving Between Records and Fields."

4 **Click Go To**
A window opens containing information on moving between records and fields. See Figure 1-12. Depending on the type and size of your monitor, the window might appear differently on your screen. Notice that when the mouse pointer is on a green underlined topic, its shape changes to 👆. You can click a green underlined topic to open a dialog box with more information about that topic.

5 **Scroll down the window, move the mouse pointer to the green underlined topic datasheet until the pointer changes to 👆, then click**
A window containing information on the datasheet opens. After reading the information, Michael closes the window.

6 **Press [Esc]**

7 **Click the underlined topic Go To, as shown in Figure 1-12**
A separate window displays information defining the Go To command. Michael decides to exit Help, then he'll move through the Products table to view the information it contains.

8 **Click File on the Help window menu bar, then click Exit**
The Help utility closes and you return to the Database window.

FIGURE 1-13: Record 15 selected

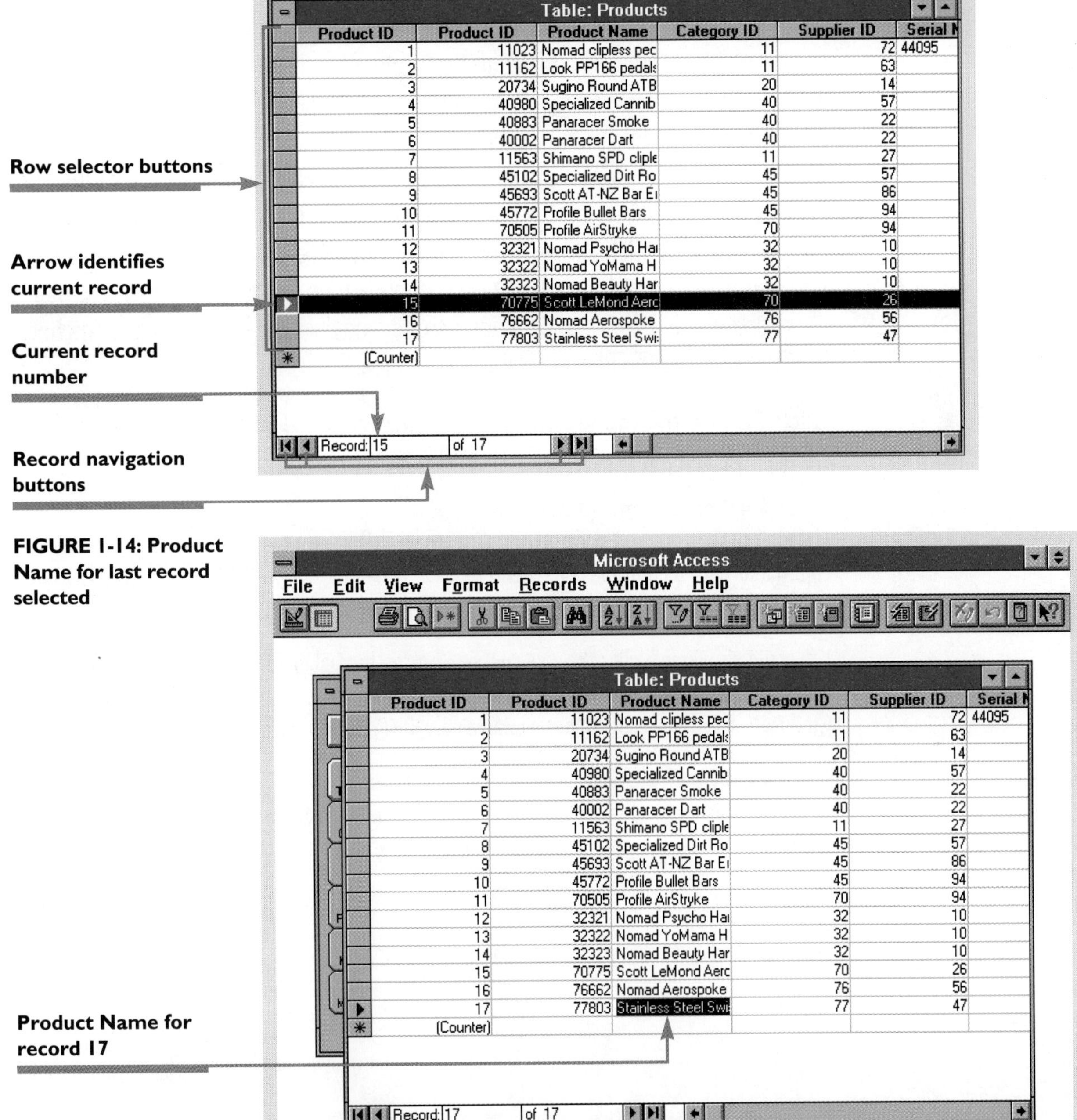

Product ID	Product ID	Product Name	Category ID	Supplier ID	Serial N
1	11023	Nomad clipless pec	11	72	44095
2	11162	Look PP166 pedal	11	63	
3	20734	Sugino Round ATB	20	14	
4	40980	Specialized Cannib	40	57	
5	40883	Panaracer Smoke	40	22	
6	40002	Panaracer Dart	40	22	
7	11563	Shimano SPD cliple	11	27	
8	45102	Specialized Dirt Ro	45	57	
9	45693	Scott AT-NZ Bar E	45	86	
10	45772	Profile Bullet Bars	45	94	
11	70505	Profile AirStryke	70	94	
12	32321	Nomad Psycho Ha	32	10	
13	32322	Nomad YoMama H	32	10	
14	32323	Nomad Beauty Har	32	10	
15	70775	Scott LeMond Aerc	70	26	
16	76662	Nomad Aerospoke	76	56	
17	77803	Stainless Steel Swi	77	47	
(Counter)					

FIGURE 1-14: Product Name for last record selected

TROUBLE?

Don't worry that the product names are **truncated**, or cut off. You will learn how to fix this in the next unit.■

Closing a database and exiting Access

When you have finished working in a database, you need to close the object you were working in, such as a table, and then close the database. If you've made changes to the database file, you need to save them before closing. To close a table, click Close on the File menu. To close a database, click Close Database on the File menu. When you have completed all your work in Access, you need to exit the application by clicking Exit on the File menu. Table 1-7 lists the different ways of exiting Access. ▶ Michael has finished exploring Access for now. He needs to close the Products table and the INVNTORY database, then exit Access. Because he didn't make changes to the INVNTORY database file, he does not have to save it. Michael begins by closing the Products table.

1. Click **File** on the menu bar, as shown in Figure 1-15, then click **Close**
   Now Michael needs to close the INVNTORY database.
2. Click **File** on the menu bar
   The File menu opens and displays the list of commands. Notice that this File menu has different commands from the previous File menu.
3. Click **Close Database**
   You could also double-click the control menu box on the Database window instead of choosing the Close Database command. Access closes the Database window and displays the startup window. Notice that the menu bar contains only the File and Help menus.
4. Click **File** on the menu bar, then click **Exit**
   You could also double-click the application control menu box to exit Access. The Access application closes, and you return to the Program Manager.

TABLE 1-7: Ways to exit Access

METHOD	KEY OR COMMAND
Menu	Choose Exit from the File menu
Keyboard	Press [Alt][F4]
Mouse	Double-click the application control menu box

FIGURE 1-15: Closing a table

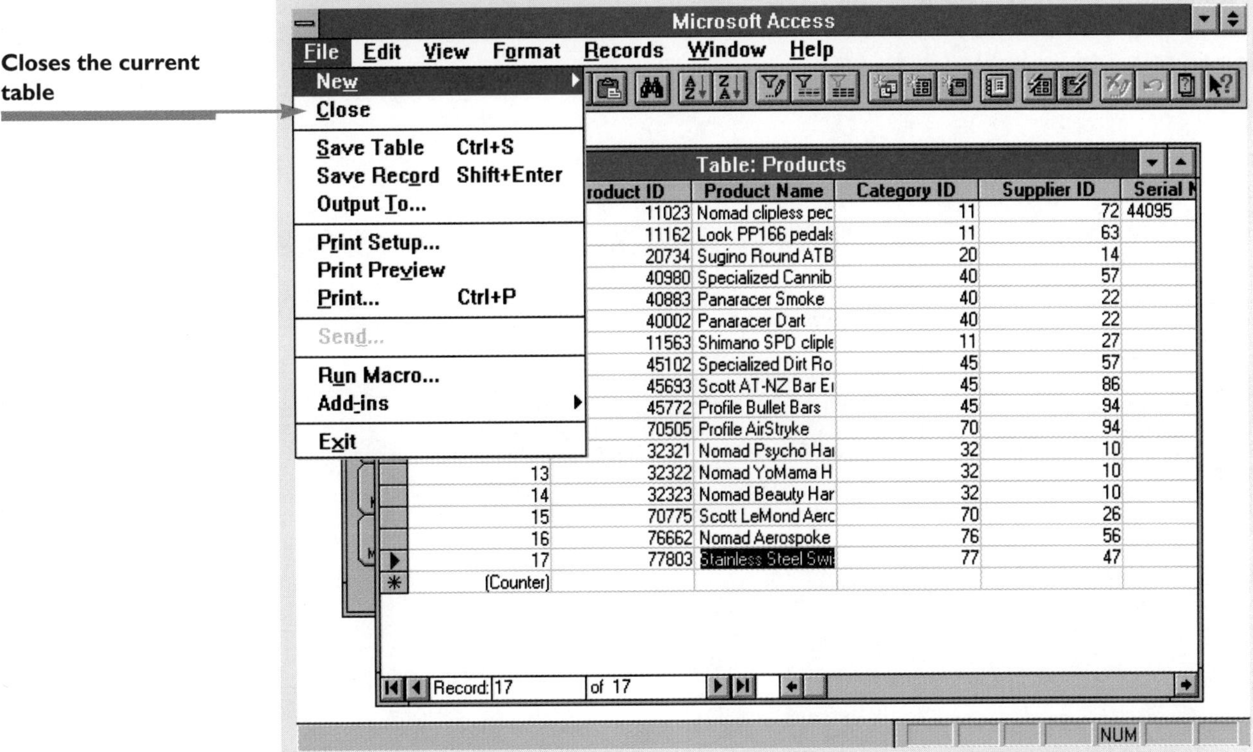

QUICK TIP

Make sure you always properly end your Access session by using the steps in this unit. Improper exit procedures can result in corruption of your data files.

CONCEPTSREVIEW

Label each of the elements of the Access window shown in Figure 1-16.

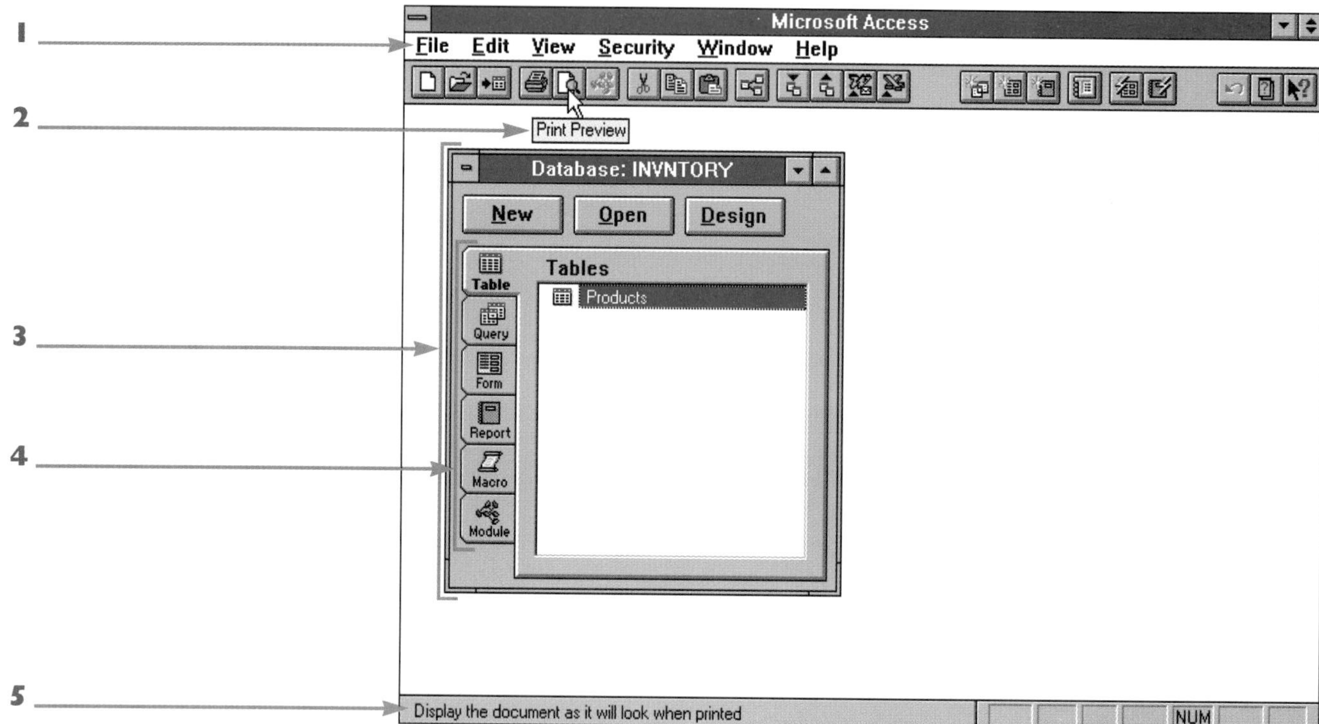

FIGURE 1-16

Match each of the following terms with the statement that describes its function.

6 A collection of data related to a particular topic or purpose

7 Combination of keys resulting in the execution of a command

8 Area that contains all database objects

9 Area in which data about a particular subject is stored

10 The name of a toolbar button

a. Database window
b. Table
c. Database
d. ToolTip
e. Shortcut keys

Select the best answer from the list of choices.

11 An electronic database can perform all of the following tasks, EXCEPT:

a. Displaying information visually
b. Calculating data accurately
c. Planning database objectives
d. Recalculating updated information

12 Which of the following is NOT a database?

a. Customer information
b. Interoffice memo
c. Telephone directory
d. Dictionary

13 Which button opens an existing database?

a. [cut button]
b. [new button]
c. [paste button]
d. [open button]

14 A menu command that is followed by an ellipsis means

a. The command is not currently available
b. Clicking the command will open a dialog box
c. Clicking the command will open a submenu
d. The command has no shortcut key

15 You can get Help in any of the following ways, EXCEPT:

a. Clicking Help on the menu bar
b. Pressing [F1]
c. Clicking the Help button
d. Minimizing the Database window

16 Which Help command displays a dialog box in which you can type the word or term for which you want Help?

a. History
b. Glossary
c. Search
d. Back

17 Which of the following is NOT a method of exiting Access?

a. Choose Exit from the File menu
b. Click the Exit button on the Database toolbar
c. Double-click the Access window control menu box
d. Press [Alt][F4]

APPLICATIONS REVIEW

1 Start Access then identify the parts of the window.

a. Make sure your computer is on and Windows is running.
b. Double-click the Microsoft Office program group icon.
c. Double-click the Microsoft Access application icon.
d. Try to identify as many components of the Access window as you can without referring to the unit material.

2 Open a database table.

a. Make sure your Student Disk is in the appropriate disk drive.
b. Click the Open Database button on the Database toolbar.
c. Open the database named STATS-1.MDB from your Student Disk.
d. Open the Statistical Data table.
e. Click the object buttons in the Database window to see the contents of each object.

3 Use dialog boxes, toolbars, and buttons.

a. Click the Print button on the Database toolbar to display the Print dialog box.
b. Click Setup to see what printer is currently active.
c. Click Cancel in the Print Setup dialog box, then click Cancel in the Print dialog box.
d. Move the mouse pointer over each toolbar button and view its ToolTip and status bar description.

4 Move through a database table.

a. Press [Tab] to move across record 1.
b. Click the Next Record button to move to record 2.
c. Click the Last Record button to move to record 51.
d. Click the Previous Record button until you have reached record 49.

5 Get Help.

a. Click Help on the menu bar, then click Search.
b. Type "exi" in the search text box.
c. Click the topic "Exit" in the list of search topics.
d. Click Show Topics.
e. Select the topic "Exit Command (File Menu)," then click Go To.
f. After reading the information, double-click the control menu box on the Help window to close Help.

6 Close a database and exit Access.

a. Click File on the menu bar, then click Close to close the Statistical Data table.
b. Click File on the menu bar, then click Close Database to close the STATS-1.MDB database file.
c. Click File on the menu bar, then click Exit to exit Access.

INDEPENDENT CHALLENGE 1

Ten examples of databases are given below. Using each of these examples, write down one sample record for each database and describe the fields you would expect to find in each.

1 Telephone directory

2 College course offerings

3 Restaurant menu

4 Cookbook

5 Movie listing

6 Encyclopedia

7 Shopping catalog

8 Corporate inventory

9 Party guest list

10 Members of the House of Representatives

INDEPENDENT CHALLENGE 2

Access provides on-line Help that explains procedures and gives you examples and demos. Help covers such elements as the Database window, the status bar, toolbar buttons, dialog boxes, and Access commands and options. Start Access then explore on-line Help by clicking Cue Cards on the Help menu. Read all the topics in "See a quick overview." Use the Back or Contents button to return to your starting point. Double-click the control menu box on the Help window to close Help, then exit Access.

UNIT 2

OBJECTIVES

- ▶ Plan a database
- ▶ Create a database
- ▶ Create a table
- ▶ Modify a table
- ▶ Enter records
- ▶ Edit records
- ▶ Preview and print the datasheet

Creating A DATABASE

Now that you are familiar with some of the basic Access features, you are ready to plan and build your own database. When you build a database, you create one or more tables containing the fields that hold the data. After you create a database, you can save, print, and manipulate the data within it. ▶ Michael wants to build and maintain a database containing information about all Nomad customers who have booked tours since 1990. The information in the database will be useful when Michael budgets for the future and when he prepares the company's Annual Report. ▶

Planning a database

Planning a Database

Before you start entering records in the database, you need to identify the goal of the database and plan how you want data stored in it. Your database might contain more than one table; the planning stage is when you decide how many tables the database will include and what data will be stored in each table. Although you can modify a database at any time, adding a new field after any records have been entered means additional work. It's impossible to plan for all potential uses of a database, but any up-front planning makes the process go more smoothly. ▶ Michael has done some preliminary planning on how the database can be used, but he knows from experience that other Nomad employees might have additional uses for the same customer information. Michael uses the following guidelines to plan his database:

1. **Determine the purpose of the database and give it a meaningful name.**
   Michael needs to store information on customers who have taken a Nomad tour. Michael names the database "CUSTOMRS," and names the table containing the customer data "Customers." He decides that the database will contain only one table because all the customer information needed can be stored there.

2. **Determine the results, called output, that you want to see, using the information stored in the database.**
   Michael needs to sort the information in a variety of ways: alphabetically by tour to measure popularity, by tour date to gauge effective scheduling dates, and by postal code for promotional mailings. He will also need to create specialized lists of customers, such as customers who took a bike tour since 1994.

3. **Collect all the information, called input, that will produce the results you want to see, talking to all the possible database users for additional ideas that might enhance the design.**
   Michael thinks that the current customer information form, as shown in Figure 2-1, is a good basis for his database table. The form provides most of the information Nomad wants to store in the database for each customer, making it a good starting point.

4. **Sketch the structure of the table, including each field's data type.**
   Using all the information on the original customer information form, Michael plans each field, the type of data each field contains (such as whether the field contains text or values to be used in calculations), and a brief description of each field's purpose. Table 2-1 lists common data types. Figure 2-2 is a sketch of the Customers table, including several new fields not included in the original customer information form.

FIGURE 2-1: Original customer information form

Nomad Ltd
Customer Information Form

Customer Name: Ginny Braithwaite
3 Which Way, Apt. 2
Salem, MA 01970

Tour: Road Bike
Date: June 15, 1994

FIGURE 2-2: Plan for Customers table

Fields	Data type	Description
CustomerID	Unique number for each record	Identifies each record
FirstName	Text	Customer's first name (+ optional middle initial)
LastName	Text	Customer's last name
Address	Text	Customer's street address
City	Text	Customer's city
State	Text	Customer's state
PostalCode	Text	Customer's zip code
Tour	Text	Type of tour
Date	Date/Time	Starting date of tour
Age	Number	Customer's age

TABLE 2-1: Common data types

DATA TYPE	DESCRIPTION OF CONTENTS
Text	Alphanumeric characters (up to 255 characters per field)
Number	Numeric values that can be used in calculations
Date/Time	Date and time values
Counter	A numeric value that automatically increases
Memo	Alphanumeric characters of unlimited length

Creating a database

After planning the structure of the database, the next step is to create the database file. This file will contain all the objects—such as tables, forms, reports, and queries—that will be used to enter and manipulate the data. When you create a database, you assign it a name. This filename can contain up to eight characters, consisting of lowercase or uppercase letters, numbers, and most symbols, but no spaces or commas. Access automatically adds the file extension .MDB to the filename. For more information on protecting a database file, see the related topic "Creating a backup." ▶ With his plan complete, Michael is ready to create the CUSTOMRS database file.

1. **Start Access then insert your Student Disk in the disk drive**
   Make sure you have made a copy of your Student Disk, as instructed on the "Read This Before You Begin Microsoft Access 2.0" page, before you use your Student Disk.
2. Click the **New Database button** on the Database toolbar
   The New Database dialog box opens, as shown in Figure 2-3.
3. Type **customrs** in the File Name text box to replace the selected default filename
4. Click the **Drives list arrow**, then click **a:**
   These lessons assume that your Student Disk is in drive A. If you are using a different drive or storing your practice files on a network, click the appropriate drive. If you are not saving files to the MY_FILES directory of your Student Disk, or if you did not complete the exercises in "Microsoft Windows 3.1," skip the next step.
5. Double-click the **MY_FILES** directory
   The CUSTOMRS database file will be saved on your Student Disk in the MY_FILES directory, as shown in Figure 2-4.
6. Click **OK**
   The Database window opens, displaying the new, empty database, as shown in Figure 2-5.

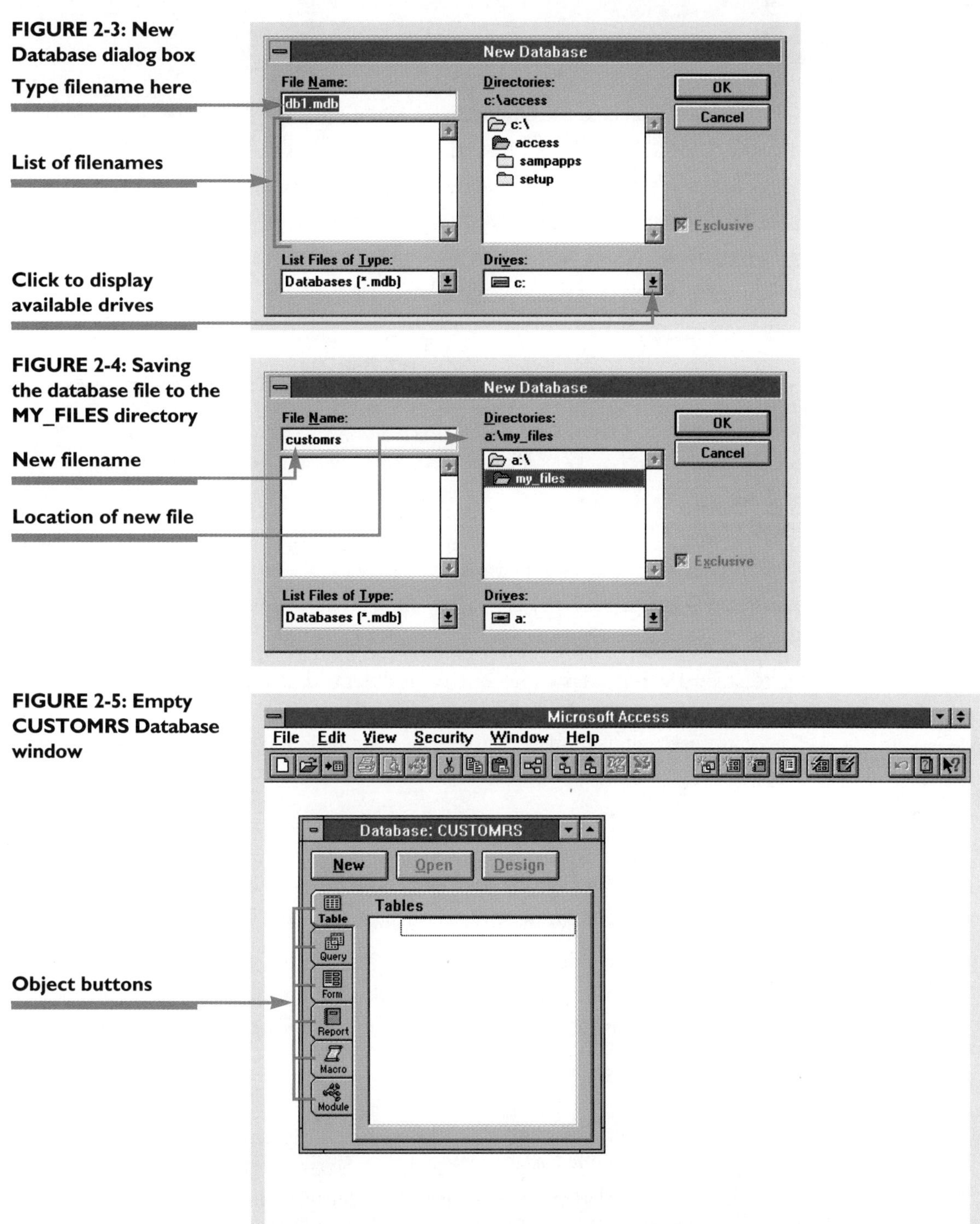

FIGURE 2-3: New Database dialog box

FIGURE 2-4: Saving the database file to the MY_FILES directory

FIGURE 2-5: Empty CUSTOMRS Database window

Creating a backup

The information in your database is very important. You should protect your investment of time spent planning the database and entering data in it by creating backup copies of the database file. The database file, which has the extension .MDB, should be copied to a disk or tape on a daily or weekly basis.

TROUBLE?

If you need help starting Access, refer to the lesson, "Starting Access 2.0 for Windows" in Unit 1.

Creating a table

Now that you've created the database file, you are ready to create the table (or tables) in the database. Creating a table is easy using the Access Table Wizard. The **Table Wizard** guides you through the process of creating a simple table, prompting you to choose the fields and options for your table. For more information on creating a table, see the related topic "Creating a table manually." ▶ Using his sketch as a guide, Michael will use the Table Wizard to create his Customers table.

1 **In the Database: CUSTOMRS dialog box, click the Table object button, if necessary, then click New**
The New Table dialog box opens. Michael uses the Table Wizard to create the new table.

2 **Click Table Wizards**
The Table Wizard dialog box opens, as shown in Figure 2-6. The Table Wizard offers 26 business and 19 personal sample tables from which you can choose. Each sample table provides sample fields related to the specific table type. Michael will choose fields from the Customers sample table to include in his Customers table.

3 **Make sure the Business radio button is selected, then click Customers in the Sample Tables list box**
The Sample Fields entries listed relate to customer information. Michael will choose the fields from this list that match his plan.

4 **Click CustomerID in the Sample Fields list box, then click the Single Field button**
The CustomerID field moves into the Fields in my new table box. Michael proceeds to add all the necessary fields for his table. (*Hint:* When a field name is selected, it is not necessary to click it before clicking.)

5 **Repeat Step 4 to enter the following fields in the table: FirstName, LastName, Address, City, State, and PostalCode**
Compare your Table Wizard dialog box to Figure 2-7.

6 **Click Next**
The second Table Wizard dialog box opens. Michael intended to name the table "Customers," which Access suggests in this dialog box. He also wants Access to set the **primary key**, a field that qualifies each record as unique. Every record in a database table must be unique to ensure the integrity of the data. The primary key prevents more than one record from having the same value in the field designated as the primary key. For example, if the CustomerID field is the primary key, there could be only one CustomerID with the value 101. If you do not specify a primary key, Access will create one for you.

7 **Click Next**
The third Table Wizard dialog box opens, as shown in Figure 2-8. Michael thinks he might want to modify the table's design.

8 **Click the Modify the table design radio button, then click Finish**
The table opens in Design view, which allows you to add, delete, or modify the table's structure.

FIGURE 2-6: First Table Wizard dialog box

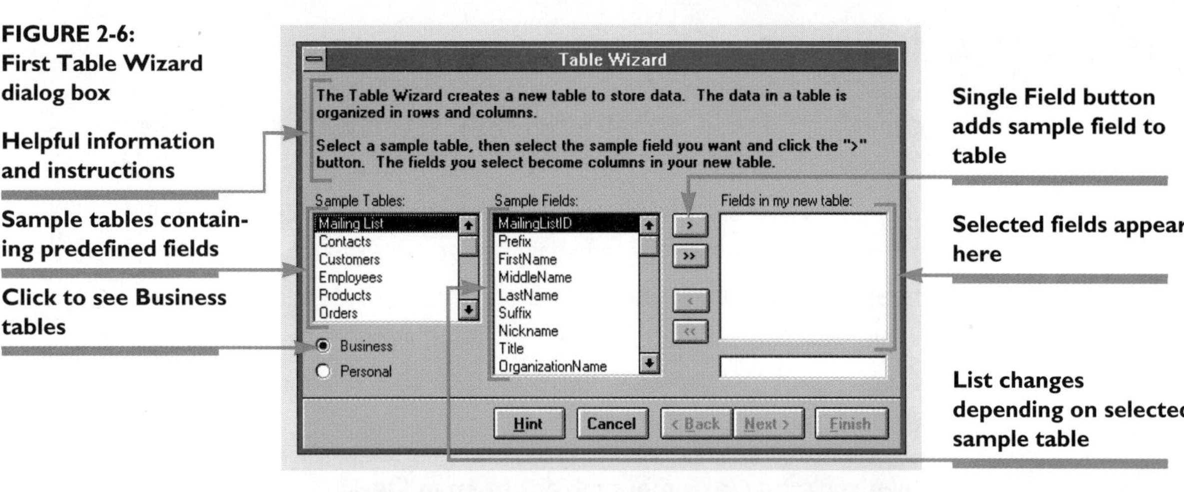

FIGURE 2-7: Completed Fields in my new table list

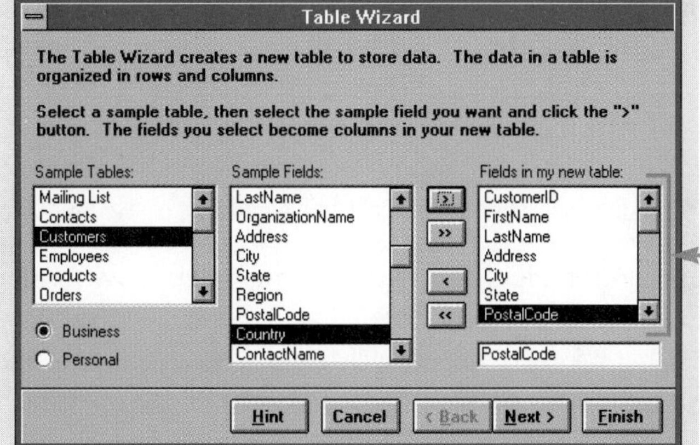

Fields selected for table

FIGURE 2-8: Third Table Wizard dialog box

Click to modify table

Creating a table manually

You can create a table manually, without using the Table Wizard, by clicking the New Table button in the New Table dialog box. No sample tables or sample fields are available; you create any field names you want. Field names can contain up to 64 characters including letters, numbers, spaces, and some special characters. You might want to create a table manually if your application is unique or your fields are unusual.

TROUBLE?

If you inadvertently add the wrong sample field while in the first Table Wizard dialog box, select the field then click the Remove Field button to return the field to the Sample Fields list box.

Modifying a table

After creating a table, you can modify it in Design view. **Design view** allows you to modify the structure of a table by adding and deleting fields, and adding **field descriptions**, which clarify the purpose or function of a field and appear in the status bar when you enter data. You can also define **field properties**, such as the number of decimal places in a number field, in Design view. ▶ Using the Table Wizard, Michael was able to add all but three of the fields in his table. Now, in Design view, he'll add the three remaining fields, add field descriptions, and modify certain field properties.

1. Make sure the Customers table is open in Design view, as shown in Figure 2-9
   If you closed the table at the end of the previous lesson, click the table name in the Database window, then click Design. Notice the row selectors at the left edge of the table. The selectors can contain **indicators**, which are described in Table 2-2, that identify the current record and indicate if the record is new or is being edited. Michael begins by adding a new field, Tour, in the first available blank row. This field will identify the type of tour taken by each Nomad customer.
2. Click in the Field Name box in the eighth row (under PostalCode), type **Tour**, then press **[Enter]**
   The Data Type field becomes highlighted and displays the word "Text." The Tour field will contain text information, so Michael accepts this suggested data type and enters a description for the field.
3. Press **[Enter]**, type **Type of tour**, then press **[Enter]**
   The next field Michael enters is a date field, which will contain the date the tour was taken. A date field has a data type of Date/Time, which Michael specifies by typing the letter "d."
4. Type **Date**, press **[Enter]**, type **d**, press **[Enter]**, type **Starting date of tour** in the Description column, then press **[Enter]**
   When you type "d" the Data Type field changes to Date/Time. The last field Michael must enter is the Age field. This field will contain the age of the tour participant. Michael specifies the data type for a number field by typing the letter "n."
5. Type **Age**, press **[Enter]**, then type **n**
   By default, number fields are displayed with two decimal places. Because this is not an appropriate format for a person's age, Michael needs to change the format of the number. To do so he presses [F6] to move to the Field Properties section of the window.
6. Press **[F6]** to switch panes to the Field Properties section
   Currently the Decimal Places box displays the option "Auto," which specifies the default two decimal places. Michael needs to change the number of decimal places too so that the ages will appear as whole numbers.
7. Click in the Decimal Places box, click the **list arrow**, then click **0** to specify whole numbers

FIGURE 2-9: Table in Design view

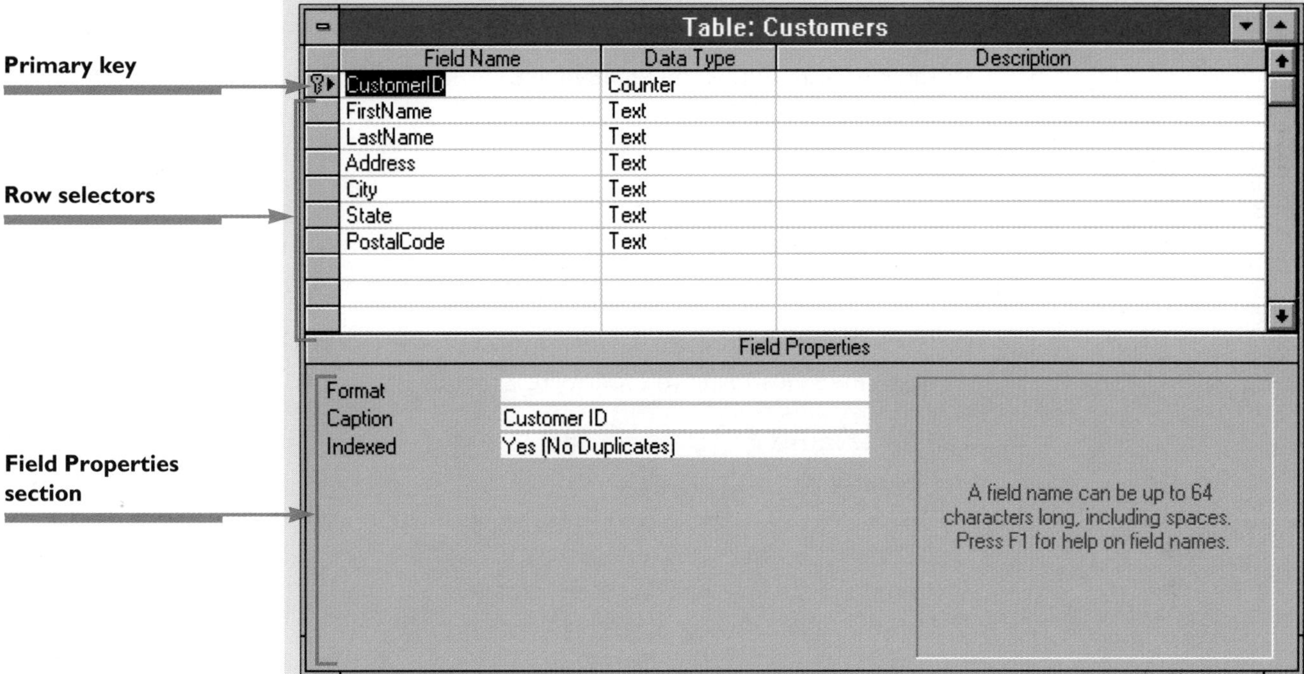

TABLE 2-2: Indicators in row selectors

SYMBOL	DESCRIPTION
▶	Current record indicator
*	New record indicator
✎	Edit record indicator

Modifying a table, continued

Next Michael needs to add a description for each of the fields he entered. For more information on modifying table entries, see the related topic "Editing table entries."

8 Press **[F6]** to switch panes, then click in the Age field Description box

9 Type **Enter the Customer's age at the time of the tour**
Next Michael adds descriptions for each of the remaining fields.

10 Click in each field name's Description box and add a description for the first nine fields using the following entries:

Field Name	Description
CustomerID	Identification number
FirstName	Customer's first name (and optional middle initial)
LastName	Customer's last name
Address	Customer's street address
City	Customer's city
State	Customer's state
PostalCode	Customer's zip code

Your table should look like Figure 2-10. Now that he has entered and modified all the fields in the table, Michael saves the modified table structure.

11 Click **File** on the menu bar, then click **Save**

FIGURE 2-10: Table containing field descriptions

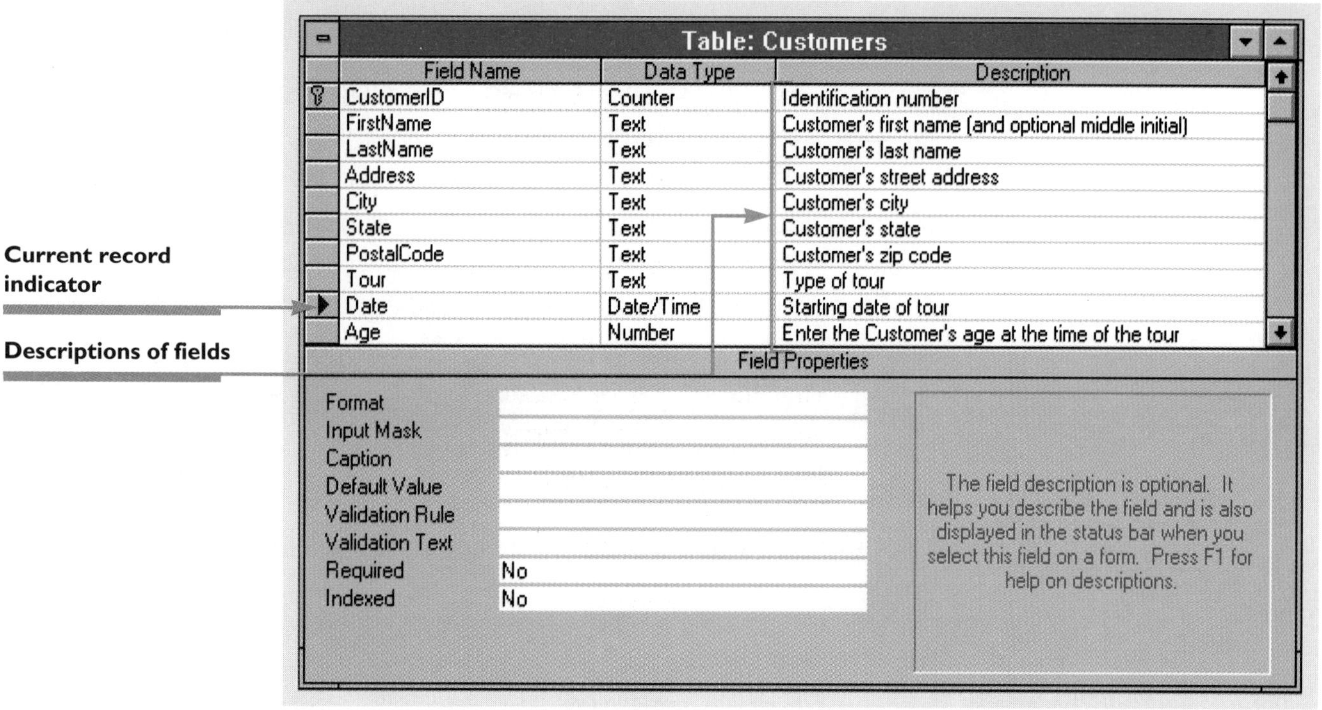

Current record indicator

Descriptions of fields

Table: Customers

Field Name	Data Type	Description
CustomerID	Counter	Identification number
FirstName	Text	Customer's first name (and optional middle initial)
LastName	Text	Customer's last name
Address	Text	Customer's street address
City	Text	Customer's city
State	Text	Customer's state
PostalCode	Text	Customer's zip code
Tour	Text	Type of tour
Date	Date/Time	Starting date of tour
Age	Number	Enter the Customer's age at the time of the tour

Field Properties

Format	
Input Mask	
Caption	
Default Value	
Validation Rule	
Validation Text	
Required	No
Indexed	No

The field description is optional. It helps you describe the field and is also displayed in the status bar when you select this field on a form. Press F1 for help on descriptions.

Editing table entries

You can edit any table entry, such as a field name, data type, or description, by selecting the entry then pressing [Delete] or [Backspace] to remove the error. You can modify the field type by selecting the current entry, then clicking the list arrow in the field type box and making another selection. Clicking the Design button on the Database window opens the table in Design view, which allows you to modify the table structure.

QUICK TIP

When entering field information in a column, you can use [↓] to complete the entry and move to the field below.

Entering records

After you create the table structure, you enter the data for the table in the **datasheet**, a grid in which each record is contained in a row and field names are listed as column headings. Careful data entry is vital to obtaining accurate reports from the database. If you enter data carelessly, the results of searches for particular information might be incorrect. See the related topic "Saving your records" for more information on entering records. ▶ Michael is now ready to enter the records for the Customers table into the datasheet. First, he will maximize the datasheet window and resize the table columns.

1 Click **View** on the menu bar, then click **Datasheet**

The Datasheet window opens. Michael wants to be able to see all the fields in the table. He begins by maximizing the Datasheet window.

2 Click the **Maximize button** in the upper-right corner of the datasheet window

The window is maximized, and all the fields are the same size, even though the fields do not require the same amount of space. Michael wants to resize the fields.

3 Move the mouse pointer between the Customer ID and First Name field names

The pointer changes to ✛, as shown in Figure 2-11.

4 Double-click the **left mouse button**

The field width for Customer ID adjusts to the width of the field name. You can also adjust the field width by dragging the mouse pointer when it is between the field names. Michael will resize all the fields in the table to the width of the field names.

5 Repeat steps 3 and 4 until all the fields are resized, as shown in Figure 2-12

When you enter a record, the word "Counter" appears below the current record. This is the primary key assigned by Access. The Counter field automatically advances to the next number. Also, when you enter data into a field that is too narrow, the data scrolls as you enter it. Michael is now ready to enter the first record into the table.

6 Click the **First Name field**, type **Ginny**, press **[Enter]**, type **Braithwaite**, press **[Enter]**, type **3 Which Way, Apt. 2**, press **[Enter]**, type **Salem**, press **[Enter]**, type **MA**, press **[Enter]**, type **01970**, press **[Enter]**, type **Road Bike**, press **[Enter]**, type **6/15/94**, press **[Enter]**, type **25**, then press **[Enter]**

The first record has been entered. Note that you can advance to the next field by pressing either [Enter] or [Tab]. Michael enters nine additional records.

7 Enter the additional records shown in Figure 2-13

Don't be concerned about making mistakes; you learn how to edit records in the next lesson.

8 Resize the Address, City, Date, and Tour fields to the largest entry in the column

9 Click **File** on the menu bar, then click **Save Table**

FIGURE 2-11: Datasheet window and resizing pointer

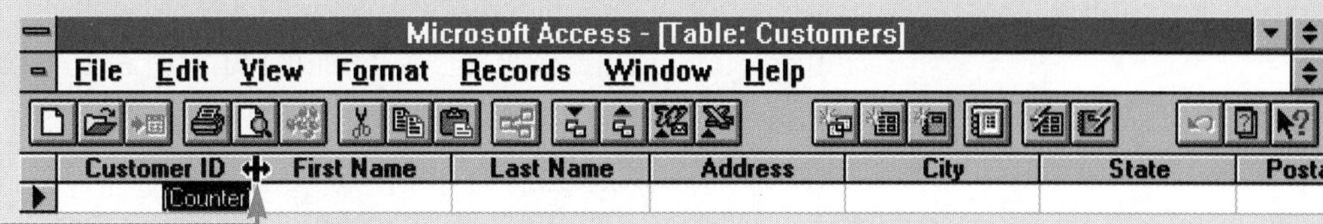

FIGURE 2-12: Resized fields

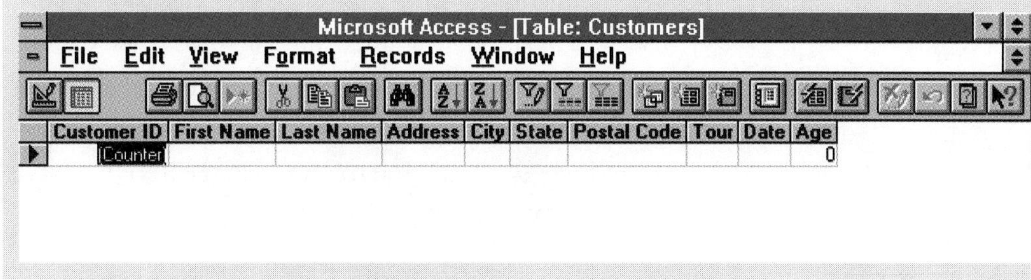

FIGURE 2-13: Records entered in Customers table

Customer ID	First Name	Last Name	Address	City	State	Postal Code	Tour	Date	Age
1	Ginny	Braithwaite	3 Which Way, Apt. 2	Salem	MA	01970-	Road Bike	6/15/94	25
2	Robin	Spencer	293 Serenity Drive	Concord	MA	01742-	Mt. Bike	9/26/93	32
3	Camilla	Dobbins	486 Intel Circuit	RioRancho	NM	87124-	Road Bike	6/15/94	30
4	Pip	Khalsa	1100 Vista Road	Santa Fe	NM	87505-	Mt. Bike	9/26/93	28
5	Kendra	Majors	1 Spring Street	Lenox	MA	02140-	Bungee	9/20/93	21
6	Tasha	Williams	1 Spring Street	Lenox	MA	02140-	Road Bike	6/15/94	28
7	Fred	Gonzales	Purgatory Ski Area	Durango	CO	81301-	Road Bike	6/15/94	26
8	John	Black	11 River Road	Brookfield	CT	06830-	Road Bike	6/15/94	29
9	Scott	Owen	72 Yankee Way	Brookfield	CT	06830-	Bungee	9/20/93	19
10	Virginia	Rodarmor	123 Main Street	Andover	MA	01810-	Bungee	9/20/93	22
(Counter)									0

Saving your records

Unlike other applications in which you must periodically choose a Save command to save your work, Access saves a record after you press [Tab] or [Enter] to advance to the next record or when you close the datasheet. However, when you modify the structure of a table or when you edit records, you need to save the table.

Editing records

You can change the contents of a field at any time. To edit a field, you first click in the field, select the information you want to change, then type the corrections. You can use any text editing techniques. To cut or copy, select the text, then choose the Cut or Copy command from the Edit menu, place the pointer where you want the text, then choose the Paste command from the Edit menu. You can also use the toolbar buttons for Cut, Copy, and Paste instead of the menu commands. Table 2-3 lists several keyboard shortcuts you can use when editing records. For information on reorganizing columns in a table, see the related topic "Moving table columns." ▶ After checking his records, Michael notices that he entered several fields incorrectly. He needs to edit the records to make the corrections. He begins with record 7 where he will change the type of tour from Road Bike to Mt. Bike.

1. **Double-click Road in the Tour field of record 7, then type Mt.**
   Notice that the Edit record indicator appears in the row selector for record 7. Michael also needs to change the date for this record.
2. **Press [Tab] to move to and highlight the date, then type 9/26/93 to change the date**
   Next Michael needs to correct the address information for records 5 and 6.
3. **Click to the right of I in the Address field in record 5, press [Backspace], then type 530**
   The Address field in record 6 should be the same as the Address field in record 5.
4. **Press [↓] then press [Ctrl][']**
   The address for both records is now 530 Spring Street, as shown in Figure 2-14. Michael saves the changes made in the table.
5. **Click File on the menu bar, then click Save Table**

TABLE 2-3: Keyboard shortcuts in tables

SHORTCUT KEY	ACTION
[F5]	Move to a specific record
[F6]	Move between window sections
[F7]	Open the Find dialog box
[Ctrl][']	Insert the value from the same field in the previous record
[Ctrl][;]	Insert the current date
[Ctrl][=]	Move to the first blank record
[Esc]	Undo changes in the current field or record
[Shift][Enter]	Save the current record

FIGURE 2-14: Modified records

Field modified to match entry in previous record

Edit record indicator

Modified entry

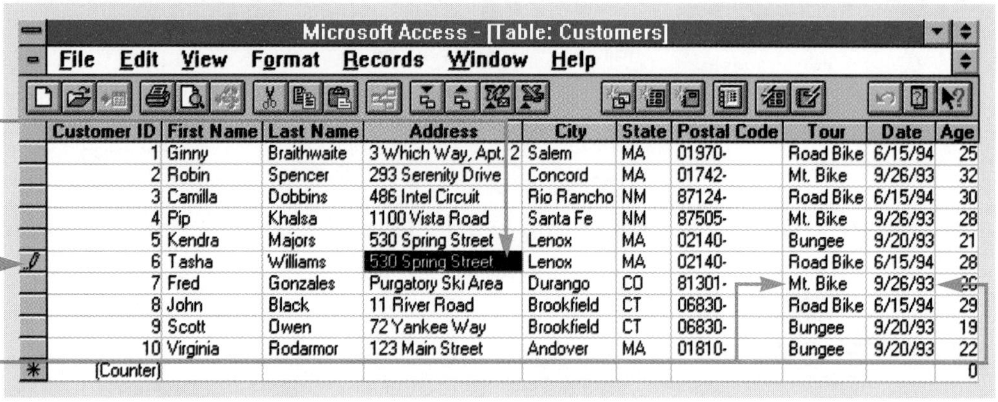

Microsoft Access - [Table: Customers]

File Edit View Format Records Window Help

	Customer ID	First Name	Last Name	Address	City	State	Postal Code	Tour	Date	Age
	1	Ginny	Braithwaite	3 Which Way, Apt. 2	Salem	MA	01970-	Road Bike	6/15/94	25
	2	Robin	Spencer	293 Serenity Drive	Concord	MA	01742-	Mt. Bike	9/26/93	32
	3	Camilla	Dobbins	486 Intel Circuit	Rio Rancho	NM	87124-	Road Bike	6/15/94	30
	4	Pip	Khalsa	1100 Vista Road	Santa Fe	NM	87505-	Mt. Bike	9/26/93	28
	5	Kendra	Majors	530 Spring Street	Lenox	MA	02140-	Bungee	9/20/93	21
✎	6	Tasha	Williams	530 Spring Street	Lenox	MA	02140-	Road Bike	6/15/94	28
	7	Fred	Gonzales	Purgatory Ski Area	Durango	CO	81301-	Mt. Bike	9/26/93	26
	8	John	Black	11 River Road	Brookfield	CT	06830-	Road Bike	6/15/94	29
	9	Scott	Owen	72 Yankee Way	Brookfield	CT	06830-	Bungee	9/20/93	19
	10	Virginia	Rodarmor	123 Main Street	Andover	MA	01810-	Bungee	9/20/93	22
*	(Counter)									0

Moving table columns

You can reorganize the columns in a table by moving them from one location to another. To move a column, click its field name so that the entire column is selected, then drag the pointer to the column's new location. As you drag, the mouse pointer changes to , as shown in Figure 2-15. A heavy vertical line represents the new location. Release the mouse button when you have correctly positioned the column.

Mouse pointer indicating column is being moved

New location of Tour column

Column to be moved

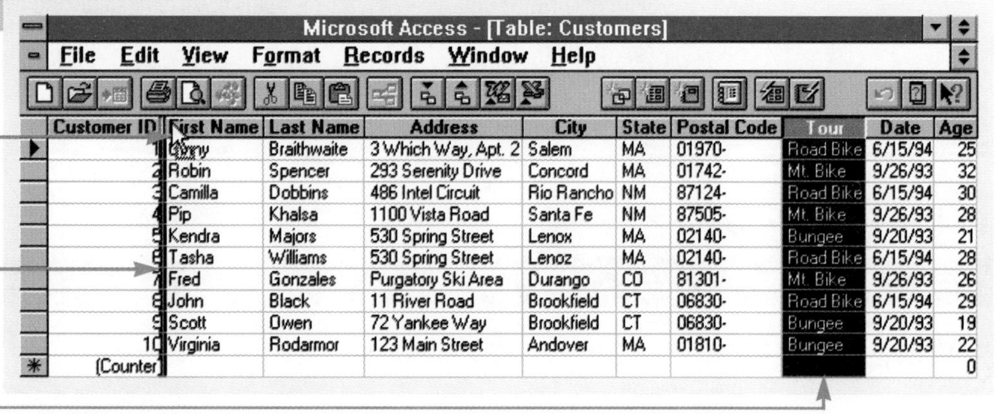

Microsoft Access - [Table: Customers]

File Edit View Format Records Window Help

	Customer ID	First Name	Last Name	Address	City	State	Postal Code	Tour	Date	Age
▶	1	Ginny	Braithwaite	3 Which Way, Apt. 2	Salem	MA	01970-	Road Bike	6/15/94	25
	2	Robin	Spencer	293 Serenity Drive	Concord	MA	01742-	Mt. Bike	9/26/93	32
	3	Camilla	Dobbins	486 Intel Circuit	Rio Rancho	NM	87124-	Road Bike	6/15/94	30
	4	Pip	Khalsa	1100 Vista Road	Santa Fe	NM	87505-	Mt. Bike	9/26/93	28
	5	Kendra	Majors	530 Spring Street	Lenox	MA	02140-	Bungee	9/20/93	21
	6	Tasha	Williams	530 Spring Street	Lenoz	MA	02140-	Road Bike	6/15/94	28
	7	Fred	Gonzales	Purgatory Ski Area	Durango	CO	81301-	Mt. Bike	9/26/93	26
	8	John	Black	11 River Road	Brookfield	CT	06830-	Road Bike	6/15/94	29
	9	Scott	Owen	72 Yankee Way	Brookfield	CT	06830-	Bungee	9/20/93	19
	10	Virginia	Rodarmor	123 Main Street	Andover	MA	01810-	Bungee	9/20/93	22
*	(Counter)									0

FIGURE 2-15: Moving a table column

Previewing and printing the datasheet

After entering and editing the records in a table, you can print the datasheet to obtain a hard copy of the table data. Table 2-4 describes some of the options available in the Print dialog box. Before printing, it's a good idea to preview the datasheet to see how it will look when printed and, if necessary, to make any adjustments to margins, page orientation, and so on. ▶ Michael is ready to preview and print the datasheet.

1. **Click the Print Preview button on the Database toolbar**
   The datasheet appears on a miniaturized page in the Print Preview window, as shown in Figure 2-16, and the Print Preview toolbar appears. Michael decides to use the Magnifier pointer to see how the datasheet looks when magnified.
2. **Click anywhere in the miniaturized datasheet**
   A magnified version of the datasheet appears. Michael returns the datasheet to its original appearance.
3. **Click anywhere in the magnified datasheet**
   Michael is satisfied with the datasheet's appearance and decides to print it.
4. **Click the Print button on the Print Preview toolbar**
   The Print dialog box opens, as shown in Figure 2-17. This dialog box provides options for printing all pages or a specified range of pages, and for printing multiple copies. Michael does not have to make any changes in this dialog box.
5. **Click OK to print the datasheet, then click the Close Window button on the Print Preview toolbar to return to the datasheet**
   With his printed datasheet, Michael is ready to save the table and exit Access.
6. **Click File on the menu bar, then click Save Table**
7. **Click File on the menu bar, then click Exit**

TABLE 2-4: Print dialog box options

OPTION	DESCRIPTION
Printer	Displays the name of the selected printer and print connection
Print Range	Specifies all pages, certain pages, or a range of pages to print
Copies	Specifies the number of copies to print
Print to File	Prints a document to an encapsulated PostScript file instead of a printer
Margins	Adjust the left, right, top, and bottom margins (available through the Setup option)
Orientation	Specifies Portrait (the default) or Landscape paper (available through the Setup option)

FIGURE 2-16: Datasheet in print preview

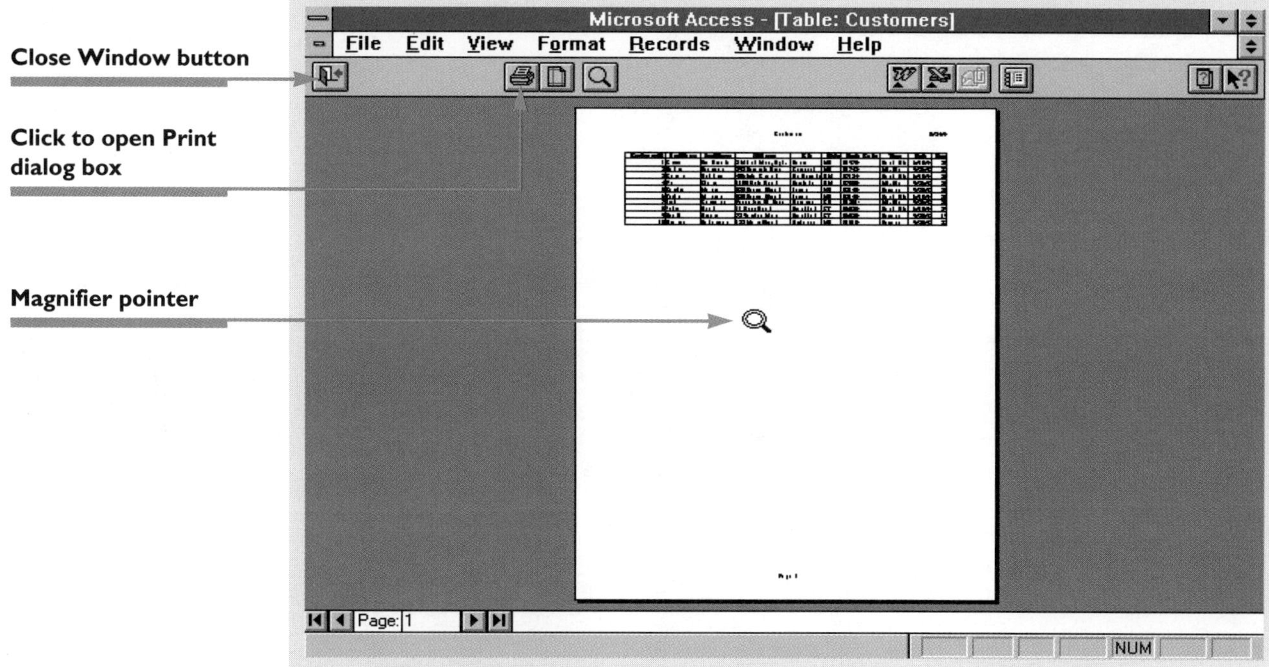

FIGURE 2-17: Print dialog box

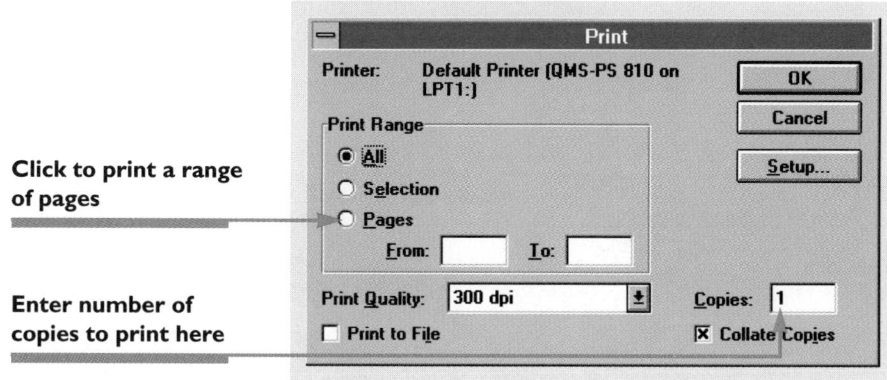

CONCEPTS REVIEW

Label each element of the Access window shown in Figure 2-18.

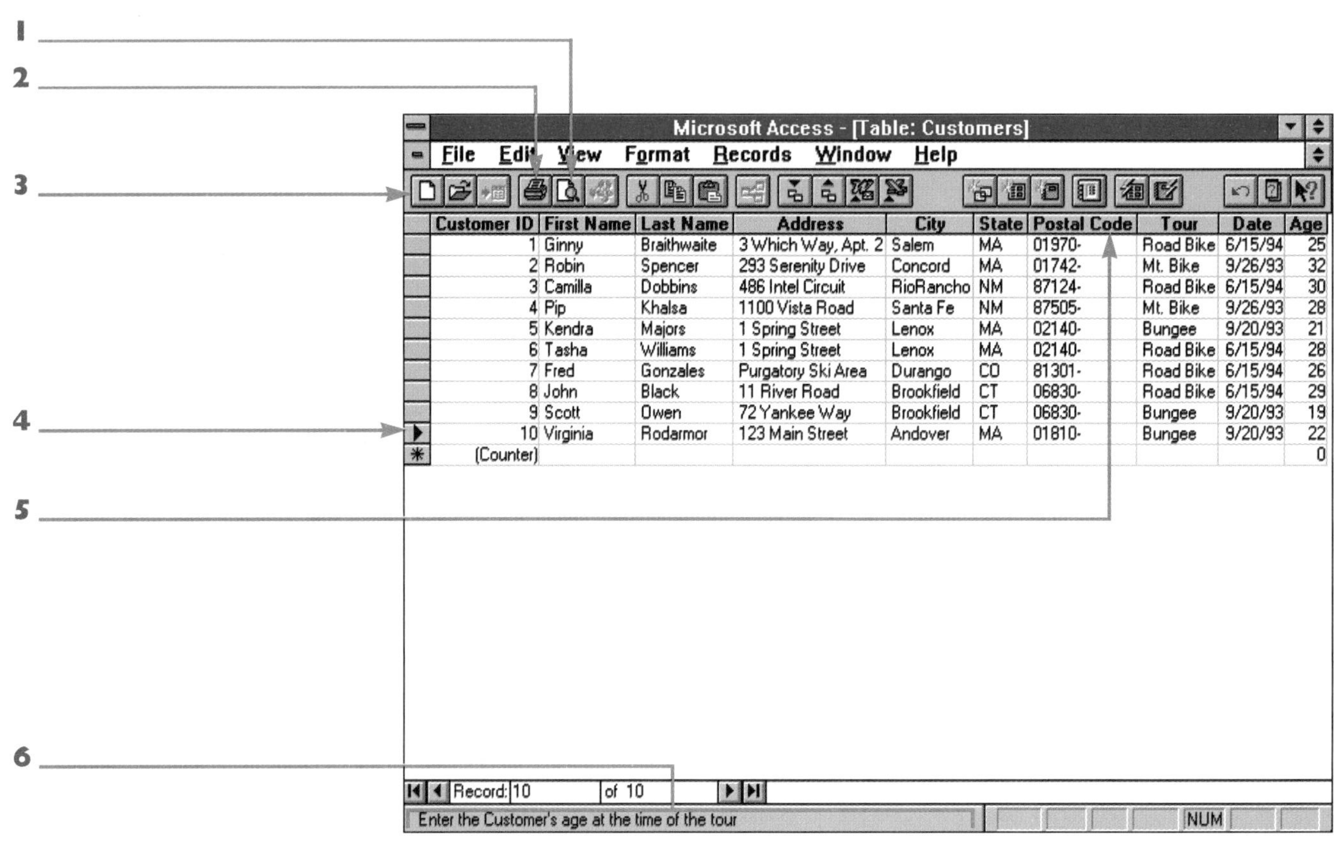

FIGURE 2-18

Match each data type with the statement that describes its function.

7 Numeric data type that automatically increases with each record

8 Alphanumeric characters of no more than 255 characters in length

9 Alphanumeric characters of unlimited length

10 Numeric values that can be used in calculations

11 Date and time values

a. Memo
b. Date/Time
c. Counter
d. Text
e. Number

Select the best answer from the list of choices.

12 All of the following procedures save a record EXCEPT:

a. Pressing [Tab] to advance to the next record
b. Pressing [Shift][Ctrl] while in the record
c. Pressing [Enter] to advance to the next record
d. Pressing [Shift][Enter] while in the record

13 When the mouse pointer is placed between two field selectors, it becomes

a.
b.
c.
d.

14 The Edit record indicator is

a. [*]
b. [▲]
c. [▶]
d. [✎]

15 The button that closes the Print Preview window is

a.
b.
c.
d.

16 The Table Wizard provides all of the following, EXCEPT:

a. Sample tables
b. Sample fields
c. Sample field descriptions
d. Business and personal tables

APPLICATIONS REVIEW

1 Plan a database.

a. Plan a database that will contain the names and addresses of your business contacts.
b. Based on your own experience, decide which fields you need to include in the database.
c. Write down the necessary fields with names and explanations for each field.

2 Create a database.

a. Start Access and insert your Student Disk in the disk drive.
b. Use the New Database button to create a new database file.
c. Save the file as CONTACTS in the MY_FILES directory on your Student Disk.

3 Create a table.

a. Click the Table object button in the Database window, then click New.
b. Click Table Wizards.
c. In the Sample Tables list box, click Contacts. Make sure the Business radio button is selected.
d. In the Sample Fields list box, choose each of the following fields for your table:
ContactID
Prefix
FirstName
LastName
Address
City
State
PostalCode
Birthdate
e. Continue through the Table Wizard. Name the table CONTACTS.
f. Click the Modify the table design radio button in the third Table Wizard dialog box, then click Finish.

4 Modify a table.

a. In the first available blank row, add a new text field called "Other."
b. Click the ContactID field Description box.
c. Type "Unique number for Contact."
d. Press [↓] to move to the next Description box. Add appropriate descriptions for the other fields.

5 Enter records.

a. Display the Datasheet window.
b. Enter the names of 10 people you consider to be associates. You can make up the data if you want.
c. Resize the columns so that all the data is displayed.

6 Edit records, then preview and print the datasheet.

a. Make at least three changes to the records.
b. Click the Print Preview button on the Database toolbar to display the datasheet in the Print Preview window.
c. After viewing the datasheet, click the Print button on the Print Preview toolbar to print the datasheet.
d. After printing, return to the Database window.
e. Save the table then exit Access.

INDEPENDENT CHALLENGE 1

As the personnel manager for Green Gardens Realty, you are responsible for maintaining an employee record for each employee. Currently, Green Gardens employs four salespeople, three secretaries, and one general manager. You need to create a database to contain the employee information. Although you can add other fields, the following fields must be included in your database table:

EmployeeID
FirstName
LastName
SocialSecurityNumber
Title
DateHired
Salary

To complete this independent challenge:

1. Sketch a sample database on paper, indicating which fields are necessary. Write down each field name and a description of the field's function.
2. Create a database file named GRNGRDNS.MDB in the MY_FILES directory on your Student Disk.
3. Use the Table Wizard to create the table, and use the Employees sample table to select the fields. Make sure the Business radio button is selected in the Table Wizard dialog box, and accept the default table name.
4. Make up data and add records for each employee.
5. Save the table, then preview and print the datasheet.
6. Close the table.
7. Submit your paper sketch with your printed datasheet.

INDEPENDENT CHALLENGE 2

Create a database that catalogs your own music collection. Be sure to include the following fields, although you can add others:

MusicCollectionID
GroupName
Title
Format
YearReleased

To complete this independent challenge:

1. Sketch a sample database on paper, indicating which fields are necessary. Write down each field name and a description of the field's function.
2. Create a database file named MYMUSIC.MDB in the MY_FILES directory on your Student Disk.
3. Use the Table Wizard to create the table, and use the Music Collection sample table (a Personal table) to select the fields.
4. Enter records for your music collection. Enter a minimum of 10 records.
5. Save the table, then preview and print the datasheet.
6. Close the table then exit Access.
7. Submit your paper sketch with your printed datasheet.

UNIT 3

OBJECTIVES

- Find records
- Sort a table
- Filter a table
- Create a simple query
- Create a complex query
- Modify a query

Manipulating DATA

After you create an Access database table and enter data in it, you can manipulate the data easily to find the information you need. In this unit, you will learn how to find and organize data to display the results you want. You will also learn techniques for retrieving information from a table based on specified criteria. ▶ Nomad Ltd's Travel Division uses its customer database to learn which tours are popular, as well as the demographic backgrounds of its clients. Michael created this database and entered all customer records in it. Now he wants to manipulate the data so he can include preliminary information on Nomad customers in the Annual Report. ▶

Finding records

Finding records in a table is an important database task. Table 3-1 lists a variety of keyboard shortcuts used to navigate a table. In addition, you can locate specific records using the datasheet. For information on finding records, see the related topic "Using wildcards in Find." ▶ Michael wants to locate the record for Carol Smith because he entered her name incorrectly when creating the table; he needs to change the last name to "Smithers." Then he needs to enter a record for a new customer.

1. **Start Access and insert your Student Disk in the disk drive**
2. **Click the Open Database button on the Database toolbar, then open the database named CUSTDATA.MDB from your Student Disk**
   Note that this is the same database as the one you created in Unit 1, which you called CUSTOMRS. A new file is provided here with complete records. Next Michael opens the Customers table and maximizes it so it fills the screen.
3. **Click the Table object button in the Database window, click Customers, click Open, then click the Maximize button to maximize the table window**
   Access displays the Customers table, which contains 30 records, as shown in Figure 3-1. If the Table Datasheet toolbar is not displayed, continue to Step 4; otherwise skip to Step 5.
4. **Click View on the menu bar, click Toolbars to display the Toolbars dialog box, click Table Datasheet, click Show, then click Close**
   Michael will use the Table Datasheet toolbar to change Carol Smith's last name to Smithers.
5. **Click the Find button on the Table Datasheet toolbar**
   The Find in field dialog box opens, as shown in Figure 3-2. By default Access searches the current field, which in this case is Customer ID. However, Michael wants to search all fields in the table for the name "Smith."
6. **Type Smith in the Find What text box, click the All Fields radio button, click Find Next, then click Close**
   Access highlights the name "Smith" in record 11, which is now the current record, for the customer Carol Smith. Michael can now replace the highlighted name with the correct name.
7. **Type Smithers**
   Next Michael wants to see the last record in the table before he enters the new record.
8. **Click Records on the menu bar, click Go To, then click Last**
   The last name of the customer in the last record is selected. Next, enter the new record.
9. **Click the New button on the Table Datasheet toolbar, then enter the following data in record 31**
   Elizabeth Michaels, 57 Beechwood Dr., Wayne, NJ, 07470, Mt. Bike, 6/20/94, 37

FIGURE 3-1: Customers table

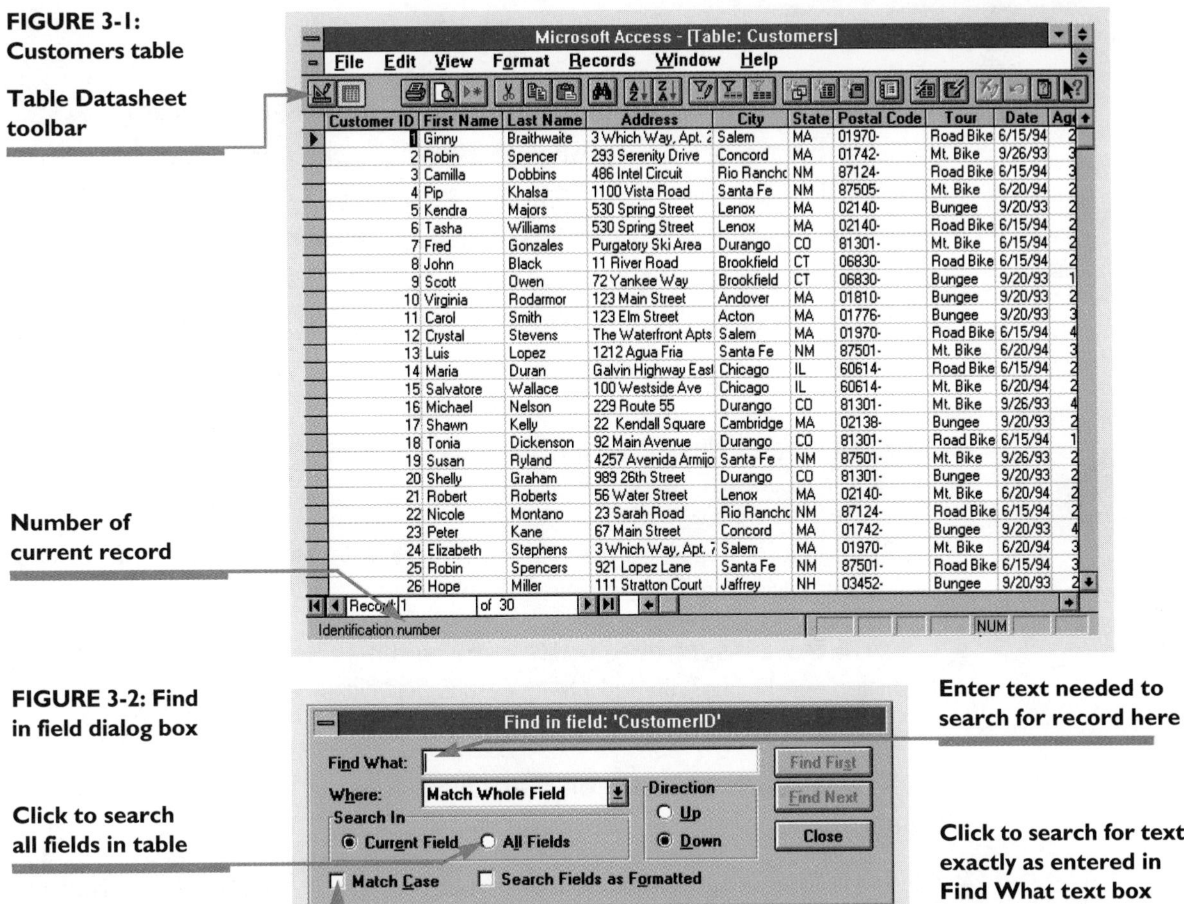

Customer ID	First Name	Last Name	Address	City	State	Postal Code	Tour	Date	Age
1	Ginny	Braithwaite	3 Which Way, Apt. 2	Salem	MA	01970-	Road Bike	6/15/94	2
2	Robin	Spencer	293 Serenity Drive	Concord	MA	01742-	Mt. Bike	9/26/93	3
3	Camilla	Dobbins	486 Intel Circuit	Rio Rancho	NM	87124-	Road Bike	6/15/94	3
4	Pip	Khalsa	1100 Vista Road	Santa Fe	NM	87505-	Mt. Bike	6/20/94	2
5	Kendra	Majors	530 Spring Street	Lenox	MA	02140-	Bungee	9/20/93	2
6	Tasha	Williams	530 Spring Street	Lenox	MA	02140-	Road Bike	6/15/94	2
7	Fred	Gonzales	Purgatory Ski Area	Durango	CO	81301-	Mt. Bike	6/15/94	2
8	John	Black	11 River Road	Brookfield	CT	06830-	Road Bike	6/15/94	2
9	Scott	Owen	72 Yankee Way	Brookfield	CT	06830-	Bungee	9/20/93	1
10	Virginia	Rodarmor	123 Main Street	Andover	MA	01810-	Bungee	9/20/93	2
11	Carol	Smith	123 Elm Street	Acton	MA	01776-	Bungee	9/20/93	3
12	Crystal	Stevens	The Waterfront Apts	Salem	MA	01970-	Road Bike	6/15/94	4
13	Luis	Lopez	1212 Agua Fria	Santa Fe	NM	87501-	Mt. Bike	6/20/94	3
14	Maria	Duran	Galvin Highway East	Chicago	IL	60614-	Road Bike	6/15/94	2
15	Salvatore	Wallace	100 Westside Ave	Chicago	IL	60614-	Mt. Bike	6/20/94	2
16	Michael	Nelson	229 Route 55	Durango	CO	81301-	Mt. Bike	9/26/93	4
17	Shawn	Kelly	22 Kendall Square	Cambridge	MA	02138-	Bungee	9/20/93	2
18	Tonia	Dickenson	92 Main Avenue	Durango	CO	81301-	Road Bike	6/15/94	1
19	Susan	Ryland	4257 Avenida Armijo	Santa Fe	NM	87501-	Mt. Bike	9/26/93	2
20	Shelly	Graham	989 26th Street	Durango	CO	81301-	Bungee	9/20/93	2
21	Robert	Roberts	56 Water Street	Lenox	MA	02140-	Mt. Bike	6/20/94	2
22	Nicole	Montano	23 Sarah Road	Rio Rancho	NM	87124-	Road Bike	6/15/94	2
23	Peter	Kane	67 Main Street	Concord	MA	01742-	Bungee	9/20/93	4
24	Elizabeth	Stephens	3 Which Way, Apt. 7	Salem	MA	01970-	Mt. Bike	6/20/94	3
25	Robin	Spencers	921 Lopez Lane	Santa Fe	NM	87501-	Road Bike	6/15/94	3
26	Hope	Miller	111 Stratton Court	Jaffrey	NH	03452-	Bungee	9/20/93	2

FIGURE 3-2: Find in field dialog box

Using wildcards in Find

Wildcards are symbols you can use as substitutes for characters in text to find any records matching your entry. Access uses three wildcards: the asterisk (*) represents any group of characters, the question mark (?) stands for any single character, and the pound sign (#) stands for a single number digit. For example, to find any word beginning with S, type "s*" in the Find What text box.

TABLE 3-1: Keystrokes for navigating a datasheet

KEYS	ACTIONS	KEYS	ACTIONS
[↑], [↓], [←], [→]	Move one field in the direction indicated	[Tab]	Move to next field in current record
[F5]	Move to Record number box on the horizontal scroll bar, then type number of record to go to	[Shift][Tab]	Move to previous field in current record
[Home]	Move to first field in current record	[Ctrl][Home]	Move to first field in first record
[End]	Move to last field in current record	[Ctrl][End]	Move to last field in last record
		[Ctrl][=]	Move to first blank record

Sorting a table

Sorting Records

The ability to sort information in a table is one of the most powerful features of a database. **Sorting** is an easy way of organizing records according to the contents of a field. For example, you might want to see all records in alphabetical order by last name. You can sort records in **ascending order**, alphabetically from A to Z, or in **descending order**, alphabetically from Z to A. For more information on sorting, see the related topic "Using the menu bar to sort." ▶ Michael sorts his table in a variety of ways, depending on the task he needs to perform. His most common tasks require a list sorted in ascending order by tour, and another list sorted in descending order by date.

1 Click the **Tour** field name
The Tour column is selected. The table will be sorted by tour. In addition to clicking the Tour field name to select the field, you can also click any record's Tour field.

2 Click the **Sort Ascending button** on the Table Datasheet toolbar
The table is sorted in ascending order by tour, as shown in Figure 3-3. Michael decides to print this sorted table for reference using the default settings.

3 Click the **Print button** on the Table Datasheet toolbar, then click **OK**
The sorted datasheet prints. Michael wants to return the table to its original order.

4 Click the **Show All Records button** on the Table Datasheet toolbar
The table returns to its original order. You can also return a table to its original order by sorting the Customer ID field in ascending order. Michael's division wants to know which tour dates are popular, so Michael decides to sort the records in descending order by the Date field.

5 Click the **Date** field name to select the Date column

6 Click the **Sort Descending button** on the Table Datasheet toolbar
The records are sorted from most recent to least recent, as shown in Figure 3-4. Michael notes that bike tours are booming, with 18 customers taking bike tours in June of 1994. This information will be important in planning the 1995 and 1996 seasons. Michael wants to print the sorted table.

7 Click the **Print button** on the Table Datasheet toolbar, then click **OK**
Next Michael returns the table to its original order.

8 Click the **Show All Records button** on the Table Datasheet toolbar

FIGURE 3-3: Table sorted in ascending order by Tour field

Records sorted by tour

Microsoft Access - [Table: Customers]

File Edit View Format Records Window Help

Customer ID	First Name	Last Name	Address	City	State	Postal Code	Tour	Date	Ag
5	Kendra	Majors	530 Spring Street	Lenox	MA	02140-	Bungee	9/20/93	2
26	Hope	Miller	111 Stratton Court	Jaffrey	NH	03452-	Bungee	9/20/93	2
9	Scott	Owen	72 Yankee Way	Brookfield	CT	06830-	Bungee	9/20/93	1
10	Virginia	Rodarmor	123 Main Street	Andover	MA	01810-	Bungee	9/20/93	2
23	Peter	Kane	67 Main Street	Concord	MA	01742-	Bungee	9/20/93	4
11	Carol	Smithers	123 Elm Street	Acton	MA	01776-	Bungee	9/20/93	3
20	Shelly	Graham	989 26th Street	Durango	CO	81301-	Bungee	9/20/93	2
17	Shawn	Kelly	22 Kendall Square	Cambridge	MA	02138-	Bungee	9/20/93	2
16	Michael	Nelson	229 Route 55	Durango	CO	81301-	Mt. Bike	9/26/93	4
2	Robin	Spencer	293 Serenity Drive	Concord	MA	01742-	Mt. Bike	9/26/93	3
4	Pip	Khalsa	1100 Vista Road	Santa Fe	NM	87505-	Mt. Bike	6/20/94	2
7	Fred	Gonzales	Purgatory Ski Area	Durango	CO	81301-	Mt. Bike	6/15/94	2
13	Luis	Lopez	1212 Agua Fria	Santa Fe	NM	87501-	Mt. Bike	6/20/94	3
15	Salvatore	Wallace	100 Westside Ave	Chicago	IL	60614-	Mt. Bike	6/20/94	2
31	Elizabeth	Michaels	57 Beechwood Dr.	Wayne	NJ	07470-	Mt. Bike	6/20/94	3
27	Martha	Fried	Hyde Park Estates	Santa Fe	NM	87501-	Mt. Bike	9/26/93	3
19	Susan	Ryland	4257 Avenida Armijo	Santa Fe	NM	87501-	Mt. Bike	9/26/93	2
30	Adelia	Ballard	3 Hall Road	Williamstow	MA	02167-	Mt. Bike	9/26/93	4
21	Robert	Roberts	56 Water Street	Lenox	MA	02140-	Mt. Bike	6/20/94	2
24	Elizabeth	Stephens	3 Which Way, Apt. 7	Salem	MA	01970-	Mt. Bike	6/20/94	3
28	Gayle	Hesh	1192 Don Diego	Santa Fe	NM	87501-	Mt. Bike	6/20/94	2
3	Camilla	Dobbins	486 Intel Circuit	Rio Ranchc	NM	87124-	Road Bike	6/15/94	3
29	Evan	Dewey	823 Northside Hgts.	Albuquerqu	NM	87105-	Road Bike	6/15/94	3
14	Maria	Duran	Galvin Highway East	Chicago	IL	60614-	Road Bike	6/15/94	2
8	John	Black	11 River Road	Brookfield	CT	06830-	Road Bike	6/15/94	2
18	Tonia	Dickenson	92 Main Avenue	Durango	CO	81301-	Road Bike	6/15/94	1

Record: 1 of 31

Type of tour FLTR NUM

FIGURE 3-4: Table sorted in descending order by Date field

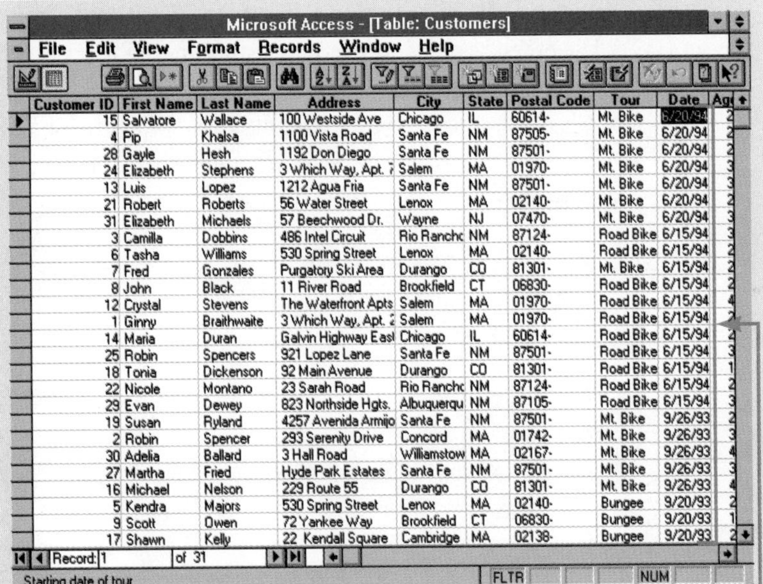

Microsoft Access - [Table: Customers]

File Edit View Format Records Window Help

Customer ID	First Name	Last Name	Address	City	State	Postal Code	Tour	Date	Ag
15	Salvatore	Wallace	100 Westside Ave	Chicago	IL	60614-	Mt. Bike	6/20/94	2
4	Pip	Khalsa	1100 Vista Road	Santa Fe	NM	87505-	Mt. Bike	6/20/94	2
28	Gayle	Hesh	1192 Don Diego	Santa Fe	NM	87501-	Mt. Bike	6/20/94	2
24	Elizabeth	Stephens	3 Which Way, Apt. 7	Salem	MA	01970-	Mt. Bike	6/20/94	3
13	Luis	Lopez	1212 Agua Fria	Santa Fe	NM	87501-	Mt. Bike	6/20/94	3
21	Robert	Roberts	56 Water Street	Lenox	MA	02140-	Mt. Bike	6/20/94	2
31	Elizabeth	Michaels	57 Beechwood Dr.	Wayne	NJ	07470-	Mt. Bike	6/20/94	3
3	Camilla	Dobbins	486 Intel Circuit	Rio Ranchc	NM	87124-	Road Bike	6/15/94	3
6	Tasha	Williams	530 Spring Street	Lenox	MA	02140-	Road Bike	6/15/94	2
7	Fred	Gonzales	Purgatory Ski Area	Durango	CO	81301-	Mt. Bike	6/15/94	2
8	John	Black	11 River Road	Brookfield	CT	06830-	Road Bike	6/15/94	2
12	Crystal	Stevens	The Waterfront Apts	Salem	MA	01970-	Road Bike	6/15/94	4
1	Ginny	Braithwaite	3 Which Way, Apt. 2	Salem	MA	01970-	Road Bike	6/15/94	2
14	Maria	Duran	Galvin Highway East	Chicago	IL	60614-	Road Bike	6/15/94	2
25	Robin	Spencers	921 Lopez Lane	Santa Fe	NM	87501-	Road Bike	6/15/94	3
18	Tonia	Dickenson	92 Main Avenue	Durango	CO	81301-	Road Bike	6/15/94	1
22	Nicole	Montano	23 Sarah Road	Rio Ranchc	NM	87124-	Road Bike	6/15/94	2
29	Evan	Dewey	823 Northside Hgts.	Albuquerqu	NM	87105-	Road Bike	6/15/94	3
19	Susan	Ryland	4257 Avenida Armijo	Santa Fe	NM	87501-	Mt. Bike	9/26/93	2
2	Robin	Spencer	293 Serenity Drive	Concord	MA	01742-	Mt. Bike	9/26/93	3
30	Adelia	Ballard	3 Hall Road	Williamstow	MA	02167-	Mt. Bike	9/26/93	4
27	Martha	Fried	Hyde Park Estates	Santa Fe	NM	87501-	Mt. Bike	9/26/93	3
16	Michael	Nelson	229 Route 55	Durango	CO	81301-	Mt. Bike	9/26/93	4
5	Kendra	Majors	530 Spring Street	Lenox	MA	02140-	Bungee	9/20/93	2
9	Scott	Owen	72 Yankee Way	Brookfield	CT	06830-	Bungee	9/20/93	1
17	Shawn	Kelly	22 Kendall Square	Cambridge	MA	02138-	Bungee	9/20/93	2

Record: 1 of 31

Starting date of tour FLTR NUM

Records sorted in descending order by date

Using the menu bar to sort

In addition to using buttons on the Table Datasheet toolbar, you can also sort using the menu bar. After you select the field you want to sort, click Records on the menu bar, then click Quick Sort. Click either Ascending or Descending on the Quick Sort menu, shown in Figure 3-5.

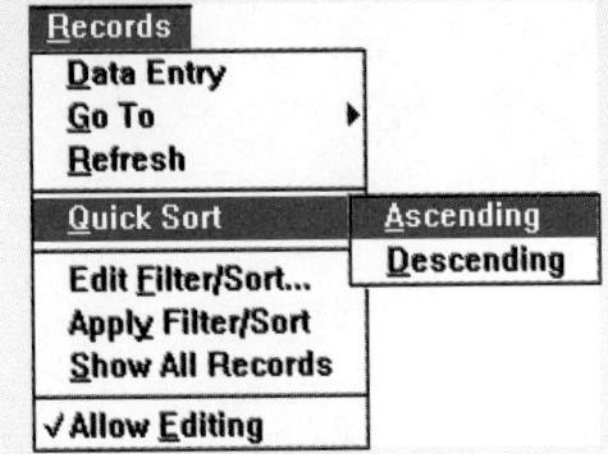

FIGURE 3-5: Quick Sort menu

Filtering a table

Filtering Records

Sorting allows you to manipulate table records in a simple way and to display them in ascending or descending order. **Filtering** is a more complex method of organizing records where you define the fields on which the table is sorted. A sort contains all the records in a table, whereas a filter shows only those records that qualify, based on your **criteria**, or parameters. For more information on filtering, see the related topic "When to use a filter." ▶ Often, Michael needs a list of customers by a specific tour. He can filter the Customers table to obtain this list.

STEPS

1. **Make sure the Customers table is open, with all records displayed**
   Michael needs to make sure there aren't any fields in the grid before filtering the table.
2. **Click Edit on the menu bar, then click Clear Grid**
   This clears any fields that appear in the grid. Now Michael wants to narrow the number of records displayed so he can see only those records for customers who took a Mt. Bike tour.
3. **Click the Edit Filter/Sort button on the Table Datasheet toolbar**
   The Filter window opens, as shown in Figure 3-6. The **Filter window** consists of two areas: the **field list** on top, containing all the fields in the table, and the **filter grid** on the bottom, where you specify the criteria for the filter. The toolbar displayed is the Filter/Sort toolbar. Michael wants to create a filter to show an unsorted list of all the records of customers who took a Mt. Bike tour.
4. **Double-click Tour in the field list**
   Access places the Tour field in the first empty Field cell in the filter grid. Next, Michael defines the criteria for the Tour field.
5. **Click the Criteria cell in the Tour column, type Mt. Bike, then press [Enter]**
   Access adds quotation marks around the entry to indicate that the entry is text, rather than a value. Your completed filter grid should look like Figure 3-7.
6. **Click the Apply Filter/Sort button on the Filter/Sort toolbar**
   Only those records containing the Mt. Bike tour appear, as shown in Figure 3-8.
7. **Click the Show All Records button on the Table Datasheet toolbar to return the table to its original order**

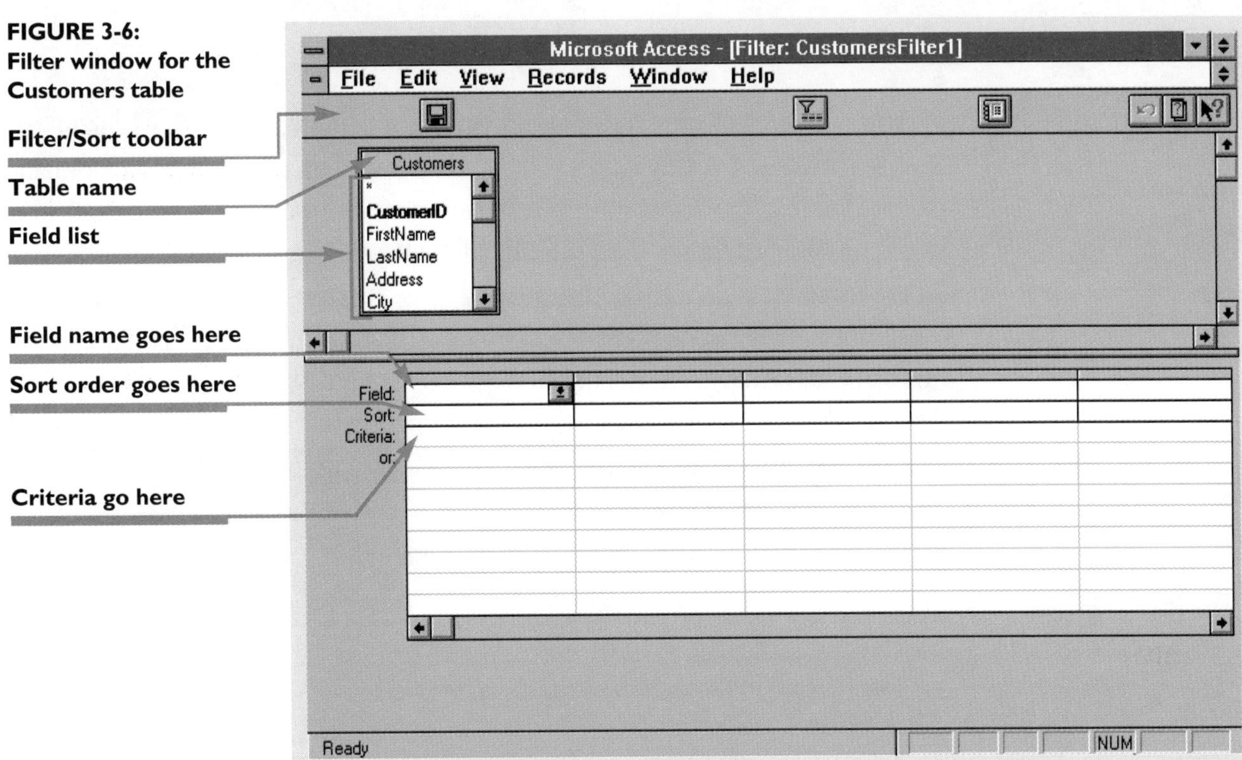

FIGURE 3-6: Filter window for the Customers table

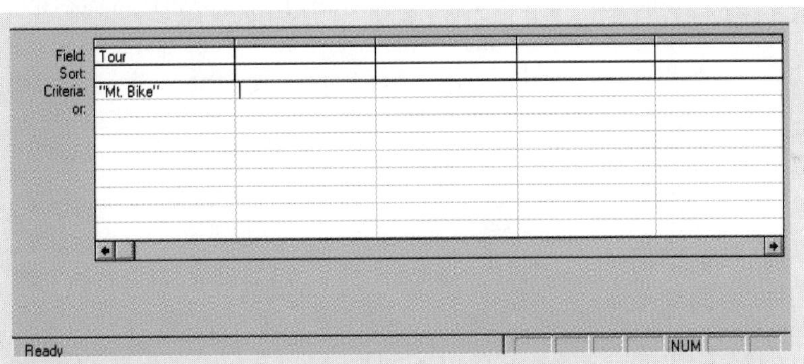

FIGURE 3-7: Completed filter grid

FIGURE 3-8: Filtered table records

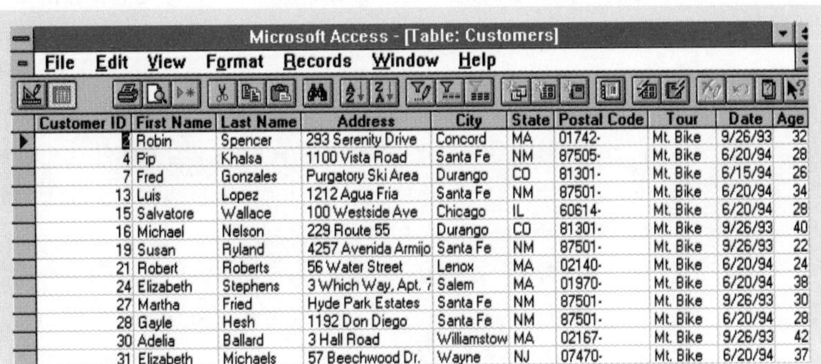

Customer ID	First Name	Last Name	Address	City	State	Postal Code	Tour	Date	Age
2	Robin	Spencer	293 Serenity Drive	Concord	MA	01742-	Mt. Bike	9/26/93	32
4	Pip	Khalsa	1100 Vista Road	Santa Fe	NM	87505-	Mt. Bike	6/20/94	28
7	Fred	Gonzales	Purgatory Ski Area	Durango	CO	81301-	Mt. Bike	6/15/94	26
13	Luis	Lopez	1212 Agua Fria	Santa Fe	NM	87501-	Mt. Bike	6/20/94	34
15	Salvatore	Wallace	100 Westside Ave	Chicago	IL	60614-	Mt. Bike	6/20/94	28
16	Michael	Nelson	229 Route 55	Durango	CO	81301-	Mt. Bike	9/26/93	40
19	Susan	Ryland	4257 Avenida Armijo	Santa Fe	NM	87501-	Mt. Bike	9/26/93	22
21	Robert	Roberts	56 Water Street	Lenox	MA	02140-	Mt. Bike	6/20/94	24
24	Elizabeth	Stephens	3 Which Way, Apt. 7	Salem	MA	01970-	Mt. Bike	6/20/94	38
27	Martha	Fried	Hyde Park Estates	Santa Fe	NM	87501-	Mt. Bike	9/26/93	30
28	Gayle	Hesh	1192 Don Diego	Santa Fe	NM	87501-	Mt. Bike	6/20/94	28
30	Adelia	Ballard	3 Hall Road	Williamstow	MA	02167-	Mt. Bike	9/26/93	42
31	Elizabeth	Michaels	57 Beechwood Dr.	Wayne	NJ	07470-	Mt. Bike	6/20/94	37

When to use a filter

A filter is temporary and cannot be saved; however, you can print the results of a filter just as you print any datasheet. A filter is best used to narrow the focus of the records temporarily in the current table.

Creating a simple query

A **query** is a set of criteria you specify to retrieve certain data from a database. Unlike a filter, which only allows you to manipulate data temporarily, a query can be saved so that you do not have to recreate it. A query also displays only the fields you have specified, rather than showing all table fields. Records resulting from a query are collected in a temporary area called a **dynaset**, which looks like a table, but is merely a view based on the query. The most commonly used query is the **select query**, in which records are collected, viewed, and can be modified later. ▶ The Nomad employee responsible for setting up Mt. Bike tours often asks Michael for a list of customers who have participated in these tours. Michael needs to create a query that displays the names of all Mt. Bike customers in ascending order. He does not need to see any other information.

1. Click the **New Query button** on the Table Datasheet toolbar
   The New Query dialog box opens and displays options for using the Query Wizard and for designing a new query. Michael decides to design a new query.
2. Click **New Query**
   The Select Query window opens, as shown in Figure 3-9. The Select Query window is similar to the Filter window; however, the Query Design toolbar provides more buttons than the Filter/Sort toolbar. Michael adds the first field, sort, and criteria specifications to the grid area.
3. Double-click **Tour** in the field list, then click the **Show box** if it is checked to deselect it
   The Tour field name appears in the Field cell in the query grid. The Show box indicates whether or not the field will be displayed in the query results. Michael does not need to see the contents of this field—only the customer names. Michael does need to specify the criteria for the query.
4. Click the **Criteria cell**, type **Mt. Bike**, then press **[Enter]**
   Michael wants the query results to show the last name, in ascending order, of each customer who participated in a Mt. Bike tour.
5. Double-click **LastName** in the field list, click the **Sort cell**, then type **a** (make sure the Show box is selected for the LastName field)
   Typing "a" in the Sort cell displays the word "ascending" in the cell. Compare your grid to Figure 3-10. Michael wants to view the results of the query.
6. Click the **Datasheet View button** on the Query Design toolbar
   The results of the query are shown in Figure 3-11. The results show that 13 customers took Mt. Bike tours. Michael returns to Design View.
7. Click the **Design View button** on the Query Datasheet toolbar
   The query grid is redisplayed. Michael wants to save the query results.
8. Click the **Save button** on the Query Design toolbar, type **Mt Bike customers** in the Query Name text box of the Save As dialog box, as shown in Figure 3-12, then click **OK**
   The query is saved as part of the database file
9. Click **File** on the Query menu bar, then click **Close** to close the query

FIGURE 3-9:
Select Query window

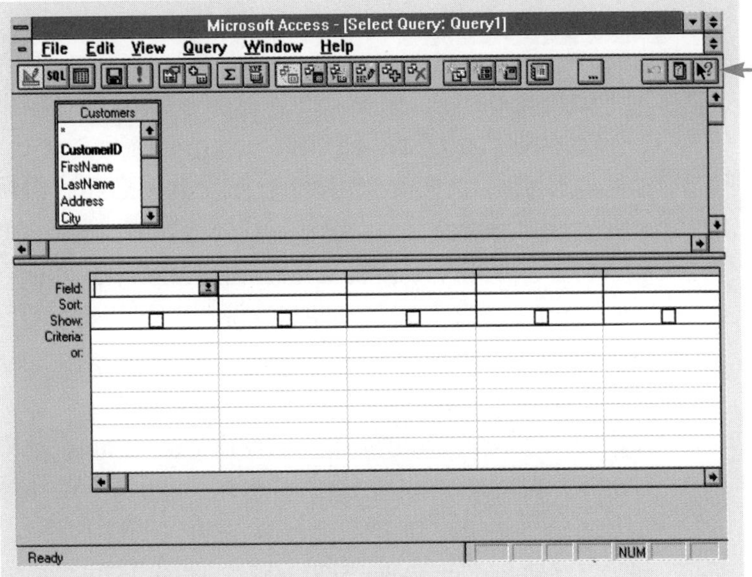

Query Design toolbar

FIGURE 3-10:
Simple query grid

Field data will not appear in query results

"ascending" appears when "a" is typed

Field data will appear in query results

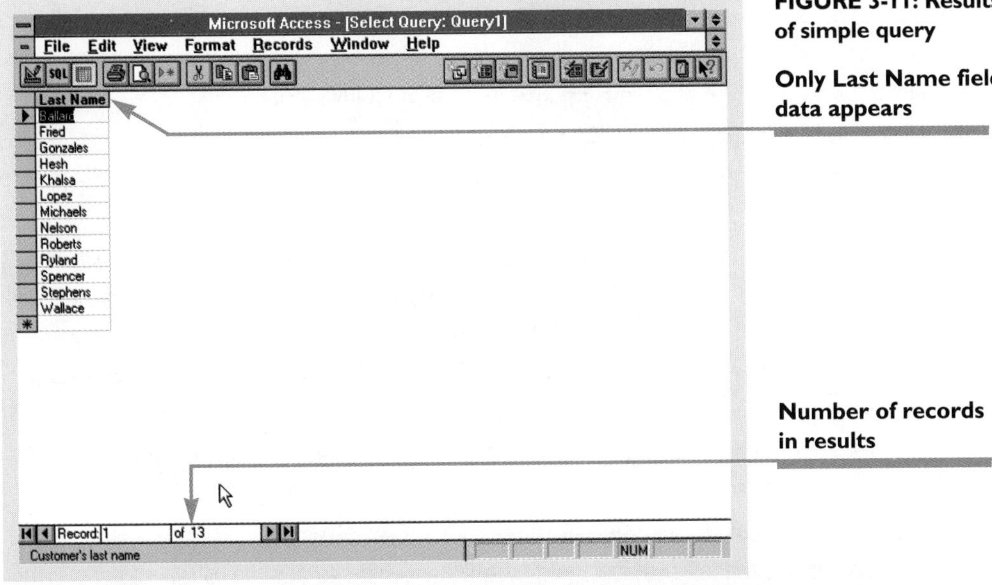

FIGURE 3-11: Results of simple query

Only Last Name field data appears

Number of records in results

FIGURE 3-12: Save As dialog box for query

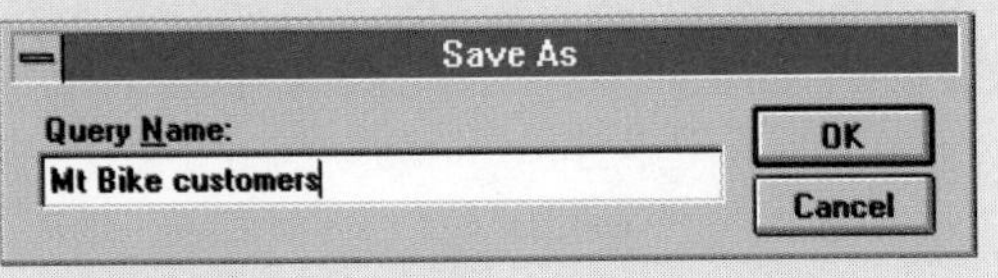

TROUBLE?

If you enter a field in the query grid in error, select the field then press [Delete] to delete it.

Creating a complex query

The criteria you specify for a query can be as simple as a list of all customer names, or as complex as a list of all customers over the age of 30, who live in New Mexico and took a tour in June. You can specify **AND** and **OR** criteria to broaden or narrow the number of records selected in a query. For example, a query of customers who took a Mt. Bike tour *or* a Road Bike tour gives different results from a query of customers who took a Mt. Bike tour *or* a Road Bike tour *and* live in New Mexico. Because a great deal of thought goes into creating more complex queries, it is important that you save such queries if you plan on using them again. Table 3-2 lists the most commonly used Query Design buttons, which can help you design complex queries easily. ▶ Each month, Michael wants to see a list of all customers, in descending order by last name, who took a Mt. Bike *or* Road Bike tour *and* who have a postal code greater than 50000. The list will also include the customers' first names. He decides to create and save a query that will display this data.

1. **Click the New Query button on the Table Datasheet toolbar**
   The New Query dialog box opens. Michael decides to design a new query.
2. **Click New Query**
   The Select Query window opens. Michael adds the first field, sort, and criteria specifications to the query grid.
3. **Double-click Tour in the field list**
   The Tour field name appears in the Field cell in the grid. Michael wants the tours displayed in ascending order.
4. **Click the Sort cell, then type a to display the word "ascending"**
   You could also click the list arrow in the cell to display a list of choices, then choose Ascending. Michael wants the Tour field data displayed in the query results.
5. **Make sure the Show box is checked**
   Michael wants to display the records of customers who took either a Mt. Bike *or* Road Bike tour. He enters this information in the Criteria cell.
6. **Click the Criteria cell, type Mt. Bike Or Road Bike, then press [Enter]**
   The entry "Mt. Bike" Or "Road Bike" appears in the Criteria cell. See Figure 3-13. Next, Michael adds the FirstName and LastName fields to the query grid.
7. **Double-click FirstName in the field list, then double-click LastName in the field list**
   The FirstName and LastName fields are added to the grid. Michael wants to sort the LastName field in descending order.
8. **Click the Sort list arrow, then click Descending**
   With the "Or" criteria for the query specified, Michael decides to view the datasheet.
9. **Click the Datasheet View button on the Query Design toolbar**
   The results of the query are displayed in the datasheet. See Figure 3-14. Notice that customers who took either a Mt. Bike or Road Bike tour are listed. The last names are sorted in descending order and grouped by each tour type.

FIGURE 3-13: "Or" specification in query grid

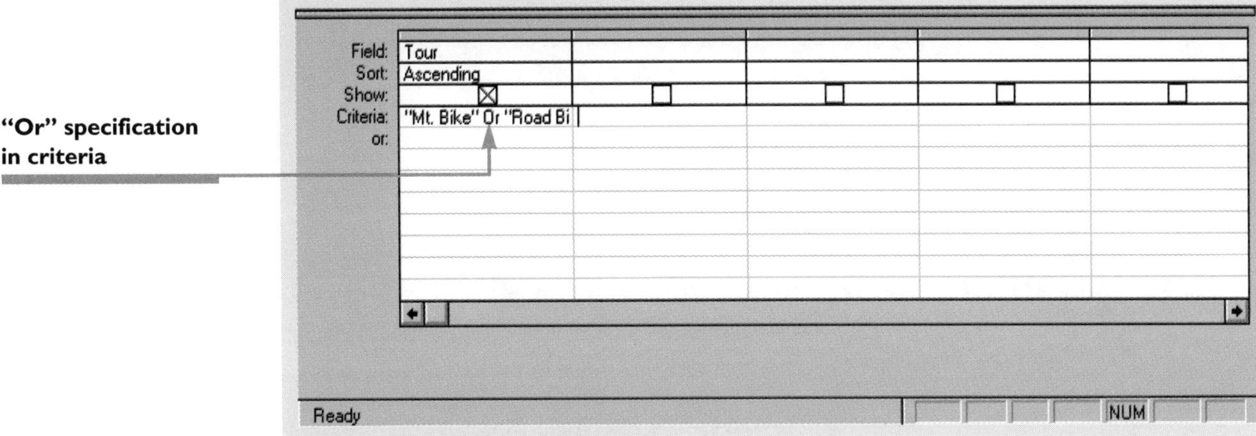

FIGURE 3-14: Datasheet showing results of "Or" query

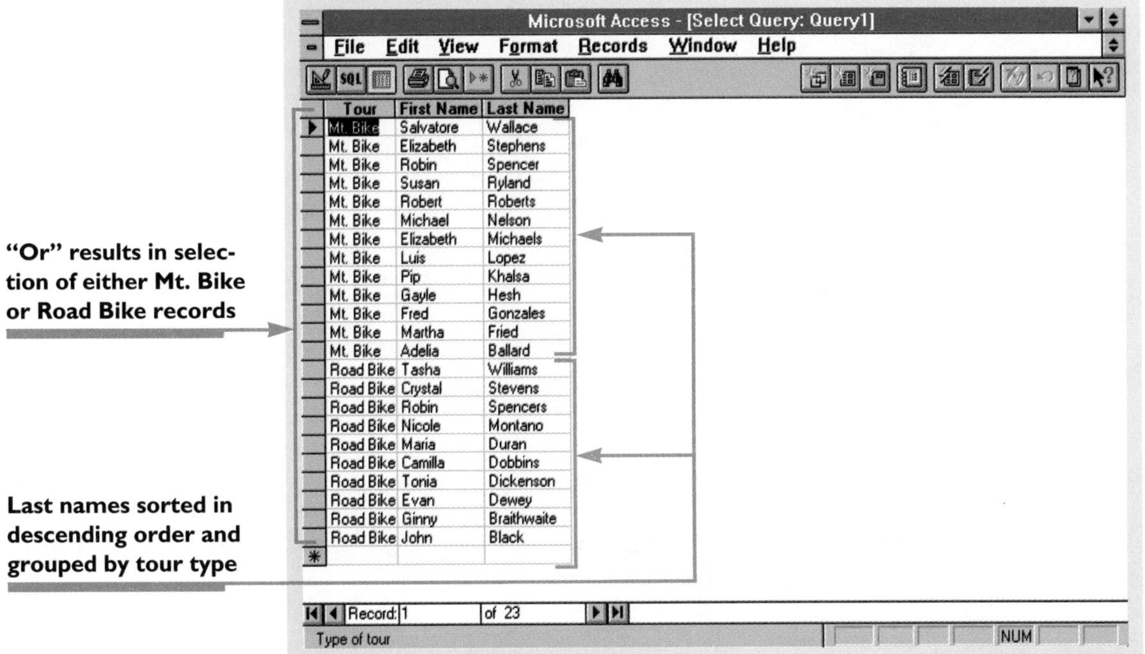

TABLE 3-2: Commonly used Query Design buttons

BUTTON	DESCRIPTION	BUTTON	DESCRIPTION
	Design View		Apply Filter/Sort
	Datasheet View		Show All Records
	Sort Ascending		New Query
	Sort Descending		Undo Current Field/Record
	Edit Filter/Sort		Save

Creating a complex query, continued

To complete his query, Michael needs to specify that the list include only those customers with a postal code greater than 50000. This is the "And" specification for the query.

10 **Click the Design View button** on the Query Datasheet toolbar
The query grid is redisplayed. Michael adds the PostalCode field to the query grid, and does not sort it because the query is being sorted by the LastName field.

11 Double-click **PostalCode** in the field list
Next Michael adds the criteria for the PostalCode field.

12 Click the **Criteria cell**, type **>50000**, then press **[Enter]**
After you press [Enter], the Tour field might scroll out of view. If necessary, scroll the window to view the completed query grid, shown in Figure 3-15. Michael views the datasheet for the completed query.

13 Click the **Datasheet View button** on the Query Design toolbar
The query results are narrowed from 23 records to 14 records with the addition of the "And" specification, as shown in Figure 3-16. Michael prints the datasheet so he can have a record of the results.

14 Click the **Print button** on the Query Datasheet toolbar, then click **OK**
Michael returns to Design view to save the query.

15 Click the **Design View button** on the Query Datasheet toolbar

16 Click the **Save button** on the Query Design toolbar
The Save As dialog box opens.

17 Type **Mt Bike OR Road Bike AND PostalCode > 50000**, then click **OK**
The query is saved for future use. Michael closes the query and the table.

18 Click **File** on the Query menu bar, then click **Close**; click **File** on the Datasheet menu bar, then click **Close**

FIGURE 3-15: Query grid with PostalCode field added

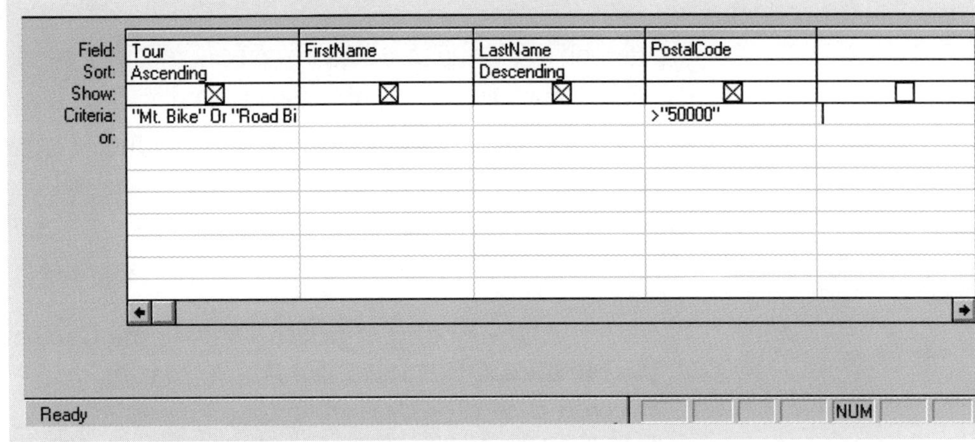

FIGURE 3-16: Results of complex query

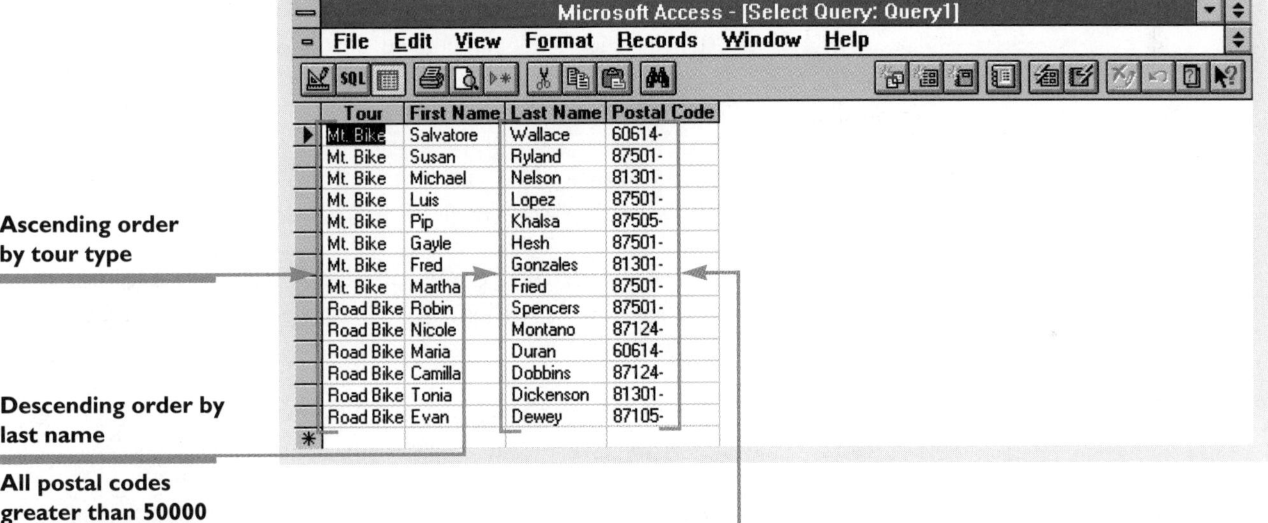

Tour	First Name	Last Name	Postal Code
Mt. Bike	Salvatore	Wallace	60614-
Mt. Bike	Susan	Ryland	87501-
Mt. Bike	Michael	Nelson	81301-
Mt. Bike	Luis	Lopez	87501-
Mt. Bike	Pip	Khalsa	87505-
Mt. Bike	Gayle	Hesh	87501-
Mt. Bike	Fred	Gonzales	81301-
Mt. Bike	Martha	Fried	87501-
Road Bike	Robin	Spencers	87501-
Road Bike	Nicole	Montano	87124-
Road Bike	Maria	Duran	60614-
Road Bike	Camilla	Dobbins	87124-
Road Bike	Tonia	Dickenson	81301-
Road Bike	Evan	Dewey	87105-

QUICK TIP

You can save a filter as a query by choosing Save As Query from the File menu (while in the Filter window), then name the query and click OK.

Modifying a query

After you create and save a query, you can modify it by adding and deleting fields, or changing field specifications. For example, you could change the sort order for a field or add new criteria for a field. For information on saving a query, see the related topic "Using Save As with queries." ▶ Michael wants to add a field indicating customer age to the Mt Bike OR Road Bike AND PostalCode > 50000 query, and modify the sort specification for the LastName and PostalCode fields.

1 Click the **Query object button** in the Database window, make sure the **Mt Bike OR Road Bike AND PostalCode >50000** query is selected, then click **Design**
The Select Query: Mt Bike OR Road Bike AND PostalCode >50000 window opens. Michael wants to include the Age field in the query results.

2 Double-click **Age** in the field list, then click the **Show box** to select it
The Age field is included in the query for display purposes only. Michael will not specify any criteria for this field. Next, Michael needs to change the specifications for the LastName field so that it is not sorted.

3 Click the **Sort list arrow** for the LastName field, then click **(not sorted)**
Next, Michael changes the sort order for the PostalCode field to Descending.

4 Click the **Sort list arrow** for the PostalCode field, then click **Descending**
All the necessary changes have been made to the query. Compare your query grid to Figure 3-17. Michael needs to save his changes.

5 Click the **Save button** on the Query Design toolbar
The query with modifications is saved. Now Michael views the results of the modified query.

6 Click the **Datasheet View button** on the Query Design toolbar
The results of the modified query are shown in Figure 3-18. Notice that the Tour field data is still in ascending order, the LastName field data is no longer sorted, and the order of records within each tour type is sorted in descending order by postal code. The age of each customer is also displayed. Michael is finished with his modifications and returns to the Database window.

7 Click **File** on the menu bar, then click **Close**

8 Click **File** on the menu bar, then click **Exit**

FIGURE 3-17: Modified query grid

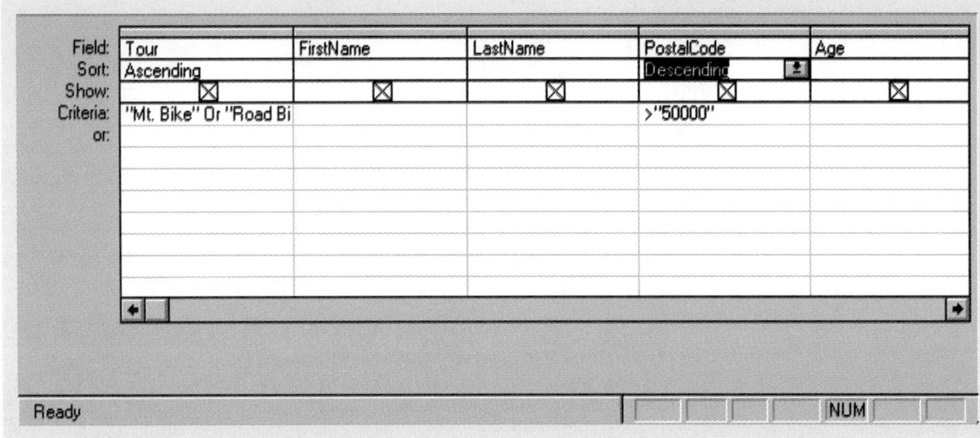

FIGURE 3-18: Results of modified query

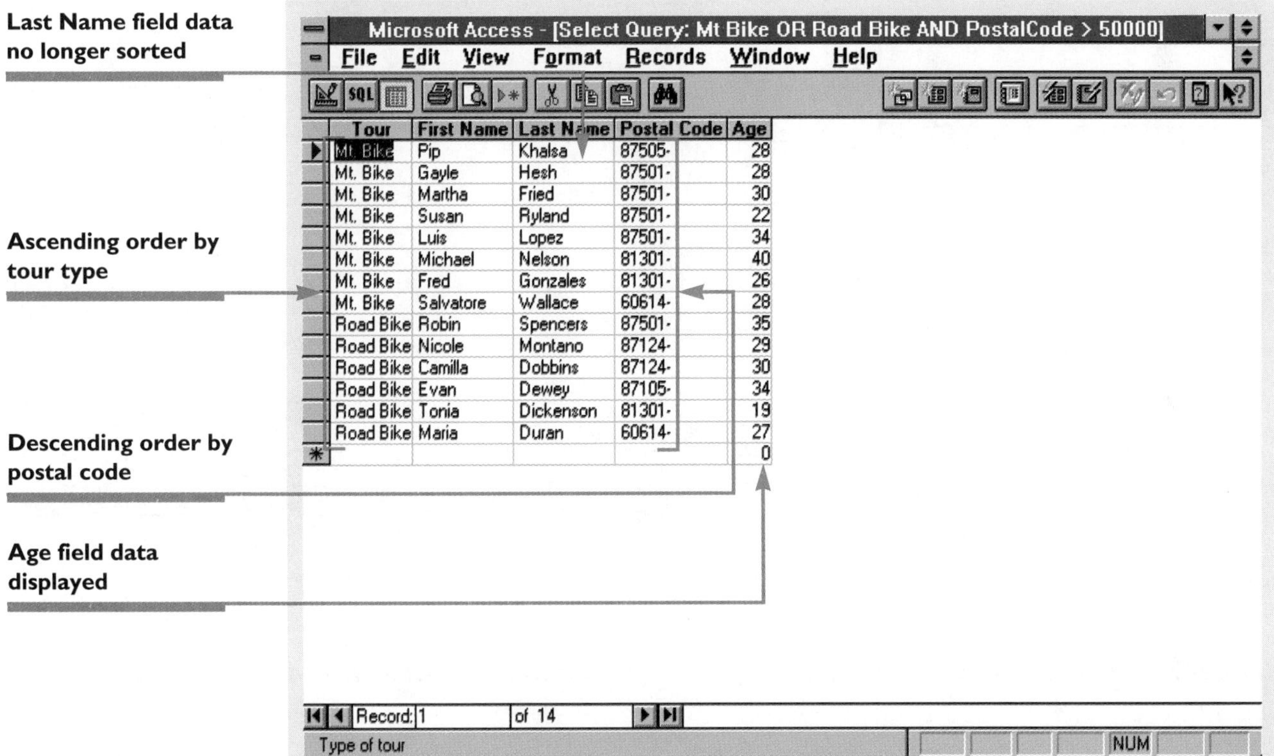

Using Save As with queries

You might want to create several queries that are similar. Rather than having to make minor adjustments in a query each time you use it, use Save As to create individual queries for each of your needs. Click File on the menu bar, click Save As, then supply a new name for each query.

CONCEPTS REVIEW

Label each of the elements of the Select Query window shown in Figure 3-19.

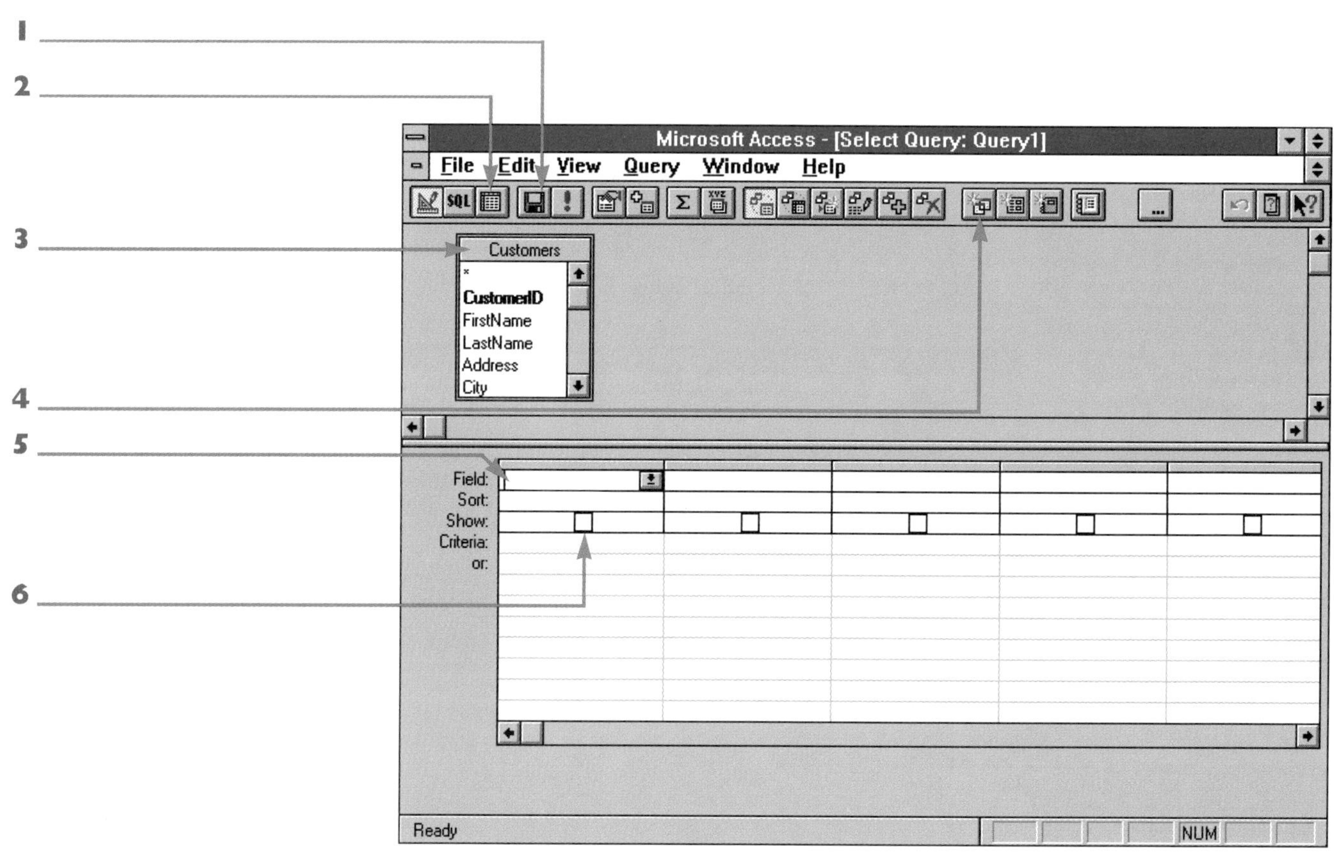

FIGURE 3-19

Match each button with its correct description.

7

8

9

10

11

12

a. Open Database

b. Print

c. Show All Records

d. Edit Filter/Sort

e. Datasheet View

f. Save

Select the best answer from the list of choices.

13 You can move to the first blank record by pressing

a. [Ctrl][*]

b. [Home][End]

c. [Ctrl][=]

d. [Home]

14 The button that sorts a table from A to Z is

a.

b.

c.

d.

15 Which button searches for text?

a. [button]
b. [button]
c. [button]
d. [button]

16 The method of organizing records to display only qualifying records is called

a. Sorting
b. Filtering
c. Sifting
d. Flexing

17 Specifications that define which records will be displayed are called

a. Extractions
b. Gauges
c. Properties
d. Criteria

18 The results of a query are placed in a temporary holding area called a

a. Dynaset
b. Filter
c. Datasheet
d. Design query

APPLICATIONS REVIEW

1 Find records.

a. Start Access and insert your Student Disk in the disk drive.
b. Open the database BICYCLE.MDB from your Student Disk.
c. Use the Find button to locate all records in all fields that match any part of a field and contain the text "bar."
d. How many occurrences are there?

2 Sort a table.

a. Sort the Products table in ascending order using the Product ID field containing the five-digit numbers. Print the datasheet.
b. Return the datasheet to its original order by clicking the Show All Records button.
c. Create and print a list of products in descending order by Units In Stock.
d. Return the datasheet to its original order.

3 Filter a table.

a. Create a filter that shows all products on order. A product on order has a value larger than 0 in the Units On Order field. (*Hint:* Set the criteria in the filter grid to ">0" for Units On Order.)
b. Print the datasheet, showing only the Product ID field data containing the five-digit numbers and the product name for the items on order.
c. Return the datasheet to its original order.

4 Create a simple query.

a. Create a query for Step 3a above. Name this query "Products on Order."
b. Create another query that lists all products with a unit price greater than $50. Name this query "Products costing >$50."
c. Display the ProductName, ProductID1, UnitsInStock, and UnitPrice field data in the query for Step 4b.

5 Create a complex query.

a. Create a query that shows the Product Name of all products with a DiscoStatus = Yes field AND that are sold by the pair (the Units field). Sort the query in ascending order by units. Name this query "Discoed, by Unit."
b. Print the datasheet for the query.

6 Modify a query.

a. Modify the Products on Order query so that the results are sorted in ascending order by the Supplier ID field. Make sure the Supplier ID field data is displayed. Save the modified query. Print the query results.
b. Modify the Products costing >$50 query to include the following fields: Product ID containing the five-digit number, Reorder Level, and Reorder Amount. Save the modified query. Print the query results.
c. Modify the Discoed, by Unit query so that the results are sorted in descending order by units, and so that the data for the Unit Price field is displayed. Save the modified query. Print the query results.
d. Close the file and exit Access.

INDEPENDENT CHALLENGE 1

The Melodies Music Store has hired you as the customer service manager. The store attracts a variety of customers with different tastes in music. To provide your customers with lists of the types of music available, you need to create queries in the store's music database, which is contained in the file MELODIES.MDB on your Student Disk. The database includes one table, called Available titles. This table divides data into eight musical classifications: Classic, Alternative, Rock, World Music, Jazz, Blues, Pop, and Metal.

To complete this independent challenge:

1. Using the Available titles table, find out how many records are in the Classic group. Should this classification be its own subgroup?
2. Sort the records by Category ID, then by Product Name. Print the results.
3. Create a filter that examines records with a Serial Number lower than 400000. Print this list.
4. Because musical categories overlap, group the eight classifications into three subgroups. You might, for example, include Alternative and Metal into a group called Grunge; Classic, Pop, and Rock into a group called Rock N Roll; and World Music, Jazz, and Blues into a group called Easy Listening.
5. Create a query for each of the three subgroups that finds all of the titles in that subgroup. Each query must use an "Or" specification in the query grid. Name each query for its classification.
6. Query the Available titles table using each query created in Step 5, and print the results of each query.
7. Modify one of the subgroup queries to include a musical classification already included in another subgroup. For example, you could include Pop in Easy Listening as well as Rock N Roll.
8. Print the results of the modified query.
9. Submit all printouts.

INDEPENDENT CHALLENGE 2

You work in the US Census Office for your city. Using the database STATS-1.MDB from your Student Disk, create several queries that examine the data in the Statistical Data table. The records in the Statistical Data table contain marriage information by state. Each state is assigned a geographical area.

To complete this independent challenge:

1. Find the states in the same geographical area as your state. For example, if your state is Utah, other states in the Mountain Region are New Mexico, Colorado, Nevada, Montana, Arizona, Idaho, and Wyoming.
2. Create a query that selects records in your geographical area and sorts them in ascending order by state. Display the State and Marriages fields.
3. On paper, write down at least three additional queries that would extract meaningful data and give different outputs.
4. Create each of these queries.
5. Print a sample of each query's dynaset.
6. Submit each of the samples with the handwritten work.

UNIT 4

OBJECTIVES

- Create a form
- Modify a form
- Modify controls
- Use a form to add a record
- Create a report
- Modify a report
- Add an expression to a report
- Create a report from a query

Creating FORMS AND REPORTS

The Datasheet View gives you an overall look at the records in a table. Often, however, all the fields in the table are not visible without scrolling left or right. Access allows you to create attractive screen forms that make it easy to view the fields in each record. You can design a screen form to match the design of a particular paper form to facilitate data entry. You can also create reports, which can display query results in different ways, both on the screen and in printed output. ▶ Because Nomad Ltd's Travel Division has been so successful with its bicycle tours, it keeps an inventory of supplies, which it then sells to tour customers. Michael wants to create a form to make it easier to enter inventory data. He also wants to produce reports on the data to distribute to other Nomad employees. Michael plans to submit a sample form and report to the Board of Directors as part of the Annual Report. ▶

Creating a form

You can create a form from scratch, or you can use the Form Wizard. The **Form Wizard** provides sample form layouts and gives you options for including specific fields in a form. For information on creating a simple form automatically, see the related topic "Using the AutoForm button." ▶ Currently, the Travel Division fills out a paper form for each product in its bicycle inventory. Michael needs to create an Access form for the bicycle inventory data. He wants to design the form so that it looks similar to the original paper form. He also wants the form to display one record at a time and display all the fields in the table.

1. Start Access and insert your Student Disk in drive A
2. Click the **Open Database button** on the Database toolbar, then open the file BIKEINV.MDB from your Student Disk
   This database file contains the bicycle inventory data. Michael wants to create a new form for the Bicycle Products table.
3. Click the **Form object button** in the Database window, then click **New**
   The New Form dialog box opens, as shown in Figure 4-1. Michael needs to identify the table on which the form will be based, then he can choose the Form Wizards option to create the form.
4. Click the **Select A Table/Query list arrow**, click **Bicycle Products**, then click **Form Wizards**
   A dialog box opens and lists possible form layouts. Michael chooses the Single-Column Wizard.
5. Click **Single-Column**, if necessary, then click **OK**
   The Single-Column Form Wizard dialog box opens, as shown in Figure 4-2. This dialog box allows you to select which fields you want to include in the form, and to determine the order in which they appear.
6. Click **ProductID** in the Available fields list box, then click the **Single Field button**
   ProductID appears in the Field order on form box. Michael wants all the fields to appear in the form. Instead of selecting each field individually, he decides to select all the fields at one time.
7. Click the **All Fields button**
   All the fields appear in the Field order on form box. Michael is ready to choose a style for his form. He decides to accept the default style suggested by the Form Wizard.
8. Click **Next**, click **Embossed**, then click **Next**
   The final dialog box suggests the table name as the title for the form. Michael accepts the title suggestion and wants to see the form with data in it.
9. Click **Finish**
   The Bicycle Products form opens in Form View, as shown in Figure 4-3. The fields are listed in a single column in the form, and the data for the first record in the table is displayed. The navigation buttons at the bottom of the form allow you to move from record to record, and the vertical scroll bar allows you to move to areas of the form that currently are not visible.

FIGURE 4-1: New Form dialog box

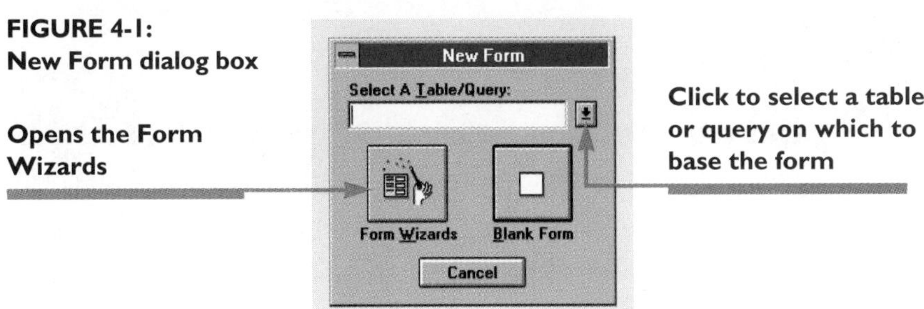

FIGURE 4-2: Single-Column Form Wizard dialog box

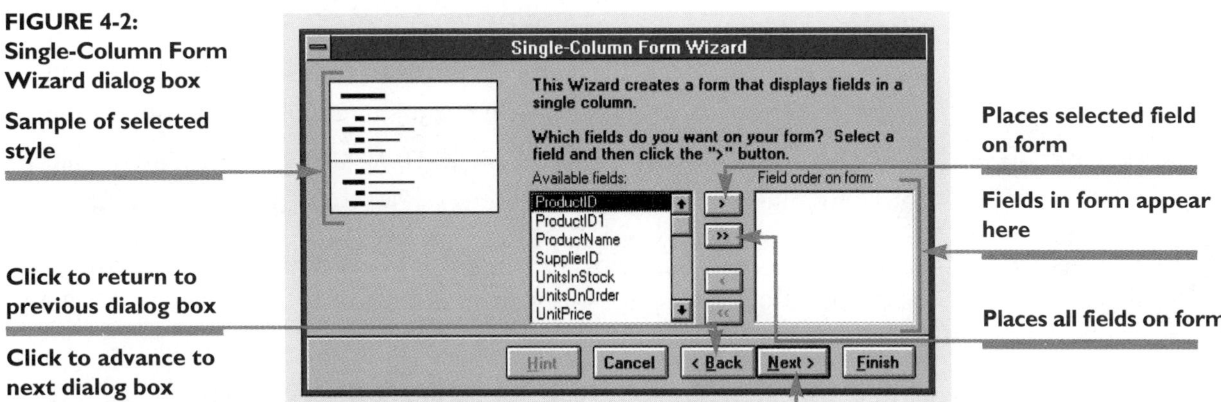

FIGURE 4-3: Bicycle Products form

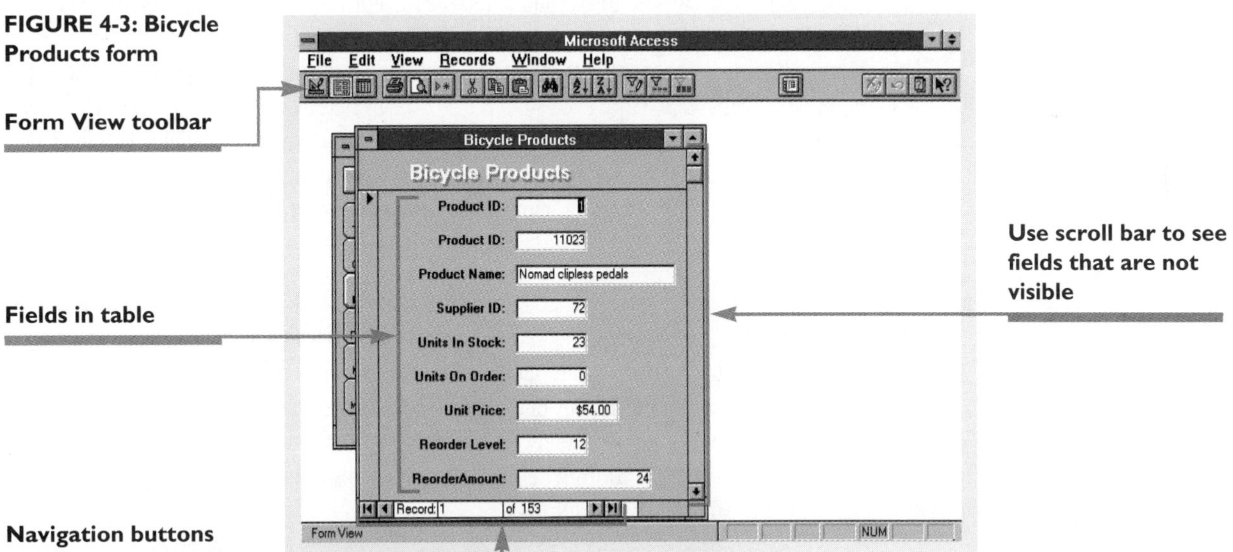

QUICK TIP

The Back button in the Form Wizard dialog boxes allows you to move to the previous dialog box and make changes, as necessary, before completing the form.■

Using the AutoForm button

You can create a simple form using the AutoForm button on the Database toolbar. This button offers no prompts or dialog boxes; it instantly creates a single-column form that displays all fields in the table or query.

Modifying a form

After you create a form, you can modify it easily by changing the locations of fields, adding or deleting fields, adding graphics, and changing the color of text and field data. You modify a form in Design View, which is divided into three sections: Form Header, Detail, and Form Footer. The **Form Header** appears at the beginning of each screen form and usually contains a form title or logo. The **Detail** displays the fields and data for each record. The **Form Footer** appears at the bottom of each screen form and can contain totals, instructions, or command buttons. In Design View, a field is called a control. A **control** consists of the field text and the data it contains. ▶ Michael wants to reposition the fields in the form to match the design of the paper form. This will make it easier to enter data from the paper-based forms into the screen form. Figure 4-4 shows a completed paper form.

1 **Click the Maximize button to maximize the Bicycle Products form**
Maximizing the form gives Michael a larger work area in which to change the form design. Next he changes to Design View, where he can make modifications.

2 **Click the Design View button on the Form View toolbar**
The screen changes to Design View, as shown in Figure 4-5. Only the Form Header and Detail sections are visible (you can use the scroll bars to see the Form Footer section). The form background changes to a grid, which helps keep fields aligned horizontally and vertically. The **Toolbox**, which might appear in a different area on your screen, contains buttons you can use to modify the form. Notice that each field name is displayed twice: the name on the left is a label that identifies the field; and the name on the right is the control for the field, which represents where the actual data for the field will be displayed. Before moving any fields, Michael wants to expand the size of the work area by placing the pointer on the right edge of the form, as shown in Figure 4-5, and dragging to the right.

3 **Place the pointer on the right edge of the form until the pointer changes to ✛, then drag the right edge to the 6" mark on the ruler**
Compare your results to Figure 4-6. Michael is ready to reposition fields on the form. To do this, he first needs to **select** a field by clicking the control for the field. Black squares, called **handles**, appear around the perimeter of a selected control. You can reposition a control by dragging a handle to a new location. When you work with controls, the pointer assumes different shapes, which are described in Table 4-1.

4 **Click the ProductName control then, when the pointer is ✋, drag the control to the right of the ProductID1 control at 2.5" on the horizontal ruler, then release the mouse button**
The Product Name field is now on the same line as the ProductID1 field.

TABLE 4-1: Mouse pointer shapes

SHAPE	ACTION	SHAPE	ACTION
↖	Selects a control	☝	Moves the control where pointer is currently positioned
✋	Moves all selected controls	↔	Changes a control's size

FIGURE 4-4: Bicycle Products paper form

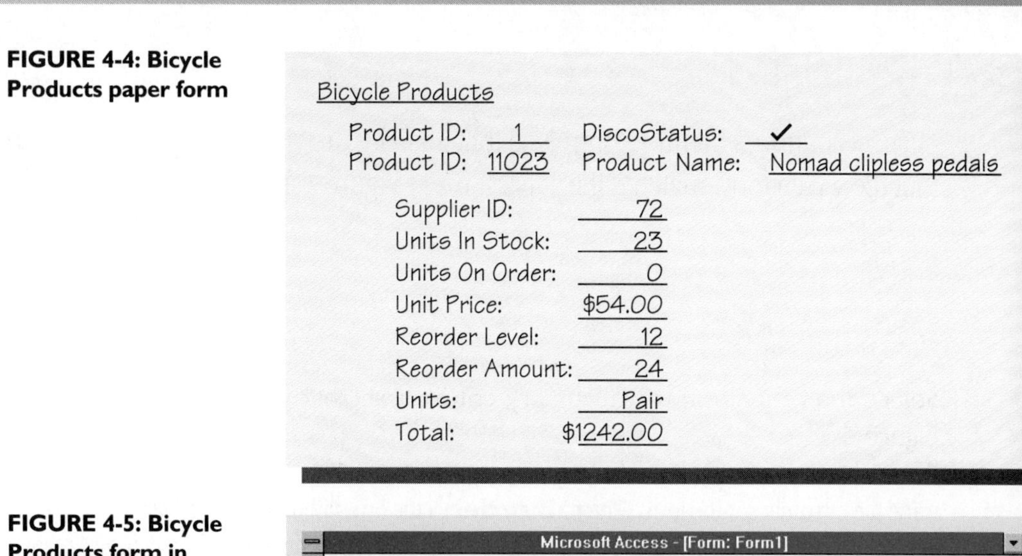
Bicycle Products
Product ID: 1
DiscoStatus: ✓
Product ID: 11023
Product Name: Nomad clipless pedals
Supplier ID: 72
Units In Stock: 23
Units On Order: 0
Unit Price: $54.00
Reorder Level: 12
Reorder Amount: 24
Units: Pair
Total: $1242.00

FIGURE 4-5: Bicycle Products form in Design View

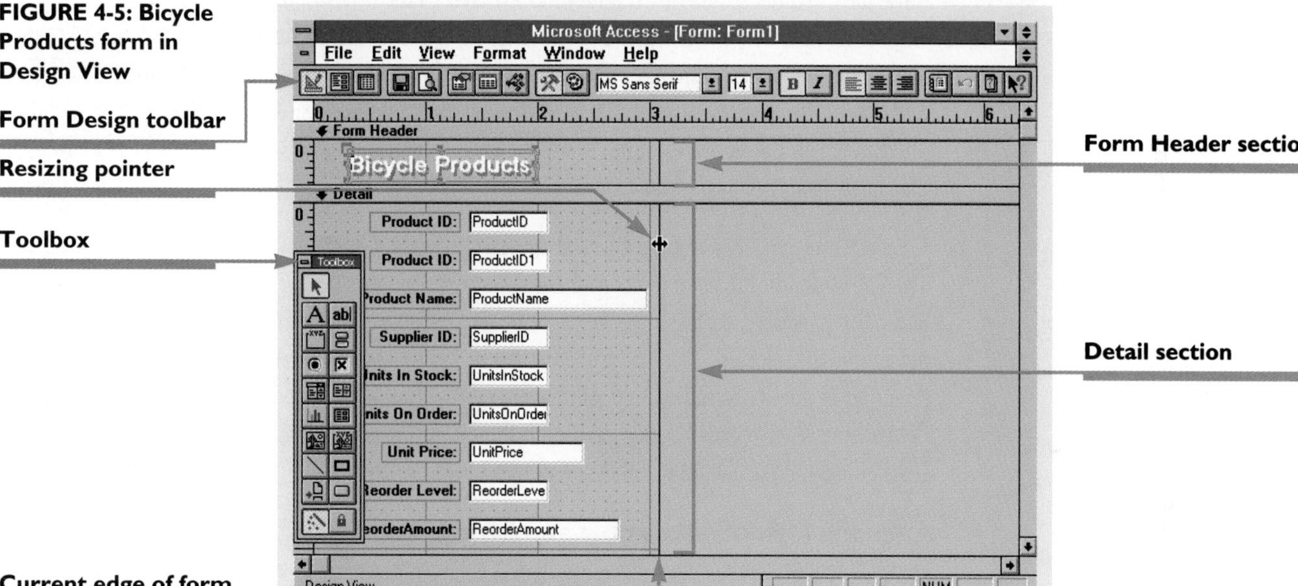

FIGURE 4-6: Bicycle Products form with enlarged work area

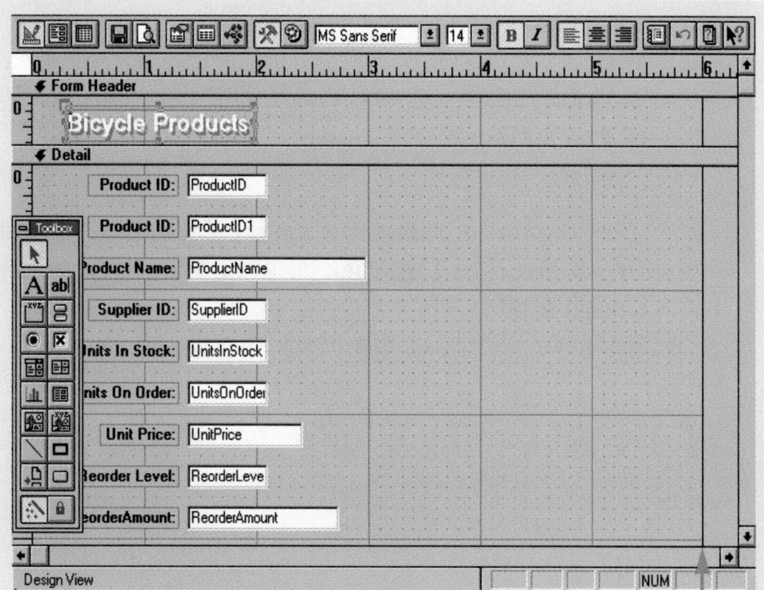

Modifying a form, continued

Michael continues to move controls so that all fields are visible on the form, and so that the screen form matches the paper form in Figure 4-4.

5 **Select and reposition the necessary controls so that your form matches Figure 4-7**
You might need to use the scroll bar to see the remaining controls. Next, Michael needs to determine the tab order for the form. The **tab order** is the order in which you advance from one field to the next when you press [Tab] to enter data in the form. The order of the fields in a table determines the default tab order. Even when controls are repositioned in a form, the tab order remains in the original order of the fields in the table. Michael wants the tab order to reflect the order in which the fields now appear on the form, which matches the paper form, to facilitate data entry from the paper form.

6 **Click Edit on the menu bar, then click Tab Order**
The Tab Order dialog box opens. In this dialog box you can change the order of fields in any of the three sections on the form. Because fields are usually in the Detail section, this section is automatically selected. The Custom Order list box shows the current tab order, which still reflects the order of the fields in the table. Michael needs to change the tab order so that the DiscoStatus field follows the Product ID field, to match the new arrangement of fields in the form. The DiscoStatus field indicates whether the product is currently offered or has been discontinued.

7 **Click the DiscoStatus row selector in the Custom Order list box, drag it until it is below ProductID, as shown in Figure 4-8, then release the mouse button**

8 **Click OK**
Although nothing visibly changes on the form, the tab order changes to reflect the order of the fields on the form. When Michael uses the screen form to enter data from a paper form, the order in which he moves from field to field by pressing [Tab] will match the order in the paper form. Michael saves his work and views the form in Form View.

9 **Click the Save button on the Form Design toolbar, type Bicycle Products, click OK, then click the Form View button on the Form Design toolbar**
The form is saved as part of the database file. Compare your form to Figure 4-9.

FIGURE 4-7: Repositioned controls

Handles

Selected control

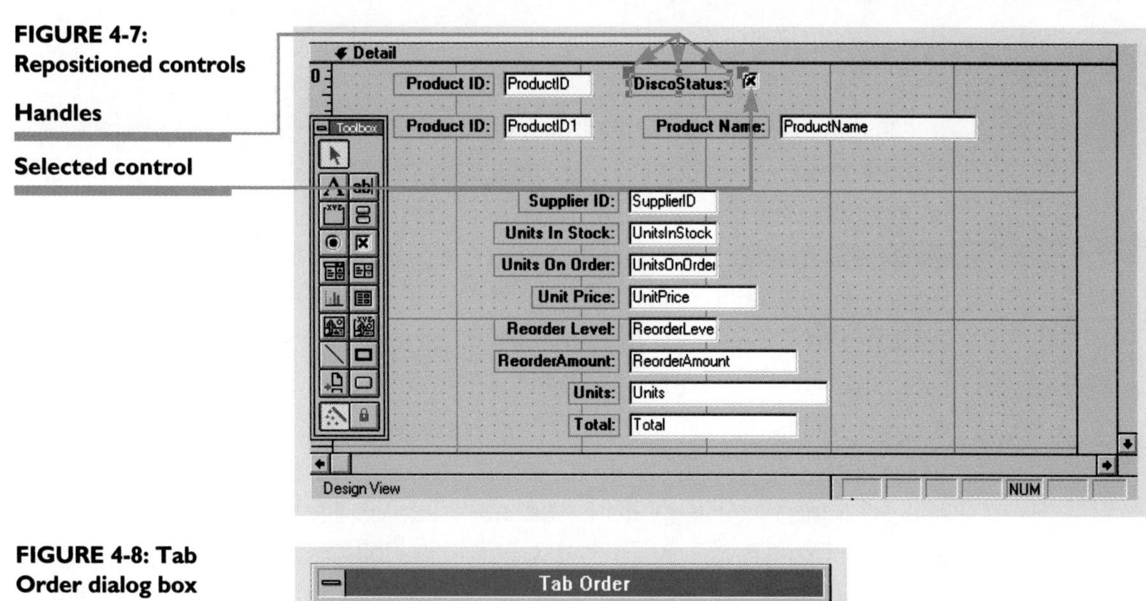

FIGURE 4-8: Tab Order dialog box

Indicates form section being displayed

Row selectors

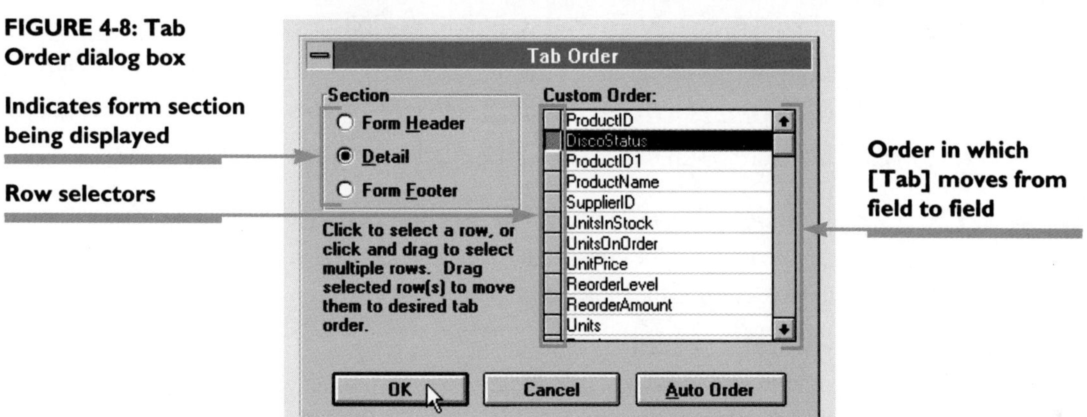

Order in which [Tab] moves from field to field

FIGURE 4-9: Form displayed in Form View

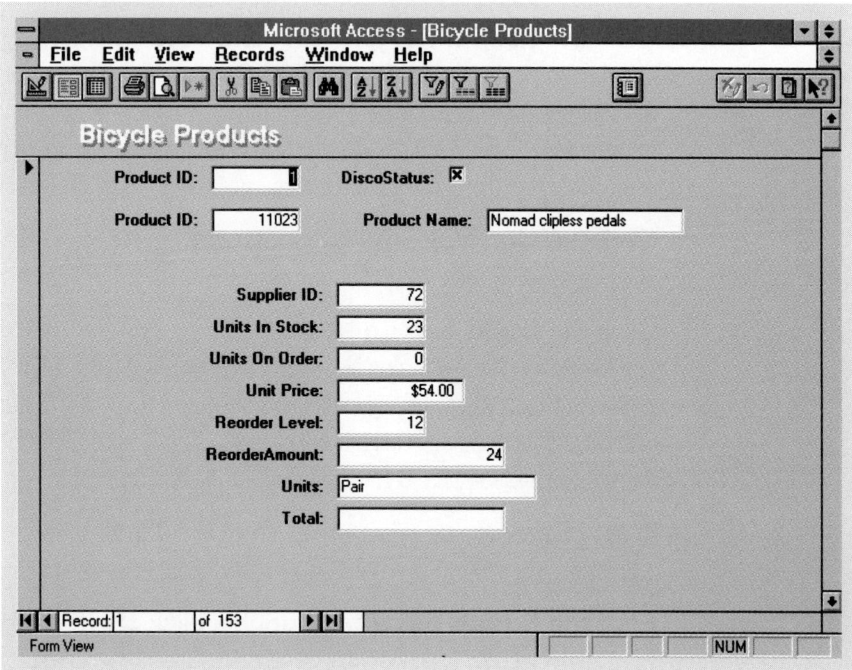

Modifying controls

In addition to repositioning controls, you can also modify the **properties**, or characteristics, of a control to make data entry more efficient. Controls are either bound, unbound, or calculated. A **bound control** has a field in a table or query as its source of data. An **unbound control** has no source for its data (for example, an unbound control could be a title above a group of controls). A **calculated control** has a mathematical expression as its data source. By default, all controls occur as text boxes; however, you can create several types of controls, including toggle buttons and check boxes, using the Toolbox. See the related topic "Formatting a control" for information on enhancing a control. ▶ Michael wants to create a calculated control that will display an in-stock value for each item in the inventory. To do this, he will use the Expression Builder to create an equation that multiplies the Units In Stock field value by the Unit Price field value. The **Expression Builder** displays fields and mathematical symbols you can use to create an expression. First, Michael returns to Design View.

1. **Click the Design View button on the Form View toolbar**
   Michael wants the results of the expression to appear in the Total field. He must select the control for this field before creating the equation.
2. **Click the Total control**
   Handles appear around the control to indicate it is selected. Although Michael could type an expression directly into the text box, he chooses to use the Expression Builder. You access the Expression Builder through the Properties Sheet.
3. **Click the Properties button on the Form Design toolbar**
   The Properties Sheet opens for the selected Total control. The Properties Sheet shows the control's name and source, the field description as it appears in the status bar, and other relevant information. Because Michael wants to change the Total control to a calculated control, he needs to modify the Control Source property.
4. **Click the Control Source property**
   The Expression Builder's Build button appears, as shown in Figure 4-10.
5. **Click the Build button**
   The Expression Builder dialog box opens, as shown in Figure 4-11. This dialog box contains a section in which you build the expression, the buttons you use to build the expression, and the fields available in the selected table. The word "Total" appears in the expression list box because that control was selected. Before building the expression Michael must erase the word Total.
6. **Press [Backspace] five times to erase Total**
   The expression will multiply the Units In Stock field value by the Unit Price field value.
7. **Click the Equals button, double-click UnitsInStock, click the Multiplication button, then double-click UnitPrice**
   The completed expression appears in the expression text box. See Figure 4-12. If your expression does not match the one in the figure, use [Backspace] to erase the expression, then repeat step 7.
8. **Click OK to return to the Properties Sheet for the Total control**

FIGURE 4-10: Properties Sheet for Total control

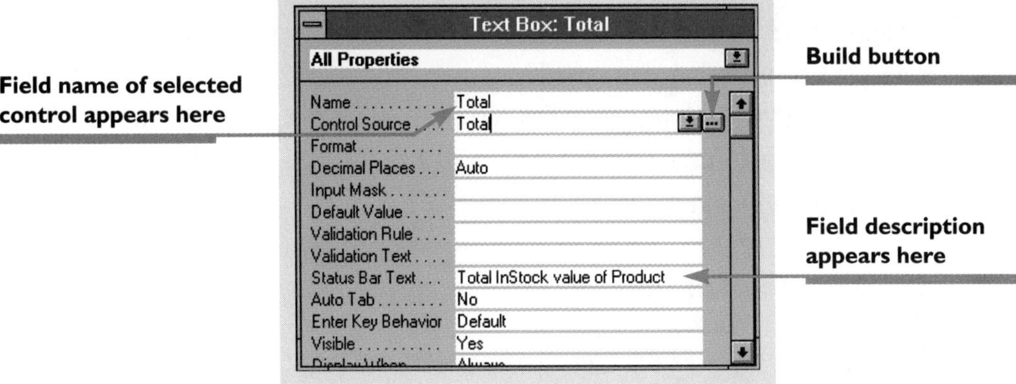

FIGURE 4-11: Expression Builder dialog box

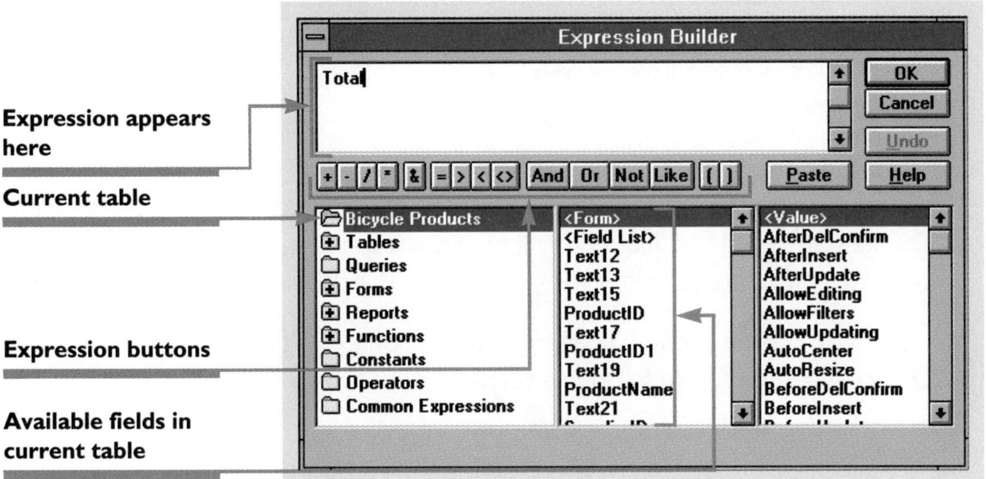

FIGURE 4-12: Completed Expression Builder dialog box

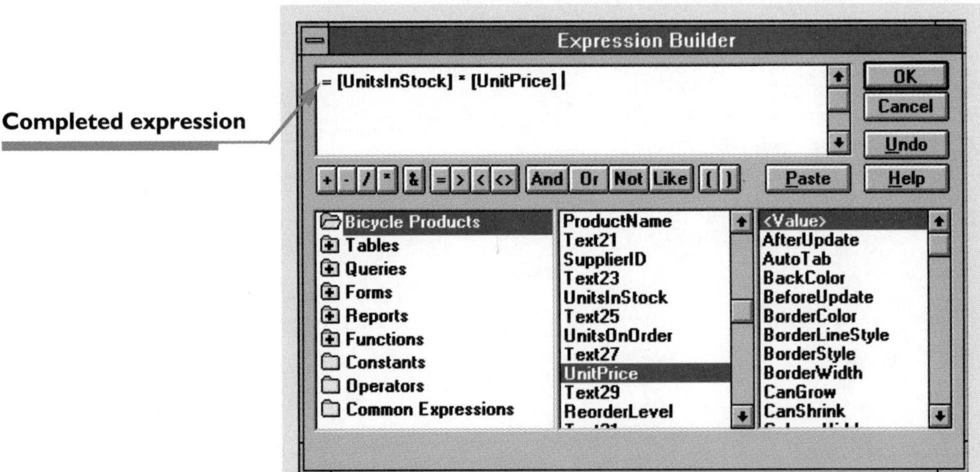

Formatting a control

You can bold, italicize, or underline a control by selecting it then clicking the appropriate attribute button on the Form Design toolbar.

Modifying controls, continued

Michael wants the calculated value to be displayed with the Currency format, which specifies a dollar sign, two decimal places, and commas separating thousands. Changing the format of a field's control only affects the appearance of the field data in the form; it does not affect how data is stored in the database. For more information on modifying controls, see the related topic "Aligning controls."

9 **Click the Format property in the Properties Sheet, click the list arrow, then click Currency**

The Format property now specifies the Currency format. See Figure 4-13. Note also that the Control Source property shows the expression as the source for the Total control.

10 **Double-click the control menu box on the Properties Sheet to close it**

The form is displayed in Design View. Note that the equation you created using the Expression Builder appears in the Total control. See Figure 4-14. Michael wants to view the completed form in Form View.

11 **Click the Form View button on the Form Design toolbar**

Compare your completed form to Figure 4-15. It is alright if your controls are spaced differently. The calculated result of the Total field for the first record appears in Currency format. Michael closes the form, saving his modifications, and returns to the Database window.

12 **Click File on the menu bar, click Close, then click Yes to save the changes to the Bicycle Products form**

FIGURE 4-13: Completed Properties Sheet

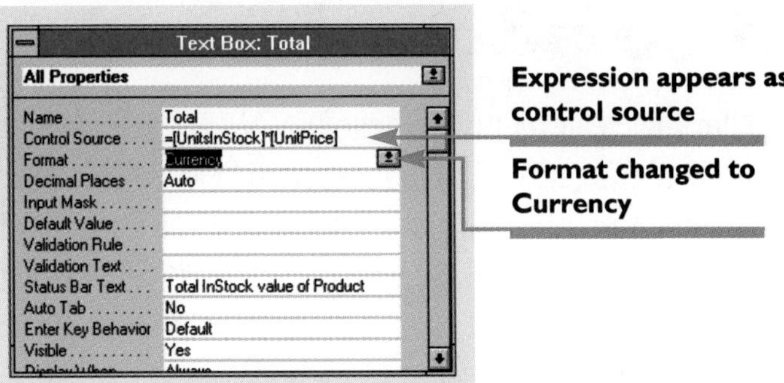

Expression appears as control source

Format changed to Currency

FIGURE 4-14: Equation created by Expression Builder

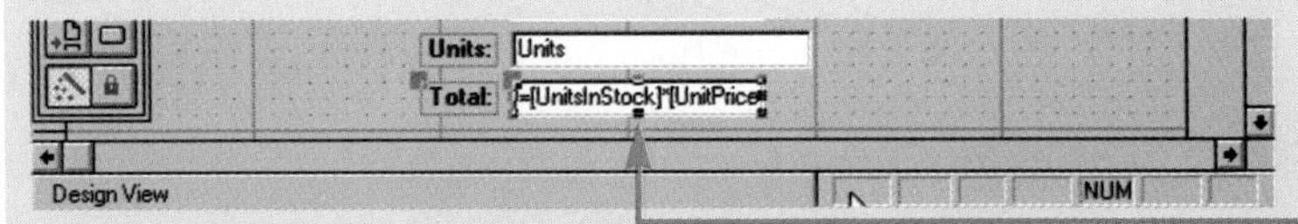

Equation

FIGURE 4-15: Completed form in Form View

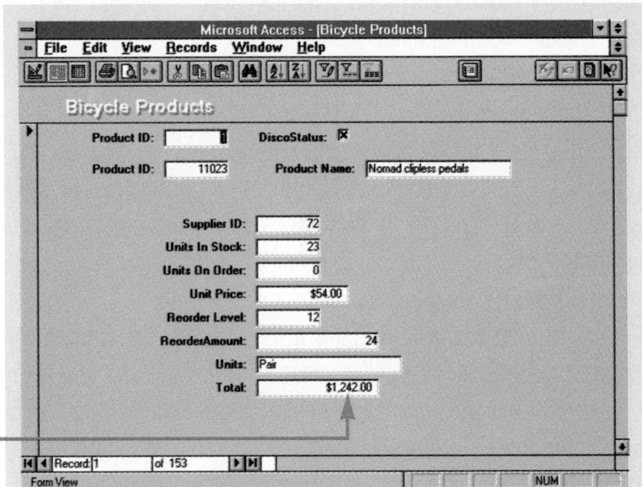

Result of expression

Aligning controls

In Design View, you can align controls with other controls. First, you must select the controls you want to align by pressing [Shift] while clicking the controls. After selecting all the necessary controls, click Format on the menu bar, click Align, then click the alignment position you want, as shown in Figure 4-16.

FIGURE 4-16: Aligning controls

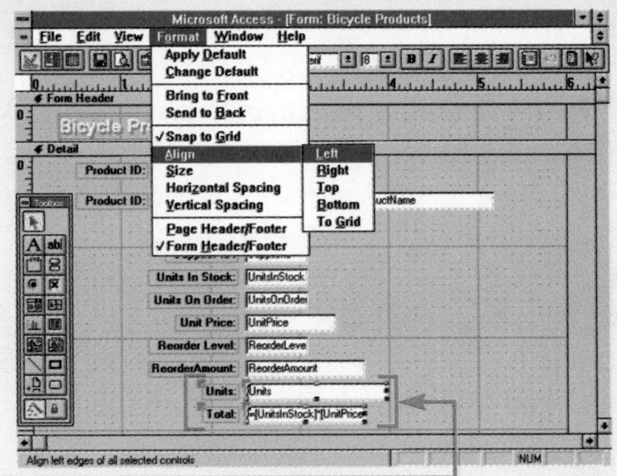

Selected controls

QUICK TIP

You can delete a control by selecting it with the mouse, then pressing [Delete].

Using a form to add a record

After you create a form, you can use it to add records to the database table. To add a record you press [Tab] to move from field to field, entering the appropriate information. You can also print a form to obtain a hard copy for sharing with others. ▶ Michael will use the Bicycle Products form to add a new record to the Bicycle Products table. Then he'll print the form with the data for the new record, and distribute the form to other Nomad employees so that they can see how to use the form to enter data. Because the Bicycle Products table is already selected in the Database window, Michael begins by opening the form.

1. **Click the Open button in the Database window**
   Michael maximizes the form to make it easier to see all the fields.
2. **Click the Maximize button to maximize the form**
   Now Michael can add the new record.
3. **Click the New button on the Form View toolbar**
   A new, blank record is displayed. The text "(Counter)" appears in the first Product ID field. (Recall that the first Product ID field is the Counter field for the table; the second Product ID field contains the actual product identification numbers for the items in the bicycle inventory.) Record 154 of 154 appears in the status bar. See Figure 4-17. Michael begins to enter the data for the new record.
4. **Press [Tab] to advance to the next field**
   The cursor moves to the DiscoStatus field. Remember that when you created the form, you changed the tab order so that DiscoStatus would be the second field moved to in the form. Michael will leave the DiscoStatus field blank to indicate that the product is currently offered (he would enter an "x" in this field for a product that is discontinued). Michael continues to enter the data for the record, pressing [Tab] to move from field to field.
5. **Press [Tab] to advance to the second Product ID field, type 57129, press [Tab], type Nomad FinneganFast Tire, press [Tab], type 22, press [Tab], type 14, press [Tab], type 20, press [Tab], type 15.50, press [Tab], type 15, press [Tab], type 20, press [Tab], type Each, then press [Enter]**
   Compare your completed record to Figure 4-18. Notice that the Total field shows the calculated result. Michael saves the new record.
6. **Click File on the menu bar, then click Save Record**
   The new record is stored in the Bicycle Products table. Next Michael wants to print the form containing the new record.
7. **Click the Print Preview button on the Form View toolbar, then click the Last Record button**
   The status bar indicates that the last record, the one Michael just added, is on page 68. Michael wants to print only page 68.
8. **Click the Print button on the Print Preview toolbar, type 68 in the From text box, then click OK**
   Michael closes the Print Preview window, then closes the form and returns to the Database window.
9. **Click the Close Window button on the Print Preview toolbar, click File on the menu bar, then click Close**

FIGURE 4-17: Blank form for new record

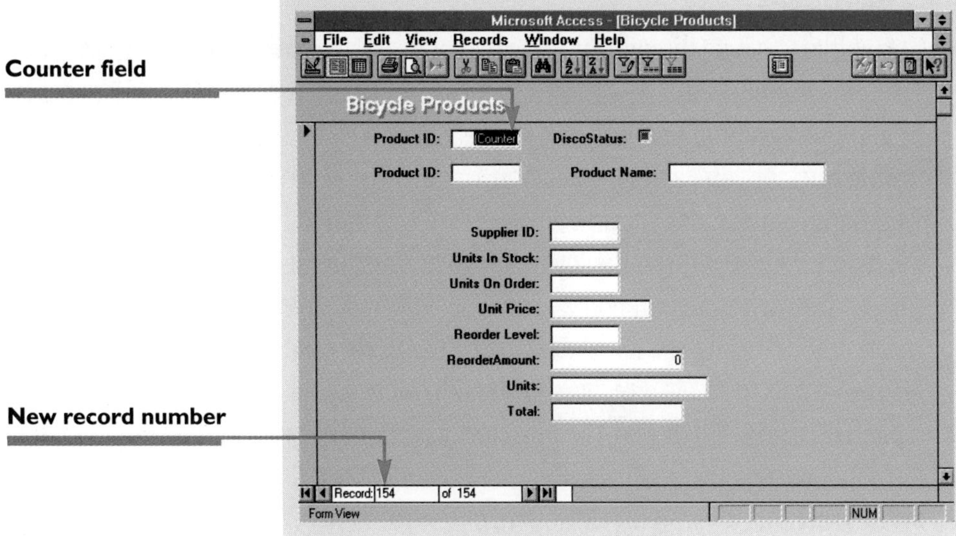

FIGURE 4-18: Completed record 154

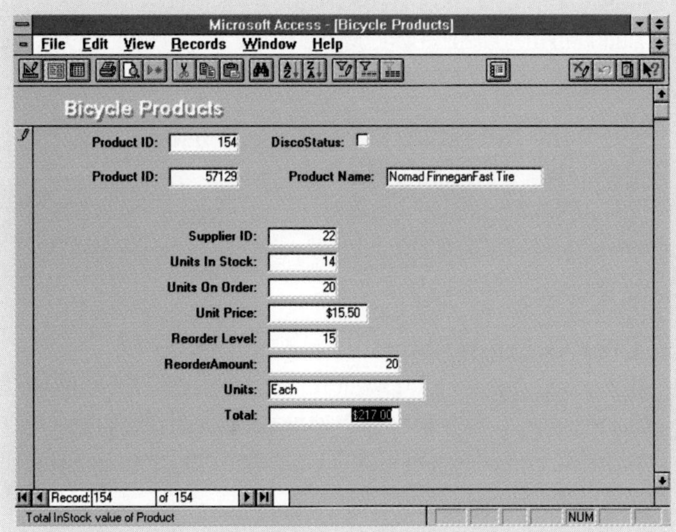

Creating a report

The ability to create thoughtful, concise reports enables you to share data with others in meaningful ways. The most significant data can lose its impact if it appears in an unprofessional or poorly laid out report. You can create reports in Access from scratch or you can use the Report Wizard. The **Report Wizard** provides sample report layouts and gives you options for including specific fields in the report. As with a form, the layout of a report includes sections for a Report Header, Detail, and Report Footer. For more information on creating a simple report automatically, see the related topic "Using the AutoReport button." ▶ Michael wants to create a report showing all but two fields in the Bicycle Products table. The report will display the inventory in groups by product name so that all of the data for the same products will be listed and totaled together. Michael plans on distributing this report to other Nomad employees and to customers.

1 Click the **New Report button** on the Database toolbar
The New Report dialog box opens. You could also create a report by clicking the Report object button in the Database window, then clicking New. Michael uses the Bicycle Products table for his report, which he'll create using the Report Wizard.

2 Click the **Select A Table/Query list arrow**, click **Bicycle Products**, then click **Report Wizards**
The Report Wizards dialog box opens and prompts you to select the type of report you want to create, as shown in Figure 4-19. Michael selects the Groups/Totals report because he will be grouping data in his report.

3 Click **Groups/Totals** then click **OK**
The Groups/Totals Report Wizard dialog box opens. This dialog box allows you to select which fields appear in the report. Michael wants all fields except the Product ID and Total fields to be included. Rather than individually select all but these two fields, Michael selects all the fields and then deletes the two he doesn't want.

4 Click the **All Fields button** to move all the fields to the Field order on report list box
All fields in the Available fields list move to the Field order on report list. Now Michael can remove the fields he doesn't want included in the report.

5 Click **Total** in the Field order on report list box, click the **Remove Field button**, click **ProductID** in the Field order on report list box, then click the **Remove Field button**
Your Field order on report list box should look like the one in Figure 4-20.

6 Click **Next** to display the next dialog box
This dialog box determines how the data in the report will be grouped.

FIGURE 4-21: Previewing the report

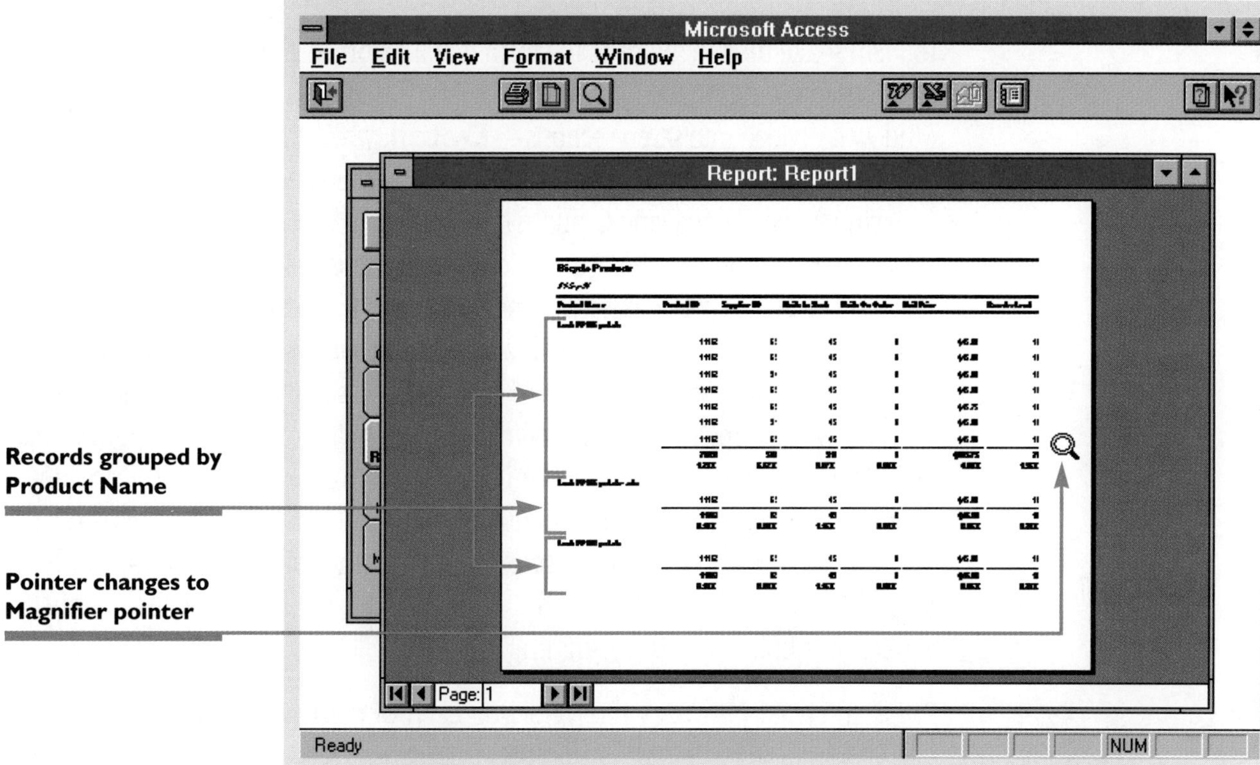

FIGURE 4-22: Printed report

Bicycle Products

17-Oct-94

Product Name	Product ID	Supplier ID	Units In Stock	Units On Order	Unit Price	Reorder Level
Look PP166 pedals						
	11162	63	45	0	$45.00	10
	11162	63	45	0	$45.00	10
	11162	94	45	0	$45.00	10
	11162	63	45	0	$45.00	10
	11162	63	45	0	$45.75	10
	11162	91	45	0	$45.00	10
	11162	63	45	0	$45.00	10
	78134	**500**	**315**	**0**	**$315.75**	**70**
	1.23%	**6.62%**	**8.07%**	**0.00%**	**4.63%**	**1.96%**
Look PP166 pedals - adv						
	11162	63	45	0	$45.00	10
	11162	**63**	**45**	**0**	**$45.00**	**10**
	0.18%	**0.83%**	**1.15%**	**0.00%**	**0.66%**	**0.28%**
Look PP168 pedals						
	11162	63	45	0	$45.00	10
	11162	**63**	**45**	**0**	**$45.00**	**10**
	0.18%	**0.83%**	**1.15%**	**0.00%**	**0.66%**	**0.28%**

Modifying a report

You can make modifications to the format of a report, such as bolding column headings or changing the alignment of fields in a column. The Report Design window is divided into seven sections—**Detail**, which contains controls and the compiled data from the table, and a Header and Footer section for each of the following: Report, Page, and Group. The **Group Header** references the field on which each group is based (in this case, the groups are based on Product Name). The **Report Header** and **Report Footer** print only on the first and last page of the report; the **Page Header** and **Page Footer** print on every page. ▶ Although the Products by DiscoStatus report is adequate, Michael wants to make several modifications to give the report a more professional look. The Product ID, Supplier ID, Units In Stock, Units On Order, Unit Price, and Reorder Level field headings are not aligned with the data below them, as shown in Figure 4-23. Because Michael's screen is already in Design View, he can easily align the field headings with their data to format the report. Michael uses [Shift] to select multiple controls for aligning.

1. **Press and hold [Shift] while selecting each of the control headings in the Page Header section, *except* Product Name**
   While pressing and holding [Shift] and selecting controls, you might need to scroll the window to select all the desired controls. Each selected control has handles surrounding it. First Michael centers the selected controls.
2. **Click the Center button ▤ on the Report Design toolbar**
   Access centers the headings for the selected controls in the Page Header section. See Figure 4-24. Michael wants to center align the controls in the Detail section of the report.
3. **Select the ProductIDI control**
   Selecting this control without holding [Shift] deselects the previously selected controls. Michael continues to make multiple selections in the Detail section.
4. **Press and hold [Shift] while selecting each of the control headings in the Detail section, then click ▤ on the Report Design toolbar**
   Access centers the headings for the selected controls in the Detail section. Michael decides that the information in the ProductName Footer section is unnecessary and wants to delete it, but first deselects the controls in the Detail section.
5. **Select the first control in the ProductName footer section**
6. **Press [Shift] while selecting each of the controls in the ProductName Footer section, including the underscores, as shown in Figure 4-25, then press [Delete]**
   The report now has a gap in it created by the deleted controls. Michael will close the gap by changing the row width using the Page Footer divider. The **Page Footer divider** is the bar containing the section name "Page Footer." He can drag the divider up to narrow the gap.
7. **Drag the Page Footer divider up toward the ProductName Footer section to the 1/4" mark on the ruler, as shown in Figure 4-26**
   You might have to move the Toolbox toolbar in order to see the ruler.

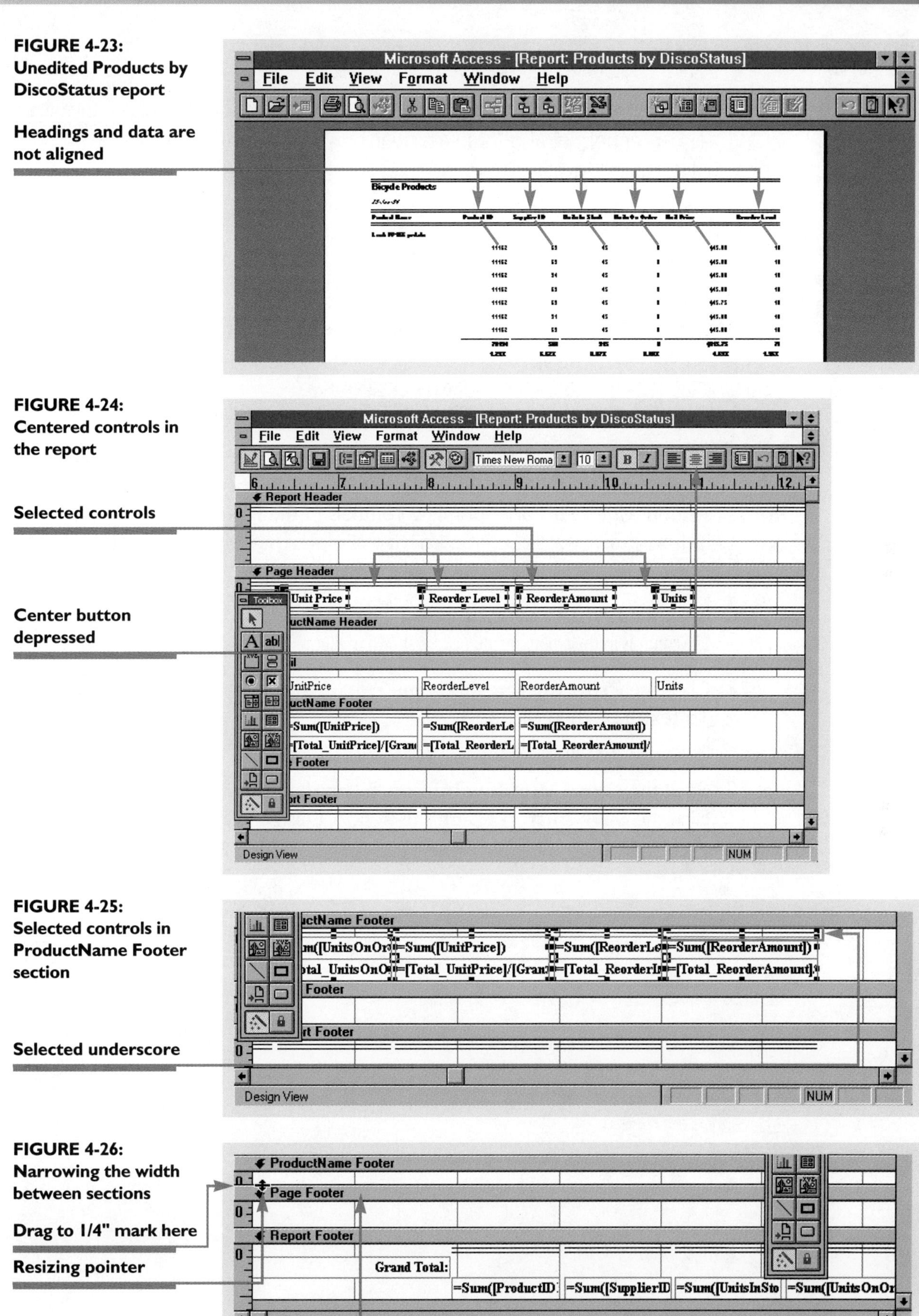

FIGURE 4-23: Unedited Products by DiscoStatus report

FIGURE 4-24: Centered controls in the report

FIGURE 4-25: Selected controls in ProductName Footer section

FIGURE 4-26: Narrowing the width between sections

Modifying a report, continued

Next Michael needs to resize the Detail control widths so that they match the Page Header controls. ▶ Also, for information on saving a form as a report, see the related topic "Saving a form as a report" on the next page.

8 Click the **ProductIDI** control in the Detail section, move the pointer to the right middle handle until the pointer changes to ↔, then drag the handle until it is aligned with the width of the ProductID control in the Page Header section, as shown in Figure 4-27
This process must be repeated for the remaining controls in the Detail section.

9 Repeat Step 8 to resize the SupplierID, UnitsInStock, UnitsOnOrder, UnitPrice, ReorderAmount, Units, and DiscoStatus controls in the Detail section with their corresponding controls in the Page Header section
Each of the controls in the Detail section is now aligned and resized with its control in the Header section. Michael wants to preview the report and print a sample page of the report.

10 Click the **Print Preview button** on the Report Design toolbar
The controls in the report are aligned, as shown in Figure 4-28.

11 Click the **Print button** on the Print Preview toolbar, click **1** in the To text box, then click **OK**
Michael closes the Print Preview window and saves the report.

12 Click the **Close Window button** on the Print Preview toolbar, then click the **Save button** on the Report Design toolbar

FIGURE 4-27: Resizing a control

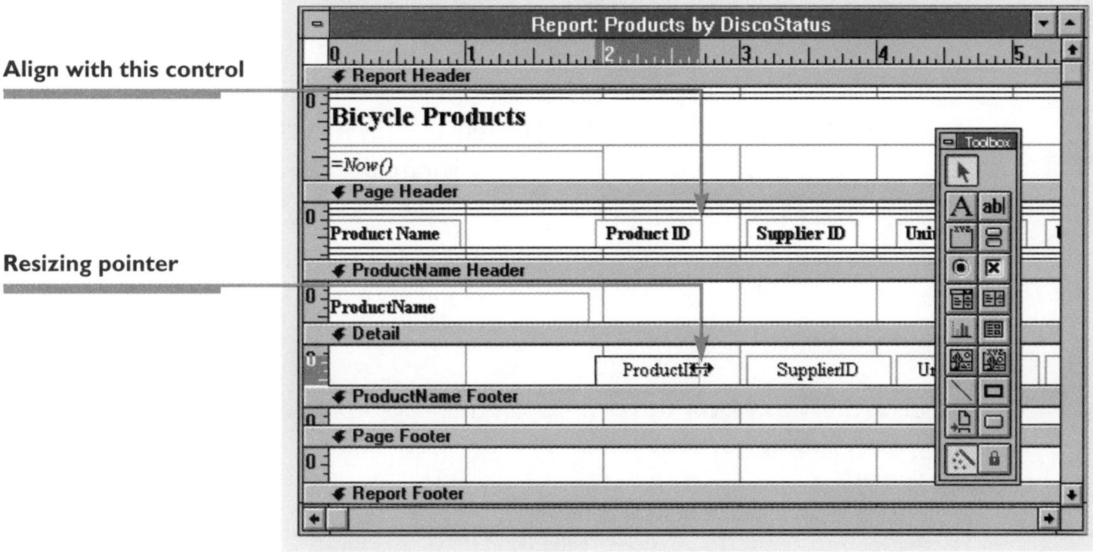

FIGURE 4-28: Report in Print Preview

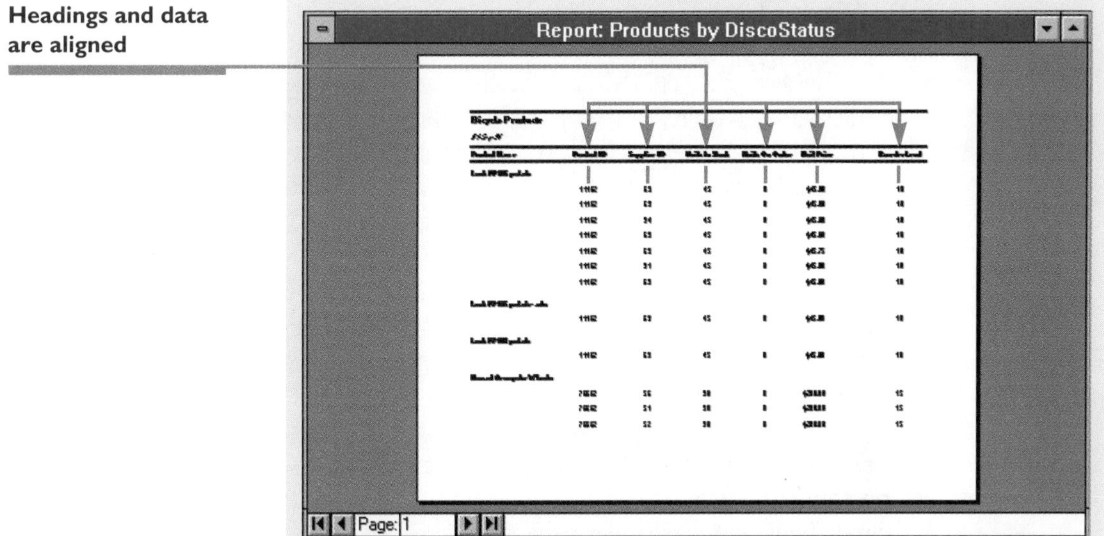

Saving a form as a report

You can save a form as a report, which saves you the time and effort of having to recreate an existing format. To save a form as a report, open the form in Design View, click File on the menu bar, click Save As Report, then supply a new name for the report.

Adding an expression to a report

You have already seen how an expression can be incorporated in a form. You can also add an expression to a report to perform calculations. The expression can include field names, table names, and functions. A **function** is an easy-to-use preprogrammed mathematical equation. For more information on functions, see the related topic "Using functions in expressions." ▶ Michael wants to add an expression to the Products by DiscoStatus report. The expression will count the number of products in each group, by product identification number (as specified by the ProductID1 field).

1. Click the **Text box button** on the Toolbox toolbar, then click in the ProductName Footer section directly under the ProductID1 control at the 2" mark
   This places an unbound control in the ProductName Footer section, into which Michael will type the expression. The expression will include the Count function, which counts the number of occurrences of a specified field in a column.
2. Click inside the unbound control, type **=Count([ProductID1])**, then press **[Enter]**
   The expression appears in the control, as shown in Figure 4-29, although some of its contents might be truncated, or cut off. This does not affect the display of the expression results in the report. Michael wants to preview the report to see the results of the expression.
3. Click the **Print Preview button** on the Report Design toolbar
   The number of records in each group has been counted, although the values need to be aligned with the values in the ProductID1 column. Michael needs to close the Print Preview window, then use the Left-Align button to align the selected control.
4. Click the **Close Window button** on the Print Preview toolbar, then click the **Left-Align button** on the Report Design toolbar
   The expression will be left-aligned when previewed and printed. Michael decides to preview the report again to check the results of this modification.
5. Click the **Print Preview button** on the Report Design toolbar, view the results of the modified control, then click the **Close Window button** on the Print Preview toolbar
   As shown in Print Preview, the value in the expression is left-aligned in the Product ID column. Michael needs to add a label to describe what the values represent in the report. He decides to add the label "Items in Category."
6. Click the **Label button** on the Toolbox toolbar, click 3/4" from the left edge of the ProductName Footer section, type **Items in Category:** then press **[Enter]**
   The label is added to the report, as shown in Figure 4-30. Michael again previews his report.
7. Click the **Print Preview button** on the Report Design toolbar
   The completed report appears with the expression results and corresponding labels. Compare your previewed report with Figure 4-31. Michael prints the first page of the report, then closes the Print Preview window and saves his modifications.
8. Click the **Print button** on the Print Preview toolbar, type **1** in the To text box, click **OK**, click the **Close Window button** on the Print Preview toolbar, then click the **Save button** on the Report Design toolbar
9. Click **File** on the menu bar, then click **Close**

FIGURE 4-29: Truncated expression in control

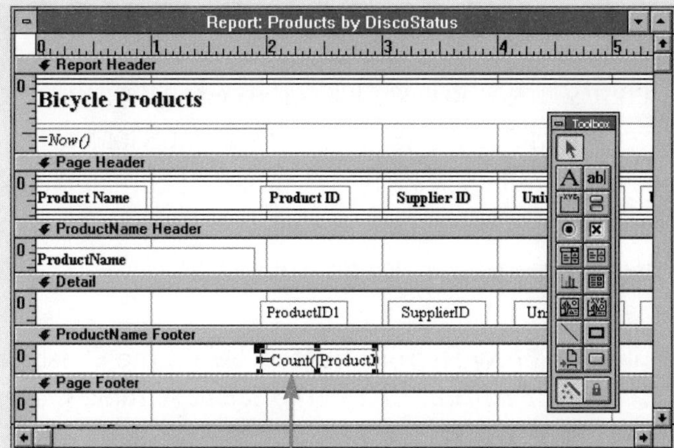

Expression indicating Count function

FIGURE 4-30: Descriptive label added to expression

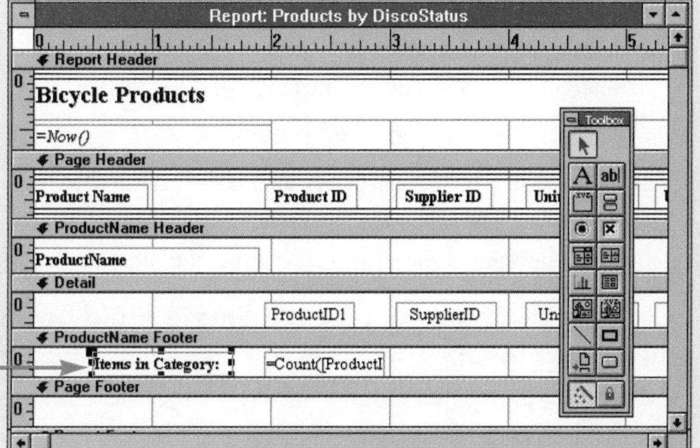

Label identifies results of expression

FIGURE 4-31: Completed report with expression and label

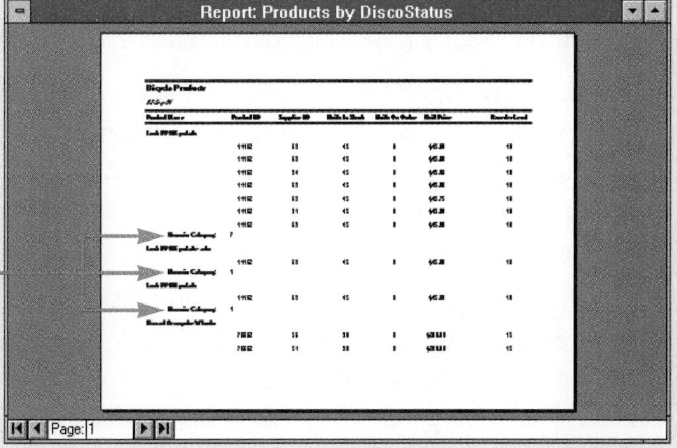

Labels and results of expression

Using functions in expressions

In addition to Count, Access provides many other functions for use in expressions. Using Access Help, you can search for the topic "Functions" to display a list of available functions and how to use them.

Creating a report from a query

You've seen how to create a report based on the fields in a table. Many times, however, you will want to use a query as the basis for a report. ▶ Michael has created a query for the Bicycle Products table called Current Product List to display only current products. He wants to use this query as the basis for a new report. Again, he'll use the Report Wizard to create this report.

1. Click the **New Report button** on the Database toolbar, click **Current Product List** in the Select A Table/Query list box, then click **Report Wizards**
   Michael wants this report to have a tabular layout, in which data is presented in columns and rows.
2. Click **Tabular** then click **OK**
   The Tabular Report Wizard dialog box opens, as shown in Figure 4-32. The Available fields list box displays all the fields used in the query (not all the fields in the table). Michael wants to include all the fields in the report.
3. Click the **All Fields button**, then click **Next**
   Michael wants the records sorted by ProductName. The next two dialog boxes contain default settings for the report's appearance, paper orientation, and title, which Michael accepts.
4. Click **ProductName**, click the **Single Field button**, click **Next**, then click **Finish**
   Access creates the report and displays it in Print Preview. Michael needs to make a few minor modifications to the alignment of controls.
5. Click the **Close Window button** on the Print Preview toolbar
   Michael wants to center the headings for Product ID, Supplier ID, Units In Stock, and Unit Price. He does this by selecting these controls and then using the Center button.
6. Click the **ProductID control**, press and hold **[Shift]**, click the controls for **SupplierID**, **UnitsInStock**, and **UnitPrice** in the PageHeader section, then click the **Center button** on the Report Design toolbar
   Access centers the headings for the selected controls in the Page Header section. Michael wants to center align the controls in the Detail section of the report.
7. Click the ProductID1 control, press and hold **[Shift]** while clicking the **ProductID1**, **SupplierID**, **UnitsInStock**, and **UnitPrice controls** in the Detail section, then click on the Report Design toolbar
   Michael previews and prints the report to see his modifications.
8. Click the **Print Preview button** on the Report Design toolbar, click the **Print button** on the Print Preview toolbar, then click **OK**
   Compare page 1 of your printed report with Figure 4-33. Michael closes the Print Preview window, saves his modifications, and closes the report.
9. Click on the Print Preview toolbar, click the **Save button** on the Report Design toolbar, type **Current Product List**, click **OK**, click **File** on the menu bar, then click **Exit**

FIGURE 4-32: Tabular Report Wizard dialog box

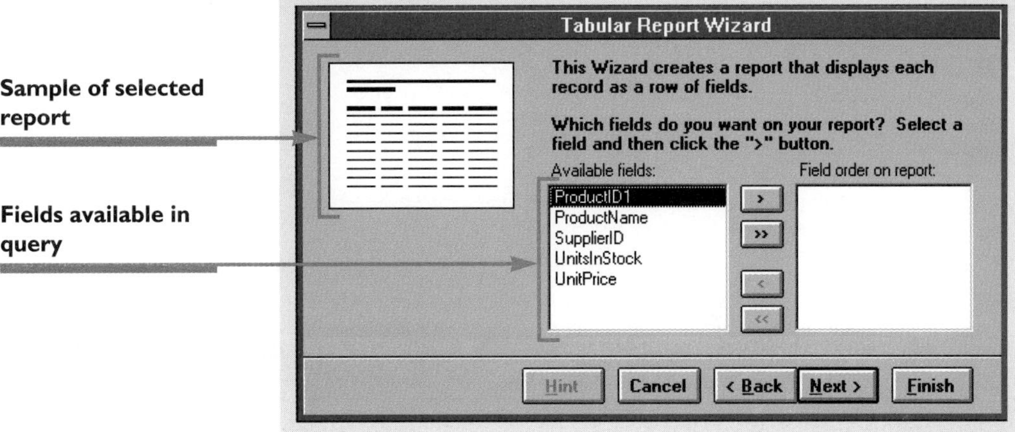

FIGURE 4-33: Completed report created from a query

Current Product List

30-Sep-94

Product ID	Product Name	Supplier ID	Units In Stock	Unit Price
11162	Look PP166 pedals	63	45	$45.75
11162	Look PP166 pedals	63	45	$45.00
11162	Look PP166 pedals	94	45	$45.00
11162	Look PP166 pedals	63	45	$45.00
11162	Look PP166 pedals	91	45	$45.00
11162	Look PP166 pedals - adv	63	45	$45.00
11162	Look PP168 pedals	63	45	$45.00
76662	Nomad Aerospoke Wheels	56	30	$200.00
76662	Nomad Aerospoke Wheels	56	30	$200.00
76662	Nomad Aerospoke Wheels	56	30	$200.00
76662	Nomad Aerospoke Wheels	56	30	$200.00
76662	Nomad Aerospoke Wheels - Pro	56	30	$200.00
32323	Nomad Beauty Handlebar tape	10	27	$3.00
32323	Nomad Beauty Handlebar tape	10	27	$2.00
11023	Nomad clipless pedals	54	20	$54.50
11023	Nomad clipless pedals	72	23	$54.00
11023	Nomad clipless pedals	72	23	$54.00

When basing a report on a query, give the report the same name as the query name; this will remind you that the report and the query are related.

CONCEPTSREVIEW

Label each of the elements of the Report Design window shown in Figure 4-34.

1
2
3
4
5
6

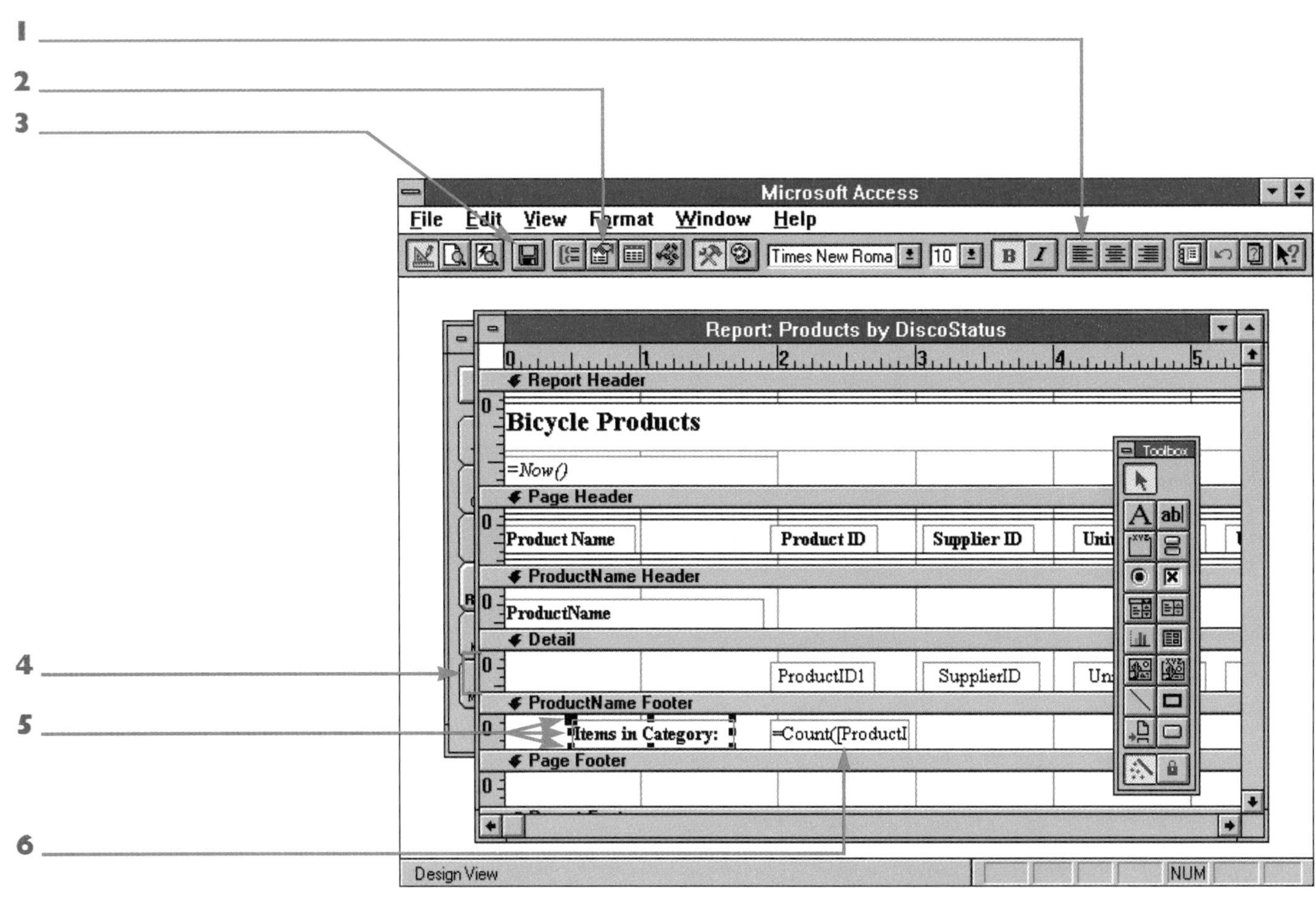

FIGURE 4-34

Match each button to its correct description.

7
8
9
10
11
12

a. Print Preview
b. Zoom
c. Close Window
d. Form View
e. Properties
f. New Report

Select the best answer from the list of choices.

13 Objects in a form or report are called
a. Properties
b. Controls
c. Pieces
d. Handles

14 The pointer used to resize a control is
a.
b. ↔
c.
d.

15 Black squares that surround a selected control are called

a. Queries

b. Quotes

c. Handles

d. Markers

16 The button used to open the Expression Builder is

a. [button]

b. [button]

c. [button]

d. [button]

17 Select multiple controls by clicking each control while pressing

a. [Ctrl]

b. [Enter]

c. [Shift]

d. [Alt]

18 A control is considered to be bound when

a. It is displayed in a form or report

b. It is used to sort a table

c. Its data source is found in a table

d. Its data source is the result of an expression

APPLICATIONSREVIEW

1 Create a form.

a. Start Access and make sure your Student Disk is in drive A. Open the file PARTS.MDB from your Student Disk.

b. Create a new form for the Products table.

c. Use the Form Wizard to create a single-column form.

d. Include all fields in the form.

e. Use the Embossed style.

f. Display the form with data.

2 Modify a form.

a. Maximize the Form window and change the form's dimensions so that it is at least 6" wide.

b. Select controls and position them so that all controls are displayed on the screen in an order you feel makes sense.

c. Modify the tab order so that pressing [Tab] moves sequentially through the fields as you have arranged them.

d. Save your form as Product Entry Form.

3 Modify controls.

a. Change the format of the UnitsOnOrder control so that it has one decimal place.

b. Change the number contained in the UnitsInStock field so that it appears in italics.

c. View the changes in Form View.

d. Save your changes.

4 Add a record using a form.

a. Open the Product Entry Form.

b. Enter the following new record: Product ID: 70701, Product Name: Nomad Honey Handlebar tape, Category ID: 32, Supplier ID: 10, Units In Stock: 52, Units On Order: 0, Unit Price: 2, Reorder Level: 30, Reorder Amount: 35, Units: Each, DiscoStatus: No.

c. Save the record.

d. Print the form containing the new record.

5 Create a report.

a. Create a Groups/Totals report based on the Products sold as "Each" query using the table Report Wizard. Sort the report by Product Name.

b. Include all the fields in the report.

c. Sort the report by SupplierID.

d. Preview the report with the data in it.

e. Print the report.

f. Save the report as Products by Supplier.

6 Modify a report.

a. Align the fields so that the values are centered with the headings above them.

b. Delete any calculated summaries you feel detract from the report.

c. Preview and print the report.

d. Save your changes.

7 Add an expression to a report.

a. Create an expression in the Product Name Footer under Product Name that counts the number of items for each supplier.

b. Add the descriptive label "Items from Supplier:" to the left of the expression.

c. Preview and print the report.

d. Save your changes.

8 Create a report from a query.
   a. Create a Tabular report using the Report Wizard based on the query Products sold as "Each."
   b. Center the controls with their heading controls, where necessary.
   c. Save the report using the query name.
   d. Preview and print the report.
   e. Close the Print Preview window, then exit Access.

INDEPENDENT CHALLENGE 1

As the Customer Service Manager of the Melodies Music Store, you must continue your work on the music database. Several of the store's employees will be using the database to enter data, and you need to design a form to facilitate this data entry. The employees will be entering data from a paper-based form, shown in Figure 4-35. You also need to generate reports for output requests by management as well as customers.

Product ID: Category ID:
Artist:
Title:
Serial Number:
Units in Stock:
Unit Price:

FIGURE 4-35

To complete this independent challenge:

1 Open the file MELODY.MDB from your Student Disk.

2 Create a single-column form that includes all the fields in the table, then save it as Title Input.

3 The controls should be positioned so that they all fit on the screen. Make sure the tab order reflects any fields that you moved.

4 Use the newly created form to add three new records of your favorite artists.

5 Print the form containing one of the new records.

6 Add an expression that calculates a new field called OnHand that multiplies the UnitsInStock field value by the UnitPrice field value.

7 Create a report based on the Available titles table query, which displays all fields in a Groups/Totals format.

8 Save the report as MUSICTITLES then print the report.

INDEPENDENT CHALLENGE 2

You work in the U.S. Census Office for your city. The records in the Statistical Data table, which is in the database file STATS-1.MDB on your Student Disk, contain marriage information by state. Each state is assigned a geographical area. Using the Statistical Data table, create a form to facilitate data entry, and create at least two reports showing different groupings of this information.

To complete this independent challenge:

1 Create a single-column form containing all the fields in the table.

2 Modify the form by repositioning the controls, then adjusting the tab order.

3 Save the form using a name of your choice.

4 Preview the form after each of your modifications.

5 Create at least two forms based on information in the table. Save each form using a name of your choice. Try saving each form as a report.

6 Print a sample of each report.

7 Create reports of your choosing based on each of the queries saved in the STATS-1.MDB database file. Each report should show all the fields in each query, and use a format you feel best shows the data.

8 Print the reports.

Glossary

AND and OR criteria Parameters used to qualify records selected in a query or filter. AND is used to narrow the number of selected records, whereas OR is used to broaden the number of selected records.

Ascending order A sort order in which fields are alphabetized from A to Z.

AutoReport Button that automatically creates a report that displays all fields in a single-column format.

Bound control A control on a form that is linked to a specific field in the database. *See also* Control.

Calculated control A control that has a mathematical expression as its data source.

Cell The intersection of a column and a row.

Control A graphical object that consists of the field text and the data in it. Controls are either bound, unbound, or calculated.

Counter field A field that automatically assigns the next consecutive number each time a record is added.

Data The information contained in a database table.

Database A collection of data related to a particular topic or purpose.

Database window The window that opens when you start Access. It provides access to the objects in the database.

Datasheet A grid in which each record is contained in a row, and field names are listed as column headings. You enter data for a table in the datasheet.

Datasheet View A window that displays records in a grid format of columns and rows, which you can use to navigate through the records quickly.

Descending order A sort order in which fields are alphabetized from Z to A.

Design View A window that shows the structure of a table, form, query, or report. You use this view to modify the structure of a table by adding and deleting fields and adding field descriptions and field properties.

Detail Section of a form that appears on the screen form and displays the fields and data for each record visible in Design View. Detail section also appears in Report Design window, in which you can make modifications to the format of a report.

Dynaset Collection of records resulting from a query; looks and acts like a table, but is merely a view based on the query.

Expression A mathematical equation created within a form or report's control.

Expression Builder A feature that displays helpful fields and mathematical symbols you use to create expressions.

Field Category of information in a database table, such as a customer's last name.

Field description Optional text that clarifies the purpose or function of a field. The field description appears in the status bar when you enter data.

Field properties Information you can define that affects the data entered in a field, such as the number of decimal places in a number. You define field properties in the Design view.

Filter window A window that consists of two areas: the field list on top, containing all the fields in the table, and the filter grid on the bottom, into which fields are dragged and filtering criteria are defined.

Filtering A more complex method of organizing records, in which you define the fields on which the table is sorted.

Form An object used to enter, edit, and display records one at a time.

Form Footer A section of a form that appears at the bottom of each screen form and can contain totals, instructions, or command buttons.

Form Header A section of a form that appears at the beginning of each screen form and can contain a title or logo.

Form View Screen in which table data can be viewed, entered, or changed one record at a time.

Form Wizard A feature that guides you through the process of creating a form by providing sample form layouts and form-specific options.

Function An easy-to-use preprogrammed mathematical equation that can be used in forms and reports to make calculations.

Handles Black squares that appear around the perimeter of a control, indicating the control is selected.

Help On-line system that gives you immediate access to definitions, explanations, and useful tips as they related to Access.

Input Materials necessary to produce the results you want.

Mouse pointer An arrow indicating the location of the mouse on the desktop. The mouse pointer changes shape at times, depending on the application and task being executed or performed.

Object The principal component of an Access database. Tables, queries, forms, and reports are all referred to as objects in Access.

Object buttons Buttons on the left side of the database window that allow you to open, create, and modify database components.

Output The desired results of a database, often printed reports or screen forms.

Page Footer Material that appears at the bottom of each page in printed output.

Page Header Material that appears at the top of each page in printed output.

Primary key A field that qualifies each record as unique. If you do not specify a primary key, Access will create one for you.

Print Preview A window that displays a view of how a page will appear when printed.

Property Quality or characteristic of a control that makes data entry more efficient.

Property Sheet A window that displays the control's name and source and that lists the qualities for the selected control that can be edited.

Query A set of qualities, or criteria, that you specify to retrieve certain data from a database. You can save a query to use at a later time.

Query grid Area in which fields and query instructions are contained.

Record A group of related fields, such as all information on a particular customer.

Relational database A database that contains more than one table and allows information within its tables to be shared.

Report An Access object that presents data selected and formatted for printing.

Report Footer Material that appears at the bottom of the last printed page of a report.

Report Header Material that appears at the top of the first printed page of a report.

Report Wizard A feature that guides you through the process of creating a report by providing sample report layouts and options for including specific fields in the report.

Row selector A gray box at the left edge of a datasheet that is used to select an entire row.

Select query A query that created a dynaset in which records are collected and viewed, and can be modified.

Shortcut keys A key or key combination that allows you to select a command without using the menu bar or toolbar.

Sort A feature that organizes records from A to Z or Z to A, based on one or more fields in a table or query.

Source document The document from which information will be copied into the clipboard.

Startup window The window that appears when you start Access; the area from which you carry out database operations.

Status bar A horizontal bar at the bottom of the screen that displays information about commands or actions and descriptions of ToolTips.

Tab order Determines the order in which you advance from one field to the next when you press [Tab] to enter data in a form.

Table A collection of related records in a database.

Table Wizard A feature that guides you through the process of creating a simple table, prompting you to choose from a variety of fields and options.

Toolbar A horizontal bar with buttons that provide access to the most commonly used Access commands.

ToolTip When you move the pointer over a button, the name of the button appears under the pointer and a description of the button appears in the status bar.

Unbound control A control that is entirely stored in the design of a form or report. There is no link to data in a table. For example, a title above a group of controls is an unbound control.

Wildcards Symbols that can be used to substitute for characters in text.

Wizard A feature that provides a series of dialog boxes that guide you through the process of creating a table, form, report, query, or other Access object; unique to Microsoft products.

Index

UNIT 2

OBJECTIVES

- Use Mail Merge to create a form letter
- Export an Access table to Excel

Integrating WORD, EXCEL, AND ACCESS

ou have learned how to use Word, Excel, and Access individually to accomplish specific tasks more efficiently. Now you will learn how to integrate files created using these applications so that you can use the best features of each one. ▶ In preparation for the upcoming Annual Report, Andrew Gillespie, the national sales manager for Nomad Ltd, wants to establish a tour customer profile that he can incorporate into the report. To do this, he will mail a survey to Nomad Ltd's tour customers. He also wants to export the Access database of customer names and addresses into an Excel worksheet so that he can create an Excel chart showing from which areas of the country Nomad attracts the most customers. ▶

Using Mail Merge to create a form letter

Companies often keep a database of customer names and addresses, then send form letters to their customers. With Microsoft Office, you can combine, or **merge**, data from an existing Access table with a Word document to automatically create personalized form letters. ▶ Andrew wants to survey customers who have taken tours with Nomad during the last two years. He wrote a form letter using Word. He wants to merge the letter with the customer names and addresses that already exist in an Access table.

1 Double-click the **Microsoft Word application icon** in the Program Manager window, open the file INT_2-1.DOC from your Student Disk, then save it as SURVEY.DOC to your MY_FILES directory
The document SURVEY.DOC appears in the document window. To merge this letter with the data in the Access table, Andrew uses Word's Mail Merge feature.

2 Click **Tools** on the menu bar, then click **Mail Merge**
The Mail Merge Helper dialog box opens, as shown in Figure 2-1. This dialog box contains three list boxes to help you perform the mail merge operation. Andrew begins by naming the **main document**—the letter that the data will be merged with.

3 Click **Create** then click **Form Letters**
A dialog box opens, asking if the document in the active window or a new document should be used as the main document. See Figure 2-2. Andrew wants to use SURVEY.DOC as his main document, so he chooses Active Window.

4 Click **Active Window**
Step 1 of the Mail Merge Helper dialog box now lists SURVEY.DOC as the main document. Next, Andrew uses Step 2 to identify the data source. The **data source** file contains the variable information that will be inserted into the main document during the merge process.

5 Click **Get Data** then click **Open Data Source**
The Open Data Source dialog box opens. Andrew uses an Access database as the data source.

6 Click the **List Files of Type list arrow**, click **MS Access Databases (*.mdb)**, click **CUSTINFO.MDB** in the File Name list box, then click **OK**
If a Confirm Data Source dialog box opens, click MS Access Databases via DDE (*.mdb). If CUSTINFO.MDB is not listed in the File Name list box, make sure that the current drive and directory is a:\. Access is started automatically, and a Microsoft Access dialog box opens, listing the tables in CUSTINFO.MDB, as shown in Figure 2-3. Andrew chooses the Customers table from the database.

7 Click the **Tables tab** if necessary, click **Customers**, then click **OK**
If you wanted to choose a query, you would click the query tab to see the list of queries in the database. A dialog box opens, displaying a warning that no merge fields were found in your main document. **Merge fields** identify which fields in each record of the database will be merged with the form letter. Andrew needs to edit the main document so he can insert these merge fields in it.

8 Click **Edit Main Document**
You are returned to the document window, and the Mail Merge toolbar appears under the Formatting toolbar. Buttons in the Mail Merge toolbar are described in Table 2-1. In the next lesson, you will continue setting up the mail merge.

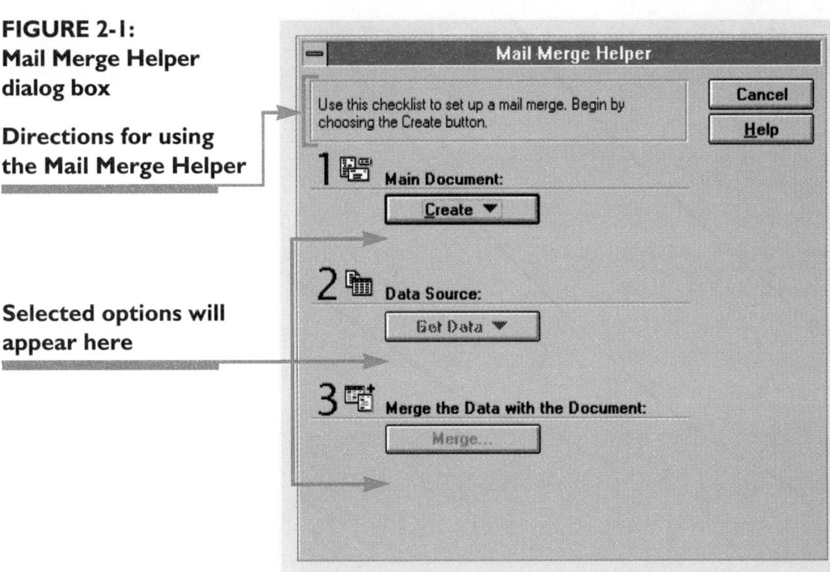

FIGURE 2-1: Mail Merge Helper dialog box

Directions for using the Mail Merge Helper

Selected options will appear here

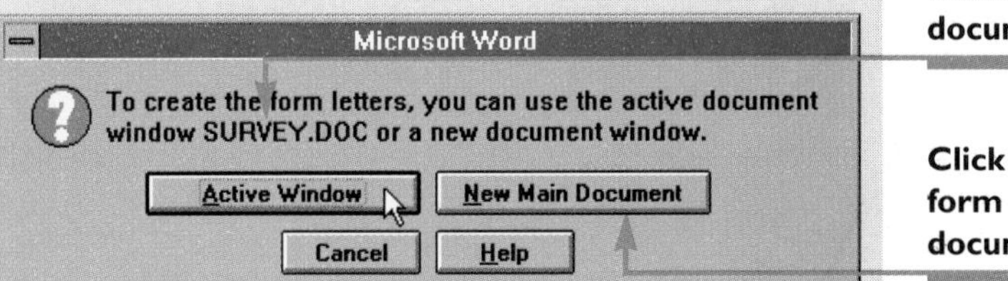

FIGURE 2-2: Select a main document dialog box

Indicates active document

Click to create the form letter in a new document

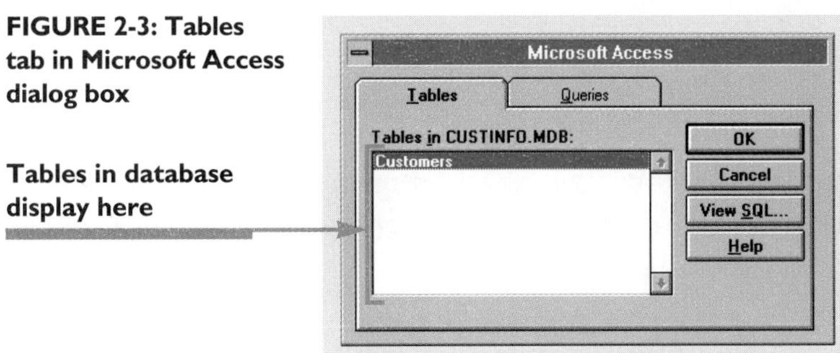

FIGURE 2-3: Tables tab in Microsoft Access dialog box

Tables in database display here

TABLE 2-1: Mail Merge buttons

BUTTON	NAME	BUTTON	NAME
	View Merged Data		Check for Errors
	First Record		Merge to New Document
	Previous Record		Merge to Printer
	Next Record		Mail Merge
	Last Record		Find Record
	Mail Merge Helper		Edit Data Source

TROUBLE?

If a message box appears telling you that there isn't enough memory to open the database file, try launching Access prior to Step 1 on the previous page.

Using Mail Merge to create a form letter, continued

After identifying the main document and the data source, Andrew needs to insert merge fields into the main document.

9 Position the pointer in the second empty paragraph below the date, then click **Insert Merge Field** on the Mail Merge toolbar
A list of fields in the Access database appears, as shown in Figure 2-4. The first merge field Andrew wants to insert is the FirstName field in the inside address.

10 Click **FirstName** in the fields list
The FirstName field is inserted between brackets in the form letter.

11 Press **[Spacebar]**, click **Insert Merge Field** on the Mail Merge toolbar, click **LastName** in the list, then press **[↓]**

12 Continue inserting the merge fields and typing the text shown in Figure 2-5
Make sure you put a comma and a space after the City merge field. After all the merge fields are entered, Andrew saves the main document.

13 Click the **Save button** on the Standard toolbar
Now Andrew wants to merge the two files.

14 Click the **Mail Merge Helper button** on the Mail Merge toolbar
The Mail Merge Helper dialog box opens. Compare your screen with Figure 2-6. Andrew makes sure the correct files are listed and is now ready to perform the merge.

15 Click **Merge**
The Merge dialog box opens, as shown in Figure 2-7. If you wanted to merge the main document with records that met certain criteria you would click Query Options. If you wanted to merge the files directly to the printer, you would click the Merge To list arrow, then choose the printer. It's a good idea to merge the documents into one new document so that you can examine the final product and make any necessary corrections before you print. Andrew accepts the dialog box defaults.

16 Click **Merge**
As Word merges the document with the table, messages appear in the status bar indicating which records are currently being processed. "Microsoft Word – Form Letters 1" appears in the title bar when the merge is complete. You should see the first form letter with Ginny Braithwaite's data on your screen. Andrew saves the merged document.

17 Click the **Save button** on the Standard toolbar, then save the document as FORMLET.DOC to the MY_FILES directory on your Student Disk
Andrew is satisfied with his merge project and prints the document.

18 Click **File** on the menu bar, click **Print** and specify pages 1 through 3 to print only the first three form letters, then click **OK** and close FORMLET.DOC
The first three of the thirty form letters print.

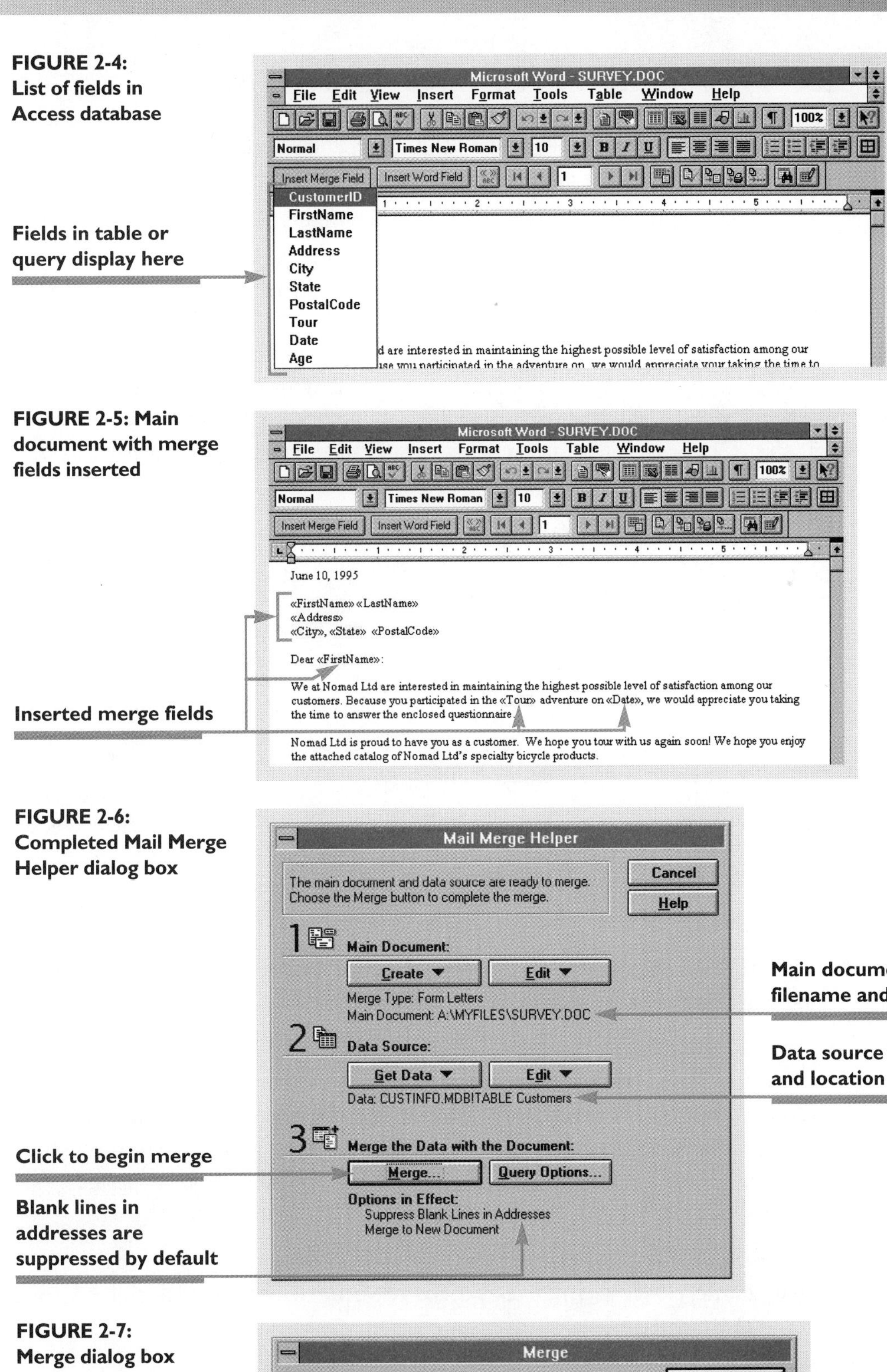

FIGURE 2-4: List of fields in Access database

FIGURE 2-5: Main document with merge fields inserted

FIGURE 2-6: Completed Mail Merge Helper dialog box

FIGURE 2-7: Merge dialog box

QUICK TIP

To eliminate the Mail Merge toolbar from a document, click the Mail Merge Helper button, click Create under Main Document, then click Restore to Normal Word Document.

Exporting an Access table to Excel

Data in an Access table can be exported to Excel and several other applications. When a table is **exported**, a copy of the data is created in a format acceptable to the other application, and the original data remains intact. ► Andrew wants to export the Customer table in the CUSTINFO.MDB database into Excel so that he can analyze the data and create a chart that shows the distribution of Nomad's customers by tour type.

1. **Press and hold [Alt] then press [Tab] as many times as necessary until the Microsoft Access application icon appears in the middle of the screen**
   The blank Access application window appears. Andrew opens the database containing the table he wants to export to Excel.
2. Click the **Open Database button** on the Database toolbar, select CUSTINFO.MDB from your Student Disk, click **OK**, then click the **Export button** on the Database toolbar
   The Export dialog box opens, as shown in Figure 2-8. Note that your list of Data Destinations might be different. Andrew needs to select the file type of the exported data.
3. Click **Microsoft Excel 5.0** in the Data Destination list box, then click **OK**
   The Select Microsoft Access Object dialog box opens, with the Customers table already selected. Andrew wants to export the Customers table.
4. Click **OK**, double-click the MY_FILES directory to open it, then click **OK** in the Export to File dialog box to accept the default name CUSTOMER.XLS
   The table has been exported and saved as an Excel file. Andrew no longer needs Access so he exits the program. Andrew wants to see the exported file. First he opens Excel.
5. Click **File** on the menu bar, then click **Exit** to exit Access, then double-click the **Microsoft Excel application icon** in the Program Manager Window
   A new, blank Excel workbook opens. Andrew opens the exported file.
6. Click the **Open button** on the Standard toolbar, then open the file CUSTOMER.XLS from the MY_FILES directory on your Student Disk
   The exported data appears in a workbook that contains only one worksheet instead of sixteen, as shown in Figure 2-9. When data is imported into Excel, only one worksheet is supplied, although more can be added. Andrew resizes the columns so that he can see all the data.
7. Select the A through J **column selector buttons**, click **Format** on the menu bar, click **Column**, click **AutoFit Selection**, then click cell **A1** to deselect the columns
   Compare your screen to Figure 2-10. Andrew is satisfied with the exported file. He decides to save his work and print the worksheet.
8. Click the **Save button** on the Standard toolbar, then click the **Print button** on the Standard toolbar
   Satisfied with the printed worksheet, Andrew exits Excel.
9. Click **File** on the menu bar, click **Exit** to exit Excel, then exit any other open applications

FIGURE 2-8: Export dialog box

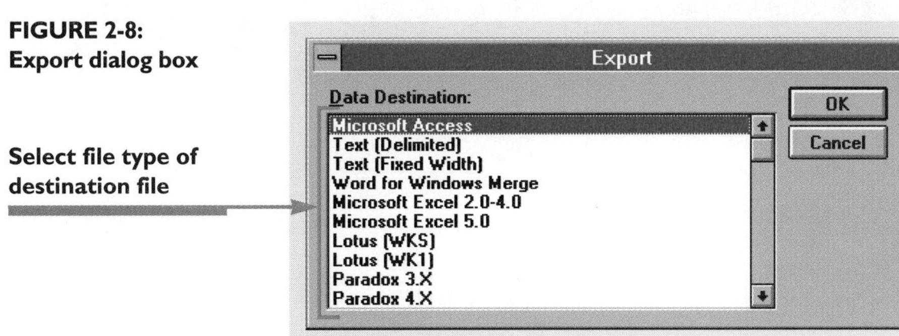

Select file type of destination file

FIGURE 2-9: Exported Access data in an Excel worksheet

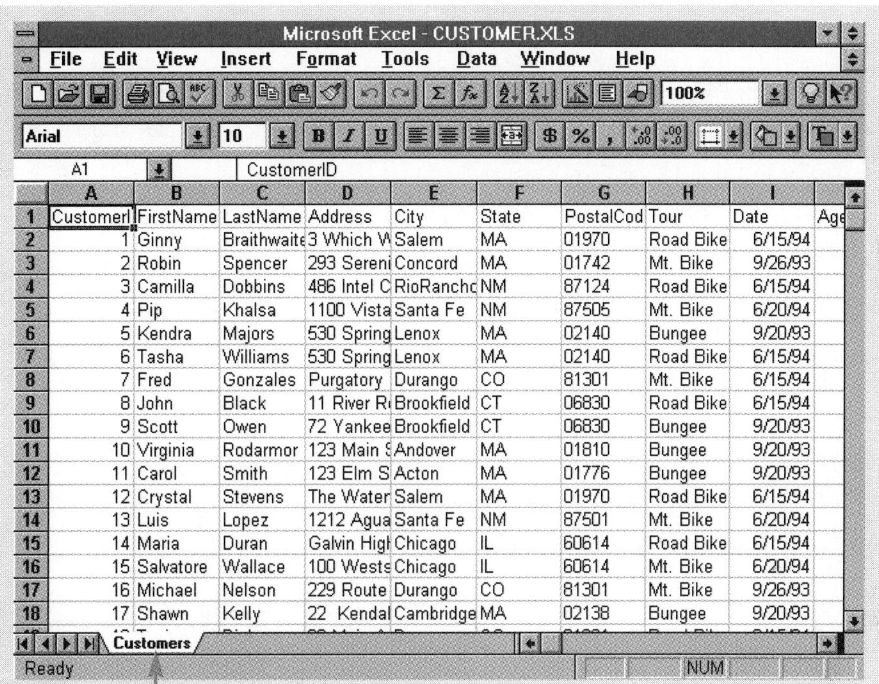

	A	B	C	D	E	F	G	H	I	
1	Customerl	FirstName	LastName	Address	City	State	PostalCod	Tour	Date	Age
2	1	Ginny	Braithwaite	3 Which W	Salem	MA	01970	Road Bike	6/15/94	
3	2	Robin	Spencer	293 Sereni	Concord	MA	01742	Mt. Bike	9/26/93	
4	3	Camilla	Dobbins	486 Intel C	RioRancho	NM	87124	Road Bike	6/15/94	
5	4	Pip	Khalsa	1100 Vista	Santa Fe	NM	87505	Mt. Bike	6/20/94	
6	5	Kendra	Majors	530 Spring	Lenox	MA	02140	Bungee	9/20/93	
7	6	Tasha	Williams	530 Spring	Lenox	MA	02140	Road Bike	6/15/94	
8	7	Fred	Gonzales	Purgatory	Durango	CO	81301	Mt. Bike	6/15/94	
9	8	John	Black	11 River R	Brookfield	CT	06830	Road Bike	6/15/94	
10	9	Scott	Owen	72 Yankee	Brookfield	CT	06830	Bungee	9/20/93	
11	10	Virginia	Rodarmor	123 Main S	Andover	MA	01810	Bungee	9/20/93	
12	11	Carol	Smith	123 Elm S	Acton	MA	01776	Bungee	9/20/93	
13	12	Crystal	Stevens	The Water	Salem	MA	01970	Road Bike	6/15/94	
14	13	Luis	Lopez	1212 Agua	Santa Fe	NM	87501	Mt. Bike	6/20/94	
15	14	Maria	Duran	Galvin High	Chicago	IL	60614	Road Bike	6/15/94	
16	15	Salvatore	Wallace	100 Wests	Chicago	IL	60614	Mt. Bike	6/20/94	
17	16	Michael	Nelson	229 Route	Durango	CO	81301	Mt. Bike	9/26/93	
18	17	Shawn	Kelly	22 Kendal	Cambridge	MA	02138	Bungee	9/20/93	

Single worksheet

FIGURE 2-10: Excel worksheet with resized columns

Microsoft Excel - CUSTOMER.XLS

File Edit View Insert Format Tools Data Window Help

A1 CustomerID

	A	B	C	D	E	F	G	H
1	CustomerID	FirstName	LastName	Address	City	State	PostalCode	Tour
2	1	Ginny	Braithwaite	3 Which Way, Apt. 2	Salem	MA	01970	Road Bike
3	2	Robin	Spencer	293 Serenity Drive	Concord	MA	01742	Mt. Bike
4	3	Camilla	Dobbins	486 Intel Circuit	RioRancho	NM	87124	Road Bike
5	4	Pip	Khalsa	1100 Vista Road	Santa Fe	NM	87505	Mt. Bike
6	5	Kendra	Majors	530 Spring Street	Lenox	MA	02140	Bungee
7	6	Tasha	Williams	530 Spring Street	Lenox	MA	02140	Road Bike
8	7	Fred	Gonzales	Purgatory Ski Area	Durango	CO	81301	Mt. Bike
9	8	John	Black	11 River Road	Brookfield	CT	06830	Road Bike
10	9	Scott	Owen	72 Yankee Way	Brookfield	CT	06830	Bungee
11	10	Virginia	Rodarmor	123 Main Street	Andover	MA	01810	Bungee
12	11	Carol	Smith	123 Elm Street	Acton	MA	01776	Bungee
13	12	Crystal	Stevens	The Waterfront Apts.	Salem	MA	01970	Road Bike
14	13	Luis	Lopez	1212 Agua Fria	Santa Fe	NM	87501	Mt. Bike
15	14	Maria	Duran	Galvin Highway East	Chicago	IL	60614	Road Bike
16	15	Salvatore	Wallace	100 Westside Ave	Chicago	IL	60614	Mt. Bike
17	16	Michael	Nelson	229 Route 55	Durango	CO	81301	Mt. Bike
18	17	Shawn	Kelly	22 Kendall Square	Cambridge	MA	02138	Bungee

Customers

Ready NUM

INDEPENDENT CHALLENGE 1

As the owner of MEGA-BYTES, a new computer hardware and software supplier, you want to invite area businesses to an open house. You need to create a database containing the names of potential customers. The database will be maintained to include current, potential, and past customers. (Potential customers are those who have visited the store but have not yet made a purchase.) Once the database table is complete, create a form letter in which you will merge the data stored in the table.

To complete this independent challenge:

1 Decide what fields should be included in the database. Write your fields down on paper. Include fields for type of customer (current, potential, or past). Create this database based on your plan.

2 Save the new database file as MEGABYTE.MDB to the MY_FILES directory on your Student Disk, then create the customer table called CUSTOMERS.

3 Create a form to facilitate the entry of your records.

4 Print one record to show a sample of the form.

5 Add 15 records to your table drawing on businesses in your local area.

6 Print out the datasheet for the CUSTOMERS table, showing all 15 records.

7 Create a main document in Word using all the fields you feel are necessary; save the main document as PARTY.DOC to the MY_FILES directory on your Student Disk.

8 Merge the document PARTY.DOC and the CUSTOMERS table into a new document named OPENHSE.DOC.

9 Print the last five merged documents in OPENHSE.DOC, then submit them with the other printed materials.

INDEPENDENT CHALLENGE 2

Your client, the Melodies Music Store, has hired you, a computer consultant, to analyze their product database. They want to see a chart showing how much inventory they have in each music category. They supplied you with an Access database, MUSIC.MDB, that contains all of their products. Using the MUSIC.MDB database on your Student Disk, export the Available titles table, analyze it, then create a chart using Excel.

To complete this independent challenge:

1 Open the MUSIC.MDB database in Access. Sort the data in the Available titles table by Category ID.

2 Export the Available titles table in the MUSIC.MDB database to an Excel worksheet.

3 Save the worksheet as MUSICLST.XLS to the MY_FILES directory on your Student Disk.

4 Resize columns and add formatting to make the worksheet more attractive and easy to read.

5 Preview and print the worksheet.

6 Add a new worksheet to the workbook. Name this new sheet "Charts."

7 Using the AutoSum button, determine how many units in each category are in stock.

8 Create a column chart and a pie chart of the units in stock.

9 Print the charts and the worksheets, then save your work.

10 Submit all printed materials from this challenge.

Microsoft® PowerPoint® 4.0

for Windows™

UNIT 1 **Getting Started with Microsoft PowerPoint 4.0**

UNIT 2 **Creating a Presentation**

UNIT 3 **Modifying a Presentation**

UNIT 4 **Enhancing a Presentation**

Read This Before You Begin Microsoft PowerPoint 4.0

To the Student

The lessons and exercises in this book feature several PowerPoint presentation files provided to your instructor. To complete the step-by-step lessons, Applications Reviews, and Independent Challenges in this book, you must have a Student Disk. Your instructor will do one of the following: 1) provide you with your own copy of the disk; 2) have you copy it from the network onto your own floppy disk; or 3) have you copy the lesson files from a network into your own subdirectory on the network. Always use your own copies of the lesson and exercise files. See your instructor or technical support person for further information.

Using Your Own Computer

If you are going to work through this book using your own computer, you need a computer system running Microsoft Windows 3.1, Microsoft PowerPoint 4.0 for Windows, and a Student Disk. *You will not be able to complete the step-by-step lessons in this book using your own computer until you have your own Student Disk.* This book assumes the default settings under a complete installation of Microsoft PowerPoint 4.0 for Windows.

To the Instructor

Bundled with the instructor's copy of this book is a Student Disk. The Student Disk contains all the files your students need to complete the step-by-step lessons in the units, Applications Reviews, and Independent Challenges. As an adopter of this text, you are granted the right to distribute the files on the Student Disk to any student who has purchased a copy of the text. You are free to post all these files to a network or standalone workstations, or simply provide copies of the disk to your students. The instructions in this book assume that the students know which drive and directory contain the Student Disk, so it's important that you provide disk location information before the students start working through the units. This book also assumes that PowerPoint 4.0 is set up using the complete installation procedure.

Using the Student Disk files

To keep the original files on the Student Disk intact, the instructions in this book for opening files require two important steps: (1) Open the existing file and (2) Save it as a new file with a new name. This procedure, covered in the lesson entitled "Opening an existing presentation," ensures that the original file will remain unmodified in case the student wants to redo any lesson or exercise.

To organize their files, students are instructed to save their files to the MY_FILES directory on their Student Disk that they created in *Microsoft Windows 3.1 Illustrated*. In case your students did not complete this lesson, it is included in the Instructor's Manual that accompanies this book. You can circulate this to your students or you can instruct them to simply save to drive A or drive B.

UNIT 1

OBJECTIVES

- Define presentation software
- Start PowerPoint 4.0 for Windows
- Use the AutoContent Wizard
- View the PowerPoint window
- View your presentation
- Work with toolbars
- Get Help
- Close a file and exit PowerPoint

Getting Started WITH MICROSOFT POWERPOINT 4.0

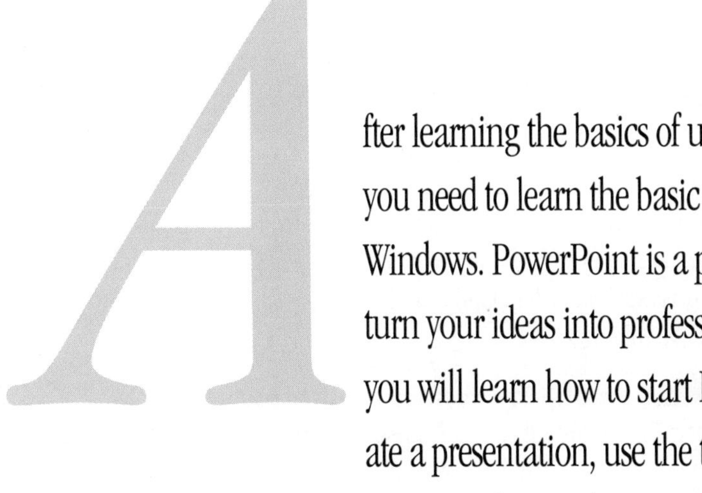

fter learning the basics of using Microsoft Windows, you have the skills you need to learn the basic features of Microsoft PowerPoint 4.0 for Windows. PowerPoint is a presentation graphics application that helps turn your ideas into professional, compelling presentations. In this unit, you will learn how to start PowerPoint, use the AutoContent Wizard to create a presentation, use the toolbars, get Help, and close a presentation file. ▶ Lynn Shaw is the executive assistant to the president of Nomad Ltd, an outdoor sporting gear and adventure travel company. To create more effective presentations, she wants to familiarize herself with the basics of PowerPoint and learn how to use PowerPoint. ▶

Defining presentation software

A **presentation graphics application** is a computer program you use to organize and present information. Whether you are giving a sales pitch or promoting a product, a presentation graphics application can help make your presentation effective and professional. You can use PowerPoint to create 35-mm slides, overheads, speaker's notes, audience handouts, outline pages, or on-screen presentations, depending on your specific presentation needs. Table 1-1 explains the PowerPoint output capabilities. ▶ Nomad's president has asked Lynn Shaw to create a brief presentation on the company's annual report. Lynn is not that familiar with PowerPoint so she gets right to work exploring PowerPoint. Figure 1-1 shows an overhead Lynn created using a word processor for the president's most recent presentation. Figure 1-2 shows how the same overhead might look in PowerPoint.

These are some of the benefits Lynn will gain by using PowerPoint:

- **Enter and edit data easily**
  Using PowerPoint, Lynn can enter and edit data quickly and efficiently. When Lynn needs to change a part of her presentation, she can use PowerPoint's advanced word processing and outlining capabilities to edit her content rather than re-create her presentation.

- **Change the appearance of information**
  By exploring PowerPoint's capabilities, Lynn will discover how easy it is to change the appearance of her presentation. PowerPoint has many features that can transform the way text, graphics, and slides appear.

- **Organize and arrange information**
  Once Lynn starts using PowerPoint, she won't have to spend a lot of time making sure her information is correct and in the right order. With PowerPoint, Lynn can quickly and easily rearrange and modify any piece of information in her presentation.

- **Incorporate information from other sources**
  When Lynn creates presentations, she often uses information from other people in the company. Using PowerPoint, she can import information from a variety of sources, including spreadsheets, graphics, and word processed files from applications such as Microsoft Word, Microsoft Excel, Microsoft Access, and WordPerfect.

- **Show a presentation on any Windows computer**
  PowerPoint has a powerful feature called the **PowerPoint Viewer** that Lynn can use to show her presentation on computers that do not have PowerPoint installed. The PowerPoint Viewer displays a presentation as an on-screen slide show.

FIGURE 1-1: Traditional overhead

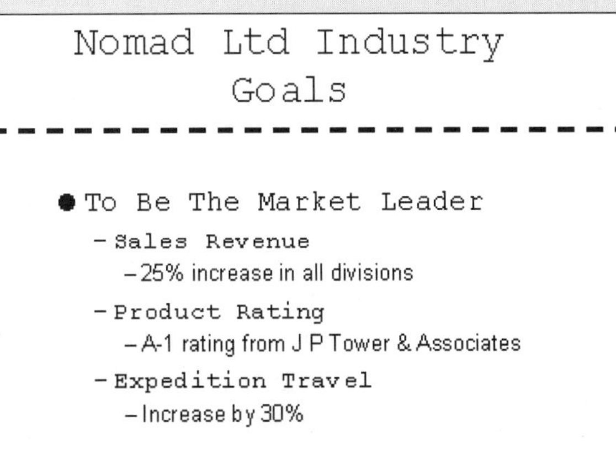

FIGURE 1-2: PowerPoint overhead

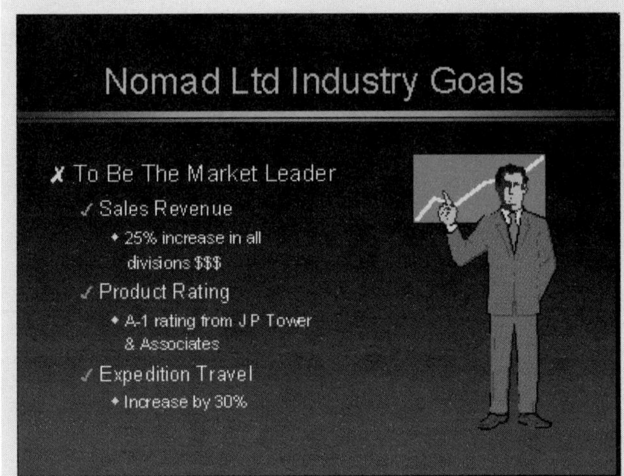

TABLE 1-1: PowerPoint output capabilities

OUTPUT	METHOD
35-mm slides	Use a film processing bureau to convert PowerPoint slides to 35-mm slides
B&W overheads	Print PowerPoint slides directly to transparencies on your B&W printer
Color overheads	Print PowerPoint slides directly to transparencies on your color printer
On-screen presentations	Run a slide show directly from your computer monitor or projector
Speaker notes	Print notes that help you remember points about each slide when you speak
Audience handouts	Print handouts with 2, 3, or 6 slides on a page
Outline pages	Print the outline of your presentation to show the main points

Starting PowerPoint 4.0 for Windows

To start PowerPoint, you first start Windows, as described in "Microsoft Windows 3.1." Then, you open the program group window that contains the PowerPoint application icon. This is usually the Microsoft Office program group, though your computer could have PowerPoint in its own program group. If you have trouble finding the program group that contains the PowerPoint application icon, check with your instructor or technical support person. If you are using a computer on a network, you might need to use a different starting procedure. You can also customize your starting procedure. See the related topic "Assigning a shortcut key to start PowerPoint" for more information. ▶ Lynn starts PowerPoint to familiarize herself with the application.

1 Make sure the Program Manager window is open
The Program Manager icon might appear at the bottom of your screen. Double-click it to open it, if necessary.

2 Double-click the **Microsoft Office program group icon**
The Microsoft Office program group window opens, displaying icons for PowerPoint and other Microsoft applications, as shown in Figure 1-3. Your screen might look different, depending on which applications are installed on your computer. If you cannot locate the Microsoft Office program group, click Window on the Program Manager menu bar, then click Microsoft Office.

3 Double-click the **Microsoft PowerPoint application icon**
PowerPoint opens. Unless a previous user has **disabled** (turned off) it, the Tip of the Day dialog box opens, as shown in Figure 1-4. This dialog box presents a new tip each time you start PowerPoint. The tips explain how to use PowerPoint features more effectively. If you don't want to see a tip every time you start PowerPoint, click the Show Tips at Startup check box to remove the "x" and turn the feature off. The rest of the book assumes you are familiar with the Tip of the Day dialog box.

4 If necessary, click **OK** to close Tip of the Day dialog box
The Tip of the Day dialog box closes, and the PowerPoint startup dialog box opens, allowing you to choose how you want to create your presentation. In the next lesson, Lynn chooses the AutoContent Wizard option in the PowerPoint startup dialog box to see how wizards can help her develop a presentation.

FIGURE 1-3: Microsoft Office program group

Microsoft PowerPoint application icon

List of available applications might vary

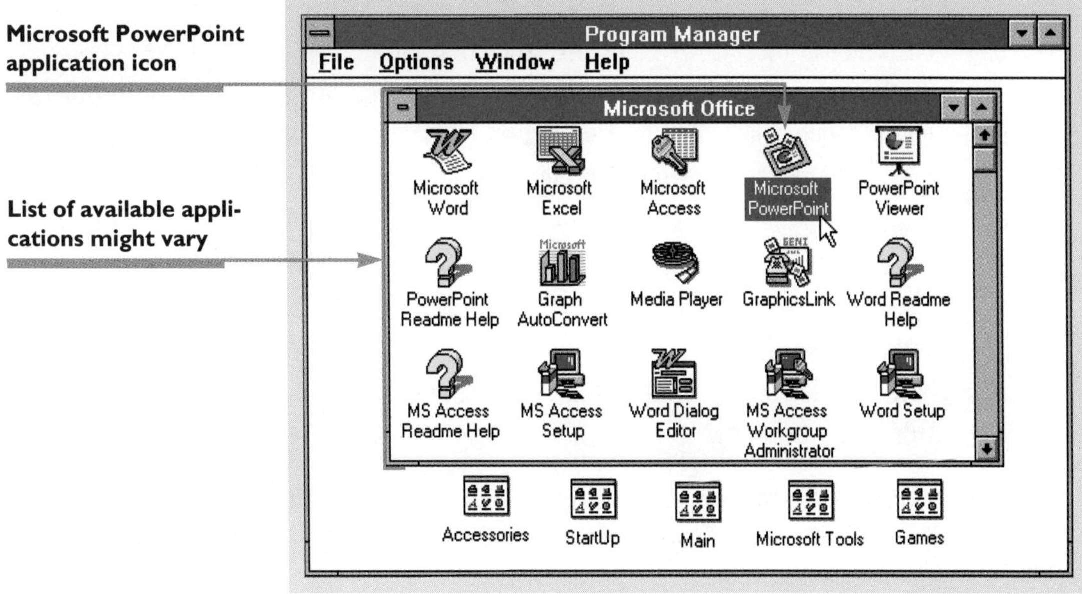

FIGURE 1-4: Tip of the Day dialog box

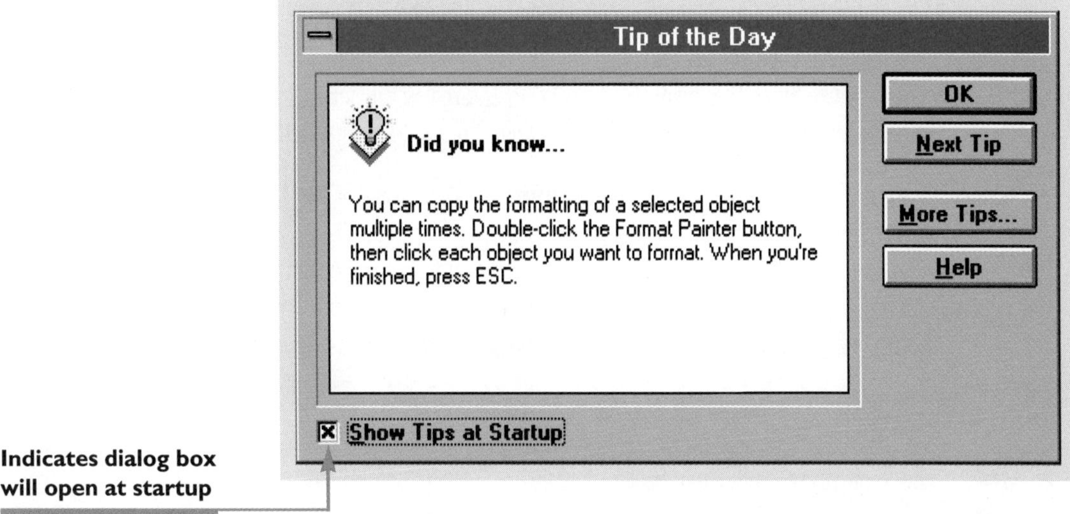

Indicates dialog box will open at startup

Assigning a shortcut key to start PowerPoint

To assign a shortcut key that starts PowerPoint automatically from the Program Manager, click the PowerPoint icon in Program Manager, click File on the menu bar, then click Properties. Click the Shortcut Key text box, press the keys you want to use, like [Ctrl] [Alt] [P], then click OK. You can then start PowerPoint without having to navigate a group window by simply pressing that key combination.

Using the AutoContent Wizard

The PowerPoint startup dialog box, shown in Figure 1-5, gives you five options for starting your presentation. The first option, the AutoContent Wizard, is the quickest way to create a presentation. A **wizard** is a series of steps that guides you through a task (in this case, creating a presentation). Using the AutoContent Wizard, you first create a title slide, then you choose a presentation category from the wizard's list of sample presentations. The AutoContent Wizard then creates an outline with sample text you can use as a guide to help formulate the major points of your presentation. See Table 1-2 for an explanation of all the options in the PowerPoint startup dialog box. ▶ Lynn continues to explore PowerPoint by opening the AutoContent Wizard.

1. **Click the AutoContent Wizard radio button, then click OK**
   The AutoContent Wizard opens and displays the Step 1 of 4 dialog box, which explains what the wizard is going to do.

2. **Click Next**
   The Step 2 of 4 dialog box opens, requesting information that will appear on the title slide of the presentation. Lynn types the title of her presentation in the first text box.

3. **Type Annual Report**
   The next two text boxes display information entered by the person who installed PowerPoint. Lynn enters the president's name and company name to complete the dialog box.

4. **Press [Tab] then type Bill Davidson; press [Tab], type Nomad Ltd, then click Next**
   The Step 3 of 4 dialog box opens, giving you six different presentation categories to choose from. Each presentation category generates a different sample outline. The president's presentation is going to be on the company's annual report so she chooses the Reporting Progress option.

5. **Click the Reporting Progress radio button**
   Notice that the sample outline in the view box on the left side of the dialog box changes to reflect the Reporting Progress category.

6. **Click Next, read the information in the dialog box, then click Finish**
   The AutoContent Wizard creates an outline with sample text based on the Reporting Progress category. Unless another user disabled it, PowerPoint displays **Cue Cards**, a step-by-step guide, on the right side of your window, as shown in Figure 1-6. See the related topic "Cue Cards" for more information. Lynn reads the information presented by Cue Cards, then closes the Cue Cards window in order to view her entire outline.

7. **If necessary, double-click the control menu box in the Cue Cards window to close it**
   The Cue Cards window closes, and the outline created by the AutoContent Wizard appears in full view.

FIGURE 1-5: PowerPoint startup dialog box

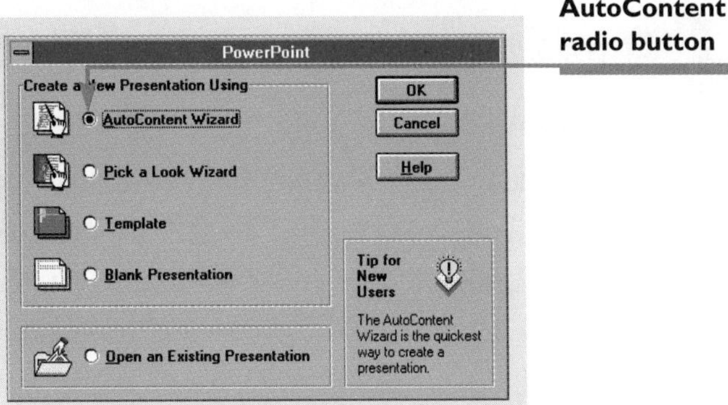

FIGURE 1-6: Presentation window with Cue Cards window

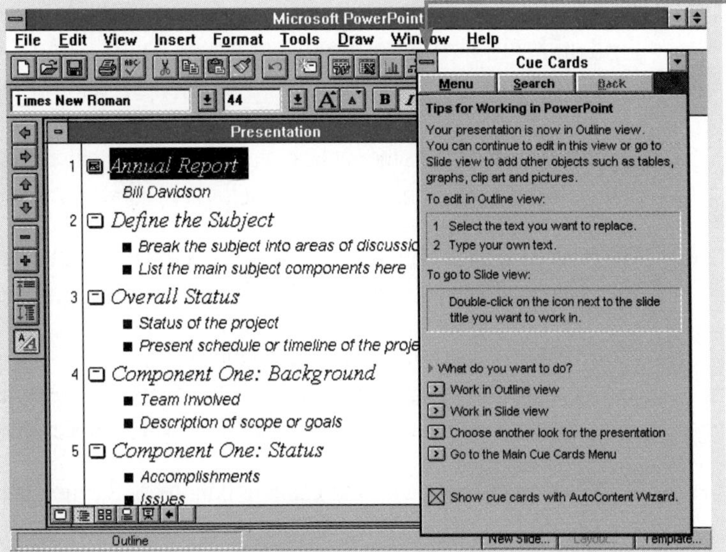

Cue Cards

PowerPoint Cue Cards walk you through simple and advanced tasks. You can open Cue Cards at any time by clicking Help on the menu bar, then clicking Cue Cards. The Cue Cards window stays on your screen while you perform the steps of the chosen task. Close the Cue Cards window by double-clicking its control menu box.

TABLE 1-2: PowerPoint startup dialog box options

OPTION	DESCRIPTION
AutoContent Wizard	Helps you determine the content and organization of your presentation by creating a title slide and outline using ready-made text for the category you choose
Pick a Look Wizard	Offers different visual formats to help you select a look and feel for your presentation
Template	Opens the Apply Template dialog box, displaying PowerPoint's preformatted templates
Blank Presentation	Opens the New Slide dialog box, allowing you to choose a predesigned slide layout
Open an Existing Presentation	Opens the File Open dialog box, allowing you to open a previously created presentation

Viewing the PowerPoint window

After you make your selection in the PowerPoint startup dialog box, the Presentation window appears within the PowerPoint window, displaying the presentation you just created or opened. You use the toolbars, buttons, and menu in the PowerPoint window to view and develop your presentation. PowerPoint has different **views** that allow you to see your presentation in different forms. You'll learn more about PowerPoint views in the next lesson. You move around in these views by using the scroll bars. See the related topic "Using the scroll bars" for more information. This lesson introduces you to elements of the PowerPoint window. Find and compare the elements described below using Figure 1-7. If you do not see a Presentation window as shown in Figure 1-7, see the Trouble? on the next page.

- The **title bar** displays the application name and contains a control menu box and resizing buttons, which you learned about in "Microsoft Windows 3.1."
- The **menu bar** lists the names of the menus you use to choose PowerPoint commands. Clicking a menu name on the menu bar displays a list of commands from which you might choose.
- The **Standard toolbar** contains buttons for the most frequently used commands, such as copying and pasting. Clicking buttons on a toolbar is often faster than using the menu. However, in some cases, using the menu offers additional options not available by clicking a button.
- The **Formatting toolbar** contains buttons for the most frequently used commands, such as changing font type and size.
- The **Outlining toolbar** appears only in Outline view, the current view. The Outlining toolbar contains buttons for the most frequently used outlining commands, such as moving and indenting text lines.
- The **Presentation window** is the "canvas" where you type text, work with lines and shapes, and view your presentation.
- The **status bar**, located at the bottom of the PowerPoint window, displays messages about what you are doing and seeing in PowerPoint.

FIGURE 1-7: PowerPoint window in Outline view

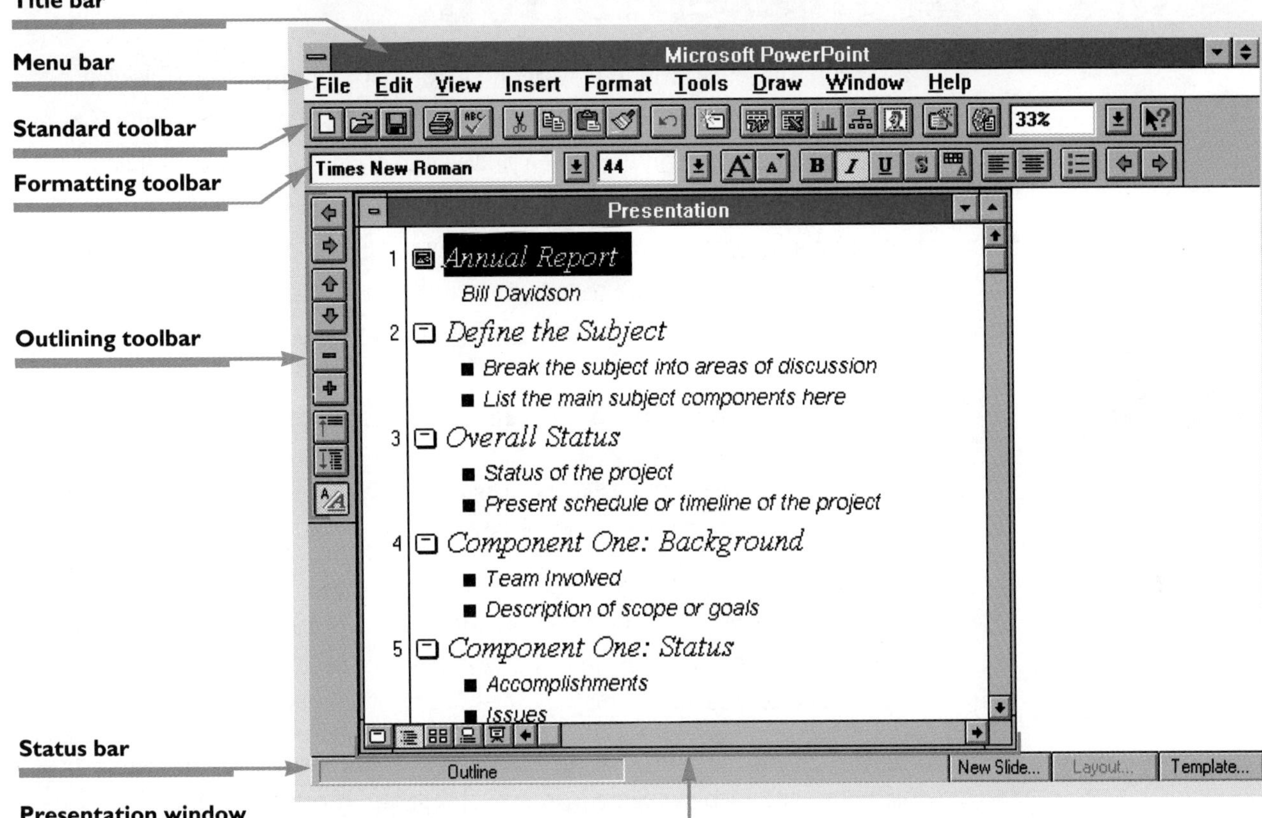

Using the scroll bars

Sometimes you need to **scroll**, or move, within a window to see more of the window contents. There are three ways to scroll in PowerPoint: click the vertical scroll arrows to move one line at a time; click above or below the vertical scroll box to move one screen at a time; or drag the vertical scroll box to move quickly to any point in the window. The scroll box for the vertical scroll bar is called the **elevator**. Use the horizontal scroll bar to move the screen to the left or the right.

TROUBLE?

If your PowerPoint window doesn't look similar to Figure 1-7, your Presentation window might be maximized to fill the entire PowerPoint window. Click the lower Restore button to return the Presentation window to its original size. Size it to look like Figure 1-7, if necessary.■

Viewing your presentation

This lesson introduces you to PowerPoint's five views: Outline view, Slide view, Notes Pages view, Slide Sorter view, and Slide Show view. Each PowerPoint view displays your presentation in a different way and allows you to manipulate your presentation differently. See Table 1-3 for a brief description of the PowerPoint view buttons. To easily move between the PowerPoint views, you use view buttons located at the bottom of the Presentation window, as shown in Figure 1-8. ▶ Follow Lynn as she moves between each PowerPoint view.

1 Click the **down scroll arrow** repeatedly to scroll through your presentation outline
As you scroll through the presentation, notice that each of the nine slides in the presentation is identified by a number along the left side of the outline.

2 Click the **Slide View button** on the status bar
PowerPoint switches to Slide view and displays the first slide in the presentation, which corresponds to the slide title and main point on the first slide in Outline view. To see what some of her slides look like, Lynn decides to scroll through her presentation by dragging the elevator.

3 Drag the elevator down the vertical scroll bar until the Slide Indicator box, which appears, displays Slide 3, then release the mouse button
The **Slide Indicator box** tells you which slide will appear when you release the mouse button, as shown in Figure 1-9. To return to Slide 1, Lynn uses the Previous Slide button instead of the elevator.

4 Click the **Previous Slide button** twice to move back to Slide 1
The elevator moves back up the scroll bar, and PowerPoint returns Lynn to Slide 1.

5 Click the **Notes Pages View button**
Slide view changes to Notes Pages view, showing you a reduced image of the title slide above a large box. Lynn can enter text in this box and then print the notes page to help her remember important points of her presentation.

6 Click the **Slide Sorter View button**
A miniature image of each slide in the presentation appears in this view. Lynn can examine the flow of her slides and easily move them if they need to be rearranged.

7 Click the **Slide Show button**
The first slide fills the entire screen. In this view, Lynn can practice running through her slides and set special effects so the presentation can be shown as an electronic slide show.

8 Click the **left mouse button** to advance through the slides one at a time until you return to Slide Sorter view.

FIGURE 1-8: Outline view

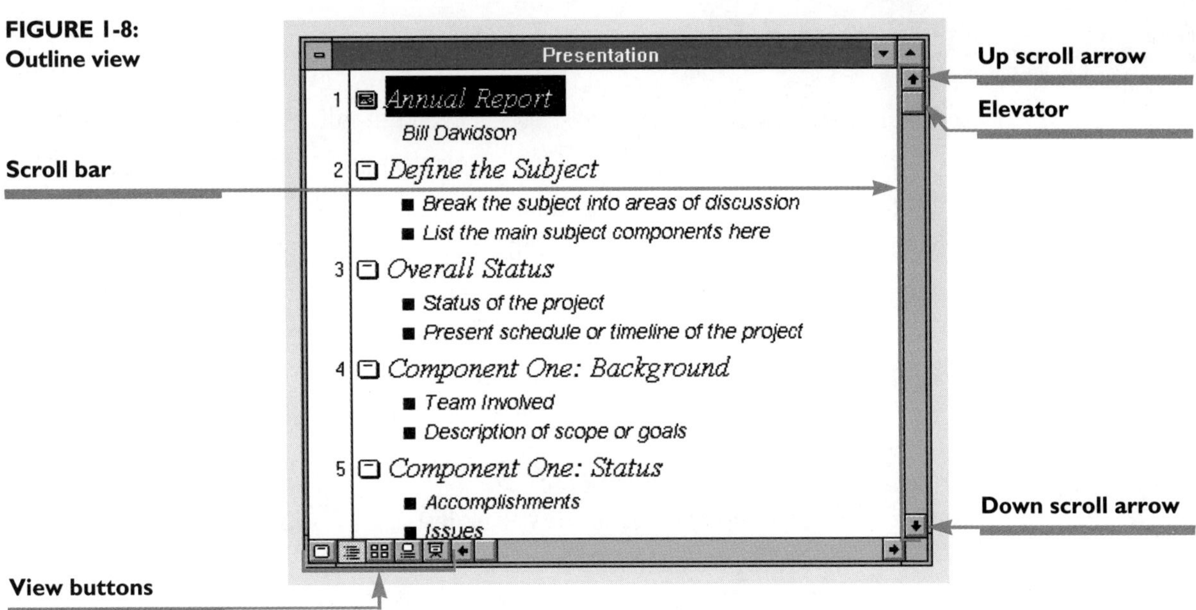

FIGURE 1-9: Slide view

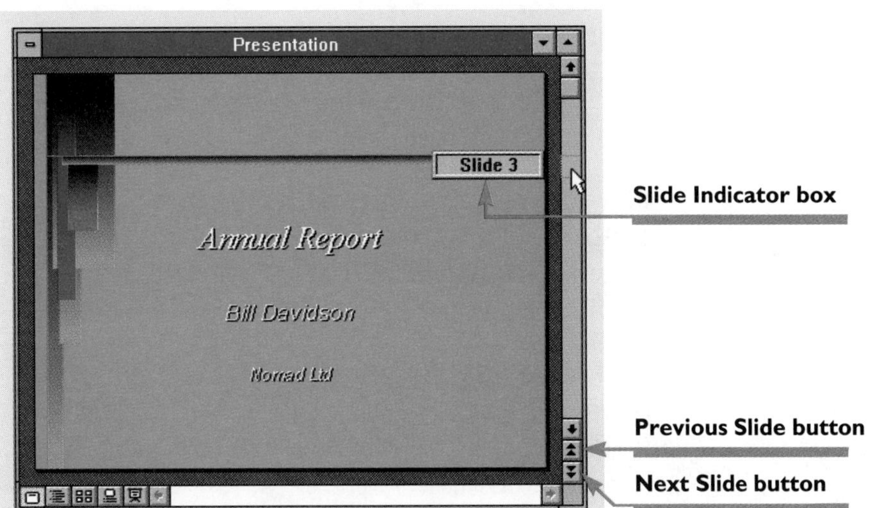

TABLE 1-3: View buttons

BUTTON	BUTTON NAME	DESCRIPTION
	Outline View	Displays the title and main topics in the form of an outline. Use this view to enter and edit the text of your presentation.
	Slide View	Displays one slide at a time. Use this view to modify and enhance a slide's appearance.
	Notes Pages View	Displays a reduced slide image and a box to type notes. Use this view to take notes on your slides, which you can use during your presentation.
	Slide Sorter View	Displays a miniature picture of each slide in the order they appear in your presentation. Use this view to rearrange and add special effects to your slides.
	Slide Show	Displays your presentation as an electronic slide show.

Working with toolbars

The PowerPoint toolbars offer easy access to commonly used commands. Each PowerPoint view displays different toolbars containing toolbar buttons appropriate for the tasks you perform in that view. You can place the toolbars anywhere on your screen or remove them, depending on your needs. If you have a small monitor, you might want to remove a toolbar so you can see more of your presentation. See the related topic "Arranging toolbars" for more information. PowerPoint has eight ready-made toolbars that you can add, remove, or modify at any time. ▶ In this lesson, Lynn uses the Formatting toolbar to format a slide title.

1 Click the **Outline View button**

The outline fills the Presentation window with the first slide title selected. In Outline view, text such as the slide title must be selected before you move or change it. Lynn decides to change the title slide font attributes (the appearance of the typeface) from italic to bold italic.

2 On the Formatting toolbar, move the mouse pointer over the Bold button *but do not click*

The Formatting toolbar appears below the Standard toolbar, as shown in Figure 1-10. Notice that as the mouse pointer rests over the Bold button, a small box, called a **ToolTip**, appears, identifying the Bold button.

3 Move the mouse pointer over other toolbar buttons on the Formatting toolbar to display their ToolTips

Notice that a brief description of the button also appears in the status bar. ToolTips also appear for the view buttons and the Next and Previous Slide buttons.

4 Click on the Formatting toolbar

PowerPoint bolds the slide title, Annual Report. The Bold button is a **toggle button**, which you click to turn the bold attribute on or off. Now that the title is bold, Lynn decides to increase its font size so it is more visible.

5 Click the **Increase Font Size button** on the Formatting toolbar

The font size for the title increases from 44 to 48. The Font Size list box displays the font size change.

FIGURE 1-10: PowerPoint window showing ToolTip

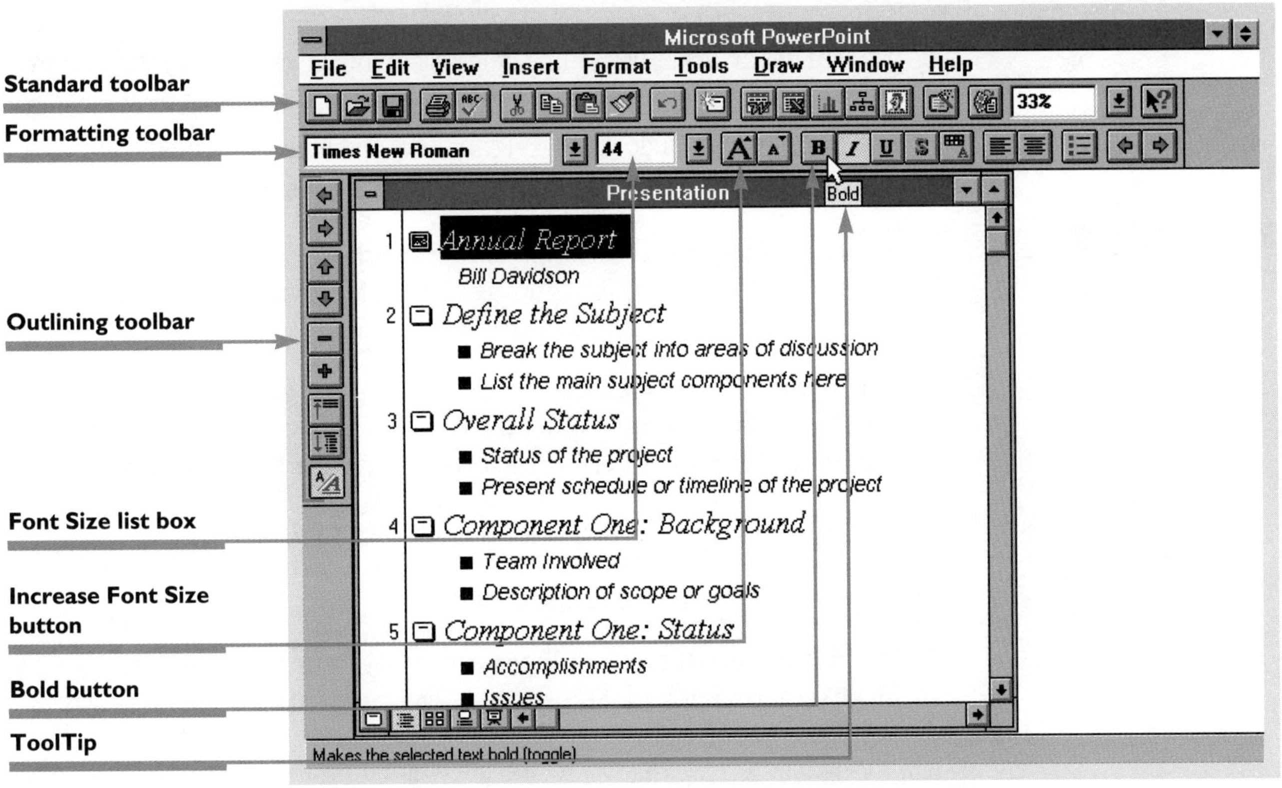

Standard toolbar

Formatting toolbar

Outlining toolbar

Font Size list box

Increase Font Size button

Bold button

ToolTip

Microsoft PowerPoint

File Edit View Insert Format Tools Draw Window Help

Times New Roman 44

Presentation

Bold

1 Annual Report
Bill Davidson
2 Define the Subject
■ Break the subject into areas of discussion
■ List the main subject components here
3 Overall Status
■ Status of the project
■ Present schedule or timeline of the project
4 Component One: Background
■ Team Involved
■ Description of scope or goals
5 Component One: Status
■ Accomplishments
■ Issues

Makes the selected text bold (toggle)

Arranging toolbars

You can move or hide PowerPoint toolbars at any time. Move a toolbar by clicking an open space on the toolbar and dragging it to a new location. An outline of the toolbar appears so you can see how the toolbar will look when you release the mouse button. You can hide a toolbar by double-clicking its control menu box.

You can add or delete toolbar buttons using the Customize command from the Tools menu.■

Getting Help

PowerPoint has an extensive on-line Help system that gives you immediate access to definitions, reference information, and feature explanations. Help information appears in a separate window that you can move and resize. ▶ Lynn likes the flexibility of the toolbars and decides to find out more about them.

1 **Click Help on the menu bar, then click Search for Help on**
The PowerPoint Help window opens displaying the Search dialog box. Lynn decides to use the Search dialog box to find out more about toolbars.

2 **Type toolbar in the search text box containing the blinking insertion point**
Notice that as you type each character in this text box, the list of topics scrolls. The list box displays three toolbar categories: toolbar buttons, toolbar commands, and toolbars.

3 **Click toolbars in the list box, then click Show Topics**
Help displays all the toolbar-related topics in the lower list box, as shown in Figure 1-11. To view all the topics in this box, click the down scroll arrow.

4 **Click Adding buttons to toolbars in the lower list box, then click Go To**
The Search dialog box closes. The Help window displays the steps to add buttons to toolbars, as shown in Figure 1-12. Your Help window might look different than Figure 1-12, so use the scroll arrows to move up and down the Help window to view all the information, if necessary. Refer to Table 1-4 for a description of the available Help buttons.

5 **If necessary, click the down scroll arrow in the Help window until the "See also" section appears**

6 **Click The Toolbars when the pointer changes to** 👆
Related information on toolbars appears in the Help window. Lynn reads this information and decides to close the Help window.

7 **Double-click the control menu box in the Help window to close it**
The Help window closes and you return to your presentation.

TABLE 1-4: The Help buttons

BUTTON	DESCRIPTION
Contents	Displays Help topic categories
Search	Opens a dialog box where you specify a topic you want help with
Back	Returns you to the previous topic
History	Shows you a list of the Help topics to which you have referred
<<	Moves to the previous Help topic
>>	Moves to the next Help topic

FIGURE 1-11: Search dialog box

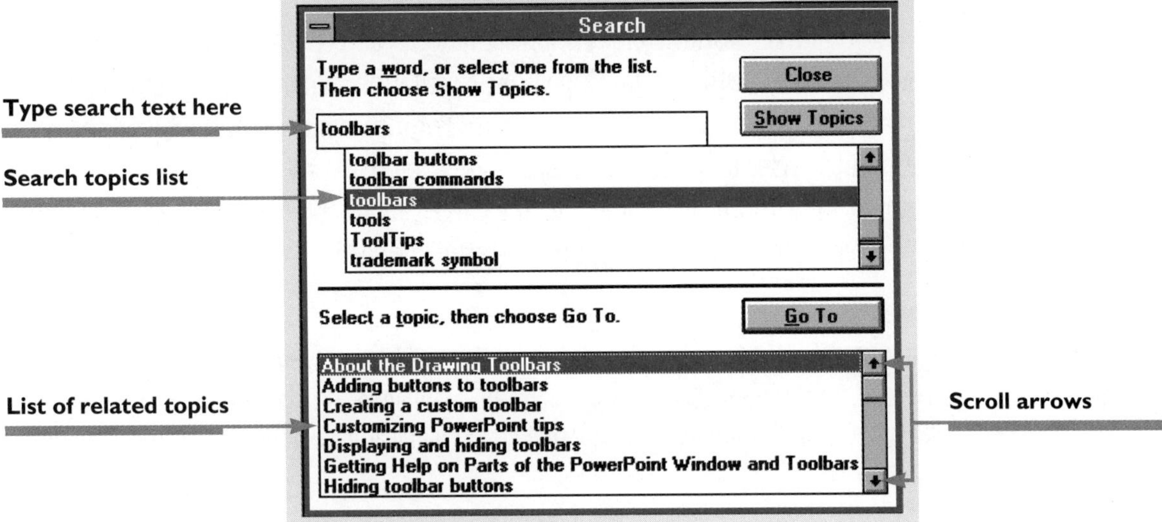

FIGURE 1-12: Help window

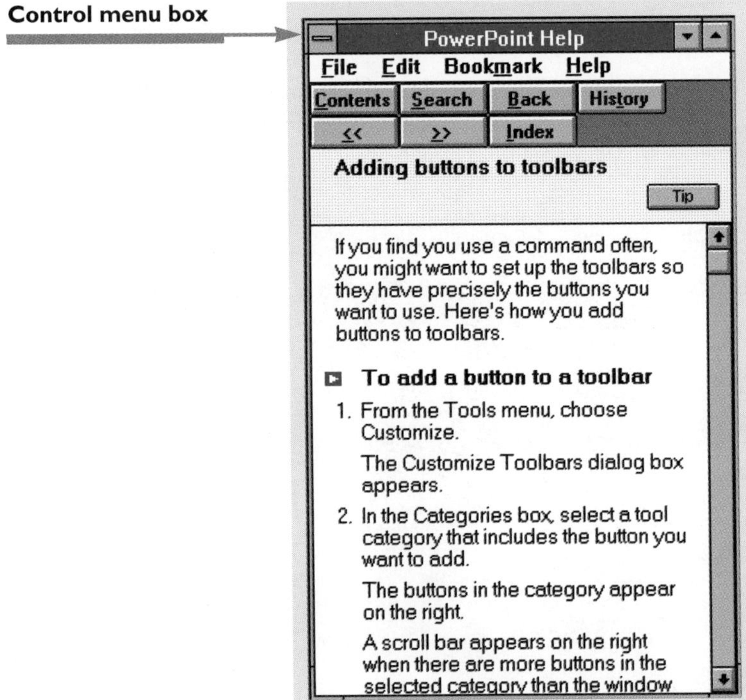

QUICK TIP

On the Standard toolbar, click the Help button and then click a window item to jump to the Help topic for that item.

Closing a file and exiting PowerPoint

When you finish working on your presentation, you generally save your work and then close the file containing your presentation. When you are done using PowerPoint, you need to exit the program. For a comparison of the Close and Exit commands, refer to Table 1-5. ▶ Lynn needs to go to a meeting, so she exits PowerPoint without saving the file. She can easily re-create this presentation later and use it as the basis of her annual report if she so chooses.

1 **Click File on the menu bar, then click Close, as shown in Figure 1-13**
A Microsoft PowerPoint dialog box opens, as shown in Figure 1-14, asking you to save your presentation. Because Lynn was just exploring PowerPoint features, she does not want to save this presentation.

2 **Click No**
The Presentation window closes.

3 **Click File on the menu bar, then click Exit**
The PowerPoint application closes, and you return to the Program Manager.

If you want to exit PowerPoint without saving your work and closing the presentation, click File on the menu bar, click Exit, then click No when asked if you want to save your changes.

TABLE 1-5: Understanding the Close and Exit commands

CLOSING A FILE	EXITING POWERPOINT
Puts a file away	Puts all files away
Leaves PowerPoint loaded in computer memory	Frees computer memory up for other uses

FIGURE 1-13: File menu

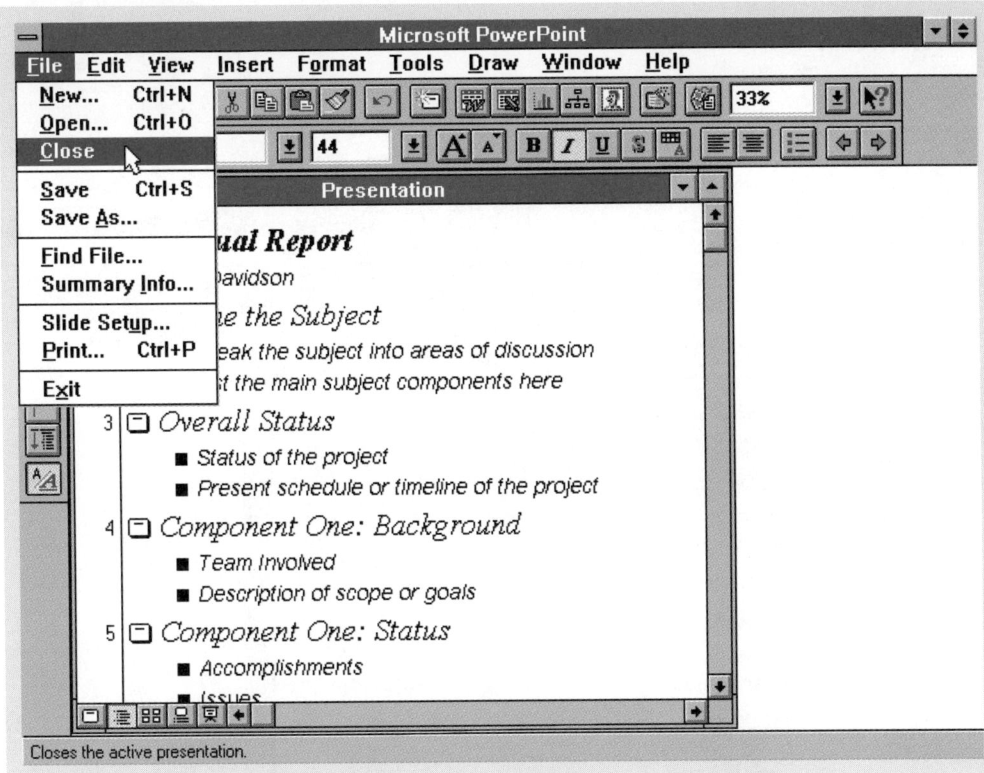

FIGURE 1-14: Microsoft PowerPoint dialog box

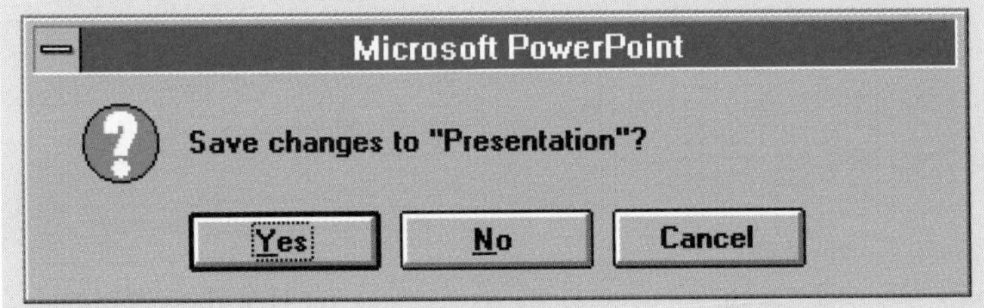

QUICK TIP

Double-clicking the control menu box next to the menu bar closes the presentation. Double-clicking the control menu box in the title bar exits the application.■

CONCEPTS REVIEW

Label the PowerPoint window elements shown in Figure 1-15.

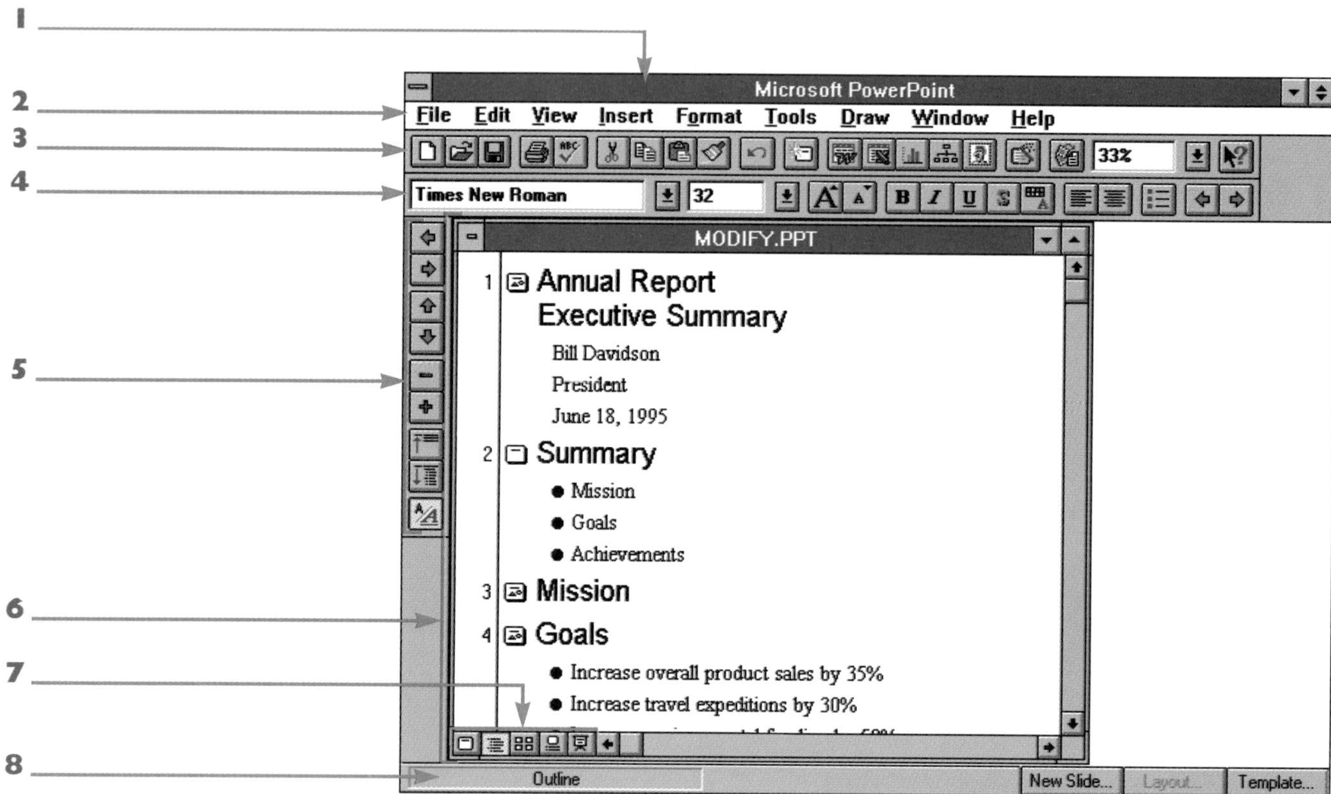

FIGURE 1-15

Match each term with the statement that describes its function.

9 The area where you work on your presentation

10 An on-screen step-by-step guide

11 Small box that identifies a tool button

12 Dialog box that contains PowerPoint hints

13 Small box in the vertical scroll bar

a. ToolTip
b. Tip of the Day
c. Presentation window
d. Elevator
e. Cue Cards

Select the best answer from the list of choices.

14 PowerPoint can help you create all of the following, EXCEPT:
a. 35-mm slides
b. Movies
c. An on-screen presentation
d. Outline pages

15 The buttons that you use to switch between the PowerPoint views are called
a. PowerPoint buttons
b. View buttons
c. Screen buttons
d. Toolbar buttons

16 All of these are PowerPoint views, EXCEPT:

a. Slide view
b. Notes Pages view
c. Outline view
d. Current Page view

17 The term for moving to different parts of your slide or outline is

a. Scrolling
b. Aligning
c. Moving
d. Shifting

18 This view shows your presentation electronically:

a. Electronic view
b. Slide Sorter view
c. Presentation view
d. Slide Show view

19 Which wizard helps you organize and outline your presentation?

a. Pick a Look Wizard
b. Presentation Wizard
c. AutoContent Wizard
d. OrgContent Wizard

APPLICATIONS REVIEW

1 Start PowerPoint and use the AutoContent Wizard to create a sample presentation on a topic of your choice.

a. Double-click the PowerPoint application icon in the Microsoft Office program group window.
b. Click the AutoContent Wizard radio button, then click OK.
c. Fill in the necessary information in the Step 2 of 4 dialog box.
d. Choose a presentation category in the Step 3 of 4 dialog box, then click Finish.

2 Work with Cue Cards and view the PowerPoint window.

a. If necessary, click Cue Cards on the Help menu. Click one of the menu buttons located at the bottom of the Cue Cards window.
b. Read through the Cue Card steps at the top of the window on the subject you chose.
c. Double-click the control menu box on the Cue Cards window to close it.
d. Your outline is in full view. Examine the content of the sample outline.
e. Identify as many elements of the PowerPoint window as you can without referring to the unit material.

3 Explore the PowerPoint views.

a. Use the scroll arrows to move up and down the outline to view its content.
b. Click the Slide View button. Notice that a description of the view button appears in the status bar.
c. Click the Next Slide button to view your slides.
d. Click the Notes Pages View button, and drag the elevator up and down to view your notes pages. After you finish exploring, drag the elevator to slide.
e. Click the Slide Sorter View button, and examine your slides.
f. Click the Slide Show button. The first slide of your presentation fills the screen. Advance through the slide show by clicking the left mouse button.

4 Explore the PowerPoint toolbars.

a. Click the Outline View button.
b. Click the Increase Font Size button.
c. Click the Underline button to underline the title.

5 Explore PowerPoint Help.

a. Click Help on the menu bar, then click Contents. The Help window opens.
b. Click the Reference Information icon.
c. Click Getting Help on Menu Commands and read the Help information on menu commands.
d. Double-click the control menu box to close the Contents window.
e. Double-click the control menu box to close the PowerPoint Help window.

6 Close your presentation and exit PowerPoint.

a. Click File on the menu bar, then click Close.
b. Click No if you see a message asking if you want to save the changes.
c. Click File on the menu bar, then click Exit.

INDEPENDENT CHALLENGE 1

PowerPoint offers an interactive tutorial called Quick Preview, which gives you an overview of PowerPoint's features. The Quick Preview covers the PowerPoint Wizards, adding a new slide, and adding graphs, tables, templates, and clip art. To work through the Quick Preview, click Help on the menu bar, then click Quick Preview. Click the appropriate buttons to proceed through the preview, and then click Quit when you are finished.

INDEPENDENT CHALLENGE 2

You are in charge of marketing for AllSigns, Inc., a medium size company that produces all types of business and professional signs. The company has a regional sales area that includes three neighboring Northeast states. You found out today that AllSigns' president just confirmed a deal with American Hotels, a national hotel chain, to present a proposal for a large contract to make signs for all of their hotels.

Because you are in charge of marketing, you are given the responsibility of planning and creating the outline of the proposal the president will present to American Hotels.

Create an outline that reflects the major issues AllSigns needs to convey to American Hotels to secure a large contract. Assume the following: AllSigns needs to promote their company and products to American Hotels; AllSigns make all types of signs from outdoor advertising signs to indoor informational and directional signs; the AllSigns proposal includes outdoor advertising signs and indoor informational signs.

To complete this independent challenge:

1. Use the AutoContent Wizard to help you create a promotional outline.
2. Plan how you would change and add to the sample text created by the wizard. What information do you need to promote AllSigns to a large company?
3. Take notes on how you might change the outline text. In the next unit, you'll learn how to enter your own text into a presentation.

UNIT 2

OBJECTIVES

- Plan an effective presentation
- Choose a look for a presentation
- Enter slide text
- Create a new slide
- Work in Outline view
- Enter text in Notes Pages view
- Save a presentation
- Print a presentation

A PRESENTATION

Now that you are familiar with the basics of PowerPoint, you are ready to plan and create your own presentation. The two fundamental aspects of creating a presentation are entering and editing text and choosing a slide design. PowerPoint provides two wizards that guide you through the steps you take to accomplish these tasks: the AutoContent Wizard, which as you saw in Unit 1, creates sample text for a number of different presentation situations, and the Pick a Look Wizard, which helps you choose a slide design. In this unit, you will use the Pick a Look Wizard to select a design from a large gallery of slide designs you can use for your presentation. After choosing a look, you'll enter text in different PowerPoint views, create a new slide, then save and print the presentation. ▶ Lynn Shaw from Nomad Ltd begins to create the presentation the president will give at a shareholders' meeting later in the month. ▶

Planning an effective presentation

Before you begin a presentation, you need to plan and outline the message you want to communicate and consider how you want it to look. In preparing the outline, you need to consider where you are giving the presentation and who your primary audience is going to be. It's also important to know what resources you might need, such as a computer or projection equipment. ▶ Using Figure 2-1 and Figure 2-2 and the planning guidelines below, follow Lynn as she outlines the presentation message.

1. **Determine the purpose of the presentation and the location and audience.**
   The president needs to present the highlights of Nomad's Annual Report at a shareholders' meeting at the Plaza Center Inn in a large hall.
2. **Determine the type of output, either black and white (B&W) or color overhead transparencies, on-screen slide show, or 35-mm slides, that best conveys your message, given time constraints and hardware availability.**
   Since the president is speaking in a large hall and has access to a computer and projection equipment, Lynn decides to produce an on-screen slide show.
3. **Determine a look for your presentation that will help communicate your message. You can choose a professionally designed template quickly and easily with PowerPoint's Pick a Look Wizard.**
   Lynn needs to choose a template that will appeal to the audience and help reinforce a message of confidence and accomplishment.
4. **Determine the message you want to communicate. Give the presentation a meaningful title and then outline your message and organize your thoughts.**
   Lynn titles the presentation "Annual Report Executive Summary" and then outlines the message with the information given her by the president, who wants to highlight the previous year's accomplishments and set the goals for the coming year (Figure 2-1).
5. **Determine what you want to produce when the presentation is finished. You need to prepare not only the slides themselves, but supplementary materials, including notes for the speaker, handouts for the audience, and an outline of the presentation.**
   Lynn knows the president wants speaker's notes to refer to during his presentation. Speaker's notes allow the president to stay on track and deliver a concise message.
6. **Roughly sketch on paper how you want the slides and words on the slides to look. Use this sketch to help guide your choices as you progress through the Pick a Look Wizard.**
   Lynn wants a bold and bright look to convey a sense of accomplishment and excitement. Her sketch looks like Figure 2-2.

FIGURE 2-1: Outline of text for presentation

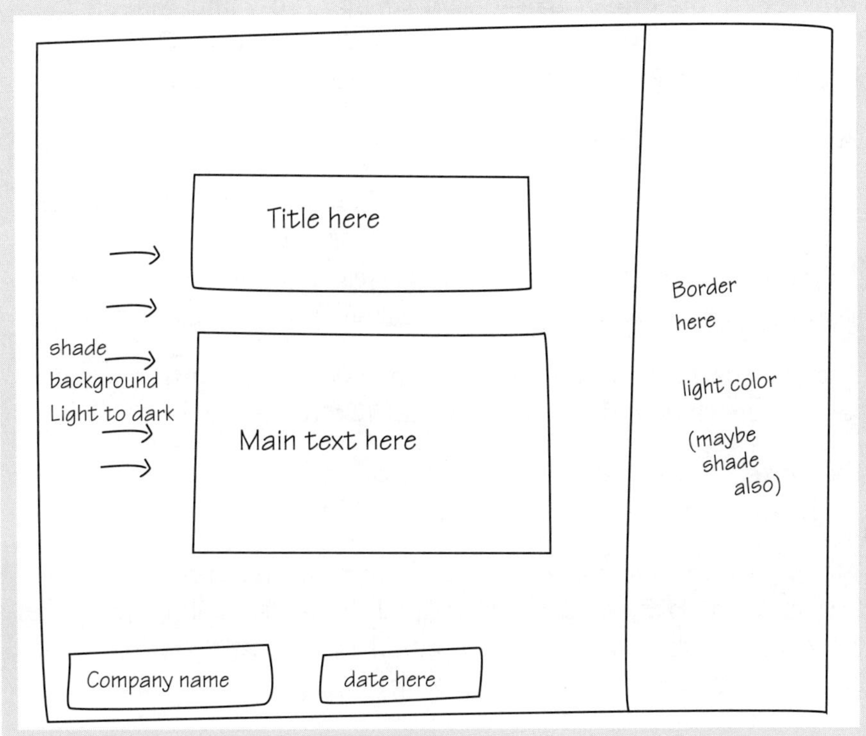

FIGURE 2-2: Presentation slide design sketch

Choosing a look for a presentation

With PowerPoint's Pick a Look Wizard, you don't have to be an artist or spend hours to create a great looking presentation. The **Pick a Look Wizard** is a series of steps that leads you through choosing a look for your presentation. The PowerPoint software comes with a collection of prepared slide designs that have borders, colors, text attributes, and other elements arranged in a variety of formats. You can also create your own design if you have time. ▶ Lynn doesn't have a lot of time but wants to create a good-looking presentation, so she uses the Pick a Look Wizard to help her choose the slide design for the president's presentation.

1. Start PowerPoint, click the **Pick a Look Wizard radio button** in the PowerPoint startup dialog box, then click **OK**
   The Pick a Look Wizard opens and displays the Step 1 of 9 dialog box, which explains what the Wizard is going to do.
2. Click **Next**
   The Step 2 of 9 dialog box opens, giving you four different output options that determine the color and style of your presentation. Lynn decides to develop the presentation on a white background and add the color and shading later so she chooses the Color Overheads option.
3. Click the **Color Overheads radio button**, then click **Next**
   The Step 3 of 9 dialog box opens, as shown in Figure 2-3, giving you a choice of four slide background designs, called **templates**. To view additional templates, click the More button.
4. Click **More**, click the **File Name down scroll arrow** until the SOARINGC.PPT template appears, then click **SOARINGC.PPT**
   A sample of the SOARINGC.PPT template appears in the Preview box. See Figure 2-4.
5. Click **Apply** then click **Next**
6. Click the **Audience Handout Pages check box** and click the **Outline Pages check box** to deselect them, then click **Next**
   The Slide Options dialog box gives you three options that you can place on every slide: Name, Date, and Page Number. Lynn decides to include the company name and the date on the slides.
7. If necessary, highlight the text in the text box below the Name, company, or other text check box, then type **Nomad Ltd** to replace it
8. Click the **Date check box**, then click **Next**
   For the speaker's notes, Lynn just wants the page number, selected by default.
9. Click **Next**, read the information in the dialog box, then click **Finish**
   The Pick a Look Wizard closes and creates a title slide with the presentation design you selected, shown in Slide view with the Drawing toolbar available. The special characters (//) on the bottom of the slide indicate where PowerPoint will print the current date. See Figure 2-5.

FIGURE 2-3: Pick a Look Wizard - Step 3 of 9 dialog box

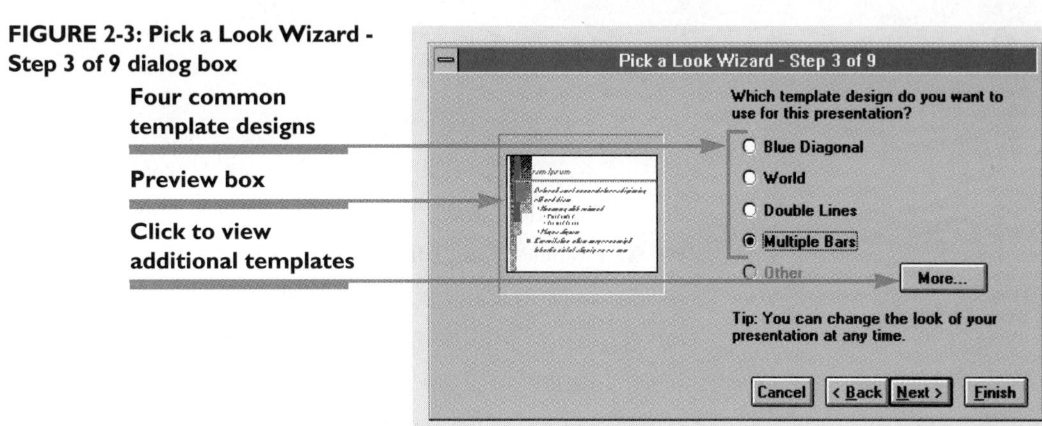

FIGURE 2-4: Presentation Template dialog box

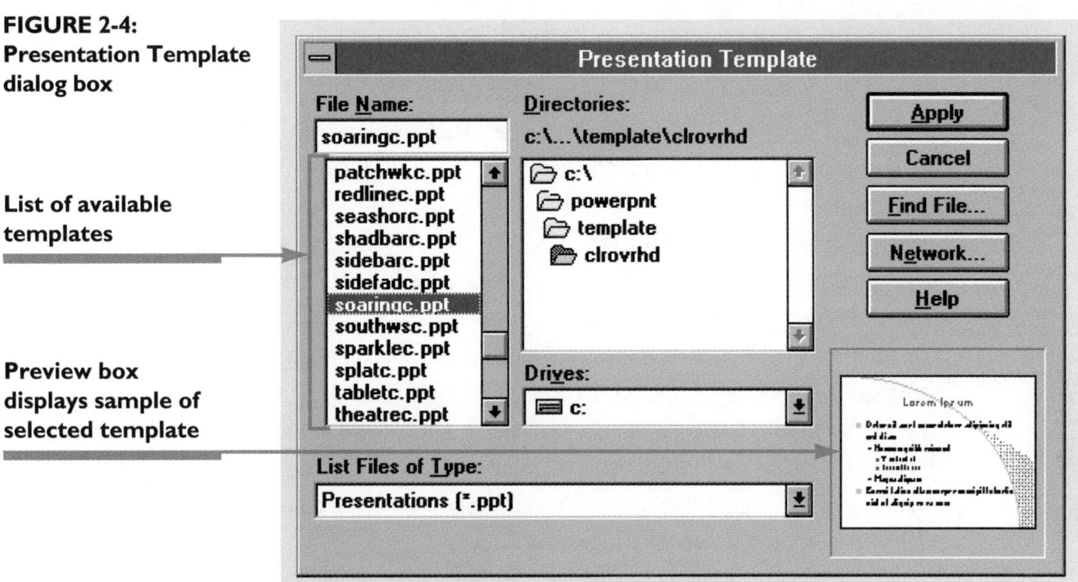

FIGURE 2-5: Presentation title slide

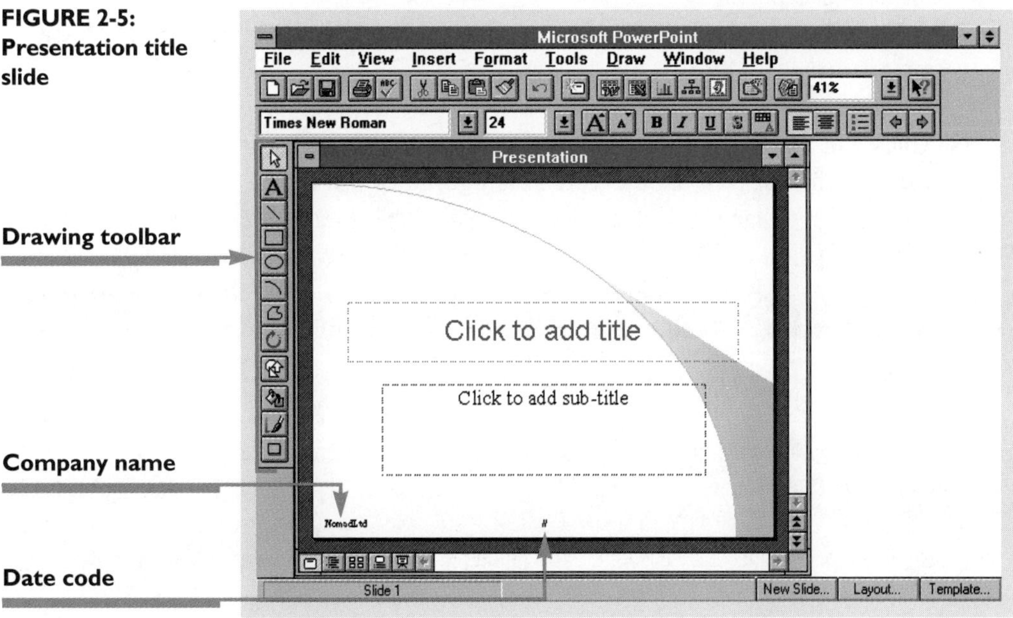

TROUBLE?

If you need help starting PowerPoint, refer to the lesson "Starting PowerPoint 4.0 for Windows" in Unit 1.

Entering slide text

Once the Pick a Look Wizard finishes, PowerPoint creates the **title slide**, the first slide in your presentation. The title slide has two **placeholders**, boxes with dashed line borders where you enter text. The title slide has a **title placeholder** labeled "Click to add title" and **a main text placeholder** labeled "Click to add sub-title" where you enter additional information, such as your company name or department. To enter text in a placeholder, simply click the placeholder and then type your text. After you enter text in a placeholder, the placeholder becomes a **text object**. Objects are the building blocks that make up a presentation slide. ▶ Lynn begins working on the president's presentation by entering the title of the presentation in the title placeholder.

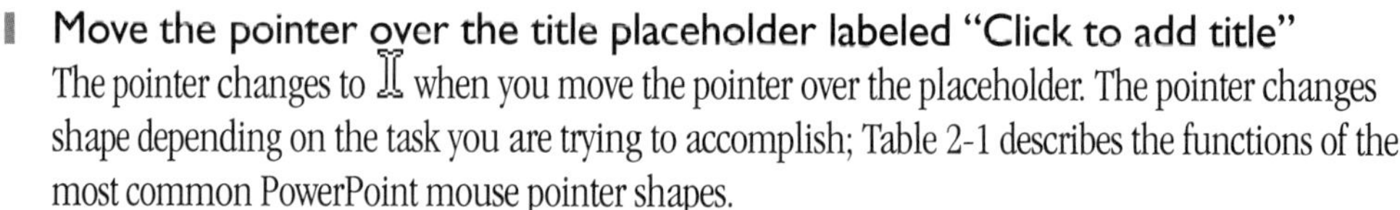

1. **Move the pointer over the title placeholder labeled "Click to add title"**
   The pointer changes to I when you move the pointer over the placeholder. The pointer changes shape depending on the task you are trying to accomplish; Table 2-1 describes the functions of the most common PowerPoint mouse pointer shapes.
2. **Click the title placeholder**
   The blinking vertical line, called the **insertion point**, indicates where your text will appear in the title placeholder. A slanted line border, called a **selection box**, appears around the title placeholder, indicating that it is selected and ready to accept text, as shown in Figure 2-6. Lynn enters the title for the presentation.
3. **Type Annual Report, press [Enter], then type Executive Summary**
   PowerPoint centers the title text within the title placeholder, now called a text object. Pressing [Enter] in a text object moves the insertion point down to begin a new line of text.
4. **Click the main text placeholder**
   In the same way, Lynn enters the president of Nomad's name, job title, and meeting date in the main text placeholder.
5. **Type Bill Davidson, press [Enter], type President, press [Enter], then type June 18, 1995**
   Compare your title slide to Figure 2-7.
6. **Click the Selection Tool button on the Drawing toolbar, or click outside the main text object in a blank area of the slide**
   Clicking the Selection Tool button or a blank area of the slide deselects all selected objects on the slide.

TABLE 2-1: PowerPoint mouse pointer shapes

SHAPE	DESCRIPTION
↖	Appears when you select the Selection tool. Use this pointer to select one or more PowerPoint objects.
I	Appears when you move the pointer over a text object. Use this pointer, referred to as the I-beam, to place the insertion point where you want to begin typing or select text.
✥	Appears when you move the pointer over a bullet or slide icon. Use this pointer to select title or paragraph text.
↓	Appears when you select the Text tool. Use this pointer, referred to as the text cursor, to create text objects.
+	Appears when you select a drawing tool. Use this pointer, referred to as the crosshair cursor, to draw shapes.

FIGURE 2-6: Selected title placeholder

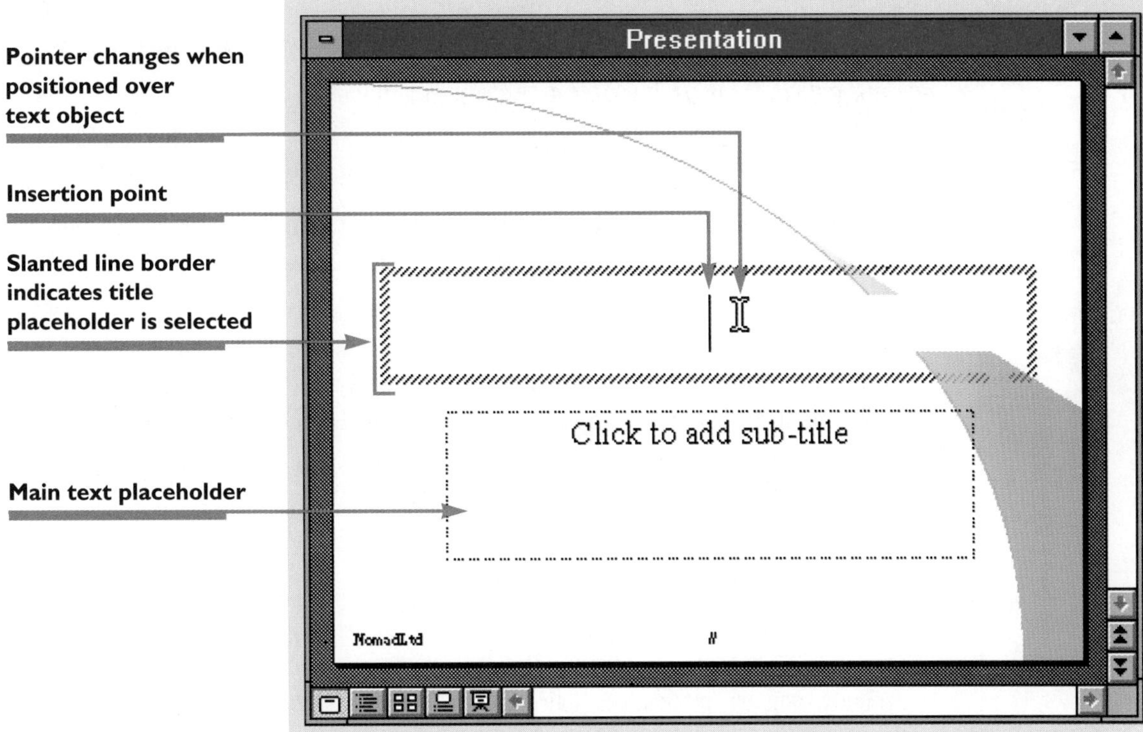

FIGURE 2-7: Title slide with text

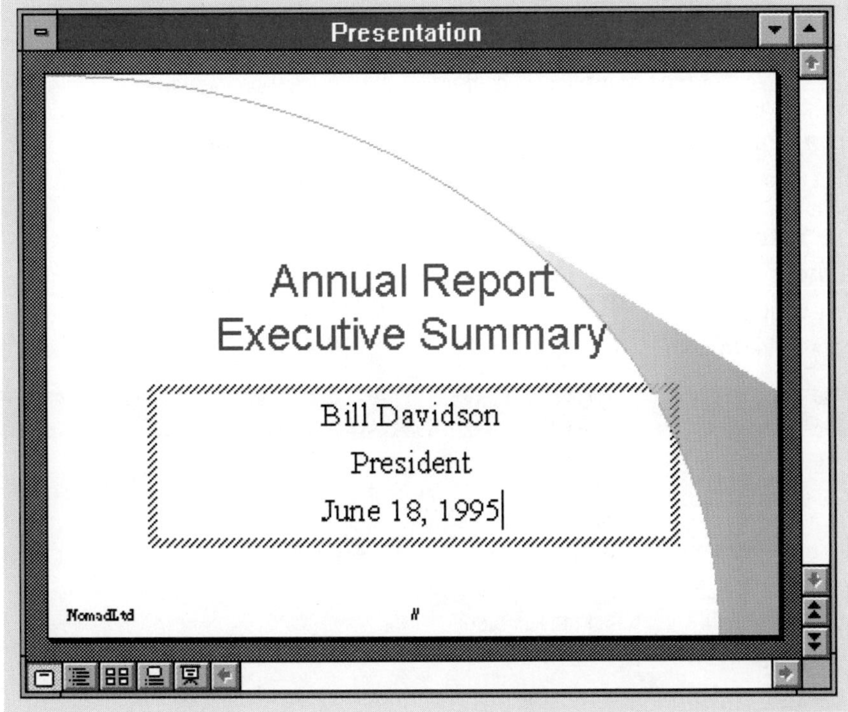

TROUBLE?

If you press a wrong key by mistake, press [Backspace] to erase the character, then continue to type.

Creating a new slide

To help you create a new slide easily, PowerPoint offers 21 predesigned slide layouts, called **AutoLayouts**, that include a variety of placeholder arrangements for titles, main text, and objects such as clip art, graphs, and charts. See Table 2-2 for an explanation of the different placeholders you'll find in the list of AutoLayouts. ▶ To continue developing the presentation, Lynn needs to create a slide that displays the topic headings for the president's presentation.

1 **Click the New Slide button** [New Slide...] **on the status bar, or click the Insert New Slide button on the Standard toolbar**
The New Slide dialog box opens, displaying the different AutoLayouts (click the down scroll arrow to see more). You can choose the layout that best meets your needs by clicking it in the AutoLayout list. The title for the selected AutoLayout appears in a Preview box to the right of the list, as shown in Figure 2-8. Lynn decides to use the default Bulleted List AutoLayout to enter the topic headings.

2 Click **OK**
A new empty slide appears after the current slide in your presentation and displays a title placeholder and a main text placeholder. Notice that the status bar displays Slide 2. Lynn enters a title for this slide.

3 Click the **title placeholder** then type **Summary**

4 Click the **main text placeholder**
This deselects the title text object. The insertion point appears next to the bullet in the main text placeholder. Lynn enters the first two topic headings for the president's presentation.

5 Type **Goals**, press **[Enter]**, then type **Accomplishments**
A new bullet automatically appears when you press [Enter].

6 Click the **Selection Tool button** on the Drawing toolbar, or click outside the main text object in a blank area of the slide to deselect the main text object
Compare your slide to Figure 2-9.

TABLE 2-2: AutoLayout placeholder types

PLACEHOLDER	DESCRIPTION
Bulleted List	Displays a short list of related points
Clip Art	Inserts a picture, such as PowerPoint clip art
Graph	Inserts a graph that uses standard Microsoft graph techniques
Org Chart	Inserts an organizational chart
Table	Inserts a table from Microsoft Word
Object	Adds an external object such as a media clip, sound, or WordArt to a PowerPoint slide

FIGURE 2-8: New Slide dialog box

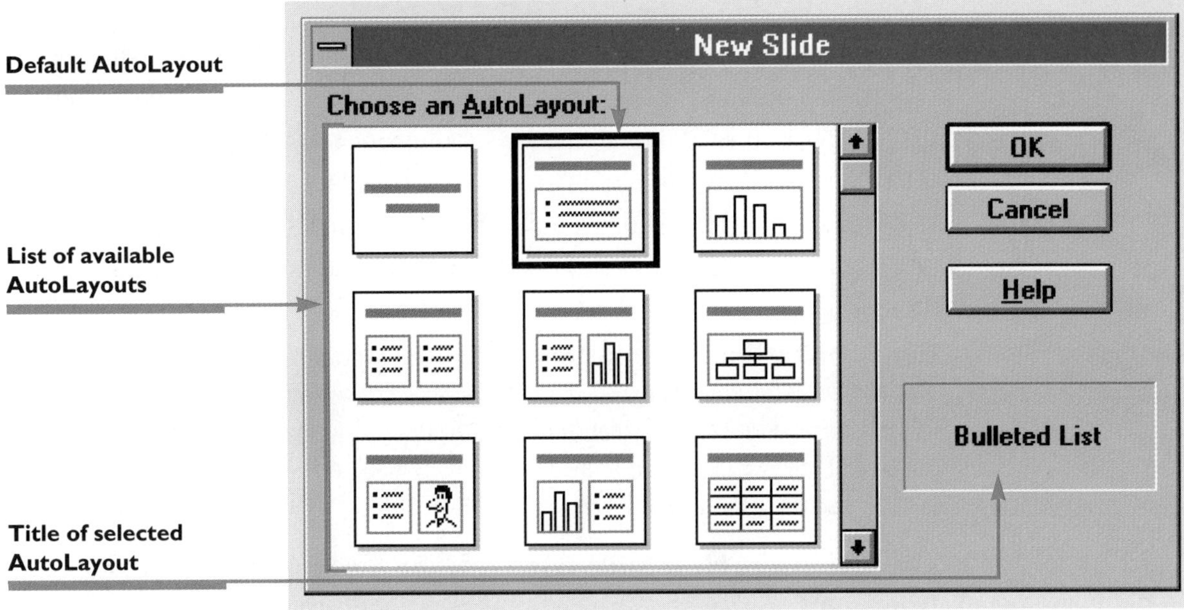

FIGURE 2-9: New slide with bulleted list

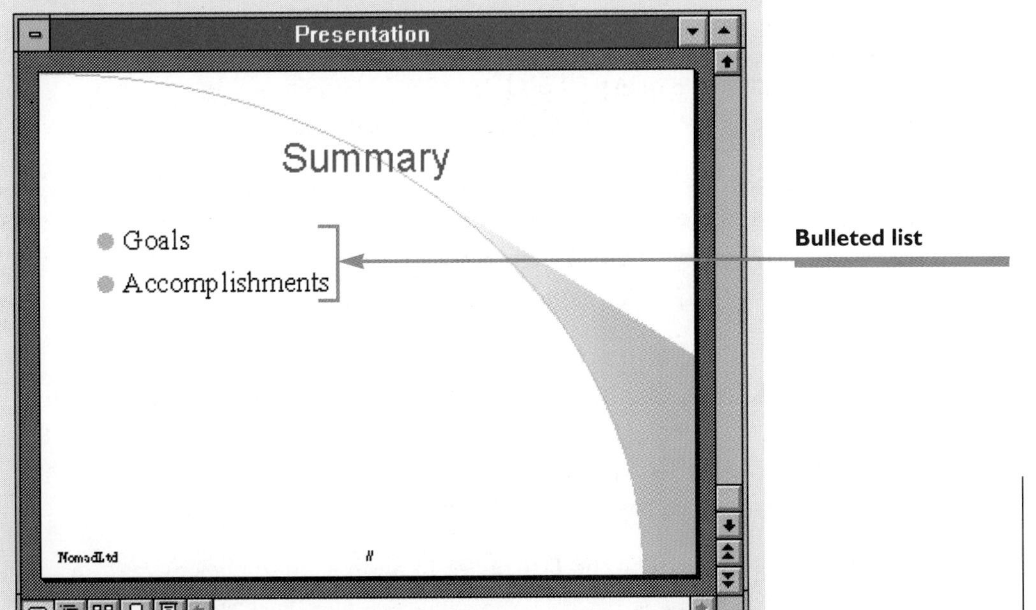

QUICK TIP

You can move from one text object to the next using the shortcut key [Ctrl][Enter]. ▶ To add a new slide with the same layout as the current slide, press and hold [Shift] then click the New Slide button New Slide... on the status bar.■

Working in Outline view

In PowerPoint, you can enter your presentation text in Slide view or Outline view. Outline view displays the titles and main text of all the slides in your presentation in one view. As in a regular outline, the headings, or **titles**, appear first, then under them, the sub points, or **main text**. The main text appears as one or more lines of bulleted text under a title. ▶ Lynn entered the first two slides of her presentation in Slide view. Now, she switches to Outline view to enter text for two more slides.

1. **Click the Outline View button on the status bar**
   The outline fills the Presentation window with the Slide 2 title selected (the one you just created). Notice that the Outlining toolbar replaces the Drawing toolbar on the left side of the PowerPoint window. Table 2-3 describes the buttons available on the Outlining toolbar. Now, Lynn enters the text for her third slide.

2. Click the **Insert New Slide button** on the Standard toolbar, then type **Goals**
   A symbol called a **slide icon** appears when you add a new slide to the outline. Text you enter next to a slide icon becomes the title for that slide. Now Lynn enters the main text for the Goals slide.

3. Press **[Enter]** then click the **Demote (Indent More) button** on the Outlining toolbar, or press **[Tab]**
   The slide icon changes to a bullet and indents one level to the right.

4. Type **Increase overall product sales by 35%**, then press **[Enter]**; type **Increase travel expeditions by 30%**, then press **[Enter]**; type **Increase environmental funding by 50%**, then press **[Ctrl] [Enter]**
   Notice that pressing [Ctrl] [Enter] creates a new slide.

5. Type **Accomplishments** then press **[Ctrl] [Enter]**; type **Product sales up by 53.4%**, then press **[Enter]**; type **Environmental funding up by 5.4%** then press **[Enter]**; type **Travel expeditions up by 26.9%**
   Lynn discovers that two of the bullet points she just typed for slide four are out of order so she moves them into the correct position.

6. Position the pointer over the last bullet in Slide 4, then click
   The pointer changes from I to ✥, and PowerPoint selects the entire line of text.

7. Click the **Move Up button** on the Outlining toolbar
   The third bullet point moves up one line and trades places with the second bullet point, as shown in Figure 2-10. Now, Lynn wants to see the slides she just created in Slide view.

8. Double-click the **slide icon** for Slide 4, then view the slide
   PowerPoint switches to Slide view for Slide 4.

9. Click the **Previous Slide button** below the vertical scroll bar three times to view each slide until Slide 1 appears in the status bar

FIGURE 2-10: Outline view

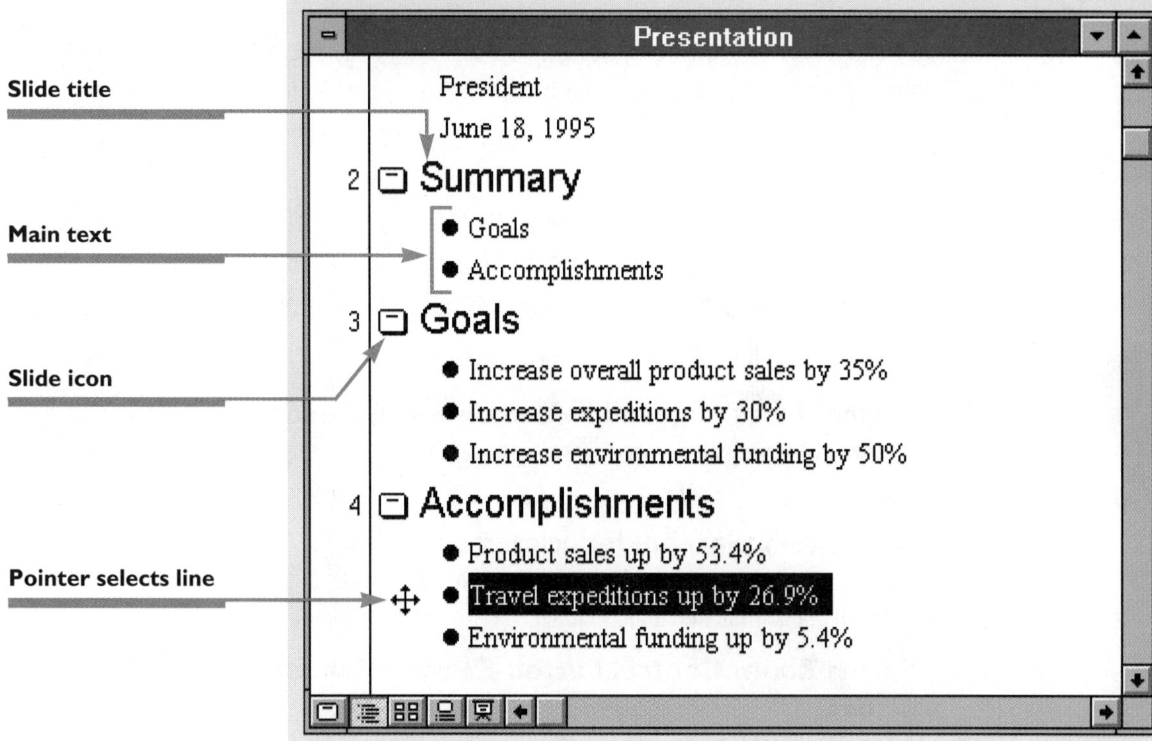

TABLE 2-3: Outlining toolbar commands

BUTTON	DESCRIPTION
Promote (Indent less)	Indents selected text one tab to the left
Demote (Indent more)	Indents selected text one tab to the right
Move Up	Moves the selection above the previous line
Move Down	Moves the selection below the next line
Collapse Selection	Displays only the titles of the selection
Expand Selection	Displays all levels of the selection
Show Titles	Displays only the titles for all slides
Show All	Displays the title and all the body text for all slides
Show Formatting	Displays all character formatting

QUICK TIP

You can use the mouse to move titles and main text by dragging slide icons or bullets to a new location.

Entering text in Notes Pages view

To help you give your presentation, you can create speaker's notes that accompany your slides so you don't have to rely on your memory. Notes Pages view displays a reduced slide image and a text placeholder where you enter the notes for each slide of your presentation. The notes you enter there do not appear on the slides themselves; they are private notes for you. You can also print these pages. See the Quick Tip and the related topic "Printing handout pages" for more information. ▶ To make sure the president doesn't forget key points of his presentation, Lynn enters notes for some of the slides.

1. Click the **Notes Pages View button** on the status bar
   The view of your presentation changes from Slide view to Notes Pages view, as shown in Figure 2-11.
2. Click the **text placeholder** below the slide image
   The insertion point appears, indicating the placeholder is ready to accept your text. The insertion point is small and difficult to see so Lynn increases the view size.
3. Click the **Zoom Control button** on the Standard toolbar, then click **66%**
   The text placeholder increases in size. Now that the text placeholder is larger and easier to see, Lynn enters her notes for Slide 1.
4. Type **Welcome to the 1994 Annual Report meeting for shareholders and employees**
5. Click the **Next Slide button** below the vertical scroll bar, click the **text placeholder**, then type **The main purpose for this meeting is to share with you the exciting accomplishments Nomad Ltd has achieved in the last year**
   As you type, text automatically wraps to the next line.
6. Click , click the **text placeholder**, then type **Our 1994 goals were aggressive yet attainable. We started 1994 with the desire to increase product sales by 35%, increase travel expeditions by 30%, and increase funding on the environment by 50%. Well, how did we do?**
7. Click , click the **text placeholder**, type **With the introduction of our award winning OutBack camping gear series, product sales jumped up by 53.4%. With the acquisition of a travel subsidiary company called New Directions, expeditions for the year increased by 26.9%. Because of new product lines and the acquisition of New Directions, environmental funding only increased by 5.4%.**; press **[Enter]**, then type **I would like to thank you all for your hard work. Congratulations!**
8. Click the **Zoom Control button** then click **33%**
   The view size decreases to 33%, as shown in Figure 2-12. Now Lynn can save her work.

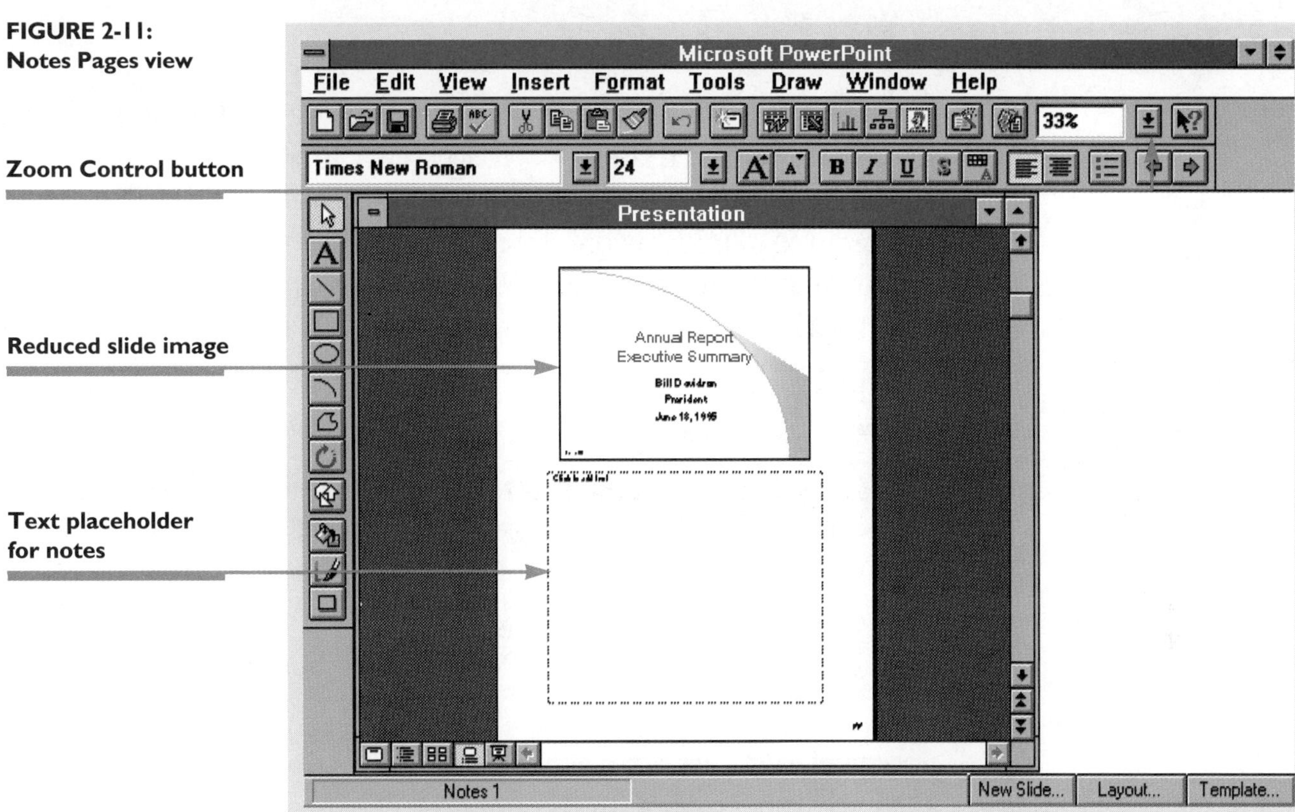

FIGURE 2-11: Notes Pages view

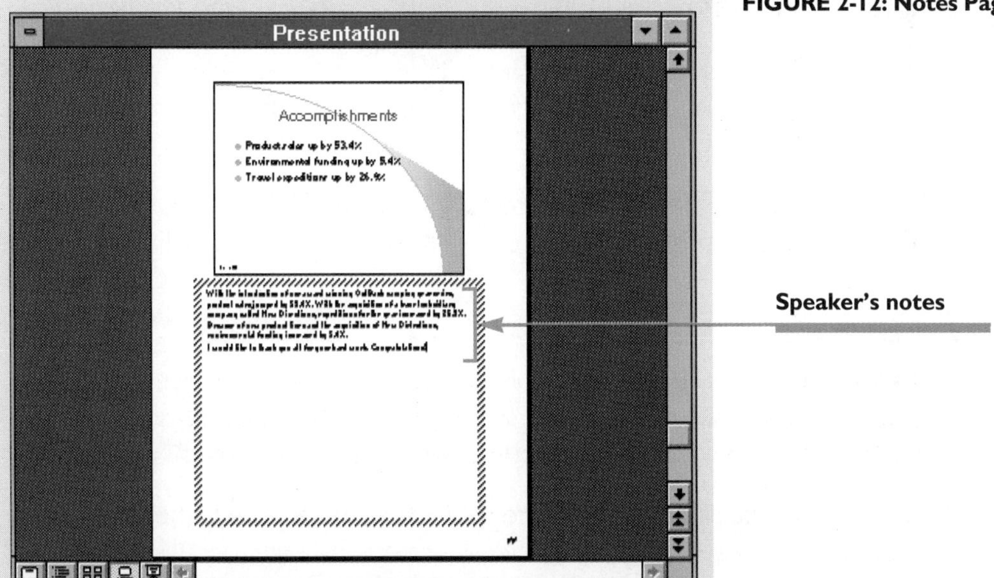

FIGURE 2-12: Notes Pages view with text

Printing handout pages

You can also print pages for your audience so they can follow along as you make your presentation. You can print handout pages that contain either two, three, or six slide pictures per page. In the Print dialog box, select the desired handout pages setting, and then print.

QUICK TIP

If you want to provide pages on which your audience can take notes, print the Notes Pages view, but leave the text placeholder blank or draw some lines.

Saving a presentation

To store a presentation permanently, you must save it to a file on a disk. As a general rule, you should save your work about every 10 or 15 minutes and before printing. ▶ Name and save the president's presentation to the MY_FILES directory you created on your Student Disk. For more information about your Student Disk, refer to "Read This Before You Begin Microsoft PowerPoint 4.0" on page 2 of PowerPoint Unit 1. Lynn saves her presentation as 94REPORT.

1 Click **File** on the menu bar, then click **Save As**
The Save As dialog box opens.

2 If necessary, double-click the **File Name text box** to select its contents
You edit the text in the File Name text box the same way you would edit text in an outline. PowerPoint accepts filenames consisting of one to eight characters.

3 Type **94REPORT** in the File Name text box
The name "94REPORT" appears in the File Name text box, replacing the PowerPoint default filename.

4 Click the **Drives list arrow**, then click the drive that contains your Student Disk
See Figure 2-13. Windows displays an error message if you select a drive that does not contain a disk. See the related topic "Select the correct drive when saving a file" for more information.

If you created a MY_FILES directory in "Microsoft Windows 3.1," you can save your files there. If you do not have a MY_FILES directory, skip Step 5 and continue with Step 6 to save the file to the a:\ directory on your Student Disk.

5 Double-click the **MY_FILES** directory on your Student Disk
The Save As dialog displays the location on your Student Disk where you will save your presentation.

6 Click **OK**
The Summary Info dialog box opens, displaying title, subject, and author information about your presentation. Closing this dialog box saves the presentation with the filename 94REPORT.PPT. The default file extension for PowerPoint presentations is PPT.

7 Click the **Subject text box**, type **1994 Annual Report**, then click **OK**
The Summary dialog box closes, and the filename appears in the title bar at the top of the Presentation window. Lynn decides she wants to save the presentation in Slide view instead of Notes Pages view so it opens to display a slide.

8 Click the **Slide View button** on the status bar
The presentation view changes from Notes Pages view to Slide view.

9 Click the **Save button** on the Standard toolbar
The Save command saves your changes to the file you designated when you used Save As. Save a file frequently while working with it to protect the presentation. Table 2-4 shows the difference between the Save and the Save As commands.

FIGURE 2-13: Save As dialog box

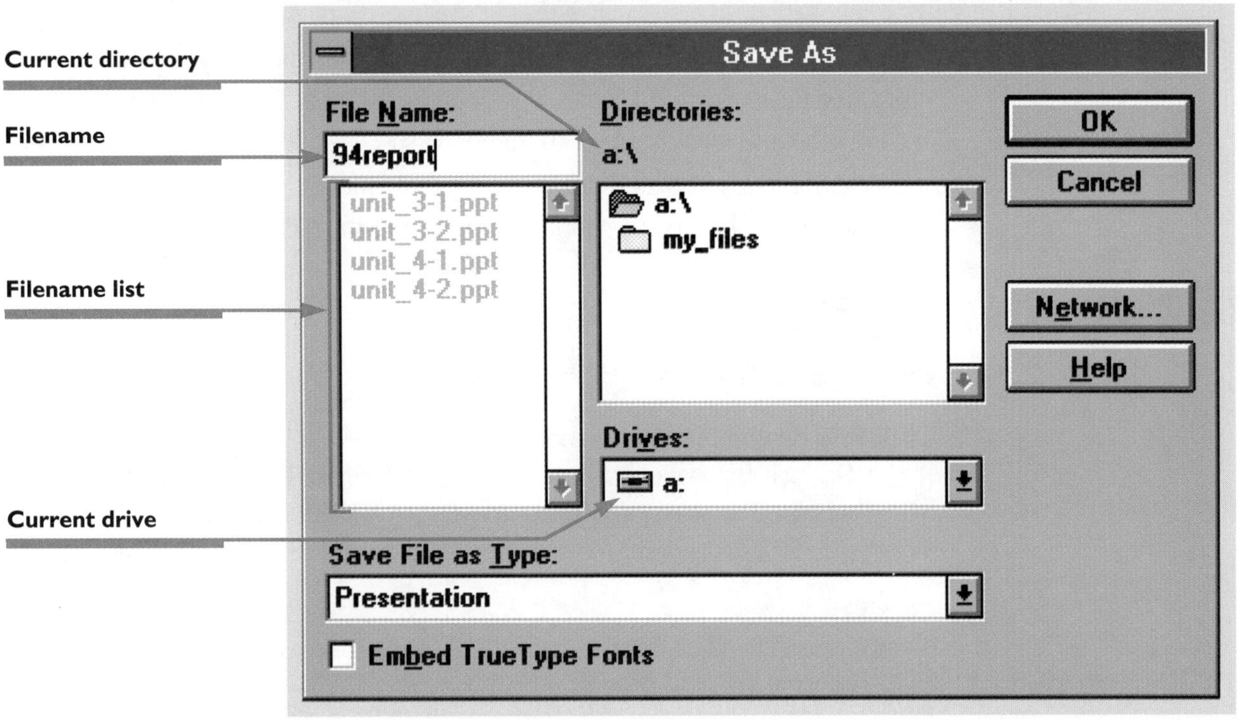

Current directory

Filename

Filename list

Current drive

Selecting the correct drive when saving a file

When you save a file, you need to select the appropriate disk drive on the computer—either drive A or drive B. You generally do not save files on the internal hard disk, drive C, or network server drive (D, E, and so on) unless you are working on your own computer. Instead, save all your work on a 3.5- or 5.25-inch disk. To create a backup copy, save the file on a second disk and store the second disk in a safe place.

Click the Save button on the Standard toolbar to save a file quickly, or use the shortcut key [Ctrl][S].

TABLE 2-4:
Save and Save As commands

COMMAND	DESCRIPTION	PURPOSE
Save As	Gives you opportunity to designate a location and name for file	Use to save a file for the first time, change the file's name or location, or save the file to use in a different application. Useful to save different versions of a presentation.
Save	Saves named file to previously specified location	Use to save any changes to the original file. Fast and easy; do this often to protect your work.

Printing a presentation

Print your presentation when you have completed it or when you want to review your work. Reviewing hard copies of your presentation at different stages of production is helpful and gives you an overall perspective of your presentation content and look. Table 2-5 provides some printing guidelines. ▶ Lynn prints the slides and notes pages of the presentation to review what she has developed so far.

1 **Check the printer**
Make sure the printer is on, has paper, and that it is on-line or ready to print. If you send a file to a printer that is not ready, an error message appears.

2 Click **File** on the menu bar, then click **Print**
The Print dialog box opens, as shown in Figure 2-14. In this dialog box, you can specify the print options you want to use when you print your presentation. With the Print What option set to Slides and the Slide Range option set to All, Lynn is ready to print all the slides of the presentation.

3 Click **OK**
PowerPoint sends the file to the printer. Note that the Cancel button displays on the screen briefly, giving you a chance to cancel the print job.

4 Click **File** on the menu bar, then click **Print**
The Print dialog box again opens. You have already printed the presentation slides. Now print the notes pages.

5 Click the **Print What list arrow**, then click **Notes Pages**
PowerPoint is ready to print the Notes Pages view of the presentation.

6 Click **OK**
The Print dialog box closes, and your presentation is printed.

7 Click **File** on the menu bar, then click **Exit**
The presentation file closes and you exit PowerPoint.

TABLE 2-5:
Presentation printing guidelines

BEFORE YOU PRINT	RECOMMENDATION
Check the printer	Make sure the printer is on and on-line, that it has paper, and there are no error messages or warning signals.
Check the Slide Setup	Make sure the slide size, orientation, and page number are acceptable for the printer by choosing the Slide Setup command from the File menu.
Check the printer selection	Check the printer entry at the top of the Print dialog box. If the incorrect printer is selected, click the Printer button to select the correct printer.

FIGURE 2-14: Print dialog box

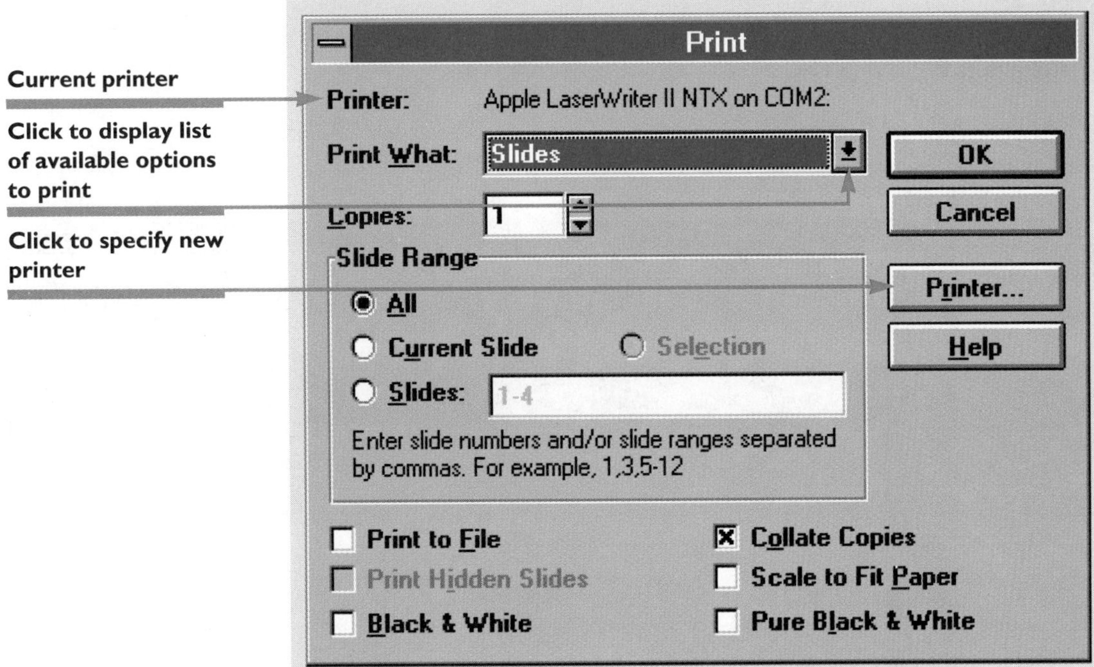

Using Slide Setup

Use the Slide Setup command on the File menu to customize the presentation output size to meet your specific needs. You can change the slide width, height, and orientation of your slides.

QUICK TIP

Click the Print button on the Standard toolbar to print quickly using the current settings.

CONCEPTS REVIEW

Label each of the elements of the PowerPoint window shown in Figure 2-15.

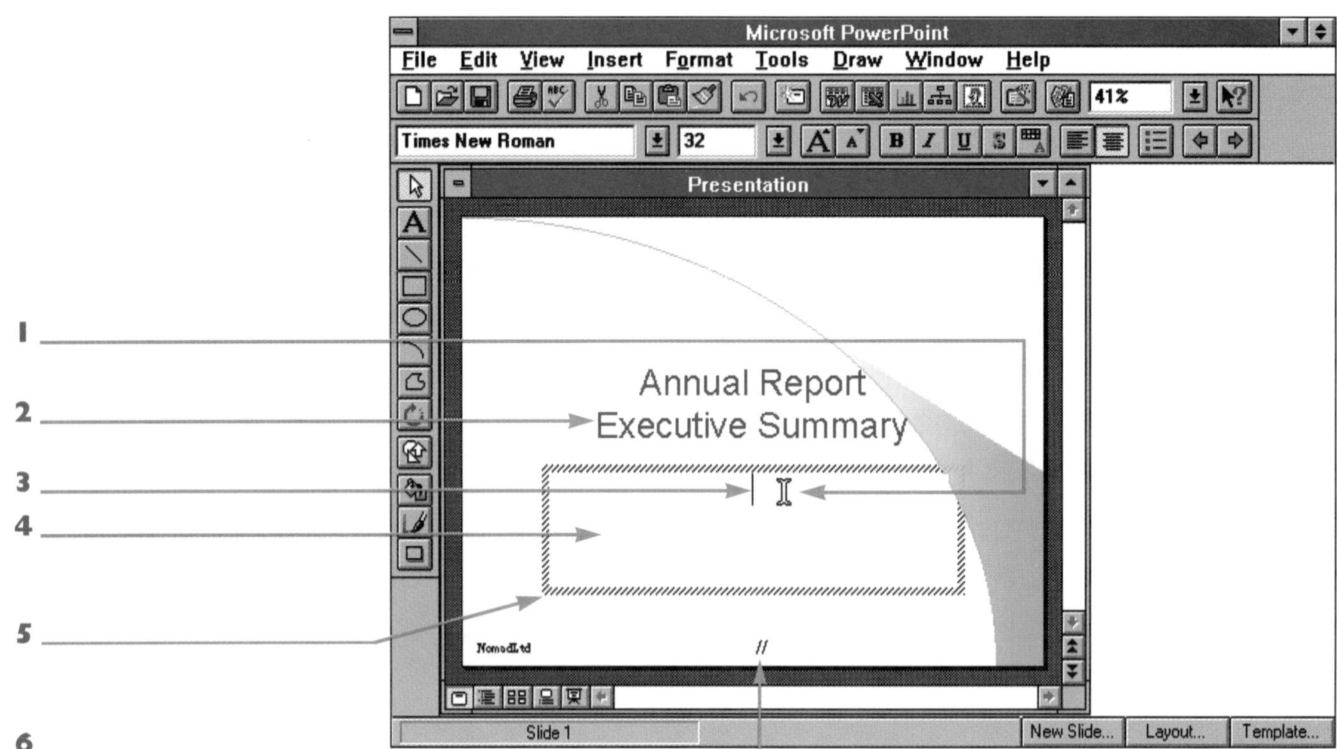

FIGURE 2-15

Match each of the terms with the statement that describes its function.

7 A symbol that initially appears after clicking the main text placeholder

8 A symbol that indicates where your text will appear in a text object

9 A slanted line selection box with text

10 A dotted box with prompt text that displays on a slide where you can enter text

11 A symbol that represents a slide

a. Placeholder
b. Insertion point
c. Text object
d. Slide icon
e. Bullet

Select the best answer from the list of choices.

12 Which of the following is NOT a presentation print option?
  a. Slides
  b. Notes Pages
  c. Handouts (4 slides per page)
  d. Outline view

13 Which of the following is NOT a slide output option?
  a. 35-mm slides
  b. B&W overheads
  c. Notes pages
  d. On-screen slide show

14 When you start a new presentation, which command do you choose from the PowerPoint startup dialog box to choose a look for your presentation?

a. AutoContent Wizard

b. Pick a Look Wizard

c. Blank Presentation

d. Current Presentation

15 You can make copy of a presentation with a different name by using which command:

a. Save

b. Open

c. Save As

d. Copy

APPLICATIONS REVIEW

1 Choose a look for your presentation.

a. Start PowerPoint.

b. Click the Blank Presentation radio button or click the New button on the Standard toolbar.

c. Click the Pick a Look Wizard radio button, click OK, then click Next.

d. Click the 35mm Slides button, click Next, click each of the template options to review the different designs or use the More button, choose a slide design, then click Apply or Next if using one of the radio button templates.

e. Click Next, click the Audience Handout Pages check box and click the Outline Pages check box to deselect these options, then click Next to continue.

f. Click the Name, company, or other text check box, enter your name in the box, click the Date check box, click the Page Number check box, then click Next.

g. Click the Name, company, or other text check box, click the Date check box, click Next, then click Finish.

2 Enter slide text.

a. Click the title placeholder then type "Product Marketing."

b. Click the main text placeholder, type "Chris Thielen," press [Enter], then type "Manager."

3 Create a new slide and work in Outline view.

a. Switch to Outline view.

b. Click the New Slide button

c. Enter the outline from Table 2-6.

TABLE 2-6

Goals for the Week
- Chris
  - Interview new candidates
- John
  - Revise product marketing report
  - Set up plan for the annual sales meeting
- April
  - Investigate advertising agencies
  - Establish advertising budget

4 Enter text in Notes Pages view.

a. Switch to Notes Pages view for Slide 2.

b. Click the notes placeholder.

c. Zoom in the view.

d. Enter the following speaker's notes:

Remember, this week I'll be interviewing new candidates for a product marketing position. I'll have each of you interview the candidates who meet initial qualifications next week.

e. Switch back to Slide view.

5 Print a handout (2 slides per page) and the notes pages.

a. Click File on the menu bar, then click Print.

b. Click the Print What list arrow, click Handouts (2 slides per page), then click OK.

c. Using the same process, print the notes pages to accompany the handouts.

d. Save the presentation as INTRVIEW.PPT in the MY_FILES directory on your Student Disk.

6 Create a new presentation.

a. Click the New button on the Standard toolbar.

b. Click the Blank Presentation radio button in the PowerPoint startup dialog box.

c. Click the Bulleted List AutoLayout, then click OK.

d. Enter the slide title and bulleted text in Table 2-7.

TABLE 2-7

Title:	Next Steps
Bulleted Text:	Develop Technology Implementation Plans
	Develop Marketing Implementation Plans

e. Print the slides and the notes pages to accompany the presentation.

f. Save the presentation as NEXTSTEP.PPT in the MY_FILES directory on your Student Disk, and close the presentation.

INDEPENDENT CHALLENGE 1

You have been asked to give a six-week basic computer course at the local adult school for adults who have never used a computer. One of your responsibilities as the instructor is to create presentation slides and an outline of the course materials for the students.

Plan and create presentation slides that outline the course material for the students. Create slides for the course introduction, course description, course requirements, course texts and grading, and a detailed course syllabus. For each slide include speaker's notes to help you stay on track during the presentation.

Create your own course material, but assume the following: the school has a computer lab with IBM compatible and Microsoft Windows software; each student has a computer on his or her desk; students are intimidated by computers but want to learn; each weekly class session lasts for 50 minutes.

To complete this independent challenge:

1 Think about the results you want to see, the information you need, and the type of message you want to communicate in this presentation.

2 Sketch a sample presentation on a piece of paper, indicating the presentation look and how the information should be laid out. What content should go on the slides? On the notes pages?

3 Create the presentation by choosing a presentation look, entering the title slide text, the outline text, and the notes pages text. Remember you are creating and entering your own presentation material.

4 Save the presentation as CLASS1.PPT in the MY_FILES directory on your Student Disk. Before printing, view each slide so you know what the presentation will look like. Adjust any items as needed, and print the slides, notes pages, and handouts.

5 Submit your presentation plan, your preliminary sketches, and the final worksheet printout.

INDEPENDENT CHALLENGE 2

You are the training director for Space Amusements, Inc., a theme park and entertainment company. One of your responsibilities is to give an introductory presentation at the weekly new employee orientation training class. The theme park, Space Amusements, is hiring 30 to 50 new employees a week for the peak season in the areas of entertainment, customer support, maintenance, cashier, and food service.

Plan and create presentation slides that outline your part of the training for new employees. Create slides for the introduction, agenda, company history, new attractions, benefits, and safety requirements. For each slide include speaker's notes that you can hand out to the employees.

Create your own presentation and company material, but assume the following: the new employee training class lasts for four hours; the training director's presentation lasts 15 minutes; the new attraction for this season is the Demon roller coaster.

To complete this independent challenge:

1 Think about the results you want to see, the information you need, and what type of message you want to communicate for this presentation.

2 Sketch a sample presentation on a piece of paper, indicating the presentation look and how the information should be laid out. What content should go on the slides? On the notes pages?

3 Create the presentation by choosing a presentation look, entering the title slide text, the outline text, and the notes pages text. Remember you are creating and entering your own presentation material.

4 Save the presentation as NEWHIRE.PPT in the MY_FILES directory on your Student Disk. Before printing, view each slide so you know what the presentation will look like. Adjust any items as needed, and print the slides and notes pages.

5 Submit your presentation plan, your preliminary sketches, and the final worksheet printout.

UNIT 3

OBJECTIVES

- Open an existing presentation
- Add and arrange text
- Format text
- Draw and modify objects
- Edit objects
- Align and group objects
- Replace text
- Check spelling

A PRESENTATION

After you create the basic outline of your presentation and enter text, you need to review your work and modify your slides to achieve the best possible look. In this unit, you will open an existing presentation, and then add and rearrange text, draw and modify objects, replace a font, and use the spell checker. ▶ Lynn Shaw continues to work on the Annual Report Executive Summary presentation for the president of Nomad Ltd. Lynn uses PowerPoint's text editing and drawing features to refine the presentation and bring it closer to a finished look. ▶

Opening an existing presentation

Sometimes it's easiest to create a new presentation by changing an existing one. Creating a new presentation from an old one saves you from having to type duplicate information. You simply open the file you want to change, then use the Save As command to save a copy of the file with a new name. In this book, whenever you open an existing presentation, the instructions tell you to save a copy of it to your Student Disk so you can keep the original file intact. Saving a copy with a new name does not affect the information in the original file. Table 3-1 lists some guidelines to follow when naming a presentation file. ▶ Follow Lynn as she opens an existing presentation and saves it using a new name.

1. Start PowerPoint and insert your Student Disk in the appropriate disk drive
2. Click the **Open an Existing Presentation radio button** in the PowerPoint startup dialog box, then click **OK**
   If PowerPoint is already running, click the Open button on the Standard toolbar to open this dialog box.

   The Open dialog box opens.
3. Click the **Drives list arrow**
   A list of drives opens. Locate the drive that contains your Student Disk. These lessons assume your Student Disk is in drive A.
4. Click **a:**
   A list of the files on your Student Disk appears in the File Name list box, as shown in Figure 3-1.
5. In the File Name list box, click **UNIT_3-1.PPT** then click **OK**
   The file named UNIT_3-1.PPT opens. Now, save a copy of this file with a new name to the MY_FILES directory on your Student Disk using the Save As command.

   For more information on the MY_FILES directory, see the lesson entitled "Saving a presentation" in Unit 1.
6. Click **File** on the menu bar, then click **Save As**
   The Save As dialog box opens. The Save As dialog box works just like the Open dialog box.
7. Make sure the Drives list box displays the drive containing your Student Disk, then double-click **MY_FILES** in the list of directories
   If you aren't saving files to the MY_FILES directory, you don't need to double-click it. Continue with Step 8.
8. If necessary, select the current filename in the File Name text box, then type **94REPRT1**
   Compare your screen to the Save As dialog box in Figure 3-2.
9. Click **OK**; if the Summary Info dialog box opens, click **OK** again
   PowerPoint creates a copy of UNIT_3-1.PPT with the name 94REPRT1.PPT and closes UNIT_3-1.PPT.

FIGURE 3-1: Open dialog box

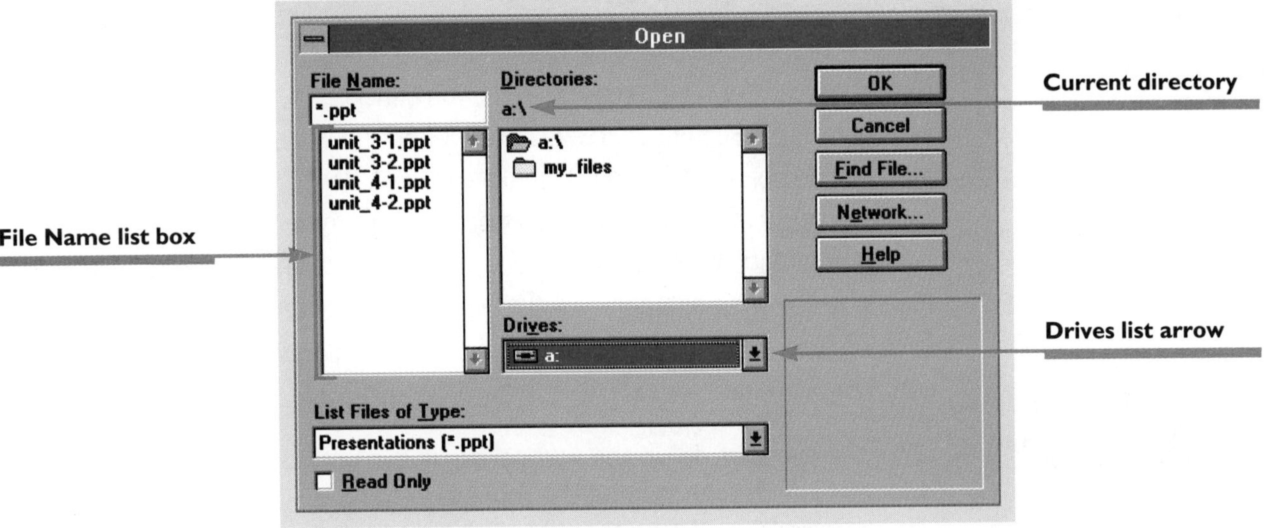

FIGURE 3-2: Save As dialog box

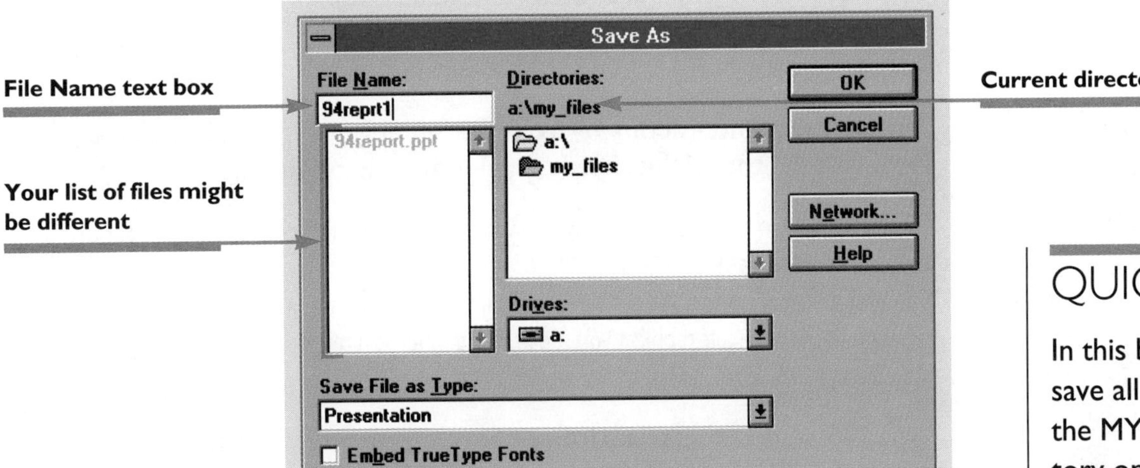

QUICK TIP

In this book, you will save all your work to the MY_FILES directory on your Student Disk that you created in "Microsoft Windows 3.1." This will help you to distinguish between the files that were provided on the Student Disk and the files you modify and save. If you did not create a MY_FILES directory, save all your work to your Student Disk in drive A or drive B.

TABLE 3-1: Filenaming guidelines

• You can use up to eight characters to name a file.
• Filenames can use uppercase, lowercase, or mixed case.
• You can't use certain special characters, such as /, \, [,], ", and =.
• Filenames can't contain spaces.

Adding and arranging text

Using PowerPoint's advanced text editing capabilities, you can easily add, insert, or rearrange text. On a PowerPoint slide, you either enter text in prearranged text placeholders or use the Text tool to create your own text objects when the text placeholders don't provide the flexibility you need. With the Text tool, you can create two types of text objects: a **text label** used for a small phrase where text doesn't automatically wrap inside a box, and a **word processing box** used for a sentence or paragraph where the text wraps inside the boundaries of a box. ▶ In this lesson, Lynn scrolls to Slide 3 and uses the Text tool to create a word processing box to enter Nomad Ltd's mission statement.

1. **Drag the elevator down the vertical scroll bar until the Slide Indicator box displays Slide 3, then release the mouse button**
   The Slide Indicator box that appears when you drag the elevator tells you which slide will appear when you release the mouse button. Now, Lynn creates a word processing box and enters the company mission statement next to the shuttle graphic.
2. **Click the Text Tool button on the Drawing toolbar, then position the pointer in the blank area of the slide**
   The pointer changes to ↓.
3. **Position the pointer about ½" from the left edge of the slide and about even with the top of the shuttle graphic already on the slide**
4. **Drag the word processing box toward the graphic so that your screen looks like Figure 3-3**
   When you begin dragging, the pointer changes from ↓ to + and an outline of the box appears, indicating how large a text object you are drawing. After you release the mouse, an insertion point appears inside the text object, ready to accept text.
5. **Type Nomad Ltd is a national sporting-goods retailer dedicated to delivering high-quality sporting gear and adventure clothing**
   Notice that the word processing box increases in size as your text wraps inside the object. Lynn discovers a mistake in the mission statement and corrects it by moving a word to its correct position.
6. **Double-click the word adventure to select it**
   When you select the word, the pointer changes from I to ↖.
7. **Drag the word adventure to the left of the word "sporting" in the mission statement, then release the mouse button**
   Notice that the dotted insertion line indicates where PowerPoint will place the word when you release the mouse button.
8. **Click a blank area of the slide outside the text object**
   The text object deselects. Your screen to should look similar to Figure to 3-4.

FIGURE 3-3: Slide showing word processing box ready to accept text

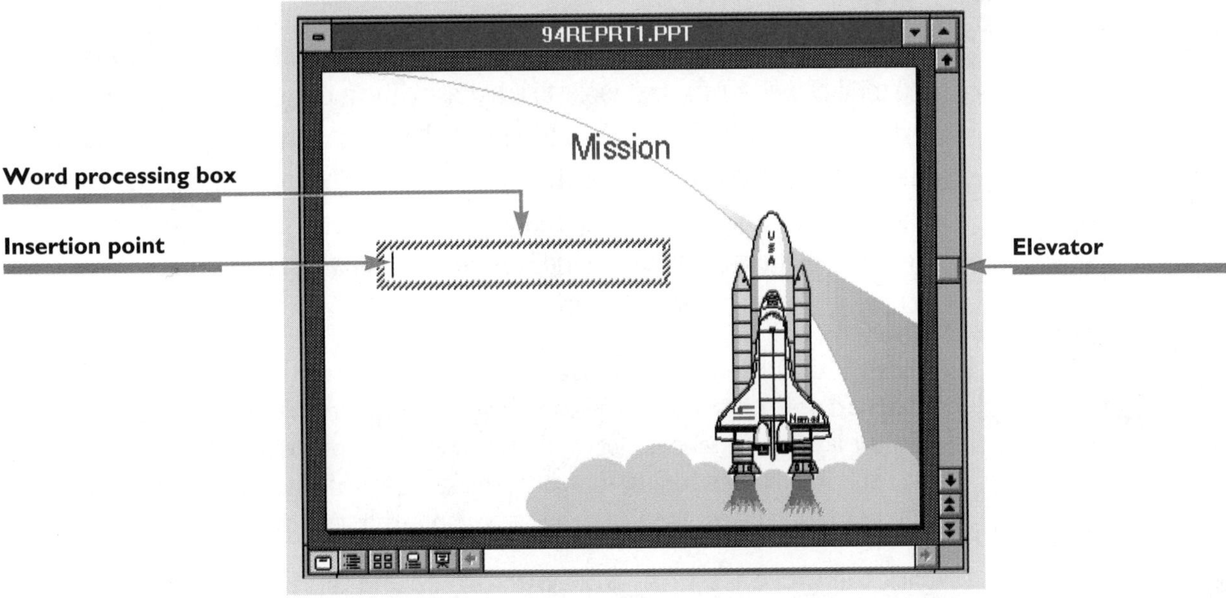

FIGURE 3-4: Slide after adding text to a word processing box

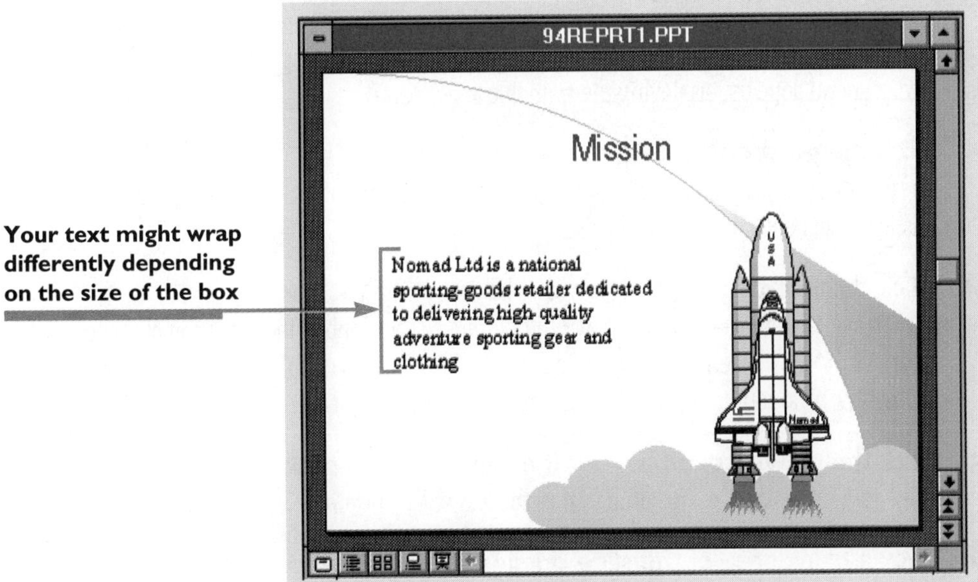

Formatting text

Once you have entered and arranged the text in your presentation, you can change and modify the way the text looks to emphasize the message you are presenting. Text that is important needs to be highlighted in some way to make it distinct from other text or objects on the slide. To change the way text looks, you need to select it, and then choose one of the Formatting commands to make the change. ▶ Lynn uses some of the commands on the Formatting toolbar to change the way the company mission statement looks.

1 Press **[Shift]** then click the **word processing box**
A **dotted selection box** appears around the word processing box, which indicates that the whole text object is selected, not just the text inside the object. Lynn selects the text object instead of individual text because she wants to make a **global change**, which changes all of the text. Now, Lynn changes the size and appearance of the text to emphasize it on the slide.

2 Click the **Increase Font Size button** and the **Italic button** on the Formatting toolbar
The text increases in size and changes from normal to italic text. The Italic button, like the Bold button, is a toggle button, which you click to turn the attribute on or off. Lynn decides to change the mission statement text color.

3 Click the **Text Color button** on the Formatting toolbar
A color menu appears, displaying the available text colors.

4 Click the **gold color cell,** as shown in Figure 3-5
The text in the word processing box changes color. Now, Lynn puts the finishing touch on the mission statement by changing the font.

5 Click the **Font button** on the Formatting toolbar
A list of available fonts opens, as shown in Figure 3-6. The double line at the top of the font list separates the most recent fonts you used from the rest of the available fonts. Lynn finds and chooses the Arial font to replace the current font in the text object.

6 Click the **down scroll arrow** if necessary, then click **Arial**
The Arial font replaces the original font in the text object. Compare your screen to Figure 3-7.

7 Click a blank area of the slide outside the text object to deselect the text object

8 Click the **Next Slide button** to move to Slide 4, which you'll work with in the next lesson

FIGURE 3-5:
Text Color menu

FIGURE 3-6:
Font list

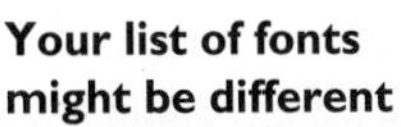

Your list of fonts might be different

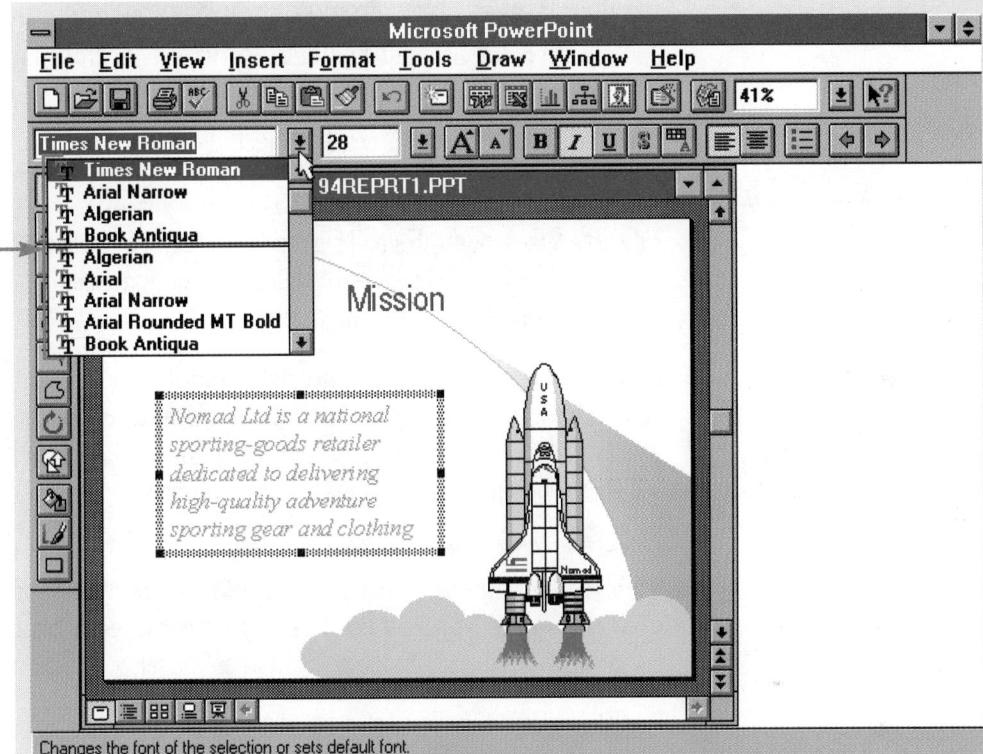

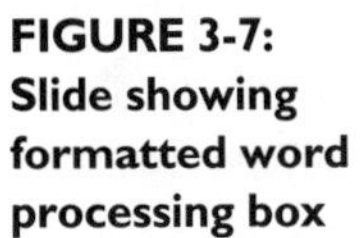

FIGURE 3-7:
Slide showing formatted word processing box

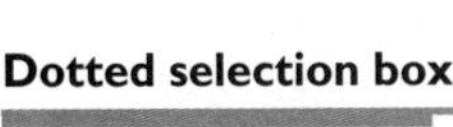

Dotted selection box

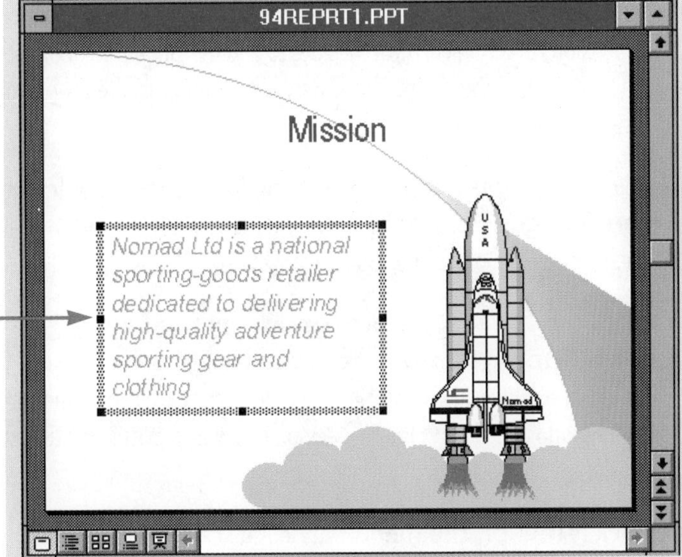

QUICK TIP

The size of your slide text should be set no lower than 18 points to be easily read by your audience.

Drawing and modifying objects

PowerPoint's drawing capabilities allow you to draw and modify lines, shapes, and pictures to enhance your presentation. Table 3-2 describes several drawing methods. Similar to the text objects you learned about in Unit 2, lines and shapes that you create with the PowerPoint drawing tools are objects that you can change and manipulate at any time. PowerPoint shapes and lines have graphic attributes, such as fill color, fill pattern, line color, line style, and shadow that you can change. ▶ Follow Lynn as she rearranges a text object on Slide 4 of the president's presentation and then draws an object to enhance the look of the slide.

1 Press **[Shift]** then click the **main text object**
A dotted selection box with small black boxes called **resize handles** appears around the text object. The resize handles let you adjust the size and shape of the object. Lynn reduces the text object so it takes up less room.

2 Position the pointer over the right middle resize handle, then drag the resize handle to the left until the text object is about half its original size
When you drag a text object's resize handle, the pointer changes to +, and an outline of the text object appears. Lynn is now ready to add a shape.

3 Click the **AutoShapes button** on the Drawing toolbar, click the **Thick Up Arrow Tool button** on the AutoShapes toolbar, then click the **AutoShapes toolbar control menu box**
Figure 3-8 shows the AutoShapes toolbar. When you select a shape, the pointer changes to +.

4 Position the pointer in the blank area of the slide to the right of the text object, press **[Shift]**, drag down and to the right to create an arrow shape similar to the one shown in Figure 3-9, then release the mouse button
When you release the mouse button, the arrow assumes its position on the slide, filled with a default color. You can use the **adjustment handle**, shown in Figure 3-9, to change the dimensions of an object. Lynn decides to add the Drawing+ toolbar to her window and change the line width of the arrow. If the Drawing+ toolbar is already on your screen, skip Step 5 and continue with Step 6.

5 Click **View** on the menu bar, click **Toolbars**, click the **Drawing+ toolbar check box** to select it, then click **OK**
The Drawing+ toolbar appears on your screen.

6 Click the **Line Style button** on the Drawing+ toolbar, then click the **third line style** down from the top
PowerPoint applies the new line style to the arrow. Now, hide the Drawing+ toolbar forthe next student, and continue to the next lesson to see how Lynn edits the arrow shape to fit the design of the slide.

7 Click **View** on the menu bar, click **Toolbars**, click the **Drawing+ toolbar check box** to deselect it, then click **OK**

FIGURE 3-8: AutoShapes toolbar

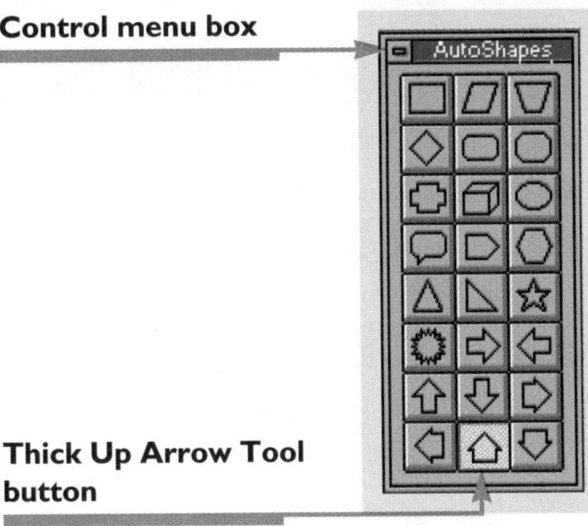

FIGURE 3-9: Slide showing arrow object

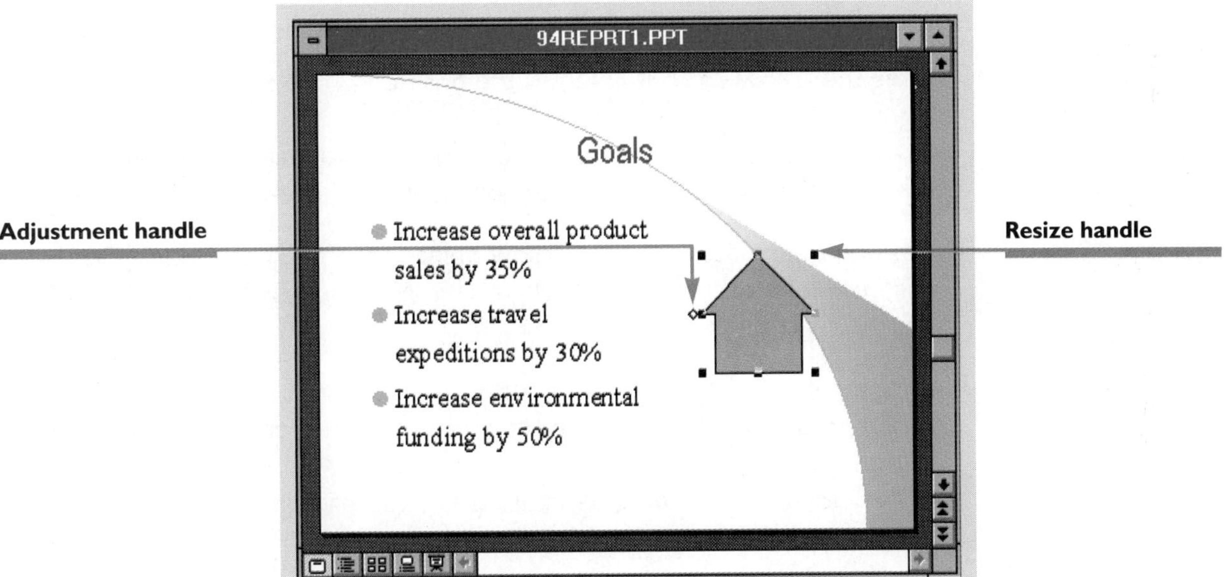

TABLE 3-2: Drawing methods

METHOD	EXAMPLE
Click any drawing tool then drag to create an unproportional object	rectangle, ellipse
Click any drawing tool, press [Shift], then drag to create a proportional object from the edge of the object	square, circle
Click any drawing tool, press [Ctrl], then drag to create a proportional object from the center of the object	square, circle

QUICK TIP

To quickly add or hide a toolbar, position the pointer over a toolbar, click the right mouse button, then click the toolbar you want to add or hide from the menu.

Editing objects

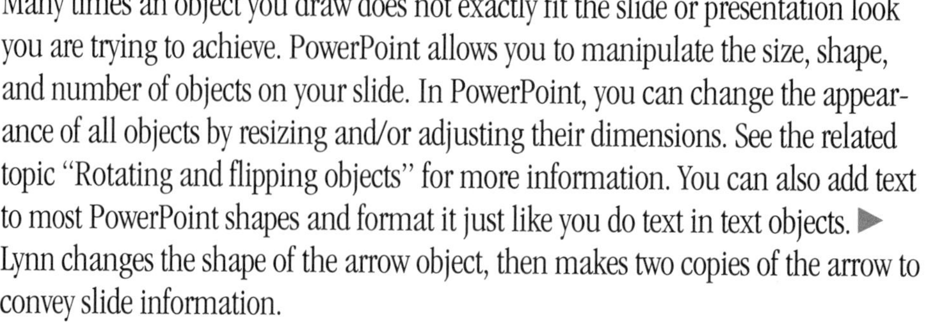

Many times an object you draw does not exactly fit the slide or presentation look you are trying to achieve. PowerPoint allows you to manipulate the size, shape, and number of objects on your slide. In PowerPoint, you can change the appearance of all objects by resizing and/or adjusting their dimensions. See the related topic "Rotating and flipping objects" for more information. You can also add text to most PowerPoint shapes and format it just like you do text in text objects. ▶ Lynn changes the shape of the arrow object, then makes two copies of the arrow to convey slide information.

1. **If the arrow object is not selected, click it**
2. **Drag the bottom middle resize handle up about ½"**
   The size and shape of your arrow should look similar to the arrow object in Figure 3-10. Lynn is satisfied with the way the arrow looks, so she decides to move the arrow into place on the slide.
3. **Drag the arrow up so it assumes the position of the arrow shown in Figure 3-10**
   An outline appears when you move the arrow object to help you position it in the correct place. Now, Lynn makes two copies of her arrow object and places them below the first object.
4. **Position the pointer over the arrow object, then press and hold [Ctrl]**
   Notice that a plus sign (+) appears next to indicating that PowerPoint will make a copy of the arrow object when you drag the pointer.
5. **Drag a copy of the arrow object down the slide so it assumes a position similar to the second arrow object in Figure 3-11, then release the mouse button**
   An exact copy of the first arrow object, including all graphic and text attributes, is made. Lynn makes a copy of the second arrow object.
6. **Press [Ctrl], drag a copy of the arrow object down the slide, then release the mouse button**
   Compare your screen to Figure 3-11. Lynn now adds some text to her arrow objects.
7. **Double-click the top arrow object, then type 35%**
   An insertion point appears in the arrow object, which indicates it is ready to accept text. The text appears in the center of the object. Now, add text to the other two arrow objects.
8. **Double-click the middle arrow object, then type 30%; double-click the bottom arrow object, type 50%, then click a blank area of the slide to deselect the object**
   In the next lesson, Lynn aligns and groups the arrow objects and then copies them to a different slide.

FIGURE 3-10:
Slide showing resized arrow object

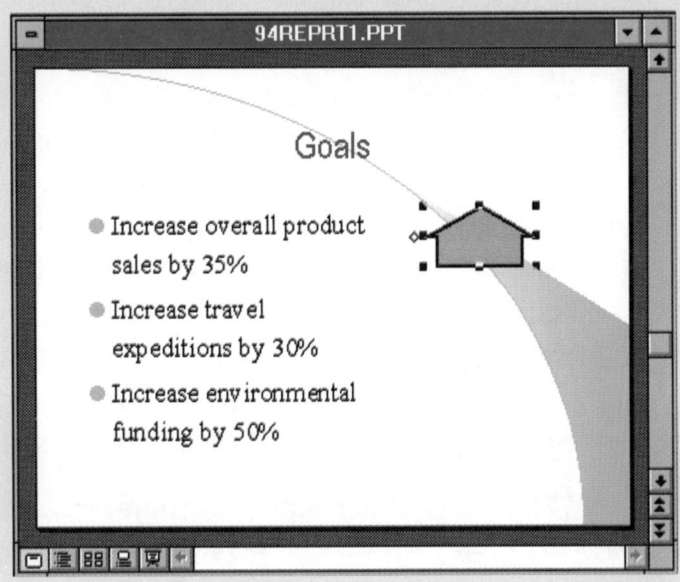

FIGURE 3-11:
Slide showing arrow objects

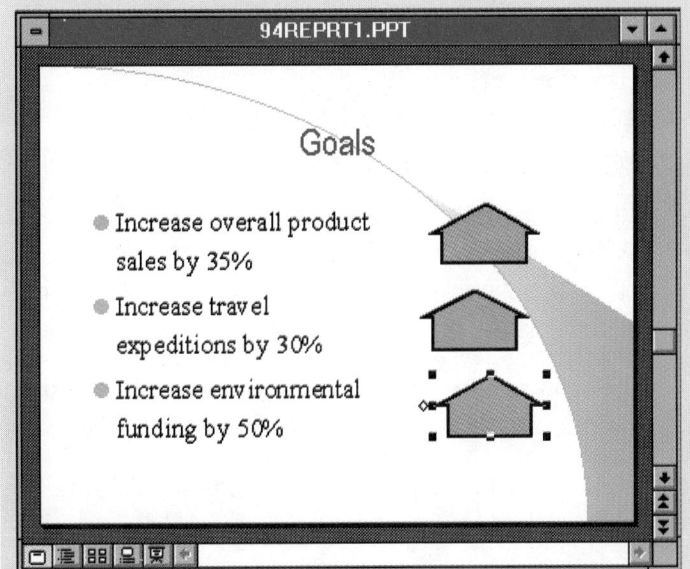

Rotating and flipping objects

Another way to change the appearance of an object is to rotate or flip it. To rotate or flip an object, select it, click Draw on the menu bar, click Rotate/Flip, then click one of the available menu commands, as shown in Figure 3-12.

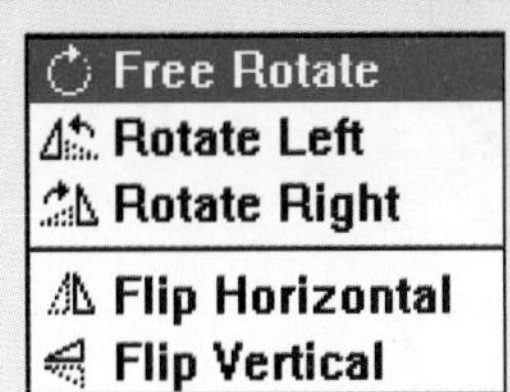

FIGURE 3-12: Rotate/Flip cascading menu

QUICK TIP

Be careful not to put too much information (text or graphics) on one slide. If possible, keep your slide text to 25 words or less.

Aligning and grouping objects

Aligning, Grouping, and Stacking Objects

After you create your objects, modify their appearance, and edit their shape and size, you can position them on the slide by aligning and grouping common objects together. The Align command aligns objects relative to each other by snapping the selected objects to an invisible grid of evenly spaced vertical or horizontal lines. You can also group objects into one object to make editing and moving much easier. In PowerPoint you can group, ungroup, or regroup objects. You can also position objects on top of each other. See the related topic "Object stacking order" for more information. ▶ Lynn aligns and groups the arrow objects and then copies and pastes the grouped object to the next slide.

1 Press **[Shift]** then click **each arrow object** to select all three
Lynn decides to leave the objects where they are on the slide but align them together vertically.

2 Click **Draw** on the menu bar, then click **Align**
A list of alignment options appears. The top three options align objects vertically, while the bottom three align objects horizontally. Lynn decides to align the arrow objects to their center.

3 Click **Centers**
The arrow objects align themselves to the center, as shown in Figure 3-13. Now, Lynn groups the objects together to maintain their exact spacing and position relative to each other.

4 Click **Draw** on the menu bar, then click **Group**
The arrow objects group together to form one object without losing their individual attributes. You can ungroup objects to restore each individual object. Lynn likes the arrow objects and decides to make a copy of them and paste them on the next slide.

5 Click the **arrow object** with the right mouse button
A shortcut menu opens, giving you access to common object commands.

6 Click **Copy** in the shortcut menu, then click the **Next Slide button**
The arrow object is copied to the Clipboard, and Slide 5 appears.

7 Click the **Paste button** on the Standard toolbar
The arrow object appears on Slide 5. Notice that the position of the pasted arrow object is the same as it was on Slide 4. Now, Lynn needs to change the text in the arrow objects to match the slide text.

8 Double-click the **top arrow object**, then type **53.4%**; double-click the **middle arrow object**, then type **26.9%**; double-click the **bottom arrow object**, type **6.3%**, then click outside the object to deselect it
Compare your screen to Figure 3-14.

FIGURE 3-13: Slide showing aligned arrow objects

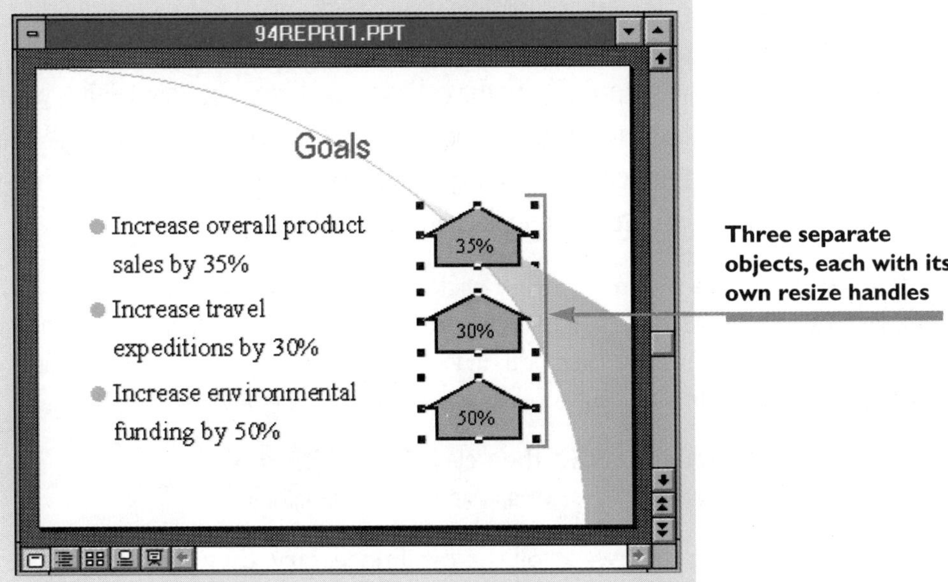

FIGURE 3-14: Slide 5 showing pasted arrow objects

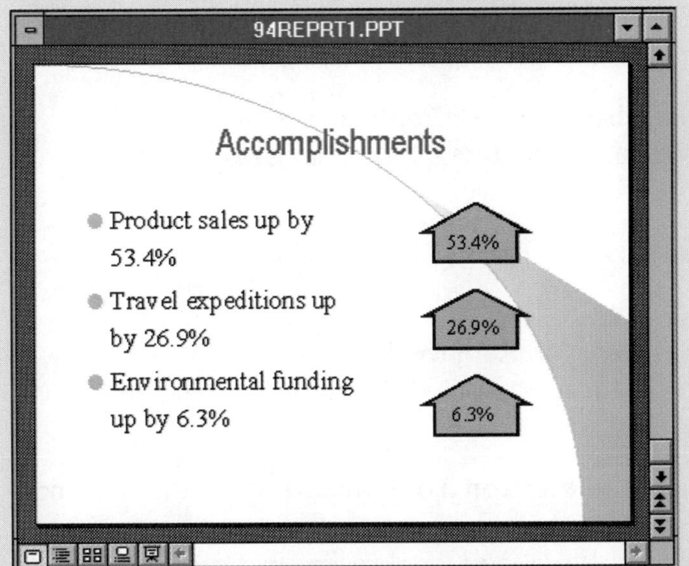

Object stacking order

A **stacking order** is how objects are placed on one another. The first object you draw is on the bottom of the stack. The last object you draw is on the top of the stack. You can change the order of the stack by using the Bring to Front, Send to Back, Bring Forward, and Send Backward commands located on the Draw menu. The stacking order of objects is important to know when you are working with layers of objects to achieve a certain look.

TROUBLE?

If the copy command on the shortcut menu is dimmed when you click the arrow object, move your pointer over the colored area of one of the arrows, not on the text, then click the right mouse button.

Replacing text

As you review your presentation, there might be certain words or fonts that you want to change or replace throughout the entire presentation. In PowerPoint, you can find and replace text case attributes, periods, words or sentences, and fonts. See the related topic "Changing text case and periods" for more information. ▶ Upon review of her work, Lynn decides to replace the slide title font and text.

1 Click **Tools** on the menu bar, then click **Replace Fonts**
The Replace Font dialog box opens. If text is selected before you open the Replace Font dialog box, the font used in the selected text appears in the Replace list box. If no text is selected, the font currently listed on the Formatting toolbar appears in the Replace list box.

2 Click the **Replace list arrow**, then click **Arial Narrow**
Arial Narrow, the font you want to replace, appears in the Replace list box.

3 Click the **With list arrow**, scroll the list if necessary, then click **Arial**
Compare your dialog box to Figure 3-15. PowerPoint will replace all of the Arial Narrow title text in your presentation with Arial when you click the Replace button.

4 Click **Replace** then click **Close**
PowerPoint replaces the title font and then closes the Replace Font dialog box. Now Lynn wants to change the word "Accomplishments" to "Achievements" throughout the presentation.

5 Click **Edit** on the menu bar, then click **Replace**
The Replace dialog box opens and displays the insertion point in the Find What text box, as shown in Figure 3-16.

6 Type **Accomplishments** then press **[Tab]**
Pressing [Tab] moves the insertion point to the Replace With text box. Now, type in the new word.

7 Type **Achievements** then click **Replace All**
PowerPoint replaces the word "Accomplishments" with "Achievements" in all views of your presentation.

8 Click **Close** then click the **Selection Tool button** on the Drawing toolbar
The Replace dialog box closes, and the title is deselected. Compare your screen to Figure 3-17.

FIGURE 3-15: Replace Font dialog box

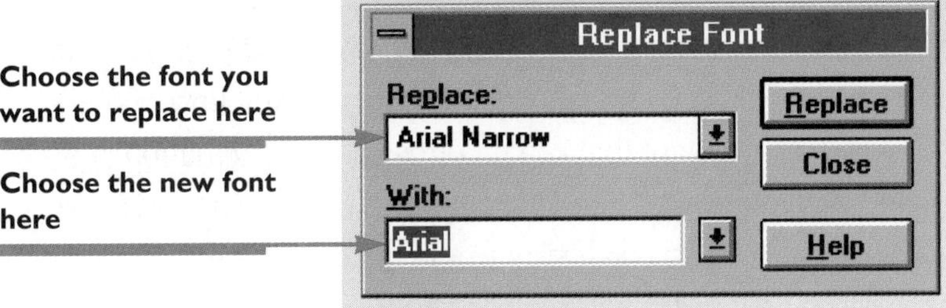

FIGURE 3-16: Replace dialog box

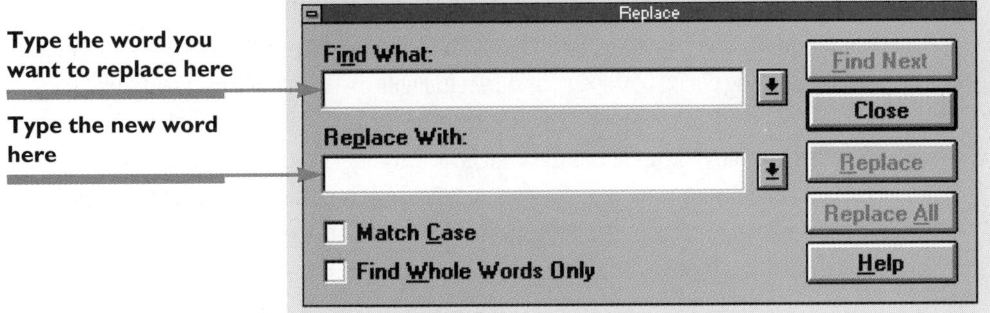

FIGURE 3-17: Slide with replaced title text

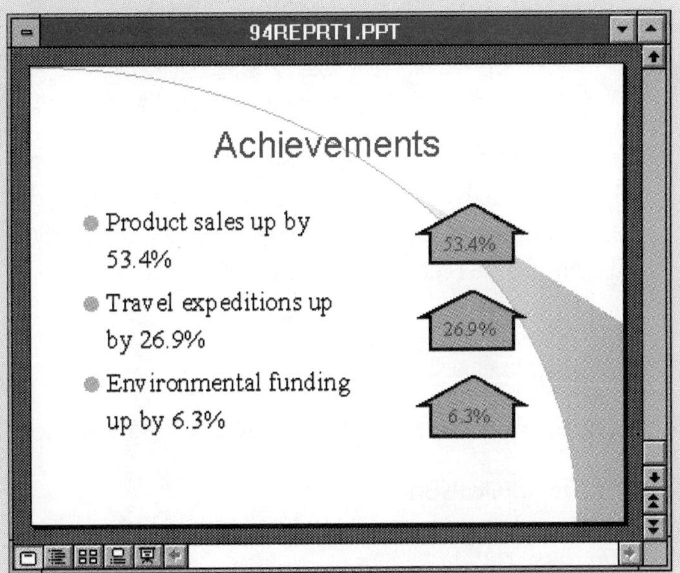

Changing text case and periods

Sometimes it is useful to change the text case of certain words or sentences in your presentation. Select the text object, click Format on the menu bar, then click Change Case to access all the text case options. PowerPoint also has a command to add or remove periods. If you add periods, PowerPoint places periods at the end of each sentence in your presentation. Click Format on the menu bar, then click Periods to access the Period dialog box.

Checking spelling

As your work nears completion, you need to review and proofread your presentation thoroughly for errors. You can check for spelling errors using PowerPoint's spell checker, but it is still important that you proofread it for punctuation and word usage errors. PowerPoint's spell checker recognizes misspelled words, not misused words. For example, the spell checker would not detect The Test even if you intended to type The Best. ▶ Lynn is finished adding and changing text in the presentation, so she checks the spelling.

1. **Click the Spelling button on the Standard toolbar**
   PowerPoint begins to check spelling. When PowerPoint finds a misspelled word or a word it doesn't recognize, the Spelling dialog box opens, as shown in Figure 3-18. In this case, PowerPoint does not recognize the president's last name on Slide 1 (if you made a typing error, another word might appear in this dialog box). Lynn knows the word is spelled correctly so she tells PowerPoint to ignore the word and continue through the presentation. You could also add this word to the dictionary so PowerPoint won't consider it misspelled. See the related topic "Adding words to the Custom dictionary" for more information.

2. Click **Ignore**
   The spell checker ignores the word. The spell checker finds the misspelled word "Outdor" on the same slide. Lynn doesn't want to ignore this word so she fixes the spelling.

3. Click **Outdoor** in the Suggestions list box, then click **Change**
   PowerPoint replaces the incorrect word and continues checking the presentation.

4. Continue checking the spelling in your presentation
   If PowerPoint finds another word it does not recognize, either change it or ignore it. When the spell checker is done checking your presentation, a Microsoft PowerPoint dialog box opens, indicating the spell checker is finished.

5. Click **OK**
   The dialog box closes.

6. Click **File** on the menu bar, click **Close**, then click **Yes** in the dialog box

7. Exit the application

FIGURE 3-18: Spelling dialog box

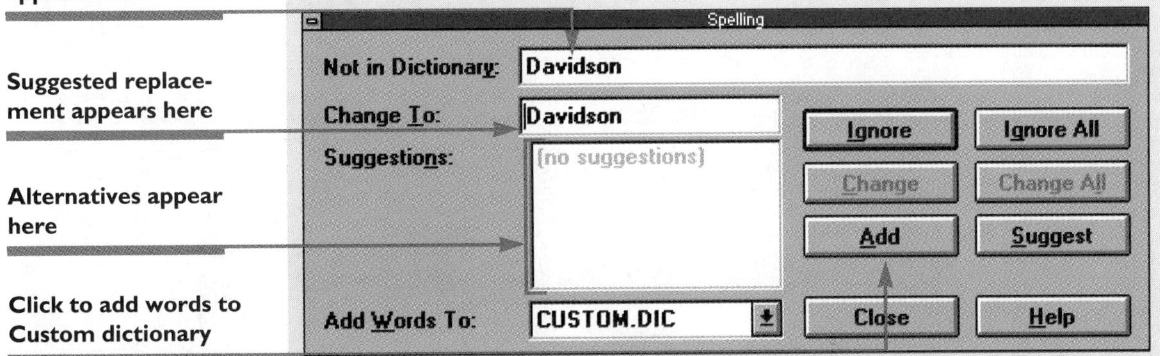

Adding words to the Custom dictionary

If there is a word you use all the time that is not included in PowerPoint's dictionary, add the word to the Custom dictionary by clicking Add in the Spelling dialog box when PowerPoint suggests the word is misspelled.

QUICK TIP

The PowerPoint spell checker does not check the text in pictures or embedded objects. You'll need to spell check text in imported objects using their original application.

CONCEPTS REVIEW

Label each of the elements of the PowerPoint window shown in Figure 3-19.

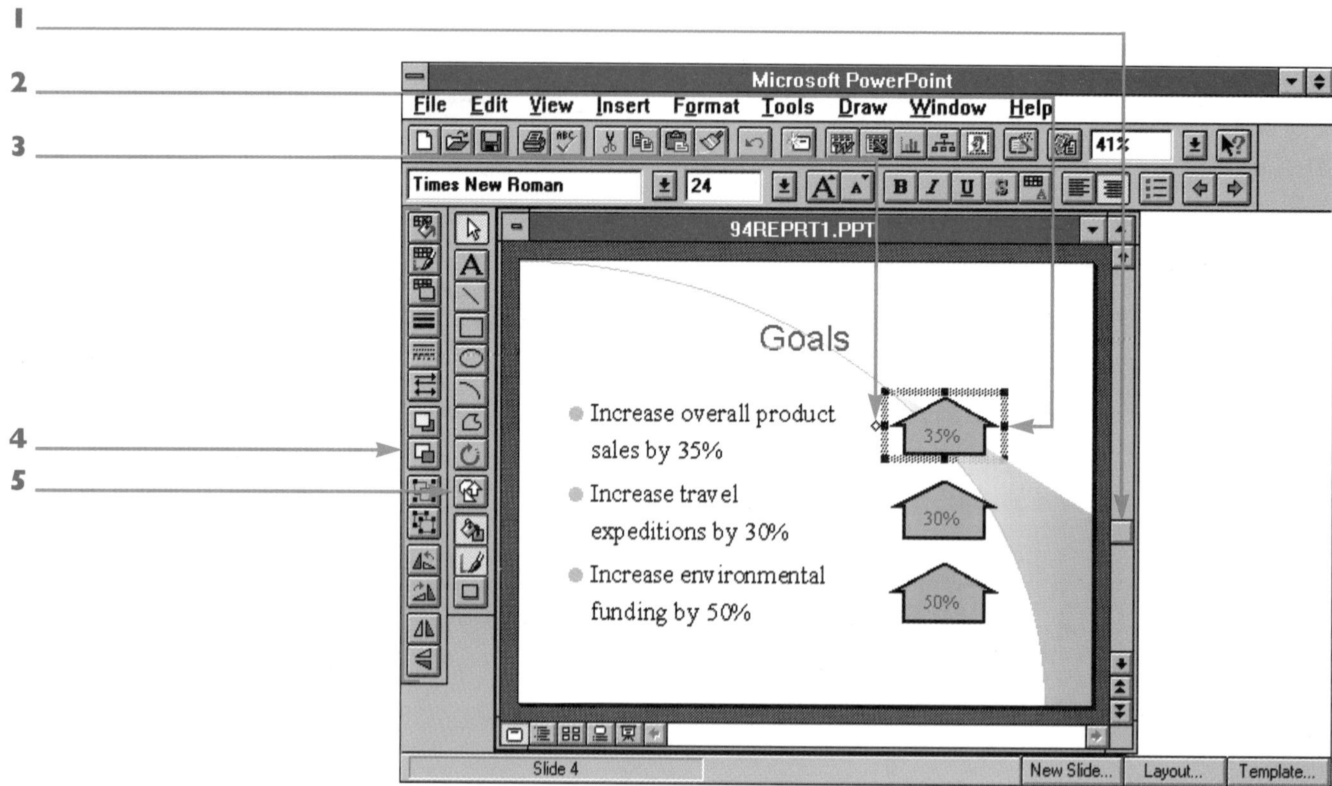

FIGURE 3-19

Match each of the terms with the statement that describes its function.

6 Turns a feature on and off

7 Use this to create a text object on a slide

8 Small box used to move between slides in the vertical scroll bar

9 A text object that does not word wrap

10 A text object you create by dragging a box with the Text tool

a. Elevator
b. Text label
c. Word processing box
d. Text tool
e. Toggle button

Select the best answer from the list of choices.

11 Saving a presentation using the Save As command
a. Opens a blank presentation
b. Saves a copy of the original presentation with a new name
c. Saves the original presentation
d. No different than the Save command

12 What objects can you create with the Text tool?
a. Text placeholder and text object
b. Word placeholder and text box
c. Text label and word processing box
d. Word processing label and text placeholder

13 You know a whole object is selected and can be moved when
a. A slanted line selection box with resize handles appears
b. An outline of the object appears
c. An object selection box appears
d. A dotted line selection box with resize handles appears

14 How do you change the shape of a PowerPoint object?
a. Move the size handle.
b. Move the resize button.
c. Move the adjustment handle.
d. You can't change the shape of a PowerPoint object.

15 All of the following statements about objects are true, EXCEPT:

a. You can add text to all objects.

b. You can resize the shape of objects.

c. You can adjust the dimension of an object.

d. You can copy and paste objects to different slides.

APPLICATIONS REVIEW

1 Open an existing presentation and save it with a new name.

a. Start PowerPoint from the Program Manager window.

b. Click the Blank Presentation radio button or click the Open button on the Standard toolbar.

c. Click the Drives list arrow, then select the drive containing your Student Disk.

d. Click UNIT_3-2.PPT in the File Name list box, then click OK.

e. Click File on the menu bar, then click Save As.

f. Click the Drives list arrow, then select the MY_FILES directory on your Student Disk.

g. Select the current filename, type PROGRESS in the File Name text box, then click OK. Click OK in the Summary Info box, if necessary.

2 Add a word processing box and arrange text.

a. Move to Slide 2 and click the Text Tool button on the Drawing toolbar.

b. Position the pointer near the bottom of the slide, then drag to create a box about 3" wide.

c. Type "Department product managers have 20 min. for line reports."

d. Double-click the word "product," then move it in front of the word "line."

e. Deselect the object.

3 Format text.

a. Press [Shift], then click the word processing box you just created to select it.

b. Click the Italic button on the Formatting toolbar to turn the italic attribute off.

c. Use the Text Color button on the Formatting toolbar to change the color of the text to red.

d. Use the Center Alignment button on the Formatting toolbar to center the text and then deselect the word processing box.

4 Draw and modify an object.

a. Move to Slide 3. If the AutoShapes toolbar is already visible, skip Step b.

b. Click the AutoShapes button on the Drawing toolbar.

c. Click the Seal Tool button on the AutoShapes toolbar, then hide the AutoShapes toolbar.

d. Position the pointer in the lower-right corner of the slide.

e. Press [Shift], then drag to create a seal shape about 1½" wide. Add the Drawing+ toolbar to your screen to change the shape attributes.

f. If the Drawing+ toolbar is not visible on your screen, move the pointer over a toolbar, click the right mouse button, then click Drawing+ in the shortcut menu.

g. Click the Fill Color button on the Drawing+ toolbar, then click the blue color cell.

h. Click the Line On/Off button and the Shadow On/Off button on the Drawing+ toolbar, then deselect the object.

i. Hide the Drawing+ toolbar.

5 Edit the shape and add text to objects.

a. Move to Slide 4 then click the arrow shape to select it.

b. Drag the right middle resize handle to the left about 1".

c. Drag the adjustment handle slightly to the right to change the shape of the arrow tip. Compare your arrow object to the arrows in Figure 3-20.

d. Make two copies of the arrow object by pressing [Ctrl] and dragging the arrow object. Try to put an even amount of space between the objects, as shown in Figure 3-20.

e. Double-click the left arrow object, then type "Teams"; double-click the middle arrow object, then type "Goals"; double-click the right arrow object, then type "Resources"; double-click the cube, type "OutBack," press [Enter], then type "Product."

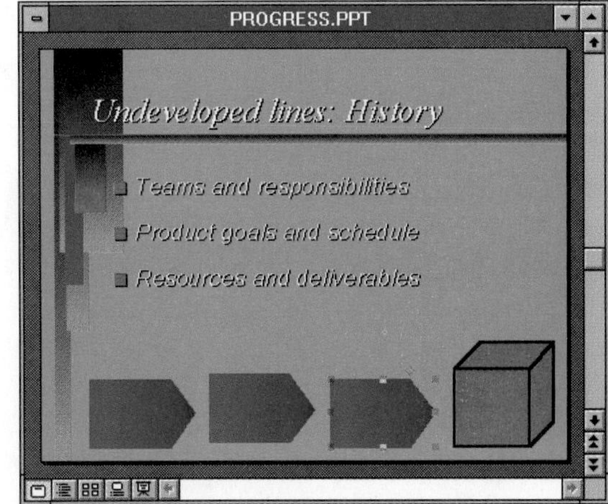

FIGURE 3-20

6 Align and group objects.
   a. Select all of the objects using the Shift key.
   b. Click Draw on the menu bar, then click Align.
   c. Click Bottoms in the list.
   d. Click Draw on the menu bar, then click Group.
   e. Press [Up Arrow] twice to move the grouped object.

7 Check spelling.
   a. Click the Spelling button on the Standard toolbar. The Spelling dialog box opens and begins to check the spelling of the presentation.
   b. Fix the misspelled word "Acomplishments," then continue through the presentation. The spell checker will stop on all words it doesn't recognize.
   c. When the spell checker finishes, click the Save button on the Standard toolbar, then click File on the menu bar.
   d. Print the presentation in Slide view and then close the presentation and exit PowerPoint.

INDEPENDENT CHALLENGE 1

The ABC Learning Company is a Silicon Valley-based corporation dedicated to the design and development of children's instructional software. As the company's main graphics designer, the marketing manager has asked you to design and develop a standardized set of graphics for the company that all the employeesccan use for their business presentations. To help promote the company, the marketing group unveiled a new company slogan: "Learning is easy as ABC."

Plan and create standard text and graphical objects for the ABC Learning Company that employees can copy and paste into their business presentations. Create three different slides with a company logo using the AutoShapes toolbar and a company slogan using the Text tool. The marketing group will decide which of the three designs looks best. Create your own presentation slides, but assume the following: the company colors are blue and red (from the default PowerPoint color scheme).

To complete this independent challenge:

1 Think about the results you want to see, the information you need to create this presentation, and the type of message you want to communicate.

2 Sketch a sample presentation on a piece of paper, indicating the presentation look and the layout of the information. What text and graphics are needed for the slides?

3 Create a new presentation by using the Blank Presentation option and choosing the Blank AutoLayout. Remember you are creating and entering your own presentation material. The logo and the marketing slogan should look good together and the logo objects should be grouped together to make it easier for other employees to copy and paste.

4 Save the presentation as ABCLRNNG.PPT in MY_FILES directory on your Student Disk. Before printing, look through the slides so you know what the presentation will look like. Adjust any items as needed, and print the slides.

5 Submit your presentation plan, preliminary sketches, and the final presentation printout.

INDEPENDENT CHALLENGE 2

You are the construction foreman for Zimmerman Engineering, a civil engineering and construction firm. One of your responsibilities is to create a process flow diagram for the construction team to follow during the building of a custom home. The process flow diagram describes the construction process from start to finish.

Plan and create a construction process flow diagram using PowerPoint's text and drawing tools. The diagram should include shapes, lines, and text labels to indicate the flow of information.

Create your own materials, but assume the following: the process includes planning, getting permits, ordering supplies, hiring subcontractors, building stages, and finishing work.

To complete this independent challenge:

1 Think about the results you want to see, the information you need to create this presentation, and the type of message you want to communicate.

2 Sketch a sample presentation on a piece of paper, indicating the presentation look and the layout of the information. What text and graphics are needed for the slides?

3 Create a new presentation by using the Blank Presentation option and choosing the Blank AutoLayout. Remember you are creating and entering your own presentation material. The diagram objects should be grouped together to make it easier for other employees to change.

4 Save the presentation as DIAGRAM.PPT in the MY_FILES directory on your Student Disk. Before printing, look through the slides so you know what the presentation will look like. Adjust any items as needed, and print the slides.

5 Submit your presentation plan, preliminary sketches, and the final presentation printout.

UNIT 4

OBJECTIVES

- Insert clip art
- Insert a graph
- Format a chart
- Work with an organizational chart
- Insert WordArt
- Work with a Slide Master
- Choose a color scheme
- Annotate slides during a slide show
- Use slide show special effects

Enhancing A PRESENTATION

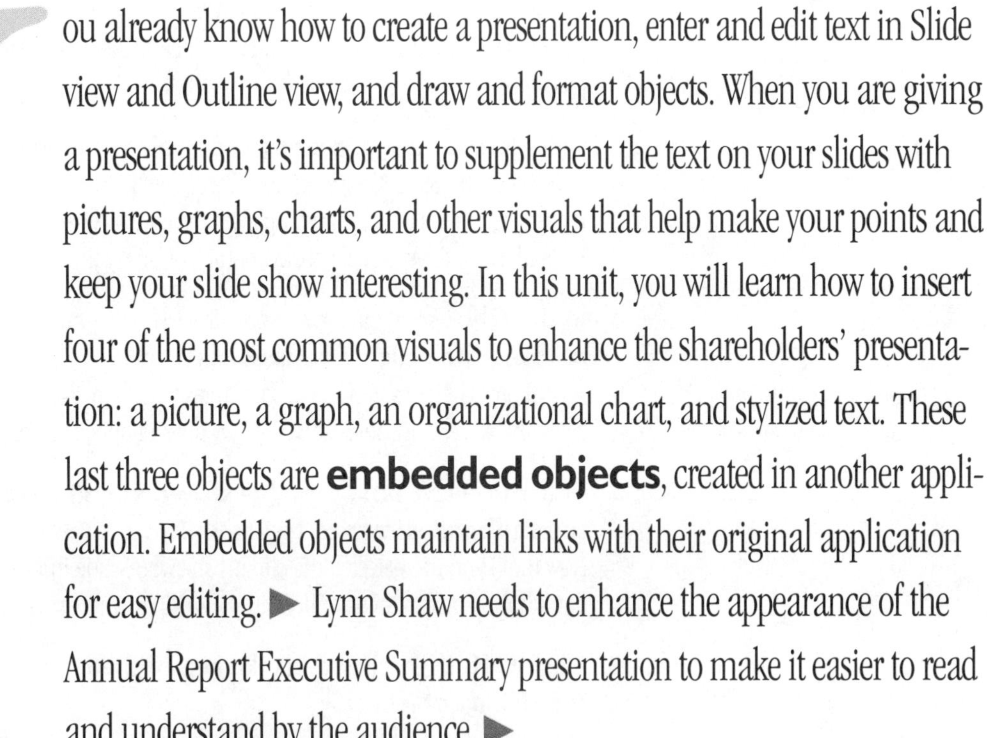

You already know how to create a presentation, enter and edit text in Slide view and Outline view, and draw and format objects. When you are giving a presentation, it's important to supplement the text on your slides with pictures, graphs, charts, and other visuals that help make your points and keep your slide show interesting. In this unit, you will learn how to insert four of the most common visuals to enhance the shareholders' presentation: a picture, a graph, an organizational chart, and stylized text. These last three objects are **embedded objects**, created in another application. Embedded objects maintain links with their original application for easy editing. ▶ Lynn Shaw needs to enhance the appearance of the Annual Report Executive Summary presentation to make it easier to read and understand by the audience. ▶

Inserting clip art

PowerPoint has over 1000 pieces of professionally designed pictures, called **clip art**, that you can import into your presentation. The clip art is stored in a file index system called a **gallery** that sorts all the clip art into categories. You can access the ClipArt Gallery in one of three ways: by double-clicking a clip art placeholder from an AutoLayout, using the Insert Clip Art button on the Standard toolbar, or choosing Clip Art from the Insert menu. You can modify PowerPoint clip art like other PowerPoint objects; for example, you can change the shape, size, fill, shading, and all other clip art style attributes. ▶ In this lesson, Lynn opens the presentation she has been working on and adds a picture from the ClipArt Gallery to one of the slides.

1. **Start PowerPoint and open the presentation UNIT_4-1.PPT from your Student Disk, save it as 94FNLRPT.PPT to the MY_FILES directory on your Student Disk, then click OK to close the Summary Info dialog box**
2. **Click the Next Slide button**
   Lynn uses PowerPoint's AutoLayout feature to add a piece of clip art to Slide 2.
3. **Click the Layout button** Layout... **on the status bar**
   The Slide Layout dialog box opens with the Bulleted List AutoLayout selected. Lynn selects the Text and Clip Art AutoLayout, which will keep the text object already on the slide intact and insert a placeholder for the clip art.
4. **Click the Text and Clip Art AutoLayout, as shown in Figure 4-1, then click Apply**
   PowerPoint applies the Text and Clip Art AutoLayout to the slide by moving the existing text object to the left and inserting a placeholder, which identifies where the clip art object will be placed on the slide.
5. **Double-click the clip art placeholder, then click Yes if necessary**
   The Microsoft ClipArt Gallery dialog box opens. The first time you open the ClipArt Gallery, PowerPoint needs to build and organize the clip art visual index. Click Yes to build the index. Depending on the speed of your computer, building the gallery index could take up to 15 minutes.
6. **In the Choose a category to view below section, drag the scroll box to the bottom, then click Transportation**
   The ClipArt Gallery's Preview box changes to display the available clip art in the Transportation category. If the Transportation category doesn't appear, select a different category.
7. **In the Preview box, click the down scroll arrow several times, then click the sailboat shown in Figure 4-2**
   Now that Lynn has selected the clip art she wants, she imports the clip art to her slide. If you don't have a picture of a sailboat in your ClipArt Gallery, select a similar picture.
8. **Click OK, then click a blank area of the Presentation window to deselect the clip art object**
   The picture of the sailboat is placed on the right side of the slide in the AutoLayout.

FIGURE 4-1: Slide Layout dialog box

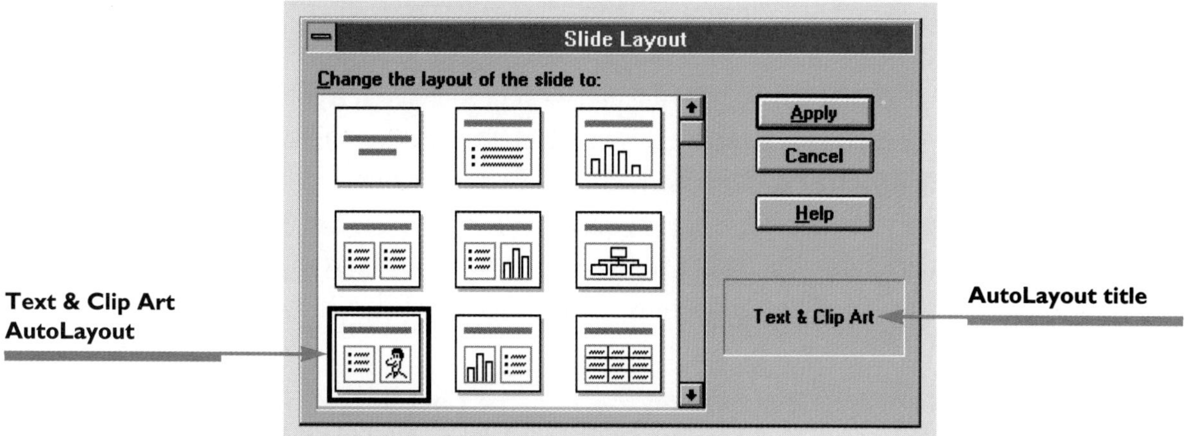

FIGURE 4-2: Microsoft ClipArt Gallery dialog box

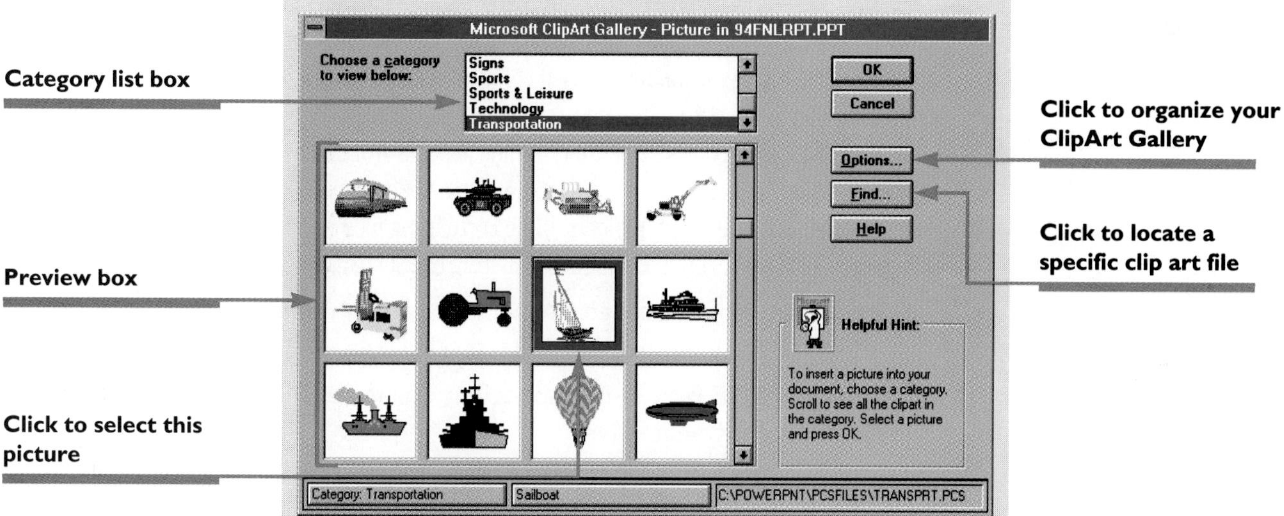

Organizing the ClipArt Gallery

Click the Options button in the Microsoft ClipArt Gallery dialog box to organize your ClipArt Gallery. The Options dialog box opens, letting you add new clip art to the gallery (Add button), rename or delete categories (Change a Category button), and edit the descriptions of the currently selected picture (Edit Picture Information button). Notice in Figure 4-2 that the description of the selected clip art appears on the status bar of the dialog box.

QUICK TIP

Click the Find button in the Microsoft ClipArt Gallery dialog box to locate a specific clip art file. See Figure 4-2.

Inserting a graph

PowerPoint includes an application called Microsoft Graph, referred to as Graph, which you use to create a graph for your slides. A **graph** is made up of two components; a **datasheet**, which contains the information you want to display, and a **chart**, which is the graphical representation of the datasheet. You can create your own graph by entering data into a Graph datasheet or you can import data from a Microsoft Excel worksheet. ▶ Follow Lynn as she imports a Microsoft Excel worksheet containing company revenue information that she needs to make into a PowerPoint graph.

1 **Drag the elevator to Slide 6, click the Layout button [Layout...], click the Graph AutoLayout (in the upper-right corner of the Slide Layout dialog box), then click Apply**
A graph placeholder replaces the bulleted list on the slide.

2 **Double-click the graph placeholder**
Graph starts and displays a default datasheet and chart. The default datasheet appears with datasheet titles along the top row and left column, such as 1st Qtr and East, and datasheet numbers below and to the right of the titles, such as 20.4 in cell A1 (a **cell** is the intersection of a row and a column). A black selection rectangle appears around a cell, indicating it is an **active cell**—selected and ready to accept data. Notice that the PowerPoint toolbars have been replaced with the Graph toolbars. If the Formatting toolbar doesn't appear, click View on the menu bar, click Toolbars, click the Formatting check box, then click OK.

3 **Click the first cell (upper-left corner) in the datasheet**
This indicates where the imported data will appear in the datasheet.

4 **Click the control box in the upper-left corner of the Datasheet window to select the entire datasheet**
Control boxes are the gray boxes located along the edges of the datasheet, as shown in Figure 4-3. The control boxes label the rows and columns in the datasheet. Clicking a row or column control box selects that entire row or column of data. Table 4-1 describes how to select and move around the datasheet.

5 **Click Edit on the menu bar, click Clear, then click All**
The default datasheet contents are deleted.

6 **Click the Import Data button on the Graph Standard toolbar**
The Import Data dialog box opens.

7 **In the File Name list box, click the worksheet UNIT_4-2.XLS from your Student Disk, click OK, then click any cell to deselect the datasheet**
The Excel data appears in the datasheet displaying Nomad sales data for the last three years. See Figure 4-4. You can click an individual cell and then type to enter data, or double-click an individual cell to edit its contents.

8 **Click the View Datasheet button on the Graph Standard toolbar**
The View Datasheet button toggles the datasheet off and out of view.

9 **Click a blank area of the Presentation window to exit Graph, then click a blank area again to deselect the graph object**
The PowerPoint toolbars and menu appear. Compare your slide to Figure 4-5.

FIGURE 4-3: Datasheet and chart in the PowerPoint window

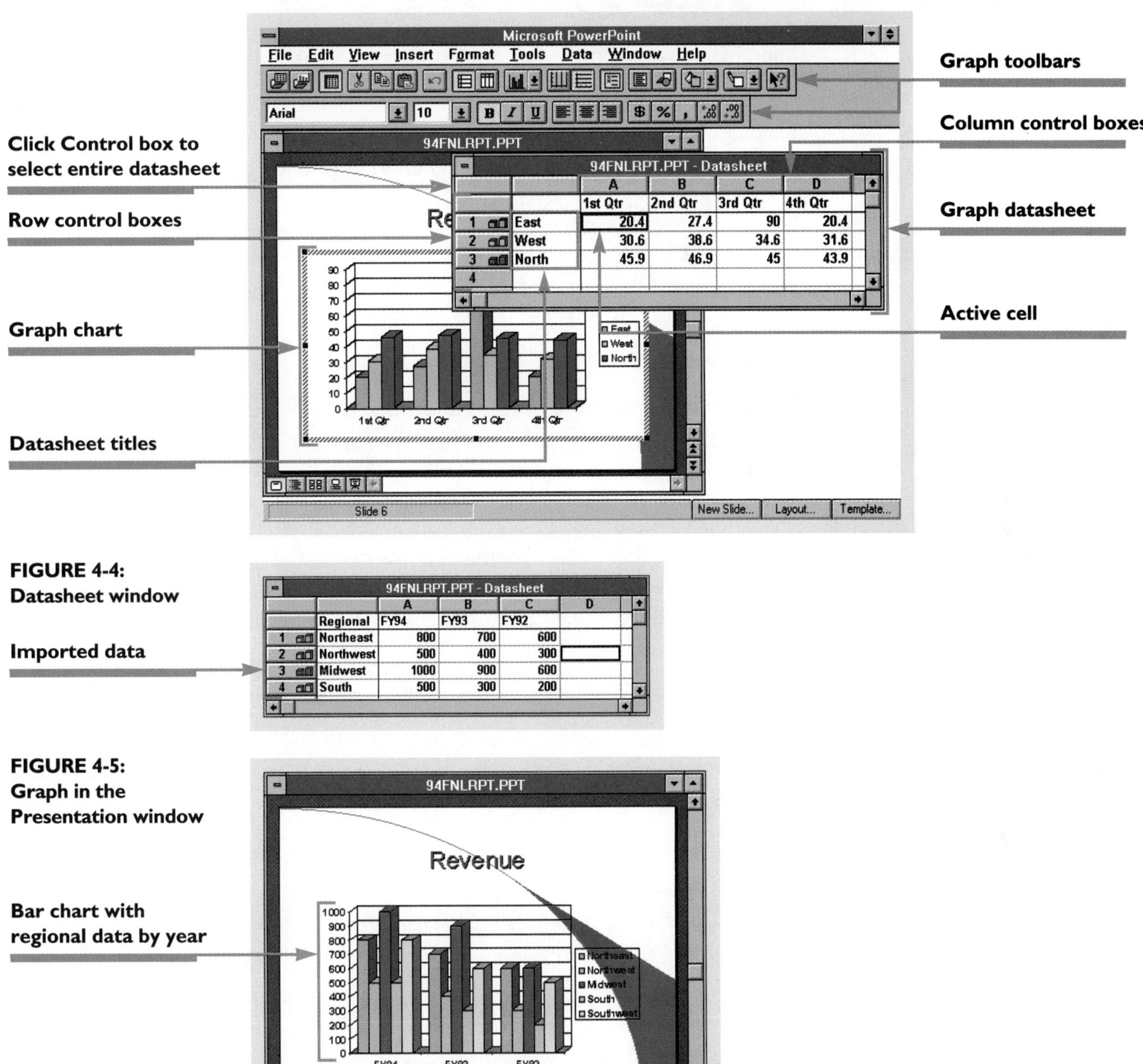

FIGURE 4-4: Datasheet window

FIGURE 4-5: Graph in the Presentation window

TABLE 4-1: Getting around the datasheet

TASK	ACTION
Select a specific cell	Click the specific cell
Select a range of cells	Click the upper-left cell then drag to the lower-right cell of the range
Select a column or row	Click the column or row control box
Select the entire datasheet	Click the upper-left corner control box

TROUBLE?

When the Graph toolbars are present, you are working in Graph. Clicking outside the graph object returns you to the Presentation window.

Formatting a chart

Graph lets you change the appearance of the chart to emphasize certain aspects of the information you are presenting. You can change the way the chart appears, create titles, format the chart labels, move the legend, or add arrows. ▶ Lynn wants to improve the appearance of her chart by displaying the data by region, formatting the x and y axes, and inserting a title.

1 Double-click the **graph object**
Graph opens and displays Lynn's chart from the previous lesson. The chart currently displays the data by year, FY94, FY93, FY92 (the rows in the datasheet). Lynn wants to change the chart to display the data by region (the columns in the datasheet).

2 Click the **By Column button** on the Graph Standard toolbar
The chart changes to display the data by region. Now Lynn wants to display the y-axis numbers in currency format with dollar signs ($).

3 Click the **sales numbers** on the y-axis, then click the **Currency Style button** on the Graph Formatting toolbar
The sales numbers change to include dollar signs, decimal points, and zeroes. Lynn doesn't like the look of the zeroes to the right of the decimal point so she decides to remove them.

4 Click the **Decrease Decimal button** on the Graph Formatting toolbar twice
The zeroes to the right of the decimal point are removed from the numbers. Lynn notices that not all the region names are displayed on the x-axis, so she decides to decrease the font size to make sure all the region names fit in the space provided.

5 Click the **region names** on the x-axis, click **Format** on the menu bar, then click **Selected Axis**
The Format Axis dialog box opens, which lets you format the pattern, scale, font, number, or alignment of the selected axis by clicking different tabs in the dialog box.

6 Click the **Font tab**, click **14** in the Size list box, as shown in Figure 4-6, then click **OK**
The font size changes from 18 points to 14 points for all the labels on the x-axis. Now Lynn adds a title to the chart.

7 Click **Insert** on the menu bar, click **Titles**, click the **Chart Title check box**, then click **OK**
A selected text object appears with the word "Title." Lynn enters the chart title.

8 Type **Annual Sales Figures by Region**, then click below the chart title
If you make a mistake while typing, press [Backspace]. Clicking outside the chart title deselects the title, so you can work on other parts of the graph. After completing the chart, Lynn exits Graph.

9 Click a blank area of the Presentation window to exit Graph, then click a blank area again to deselect the graph object
The PowerPoint toolbars and menu appear. Compare your slide to Figure 4-7. Don't worry if the legend is hard to see. You will correct this later in this Unit.

FIGURE 4-6: Format Axis dialog box

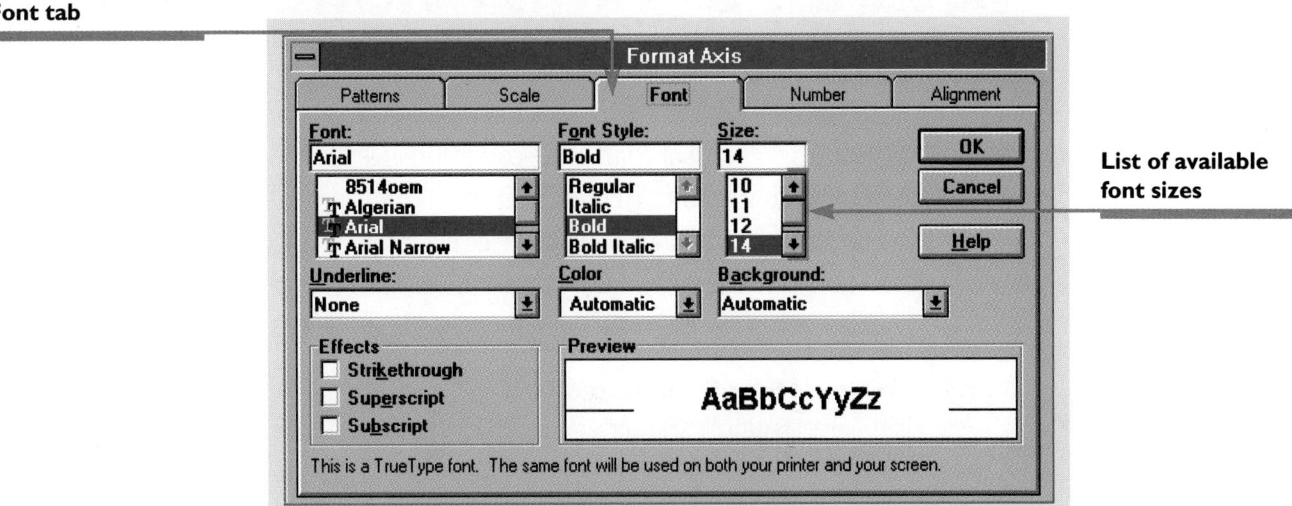

FIGURE 4-7: Slide with chart

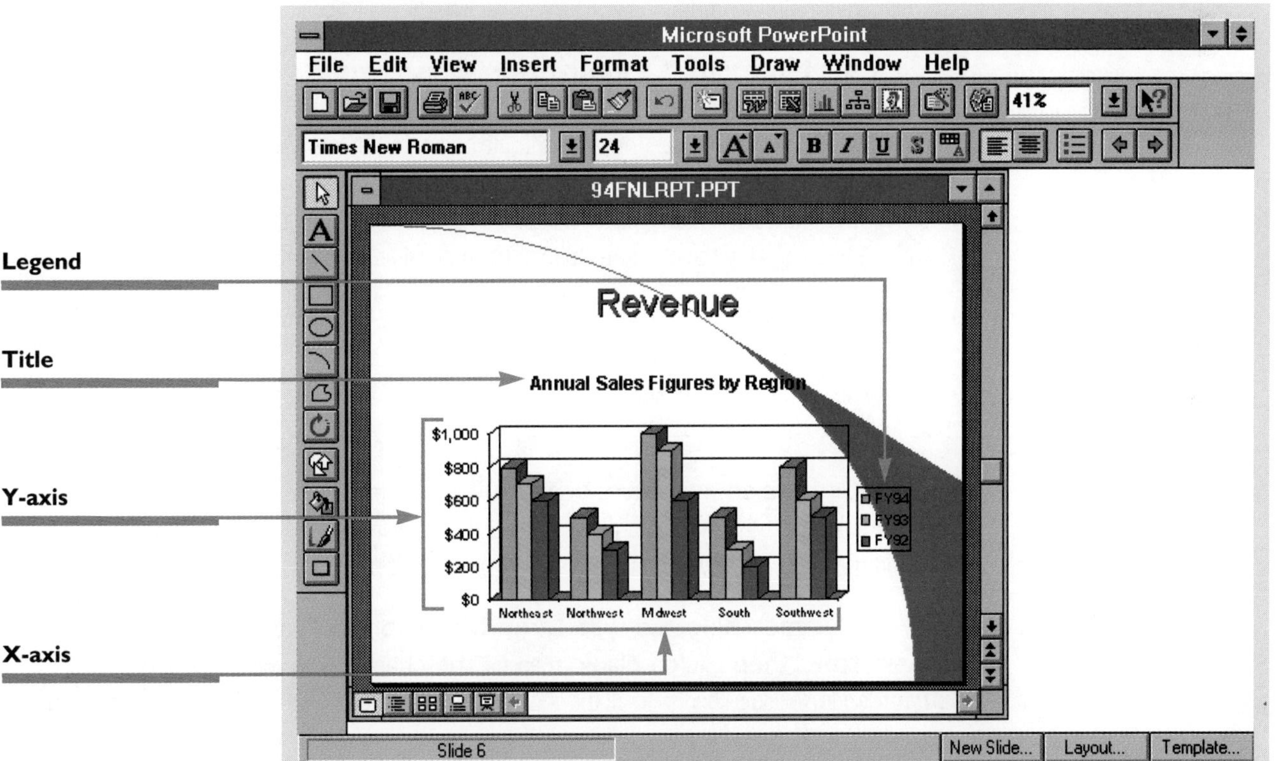

Changing graph formats

You can choose from among a number of formats for your graph. There are 12 graph categories, including two-dimensional graphs and three-dimensional graphs, for a total of 84 different formats. Click the Chart Type list arrow on the Graph Standard toolbar, and then select a chart type, such as Area, Bar, Column, Line, Pie, and Surface, from the list. To change a chart format quickly and easily, use the AutoFormat command on the Format menu.

QUICK TIP

Double-clicking any item in the Graph chart opens an editing dialog box for that item.

Working with an organizational chart

When you give presentations for the company you work for, often it's helpful to show graphically the organizational structure of your company. An **organizational chart** is a diagram of chart boxes connected together by lines that indicate a company's reporting structure. PowerPoint provides an application called Microsoft Organization Chart that you use to create chart boxes, enter chart text, and format chart boxes. ▶ The current organizational chart for Nomad Ltd needs to be updated since last year's meeting. Lynn adds her name to the current organizational chart.

1. **Click the Next Slide button**
   Slide 7 appears with Nomad's organizational chart from 1994. To edit the organizational chart, double-click the object just as you did with Graph.
2. **Double-click the organizational chart**
   The Nomad Ltd organizational chart appears in a separate window called the Microsoft Organization Chart window.
3. **Click the Microsoft Organization Chart window maximize button**
   The chart from the previous year displays the president's name, Bill Davidson, in a manager chart box. Below that box are four subordinate boxes for the four division officers who report to him. The toolbar offers five different chart box types: subordinate, co-worker (to the right), co-worker (to the left), manager, and assistant. Each of the buttons includes a small chart box with a line indicating the relationship to another chart box. Lynn adds an assistant chart box.
4. **Click the Assistant button** Assistant: **on the Org Chart Standard toolbar, then click the Bill Davidson chart box**
   A blank assistant chart box appears between the Bill Davidson's chart box and the next level of subordinate chart boxes.
5. **Click the Assistant chart box you just added**
   The blank chart box opens with placeholder text for <Name>, <Title>, <Comment 1>, and <Comment 2>, as shown in Figure 4-8. Lynn enters her name and title in the blank chart box.
6. **With <Name> selected type Lynn Shaw, press [Tab], type Executive Assistant, then click a blank area of the chart window**
   Lynn decides to add a shadow to all the chart boxes to enhance the look of the organizational chart.
7. **Click Edit on the menu bar, click Select, then click All**
   Lynn uses the Select command to quickly and accurately select all the chart boxes.
8. **Click Boxes on the menu bar, click Box Shadow, click the shadow option shown in Figure 4-9, then click a blank area of the chart window**
   Compare your screen to Figure 4-10. After making all the changes, Lynn exits and returns back to the Presentation window.
9. **Click File on the menu bar, click Exit and Return to 94FNLRPT.PPT, then click Yes to update the presentation**
   Microsoft Organization Chart updates the PowerPoint slide with the new organizational chart.

FIGURE 4-8: Blank chart box

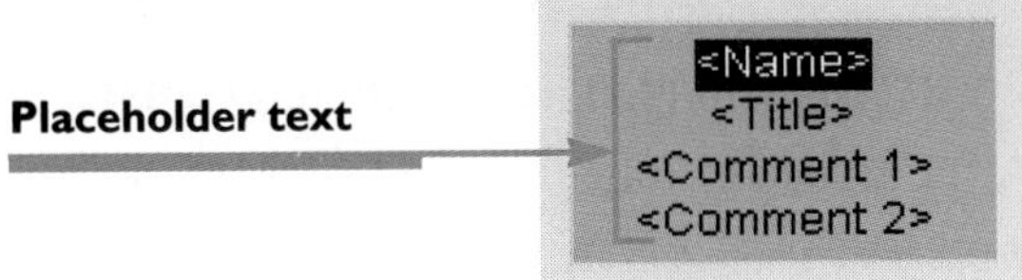

FIGURE 4-9: Box shadow options

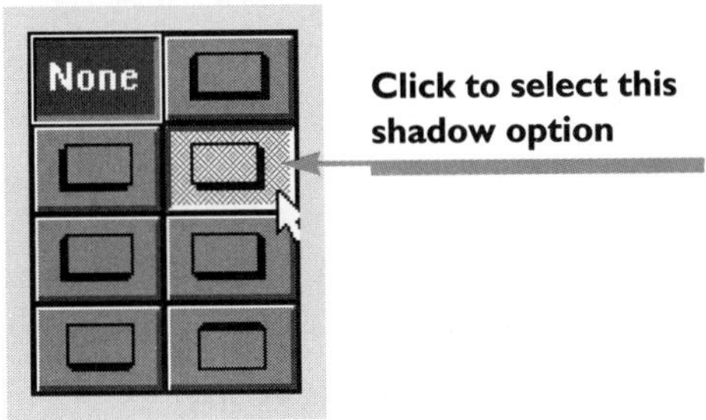

FIGURE 4-10: Slide with new organizational chart

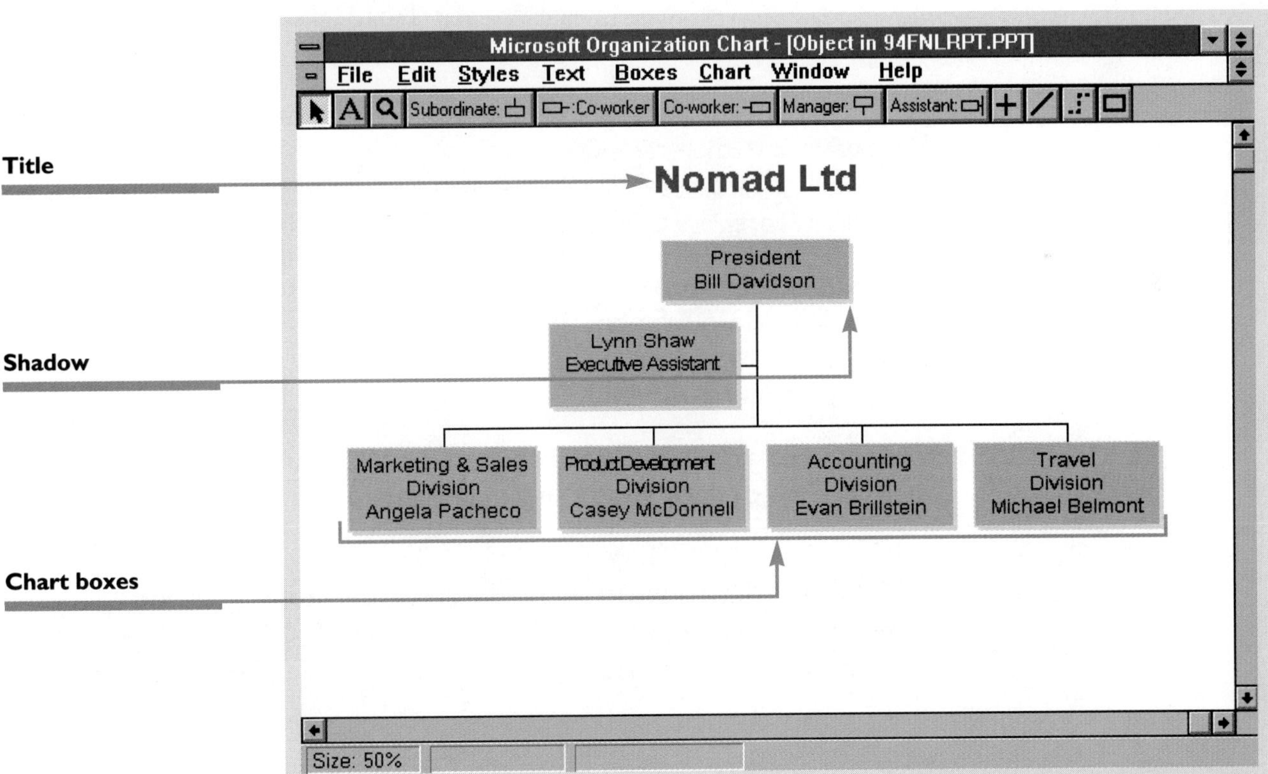

You can move a chart box to a new location by dragging it.■

Inserting WordArt

You can insert fancy or stylized text in your presentation with Microsoft WordArt. The objects you create in WordArt are embedded in your slide, and you can move and edit them like other PowerPoint objects. You can format text in a variety of shapes, create unusual alignments, and add 3-D effects using any TrueType font installed on your system. A **TrueType font** is a type of font that can be displayed or printed at any size. ▶ The president wants to end the presentation with a question and answer session. Lynn uses WordArt to enhance the last slide.

1. **Click the Next Slide button**
   Slide 8 appears. Because Lynn is going to place WordArt on this slide, she changes the slide layout to accommodate an object.

2. **Click the Layout button, click the down scroll arrow, click the Object AutoLayout, then click Apply**
   An object placeholder replaces the bulleted list on the slide.

3. **Double-click the object placeholder**
   The Insert Object dialog box opens, displaying a list of object types, from which Lynn chooses Microsoft WordArt 2.0.

4. **In the Object Type list box, click the down scroll arrow, click Microsoft WordArt 2.0, then click OK**
   WordArt starts and displays the Enter Your Text Here dialog box with sample text already selected. Notice that the PowerPoint toolbars have been replaced with the WordArt toolbar.

5. **Type Questions, press [Enter], type &, press [Enter], type Answers, then click Update Display**
   The WordArt text appears in the Presentation window. Lynn enhances the text using WordArt's powerful formatting options.

6. **Click the Format Text list arrow on the WordArt Formatting toolbar, then click the deflate shape shown in Figure 4-11**
   The text in the window changes to match the selected symbol. Lynn continues by shading the text.

7. **Click the Shading button on the Formatting toolbar, click the Foreground list arrow, click Fuchsia, then click OK.**
   The foreground color of the text changes from black to fuchsia. Lynn decides to add a shadow to the text.

8. **Click the Shadow button on the Formatting toolbar, then click the second symbol in the top row, as shown in Figure 4-12**
   A shadow appears behind the text. After completing the text styling, Lynn exits WordArt.

9. **Click a blank area of the Presentation window to exit WordArt, then deselect the WordArt object**
   The PowerPoint toolbars and menu appear. Compare your screen with Figure 4-13.

FIGURE 4-11: Format Text list

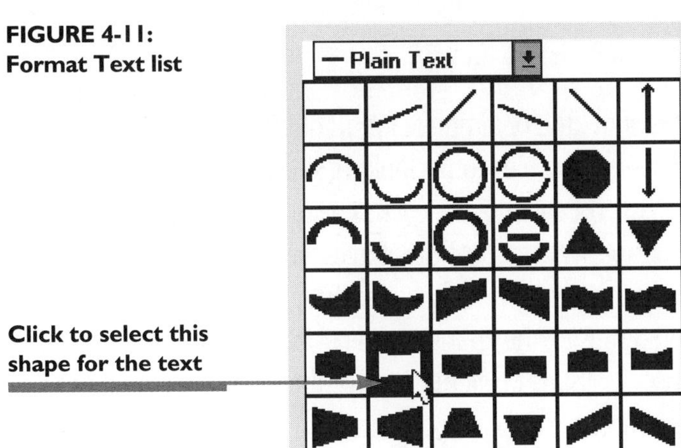

Click to select this shape for the text

FIGURE 4-12: Shadow list

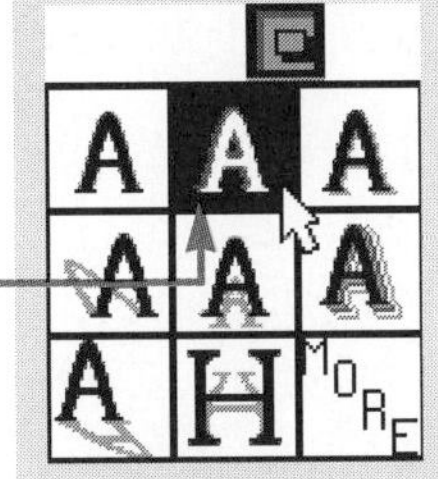

Click to select this text shadow option

FIGURE 4-13: Slide text enhanced with WordArt

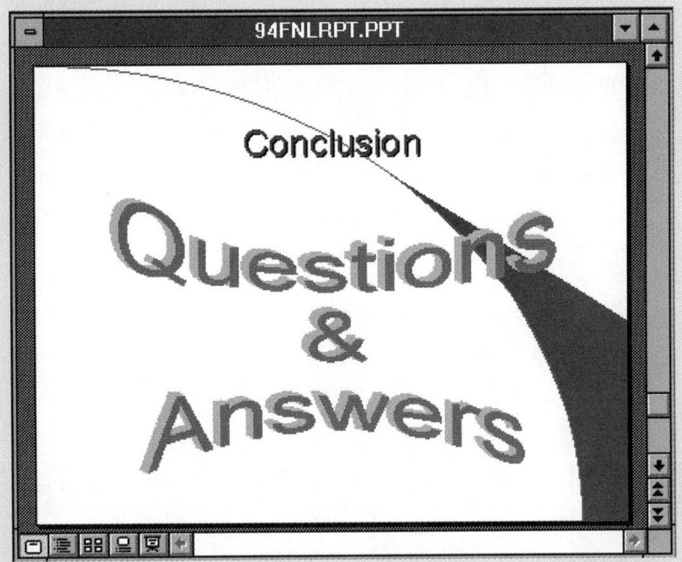

Using other presentation media

Just as you inserted Microsoft WordArt, you can also insert and play sounds and movies during your presentations. From the Insert Object dialog box, click Sound or Media Clip, then click OK. The Sound Recorder or Media Clip dialog box opens. Insert or open a file with the appropriate media type. When you are finished playing or modifying the media, exit back into PowerPoint. For sounds, a small sound icon appears, while for movies, a small screen with the first frame appears on the presentation slide. Use the Play Setting command from the Tools menu to play the sound or movie on a slide or during a slide show.

QUICK **TIP**

Use the Rotation and Effects command on the WordArt Format menu to add other special effects.

Working with a Slide Master

PowerPoint uses **masters**, a kind of template for all of the slides in the presentation, to help create consistent and professional-looking slides, audience handouts, and speaker's notes pages. Each PowerPoint view has a corresponding master—Slide Master for Slide view, Notes Master for Notes Pages view, Handout Master for Slide Sorter view, and Outline Master for Outline view. When you add an object or change the text format on a master, the changes appear in each slide in the corresponding view. ▶ Lynn uses the Slide Master to change the bullet type in all her slides and then adds the company's logo to appear in each slide of the presentation.

1. **Drag the elevator to Slide 2**
   Lynn switches to Slide 2 to make it easier to view her Slide Master changes.
2. **Click View on the menu bar, click Master, then click Slide Master**
   The status bar changes from Slide 2 to Slide Master. The Slide Master appears with the **master title placeholder** and the **master text placeholder**, as shown in Figure 4-14. The placeholders control the format of the title and main text objects for each slide.
3. **Click anywhere in the first line of text in the master text placeholder**
   The insertion point appears. PowerPoint applies any change you make to the line of text containing the insertion point to every corresponding line in the presentation. Lynn changes the round bullet on the first line of text to a checkmark.
4. **Click Format on the menu bar, click Bullet, then click the checkmark, as shown in Figure 4-15**
   This selects the checkmark as the new bullet. Because the size of the previous round bullet is larger than the checkmark, Lynn decides to increase the size of the checkmark from 75% to 100%.
5. **Click the Size % of Text up arrow until the percentage reaches 100, then click OK**
   The bullet in the first line of text changes from a round bullet to a checkmark. Lynn now inserts the company's logo.
6. **Click Insert on the menu bar, then click Picture**
   The Insert Picture dialog box opens.
7. **Click UNIT_4-6.TIF from the drive your Student Disk is in, then click OK**
   The Nomad Ltd logo appears on the Slide Master. Lynn decides to move the logo to an open place on the Slide Master.
8. **Drag the logo to the upper-left corner of the slide**
   The Nomad Ltd logo appears in the Slide Master. Lynn wants to see how the changes to the Slide Master affect her slides.
9. **Click the Slide View button**
   In Slide view, you can see the changes, as shown in Figure 4-16. You can continue to click the Next Slide button to see changes on each slide.

FIGURE 4-14: Slide Master

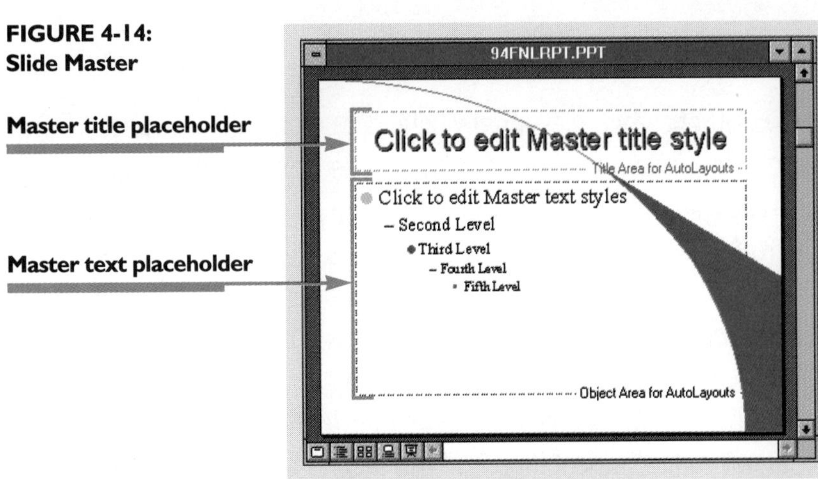

Master title placeholder

Master text placeholder

FIGURE 4-15: Bullet dialog box

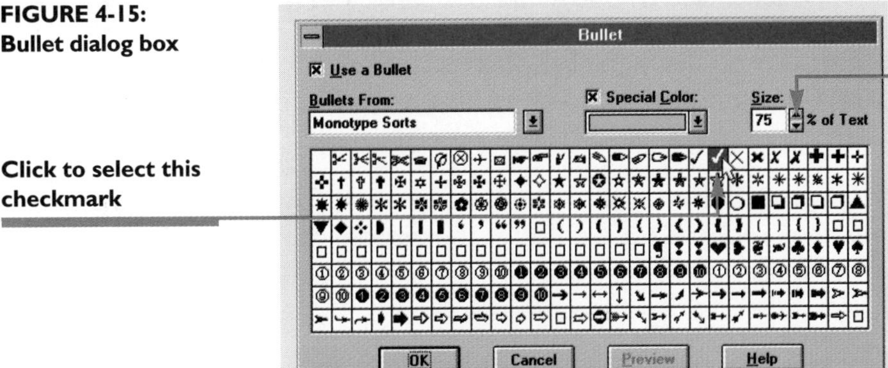

Size % of Text up arrow

Click to select this checkmark

FIGURE 4-16: Slide view

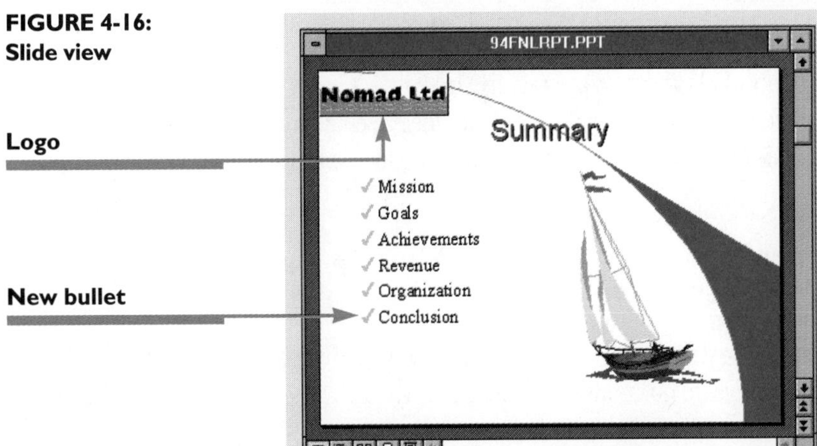

Logo

New bullet

Scaling and cropping pictures

When you insert a picture, sometimes you need to scale or crop the picture to create a desired look. **Scaling** means resizing a picture or object by a certain percentage. You can either use the resize handles on each corner of an object or the Scale command, which lets you resize an object mathematically instead of dragging its resize handles. Sometimes you only need a portion of a picture in your presentation. With the Crop Picture command, you can drag a resize handle using the Cropping tool to cover portions of a picture so you don't see all of it on the screen.

QUICK TIP

Press and hold [Shift] then click a view button to switch to the corresponding master.■

Choosing a color scheme

PowerPoint uses sets of eight professionally balanced colors called **color schemes** to help you take the guess work out of deciding which colors look good together. The color schemes determine the main colors in your presentation for slide background, text and lines, title text, shadows, fills, and accents. See Table 4-2 for color descriptions. You can create your own professional looking color schemes using the combinations of colors suggested by the Choose Scheme dialog box. You can also reuse color schemes without having to re-create them. See the related topic "Copying color schemes" for more information. ▶ The president wants to give an on-screen presentation, so Lynn decides to change the color scheme and add a shaded background to enhance the presentation for the screen.

1. Click **Format** on the menu bar, then click **Slide Color Scheme**
   The Slide Color Scheme dialog box opens, displaying the current color scheme. Lynn wants to choose a new color scheme using the Choose Scheme dialog box.
2. Click **Choose Scheme**, click the **Background Color down scroll arrow**, then click the **blue color** at the bottom of the list
   Now the background of all Lynn's slides will be blue. She next selects a complementary text and line color from the list of choices that appears.
3. Click the **white color** in the Text & Line Color list box, then click the **color scheme** in the upper-right corner of the Other Scheme Colors section
   Selecting a text and line color displays a gallery of four alternative color schemes. See Figure 4-17.
4. Click **OK** then click **Apply to All** in the Slide Color Scheme dialog box
   The new color scheme is applied to all the slides in the presentation. To apply the color scheme to the current slide only, you would click Apply. Lynn decides to add a shaded background to all the slides.
5. Click **Format** on the menu bar, then click **Slide Background**
   The Slide Background dialog box opens.
6. In the Shade Styles section, click the **Horizontal radio button**
   The shade style changes to horizontal, and four shade variants appear. Lynn uses the selected shade variant, but she wants a lighter shade.
7. Click the **Light scroll arrow** twice
   The shade variant lightens. Lynn decides to apply the shaded background, as shown in Figure 4-18, to all the slides.
8. Click **Apply to All**, then click the **Previous Slide button** to view the changes
   The new slide background is applied to all the slides in the presentation.

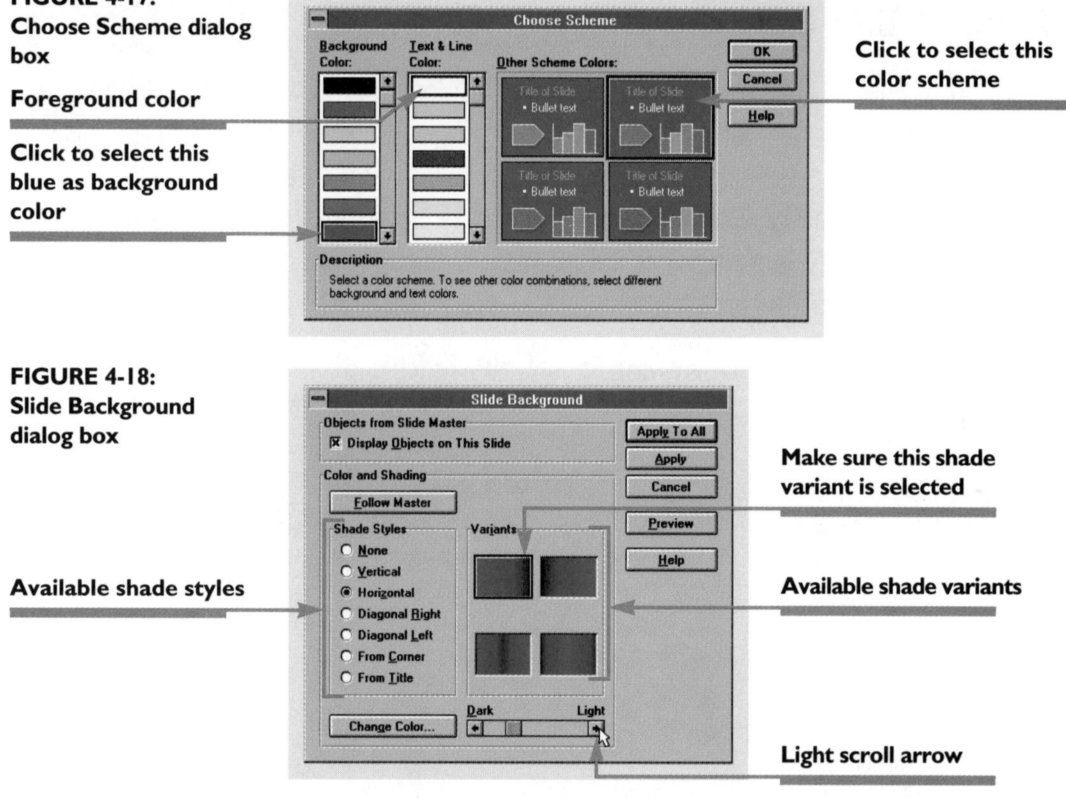

FIGURE 4-17: Choose Scheme dialog box

FIGURE 4-18: Slide Background dialog box

Copying color schemes

You can reuse color schemes without having to re-create them. Simply copy, or pick up, the color scheme from one slide and paste, or apply, the color scheme to another slide. In the Slide Sorter view, select a slide with the color scheme you want to copy, then use the Pick Up Color Scheme command on the Format menu. Select the slide you want to apply the color scheme to in Slide Sorter view from any open presentation, then use the Apply Color Scheme command.

TABLE 4-2: Color schemes

SCHEME COLORS	DESCRIPTION
Background color	Color of the slide's canvas, or background
Text and line colors	Contrast colors with the background color; used for text and drawn lines
Shadow color	Color of the shadow of text or other object; generally a darker shade of the background
Title text color	Like the text and line colors, contrast color for slide title with the background color
Fill color	Contrast color with both the background and the text and line colors
Accent colors	Colors used for other objects on slides

QUICK TIP

Click a color button on any Color palette, such as the Text Color button, then click Other Color to add a new color to the button menu.

Annotating slides during a slide show

In PowerPoint, you can show your presentation on any computer screen using Slide Show view. Slide Show view turns your computer into a projector that displays your presentation slide by slide. In Unit 1, you used the Slide Show View button to view the AutoContent slide show. ▶ Lynn runs the president's slide show and practices drawing on a slide so she can teach the president how to annotate slides during the presentation.

1. **Make sure you are viewing Slide 1, then click the Slide Show button**
   The slide show fills the screen with the first slide of the presentation. Lynn advances to the next slide.
2. **Click the mouse button then move the mouse**
   Slide 2 appears on the screen. Moving the mouse displays the pointer and the Annotation icon in the lower-right corner of the screen. You can emphasize major points in your presentation by drawing on the slide during a slide show by using the Annotation tool.
3. **Click the Annotation icon**
   The pointer changes to the Annotation tool, and the Annotation icon changes to the Exit Annotation icon. While the Annotation tool is turned on, mouse clicks do not advance to the next slide.
4. **Position under the title, then drag to draw a line**
   Compare your screen to Figure 4-19. You can draw anything on the slide when the Annotation tool is turned on. To erase the drawing, simply press [E], the letter "E" key. For other slide show controls, see Table 4-3.
5. **Press [E] to erase the annotation drawing**
   The drawing on Slide 2 is erased. Lynn now finishes using the Annotation tool.
6. **Click**
   The Exit Annotation icon changes back to . Lynn uses the mouse to advance through the rest of the presentation.
7. **Click the mouse to move through all the slides in the presentation**
   After clicking the last slide in the presentation, you return to Slide view.

TABLE 4-3: Slide show controls

CONTROL	DESCRIPTION
[E]	Erases the annotation drawing
[W]	Changes the screen to white
[B]	Changes the screen to black
[→]	Advances to the next slide
[←]	Returns to the previous slide
[Esc]	Stops the slide show

FIGURE 4-19: Presentation slide in Slide Show view

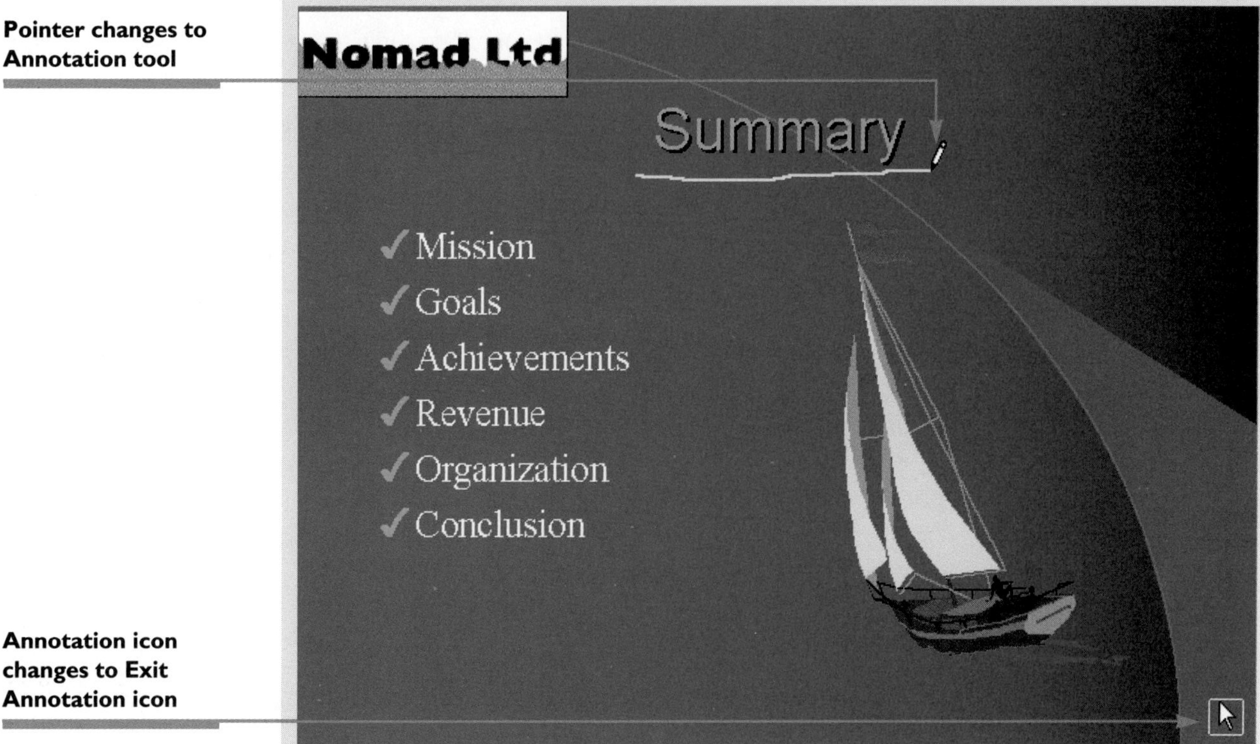

Showing slide shows on computers without PowerPoint

PowerPoint comes with a special application called **PowerPoint Viewer**. This application allows you to show a slide show on a computer that does not have PowerPoint installed. You can freely install the PowerPoint Viewer program on any compatible system. To install the program, insert the PowerPoint Viewer setup disk into a disk drive, click File on the Program Manager menu bar, click Run, type a:\vsetup (or b:\vsetup) in the File Name text box, then click OK. To run a slide show, double-click the PowerPoint Viewer icon in the Microsoft Office program group to open the Microsoft PowerPoint Viewer dialog box, click a presentation file from the list of filenames, then click Show. You can run a slide show using presentation files from PowerPoint 4.0 for Windows or PowerPoint 4.0 for the Macintosh with the PowerPoint Viewer.

QUICK TIP

Click the Slide Show button  to give a slide show beginning with the current slide.

Using slide show special effects

Screen Show Effects

You can add a dramatic element to your slide show presentation by adding special effects to an individual slide or a group of slides. Slide show special effects include transitions, timings, and builds. A **slide transition** is a visual effect applied to a slide show as it moves from one slide to another. **Slide timing** refers to the time a slide appears on the screen. With a **build slide**, you control when bulleted text appears on the screen. ▶ Using the Slide Sorter view, Lynn wants to add slide show special effects to give impact to the president's presentation.

1. Click the **Slide Sorter View button**
   The Slide Sorter view displays the slides as miniatures, and the slide you were viewing in Slide view is selected, as shown in Figure 4-20. The number of slides that appear on your screen might be different depending on the current view scale. To add a transition to all the slides, Lynn uses the Select All command to select all the slides quickly.
2. Click **Edit** on the menu bar, then click **Select All**
3. Click the **Transition Effects list arrow** on the Slide Sorter toolbar, then click **Checkerboard Across**
   Now, when you move from slide to slide, the Checkerboard Across transition effect will make the transition more interesting. Notice that a transition symbol appears below each slide miniature. Now Lynn applies a build to the two slides that have bulleted lists.
4. Click between the slides to deselect them, click **Slide 4**, press **[Shift]** and click **Slide 5**, click the **Build Effects list arrow** on the Slide Sorter toolbar, then click **Fly From Bottom**
   A build symbol appears for Slides 4 and 5. Now she rehearses the timings of the show.
5. Click **Slide 1**, then click the **Rehearse Timings button** on the Slide Sorter toolbar
   A small timing box appears in the lower-left corner of the screen with a current accumulated time for the slide. You can click the timing box or the slide to accept the time and continue to the next slide.
6. Click **each slide** to give it a slide time
   As you proceed through the show, the time you spent on each slide appears in the timing box. When you reach the build slides, the bullets appear one at a time as you click the slide. At the end of the rehearsal, PowerPoint asks if you want to record the new timings.
7. Click **Yes** to record the new slide timings
   Notice that each slide has a timing below it, as shown in Figure 4-21. You can change any slide time later using the Transition command on the Tools menu. Lynn previews the final presentation.
8. Click **View** on the menu bar, click **Slide Show**, click the **Use Slide Timings radio button** in the Advance section, then click **Show**
   Looks great! Lynn gives the presentation to Bill Davidson for his review
9. Save and close the presentation, then exit PowerPoint

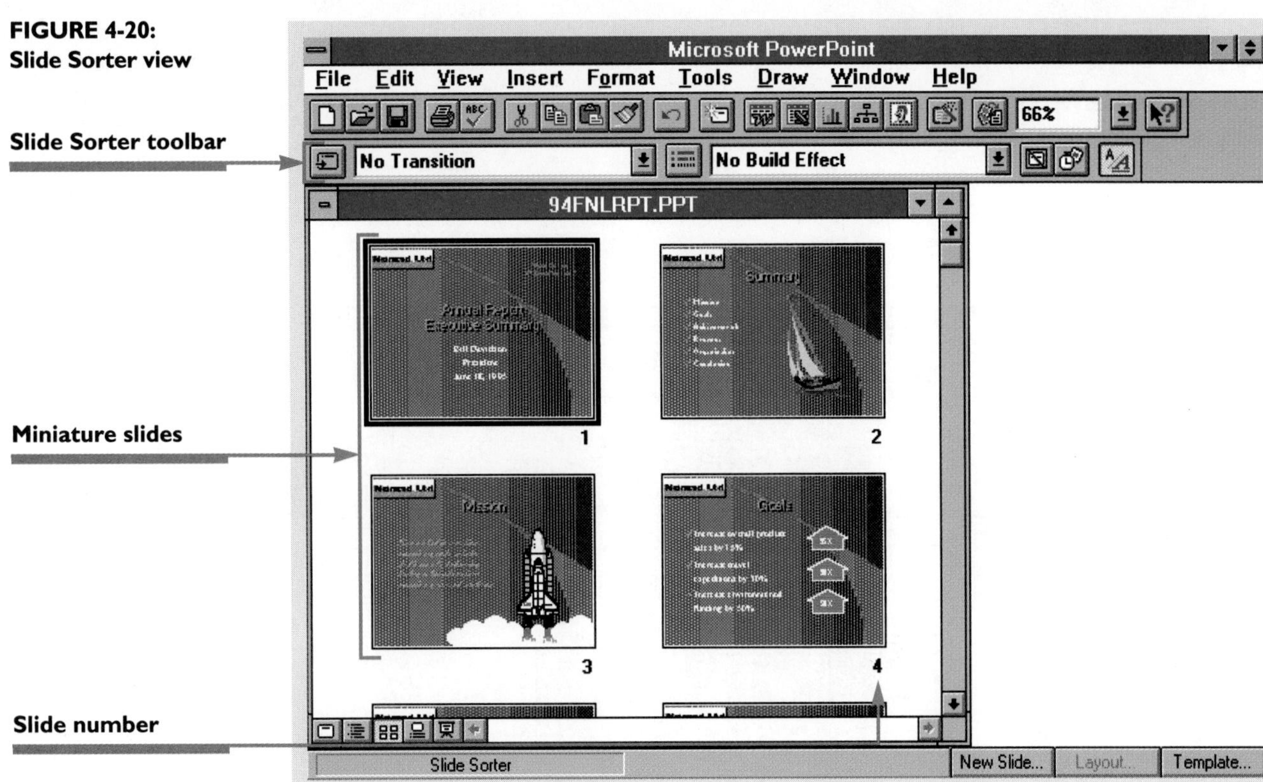

FIGURE 4-20:
Slide Sorter view

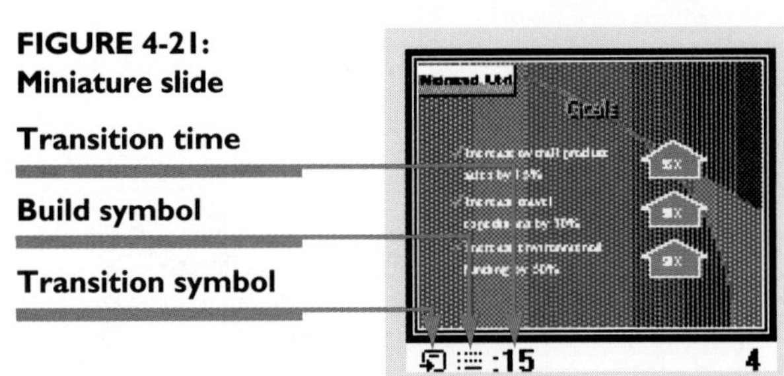

FIGURE 4-21:
Miniature slide

Customizing a slide show

You might want to customize a slide show for a specific audience. With PowerPoint, you can hide the slides you don't want to use during a slide show by using the Hide Slide command. In Slide Sorter view, select the slide or slides you want to hide, then click the Hide Slide button on the Slide Sorter toolbar. A small hide symbol appears over the slide number. During a slide show, a Hide icon appears in the lower-right corner of the screen. If you want to see the hidden slide, click the Hide icon; otherwise continue normally.

QUICK TIP

In Slide Sorter view, click the Transition symbol under the miniature slide to see the transition for the slide. See Figure 4-21.

CONCEPTS REVIEW

Label each of the elements of the PowerPoint window shown in Figure 4-22.

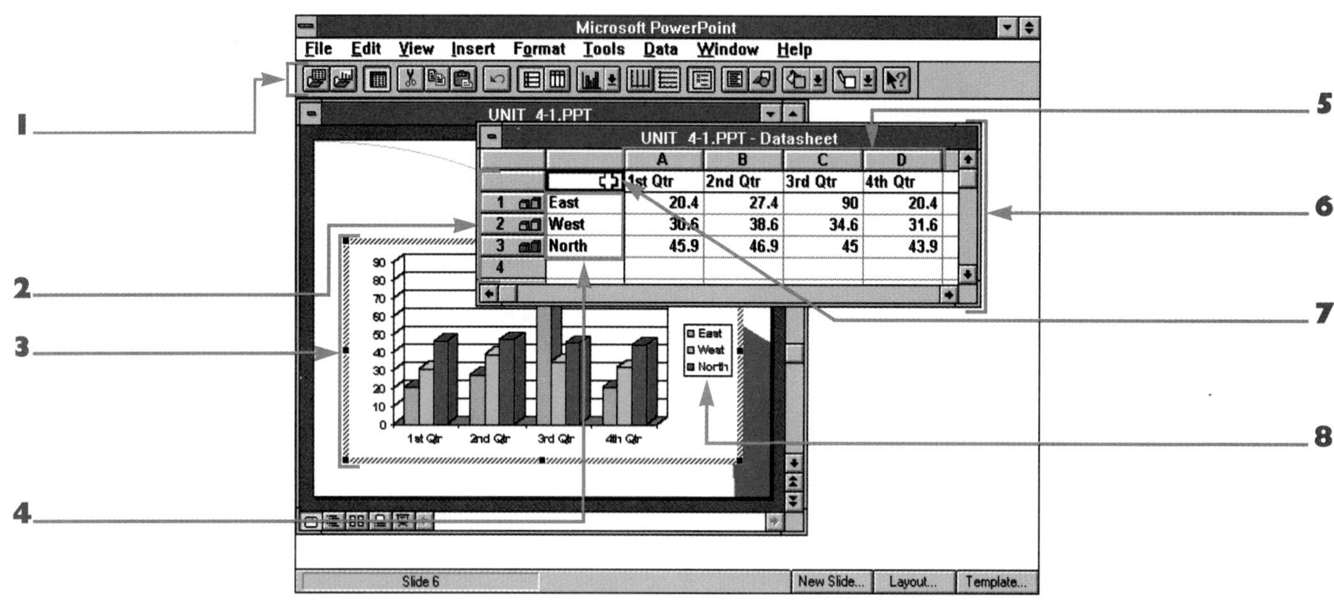

FIGURE 4-22

Match each of the terms with the statement that describes its function.

9 A selected cell in a datasheet

10 A graphical representation of a datasheet

11 The way information appears

12 Contains the data displayed in a chart

13 Maintains a link to another application

a. Chart

b. Embedded object

c. Datasheet

d. Format

e. Active cell

Select the best answer from the list of choices.

14 The PowerPoint clip art is stored in a

a. Folder

b. Gallery

c. Card Catalogue

d. Floppy disk

15 Which is NOT a way to access PowerPoint clip art?

a. Double-click a clip art placeholder

b. Click the Insert Clip Art button

c. Click Clip Art from the Insert menu

d. Double-click the Clip Art icon

16 Which of the following is NOT true about a PowerPoint graph?

a. A graph is made up of a datasheet and chart.

b. You can select a whole row or column by clicking a control box.

c. An active cell has a black selection rectangle around it.

d. You can click a control box to edit the contents of an individual cell.

17 An organizational chart is

a. A PowerPoint slide

b. An embedded object

c. A WordArt box

d. An object

APPLICATIONS REVIEW

1 Insert clip art.

a. Start PowerPoint and open the presentation UNIT_4-2.PPT from your Student Disk, save it as 94SALES.PPT in the MY_FILES directory, then click OK to close the Summary Info dialog box.

b. Click the Next Slide button.

c. Double-click the clip art placeholder.

d. In the Choose a category to view below section, scroll down the list, then click Maps - U.S. If the Maps - U.S. category doesn't appear, select a different category.

e. Click the 3-D U.S. Map with State Boundaries clip art, then click OK.

2 Insert a graph.

a. Click the Next Slide button.

b. Click the Layout button. The Slide Layout dialog box opens.

c. Click the Graph AutoLayout, then click Apply.

d. Double-click the graph placeholder to start Graph.

e. Click the first cell in the datasheet.

f. Click the Import Data button on the Graph Standard toolbar. The Import Data dialog box opens.

g. In the File Name list box, click the worksheet UNIT_4-3.XLS from your Student Disk, then click OK. A Microsoft Graph dialog box opens.

h. Click OK to overwrite the existing data. The data from the Microsoft Excel worksheet overwrites the default data in the Graph datasheet.

i. Click a blank area of the Presentation window to exit Graph.

3 Format a graph.

a. Double-click the graph object.

b. Click the By Column button on the Graph Standard toolbar.

c. Click the datasheet title names on the x-axis, click the Font Size list arrow on the Formatting toolbar, then click 14.

d. Click Insert on the menu bar, click Titles, click the Chart Title check box, then click OK.

e. Type "1994 Regional Sales Figures," then click a blank area below the title.

f. Click a blank area of the Presentation window to exit Graph.

4 Edit an organizational chart.

a. Click the Next Slide button and double-click the organizational chart, then click the maximize button.

b. Click the Subordinate button on the Org Chart toolbar.

c. Click the Production Dept. Manager chart box.

d. In the blank chart box, type "Jordan Shays," press [Tab], then type "Group Lead."

e. Click Edit on the menu bar, click Select, then click All.

f. Click Boxes on the menu bar, click Box Shadow, then click the second shadow option down in the second column.

g. Click File on the menu bar, click Exit and Return to 94SALES.PPT, then click Yes to update the presentation.

5 Work with WordArt to enhance slide text.

a. Click the Next Slide button and click the Layout button, click the Object AutoLayout, then click Apply.

b. Double-click the object placeholder.

c. In the Insert Object dialog box, click the down scroll arrow, click Microsoft WordArt 2.0, then click OK.

d. Type "The OutBack Series," press [Enter], type "by," press [Enter], type "Nomad Ltd," then click Update Display.

e. Click the Format Text list arrow, then click the Slant Up symbol on the bottom row.

f. Click the Shading button on the Formatting toolbar, click the Foreground list arrow, click Red, then click OK.

g. Click the Shadow button on the Formatting toolbar, click the top middle symbol.

h. Click a blank area of the Presentation window to exit WordArt.

6 Change a Slide Master.

a. Click the Next Slide button and click View on the menu bar, click Master, then click Slide Master.

b. Click the first line of text in the master text placeholder.

c. Click Format on the menu bar, click Bullet, then click the "X" in the top row, fourth from the right.

d. Click the Size % of Text up arrow until the percentage reaches 100, then click OK.

e. Click the Slide View button.

7 Change a color scheme.

a. Click Format on the menu bar, then click Slide Color Scheme.

b. Click the Blue Accent color in the Change Scheme Colors section.

c. Click Change Color. The Accent Color dialog box opens.

d. Click the fourth blue color down in the ninth column. Click OK then click Apply to All.

e. Click Format on the menu bar, then click Slide Background.

f. In the Shaded Styles section, click the Vertical radio button.

g. Click the Light scroll arrow three times, then click Apply to All.

8 Add slide show effects.

a. Click the Slide Sorter View button.

b. Click Edit on the menu bar, then click Select All.

c. Click the Transition Effect list arrow on the Slide Sorter toolbar, then click Random Transition.

d. Click the Rehearse Timings button on the Slide Sorter toolbar.

e. Click each slide to give it a time, then click Yes to record the new times.

f. Click between slides to deselect all the slides.

g. Click Slide 2, press [Shift], click the scroll down arrow a few times, then click Slide 6.

h. Click the Build list arrow on the Slide Sorter toolbar, then click Dissolve.

i. Double-click Slide 1.

j. Click View on the menu bar, then click Slide Show.

k. Click the Use Slide Timings radio button in the Advance section, then click Show.

l. Save, print, and then close the presentation.

INDEPENDENT CHALLENGE 1

You are the communications director at Pyles & Todd Design, Inc., an international advertising agency. One of your responsibilities is to create an on-screen presentation to promote the company at the National Association of Advertising Agencies (NAAA) convention. Use Green Pasture Farms quality products and the company's long history as the basis for your presentation.

Plan and create a slide show presentation for the marketing staff to use at the NAAA convention.

Create your own company information, but assume the following: the marketing staff will be using a color monitor with 256 colors.

To complete this independent challenge:

1 Think about the results you want to see, the information you need to create the slide show presentation, and the message you want to communicate.

2 Plan and create the color slide show presentation using slide transitions, build slides, slide timings, and shaded backgrounds. Use the Slide Show command from the View menu to make the slide show presentation run continuously.

3 Save the presentation as NAAA.PPT in the MY_FILES directory on your Student Disk. Make sure you preview the slide show presentation on the computer the marketing staff will use at the convention using PowerPoint or the PowerPoint Viewer.

4 Submit your presentation plan and the final slide show presentation.

INDEPENDENT CHALLENGE 2

You are the teacher at an elementary school. To help your 4th grade class understand the major holidays celebrated throughout the year, you want to create color slides with fun information and art for the students.

Plan and create a color slide presentation for the classroom. Create slides for the major holidays of the school year. Create your own holiday material.

To complete this independent challenge:

1 Think about the results you want to see, the information you need to create the slide show presentation, and the message you want to communicate.

2 Plan and create the color slide presentation using Microsoft ClipArt Gallery and Microsoft WordArt. Use the AutoLayout to help you create slides with the title text, bulleted text, and art. Remember you are creating and entering your own presentation material.

3 Save the presentation as HOLIDAYS.PPT in the MY_FILES directory on your Student Disk. Before printing, preview the file so you know what the presentation will look like. Adjust any items, and then print the slides.

4 Submit your presentation plan and the final slide show presentation.

Glossary

Active cell A selected cell in a Graph datasheet.

Adjustment handle A small diamond positioned next to a resize handle that changes the dimension of an object.

Annotation A freehand drawing on the screen using the Annotation tool. You can annotate only in Slide Show view.

Application A software program, such as Microsoft PowerPoint.

AutoContent wizard Helps you get your presentation started by creating a sample outline using information you provide.

AutoLayout A predesigned slide layout that contains placeholder layouts for titles, main text, clip art, graphs, and charts.

Blinking insertion point Vertical blinking line in a text object that shows your current location and where text can be entered.

Build slide Known as a progressive disclosure slide, a build slide reveals bullet points separately during a slide show.

Bullet A small graphic symbol, often used to identify a line of text in a list.

Cell A rectangle in a Graph datasheet where you enter data.

Chart The component of a graph that graphically portrays your Graph datasheet information.

Clip Art Professionally designed pictures that come with PowerPoint.

Color scheme The basic eight colors that make up a PowerPoint presentation. For example, a color scheme has a separate color for text, lines, and background color. You can change the color scheme on any presentation at any time.

Control boxes The gray boxes located along the left and top of a Graph datasheet.

Cue Cards A step-by-step instruction guide that gives you information on how to accomplish a specific task. Cue Cards appear in a separate window and stay on your screen while you work through the task instructions.

Datasheet The component of a graph that contains the information you want to display on your Graph chart.

Dialog box A box that displays the available command options for you to review or change.

Directory A subdivision of a disk that works like a filing system to help you organize files.

Disable To turn an option or feature off.

Drive The mechanism in a computer that turns a disk to retrieve and store information. Personal computers often have one hard drive labeled C and two drives labeled A and B that read removable floppy disks.

Dotted selection box Indicates that an object is selected and can be modified.

Elevator The scroll box in the vertical scroll bar.

Embedded object An object that is created in another application but is stored in PowerPoint. Embedded objects maintain a link to their original application for easy editing.

Formatting toolbar The toolbar that contains buttons for the most frequently used formatting commands, such as font type and size.

Gallery A visual index that stores the PowerPoint clip art into categories.

Global change A change made to an entire selection.

Graph The datasheet and chart you create to graphically display information.

Grid Evenly spaced horizontal and vertical lines that do not appear on the slide.

Main text Sub points or bullet points under a title in Outline view.

Main text placeholder A reserved box on a slide for the main text points.

Master text placeholder The placeholder on the Slide Master that controls the formatting and placement of the Main text placeholder on each slide. If you modify the Master text placeholder, each Main text placeholder is affected in the entire presentation.

Master title placeholder The placeholder on the Slide Master that controls the formatting and placement of the Title placeholder on each slide. If you modify the Master title placeholder, each Title placeholder is affected in the entire presentation.

Menu bar The horizontal bar below the title bar that contains the PowerPoint commands. Click a menu name to display a list of commands.

Object The component you place or draw on a slide. Objects are drawn lines and shapes, text, clip art, imported pictures, and embedded objects.

Organizational chart A diagram of connected boxes that shows reporting structure.

Outlining toolbar The toolbar that contains buttons for the most used outlining commands, such as moving and indenting text lines.

Pick a Look Wizard Helps you choose a professional look for your presentation. You can use the Pick a Look wizard at any time.

Placeholder A dashed line box where you place text or objects.

PowerPoint Viewer A special application designed to run a PowerPoint slide show on any compatible computer that does not have PowerPoint installed.

PowerPoint window A window that contains the running PowerPoint application. The PowerPoint window displays the PowerPoint menus, toolbars, and Presentation window.

Presentation graphics application A software program used to organize and present information.

Presentation window The area or "canvas" where you work and view your presentation. You type text and work with objects in the Presentation window.

Resize handle The small square at each corner of a selected object. Dragging a resize handle resizes the object.

Scale To resize a picture or object by a specified percentage.

Scroll To move within a window to see more of the window contents.

Slanted line selection box A box that appears around a text object indicating it is selected and ready to enter or edit text.

Slide icon A symbol used to identify a slide title in Outline view.

Slide Indicator box A small box that appears when you drag the elevator in Slide and Note Pages view. This box identifies which slide you are on.

Stacking order The order in which objects are placed on the slide. The first object placed on the slide is on the bottom while the last object placed on the slide is on the top.

Standard toolbar The row of buttons, or toolbar, that perform the most frequently used commands, such as copy and paste.

Status bar Located at the bottom of the PowerPoint window, it displays messages about what you are doing and seeing in PowerPoint, such as the current slide number or a description of a command or button.

Text box A box within a dialog box where you type information needed to carry out a command.

Text object Any text you create with the Text Tool or enter into a placeholder. Once you enter text into a placeholder, the placeholder becomes a text object.

Text label A text object you create with the Text Tool that does not automatically wrap text inside a box.

Timing The time a slide stays on the screen during a slide show.

Title The first line or heading in Outline view.

Title bar The horizontal bar at the top of the window that displays the name of the document or the application.

Title placeholder A reserved box on a slide for a presentation or slide title.

Title slide The first slide in your presentation.

Toggle button A button that turns a feature on and off.

Toolbar A graphical bar with buttons that perform certain PowerPoint commands, such as opening and saving.

ToolTip When you place the pointer over a button, a small box appears that identifies the button by name.

Transition The effect that moves one slide off the screen and the next slide on the screen during a slide show. Each slide can have its own transition effect.

TrueType font A font that can be displayed or printed at any size.

View PowerPoint has five views that allow you to look at your presentation in different ways. Each view allows you to change and modify the content of your presentation differently.

View buttons Appear at the bottom of the Presentation window. Allow you to switch between PowerPoints' five views.

Window A rectangle area on your screen where you view and work on presentations.

Wizard A guided approach that steps you through creating a presentation. PowerPoint has two wizards, the AutoContent Wizard and the Pick a Look Wizard, that help you with the content and the look of your presentation.

Word processing box A text object you draw with the Text Tool that automatically wraps text inside a box.

Index

D

E

F

G

H

I

J

L

M

R

S

W

Z

UNIT 3

OBJECTIVES

- Insert a Word outline into a PowerPoint presentation
- Insert a Word table into a PowerPoint slide
- Use embedding (OLE) to integrate an Excel chart with a PowerPoint slide

Integrating WORD, EXCEL, ACCESS, AND POWERPOINT

PowerPoint is the fourth component of Microsoft Office, and it can be integrated easily with the other three Office applications. This means that when preparing a PowerPoint presentation, you can insert Word documents and link or embed Excel charts into PowerPoint slides. **Embedding** an object is similar to linking an object, but the entire source file is included with the embedded object in the target file. ▶ As the Annual Meeting draws near, Lynn Shaw, the executive assistant to the president, is collecting data from Angela Pacheco, Michael Belmont, and others at Nomad Ltd. Lynn is going to prepare 35-mm slides that will be shown at the meeting. Since everyone at Nomad uses Microsoft Office, Lynn knows all the files are compatible. ▶

Inserting a Word outline into a PowerPoint presentation

While it is very easy to create an outline in PowerPoint, it is unnecessary if the outline already exists in a Word file. You can insert a Word outline into a PowerPoint outline. PowerPoint assumes that each hard return followed by a tab indicates a new heading level, and each hard return not followed by a tab indicates a new heading 1 level in the outline and needs a new slide. ▶ Angela Pacheco, in the Marketing Department, put together a few ideas for the slide presentation in a Word outline. Lynn, who has already started preparing the slide presentation, will insert Angela's outline into her existing presentation file.

1 Double-click the **Microsoft PowerPoint application icon** in the Program Manager window
PowerPoint starts and the PowerPoint dialog box opens. Lynn opens her presentation file.

2 Click **OK** to open an existing presentation

3 Open the file INT_3-1.PPT from your Student Disk, then save it as EXECSMRY.PPT in your MY_FILES directory
The first slide of Lynn's presentation appears, as shown in Figure 3-1. Before inserting the Word document, Lynn changes from Slide view to Outline view.

4 Click the **Outline View button** on the status bar
The text used in the slides appears as an outline, as shown in Figure 3-2. The presentation contains five slides.

Angela's outline contains ideas about Nomad Ltd and its corporate goals. Lynn wants these new slides to begin after the Corporate Mission Statement in Slide 2, so she makes Slide 2 the current slide.

5 Click **Slide 2**
The text in Slide 2 is selected. Lynn wants to insert the outline next.

Continue with the next lesson to insert the Word outline into the PowerPoint presentation.

FIGURE 3-1: Lynn's slide presentation

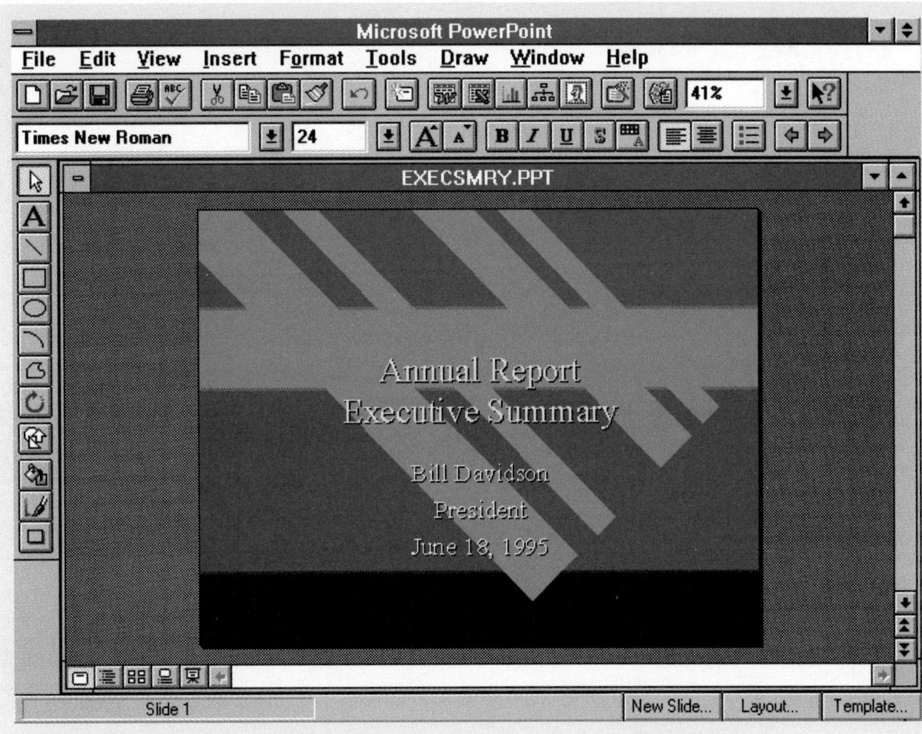

FIGURE 3-2: Existing slides in Outline view

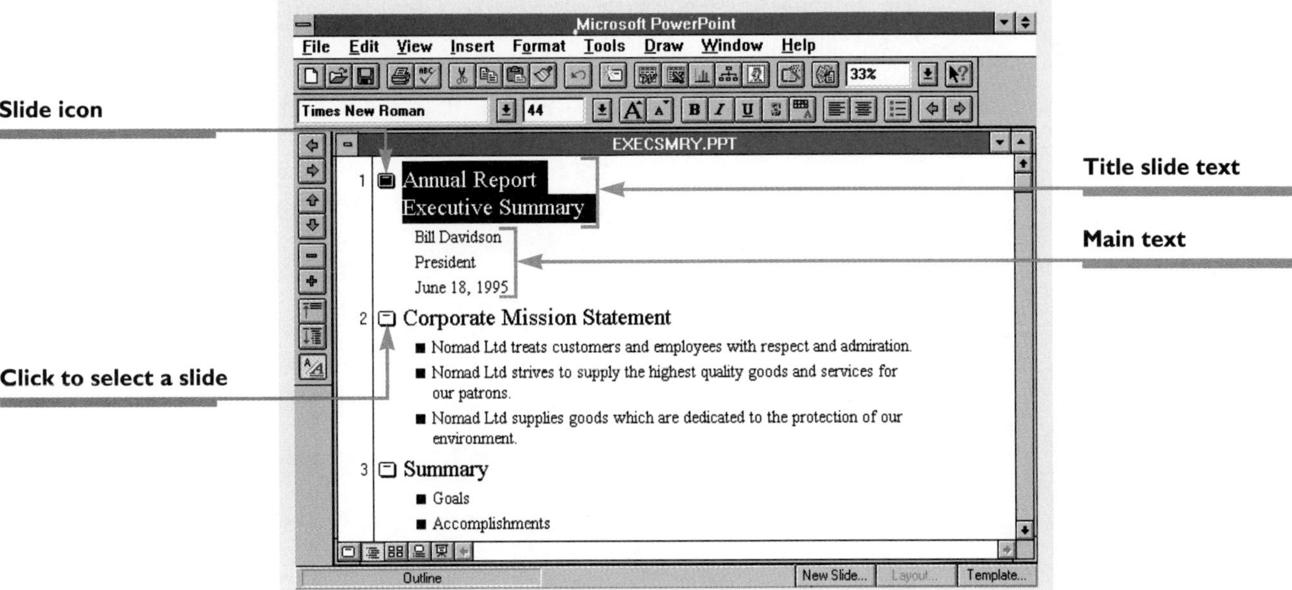

QUICK TIP

Click  on the Microsoft toolbar to quickly start PowerPoint.

Inserting a Word outline into a PowerPoint presentation, continued

After you decide where you want the new slides to begin, you insert the Word outline, and PowerPoint automatically converts the text into the slide format. The related topic "Exporting a PowerPoint presentation to Word" explains the integration feature, exporting. Lynn continues the process of inserting the outline.

6 **Click Insert on the menu bar, then click Slides from Outline**
The Insert Outline dialog box opens.

7 **Select the file OUTLINE.DOC from your Student Disk, then click OK**
A message box appears, telling you that PowerPoint is reading the outline from OUTLINE.DOC. When PowerPoint is finished, four new slides appear as slides 3, 4, 5, and 6, as shown in Figure 3-3. Once an outline is inserted into a presentation, you can edit and manipulate it as if it had been created in PowerPoint. Lynn decides to view the slides in the Slide Sorter view.

8 **Click the Slide Sorter View button on the status bar**
Use the elevator and scroll bars to see all the slides. Compare your screen to Figure 3-4. Lynn is pleased that she has saved so much time by inserting the outline. Now she saves her work.

9 **Click the Save button in the Standard toolbar**
Lynn minimizes PowerPoint so she can have use of her desktop until she needs to use PowerPoint again.

10 **Click the PowerPoint window Minimize button**

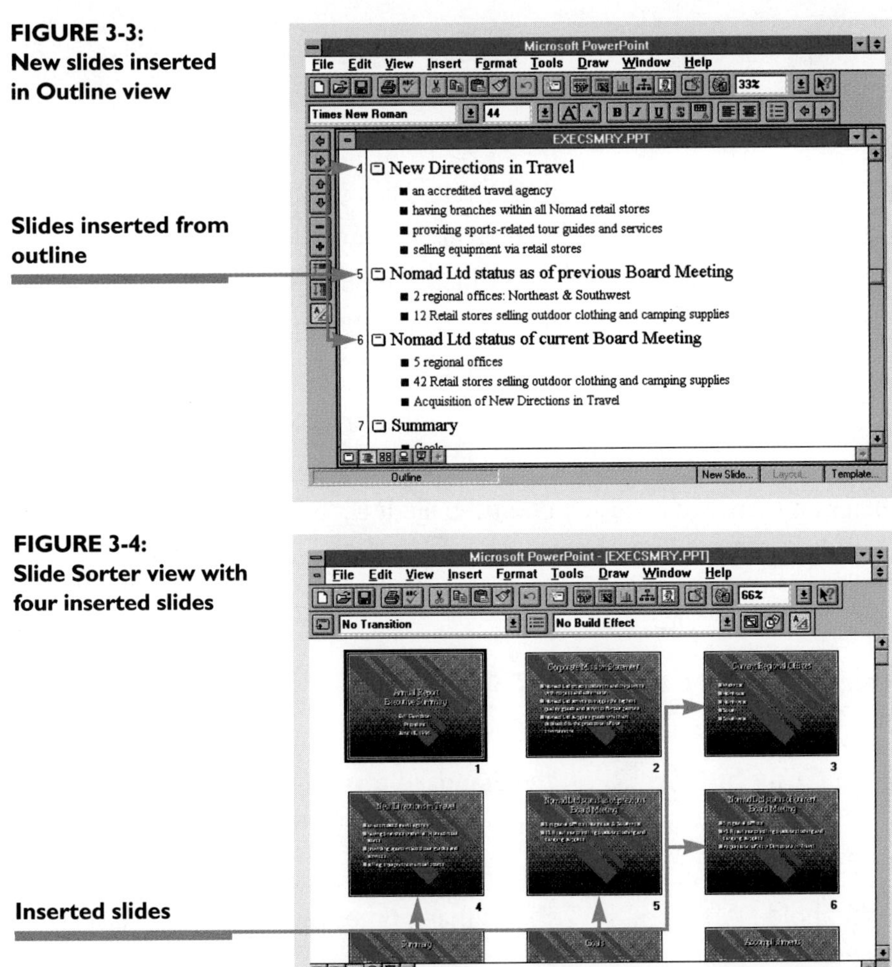

FIGURE 3-3: New slides inserted in Outline view

Slides inserted from outline

FIGURE 3-4: Slide Sorter view with four inserted slides

Inserted slides

Exporting a PowerPoint presentation to Word

You can export a PowerPoint presentation to Word. When you click the Report It button on the PowerPoint Standard toolbar, Word starts and the current PowerPoint presentation's outline is exported to Word as a Word document in Normal view. In the new Word document, a title slide becomes a centered paragraph in a larger point size, and the main text of a slide appears in a bulleted list. Once the PowerPoint outline is in Word, you can save and edit the document. See Figure 3-5.

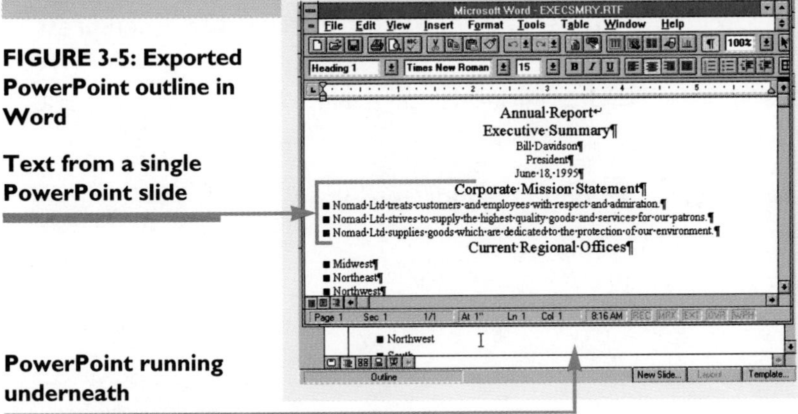

FIGURE 3-5: Exported PowerPoint outline in Word

Text from a single PowerPoint slide

PowerPoint running underneath

QUICK TIP

Outlines imported into PowerPoint can have up to nine indented levels, while outlines created in PowerPoint can have only six.

Inserting a Word table into a PowerPoint slide

If information already exists in a file from one Microsoft Office application, you can usually paste or link that information faster than retyping it. You can insert a Word table in a PowerPoint slide by copying and pasting the selected table. ▶ Lynn received a memo from Angela that contains a table illustrating the status of the previous and current years. Lynn copies the Word table directly to the PowerPoint slide.

1. Start Word by double-clicking the **Microsoft Word application icon** in the Program Manager window; open the file INT_3-2.DOC from your Student Disk, then save it as TABLE.DOC to the MY_FILES directory
   Angela's document containing the table opens, as shown in Figure 3-6. Lynn selects the table and copies it to the Clipboard.
2. Click anywhere in the table, click **Table** on the menu bar, then click **Select Table**
3. Click the **Copy button** on the Standard toolbar
   The table is copied to the Clipboard. Next Lynn opens PowerPoint, which is running but minimized.
4. Press and hold **[Alt]**, press **[Tab]** as many times as necessary to display the PowerPoint application, then release **[Alt]**
   PowerPoint opens in the Slide Sorter view, while Word runs in the background.

   Lynn wants to copy the Word table to Slide 7, which contains summary information.
5. Double-click Slide 7
   The slide opens in Slide view.
6. Click the **Paste button** on the PowerPoint Standard toolbar
   The table appears on the slide, but it's too small. Lynn enlarges it using the Scale command.
7. Click **Draw** on the menu bar, then click **Scale**
   The Scale dialog box opens, as shown in Figure 3-7.
8. Click the **Best Scale for Slide Show check box**, click **OK**, then press **[Esc]** to deselect the table
   The table appears on the slide 50% larger than originally shown. See Figure 3-8. Lynn is pleased with the presentation and saves the changes.
9. Click the **Save button** on the Standard toolbar

FIGURE 3-6: Table in Word document

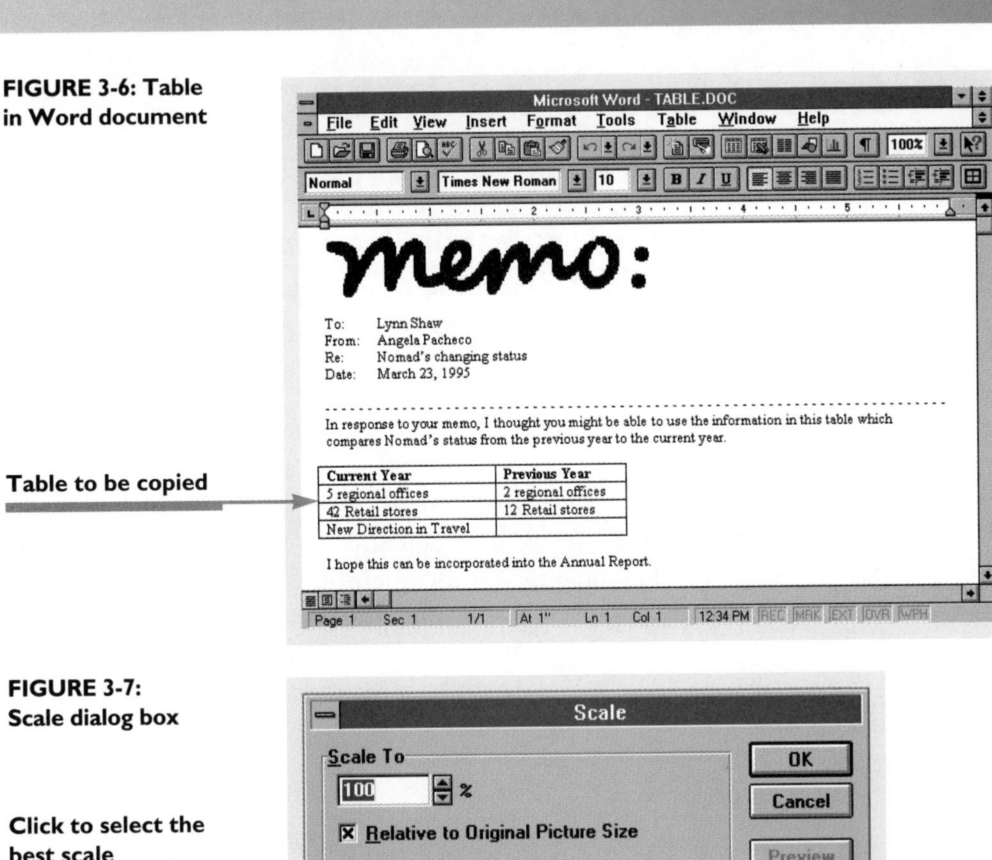

Table to be copied

FIGURE 3-7: Scale dialog box

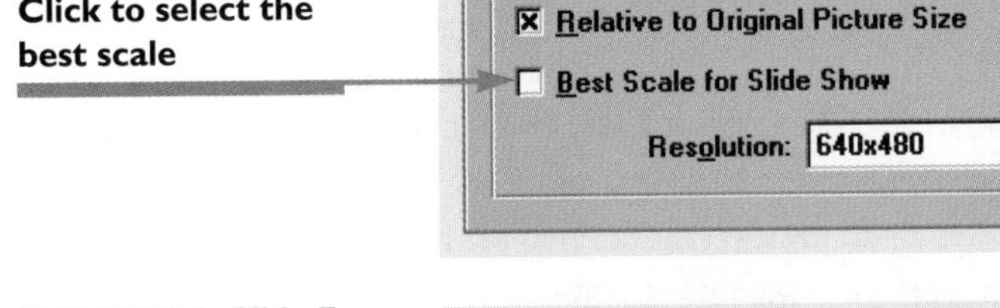

Click to select the best scale

FIGURE 3-8: Slide 7 with Word table

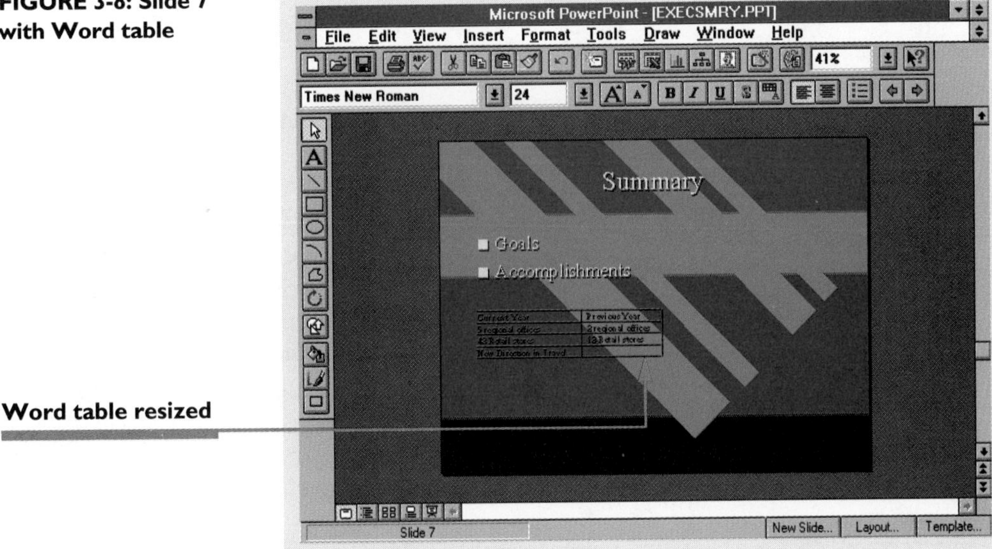

Word table resized

QUICK **TIP**

Click [Word icon] on the Microsoft toolbar to quickly start Word.

Using embedding (OLE) to integrate an Excel chart with a PowerPoint slide

Using Object Linking and Embedding

Embedding (also known as **object linking and embedding** or **OLE**) is a powerful tool that, like linking, allows you to share information from one file to another. When you embed an object, however, you put a copy of the entire source file in the target file. You can then open and make changes to the copy of the source file directly from within the target file; the original source file remains unchanged. Table 3-1 lists the advantages and disadvantages of linking and embedding. ▶ Lynn needs to include an Excel chart in the presentation. Evan Brillstein gave Lynn the Excel file containing preliminary sales data and a chart of that data. Because the data is preliminary and might change, Lynn decides to embed the data in the Excel file in her PowerPoint slide.

1 Drag the elevator to Slide 3, click **Insert** on the menu bar, then click **Object**
The Insert Object dialog box opens, as shown in Figure 3-9. Lynn wants to create an embedded object from an existing file.

2 Click the **Create from File radio button**, click **Browse**, select the file SALES.XLS from your Student Disk, click **OK**, then click **OK** to close the Insert Object dialog box
The worksheet data and chart appear on the slide, as shown in Figure 3-10. Notice that the data and chart obscure the bulleted items. Lynn wants to display only the chart, so she crops the object. **Cropping** allows you to hide areas of an object; the hidden areas are still there, they are just not visible.

3 Click **Tools** on the menu bar, then click **Crop Picture**
The pointer changes to ⌗.

4 Position the pointer over the upper-left selection handle above the word "Midwest," then drag the pointer down until only the chart remains visible
Once the object is cropped, you can move it by selecting it and dragging it to a new location.

5 With the chart still selected, drag it to the right of the bulleted items, then press **[Esc]** to deselect the object
Compare your slide to Figure 3-11. Lynn saves her work.

6 Click the **Save button** 💾 on the Standard toolbar

TABLE 3-1: Relationships between objects

METHOD	ADVANTAGES	DISADVANTAGES
Linking	File size of target file remains small, as the target file contains only a link and not the actual object	Renamed files can disrupt links
Embedding	The copy of the source file can be quickly changed, if necessary, from within the target file	Target file becomes significantly larger because the object is actually contained in the target file

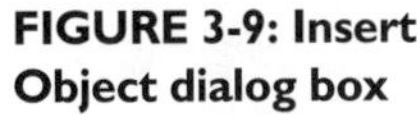

FIGURE 3-9: Insert Object dialog box

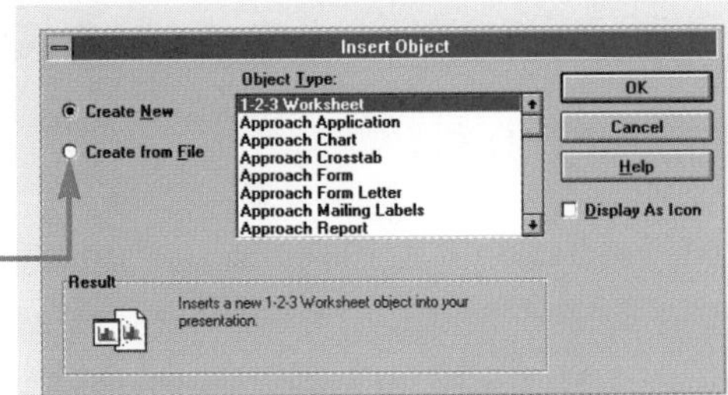

Click to embed an existing file

FIGURE 3-10: Excel object embedded in slide

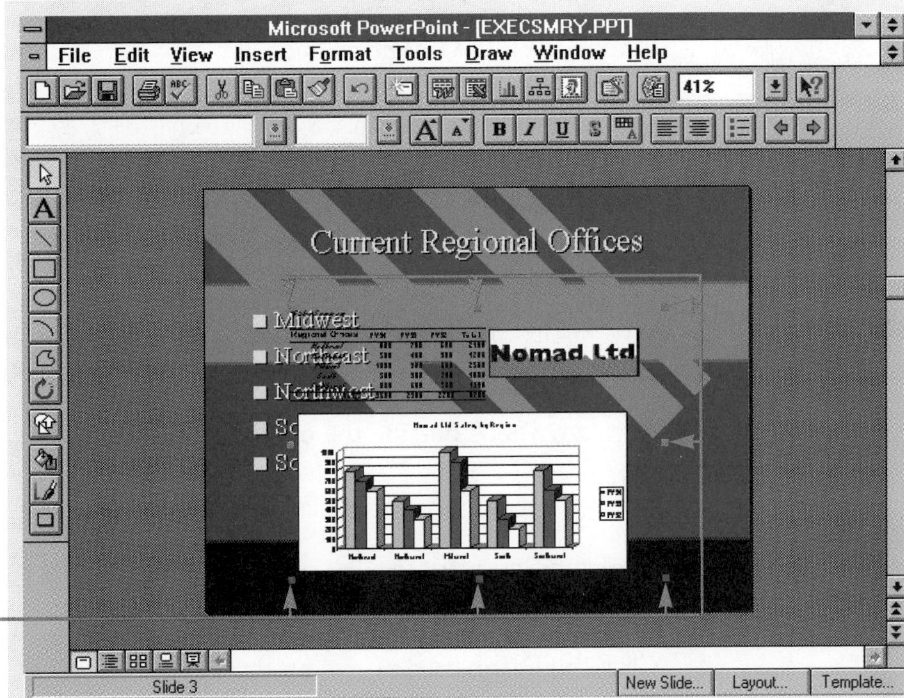

Handles on embedded object

FIGURE 3-11: Cropped object moved to new location

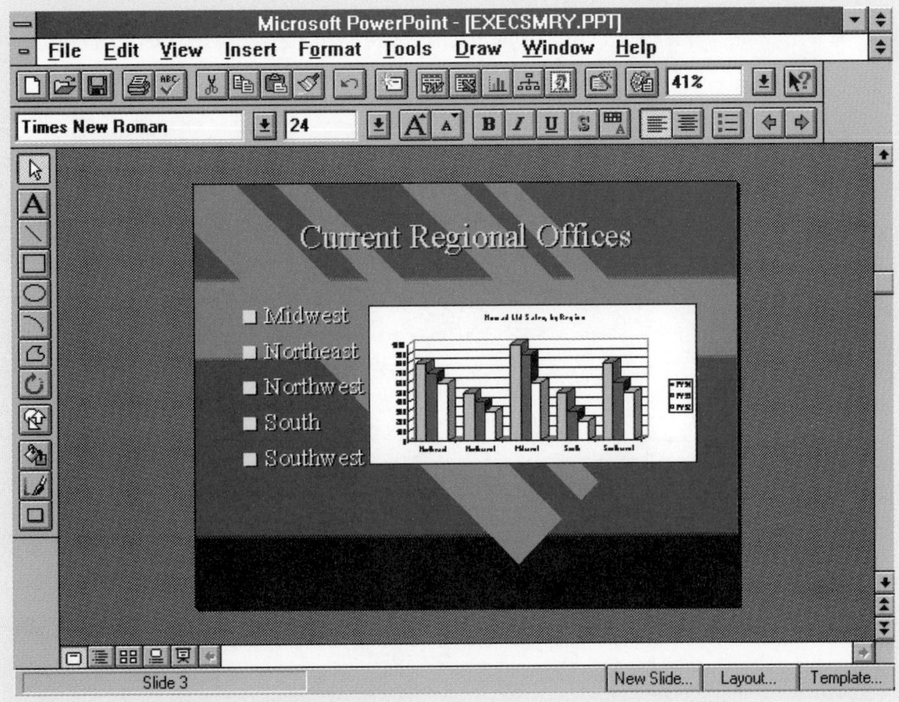

Using embedding (OLE) to integrate an Excel chart with a PowerPoint slide, continued

Because Lynn embedded the chart in the slide, she can make any changes necessary to the Excel worksheet from within PowerPoint. Evan Brillstein has given Lynn new figures for the Northeast and Southwest sales summary. Lynn opens Excel by double-clicking the embedded SALES.XLS file.

7 Double-click the **chart** on Slide 3

The entire embedded file opens, and Excel's menu bar and toolbar appear, as shown in Figure 3-12. Notice that when the pointer is over the open Excel object, it changes to ✚. Cells can be edited as if you were in Excel. Although it might be difficult to read the cells themselves, their contents appear in the formula bar.

8 Click cell **B4**, type **950**, press **[Enter]**, click cell **B8**, type **900**, then press **[Enter]**

Notice that the columns in the Excel chart change to reflect the new data. Lynn closes Excel to see the finished slide.

9 Click anywhere outside the embedded object, then press **[Esc]** to deselect the object

Figure 3-13 shows the changes in the chart on the slide. Lynn saves her PowerPoint presentation.

10 Click the **Save button** on the Standard toolbar

Lynn prints her PowerPoint slides.

11 Click the **Print button** on the Standard toolbar

12 Click **File** on the menu bar, then click **Exit** to exit PowerPoint

13 Exit all applications, saving changes, as necessary

FIGURE 3-12: Embedded Excel object open in PowerPoint

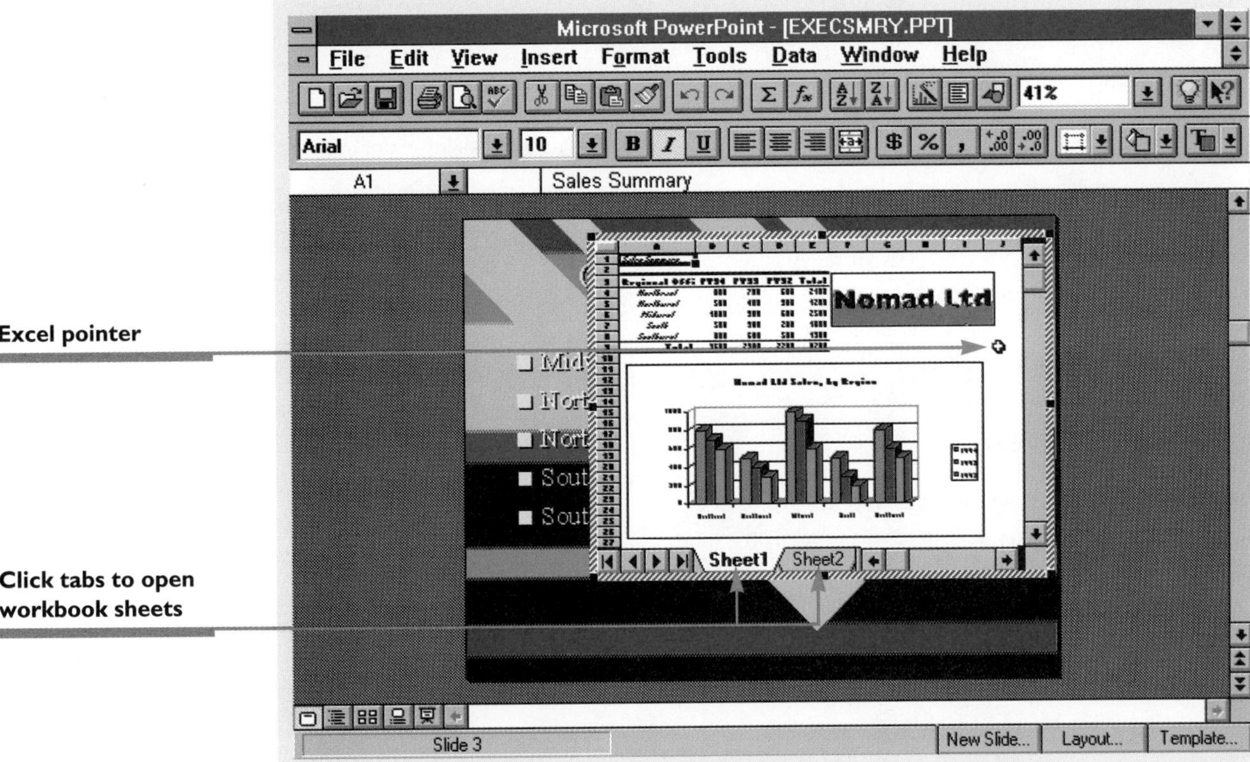

FIGURE 3-13: Modifications reflected in linked chart

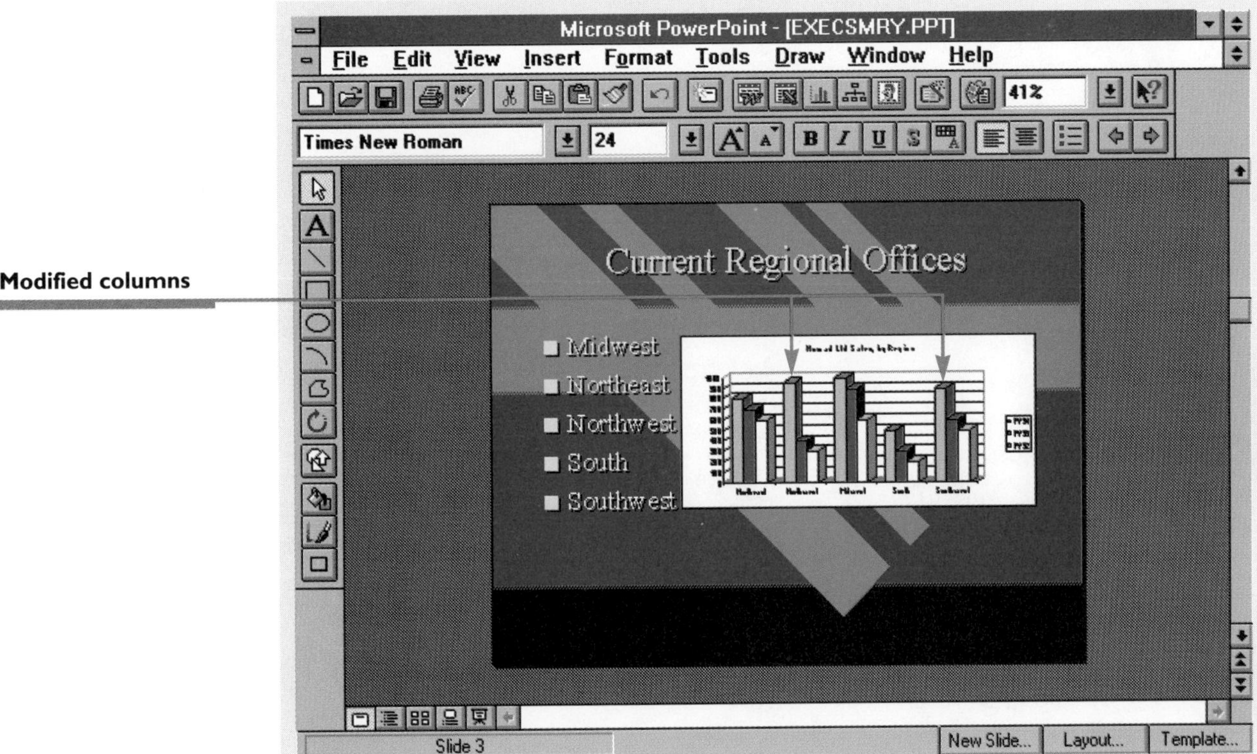

INDEPENDENT CHALLENGE I

You are the person in your company who recommends which software packages should be purchased. You have decided to recommend Microsoft Office. Create a PowerPoint presentation illustrating the advantages of each application in the Office suite. Your presentation should also contain slides that show how first-time computer users feel about computers and why Microsoft Office is a good choice for them. This information is provided in the file USERS.DOC on your Student Disk. Think about what you would like the presentation to say, and what graphics you will use. Be prepared to make an on-screen presentation to the class.

To complete this independent challenge:

1. Plan your presentation, determining its purpose and the look you want that will help communicate your message. Sketch on paper how you want the slides to look.
2. Create a PowerPoint presentation and save it as APPS.PPT to the MY_FILES directory on your Student Disk.
3. Type your outline. Your presentation should contain a total of at least 10 slides.
4. Create the title slide for your presentation, then save your work.
5. Insert the Word document USERS.DOC from your Student Disk into your presentation outline. USERS.DOC contains information about how first-time computer users feel about computers.
6. Add slide show special effects, such as builds and transitions, into the presentation.
7. Save your presentation.
8. Print the slides and the outline of your presentation. Be prepared to present your slide show to the class.

INDEPENDENT CHALLENGE 2

To augment the Census Bureau's data on marriage and birth rate statistics, you have been asked to prepare a PowerPoint presentation that will run continuously at the local census office. Charts on the data need to be linked to the PowerPoint slides, because data is updated occasionally.

Use the data found in the two worksheets in the Excel file INT_3-3.XLS on your Student Disk. Create a presentation that explains this data.

To complete this independent challenge:

1. Open the file INT_3-3.XLS from your Student Disk, then save it as BUREAU.XLS to the MY_FILES directory.
2. Create at least four charts using the data in the Marriages worksheet.
3. Create one chart using the data in the Birth rates worksheet.
4. Decide which aspects of the data you want to highlight, and write two to three paragraphs describing how your presentation will illustrate the importance of the data.
5. Create a new Word document containing an outline for your presentation, then save it as BUR-OUT.DOC to the MY_FILES directory on your Student Disk. Print this outline.
6. Open a new PowerPoint presentation. Save it as BUREAU.PPT on your Student Disk.
7. Create a title slide for the presentation.
8. Insert the Word outline into the presentation.
9. Add slide show special effects, such as builds and transitions, to the slides.
10. Link the four charts in the Marriages worksheet to slides in the presentation. (*Hint:* Use the Paste Special command on the Edit menu.)
11. Embed the chart in the Birth rates worksheet in a slide in the presentation.
12. Save your presentation.
13. Print the slides. Be prepared to make your presentation to the class.
14. Close all open applications.

COMPREHENSIVE **INDEPENDENT** CHALLENGE

You have been hired as an associate in the Marketing Department at Nomad Ltd. Nomad recently completed a big marketing campaign promoting its bicycle tours but neglected its non-bicycle tours. Sales of the bungee jumping tours especially have fallen off. It is your job to develop a marketing strategy to restore the sales levels of non-bicycle tours. The Nomad Board of Directors, concerned about the falling sales, have suggested adding rock climbing and jeep tours to the Nomad tour line to broaden Nomad's customer base.

You decide to send a questionnaire to customers who have taken the bungee jumping tour asking how this tour can be improved. You also decide to create a PowerPoint presentation that suggests advertising strategies for promoting the new tours. You will need several charts to show the current non-bicycle tour trends and the potential sales for the new tours.

To complete this independent challenge:

Pasting a graphics file into a Word document

1. Start Word and open the file INT_3-4.DOC from your Student Disk. Save it as COVERLTR.DOC to the MY_FILES directory. This is the cover letter to the questionnaire.
2. Use the Insert Picture command to add the Nomad Ltd logo to the header of the memo. The logo is in the file NOMAD.TIF on your Student Disk.

Using Mail Merge with Word and Access

3. Start Access and open the file CUSTDATA.MDB from your Student Disk.
4. Create a query that lists customers who have taken the bungee tour.
5. Use Word's Mail Merge feature to merge the cover letter and the Access query you have created. Print the resulting letters.

Using Excel

6. Start Excel and open the file INT_3-5.XLS from your Student Disk. Save it as TOURTYPE.XLS to the MY_FILES directory. This worksheet contains data for Road Bike, Mt. Bike, and Bungee tour sales.
7. Create two charts: one that compares the sales numbers of the tours, and the second that shows the tours as a percentage of all tours. Use drawing tools and color, if appropriate, to point out weak sales. Name this worksheet Current.

8 Copy the data from the Current worksheet to a new worksheet. In the new worksheet, add a formula that calculates an increase in the Bungee tour sales by 20%, then show this increase in your charts. Use drawing tools and color, if appropriate, to indicate which figures are speculative. Name this worksheet Bungee increase.

9 Copy the increased Bungee tour sales data to another new worksheet, then add two more rows for the Rock Climbing and Jeep tours. Assume their sales equal the sales of the increased Bungee tour sales. Create two more charts to show the new tours. Use drawing tools and color, if appropriate, to indicate which figures are speculative and to point out the new tours. Name this worksheet New tours.

10 Add titles to all three charts to identify them. Use drop shadows and other formatting effects to make them more attractive.

11 Print the data and the charts on all three worksheets.

Pasting a graphics file into a PowerPoint slide

12 Start PowerPoint and create a new presentation. Save it as NMD_PRES.PPT to the MY_FILES directory on your Student Disk. This presentation will illustrate your marketing ideas to increase sales.

13 Copy the Nomad logo to the Master slide.

Inserting a Word outline into a PowerPoint presentation

14 Create a title slide.

15 Insert the Word outline PROMO.DOC from your Student Disk after the title slide.

16 Add to the outline your own ideas on how to strengthen Bungee tours sales and for the new tours. You can suggest additional tours, too.

Inserting Excel charts into PowerPoint slides

17 Include the Excel charts on your slides by using the method you feel is best: pasting, linking, or embedding, or a combination of the three.

18 Use templates, clip art, builds, and any other PowerPoint features you want to create an effective and professional-looking presentation.

19 Print the presentation with six slides per page.

20 Submit all your work.

UNIT 1

OBJECTIVES

- Understand electronic mail
- Start Learning Mail
- View the Learning Mail window
- Reply to messages
- Create and send new messages
- Forward messages
- Manage your Inbox
- Create a group
- Send mail to a personal group

Getting Started WITH MICROSOFT MAIL

Microsoft Mail is an electronic mail program that lets you send and receive electronic messages to and from other users connected to your network. In this unit, you'll work with a program called "Learning Mail" that looks and feels like Microsoft Mail, but is actually a simulation of Microsoft Mail. Learning Mail was specially designed to be used with this book to teach you the basics of sending, receiving and managing electronic mail messages. **case** You'll use Learning Mail to communicate with a group of users at the fictional company, Nomad Ltd. The messages you send throughout this unit are not actually being sent to "real" people. Likewise, the messages you receive are not from "real" people—they are simulations, to show you how the real Mail program works. You'll be able to use the skills learned in this unit to work with the actual Microsoft Mail program.

Understanding electronic mail

Electronic mail, popularly known as **e-mail**, is software that lets you send and receive electronic messages over a network. A **network** is a group of computers connected to each other with cables and software. Figure 1-1 illustrates how e-mail messages can travel over a network. Because of its speed and ease of use, e-mail is often a more effective way to communicate than using pencil and paper, or even speaking to someone directly. Note that each computer network or workplace could have unique e-mail policies. See the related topic "Electronic mail guidelines."

Here are some of the benefits of using electronic mail:

- **Provides convenient and efficient way to communicate**
  You can send messages whenever you wish; the recipient does not have to be at the computer to receive your message. Other users on your network can also send you electronic messages, even if you are not currently running the mail application. Any new messages sent to you will be waiting when you open your mailbox.

- **Lets you send large amounts of information**
  Your messages can be as long as you wish, so you are not limited to the short time typically allowed on some voice mail systems. You can also attach a file (such as a spreadsheet or word processing document) to a message.

- **Lets you communicate with several people at once**
  You can send (or forward) the same message to multiple individuals at one time (without going to the copy machine first). You can also create your own electronic address book containing the names of people with whom you communicate frequently.

- **Ensures delivery of information**
  Electronic messages cannot be "lost" so no one can claim not to have received a message you sent. You even have the option to be notified when a message has been read by another user.

- **Communicate from a remote place**
  If you have a modem and communications software, you can connect your computer at home to the computers at your office over the phone lines. This gives you the flexibility to send and receive messages when you are not at the office. You can also join a commercial online service and send e-mail to people on the **Internet**, which is a network that connects millions of computer users around the world.

- **Provides a record of communications**
  You can organize your sent and received messages in a way that best suits your work style. Organizing your saved messages lets you keep a record of communications, which can be very valuable in managing a project or business.

FIGURE 1-1: Sending messages with electronic mail

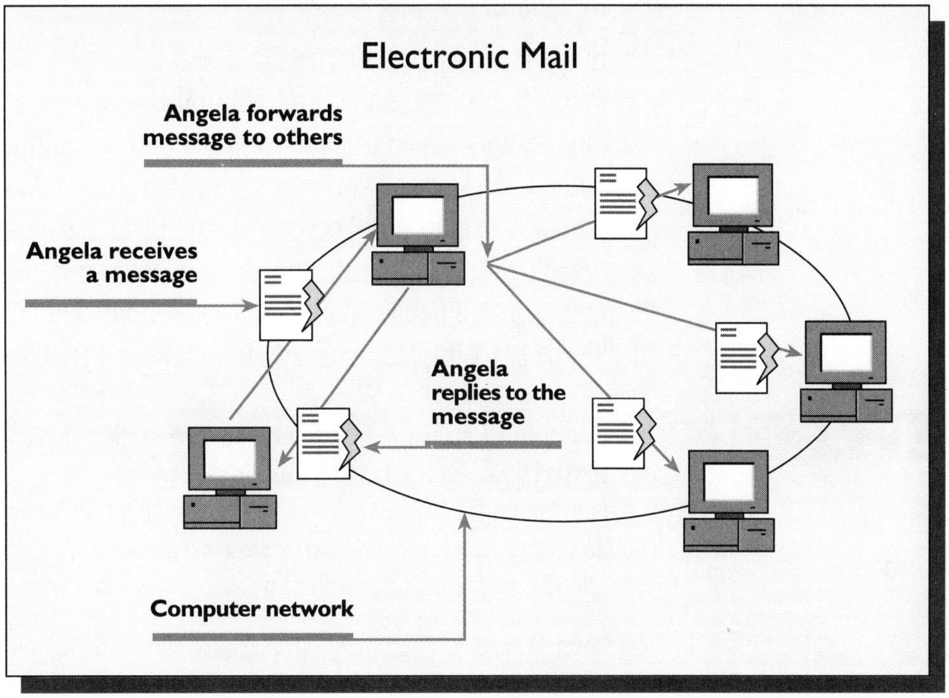

Electronic mail guidelines

It's a good idea to learn whether your company permits sending personal messages. Keep in mind that all messages you send have been legally interpreted as property of the company you work for, so never assume that your messages are private. Be sure to carefully consider the content of your messages before you send them, and never send confidential or sensitive material. When you compose a message, remember that the recipient can't use your voice, your facial expressions, or your body language to help understand the intent of your message. Therefore, you need to take extra care in what you say and how you say it in your messages. For example, using all capital letters in the text of a message is the e-mail equivalent of screaming and is not appropriate. If a message upsets you, wait a few moments to calm down before you reply. Once you send a message, you cannot prevent it from being delivered.

Starting Learning Mail

Before you can read or send messages, you must start Mail and enter a secret password. In this lesson and throughout this unit, you'll work with the Learning Mail application, which is installed in the Course Programs program group on the Windows desktop. (If you were using Microsoft Mail, it would be installed in a different program group.) You need to complete this unit in one sitting; do not exit Learning Mail until instructed. You will be using the mailbox of Angela Pacheco, who is a marketing manager at Nomad, Ltd. Case In the steps below, you'll start Learning Mail and sign in to Angela's Mail account using a password.

1 Starting from Program Manager, double-click the **Course Programs program group icon** on your desktop
If you are running Learning Mail under Microsoft Windows 95, click the **Start button**, point to **Programs**, point to **Course Programs**, then click **Learning Mail**. Then, skip Step 2 and continue with Step 3.

The Course Programs program group appears as shown in Figure 1-2. Note that the actual Microsoft Mail program would be stored in a different program group on your computer.

2 In the Course Programs window, double-click the **Learning Mail** icon
You see a message box describing the Learning Mail simulation program. Angela closes this message box to continue.

3 Click **Continue**
The Learning Mail application starts, and the Sign In dialog box appears. Here you see the name "Angela Pacheco." Angela is a fictional manager at Nomad, Ltd. You'll be using her electronic mailbox to complete the lessons in this unit. Before Angela can use Mail, she must sign in and enter a secret password identifying herself.

4 Click in the Password box
Because you are opening Angela's mailbox, do not change the default mailbox name "Angela Pacheco." If this were your Microsoft Mail account, you would enter a mailbox name provided by your system administrator. Next you must enter the password.

5 In the Password text box, type any password you wish, using up to 19 characters, then press **[Enter]**
To learn more about passwords, see the related topic "Keeping your password secure." In the next lesson, you'll examine the Learning Mail window.

FIGURE 1-2: Course Programs program group

FIGURE 1-3: Sign In dialog box

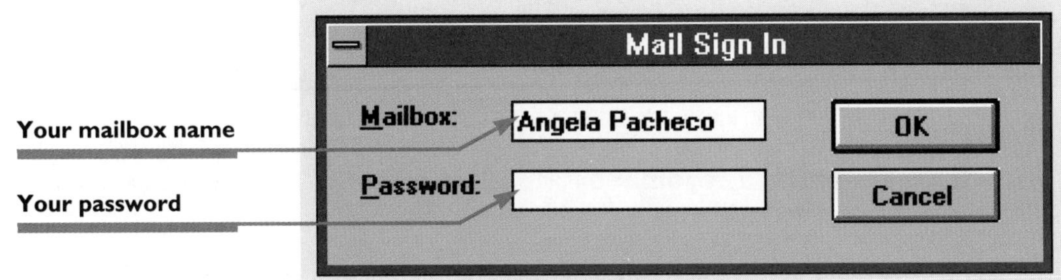

Keeping your password secure

In Learning Mail, you can enter any password you wish up to 22 characters. In Microsoft Mail, however, your system administrator will probably provide you with your own unique and secret password. After you've been assigned a password, you can then change it to one of your own choosing. It's a good idea to change your password every two months, to keep it secure. Make sure you choose a password that's easy for you to remember, but difficult for others to guess. As a security benefit, your password does not appear in the Sign in dialog box as you type it in. Instead, you see "*" as you type each letter.

QUICK TIP

To keep your password secret, do not write it down in a visible place, share it with others, or use a pet's or child's name as a password. Such passwords are easy for others to guess.■

Viewing the Learning Mail window

Before you can use Mail, you need to understand the key parts of the Mail window. Use the list below and Figure 1-4 to learn about each part of the window.

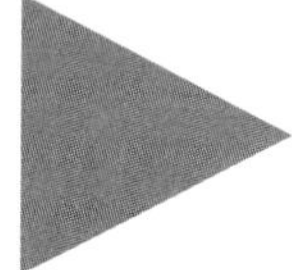

- In the Learning Mail window, you see Angela's **Inbox**, which shows a list of message headers of e-mail she has received. Each **message header** identifies the sender of the message, the subject, and the date and time the message was sent.
- An icon to the left of the sender's name represents the status of the message. For example, an icon that looks like a closed envelope indicates that the message has not been read. See Table 1-1 for a description of the icons you might see in the Inbox.
- On the left side of the Inbox you see a list of **folders**. The Deleted mail folder contains messages you have deleted. The Sent mail folder contains messages you have sent. The Inbox folder contains all the messages other users have sent to you. The Inbox folder is currently open. To open a different folder, you simply double-click the folder icon.
- Behind the Inbox folder window is another window that contains the Outbox. The **Outbox** contains messages you have sent, but which Learning Mail has not yet delivered. If your mail server is very quick, you might not see messages in the Outbox at all. If messages do appear in the Outbox, you can view the messages by clicking anywhere on the Outbox window.
- At the top of the window, the **title bar** displays the name of the application, Learning Mail. When you are reading messages the subject of the message appears in the title bar.
- The **menu bar** (as in all Windows applications) contains the names of the menu items. Clicking a menu item on the menu bar displays a list of related commands. For example, you use the commands on the Edit menu to edit the text of your message.
- Under the menu bar, the **toolbar** contains buttons that give you quick access to the most frequently used commands.
- The **status bar** at the bottom of the window informs you when you receive a new message. It also displays the current time.

FIGURE 1-4: Learning Mail window

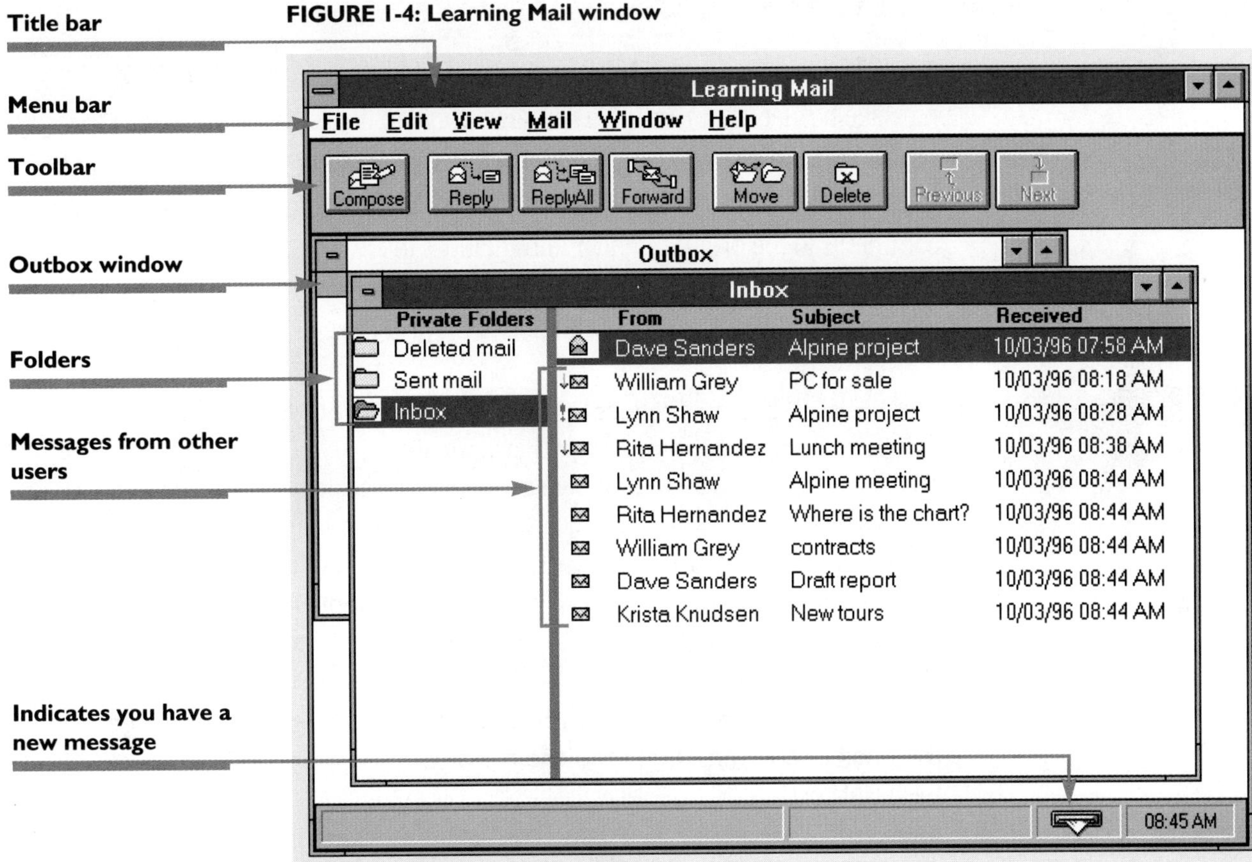

TABLE 1-1: Message header icons

ICON	DESCRIPTION
	High priority unread message
	High priority read message
	Low priority unread message
	Low priority read message
	Normal priority unread message
	Normal priority read message

Replying to messages

To read a message in your Inbox, you simply double-click anywhere in the message header. After reading a message, you can delete it or keep it in your Inbox. You can also send a response back to the sender of the message, using the Reply button on the toolbar. The Reply command automatically addresses your comments to the original sender and includes the text of the original sender's message. For more information on the text of the message, see the related topic "Emoticons." case Angela will read a few messages and send a reply.

1. **Double-click the message containing Lunch meeting in the Subject column, then read the message that appears**
   The message appears in the message window, as shown in Figure 1-5. After reading the message, Angela wants to close this message window.
2. **Double-click the Control menu box in the upper-left corner of the Lunch meeting message window (not the mail application window)**
   If you are using Windows 95, click the Close button in the Lunch meeting message window. The message window closes. Now Angela can read another message in the Inbox.
3. **Double-click the message from Lynn Shaw containing Alpine project in the Subject column, then read the message**
   You might need to scroll to see all of the message. After reading this message, Angela wants to send a reply.
4. **Click the Reply button on the toolbar**
   A new message window appears, as shown in Figure 1-6. Next, Angela enters the text of her reply.
5. **Type I prefer the Friday 4:00 time. I am working on an outline of my presentation right now and will send a draft to you soon. Because I will be relying on my assistant for a good part of this project, I think he should be at the meeting as well. What do you think?**
   After entering the reply, Angela can send the reply back to the original sender.
6. **Click the Send button in the message window**
   The message window closes, and the reply is sent. In addition, Mail stores a copy of the message in your Sent Messages folder. This folder is a permanent log of all of the messages that you have sent; the messages stay in this folder until you delete them. Next, Angela replies to a message she already read, indicated with an icon that looks like an opened envelope.
7. **Select the Alpine project message from Dave Sanders and click the Reply button**
   You do not need to open a message to reply to it. The message window appears. Next, Angela enters the text of her reply to the message.
8. **Type I am pleased that you are on the Alpine team. I will research your questions and get back to you.**
   After entering the reply, Angela can send the reply back to the original sender.
9. **Click the Send button**
   Mail sends Angela's reply back to the original sender, Dave Sanders, and the message closes.

FIGURE 1-5: Message window for reading messages

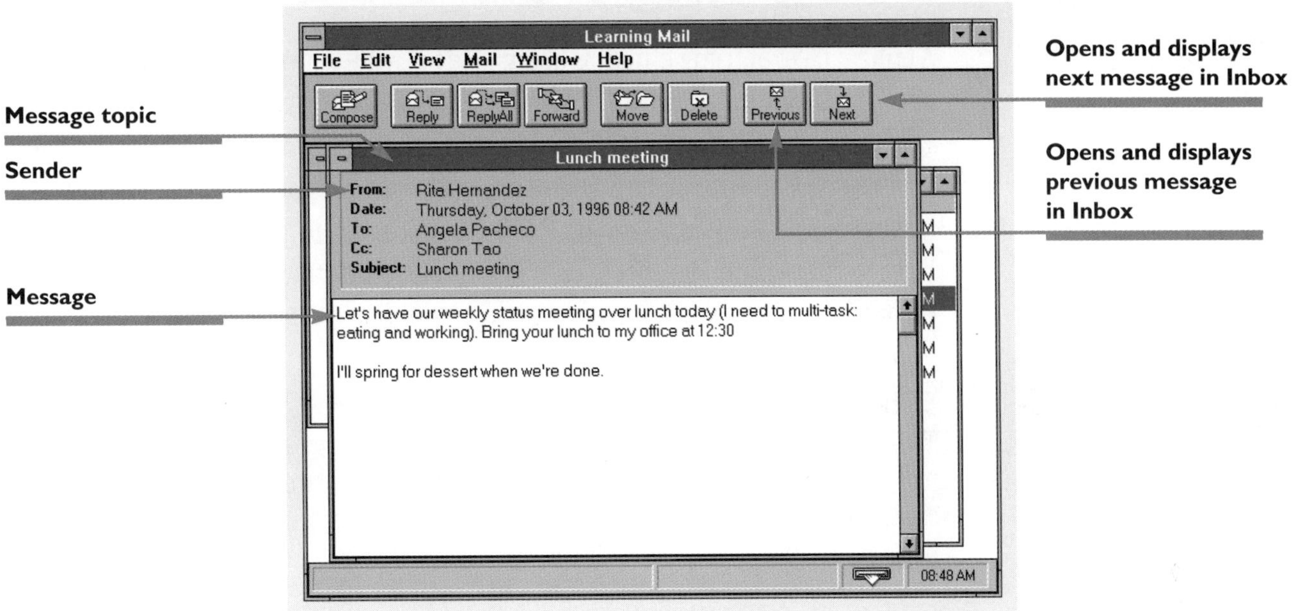

FIGURE 1-6: Message window for replying to messages

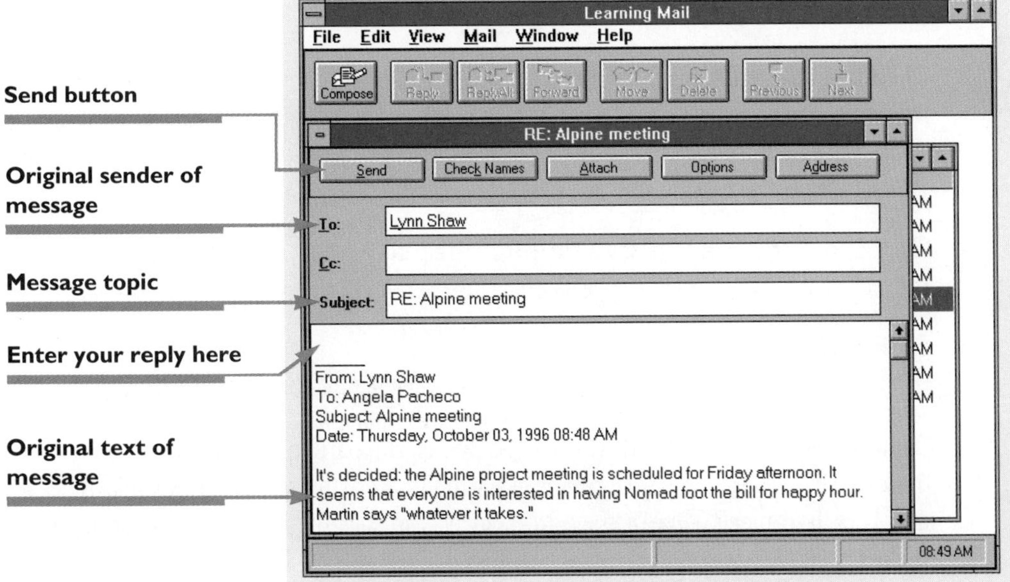

Emoticons

If you see something like this :-) in an e-mail message, you're looking at an emoticon. **Emoticons** are faces created by simple keyboard characters (in this example the colon, dash, and end parenthesis) to express an emotion or mood. The possibilities are endless and they're a fun way to get your point across.

QUICK TIP

The Next button and the Previous button in the toolbar provide a fast way to scroll through your messages. Clicking the Next or Previous button closes the currently opened message, and then opens the next or previous message in the Inbox. When you reach the top or bottom of the Inbox, the Next or Previous buttons respectively appear dimmed.

Creating and sending new messages

A critical facet of using e-mail is being able to create new messages and send them to other users on your network. When you create a message, you must indicate who the message is for and specify any other recipients who should receive a copy. You also need to enter a meaningful subject for the message. Then you write the text of your message and send it. **case** Angela wants to know if her assistant, Dave Sanders, might be able to complete an assignment earlier than originally planned, so she sends him a message.

1 Click the **Compose button** on the toolbar
The Send Note window appears as shown in Figure 1-7. In this window, you enter address information and compose your message. Although Angela could type a name directly in the To: box, she cannot recall if her assistant's user name is "Dave" or "David." To ensure that she addresses the message properly, Angela uses the Address feature to look up the correct name.

2 Click the **Address button** on the Send Note toolbar
The Address dialog box opens as shown in Figure 1-8. In this dialog box, you can view the user names of all the users connected to the mail system. These names belong to a **directory** (which is simply a collection of names) called the Postoffice List. Angela locates her assistant's name from the Postoffice List.

3 Click the name **Dave Sanders** to select it, then click the **To button**
The name "Dave Sanders" appears in the To: box in the Address dialog box. Angela wants to send a copy of this message to her supervisor, Martin, to let him know she is following up on his request to accelerate the project.

4 Click the name **Martin C. Danello**, then click the **Cc button**
The name "Martin C. Danello" appears in the Cc: area (for Courtesy Copy).

5 Click **OK**
The Send Note window appears again. Now Angela will enter the subject of the message.

6 Click in the **Subject box**, then type **New deadline**
The text in the Subject box appears in the recipient's Inbox so that the reader can quickly get an idea about the contents of the message. Next, Angela can enter the text of her message to Dave Sanders.

7 Press **[Tab]** and type **There is an important Alpine project meeting Friday, and I would like to show our ideas at that time. Let me know what I can do to facilitate your work.**
Angela is now ready to send her message.

8 Click the **Send button**
Mail sends the message with the default options in effect. If you would like confirmation that the message has been read, or if you'd like to use other options when you send a message, you can click the Options button before sending the message. See the related topic "Options when sending messages."

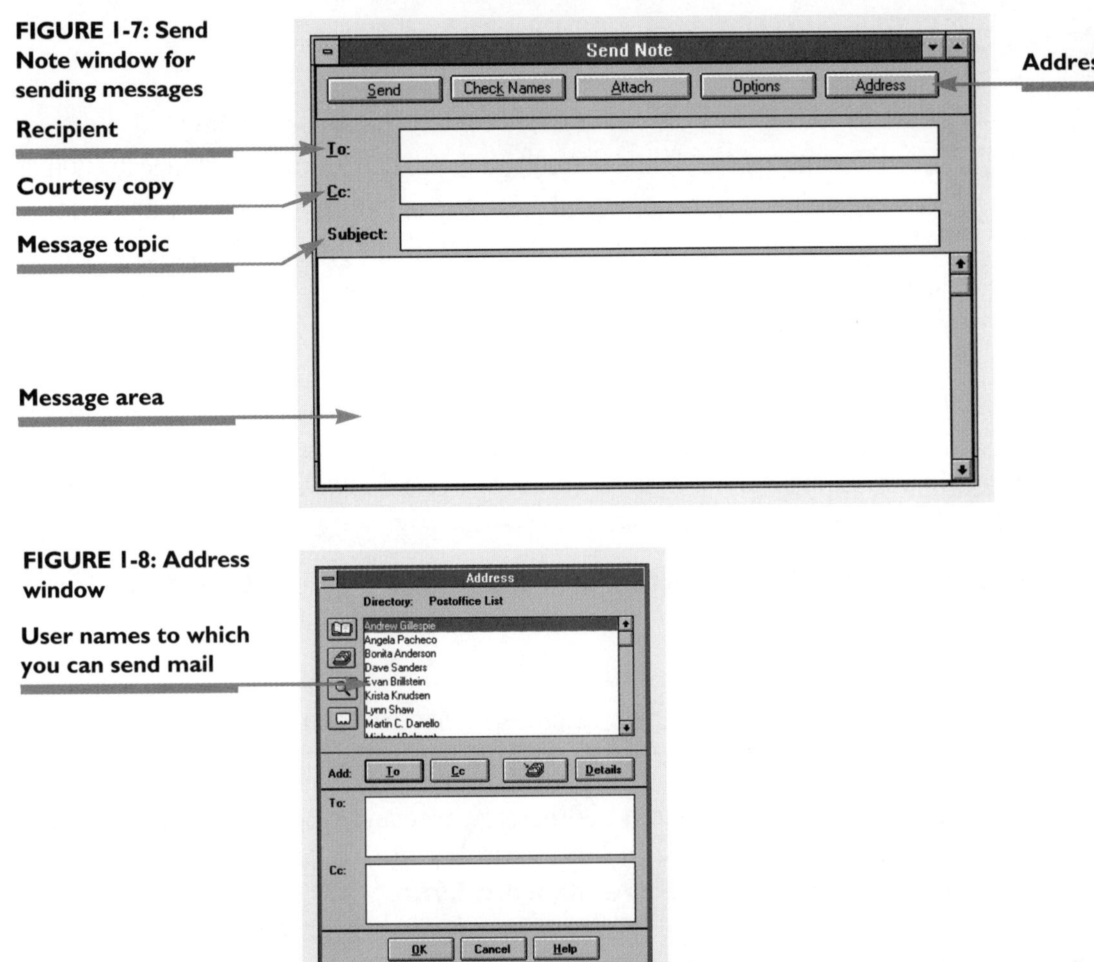

FIGURE 1-7: Send Note window for sending messages

FIGURE 1-8: Address window

Options when sending messages

There are several options that affect how messages are delivered. In the Send Note window, click the Options button to display the Options dialog box shown in Figure 1-9. When you want to know when an important message has been read you can click the Return receipt check box. When the recipient opens the message you get a **return receipt** message in your Inbox. By default, this option is not checked. Messages you send are automatically saved in the sent mail folder. If you would prefer to have Mail delete the messages, disable the Save sent messages check box. You can also assign a level of importance to the message, so that the reader can easily prioritize messages by looking at the Inbox.

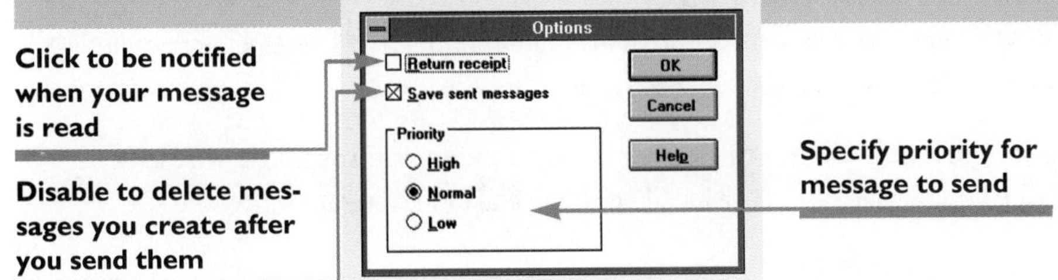

FIGURE 1-9: Options dialog box

QUICK TIP

In the Address window, double-clicking a name is a fast way to enter a name in the To: box.

Forwarding messages

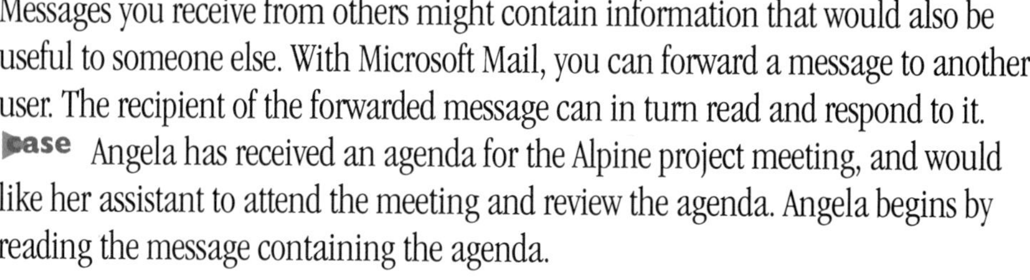

Messages you receive from others might contain information that would also be useful to someone else. With Microsoft Mail, you can forward a message to another user. The recipient of the forwarded message can in turn read and respond to it.

Case Angela has received an agenda for the Alpine project meeting, and would like her assistant to attend the meeting and review the agenda. Angela begins by reading the message containing the agenda.

1. **In the Inbox window, double-click the message with Agenda in the Subject heading, then click the Forward button on the toolbar**
   The Forward message window appears, as shown in Figure 1-10. First, Angela specifies to whom she will forward the message.

2. **Click the Address button, then double-click the name Dave Sanders**
   The name "Dave Sanders" appears in the To: box in the Address dialog box.

3. **Click OK**
   Angela returns to the Forward message window. Because the subject is already completed, she continues by composing a brief introduction to the message she is forwarding.

4. **Click the insertion point in the message area and type Glad to hear you are making progress. In fact, I think you should attend Friday's meeting. Here is the agenda from Lynn.**
   Angela has finished writing her message. However, before sending it, she wants to tell Mail to notify her when Dave has read the message.

5. **Click the Options button then click the Return receipt check box**
   The Return Receipt option is enabled, as shown in Figure 1-11.

6. **Click OK**
   Now Angela sends the message.

7. **Click the Send button**
   The message is now forwarded to Dave Sanders. After a few moments you see a message indicating the message was read. Depending on the size of the window, not all of the text in the header is visible. You can adjust the column width by dragging near the column heading. Angela opens the Read Receipt message.

8. **Double-click the message from Dave Sanders with the subject Registered: Dave Sanders**
   The Read Receipt message opens as shown in Figure 1-12. The Read Receipt message displays the details of the message and when it was read.

9. **Double-click the Control menu box to close the message window**
   If you are using Windows 95, click the Close button in the message window.

   The message window closes.

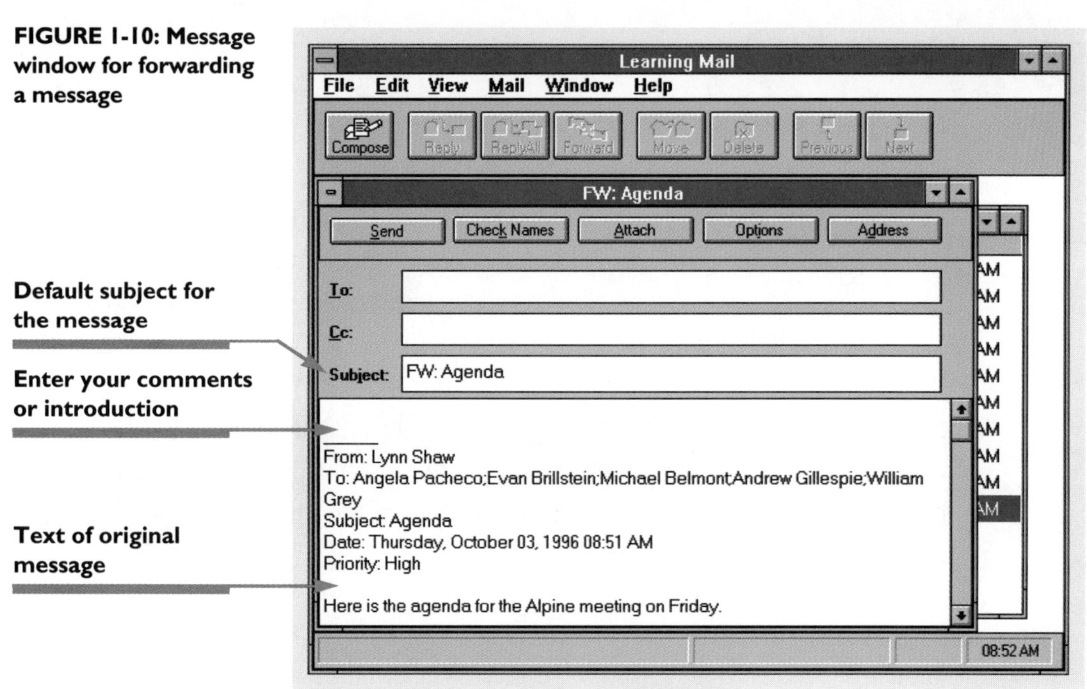

FIGURE 1-10: Message window for forwarding a message

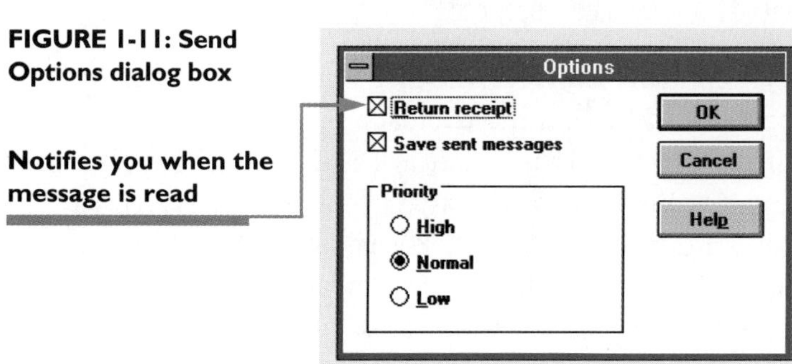

FIGURE 1-11: Send Options dialog box

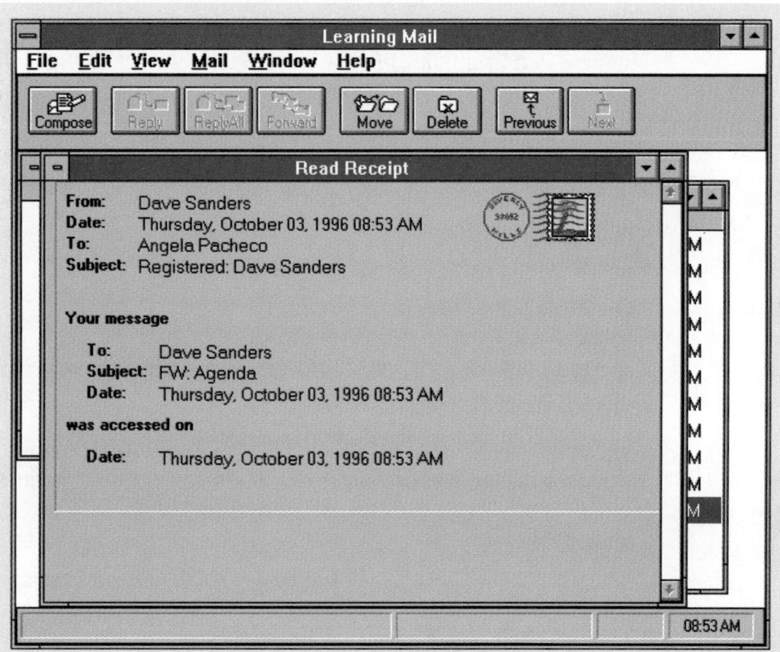

FIGURE 1-12: Read Receipt message

Managing your Inbox

As you work with Mail, your Inbox accumulates the messages you receive and read. To keep track of important messages and prevent the Inbox from becoming too big and inefficient, Microsoft Mail offers several options. For example, you can sort messages to quickly identify the messages you need. You can print messages that you need to keep on paper and you can delete messages you have read and no longer need. Mail also lets you store messages in folders, which you can create. See the related topic "Using folders to manage your Inbox" to learn about the folder feature. case Currently the messages in the Inbox are sorted by date (the default) with the oldest messages appearing at the top of the Inbox. So that she can identify the topic of each message, Angela sorts the Inbox by subject. Later she will sort the messages by priority.

1. **Click View on the menu bar, then click Sort by Subject**
   The messages in the Inbox are sorted alphabetically by the subject headings. She decides to delete a message she has read earlier and no longer needs to keep.
2. **Click the message that contains Lunch meeting in the subject column and click the Delete button on the toolbar**
   The message is removed from the Inbox and is now stored in the Deleted mail folder. If you accidentally delete a message you intended to retain, you can open the Deleted mail folder and retrieve the message. The messages in the Deleted mail folder are automatically deleted when you exit Microsoft Mail (however, you have additional options for managing the Deleted Messages folder). So that she can quickly locate important messages, Angela next sorts the Inbox by priority.
3. **Click View on the menu bar, then click Sort by Priority**
   Messages with the highest priority "!" appear in the beginning of the Inbox and messages with the lowest priority "↓" appear at the bottom of the Inbox, as shown in Figure 1-13. Angela decides she can delete the lowest priority message.
4. **Click the last message displayed in the Inbox (with a priority of "↓") then click**
   One of the messages displayed provides information Angela would like to have on paper (it contains the directions to Friday's meeting).
5. **Double-click the directions to meeting message in the Inbox, click File, then click Print**
   This command displays the Print dialog box, as shown in Figure 1-14. In this dialog box you can specify the number of copies to print and other printing options.
6. **Click OK**
   After you click OK, the dialog box closes and Mail prints the message on your printer.
7. **Double-click the Control menu box to close the message window**
   If you are using Windows 95, click the Close button in the message window.

FIGURE 1-13: Messages sorted by priority

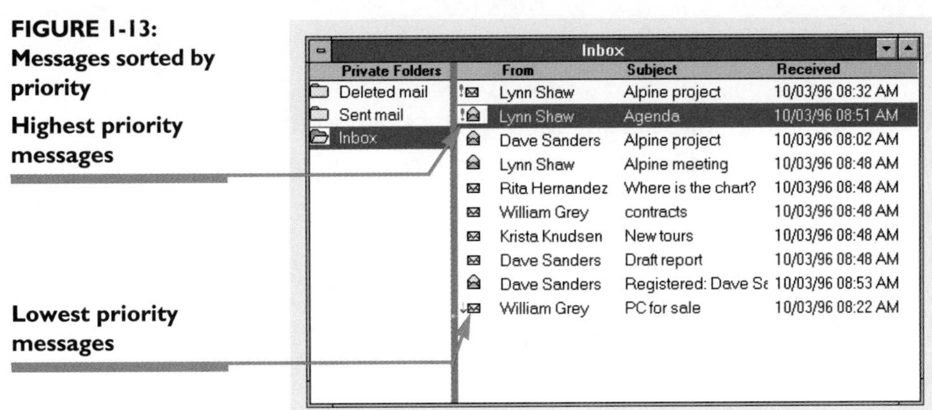

Highest priority messages

Lowest priority messages

FIGURE 1-14: Print dialog box

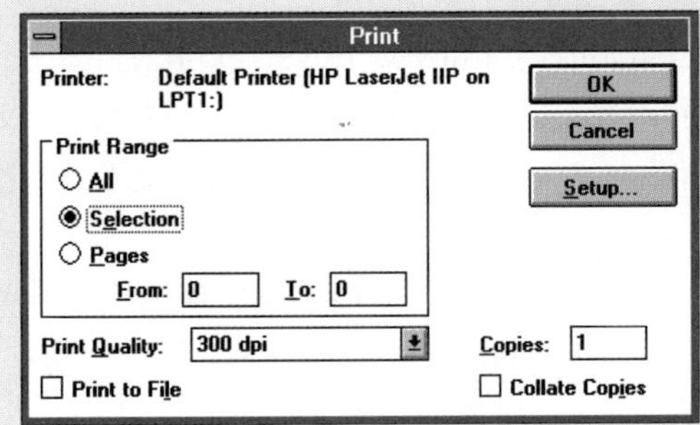

Using folders to manage your Inbox

In the actual Microsoft Mail application you can use folders to organize the messages in your Inbox. You use the New Folder command on the File menu to create folders to help you organize your messages. For example, you might want to create a folder called "Technical" and store in it messages related to system procedures or using your PC for easy reference. In addition, you can create folders within folders, allowing you to create a hierarchical structure for your Inbox. For instance, the "Technical" folder could contain the additional folders "Network" and "PC" so that you can further categorize your messages, as shown in Figure 1-15. After creating a folder, you simply drag (or use the Cut, Copy, and Paste commands) to place messages in the folder you want. Note that the ability to create folders is not available in the Learning Mail application.

FIGURE 1-15: Folders in Microsoft Mail

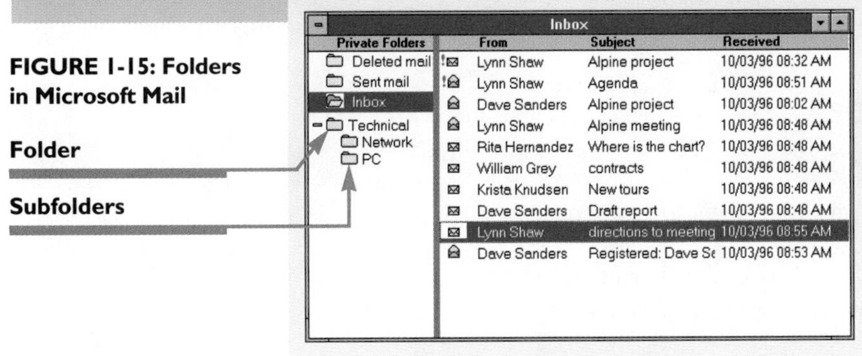

Folder

Subfolders

QUICK TIP

You can also delete messages from the Inbox by pressing [Delete]. It is a good idea to delete all unwanted messages immediately since they take up disk storage.■

Creating a group

When you address a message you must choose a name from the Postoffice List. If there are many names in the Postoffice List, it can be time consuming to scroll through all the names to select the ones you want. Fortunately, Mail provides two ways to manage the user names you use most often. You can create a **group**, which is a collection of names to whom you regularly send the same messages. For example, if you send messages reminding your staff of a weekly meeting, you can create a group that contains the names of your staff, called "Team." When you want to send a message to everyone on the team, you simply select "Team" from the Address Book, instead of selecting each user name. You can also create a **personal list** of names, containing only those which you use frequently. See the related topic "Adding names to the Personal Address Book." **case** Angela finds that she regularly sends the same message to members of her Alpine project team. She will create a personal group containing these names.

1. **Click Mail on the menu bar, then click Personal Groups**
   The Personal Groups dialog box opens, as shown in Figure 1-16. In this dialog box you can create new groups, add and delete names in groups, and remove groups entirely. Currently Angela has no groups, so she creates one.
2. **Click New**
   Clicking the New button displays the New Group dialog box in which you enter the name of a new group.
3. **In the New Group dialog box, type Alpine and then click Create**
   Mail displays the list of names from the Postoffice List. Notice the name "Andrew Gillespie" is already selected. From this list, Angela selects the additional names she wants to include in her Alpine group.
4. **Click the name Andrew Gillespie (if it is not already selected), then press and hold [Ctrl] as you click each of the following names: Dave Sanders, Krista Knudsen, and Steve Nicholas**
   With the names Andrew Gillespie, Dave Sanders, Krista Knudsen, and Steve Nicholas selected, Angela adds them to the list.
5. **Click the Add button**
   Verify that all four names appear in the Group Members area of the dialog box, as shown in Figure 1-17.
6. **Click OK**
7. **Click Close**
   Mail adds the group name to the Personal List.

FIGURE 1-16: Personal Groups dialog box

No personal groups created

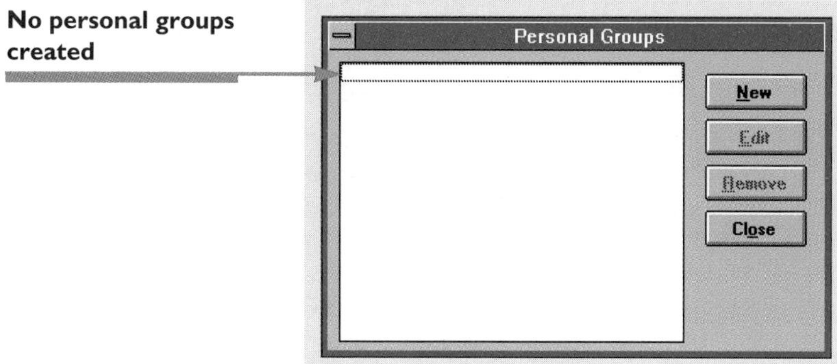

FIGURE 1-17:
Personal Groups dialog box with group entry

User names in new group

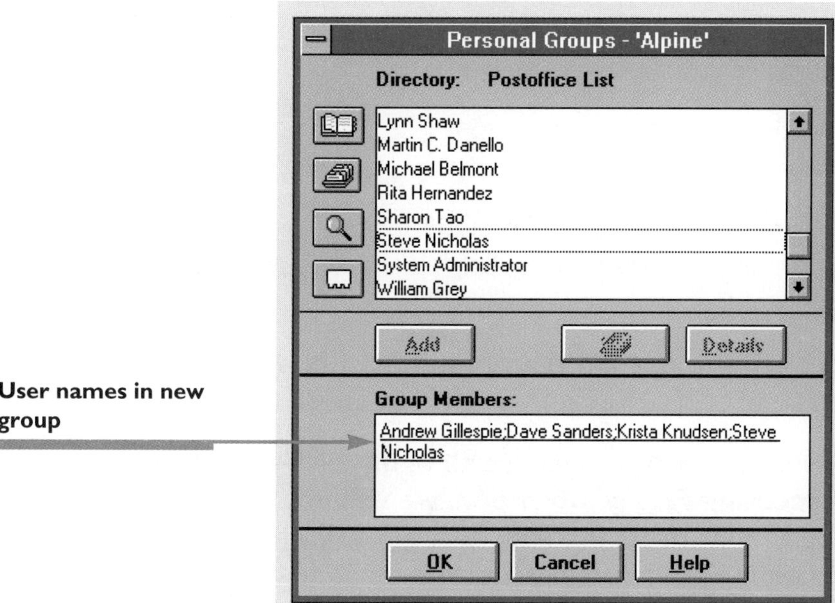

Adding names to the Personal Address Book

The names of the people in your groups are automatically added to your Personal Address Book, so that you can send individual messages to members without necessarily sending it to all the members of the group. You can also add individual names to your Personal Address Book without adding them to a group. Click Mail on the menu bar, then click Address Book. In this dialog box, you can specify the names of the users you want to appear in your Personal Address Book. Select the names you want, then click the Add to Personal Address Book button. To see the contents of the Personal Address Book, click the Personal Address Book button.

TROUBLE?

If a name you want to include in a group does not appear in the Group Members area of the Personal Groups dialog box, simply choose the name from the Postoffice list and click the Add button.

Sending mail to a personal group

In the same way you can send a message to an individual user, you can send a message to several users at once using a personal group. Case Now that Angela has created a personal group consisting of her team members, she can send a single message to all of her team using one easy-to-remember group name.

1 Click the **Compose button** on the toolbar
Angela would like to send a message to all the people on her team.

2 In the Send Note window, click **Address**
Because Angela wants to send this message to members of a group, she needs to switch to the Personal Address Book directory.

3 Click the **Personal Address button**
Clicking this button displays the Personal Address Book in the dialog box, as shown in Figure 1-18. Notice that Learning Mail displays the group name in a different color from the names of individual users. In Microsoft Mail, group names appear in bold.

4 Double-click **Alpine** from the list
It should be at the top of the list.

5 Click **OK** to return to the Send Note dialog box
The Send Note dialog box contains the name of the Alpine group. Angela enters the subject of her message.

6 In the Subject box, type **No team meeting this week**
After typing the subject of the message, Angela enters the text of her message.

7 In the message area, type **Because all of us will be attending the Alpine meeting Friday afternoon, we will not have our usual staff meeting at that time. Instead, let's get together to go over project status at 3:00 Thursday. Let me know if anyone has a problem with that.**

8 Click **Send**
Clicking this button sends the message to all the people in the Alpine group.

9 Click **File** on the menu bar, then click **Exit** to exit Learning Mail

FIGURE 1-18: Group in Personal Address Book

New group

Personal Address Book button

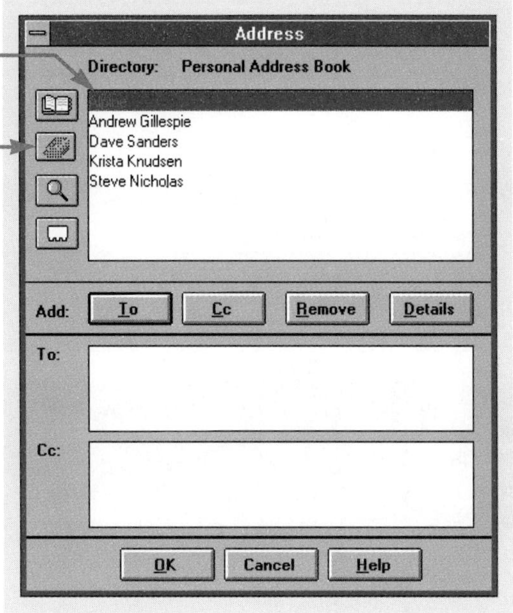

Address

Directory: Personal Address Book

Andrew Gillespie
Dave Sanders
Krista Knudsen
Steve Nicholas

Add: To Cc Remove Details

To:

Cc:

OK Cancel Help

CONCEPTSREVIEW

Label the parts of the Learning Mail window shown in Figure 1-19.

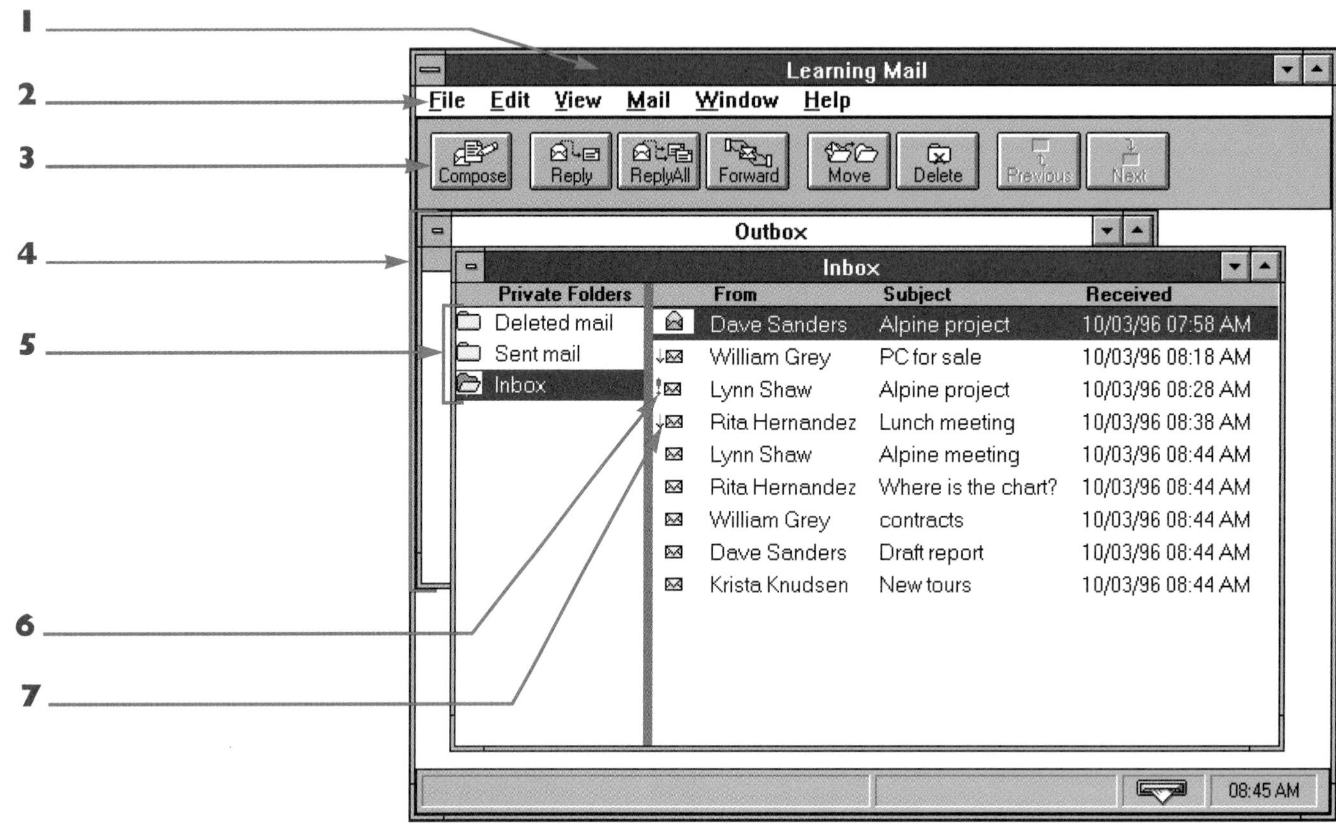

FIGURE 1-19

Match each of the following terms with the statement that best describes it.

8 Electronic mail

9 Personal group

10 Postoffice List

11 Return receipt

12 Inbox

13 Header

a. Identifies the sender, subject, and date of the message

b. All of the user names to whom you can send messages

c. A list of users to which you have assigned a name

d. Message you receive when someone reads the message you sent

e. Ability to send and receive messages over a computer network

f. Contains all the messages you have received

14 Which of the following is the popular abbreviated name for "electronic mail"?

a. Mail-net

b. Electro-mail

c. Learning Mail

d. E-mail

15 After signing into Mail, you see your messages in the:

a. Inbox

b. Message window

c. Mail window

d. Display window

16 To read a message, you:
- a. Click Mail, then click Read
- b. Double-click a message
- c. Click the Read button on the toolbar
- d. Click Mail, then click Open

17 After reading and closing a message,
- a. The next message opens so you can read it.
- b. You can click the Read button to open the next message.
- c. An icon in the header indicates you have read the message.
- d. The message is automatically deleted from the Inbox.

18 To forward a selected message to another user, you:
- a. Click File, then click Forward
- b. Click the Forward button
- c. Click the Send button
- d. Click the Reply button

19 To create a new message, you:
- a. Click the Compose button
- b. Click the Create button
- c. Click the Mail button
- d. Click the Send button

20 To send the same message to multiple users, which of the following is not an option?
- a. Drag the message to each of the user names.
- b. In the Address Book dialog box, you can select multiple names from the Postoffice List.
- c. You can enter multiple names in the Add field.
- d. Create a personal group containing the names of the users.

APPLICATIONS REVIEW

If you exited from the Learning Mail application before continuing on to this Applications Review, you will need to practice sending and deleting a few messages before you continue. You do not need to perform these steps if you did not exit Learning Mail at the end of the unit exercises.

1 Start Learning Mail.

2 Send three different messages to any three different users.

3 Delete any two messages from any two users.

4 Send one more message to any user.

After a minute or so, the messages described in the Applications Review exercises will begin to appear, so you can continue.

1 Read and reply to messages.
- a. Double-click the message containing "contracts" in the Subject column.
- b. Double-click the Control menu box in the upper-left corner of the message window (not the application window).
- c. Double-click the message from Krista Knudsen containing "New tours" in the Subject column.
- d. Click the Reply button on the toolbar.
- e. Type "Here are some ideas: Donner Challenge, Tahoe Trails, and Nevada Nirvana. What do you think?"
- f. Click the Send button in the message window.

2 Create and send new messages.
- a. Click the Compose button on the toolbar.
- b. Click the Address button on the toolbar.
- c. Click the name "Dave Sanders" to select it, then click the To button.
- d. Click the name "Rita Hernandez," then click the Cc button.
- e. Click OK.
- f. Click in the Subject box, and type "New chart."
- g. Press [Tab] and type "I think the Results chart for Rita should include a pie chart as well as a bar graph."
- h. Click the Send button.

3 Forward a message.

a. In the Inbox window, double-click the message with "Where is the chart" in the Subject heading, then click the Forward button on the toolbar.

b. Click the Address button, then double-click the name "Dave Sanders."

c. The name "Dave Sanders" appears in the To: box in the Address dialog box.

d. Click OK.

e. Click the insertion point in the message area and type "Glad to hear you are making progress on the charts. I am passing along a message from Rita. You can respond directly to her."

f. Click the Options button and click the Return receipt check box.

g. Click OK.

h. Click the Send button.

i. Double-click the message from Dave Sanders with the subject "Registered: Dave Sanders."

j. Double-click the Control menu box to close the message window. If you are using Windows 95, click the Close button in the message window.

4 Manage your Inbox.

a. Click View on the menu bar, then click Sort by Date.

b. Click the message that contains "Alpine meeting" in the subject column and click the Delete button on the toolbar.

c. Click View on the menu bar, then click Sort by Priority.

d. Double-click the message that contains "Draft report" in the subject column, click File, then click Print.

e. Click OK.

f. Double-click the Control menu box to close the message window. If you are using Windows 95, click the Close button in the message window.

5 Create a personal group.

a. Click Mail on the menu bar, then click Personal Groups.

b. Click New.

c. In the New Group dialog box, type Systems Committee and then click Create.

d. Click Evan Brillstein, then choose the following names by pressing [Ctrl] as you click each name: Lynn Shaw and William Grey.

e. Click the Add button.

f. Click OK.

g. Click Close.

6 Send mail to a personal group.

a. Click the Compose button.

b. In the Send Note window, click Address.

c. Click the Personal Address button.

d. Double-click "Systems Committee" from the list.

e. Click OK to return to the Send Note dialog box.

f. In the Subject box, type "Next systems meeting."

g. In the message area, type "For next Thursday's meeting we will review the proposals from the training companies. Please come prepared to defend your preferences."

h. Click Send.

INDEPENDENT CHALLENGE 1

To help you become more comfortable using the mail application, you can start the part of the Learning Mail program that is designed to give you the freedom to experiment with Mail features and procedures.

To complete this independent challenge:

Send a message (composed of any text) to the user called System Administrator. Shortly after you send a message to the System Administrator, you will receive a number of messages at random over the next few minutes. You can reply to, forward, delete, sort, and print these messages. You can also create and send new messages of your own. Be sure to explore using the different send options described in this unit. When you have finished working with the new messages, you can exit the mail application.

Glossary

Cc: An abbreviation for Carbon Copy or Courtesy Copy, which is a copy of a message you send or receive.

Delete folder A folder that contains messages you have deleted. Deleted messages remain in the folder until you exit the mail application.

Directory A collection of names to whom you can send messages. The Postoffice List and your Personal Address Book are examples of directories.

E-mail A popular abbreviation for electronic mail.

Electronic mail The ability to send and receive electronic messages over a network.

Folder A storage location for messages such as the Inbox folder or the Delete folder. You can also create your own folders where you can store messages yourself.

Group A collection of names to whom you regularly send the same message

Inbox folder A folder that contains messages you have received.

Message A form of communication you send or receive from other electronic mail users.

Network A group of computers connected to each other with cables and software to allow users to share applications, disk storage, printers, and send and receive electronic messages from one another.

Personal Address Book A collection of names with whom you frequently communicate using electronic mail.

Postoffice List A list that contains the names of users to whom you can send messages on your electronic mail system.

Priority The importance you assign to a message indicated with an icon.

Re: An abbreviation for reference, which identifies the subject of the message.

Return receipt The message you receive informing you that a message you sent has been read.

Index

Microsoft® Office Professional for Windows®
Additional Exercises

Word 6.0

Excel 5.0

Access 2.0

PowerPoint 4.0

Read This Before You Begin the Additional Exercises

To the Student

The additional exercises in this book feature several files provided to your instructor. To complete the exercises you must have a Student Disk for each section. See the inside front or inside back cover for more information on the Student Disks. See your instructor or technical support person for further information.

Additional materials especially designed for you are available on the World Wide Web. Go to http://www.vmedia.com/cti.

Using Your Own Computer

If you are going to work through these exercises using your own computer, you need a computer system running Microsoft Windows 3.1, Microsoft Word 6, Microsoft Excel 5, Microsoft Access 2, Microsoft PowerPoint 4, and a Student Disk. *You will not be able to complete the exercises using your own computer until you have your own Student Disk.*

To the Instructor

As an adopter of this text, you will receive the Student Disks. The Student Disks contain all the files your students need to complete the Additional Exercises. Your students must have the Student Disks to complete the Additional Exercises. See the inside front or inside back cover for more information on the Student Disks. You are free to post all these files to a network or standalone workstations, or simply provide copies of the disk to your students. The instructions in this book assume that the students know which drive and directory contain the Student Disk, so it's important that you provide disk location information before the students start working through the units.

WORD—Unit 2

APPLICATIONS REVIEW

1 Create a new document and save it.

a. Start Word and complete the Word screen check procedure described on the "Read This Before You Begin Microsoft Word 6.0" page. Make sure you insert your Student Disk in the disk drive.

b. At the insertion point, type a short letter to a local office supply company requesting a copy of their catalog.

c. Don't type the date or the inside address yet. For a salutation, type "Dear Catalog Dept.".

d. State that you are in charge of ordering supplies for your company. You want a copy of their catalog so you can compare prices. Spell the word "catalog" as "catalog." Ask if they offer discounts for large orders.

e. For a closing, type "Sincerely," press [Enter] once, then type your name.

f. Click File on the menu bar, then click Save As.

g. Make the MY_FILES directory active on your Student Disk.

h. In the File name text box, type CATREQU then click OK.

2 Insert and delete text.

a. Place the insertion point at the beginning of the document.

b. Click Insert on the menu bar, then click Date and Time. Select a date option from the list of Available Formats, then click OK. Press [Enter] twice.

c. Type the inside address. Use whatever company name and address that you want. Make sure there is one blank line between the inside address and the salutation.

d. Place the insertion point at the beginning of the company name in the inside address. Type "Catalog Supply" then press [Enter].

e. Press [Backspace] to delete "Catalog Supply" and the extra paragraph mark.

3 Select and replace text.

a. Select the text "Dear Catalog Dept.".

b. Type "To Whom It May Concern:."

c. Select the date and the paragraph mark at the end of the line, then press [Delete] to delete the entire line.

d. Click the Undo button on the Standard toolbar to restore the date.

e. Use selecting and replacing techniques to correct any mistakes in your document. Make sure you don't correct spelling mistakes.

f. Click the Save button on the Standard toolbar to save the changes.

4 Copy and move text.

a. Select the first paragraph including the paragraph mark below it.

b. Drag the selection to move it to the end of the letter.

c. Click the Undo button on the Standard toolbar to reverse the action.

d. Select the inside address including the paragraph mark below it, then click the Cut button on the Standard toolbar.

e. Click the insertion point anywhere else in the letter, then click the Paste button on the Standard toolbar.

f. Click the Undo button on the Standard toolbar to reverse the action.

5 Correct spelling in a document.

a. Click the Spelling button on the Standard toolbar and correct any spelling errors.

b. If Word identifies the company name as misspelled, click Ignore.

c. Add catalog as an AutoCorrect entry. (If this AutoCorrect entry already exists, add an AutoCorrect entry of your choice after completing the spell check using the AutoCorrect dialog box.)

d. Correct any other spelling errors in the document.

e. Click OK to close the Spelling dialog box and return to the document.

f. Save your changes.

6 Preview a document.

a. Click the Print Preview button on the Standard toolbar.

b. Click the page near your name.

c. Click the Magnifier button on the Print Preview toolbar.

d. Place the insertion point in the space between "Sincerely" and your name.
e. Press [Enter] to add one more blank line.
f. Click the One Page button on the Print Preview toolbar.
g. Click the Close button on the Print Preview toolbar.
h. Save your changes.

7 Print a document.

a. Click File on the menu bar, then click Print.
b. In the Copies box, type "2."
c. Click OK.
d. Click File on the menu bar, then click Close.
e. Click File on the menu bar, then click Exit.

INDEPENDENT CHALLENGE 1

As co-chair for the Middleburg class of 1990 planning committee, you are responsible for recruiting classmates to help with reunion activities. Open the draft letter named AEWD2-1.DOC from your Student Disk, then save it as REUNLET to the MY_FILES directory. Using Figure 2-1 as your guide, change the letter.

To complete this independent challenge:

1 Insert today's date and right-align the text (use the Align Right button on the Formatting toolbar).

2 Insert the inside address and salutation.

3 Insert the third paragraph of the text and the closing (insert your name) at the end of the document.

4 Delete the last sentence of the first paragraph.

5 Change all occurrences of "1980" to "1990."

6 Move the last sentence of the second paragraph so it's the last body paragraph.

7 Check the spelling in the document, ignoring all proper nouns.

8 Save changes to the document.

9 Preview and print the document, then close it.

FIGURE 2-1

April 13, 1996

Mr. Oliver Randall
Vice President/Marketing
InterSysData Corp.
4440 Pacific Boulevard
San Francisco, CA 94104

Dear Oliver:

As a member of the Middleburg class of 1990, I often think of the people who made Middleburg such a rewarding experience for me. Of course, there are the close friends I made and kept throughout the years, but also I think about the people I somehow lost track of since graduation. The instructors, students, and administrative staff all contribute to the richness of the memories.

Now is your opportunity to play an important role in helping bring Middleburg memories alive not only for yourself, but for your fellow classmates as well. As the co-chair of the Middleburg Reunion 1990 planning committee, I am looking for ambitious, organized alumna/e who are interested in working on various reunion activities.

We need people for the following areas: meeting coordination for all committees, computer consulting to help us use technology to work efficiently, meals and entertainment planning for the three-day event, and logistics coordination for getting everyone to Middleburg and lodging them once they return to campus. All committees need as many volunteers as they can get, so you are sure to be able to work in any area you choose.

If you are interested and available to work five hours a month for the next 10 months, please let me know. You can leave me a message at (555) 555-4321. I look forward to hearing from you soon.

[your name]
Middleburg Reunion 1990
Co-Chair

INDEPENDENT CHALLENGE 2

As a co-chair for the Middleburg class of 1990 planning committee, you received a telephone message from a classmate volunteering to serve on the entertainment committee. Create a thank-you letter to this volunteer that provides details of the entertainment committee members, meeting place, and schedule. Copy and paste the inside address and closing from the REUNLET document you created earlier. Save the document with the name THANKYOU to the MY_FILES directory on your Student Disk. Preview and print the document, then close it.

WORD—Unit 3

APPLICATIONSREVIEW

1 Format text.

a. Start Word and open the document named AEWD3-1.DOC from your Student Disk. Save the document as WINDOWMX to the MY_FILES directory.

b. Select the first occurrence of "Window Max." Click the Font list arrow on the formatting toolbar, then click Arial.

c. Click the Bold button on the Formatting toolbar.

d. Save your changes.

2 Align text with tabs.

a. Place the insertion point in front of the paragraph mark above the last sentence of the letter.

b. Click the alignment selector in the horizontal ruler until you see the left-aligned tab marker.

c. Press [Tab], then type "triple-insulated", then press [Enter].

d. Press [Tab], then type "tilt in for easy cleaning", then press [Enter].

e. Press [Tab], then type "maintenance free", then press [Enter].

f. Save your changes.

3 Format paragraphs.

a. Select the three paragraphs you just typed.

b. Click Format on the menu bar, then click Paragraph.

c. In the Spacing section, select the 0 in the Before text box, then type "2."

d. In the Spacing section, select the 0 in the After text box, then type "2."

e. Save your changes.

4 Create a numbered list.

a. Make sure the list of window features that you just typed is still selected.

b. Click the Numbering button on the Formatting toolbar.

c. Click anywhere outside the selection so the numbered list is no longer selected.

d. Save your changes.

5 Use AutoFormat and the Style Gallery.

a. Click Format on the menu bar, then click Style Gallery.

b. Select several different templates and examine your document as it would appear formatted in these templates.

c. Click Letter 1 in the list of templates, then click OK.

d. Save your changes.

6 Modify styles.

a. Select all of the text in the numbered list.

b. Click the Italic button on the Formatting toolbar.

c. Click the Style list arrow on the Formatting toolbar, then click List Number.

d. Save your changes.

7 Apply a border.

a. Select the entire document.

b. Click Format on the menu bar, click Borders and Shading, then click the Borders tab.

c. In the Presets section, click Box.

d. In the Style section, click the ¾ pt double line, then click OK.

e. Save your changes.

8 Format paragraphs with drop caps.

a. Select the first paragraph of the letter.

b. Click Format on the menu bar, then click Drop Cap.

c. In the Position section, click the Dropped icon.

d. Type "2" in the Lines to Drop text box, then click OK.

e. Click Yes in the message box to display the document in page layout view.

9 Adjust document margins.

a. Click File on the menu bar, then click Page Setup. Click the Margins tab.

b. Select the text in the Left text box, then type "1.5."

c. Click OK.

d. Select the placeholder "[your name]" at the end of the letter, then replace it with your name.

e. Save your changes.

f. Preview then print your document. Your completed document should look like Figure 3-1.

g. Exit Word.

FIGURE 3-1

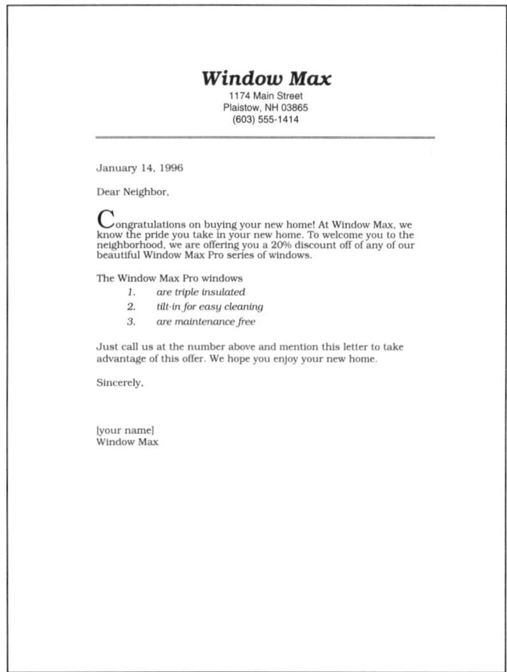

Window Max
1174 Main Street
Plaistow, NH 03865
(603) 555-1414

January 14, 1996

Dear Neighbor,

Congratulations on buying your new home! At Window Max, we know the pride you take in your new home. To welcome you to the neighborhood, we are offering you a 20% discount off of any of our beautiful Window Max Pro series of windows.

The Window Max Pro windows

1. *are triple insulated*
2. *tilt-in for easy cleaning*
3. *are maintenance free*

Just call us at the number above and mention this letter to take advantage of this offer. We hope you enjoy your new home.

Sincerely,

[your name]
Window Max

INDEPENDENT CHALLENGE 1

As co-chair for the Middleburg 1990 class reunion, you drafted a memo to the planning committee members informing them of the place and times of committee meetings. Open the document on your Student Disk named AEWD3-2.DOC and save it as SCHEDULE to the MY_FILES directory. Using Figure 3-2 as a guide, do the following to create the memo.

To complete this independent challenge:

1. Add a subject line to the memo.
2. Apply bold formatting to the meeting locations and landmark.
3. Add a tabbed schedule that provides meeting dates and topics.
4. Be sure to select the placeholder [Your Name] and replace it with your name.
5. Preview and print the document, then close it.

FIGURE 3-2

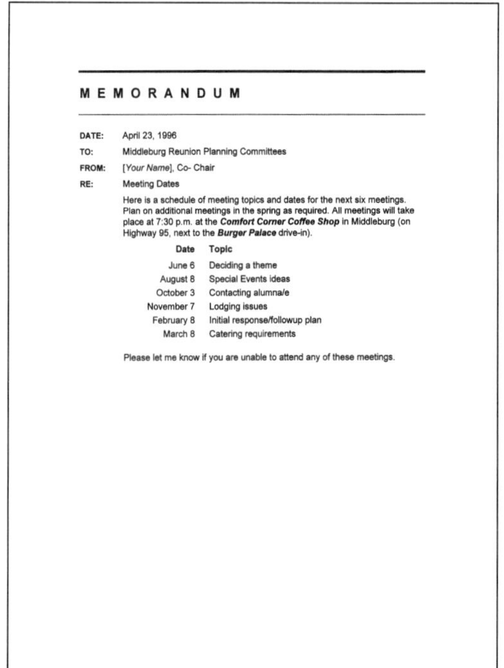

M E M O R A N D U M

DATE: April 23, 1996
TO: Middleburg Reunion Planning Committees
FROM: [*Your Name*], Co- Chair
RE: Meeting Dates

Here is a schedule of meeting topics and dates for the next six meetings. Plan on additional meetings in the spring as required. All meetings will take place at 7:30 p.m. at the ***Comfort Corner Coffee Shop*** in Middleburg (on Highway 95, next to the ***Burger Palace*** drive-in).

Date	Topic
June 6	Deciding a theme
August 8	Special Events ideas
October 3	Contacting alumna/e
November 7	Lodging issues
February 8	Initial response/followup plan
March 8	Catering requirements

Please let me know if you are unable to attend any of these meetings.

INDEPENDENT CHALLENGE 2

You are a member of the entertainment committee for the Middleburg 1990 class reunion. Another committee member drafted an announcement for a planned golf tournament. You volunteered to make the document more attractive. Open the document on your Student Disk named AEWD3-3.DOC and save it as GOLF to the MY_FILES directory. Using Figure 3-3 as a guide, complete the following formatting.

To complete this independent challenge:

1 Format the title in 18 pt bold italics, centered, with a shadow box.

2 Format all remaining text in 14 pt font size.

3 Format the first paragraph with center alignment, double-spaced, 30 pts spacing before and after, a left indent at ¾" and a right indent at 5¼". (Take care to use indent settings, not tabs.)

4 Format the lines "Where" through "How Much" with a right tab at 1¾" and a left tab at 2". Apply bold formatting to the right-tabbed information. Add 42 pts spacing after the "How Much" paragraph.

5 Format the next five "Cost/Event:" lines with a left indent at 1½" and a right indent at 4¼". Set a decimal tab at 2" for the prices. Add borders and format the text in bold and italics.

6 Center the "Complete the attached" line, add a ¾ pt dotted line as a bottom border, and add 30 pts of spacing before the paragraph.

7 Center the address information. Format the text "your name" in italics with 54 pts spacing before the paragraph.

8 Preview and print the document, then close it.

FIGURE 3-3

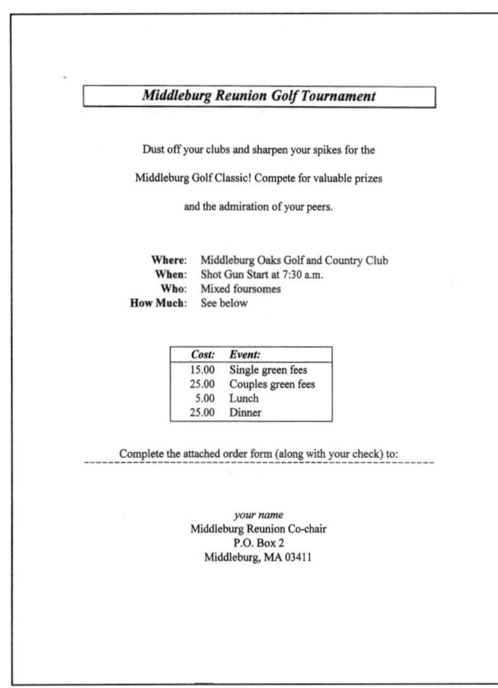

Middleburg Reunion Golf Tournament

Dust off your clubs and sharpen your spikes for the

Middleburg Golf Classic! Compete for valuable prizes

and the admiration of your peers.

Where: Middleburg Oaks Golf and Country Club
When: Shot Gun Start at 7:30 a.m.
Who: Mixed foursomes
How Much: See below

Cost:	*Event:*
15.00	Single green fees
25.00	Couples green fees
5.00	Lunch
25.00	Dinner

Complete the attached order form (along with your check) to:

your name
Middleburg Reunion Co-chair
P.O. Box 2
Middleburg, MA 03411

WORD—Unit 4

APPLICATIONS REVIEW

1 Create a table.

a. Start Word and open the document AEWD4-1.DOC. Save it to the MY_FILES directory on your Student Disk as WINTABLE.

b. Select the placeholder text "[insert table here]" then press [Delete]. (Do not select the paragraph mark at the end of the line.)

c. Click the Insert Table button on the Standard toolbar, and drag to select a grid four columns wide and four rows long.

d. Enter the information in the table using Figure 4-1 as a reference.

FIGURE 4-1

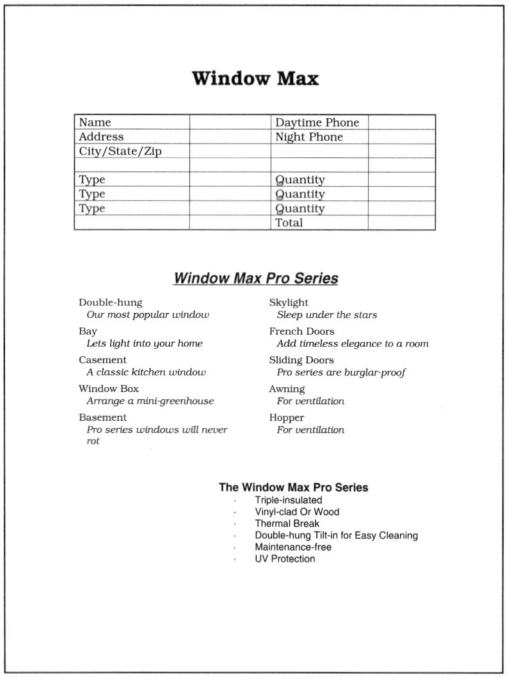

Window Max

Name		Daytime Phone	
Address		Night Phone	
City/State/Zip			
Type		Quantity	
Type		Quantity	
Type		Quantity	
		Total	

Window Max Pro Series

Double-hung
Our most popular window

Bay
Lets light into your home

Casement
A classic kitchen window

Window Box
Arrange a mini-greenhouse

Basement
Pro series windows will never rot

Skylight
Sleep under the stars

French Doors
Add timeless elegance to a room

Sliding Doors
Pro series are burglar-proof

Awning
For ventilation

Hopper
For ventilation

The Window Max Pro Series
- Triple-insulated
- Vinyl-clad Or Wood
- Thermal Break
- Double-hung Tilt-in for Easy Cleaning
- Maintenance-free
- UV Protection

2 Add rows to a table.

a. Position the insertion point in the last cell of the last row, then press [Tab].

b. Type "Type," press [Tab] twice, then type "Quantity."

c. Add two more rows with the same information as in Step b.

d. Position the insertion point in the last cell of the last row, then press [Tab] three times.

e. Type "Total," then press [Tab] once.

f. Save your changes.

3 Calculate data in a table.

a. Click Table on the menu bar, then click Formulas.

b. Press [Backspace] seven times to delete "(ABOVE)" in the Formula text box.

c. Type "(D5..D7)".

d. Click OK.

e. Save your changes.

4 Format a table.

a. Click Table on the menu bar, then click Table AutoFormat.

b. In the Formats list box, click Grid 7.

c. Click OK.

d. Save your changes.

5 Arrange text in columns.

a. Place the insertion point in front of the first occurrence of the word "Double-hung."

b. Click Insert on the menu bar, then click Break.

c. In the Section Breaks section, click the Continuous radio button, then click OK.

d. Place the insertion point on the paragraph mark below the second occurrence of the words "for ventilation," then insert another continuous section break here.

e. Press [↑] to move the insertion point inside the section you just created, click the Columns button on the Standard toolbar, then click and drag to select two columns.

f. Save your changes.

6 Position text using a frame.

a. Select the heading "The Window Max Pro Series" and the six bulleted items in the list below the heading.

b. Click Insert on the menu bar, then click Frame. Click Yes to switch to page layout view.

c. Drag the top center handle about ¼" up.

d. Drag the center handles on each of the other three sides about ¼" out.

e. Drag the framed text to the right about 3" so that the right edge of the frame is about ½" over the right margin.

f. Save your changes.

7 Insert and position a graphic.

a. Place the insertion point to the left of the framed text.

b. Click Insert on the menu bar, then click Picture.

c. In the File Name list box, scroll to and click CHECKMRK.WMF, then click OK.

d. Select the graphic, then drag the sizing handle in the lower-left corner up and to the right until the status bar indicates the graphic is 20% of its original size.

e. Click Insert on the menu bar, then click Frame.

f. Position the graphic about 1½" below the double-columns and about ½" to the left of the framed bulleted list.

g. Save your changes.

8 Create a footer.

a. Click View on the menu bar, then click Header and Footer.

b. Click the Switch Between Header and Footer button on the Header and Footer toolbar.

c. With the insertion point in the Footer-Section 1 area, type "Window Max — The Best There Is".

d. Format the footer text so it is italic and bold.

e. Click the Close button on the Header and Footer toolbar.

f. Save your changes.

g. Preview and print your work.

INDEPENDENT CHALLENGE I

You have learned many new skills since you drafted the committee memo for the Middleburg class reunion. You would now like to add some interesting visual highlights to the memo. Open the draft memo on your Student Disk called AEWD4-2.DOC and save it as REUNION to the MY_FILES directory. Using Figure 4-2 as your guide, complete the following formatting.

To complete this independent challenge:

1 Convert the tabbed text in the document to a table.

2 Delete the first column.

3 Select the entire table then use the Cell Height and Width command to center the table (on the Row Tab) and automatically adjust the column width (click AutoFit on the Column tab).

4 Use the Table AutoFormat command to format the table with the Columns 5 settings.

5 Insert the Clipart graphic file DINNER1.WMF at the end of the document.

6 Size the graphic to be approximately 160% of its original height and 300% of its original width.

7 Center the graphic between the left and right margins.

8 Preview and print the document, then close it.

FIGURE 4-2

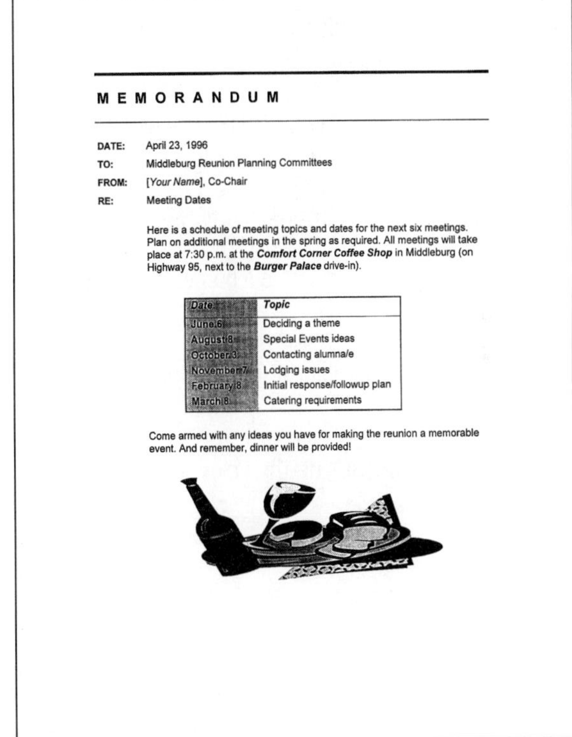

M E M O R A N D U M

DATE: April 23, 1996
TO: Middleburg Reunion Planning Committees
FROM: [*Your Name*], Co-Chair
RE: Meeting Dates

Here is a schedule of meeting topics and dates for the next six meetings. Plan on additional meetings in the spring as required. All meetings will take place at 7:30 p.m. at the ***Comfort Corner Coffee Shop*** in Middleburg (on Highway 95, next to the ***Burger Palace*** drive-in).

Date	***Topic***
June 6	Deciding a theme
August 8	Special Events ideas
October 3	Contacting alumna/e
November 7	Lodging issues
February 8	Initial response/followup plan
March 8	Catering requirements

Come armed with any ideas you have for making the reunion a memorable event. And remember, dinner will be provided!

INDEPENDENT CHALLENGE 2

You would like to further enhance the appearance of the golf announcement for the Middleburg class reunion. Open the draft announcement on your Student Disk called AEWD4-3.DOC and save it as GOLFTOUR to the MY_FILES directory. Using Figure 4-3 as your guide, complete the following formatting.

1 Convert the tabbed text ("Where" through "How Much") to a three-column table.

2 Delete the blank column in the table.

3 Use Table AutoFormat to format the table with the Columns 5 settings. (Be sure to clear the Heading Rows check box.)

4 Use the Cell Height and Width command to center the table between the left and right margins.

5 Insert the Clipart graphic file GOLF.WMF anywhere in the document.

6 Size the graphic so that it is 30% of its original size.

7 Copy and paste the graphic to create a border from the left to right margins.

8 Frame the graphic border and position it along the bottom of the document.

9 Preview and print the document, then close it.

FIGURE 4-3

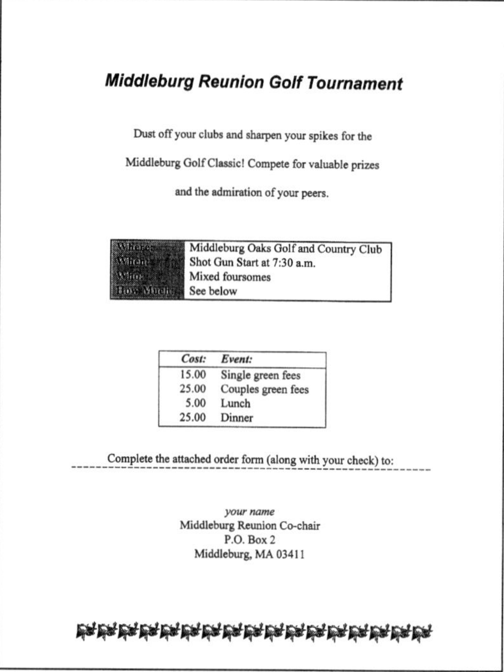

Middleburg Reunion Golf Tournament

Dust off your clubs and sharpen your spikes for the

Middleburg Golf Classic! Compete for valuable prizes

and the admiration of your peers.

Where:	Middleburg Oaks Golf and Country Club
When:	Shot Gun Start at 7:30 a.m.
Who:	Mixed foursomes
How Much:	See below

Cost:	*Event:*
15.00	Single green fees
25.00	Couples green fees
5.00	Lunch
25.00	Dinner

Complete the attached order form (along with your check) to:

your name
Middleburg Reunion Co-chair
P.O. Box 2
Middleburg, MA 03411

EXCEL—Unit 2

APPLICATIONS REVIEW

1 Design a worksheet and enter labels. Use the Excel spreadsheet to enter data for the art collection of ArtsRUs, Inc.

a. Start Excel and begin with a new worksheet in the Excel worksheet window.

b. In planning the spreadsheet, we need to anticipate the kinds of tasks the spreadsheet will be performing and lay the spreadsheet out accordingly. We will need labels going across for the broad categories. We will also need labels going down with the information for each item.

c. Click cell A1 and type "Items." Move to the cell to the right by pressing [Tab]. In cell B1, type "Unit Costs;" in cell C1, type "Number;" and in cell D1, type "Total Item Value."

d. Save the worksheet as ART to the MY_FILES directory on your Student Disk.

2 Enter labels and values.

a. Enter the following five Items of art and the values for Price Per Item and Number from Table 2-1 into the range A2:C7.

TABLE 2-1

ITEMS	UNIT COSTS	NUMBER
Mickey and Minnie Pictures	250	8
Art Deco Posters	55	15
New York City Skyline	75	18
Shallowater, TX Skyline	25	18
Mondrian Prints	159	10

b. Click cell A1 and press the Bold button. Do the same for cells B2, C2, and D2.

c. Save and print the worksheet.

3 Edit the cell entry in cell A1.

a. Click cell A1.

b. Click in the formula bar to the right of the letter "s" in Items. The blinking vertical bar, the I-beam, should appear.

c. Press [Backspace] five times and delete the word. Type the word "Objects" and press [Enter].

4 Work with ranges and enter formulas.

a. Click cell D2 and enter the formula =B2*C2.

b. Enter the formula =B3*C3 in D3.

c. Enter the formula =B4*C4 in D4.

d. Enter the formula =B5*C5 in D5.

e. Enter the formula =B6*C6 in D6.

f. Select cells D2:D6.

g. In the Name box, define this range as "Totals."

5 Use an Excel function.

a. Enter a label in cell A7 by typing "TOTAL VALUE OF COLLECTION."

b. Click cell D7, then click the AutoSum button on the toolbar. The formula =SUM(D2:D6) should appear in the formula bar. Enter the formula by clicking the Enter button on the formula bar.

c. As an alternative method you can use the range you have just defined. Click cell D7 and delete all the items in the formula bar. Type in the following =Sum(Totals). Enter the formula by clicking the Enter button.

d. Save your work.

6 Explore the Print Preview options. Click the Print Preview button on the toolbar. Notice the buttons. The Print and Setup buttons have an ellipsis following them indicating that there will be further choices.

a. Click the Setup button. Notice the tabs. Click the Page tab and select landscape orientation for your chart. You can also determine the starting page number. Replace the word "auto" with the number "5."

b. While still in Setup, click the Margins tab and notice that the page margins can be changed. In addition, you have an approximate picture of your worksheet. Without changing the margins, center your chart horizontally and vertically. Change the settings for the headers and footers to one inch.

c. Click the Header and Footer information. Change the Custom Header to read "Test File." Change the Custom Footer to read "Chapter I-Page" and add the page number symbol (#).

d. Click the Sheet tab. Deselect gridlines so that the cells in your worksheet will appear with no borders.

e. Click the Margins button. Change the size of the cells so that the labels have more room. Adjust the size of the cells with numbers so that they are approximately equal.

f. Preview, then print the worksheet and save the file.

7 More practice with formulas and functions.

a. Open a new worksheet (this will not be saved).

b. In Column A enter the following numbers on rows 1-8: 34, 56, 83, 91, 81, 12, 37, and 101.

c. Select the cells from A1:A8 and give them a range name of "Items."

d. Click cell A9 and enter the formula =SUM(Items). Press [Enter]. The answer should be 495.

e. Click cell A19 and enter the formula =Average(Items). Press [Enter]. The answer should be 61.875.

f. Edit cell A4 by changing its value from 91 to 67. Did your sum change to 471 and the average to 58.875?

g. Click cell A11 and enter the formula =(A1+A6+A9)/sum(A1:A4). Your answer should have been 2.154167.

h. Close this worksheet and do not save the changes.

INDEPENDENT CHALLENGE 1

It is time to plan the annual office party. You have been given a list of everyone's favorite foods and have to pick the right mix of party snacks and beverages. Open the workbook AEXL2-1.XLS and save it as PARTY to the MY_FILES directory on your Student Disk.

To complete this independent challenge:

1 Examine the list of items, then select from among these items until you have the mix of food and drinks that you think your group will enjoy. You need to not only select the items, but also select the quantity to determine the actual cost. You do not have to use all the items. After all, this is your chance to pick the foods you like.

2 You have a budget limit of $200. Make sure your total purchase will be less than that.

3 Once you have your list completed, be sure to save your work then preview and print the grocery list.

INDEPENDENT CHALLENGE 2

Jennifer is trying to calculate the amount of money she owes in taxes. Her taxable income is $37,000. According to the tax tables, her tax should be 28% of the amount over $22,750, plus $3412.50. She used this formula to calculate her taxes. =B1—22750*.28+3412.50. To her dismay the computer tells her that she owes $27,217.50 in taxes.

To complete this independent challenge:

1 Create a worksheet to calculate Jennifer's taxes using the above formula.

2 Edit the formula to change the order of operations until you get the correct result.

3 Save the workbook as TAXES to the MY_FILES directory on your Student Disk, then preview and print the file.

4 Close the workbook and submit your printout.

INDEPENDENT CHALLENGE 3

Chris and Olivia just got married and they are trying to create their first budget. They want to begin their marriage by investing a certain percentage of their income each month into mutual funds. Chris earns $3,000 each month. Olivia earns $5,000 each month. They decide to save 15% of their after-tax income. Chris's monthly taxes are $1000. Olivia's monthly taxes are $2300.

Will the following formula work for them? =(C2+C8)–((C3+C9)*.15 If not, how should the formula read?

To complete this independent challenge:

1 Create a worksheet to calculate the amount of money Chris and Olivia should invest in mutual funds using the above formula.

2 Edit the formula to change the order of operations until you get the correct result.

3 Save the workbook as MUTUAL to the MY_FILES directory on your Student Disk, then preview and print the file.

4 Close the workbook and submit your printout.

EXCEL—Unit 3

APPLICATIONS REVIEW

1 Insert and delete rows and columns and adjust column widths.

a. Open a new worksheet and enter the information from Table 3-1. Begin by entering the text "Disks and dats" in cell A2. Enter all information in the rows immediately below row 2.

TABLE 3-1 : Disks and dats

ITEMS SOLD IN JAN.	PRICE PER ITEM	NUMBER
3.5 inch HD Disks	1	2578
Mouse Pads	2	256
Disk Holders	12	335
28.8 Modems	159	12
Printer cables	28	535

b. Adjust all column widths using the AutoFit Feature.

c. Click the row number 6. That should be the row that Disk Holders is on. When you click, the entire row should be selected.

d. Pull down the Insert menu and click "Rows."

e. In the new row that has appeared, type "Continuous-Feed Paper" in the first column; "48" in the second; and "78" in the third.

f. Adjust the column widths again as needed so that all the text in the first column appears.

2 Copy and move cell entries and formulas.

a. Click cell A3. Drag across the block of cells to include all the items, the price, and number sold. Click the Copy button.

b. Click cell A12 and click the Paste button.

c. Edit the second chart so that it now reads "Items Sold in Feb."

d. Click cell D3 and type "Total."

e. Click cell D4 and enter the formula =B4*C4.

f. Copy the formula down for all the items sold in January by either dragging from cell D4 to cell D9 and using the Fill (down) command from the Edit menu or by dragging the fill handle.

g. Edit the numbers in the February sales to read: C13, 1789; C14, 197; C15, 225; C16, 108; C17, 22; and C18, 321.

h. Click cell D3 and copy the label. Paste it into cell D12.

i. Copy the formula in cell D4 and paste it into cell D13.

j. Fill the formula down to total all the items sold in February.

k. Save your worksheet as DISKS to the MY_FILES directory on your Student Disk.

3 Format the cells.

a. Click on the number 2 for Row 2. The entire row should be highlighted.

b. Click the Bold button.

c. Do the same for Row 3 and Row 12.

d. If necessary, adjust any column widths.

e. Click the letter B for Column B. The entire column should be highlighted. Under the format menu, select Cells. Click the Number tab. Click the Currency category and click the currency format with the dollar signs and commas.

f. Do the same thing for Column D.

4 Change the font size and attributes.

a. Click cell A2 and increase the point size to 24 point.

b. Place borders around the January sales by dragging from cell A3 to D9. Under the Format Menu, select Format Cells and click the Border tab. Click the Left, Right, Top, and Bottom boxes and press [OK].

c. Do the same thing for the February sales.

d. Click the 3 for Row 3 and center the labels in the cells by either clicking the Center button or selecting Alignment under the Format Cells menu.

e. Do the same thing for the February sales.

f. Resize the column widths if necessary.

g. Preview your work and make any changes so the data will appear neatly on a page.

h. Save and print your work.

5 Modify an existing worksheet.

a. Open the file AEXL3-1.XLS from your Student Disk.

b. Save it as BAGELS to the MY_FILES directory on your Student Disk.

c. Use the Bold button and Center button to format the column headings.

d. Resize the column widths as needed.

e. Increase the point size in row 2 to 24 point.

f. Enter the formula =B4*C4 into cell D4.

g. Fill the formula down through row 9.

h. Enter the sum of all totals into cell D10.

i. Format cells so that columns B and D are in currency format.

j. Use the Bold button to format row 10 so that all items are in bold.

k. Use any other formatting techniques you wish to change any of the attributes for the cells.

l. Preview your work. Save and print the file.

INDEPENDENT CHALLENGE 1

Congratulations—as the newest employee in your company, you have been chosen to be on the negotiating team for the next salary contract at the Lean and Mean Dream Machine. Workers are desperately seeking a one-year contract that includes a raise which is at least equal to the anticipated level of inflation (4%) plus the expected increase of 15% in their health insurance premium. Management has announced that no more than $100,000 can be added to its current payroll (which includes health insurance costs).

Open the workbook AEXL3-2.XLS and save it as CONTRACT to the MY_FILES directory on your Student Disk. Notice that certain cells have no information in them, but have a dark border. These are the cells you need to fill in.

To complete this independent challenge:

1 Create a formula to calculate the Total Current Wages by Scale. (HINT: The formula should be the number of workers times the current wages.) Fill that formula down for all pay scales (rows 3–7). Do the same thing for Total Current Health Insurance.

2 For purposes of simplicity, give workers the total health insurance benefit of 15% above their current benefit. Calculate the Ins. plus 15% Increase and fill down rows 3–7.

3 Before calculating the percent increase in column 7, calculate the Total Current Salary, the Total Current Benefits and the Total Ins. Benefits plus 15% Increase for Employees.

4 Write the formula for the Projected Increase in Wages & Benefit Cost to Employer. (HINT: that will be the sum of cells G8 and H8.)

5 When you calculate the salary increase, you will need to calculate the raise to a tenth of a percent in order to get as close as possible to the $100,000 limit that management has said it will honor. (HINT: the raise increase will be between 3.5 and 4.9%. Don't forget that you must apply the same percent increase to ALL workers.)

6 Format all cells that you have completed by selecting a number format that displays the numbers in dollar format, with commas. Adjust any columns that need to be made wider. Use any formatting enhancements necessary to make your worksheet more attractive.

7 Before printing, preview the file. Adjust any items as needed and print a copy. Save your work before closing the file.

INDEPENDENT CHALLENGE 2

The ABC Carpet company has just bought you a new laptop computer to take with you to homes and businesses to aid you in quickly calculating carpet estimates. You want to appear to be very professional, so you should try to set up all formulas in your spreadsheet before you visit each site. Your first job is to work up an estimate for Helen Smith, the owner of a condominium. Helen wants carpet for the following rooms: entry way, bedroom, den, living room, and study. The carpet in the bedroom and living room will be wall-to-wall and will not require binding. Carpet in the entry way, den, and study will be bound. The binding price for a linear foot of carpet is $1.25. When you measure the rooms, all your calculations should be put in feet, but the cost of carpet is in square yards.

Open the workbook AEXL3-3.XLS and save it as CARPET to the MY_FILES directory on your Student Disk. Notes that are important to you have been set up at the bottom of the spreadsheet. Notice that certain cells have no information in them, but have a dark border. These are the cells you will be filling in.

To complete this independent challenge:

1 Create a formula to calculate the perimeters of the entry way, den, and study. (HINT: Perimeter=(2*length) + (2*width).)

2 Create a formula to calculate the area of the entry way. Fill down the formula. Format numbers so that they are rounded to the nearest tenth of a yard. (*HINT*: Area must be calculated in square yards so the formula must be Area=(Length*Width)/9.)

3 Calculate the binding cost for the three rooms that will have bound rugs. Remember that the binding price is given in Cell D13. Total the binding cost. Format the numbers so that they are in dollar format with two decimal places.

4 Calculate the carpet cost for each room. Calculate the total cost for the owner of the condominium. Format the numbers so that they are in dollar format with two decimal places.

5 Preview your spreadsheet and make any formatting changes you need to make this estimate look as professional as possible. Look carefully at the options in the Print Preview Menu. You may also wish to eliminate the notes and add touches to make it look personal for Helen and to add vital business and address information about the ABC Company. Print a copy and save your work.

6 Because you will be using this same spreadsheet again and again with different kinds of locations and building arrangements, practice adding rows as you need to add new rooms. Remember to add rows, click the row number and go to the Insert menu and select Rows. If you make changes and wish to save them, save this file with a different name.

INDEPENDENT CHALLENGE 3

The Graphs and Graphics Company wishes to expand its present facilities and add a new computer wing to the new addition. The office manager has always been a proponent of purchasing equipment on a timely basis; however, Lindsay convinces her that leasing equipment (with a dollar buyback at the end of the three-year lease) will be a much better arrangement since all the equipment would be available in the first year. She convinces her manager that since each computer will generate a profit, the sooner all the machines are put into service, the more income the company will receive. Use the following information to help Lindsay prepare a spreadsheet that shows the cost differences between purchasing and leasing options. Make the spreadsheet as accurate as possible. Use all the formatting techniques you can to make it attractive.

- The following pieces of equipment will eventually need to be purchased: 24 computers at $1,850 each; 2 color printers at $600 each; 1 laser printer at $800; 24 software packages at $300 each; and a color scanner for $800.

- If the purchase option is used the following will be bought in year one: 8 computers, one color printer, 8 software packages and the color scanner. In year two: 8 computers, the laser printer, and 8 software packages. In year three: 8 computers, the second color printer, and 8 software packages.

- If the lease option is used, all the equipment and software will be acquired in year one. Each year the cost of the lease will be 37% of the total amount. The lease is for three years. For purposes of simplicity, assume that the lease payment is due once a year.

- Each computer has an anticipated profit of $1000 each year it is in service.

To complete this independent challenge:

1 Sketch a sample worksheet on a piece of paper, indicating how the information should be formatted.

2 Build the worksheet.

3 Format the worksheet.

4 Save the file as NEWWING to the MY_FILES directory on your Student Disk.

5 Preview the file, and make any adjustments needed, then print the worksheet.

EXCEL—Unit 4

APPLICATIONS REVIEW

1 Plan and design a chart.

a. Examine a recent newspaper. Notice the various charts that appear.

b. Look closely at the features of the charts. In most newspapers, you should find several different types of charts.

c. Ask yourself these questions. Does the author use the most appropriate chart type to depict the data? If not, what other chart type might be more appropriate? Does the chart contain labels and legends that provide you with clear information about the data? Does the chart have adequate tick marks, gridlines, and data points?

d. Make a sketch of one of these charts and use a different format for presenting the data.

2 Create a 3-D pie chart to present the results from a survey.

a. Open a new workbook.

b. Enter the labels on Row 1. In cell A1, type "Color." In B1, type "Number."

c. Click cell A2, and type "green;" cell A3, type "red;" cell A4, type "blue;" and cell A5, type "yellow." Click cell B2 and type "212;" cell B3, type "147;" cell B4, type "402;" and cell B5, type "114."

d. Select all the information (including your labels) and click the ChartWizard button.

e. Click cell A8. Confirm that you have the correct range selected and then complete the ChartWizard dialog boxes. Select the 3-D pie chart. Select the pie which gives the labels and percents.

f. The chart title should read "Comparison of Survey Results for Company Logo."

g. You do not need to include a legend.

h. Save the file as CHART to the MY_FILES directory on your Student Disk.

3 Edit the chart.

a. Use the 3-D chart you just created.

b. Double-click the chart to put it into the edit mode. Now click on the pie to change it.

c. Change all the pie colors to reflect the color in the survey. (Note: the first time you click, the entire pie will be highlighted. You must then carefully double-click on one piece at a time.) When you get a dialog box, click on the color of that wedge. Green should be green; red, red; and so on.

d. Pull out the blue wedge which should be the largest piece.

e. Double-click on this piece again and select a heavy black border on the Border menu.

4 Move and resize the chart and its objects.

a. Position the pointer on the top corner handle of the chart and drag the handle so that the chart fills the screen.

b. Double-click the chart to put it into the edit mode.

c. Move the title to the bottom of the chart.

d. Save your work.

5 Change the appearance of the chart.

a. Click the Chart Type list arrow on the Chart toolbar, and click the Column Chart button.

b. Make sure the chart is still in the edit mode.

c. Click the Gridlines button on the Chart toolbar and add gridlines to the chart.

d. Double-click on the column chart itself and select a pale color as a background for the chart.

e. Put a dark heavy border around it. (Remember that if you have a color printer, you should use color options. If not, try to make the chart more attractive by using contrasting patterns.)

f. Save your work.

6 Enhance the appearance of the chart.

a. Double-click the chart to make sure it is in the edit mode.

b. Click Insert on the Chart menu bar, click Titles, click the Category (X) Axis check box, then click OK.

c. A text box will appear. Type "Colors for Survey," then click the Enter button on the formula bar.

d. Click the Drawing button on the Standard toolbar.

e. Draw an arrow pointing to the blue column.

f. Double-click on the arrow to edit it. Select a bold line.

g. Click the text box to the right of the Chart Wizard.

h. Create a text box by dragging from the cross hatch pointer to the right. Type "The Winning Color" and click anywhere else on the chart to deselect the box.

i. Now, click on the box again and drag it close to the top of the arrow.

j. Make any other font changes you wish.

k. Save your work.

7 Preview and print the chart.

a. Make sure you are still in the edit mode, then click the Print Preview button on the Standard toolbar.

b. Carefully examine the Setup options.

c. Begin with the Page tab. Change the paper orientation to landscape.

d. Click the Chart tab and select "Scale to Fit Page."

e. Eliminate the header by clicking on Custom header and deleting the text. Do the same for the footer.

f. Save and print your work.

INDEPENDENT CHALLENGE 1

The Human Resources office has asked you to prepare a chart comparing housing costs in the various cities where your firm has offices. You need to compare average home prices for three-bedroom homes, four-bedroom homes, and two-bedroom condominiums. This information will be part of the package presented to employees who are being asked to relocate.

To complete this independent challenge:

1 Open the workbook AEXL4-1.XLS and save it as HOUSING to the MY_FILES directory on your Student Disk.

2 Determine which chart type will best present the data. Make sure that you make the work as attractive as possible by using the formatting options.

3 When your chart is completed, save and print your work.

INDEPENDENT CHALLENGE 2

In the first Excel unit you were asked to make a list of tasks that you could use spreadsheets for. Now that you have completed these four chapters, go back to that list and select a project of your own.

To complete this independent challenge:

1 Make a sketch showing how you might organize your spreadsheet.

2 Use the Excel functions that you have studied. Be sure you know how to enter data and labels, use formulas, add extra rows or columns as needed, and format your work.

3 If appropriate, create a chart.

4 Save the file as PROJECT to the MY_FILES directory on your Student Disk and print your work.

5 If you are unsure of any actions you need, take a few minutes and look over the Glossary of Terms and Index at the end of the Excel section. If these topics are not clear to you, go back and review the appropriate sections.

ACCESS—Unit 2
APPLICATIONS REVIEW

1 Plan a new database.

a. Plan a new database that will catalog important information on your friends.

b. Determine what information is important to include in this database.

c. Write the names of these important fields on paper with a brief description.

2 Create the new database.

a. Start Access and insert your Student Disk in the disk drive.

b. Use the New Database button to create a new database file.

c. Save the file as FRIENDS to the MY_FILES directory on your Student Disk.

3 Create the table.

a. Click on the Table object button in the Database window, then click New.

b. Click the Table Wizards button.

c. Select the following fields from the Sample Fields list box for your table:

FriendsID
FirstName
LastName
Address
City
State
PostalCode
HomePhone
BirthDate

d. Continue using the Table Wizard. Name this table Friends.

e. Click the Modify the table design radio button in the third Table Wizard dialog box, then click Finish.

4 Modify the Friends table.

a. Add a new text field called "Favorite Food" in the first available blank row.

b. Add a new text field called "School Address" in the next available blank row.

c. Add a new text field called "School Phone" in the next available blank row.

d. Add a new text field called "Major" in the next available blank row.

e. Add a new text field called "Notes" in the next available blank row.

f. Click the Notes field Description box.

g. Type "personal likes/dislikes."

h. Press [↓] to move to the next Description box. Enter appropriate descriptions for each of the other fields (for example, for FriendsID, type "Unique number for friend.")

5 Enter records in the Friends table.

a. Display the Datasheet window.

b. Enter the names and information about five of your friends. You can make up the data if you like.

c. Resize the columns so that all the data is visible.

6 Edit your friend's records, then preview and print the Friends datasheet.

a. Make the following changes: two of your friends change their major; three change their phone number; and one discovers that they are allergic to peanuts.

b. Click the Print Preview button on the Database toolbar. The datasheet displays in the Print Preview window.

c. After viewing the datasheet, click the Print button on the Print Preview toolbar to print the Friends datasheet.

d. After printing, return to the Database window.

e. Save the Friends table, then exit Access.

INDEPENDENT CHALLENGE 1

You are an independent computer consultant. A number of local businesses have asked you to create databases for them. Using your knowledge of Access, plan databases for the following:

- A bicycle supply shop
- A small music store
- A small advertising business

To complete this independent challenge:

1 Plan a database for Icehouse Bicycle Shop's inventory. List on paper the sort of fields you think necessary for tracking inventory. Make sure you include a reason for each field.

2 Open BICYCLE.MDB on your Student Disk. Look at the fields in this database. Compare these fields to the ones you created. Are there differences? List some reasons for the differences.

3 Plan a database for Tinbin's Music Shoppe. Tinbin needs a database to catalog inventory. List the fields you think Tinbin will need in the database and the reason for each field.

4 Open MELODIES.MDB on your Student Disk and compare the fields in that database to the fields you listed. Are there differences? List some reasons for the differences.

5 Plan a database for Madison Lane Advertisements to track their software library. List the fields required to track their software library and the reason for each field.

6 Create a new database file called MADISOFT.MDB in the MY_FILES directory on your Student Disk.

7 Use the Table Wizard to create the table and select appropriate fields. Select the Business radio button, and name your table Madison Software. Use the Invoices sample table for this purpose.

8 Save, print, then close your table.

9 Submit your plans, comparisons, and printed tables.

INDEPENDENT CHALLENGE 2

Madison Lane Advertising hires you to finish their software database. You need to modify the database you created earlier to match your employer's specifications. Include all the following fields in your database:

SoftwareID
SoftwareManufacturer
SoftwareName
SoftwareVersion
ProductNumber
Discontinued?

Add these fields to any others already included in the database.

To complete this independent challenge:

1 Open MADISOFT.MDB, the file you created earlier, on your Student Disk. Open the Madison Software table.

2 Add the additional fields to the table. If desired, you may delete earlier fields or type over them with the new fields.

3 For Data Type, use the text entry for each of the new fields except Discontinued?, which should be a (yes/no).

4 Type a brief description of each new field in the Description column. After modifying the table, click OK.

5 Type at least six entries on the table. Include any entry for Microsoft Word, Microsoft PowerPoint, and Microsoft Access, as well as any others you know. You may create data for any field. Print the datasheet.

6 Madison Lane just upgraded to the latest version of Microsoft Office. Change the SoftwareVersion and ProductNumber for Microsoft Word, Microsoft PowerPoint, and Microsoft Access, then print the datasheet.

7 Save and close the table, then submit both datasheets.

ACCESS—Unit 3

APPLICATIONS REVIEW

1 Find records.

a. Start Access and insert your Student Disk in the disk drive.

b. Open the database INVNTORY.MDB from your Student Disk.

c. Use the Find button and a wildcard to locate all records in all fields that start with the letter S.

d. How many occurrences are there?

2 Sort a table.

a. Sort the Products table in descending order using the Category ID field. Print the datasheet.

b. Return the datasheet to its original order by clicking the Show All Records button.

c. Create and print a list of products in ascending order by Unit Price.

d. Return the datasheet to its original order.

3 Filter a table.

a. Create a filter that shows all products with a unit price higher than ten dollars.

b. Print the datasheet.

4 Create a simple query.

a. Create a query for Step 3a above. Name this query "Products over ten dollars."

b. Create another query that lists all products with a unit price greater than $50. Name this query "Products costing>$50."

c. Display the ProductName, ProductID, UnitsInStock, and UnitPrice field data in the query for Step 4b.

5 Create a complex query.

a. Create a query that shows the Product Name of all products with both a unit price greater than $20 and sold only by the pair. Name this query "Pairs over $20."

b. Print the datasheet for the query.

6 Modify a query.

a. Modify the "Products over ten dollars" query to sort the results in descending order by the Product ID field. Make sure the Product ID field is visible. Save the modified query. Print the query results.

b. Modify the "Products costing>$50" query to include the following fields: Product ID1, Category ID, Supplier ID.

c. Modify the "Pairs over $20" query to sort the results in descending order by price. Save the modified query. Print the query results.

d. Close the file and exit Access.

INDEPENDENT CHALLENGE 1

You work for a Medical Consortium called Allied Surgeons and Physicians. Since three of the doctors (an Ophthalmologist, a Neurologist, and a Cardiologist) share an office suite and staff, they have hired you to create a database for their patients. Ultimately, they will need to sort, filter, and query this database to find specific patients.

To complete this independent challenge:

1 Create a database file on your Student Disk called ALLIED.MDB. Save it to the MY_FILES directory.

2 Create a table called Patient Records.

3 Add a minimum of three patient records for each physician. Patient records should include the following information: First Name; Last Name; Date of Birth; Gender; Height; Weight; Address; City; State; Postal Code; Telephone; Next of Kin; Known Allergies; Religious Affiliation; Emergency Telephone; most recent visit; and Physician Last Name.

4 Print the results of sorting the records in ascending order by Patient's Last Name.

5 Print the results of sorting the records in descending order by Physician Last Name, then in ascending order by Patient's Last Name.

6 Create a query for each physician that displays the First Name, Last Name, Gender, Date of Birth, most recent office visit date and Telephone number. Name each query "Dr XXXXXXX's Patient List" (where XXXXXXX is each physician's name).

7 Print out each list.

8 Submit all printouts.

INDEPENDENT CHALLENGE 2

Your computer consulting firm has contracted to create a database for a special effects firm called Grand Illusions. Currently, Grand Illusions is working on five films, each having a minimum of three special effects they need to track. Each special effect uses some combination of computer imaging, prosthetics, multimedia, archived footage, and an in-house tool called Black Midnight.

To complete this independent challenge:

1 Create a database file on your Student Disk called GRAND.MDB. Save it to the MY_FILES directory.

2 Create a table called Special Effects Register.

3 Create records for each special effect used in the five film projects. Each record should include the film name, special effect name, the Director's name, the tools used in the effect, and the completion date for the effect.

4 Print the results of the sort in ascending order by film name.

5 Print the results of the sort in ascending order by completion date, then in ascending order by Director's name.

6 Create a query for each film that displays the completion date, Director's name, and the tools. Call this query YYYYYYY Special Effects (where YYYYYYY is the film name).

7 Print out each list.

8 Submit all printouts.

ACCESS—Unit 4
APPLICATIONS REVIEW

1 Create a new form.
   a. Start Access with your Student Disk in drive A. Open the database called CUSTDATA.MDB from your Student Disk.
   b. Create a new form for the Customers table.
   c. Use the AutoForm button to quickly create a single column form.

2 Modify the new form.
   a. Maximize the form window and change the form's dimensions until it is at least six inches wide.
   b. Select controls and position them on the screen in an order that makes sense.
   c. Modify the tab order until the [Tab] key moves you through the fields in the order you arranged them.
   d. Save your entry as Customer Entry form.

3 Modify the controls.
   a. Change the format of the Date to automatically provide slashes between data entries (such as 12/30/96).
   b. Change the lettering in the Tour box so that it appears in boldface.
   c. View the changes in Form View.
   d. Save your changes.

4 Add a record to the table using the form.
   a. Open the Customer Entry form.
   b. Enter the following new record: First Name: John, Last Name: Peeters, Address: 805 W. Washington Ave., City: Madison, State: WI, Postal Code: 53711, Tour: Road Bike, Date: 6/15/94, Age: 32.
   c. Save the record.
   d. Print the form containing the new record.

5 Create a new report.
   a. Create a Mailing Label report based on the names and addresses using the Reports Wizard.
   b. Include the first and last name of each customer, the address on a new line, and the city, state, and postal code on a final line.
   c. Sort the labels by CustomerID.
   d. Preview the report with data in it.
   e. Print a mailing label with data on it.
   f. Save the report as MAILERS.

6 Modify a report.
   a. Align the fields until they are even.
   b. Add a comma and a space between the City and State entries. Add two spaces between the State and Postal Code entries.
   c. Preview and print the report.
   d. Save your changes.

INDEPENDENT CHALLENGE 1

The Medical Consortium, Allied Surgeons and Physicians, are very satisfied with the database you've created, and would like you to create some customized forms and reports for them. Using the ALLIED.MDB database you created earlier, create forms and reports that will make patient entry easy.

To complete this independent challenge:

1 Create a form using the Patient Records table that displays all of the fields in the table.

2 Arrange the fields in a way that seems efficient for data entry.

3 Update the tab order to reflect the new order of the fields.

4 Use the new form to add one new patient for each physician.

5 Print the form containing your new entries.

6 Add an expression that calculates each patient's current age.

7 Create a report based on each Physician's Patient List.

8 Submit all printouts.

INDEPENDENT CHALLENGE 2

To better control the expense of producing its special effects, Grand Illusions would like you to create forms, and reports with added mathematical expressions. Using the GRAND.MDB database you created earlier, create forms and reports that will help this client enter data and view its expenses.

To complete this independent challenge:

1 Create a form using the Special Effects Register table that displays all of the fields.

2 Arrange the fields in a way that seems efficient for data entry.

3 Update the tab order to reflect the new order of the fields.

4 Add a field to the table and the form for the estimated cost of the effect.

5 Add data to each record for this new field.

6 Print the form for the first record in the table.

7 Create a report based on each film's Special Effects query.

8 Add an expression that calculates Total Estimated Costs for each film.

9 Submit all printouts.

POWERPOINT—Unit 2
APPLICATIONSREVIEW

1 Plan and choose a look for a presentation.

a. Start PowerPoint.

b. Click the Pick a Look Wizard radio button, then click OK, then click Next.

c. Click the On-Screen Presentation radio button, then click Next.

d. Click the More button, in the File Name list scroll to and choose WORLDS.PPT, then click Apply, then Next.

e. Deselect the Audience Handout Pages and the Outline Pages options by clearing the check boxes.

f. Click the Name, Company, or Other text check box, enter your name in the box, click the Date check box, click the Page number check box, then click Next.

g. Click the Name, Company, or other text check box, click the Date check box, click Next, then click Finish.

2 Enter slide text.

a. Click the title placeholder, then type "International Studies Program."

b. Click the main text placeholder, type "Karen Hinrichs," press [Enter], then type "Director."

3 Create new slides in Outline view.

a. Switch to Outline View.

b. Click the Insert New Slide button.

c. Enter the text from Table 2-1.

d. Click the New Slide button.

e. Enter the text from Table 2-2.

TABLE 2-1

BENEFITS
Once in a lifetime experience
Strong Friendships
Lasting Memories
Cultural Experience

TABLE 2-2

PROGRAMS OFFERED
Italy
Sweden
Germany
China
India
And many others

4 Enter text in Note Pages view.

a. Switch to Notes Pages view.

b. Scroll to Notes 2.

c. Click the notes placeholder.

d. Change the Zoom view to 66%.

e. Enter the speaker's notes as follows:

Studying abroad is the experience of a lifetime. For the last ten years, our university has offered one of the best study abroad programs in the state. The benefits of studying abroad vary from student to student. However, all past study abroad participants agree that this experience will build strong friendships, create lasting memories, and offer a cultural experience that cannot be encountered on campus.

f. On Notes 3, enter the following notes for the speaker:

Our program offers over 25 different overseas locations. Some of the most popular programs include the Italian, Swedish, German, and Chinese programs.

g. Switch back to Slide View.

5 Save and Print a presentation.

a. Save the presentation as OVERSEAS to the MY_FILES directory on your Student Disk. Click Cancel in the Summary Info dialog box.

b. Click File on the menu bar, then click Print.

c. Click the Print What list arrow, click Handouts (3 slides per page), then click OK.

d. Using the same process, print the note pages.

INDEPENDENT CHALLENGE 1

You are an employee at Youth OutReach of America, a non-profit organization, that specializes in providing job training and education for young people, ages 16–22. One of the major funding sources for Youth OutReach of America is the Federal Government. Due to recent changes in how the government funds service programs, it is necessary to solicit local and state officials for block grants. It is your responsibility to develop the outline and basic look for a standard presentation that the president of Youth OutReach can present to various officials.

In this independent challenge, you will choose a look for the presentation, create an outline for the funding presentation, and create your own material to complete the slides of the presentation.

To complete this challenge:

1 Think about the results you want to see, the information you need, and how you want to communicate the message. Remember this presentation should be standardized so the president of Youth OutReach can use it for different audiences. Include information such as a mission statement, goals of the organization, number of young people aided by the organization, distribution of funds, and minimum funds needed.

2 Choose a look for the presentation.

3 Create new slides using the Bulleted list AutoLayout option. Enter text into the main placeholders of the slides. Use both Slide and Outline views to enter text.

4 Create a slide at the end of the presentation. Enter concluding text on the slide, summarizing the financial needs of Youth OutReach.

5 Enter notes for the speaker in Note Pages View.

6 Print the slides and note pages of the presentation.

7 Save the presentation as YOUTH to the MY_FILES directory on your Student Disk.

8 Submit your final printouts.

INDEPENDENT CHALLENGE 2

You are an independent distributor of natural juices and beverages in Denver, Colorado. Your business, Crystal Clear Waters, has progressively grown since its inception eight years ago but has recently reached a plateau over the last nine months. In an effort to turn your business around, you decide you need to acquire two major beverage accounts that would allow Crystal Clear Waters to expand its territory into surrounding states. Use PowerPoint to develop a presentation that you can use to gain more business.

In this independent challenge, you will choose a look for the presentation, complete an outline, and create your own material to complete the slides of the presentation.

To complete this independent challenge:

1 Think about the results you want to see, the information you need, and how you want to communicate the message.

2 Choose a look for the presentation.

3 Create four or five slides describing the goals and strategies your company will be using to acquire these new accounts. Enter text in the title and the main text placeholders of the slides. Use both Slide and Outline views to enter text.

4 Create a new slide at the end of the presentation. Enter concluding text on the slide, summarizing the main points of the presentation.

5 Enter notes for the speaker in Note Pages View.

6 Save the presentation as WATERS to the MY_FILES directory on your Student Disk.

7 Print the slides and speaker notes of the presentation.

8 Submit your final printouts.

POWERPOINT—Unit 3

APPLICATIONSREVIEW

1 Open an existing presentation.

a. Start PowerPoint.

b. Click the Open an Existing Presentation radio button, then click OK.

c. Click the Drives list arrow, then click a:.

d. In the File Name list box, click AEPT3-1.PPT, then click OK.

e. Click File on the menu bar, then click Save As.

f. Double-click MY_FILES in the list of directories. In the File name text box, select the current name and type CAMP.

g. Click OK, then click OK again if the Summary Info dialog box appears.

2 Add and Arrange text.

a. Drag the elevator to Slide 2 and click the Text Tool button.

b. Position the pointer to the left of the graphic and drag a 3" wide box.

c. Type the following mission statement:

Fellowship Camp is a camp for children with special needs dedicated to providing a safe, warm environment in which friendship can bloom.

d. Select the word "Camp" and move it in front of the word "Fellowship."

e. Deselect the object.

3 Format text.

a. Select the word processing box you just created by pressing [Shift] while clicking the box.

b. Increase the font size by clicking the Increase Font Size button once.

c. Click the Italic button, then click the Bold button.

d. Using the Text Color button, choose a color you find more appealing.

e. Deselect the object.

4 Draw and modify an object.

a. Display Slide 3.

b. Press [Shift] then click the main text object.

c. Resize the text object so that only the third goal appears on two lines.

d. Click the AutoShapes button on the Drawing toolbar.

e. Click the Star Tool button, then hide the AutoShapes toolbar.

f. Press [Shift] and drag a star shape that fills the empty space to the right of the text.

g. Display the Drawing+ toolbar if it is not already visible.

h. Click the Fill Color button on the Drawing+ toolbar, then choose a color that you find appealing.

i. Click the Shadow On/Off button to display a shadow.

j. Hide the Drawing+ toolbar.

5 Edit objects.

a. Select the star if it is not already selected.

b. Resize the star using the bottom corner resize handle so that the star is 1½" tall.

c. Move the star to the space below the text.

d. Press [Ctrl] and copy the star four times.

e. Create a bottom border by placing the five stars side by side below the text.

f. Double-click the first star, then type "G." Format this letter in bold using the Bold button and in black print using the Text Color button. Continue typing one letter in each star to spell the heading "GOALS."

6 Align and group objects.

a. Press [Shift] and click each of the five stars.

b. Click Draw on the menu bar, then click Align.

c. Click Middles.

d. Click Draw, then click Group.

e. Drag the stars so they appear above the text.

7 Replace text.

a. Click Tools on the menu bar, then click Replace Fonts.

b. Click the Replace list arrow and select Times New Roman.

c. Click the With list arrow and select Arial.

d. Click Replace, then click Close.

8 Check spelling.

a. Click the Spelling button on the Standard toolbar.

b. Ignore all proper names.

c. Correct any misspelled words.

d. Click OK when the spell checker has finished.

e. Click the Save button on the Standard toolbar.

f. Print the presentation in Slide view.

g. Close the presentation and exit PowerPoint.

TABLE 3-1

SLIDE TITLE	TRAINING SEMINAR AGENDA
1st bullet point	Claims Law/ Company Policy- Sept. 23rd (all day)
2nd bullet point	Insurance Policy Review-Sept. 24th (all day)
3rd bullet point	Claims Process/ Customer Relations- Sept. 25th (all day)
4th bullet point	Seminar Review- Sept. 26th (morning session)
5th bullet point	Open Q&A - Sept. 26th (afternoon session)

INDEPENDENT CHALLENGE 1

In this challenge, you are the Claims Division manager for the GlobalNet Insurance Company, a national company located in Springfield, Illinois. To keep their claims personnel up to date with new laws and company policies and procedures, GlobalNet conducts a three-day training seminar once a year for the entire claims department nationwide. It is your job to travel around the country to all of GlobalNet's regional offices and give the first day of the three-day seminar. You will give your first presentation to the claims department at the Home Office in Springfield, IL.

Add some text to various slides, then create and format some shapes to complete the slides of the presentation. Remember not to clutter the slides with too much information. To begin open the presentation provided for you on your Student Disk.

To complete this independent challenge:

1 Open the file AEPT3-2.PPT on your Student Disk.

2 After you open the presentation, look through it in Slide view and think about the results you want to see on each slide. What information is provided and what could you add? How do you want to communicate the message? Look at the organization of the presentation; you may need to make some adjustments. Enter text where you feel the presentation is weak.

3 Create a new slide with the information provided in Table 3-1. If necessary, move the slide so it flows in the presentation. (HINT: use Outline view to move the slide.)

4 Format the text throughout the presentation.

5 Use the drawing tools to add shapes to your slides. Format the objects using color and shading. Use the Align and Group commands to organize your shapes.

6 Spell check the presentation, then save the presentation as CLAIMS to the MY_FILES directory on your Student Disk.

7 Print the slides and outline of the presentation.

8 Submit your final printouts.

INDEPENDENT CHALLENGE 2

You work for Romedia Corp, a major producer of computer CD-ROM titles in the United States and Canada. Romedia's products include adventure games and elementary education titles. Twice a year, in March and in September, the Production and Acquisition departments hold a series of meetings, called Title meetings, to determine the new CD title list for the following production term. The meetings are also used to decide which current CD titles need to be revised.

It is your job, as the director of acquisitions, to chair the Title meetings and present the basic forum for discussion. You decide to create a presentation that describes the basic points you feel need to be addressed. In this challenge, you need to format text, draw and edit shapes to enhance the look of slides, then spell check and print the presentation. To begin, open the presentation provided for you on your Student Disk.

To complete this independent challenge:

1 Open the file AEPT3-3.PPT on your Student Disk.

2 After you open the presentation, look through it in Slide view and think about the results you want to see on each slide. What information is provided and what could you add? How do you want to communicate the message? Look at the organization of the presentation; you may need to make some adjustments. Enter missing text.

3 Format the text throughout the presentation.

4 Add and arrange text on Slide 6.

5 Use the drawing tools to add shapes to your slides. Format the objects using color and shading. Use the Align and Group commands to organize your shapes.

6 Spell check the presentation, then save the presentation as TITLES to the MY_FILES directory on your Student Disk.

7 Print the slides and outline of the presentation.

8 Submit your final printouts.

POWERPOINT—Unit 4

APPLICATIONS REVIEW

1 Insert clip art.

a. Start PowerPoint, open the presentation AEPT4-1.PPT, and save it as FUND to the MY_FILES directory on your Student Disk.

b. Click OK to close the Summary Info dialog box.

c. Click the Next Slide button.

d. Click the layout button on the status bar.

e. Click the Text and Clip Art AutoLayout option, then click apply.

f. Double-click the placeholder, then click Currency in the Categories list.

g. Click the Reward Accounting option, then click Insert. If this option is not available choose one that you feel will fit with this topic.

h. Deselect the object.

2 Insert a graph.

a. Click the Insert New Slide button. This should be Slide 3.

b. Click the Graph AutoLayout option, then click OK.

c. Click the title placeholder and type "Contributions."

d. Double-click the graph placeholder.

e. Click the first cell in the datasheet, then click the first control box in the Datasheet window to select the entire datasheet.

f. Click Edit on the menu bar, click Clear, then click All.

g. Click the Import Data button, then choose AEPT4-2.XLS from your Student Disk.

h. Click the View Datasheet button on the Graph Standard toolbar.

i. Click in a blank area of the presentation window to exit Graph.

j. Deselect the graph object.

3 Format a chart.

a. Double-click the graph object, then click the By Column button on the Standard toolbar.

b. Click the numbers on the y-axis, then click the Currency Style button on the Graph Formatting toolbar.

c. Click the Decrease Decimal button on the Graph Formatting toolbar twice.

d. Click Insert on the menu bar, click Titles, click the Chart Title check box, then click OK.

e. Type "Donations by Region," then click below the text.

f. Deselect the graph.

4 Work with an organizational chart.

a. Move to Slide 4.

b. Double-click the organizational chart.

c. Click the Subordinate button on the Org toolbar.

d. Click the Event Coordinator chart box.

e. In the new chart box, type Leah Kim, press [Tab] then type Assistant.

f. Click Edit on the menu bar, click Select, then click All.

g. Click Boxes on the menu bar, then click Box Color.

h. Choose a color you find visually appealing.

i. Click File on the menu bar, then click Exit and Return to FUND. Click Yes in the message box.

5 Insert WordArt.

a. Move to Slide 5.

b. Click the Layout button, click the Text & Object option, then click Apply.

c. Double-click the object placeholder.

d. Click Microsoft WordArt 2.0, then click OK.

e. Type Goals, press [Enter], type "and," press [Enter], then type "Strategies."

f. Click Update Display.

g. Click the Format Text list arrow on the WordArt Formatting toolbar, then click the Button (curve) shape.

h. Click the Shading button on the Formatting toolbar, click the Foreground list arrow, click Aqua, then click OK.

i. Click the Shadow button and choose one of the options.

j. Click a blank area in the presentation window to exit WordArt.

k. Deselect the object.

6 Work with a Slide Master.

a. Click View on the menu bar, Click Master, then click Slide Master.

b. Click the first line of text in the master text placeholder.

c. Click Format on the menu bar, click Bullet, then click one of the arrow options on the bottom row.

d. Click the Size % of Text up arrow until the percentage reaches 100, then click OK.

e. Click the Slide view button.

7 Choose a color Scheme.

a. Click Format on the menu bar, then click Slide Color Scheme.

b. Click Choose Scheme, and in the Background color list click the blue color at the bottom of the list.

c. Click the white color at the top of the list in the Text & Line Color list box.

d. Choose the color scheme in the top left hand corner of the Other Scheme Colors section.

e. Click OK, then click Apply to All.

f. Click Format on the Menu bar, then click Slide Background.

g. Click the Vertical radio button in the Shade Styles section.

h. Click Apply to All.

8 Add slide show effects.

a. Click the Slide Show Sorter View button.

b. Click Edit on the menu bar, then click Select All.

c. Click the Transition Effects list arrow on the Slide Sorter toolbar, then click Dissolve.

d. Click in a blank area, click Slide 2, then press [Shift] and click Slide 5.

e. Click the Build Effects list arrow, then click Fly From Bottom.

f. Click Slide 1, then click the Rehearse Timings button.

g. Click each slide to give it a slide time.

h. Click Yes to record the new slide timings.

i. Click the Save button on the Standard toolbar, print the presentation, then exit PowerPoint.

INDEPENDENT CHALLENGE 1

You work for Friesen, Guske & Schaffer Investment Corporation, a successful investment service company in Miami, Florida. The company provides a full set of investment opportunities, including stocks, bonds, and mutual funds. Most of the company's clients are individuals who have large estates or who are retired. In order to generate more business, you've decided that the company needs a standardized presentation promoting the company and basic investment principles.

Joe Friesen, president of the company, recently asked you to develop the company's standardized presentation. In this challenge, you'll need to enhance the look of the slides by adding and formatting embedded objects, customizing the master view, and changing the color scheme. To begin, open the presentation provided for you on your Student Disk.

To complete this independent challenge:

1 Open the file AEPT4-3.PPT on your Student Disk.

2 After you open the presentation, look through it in the Slide view and think about the results you want to see on each slide. What information is provided and what could you add? How do you want to communicate the message? Look at the organization of the presentation; you may need to make some adjustments. Enter text where you feel the presentation is weak.

3 Create a Graph chart on a new slide. This slide should be Slide 8. Import data from the file AEPT4-4.XLS. Format the chart as you feel needed.

4 Make changes to the color scheme.

5 Add clip art to the presentation. Use the align and group commands to organize your shapes.

6 Add and format objects in the presentation. Use the align and group commands to organize your shapes.

7 Shade the slide background.

8 Spell check the presentation, then save it as INVEST to the MY_FILES directory on your Student Disk.

9 Set build effects, slide transitions, and slide timings.

10 Print the slides of the presentation, then show the presentation in Slide Show view. Exit PowerPoint.

INDEPENDENT CHALLENGE 2

You are a financial management consultant for Atlantic Coast Investments, located in Washington, D.C. One of your primary responsibilities is to give financial seminars on different financial investments and how to determine which fund to invest in. In this challenge, you'll need to enhance the look of the slides by adding and formatting embedded objects, customizing the master view, and changing the color scheme. To begin, open the presentation provided for you on your Student Disk.

To complete this independent challenge:

1 Open the file AEPT4-5.PPT on your Student Disk.

2 After you open the presentation, look through it in the Slide view and think about the results you want to see on each slide. What information is provided and what could you add? How do you want to communicate the message? Look at the organization of the presentation; you may need to make some adjustments. Enter text where you feel the presentation is weak.

3 Create a Graph chart on a new slide. This slide should be Slide 6 before the conclusion. Import data from the file AEPT4-6.XLS. Format the chart as you feel needed.

4 Make changes to the color scheme.

5 Add clip art to the presentation. Use the align and group commands to organize your shapes.

6 Add and format objects in the presentation. Use the align and group commands to organize your shapes.

7 Shade the slide background.

8 Spell check the presentation, then save it as CONSULT to the MY_FILES directory on your Student Disk.

9 Set build effects, slide transitions, and slide timings.

10 Print the slides of the presentation, then show the presentation in Slide Show view. Exit PowerPoint.

TASKREFERENCE — WORD 6, UNIT 1

TASK	MOUSE/BUTTON	MENU	KEYBOARD
Borders Toolbar, display/hide	⊞	Click View, Toolbars, click Borders check box, then click OK	
Close a document	Double-click control menu box next to menu bar	Click File, Close	[Ctrl][W]
Exit Word	Double-click control menu box next to title bar	Click File, Exit	[Alt][F4]
Formatting Toolbar, display/hide		Click View, Toolbars, click Formatting check box, then click OK	
Go to a specific page	Double-click page number in status bar, type page number, then click OK	Click Edit, Go To, type page number, then click OK	[Ctrl][G]
Help, access	?	Click Help	[F1]
Move to beginning of document			[Ctrl][Home]
Nonprinting characters, display/hide	¶	Click Tools, Option, click View tab, click desired Nonprinting characters check boxes, then click OK	[Ctrl][Shift][*]
Open a document		Click File, Open, type filename, then click OK	[Ctrl][O]
Standard Toolbar, display/hide		Click View, Toolbars, click Standard check box, then click OK	
Start Word 6.0 for Windows	Double-click Microsoft Office program group icon, then double-click Microsoft Word application icon		
Tip of the Day, display/hide		Click Help, Tip of the Day, click Show Tips at Startup check box, then click OK	
Undo last action		Click Edit, Undo	[Ctrl][Z]
View, Normal		Click View, Normal	[Alt][Ctrl][N]
View, Page Layout		Click View, Page Layout	[Alt][Ctrl][P]

TASKREFERENCE — WORD 6, UNIT 2

TASK	MOUSE/BUTTON	MENU	KEYBOARD
Copy text		Click Edit, Copy	[Ctrl][C]
Cut text		Click Edit, Cut	[Ctrl][X]
Date, insert today's		Click Insert, Date and Time, click desired format, then click OK	[Alt][Shift][D]
Hard page break, insert		Click Insert, Break, select Page Break radio button, then click OK	[Ctrl][Enter]
Move to end of document			[Ctrl][End]
Overwrite mode, turn off	Double-click OVR in status bar	Click Tools, Options, click Edit tab, click Overtype Mode check box, then click OK	[Insert]
Paste text		Click Edit, Paste	[Ctrl][V]
Preview a document		Click File, Print Preview	[Ctrl][F2]
Print a document		Click File, Print, choose options, then click OK	[Ctrl][P]
Reverse an undone action		Click Edit, Redo	[Ctrl][Y]
Save document with a new name		Click File, Save As, type the filename, then click OK	[F12]
Save document with same name		Click File, Save	[Ctrl][S]
Spelling, check		Click Tools, Spelling	[F7]
Undo last action		Click Edit, Undo	[Ctrl][Z]
Window, viewing more than one		Click Window, Arrange All	

TASKREFERENCE — WORD 6, UNIT 3

TASK	MOUSE/BUTTON	MENU	KEYBOARD
AutoFormat a document		Click Format, AutoFormat, then click OK	[Ctrl][K]
Bold, toggle on or off	B	Click Format, Font, click Font tab, click Bold under Font Style, then click OK	[Ctrl][B]
Borders, apply		Click Format, Borders and Shading, click Borders tab, choose options, then click OK	
Bulleted list, create		Click Format, Bullets and Numbering, click Bulleted tab, click desired format, then click OK	
Change case		Click Format, Change Case, click desired radio button, then click OK	[Shift][F3]
Drop cap, add		Click Format, Drop Cap, click desired position, type number of lines to drop, then click OK	
Font, change	Click Font list arrow, then click Font name	Click Format, Font, click Font tab, click font name under Font, then click OK	[Ctrl][Shift][F]
Font size, change	Click Font Size list arrow, then click size	Click Format, Font, click Font tab, click font size under Size, then click OK	[Ctrl][Shift][P]
Format, copy			[Ctrl][Shift][C], then [Ctrl][Shift][V]
Italics, toggle on or off	I	Click Format, Font, click Font tab, click Italic under Font Style, then click OK	[Ctrl][I]
Margins, change		Click File, Page Setup, click Margins tab, type new margins, then click OK	
Numbered list, create		Click Format, Bullets and Numbering, click Numbered tab, click desired format, then click OK	
Paragraph, align right		Click Format, Paragraph, click Alignment list arrow, click Right, then click OK	[Ctrl][R]

TASKREFERENCE — WORD 6, UNIT 3

TASK	MOUSE/BUTTON	MENU	KEYBOARD
Paragraph, center		Click Format, Paragraph, click Alignment list arrow, click Center, then click OK	[Ctrl][E]
Paragraph indent, decrease		Click Format, Paragraph, click Indents and Spacing tab, type new indent, then click OK	
Paragraph indent, increase		Click Format, Paragraph, click Indents and Spacing tab, type new indent, then click OK	
Shading, apply		Click Format, Borders and Shading, click Shading tab, choose options, then click OK	
Style, apply	Click Style list arrow, then click style name	Click Format, Style, click style name, then click Apply	[Ctrl][Shift][S], type style name, then press [Enter]
Style, modify	After changing text, click style list arrow, click style name, then click OK	Click Format, Style, click style name, click Modify, make changes, then click OK	
Tab alignment, change	Click tab alignment selector until desired tab marker appears	Click Format, Tabs, type Tab Stop Position, click desired Alignment radio button, then click OK	
Template, apply		Click Format, Style Gallery, click Template name, then click OK	

TASKREFERENCE — WORD 6, UNIT 4

TASK	MOUSE/BUTTON	MENU	KEYBOARD
AutoFormat a table		Click Table, Table AutoFormat, click desired format, then click OK	
Columns, create	▦	Click Format, Columns, type number of columns, then click OK	
Frame, insert		In Page Layout view, click Insert, Frame	
Graphic, insert		Click Insert, Picture, click filename, then click OK	
Gridlines, display/hide		Click Table, Gridlines	
Header or footer, create		Click View, Header and Footer, type text, then click Close	
Magnification, change	Click Zoom control list arrow, then click desired magnification	Click View, Zoom, click desired magnification, then click OK	
Symbols, insert		Click Insert, Symbol, click desired symbol, click Insert, then click Close	
Table, change cell height		Click Table, Cell Height and Width, click Row tab, select Height of row(s), type desired height, then click OK	

TASKREFERENCE — WORD 6, UNIT 4

TASK	MOUSE/BUTTON	MENU	KEYBOARD
Table, change cell width		Click Table, Cell Height and Width, click Column tab, type desired width, then click OK	
Table, delete column		Highlight column, then click Table, Delete Columns	[Shift][Delete] or [Ctrl][X]
Table, delete row		Highlight row, click Table, Delete Cells, select Delete Entire Row radio button, then click OK	[Shift][Delete] or [Ctrl][X]
Table, insert		Click Table, Insert Table, type table size, then click OK	
Table, insert columns		Highlight column to left of insertion, click Table, click Insert Columns	
Table, insert rows		Highlight row below insertion, click Table, Insert Rows	

TASKREFERENCE — EXCEL 5, UNIT 1

TASK	MOUSE/BUTTON	MENU	KEYBOARD
Bold, toggle on or off	[B button]	Click Format, Cells, click Font tab, click Bold under Font Style, then click OK	[Ctrl][B]
Center cell contents	[Center button]	Click Format, Cells, click Alignment tab, click Center (Horizontal) radio button, then click OK	
Close workbook	Double-click control menu box next to menu bar	Click File, Close	[Ctrl][F4]
Exit Excel	Double-click control menu box next to title bar	Click File, Exit	[Alt][F4]
Go to specific cell		Click Edit, Go To, type cell reference, then click OK	[F5]
Help, access	[Help button]	Click Help	[F1]
Move to cell A1			[Ctrl][Home]
Move to column A in current row			[Home]
Move to last column in current row			[End] [→]
Start Excel	Double-click Microsoft Office program group icon, then double-click Microsoft Excel application icon		

TASKREFERENCE — EXCEL 5, UNIT 2

TASK	MOUSE/BUTTON	MENU	KEYBOARD
Cancel entry			[Esc]
Confirm entry			[Enter]
Function, enter		Click Insert, Function	[Shift][F3]
Preview workbook		Click File, Print Preview	
Print workbook		Click File, Print, choose options, then click OK	[Ctrl][P]
Range, name	Select range, click name box, type range name, then press [Enter]	Select range, click Insert, Name, Define, type range name, type range address under Refers to, then click OK	[Ctrl][F3]
Save with a different name		Click File, Save As, type filename, then click OK	
Save with same name		Click File, Save	[Ctrl][S]
SUM function, enter			
Undo last action		Click Edit, Undo	[Ctrl][Z]

TASKREFERENCE — EXCEL 5, UNIT 3

TASK	MOUSE/BUTTON	MENU	KEYBOARD
AutoFormat a worksheet		Select range, click Format, AutoFormat, click desired format, then click OK	
Bold, toggle on or off	[B button]	Click Format, Cells, click Font tab, click Bold in Font Style list, then click OK	[Ctrl][B]
Center data across columns	[Center Across Columns button]		
Clear data		Click Edit, Clear, Contents	[Delete]
Column, delete		Click column selector button, then click Edit, Delete	
Column, insert		Click Insert, Cells, click Entire Column radio button, then click OK	
Column widths, change		Click Format, Column, Width, type desired width, then click OK	
Comma, format	[Comma Style button]		
Copy data	[Copy button]	Click Edit, Copy	[Ctrl][C]
Currency, format	[$ button]	Click Format, Cells, click Number tab, click Currency in Category list, click desired style, then click OK	
Cut data	[Cut button]	Click Edit, Cut	[Ctrl][X]
Date, format		Click Format, Cells, click Number tab, click Date in Category list, click Desired format, then click OK	
Decimal, increase	[Increase Decimal button]		
Decimal, decrease	[Decrease Decimal button]		
Font, change		Click Format, Cells, click Font tab, click font name in Font list, then click OK	
Font size, change		Click Format, Cells, click Font tab, click size in Size list, then click OK	

TASKREFERENCE — EXCEL 5, UNIT 3

TASK	MOUSE/BUTTON	MENU	KEYBOARD
Format, copy			
Italics, toggle on or off		Click Format, Cells, click Font tab, click Italics in Font Style list, then click OK	[Ctrl][I]
Open workbook		Click File, Open, type filename, then click OK	[Ctrl][O]
Paste data		Click Edit, Paste	[Ctrl][V]
Percentage, format	%	Click Format, Cells, click Number tab, click Percentage in Category list, click desired style, then click OK	
Range, fill with series		Click Edit, Fill, Series, select desired series, then click OK	
Row, delete		Click row selector button, then click Edit, Delete	
Row, insert		Click Insert, Cells, click Entire Row radio button, then click OK	
Row height, change		Click Format, Row, Height, type new height, then click OK	
Underline, toggle on or off		Click Format, Cells, click Font tab, click Underline drop-down list arrow, click desired underline style, then click OK	[Ctrl][U]

TASKREFERENCE — EXCEL 5, UNIT 4

TASK	MOUSE/BUTTON	MENU	KEYBOARD
Arrowhead, add			
Chart, change type			
Chart, create		Click Insert, Chart, then click desired location of chart	
Chart gridlines, display/hide			
Chart titles, add		Click Insert, Titles, click appropriate axis check box, then click OK	
Drawing Toolbar, display/hide			
Drop shadow, add			
Legend, display/hide			
Margins, change		Click File, Print, Page Setup, click Margins tab, type new margins, then click OK	
Orientation of worksheet, change		Click File, Print, Page Setup, click Page tab, click desired orientation radio button, then click OK	
Worksheet gridlines, display/hide		Click File, Print Preview, Page Setup, click Sheet tab, click Gridlines check box, then click OK	

TASKREFERENCE — ACCESS 2, UNIT 1

TASK	MOUSE/BUTTON	MENU	KEYBOARD
Close a database		Click File, Close Database	
Close an object		Click File, Close	[Ctrl][F4]
Exit Access	Double-click control menu box next to title bar	Click File, Exit	[Alt][F4]
Help, access		Click Help	[F1]
Menu, close without performing action			[Esc]
Move to next record		Click Records, Go To, Next	[↓]
Move to previous record		Click Records, Go To, Previous	[↑]
Move to first record in table		Click Records, Go To, First	
Move to last record in table		Click Records, Go To, Last	
Open a database		Click File, Open Database, type filename, then click OK	[Ctrl][O]
Open an object	Click desired tab, click object name, then click Open		
Start Access	Double-click Microsoft Office program group icon, then double-click Microsoft Access application icon		
Toolbars, display/hide		Click View, Toolbars, click desired toolbar, click Show or Hide, then click Close	

TASKREFERENCE — ACCESS 2, UNIT 2

TASK	MOUSE/BUTTON	MENU	KEYBOARD
Copy data from same field in previous record			[Ctrl][‘]
Date, insert today's			[Ctrl][;]
Go to specific record	Double-click record number in status bar, type desired record number, then press [Enter]		[F5]
Move to first blank record		Click Records, Go To, New	[Ctrl][=]
New database, open		Click File, New Database	[Ctrl][N]
Preview datasheet		Click File, Print Preview	
Preview window, close		Click File, Print Preview	[Esc]
Print datasheet		Click File, Print, choose desired options, click OK	[Ctrl][P]
Save current record		Click File, Save Record	[Shift][Enter]
Table, create	Click Table button, click New, then click Table Wizards	Click File, New, Table, then click Table Wizards	
Table, save [Shift][F12]		Click File, Save Table	[Ctrl][S] or or [Alt][Shift][F2]
Undo changes in current field or record		Click Edit, Undo	[Esc]

TASKREFERENCE — ACCESS 2, UNIT 3

TASK	MOUSE/BUTTON	MENU	KEYBOARD
Filter, apply		Click Records, Apply Filter/Sort	
Filter, create		Click Records, Edit Filter/Sort	
Find specific field		Click Edit, Find	[F7]
Go to specific record	Double-click record number in status bar, type desired record number, then press [Enter]		[F5]
Move to first blank record			[Ctrl][=]
Move to first field in current record		Click Records, Go To, First	[Home]
Move to last field in current record		Click Records, Go To, Last	[End]
Move to first field in first record			[Ctrl][Home]
Move to last field in last record			[Ctrl][End]
Move to next field in current record			[Tab]
Move to previous field in current record			[Shift][Tab]
New record, add		Click Records, Go To, New	[Ctrl][+]
Query, create			

TASKREFERENCE — ACCESS 2, UNIT 3

TASK	MOUSE/BUTTON	MENU	KEYBOARD
Return sorted table to original order		Click Records, Show All Records	
Show all records		Click Records, Show All Records	
Sort records in ascending order		Click Records, Quick Sort, Ascending	
Sort records in descending order		Click Records, Quick Sort, Descending	
Toolbars, display/hide		Click View, Toolbars, click desired toolbar, click Show or Hide, then click Close	
View datasheet		Click View, Datasheet	
View query design		Click View, Query Design	

TASKREFERENCE — ACCESS, UNIT 4

TASK	MOUSE/BUTTON	MENU	KEYBOARD
AutoForm, create			
AutoReport, create			
Close form	Double-click control menu box next to form title bar	Click File, Close	
Controls, center			
Controls, left-align			
Form, create		Click Form object button, click New, click the desired table or query, then click Form Wizard	
Label, add to a report			
Record, add in a form		Click Records, Go To, then click New	
Report, create		Click View, Reports, New, click the desired table or query, then click Report Wizards	
Save form as a report		In Design View, click File, Save As Report, type report name, then click OK	
View form		Click View, Form	
View form design		Click View, Form Design	

TASKREFERENCE — POWERPOINT 4, UNIT 1

TASK	MOUSE/BUTTON	MENU	KEYBOARD
Bold, toggle on or off	B	Click Format, Font, then click Bold under Font Style, then click OK	[Ctrl][B]
Close presentation	Double-click control menu box next to presentation title bar	Click File, Close	[Ctrl][W] or [Ctrl][F4]
Cue Cards, display		Click Help, Cue Cards	
Cue Cards, hide	Double-click control menu box in Cue Cards window		
Exit PowerPoint	Double-click control menu box next to title bar	Click File, Exit	[Ctrl][Q] or [Alt][F4]
Font, increase size	A	Click Format, Font, click desired font size under Size, then click OK	[Ctrl][Shift][>]
Help, access		Click Help	[F1]
Move to previous slide			
New presentation, create		Click File, New, click AutoContent Wizard, Pick a Look Wizard, Templates, or Blank Presentation radio button, then click OK	[Ctrl][N]
Notes Pages view, display		Click View, Notes Pages	
Outline view, display		Click View, Outline	[Ctrl][Alt][O]
Slide Show, run		Click View, Slide Show, Show	
Slide Sorter view, display		Click View, Slide Sorter	[Ctrl][Alt][P]
Slide view, display		Click View, Slides	[Ctrl][Alt][N]
Start PowerPoint	Double-click Microsoft Office program group icon, then double-click Microsoft PowerPoint application icon		

TASKREFERENCE — POWERPOINT 4, UNIT 2

TASK	MOUSE/BUTTON	MENU	KEYBOARD
Demote item in Outline view			[Alt][Shift][↓]
Move item up in Outline view			[Alt][Shift][↑]
Move to next slide			
New slide, create		Click Insert, New Slide or click the New Slide button on status bar, click desired AutoLayout, then click OK	[Ctrl][M]
Print presentation		Click File, Print, click Print What list arrow, click selection, choose other options, then click OK	[Ctrl][P] or [Ctrl][Shift][F12]
Save presentation with a new name		Click File, Save As, type filename, then click OK	[F12]
Save presentation		Click File, Save	[Ctrl][S] or [Shift][F12]
Zoom control, change in Notes Pages view	Click the Zoom control list arrow	Click View, Zoom, click desired Zoom To radio button, then click OK	

TASKREFERENCE — POWERPOINT 4, UNIT 3

TASK	MOUSE/BUTTON	MENU	KEYBOARD
Align objects		Click Draw, Align, then click desired alignment	
Change case		Click Format, Change Case, click desired case, then click OK	
Color of text, change		Click Format, Font, click Color list arrow, click desired color, then click OK	
Copy an object		Click the object with right mouse button, click Copy in shortcut menu or click Edit, Copy	[Ctrl][C]
Cut an object		Click Edit, Cut	[Ctrl][X]
Drawing Toolbar, display/hide		Click View, Toolbars, click Drawing check box, click OK	
Flip object		Click Draw, Rotate/Flip, then click one of the Flip commands	
Font, change throughout presentation		Click Tools, Replace Fonts, click replace list arrow, click current font name, click With list arrow, click new font name, click Replace, then click Close	
Group objects		Select objects to group, click Draw, Group	[Ctrl][Shift][G]
Italics, toggle on or off		Click Format, Font, click Italics under Font Style, then click OK	[Ctrl][I]
Line style, change			
Open existing presentation		Click File, Open, click filename, then click OK	[Ctrl][O]
Paste an object		Click Edit, Paste	[Ctrl][V]
Periods, add throughout presentation		In Outline view, select all slides, click Format, Periods, click Add Periods radio button, click OK	
Periods, remove throughout presentation		In Outline view, select all slides, click Format, Periods, click Remove Periods radio button, click OK	

TASKREFERENCE — POWERPOINT 4, UNIT 3

TASK	MOUSE/BUTTON	MENU	KEYBOARD
Replace a word throughout presentation		Click Edit, Replace, type word to be replaced in Find What text box, type new word in Replace With text box, click Replace All, then click Close	[Ctrl][H]
Rotate an object		Click Draw, Rotate/Flip, then click one of the Rotate commands	
Shapes, add in Slide view			
Spelling, check		Click Tools, Spelling	[F7] or [Ctrl][Alt][L]
Text, add in slide view	A		
Toolbars, display/hide		Click View, Toolbars, click desired check boxes, then click OK	

TASKREFERENCE — POWERPOINT 4, UNIT 4

TASK	MOUSE/BUTTON	MENU	KEYBOARD
Annotations, erase during slide show			[E]
Background, change		Click Format, Slide Background, click desired Shade Style radio button, click desired Variant, then click Apply to All	
Builds, add	In Slide Sorter view, click Build Effects list arrow, then click desired build	In Slide Sorter view, click Tools, Build, click desired effects, then click OK	
Bullet style, change		Click Format, Bullet, click desired bullet style, then click OK	
Chart title, add		Click Insert, Titles, click Chart Title check box, then click OK	
Clip art, add	[button]	In Slides view, click Format, Slide Layout or click the Layout button in status bar, click Text and Clip Art AutoLayout or Clip Art and Text Auto-Layout, click Apply or OK, double-click clip art placeholder, click Yes, click desired category, click desired clip art, then click OK	
Color scheme, change throughout presentation		In Slides view, click Format, Slide Color Scheme, click Choose Scheme, click desired Background Color, click desired Text & Line Color, click desired color scheme in Other Scheme Colors, click OK, then click Apply to All	
Color scheme, copy		In Slide Sorter view, click Format, Pick Up Color Scheme	
Currency format in graph	$	Click Format, Selected Axis, click Number tab, click Currency under Category, select desired Format Code, then click OK	
Decrease decimal in graph	.00 →.0	Click Format, Selected Axis, click Number tab, click Number under Category, select desired Format Code, then click OK	

TASK REFERENCE — POWERPOINT 4, UNIT 4

TASK	MOUSE/BUTTON	MENU	KEYBOARD
Display hidden slide during slide show	[button]		[H]
Format axis		Select axis, click Format, Selected Axis, make desired changes, then click OK	
Graph, add		In Slides view, click Format, Slide Layout or click the Layout button in status bar, click Graph AutoLayout, click Apply or OK, then double-click graph placeholder	
Graph, display data by columns in datasheet	[button]		
Hide a slide during slide show	[button]	Click Tools, Hide Slide	
Import data to a graph	[button]		
Layout, change		In Slides view, click Format, Slide Layout or click the Layout button in status bar, choose desired AutoLayout, then click Apply or OK	
Move to previous slide in slide show			[←]
Move to next slide in slide show			[→]
Organizational chart, add	[button]	In Slides view, click Format, Slide Layout or click the Layout button in status bar, click Organizational chart AutoLayout, click Apply or OK, then double-click the organizational chart placeholder	
Picture, add		Click Insert, Picture, click filename, then click OK	
Save organizational chart and update presentation		Click File, Exit & Return to *filename*, then click Yes	
Scale objects proportionally		Click Draw, Scale, type Scale To percentage, then click OK	
Slide master, view		Click View, Master, Slide Master	

TASKREFERENCE — POWERPOINT 4, UNIT 4

TASK	MOUSE/BUTTON	MENU	KEYBOARD
Slide show, run with timings		Click View, Slide Show, click Use Slide Timings radio button, then click Show	
Sound or media, add		In Slides view, click Format, Slide Layout or click the Layout button in status bar, click Object AutoLayout, click Apply or OK, double-click the object placeholder, click Sound or Media Clip, then click OK	
Stop slide show in middle			[Esc]
Timings, add		Click Tools, Transition, select Automatically After [*blank*] Seconds radio button under Advance, type number of seconds desired, then click OK	
Transitions, add	Click Transition Effects list arrow, then click desired transition	Click Tools, Transitions, click desired transitions in Effects list, then click OK	
View datasheet			
Word Art, add		In Slides view, click Format, Slide Layout or click the Layout button in status bar, click Object AutoLayout, click Apply or OK, double-click the object placeholder, click Microsoft WordArt 2.0, then click OK	
WordArt, add shading			
WordArt, add shadow			